INVESTIGATION OF COMPETITION IN DIGITAL MARKETS

MAJORITY STAFF REPORT AND RECOMMENDATIONS

SUBCOMMITTEE ON ANTITRUST, COMMERCIAL AND ADMINISTRATIVE LAW OF THE COMMITTEE ON THE JUDICIARY

Jerrold Nadler, Chairman, Committee on the Judiciary

David N. Cicilline, Chairman, Subcommittee on Antitrust, Commercial and Administrative Law

UNITED STATES
2020

TABLE OF CONTENTS

4

I. INTRODUCTION

A. Chairs' Foreword

In June 2019, the Committee on the Judiciary initiated a bipartisan investigation into the state of competition online, spearheaded by the Subcommittee on Antitrust, Commercial and Administrative Law. As part of a top-to-bottom review of the market, the Subcommittee examined the dominance of Amazon, Apple, Facebook, and Google, and their business practices to determine how their power affects our economy and our democracy. Additionally, the Subcommittee performed a review of existing antitrust laws, competition policies, and current enforcement levels to assess whether they are adequate to address market power and anticompetitive conduct in digital markets.

Over the course of our investigation, we collected extensive evidence from these companies as well as from third parties—totaling nearly 1.3 million documents. We held seven hearings to review the effects of market power online—including on the free and diverse press, innovation, and privacy—and a final hearing to examine potential solutions to concerns identified during the investigation and to inform this Report's recommendations.

A year after initiating the investigation, we received testimony from the Chief Executive Officers of the investigated companies: Jeff Bezos, Tim Cook, Mark Zuckerberg, and Sundar Pichai. For nearly six hours, we pressed for answers about their business practices, including about evidence concerning the extent to which they have exploited, entrenched, and expanded their power over digital markets in anticompetitive and abusive ways. Their answers were often evasive and non-responsive, raising fresh questions about whether they believe they are beyond the reach of democratic oversight.

Although these four corporations differ in important ways, studying their business practices has revealed common problems. First, each platform now serves as a gatekeeper over a key channel of distribution. By controlling access to markets, these giants can pick winners and losers throughout our economy. They not only wield tremendous power, but they also abuse it by charging exorbitant fees, imposing oppressive contract terms, and extracting valuable data from the people and businesses that rely on them. Second, each platform uses its gatekeeper position to maintain its market power. By controlling the infrastructure of the digital age, they have surveilled other businesses to identify potential rivals, and have ultimately bought out, copied, or cut off their competitive threats. And, finally, these firms have abused their role as intermediaries to further entrench and expand their dominance. Whether through self-preferencing, predatory pricing, or exclusionary conduct, the dominant platforms have exploited their power in order to become even more dominant.

To put it simply, companies that once were scrappy, underdog startups that challenged the status quo have become the kinds of monopolies we last saw in the era of oil barons and railroad tycoons. Although these firms have delivered clear benefits to society, the dominance of Amazon, Apple, Facebook, and Google has come at a price. These firms typically run the marketplace while also competing in it—a position that enables them to write one set of rules for others, while they play by another, or to engage in a form of their own private *quasi* regulation that is unaccountable to anyone but themselves.

The effects of this significant and durable market power are costly. The Subcommittee's series of hearings produced significant evidence that these firms wield their dominance in ways that erode entrepreneurship, degrade Americans' privacy online, and undermine the vibrancy of the free and diverse press. The result is less innovation, fewer choices for consumers, and a weakened democracy.

Nearly a century ago, Supreme Court Justice Louis Brandeis wrote: "We must make our choice. We may have democracy, or we may have wealth concentrated in the hands of a few, but we cannot have both." Those words speak to us with great urgency today.

Although we do not expect that all of our Members will agree on every finding and recommendation identified in this Report, we firmly believe that the totality of the evidence produced during this investigation demonstrates the pressing need for legislative action and reform. These firms have too much power, and that power must be reined in and subject to appropriate oversight and enforcement. Our economy and democracy are at stake.

As a charter of economic liberty, the antitrust laws are the backbone of open and fair markets. When confronted by powerful monopolies over the past century—be it the railroad tycoons and oil barons or Ma Bell and Microsoft—Congress has acted to ensure that no dominant firm captures and holds undue control over our economy or our democracy. We face similar challenges today. Congress—not the courts, agencies, or private companies—enacted the antitrust laws, and Congress must lead the path forward to modernize them for the economy of today, as well as tomorrow. Our laws must be updated to ensure that our economy remains vibrant and open in the digital age.

Congress must also ensure that the antitrust agencies aggressively and fairly enforce the law. Over the course of the investigation, the Subcommittee uncovered evidence that the antitrust agencies failed, at key occasions, to stop monopolists from rolling up their competitors and failed to protect the American people from abuses of monopoly power. Forceful agency action is critical.

Lastly, Congress must revive its tradition of robust oversight over the antitrust laws and increased market concentration in our economy. In prior Congresses, the Subcommittee routinely examined these concerns in accordance with its constitutional mandate to conduct oversight and perform its legislative duties. As a 1950 report from the then-named Subcommittee on the Study of Monopoly Power described its mandate: "It is the province of this subcommittee to investigate factors which tend to eliminate competition, strengthen monopolies, injure small business, or promote undue concentration of economic power; to ascertain the facts, and to make recommendations based on those findings."[1]

Similarly, the Subcommittee has followed the facts before it to produce this Report, which is the product of a considerable evidentiary and oversight record. This record includes: 1,287,997 documents and communications; testimony from 38 witnesses; a hearing record that spans more than 1,800 pages; 38 submissions from 60 antitrust experts from across the political spectrum; and interviews with more than 240 market participants, former employees of the investigated platforms, and other individuals totaling thousands of hours. The Subcommittee has also held hearings and roundtables with industry and government witnesses, consultations with subject-matter experts, and a careful—and at times painstaking—review of large volumes of evidence provided by industry participants and regulators.

In light of these efforts, we extend our deep gratitude to the staff of the Subcommittee and Full Committee for their diligent work in this regard, particularly during the COVID-19 pandemic and other challenging circumstances over the past year.

Finally, as an institutional matter, we close by noting that the Committee's requests for information from agencies and any non-public briefings were solely for the purpose of carrying out our constitutionally based legislative and oversight functions. In particular, the information requested was vital to informing our assessment of whether existing antitrust laws are adequate for tackling current competition problems, as well as in uncovering potential reasons for under-enforcement. The Report by Subcommittee staff is based on the documents and information collected during its investigation, and the Committee fully respects the separate and independent decisional processes employed by enforcement authorities with respect to such matters.

Although the companies provided substantial information and numerous documents to the Subcommittee, they declined to produce certain critical information and crucial documents we requested. The material withheld was identified by the Committee as relevant to the investigation and included, primarily, two categories of information: (1) documents the companies' claimed were protected by common law privileges; and (2) documents that were produced to antitrust authorities in ongoing investigations, or that related to the subject matter of these ongoing investigations.

Institutionally, we reject any argument that the mere existence of ongoing litigation prevents or prohibits Congress from obtaining information relevant to its legislative and oversight prerogatives. We strongly disagree with the assertion that any requests for such materials and any compliance with those requests interfere with the decisional processes in ongoing investigations. Furthermore, while Congress is fully subject to constitutional protections, we cannot agree that we are bound by common

---

[1] *Aluminum: Report of the Subcomm. On Study of Monopoly Power of the H. Comm. on the Judiciary*, 82nd Cong. H. Rep. No. 255, 2 (1st Sess. 1951).

law privileges as asserted by the companies. While we determined that insufficient time exists to pursue these additional materials during this Congress, the Committee expressly reserves the right to invoke other available options, including compulsory process, to obtain the requested information in the future.

The views and conclusions contained in the Report are staff views and do not necessarily reflect those of the Committee on the Judiciary or any of its Members.

B.   Executive Summary

1. Subcommittee's Investigation

On June 3, 2019, the House Judiciary Committee announced a bipartisan investigation into competition in digital markets,[2] led by the Subcommittee on Antitrust, Commercial, and Administrative Law.[3] The purpose of the investigation was to (1) document competition problems in digital markets; (2) examine whether dominant firms are engaging in anticompetitive conduct; and (3) assess whether existing antitrust laws, competition policies, and current enforcement levels are adequate to address these issues.[4] The Committee initiated the investigation in response to broad-ranging investigative reporting, and activity by policymakers and enforcers, that raised serious concerns about the platforms' incentives and ability to harm the competitive process.[5]

---

[2] Press Release, H. Comm. on the Judiciary, House Judiciary Committee Launches Bipartisan Investigation into Competition in Digital Markets (June 3, 2019), https://judiciary.house.gov/news/press-releases/house-judiciary-committee-launches-bipartisan-investigation-competition-digital.

[3] We extend our sincere thanks to Peter Karafotas, Rich Luchette, and Francis Grubar, in the Office of Congressman David N. Cicilline, for their relentless work and selfless devotion throughout the investigation. We would also like to recognize the following staff for their significant contributions during the investigation: Dick Meltzer, Michael Tecklenburg, Kenneth DeGraff, and Victoria Houed in the Office of the Speaker of the U.S. House of Representatives; Daniel Flores, former Minority Chief Counsel, Subcommittee on Antitrust, Commercial and Administrative Law; Danny Johnson, former Minority counsel, Committee on the Judiciary; Jacqui Kappler, Legislative Director, the Honorable Henry "Hank" Johnson, Jr.; Devon Ombres, Legislative Counsel, the Honorable Jamie Raskin; Elly Kugler, Senior Counsel, the Honorable Pramila Jayapal; Jennifer Chan, Legislative Director, the Honorable Pramila Jayapal; Stuart Styron, Senior Legislative Assistant, the Honorable Val Demings; Keanu Rivera, Legislative Assistant, the Honorable Mary Gay Scanlon; Lindsey Garber, Legislative Counsel, the Honorable Joe Neguse; Miya Patel, former Legislative Assistant, the Honorable Joe Neguse; Natalie Knight, Legislative Counsel, the Honorable Lucy McBath. Staff would also like to thank Matthew Bisenius in the Office of F. James Sensenbrenner, as well as Garrett Ventry in the Office of Congressman Ken Buck, for their commitment to bipartisan cooperation. Finally, we thank Clare Cho and Mari Lee at the Congressional Research Service for their support, as well as graphics and data visualization used within this Report.

[4] Press Release, H. Comm. on the Judiciary, House Judiciary Committee Launches Bipartisan Investigation into Competition in Digital Markets (June 3, 2019), https://judiciary.house.gov/news/press-releases/house-judiciary-committee-launches-bipartisan-investigation-competition-digital.

[5] *See, e.g.*, Meehreen Khan, *EU Targets Tech Giants over Unfair Business Practices*, FIN. TIMES (Apr. 25, 2018), https://www.ft.com/content/d7228bec-4879-11e8-8ee8-cae73aab7ccb; Adam Satariano, *Google is Fined $57 Million Under Europe's Data Privacy Law*, N.Y. TIMES (Jan. 21, 2019), https://www.nytimes.com/2019/01/21/technology/google-europe-gdpr-fine.html; Richard Waters et al., *Global Regulators' Net Tightens Around Big Tech*, FIN. TIMES, (June 5, 2019), https://www.ft.com/content/973f8b36-86f0-11e9-97ea-05ac2431f453.

9

As part of the investigation, the Subcommittee held seven oversight hearings that provided Members of the Subcommittee with an opportunity to examine the state of competition in digital markets and the adequacy of existing antitrust laws. A diverse group of witnesses offered testimony on topics related to the effects of market power on the free and diverse press, on innovation, and on privacy. Other witnesses who testified included executives from businesses with concerns about the dominance of the investigated firms. The hearings also provided an opportunity for key executives from Facebook, Google, Amazon, and Apple—including the Chief Executive Officers of these firms— to address evidence that was uncovered during the investigation in a public-facing venue. After each of the hearings, Members of the Subcommittee submitted questions for the record (QFRs) to the witnesses.

The Committee requested information from the dominant platforms, from market participants, from the Federal antitrust agencies, and from other relevant parties, for the purpose of obtaining information that was not otherwise publicly available but was important to assembling a comprehensive record. The Committee also sent requests for submissions to various experts in the field, including academics, representatives of public interest groups, and practicing antitrust lawyers. The responses to these requests were indispensable to staff's ability to complete this Report and its recommendations for congressional oversight of the antitrust agencies and legislative action.

This Report is intended to provide policymakers, antitrust enforcers, market participants, and the public with a comprehensive understanding of the state of competition in the online marketplace. The Report also provides recommendations for areas of legislative activity to address the rise and abuse of market power in the digital economy, as well as areas that warrant additional congressional attention.

2. Findings

a. Overview

The open internet has delivered significant benefits to Americans and the U.S. economy. Over the past few decades, it has created a surge of economic opportunity, capital investment, and pathways for education. The COVID-19 pandemic has underscored the importance of internet access that is affordable, competitive, and widely available for workers, families, and businesses.

The online platforms investigated by the Subcommittee—Amazon, Apple, Facebook, and Google—also play an important role in our economy and society as the underlying infrastructure for the exchange of communications, information, and goods and services. As of September 2020, the combined valuation of these platforms is more than $5 trillion—more than a third of the value of the S&P 100. As we continue to shift our work, commerce, and communications online, these firms stand to become even more interwoven into the fabric of our economy and our lives.

Over the past decade, the digital economy has become highly concentrated and prone to monopolization. Several markets investigated by the Subcommittee—such as social networking, general online search, and online advertising—are dominated by just one or two firms. The companies investigated by the Subcommittee—Amazon, Apple, Facebook, and Google—have captured control over key channels of distribution and have come to function as gatekeepers. Just a decade into the future, 30% of the world's gross economic output may lie with these firms, and just a handful of others.[6]

In interviews with Subcommittee staff, numerous businesses described how dominant platforms exploit their gatekeeper power to dictate terms and extract concessions that no one would reasonably consent to in a competitive market. Market participants that spoke with Subcommittee staff indicated that their dependence on these gatekeepers to access users and markets requires concessions and demands that carry significant economic harm, but that are "the cost of doing business" given the lack of options.

This significant and durable market power is due to several factors, including a high volume of acquisitions by the dominant platforms. Together, the firms investigated by the Subcommittee have acquired hundreds of companies just in the last ten years. In some cases, a dominant firm evidently acquired nascent or potential competitors to neutralize a competitive threat or to maintain and expand the firm's dominance. In other cases, a dominant firm acquired smaller companies to shut them down or discontinue underlying products entirely—transactions aptly described as "killer acquisitions."[7]

In the overwhelming number of cases, the antitrust agencies did not request additional information and documentary material under their pre-merger review authority in the Clayton Act, to examine whether the proposed acquisition may substantially lessen competition or tend to create a monopoly if allowed to proceed as proposed. For example, of Facebook's nearly 100 acquisitions, the Federal Trade Commission engaged in an extensive investigation of just one acquisition: Facebook's purchase of Instagram in 2012.

During the investigation, Subcommittee staff found evidence of monopolization and monopoly power. For example, the strong network effects associated with Facebook has tipped the market toward

---

[6] Catherine Fong et al., *Prime Day and the broad reach of Amazon's ecosystem*, MCKINSEY & CO. (Aug. 2, 2019), https://www.mckinsey.com/business-functions/marketing-and-sales/our-insights/prime-day-and-the-broad-reach-of-amazons-ecosystem ("This ecosystem strategy in particular has significant competitive implications because McKinsey estimates that in ten years, 30 percent of the world's gross economic output will be from companies that operate a network of interconnected businesses, such as those run by Amazon, Alibaba, Google, and Facebook.").

[7] Colleen Cunningham, Florian Ederer & Song Ma, Killer Acquisitions *1 (Yale School of Management Working Paper, Mar. 2019), https://perma.cc/L6YL-YL8K (describing the practice of "acquir[ing] innovative targets solely to discontinue the target's innovative projects and preempt future competition."). *See also* C. Scott Hemphill and Tim Wu, *Nascent Competitors*, 168 U. PA. L. REV. *2 (forthcoming 2020), https://perma.cc/62HH-34ZL ("A nascent competitor is a firm whose prospective innovation represents a serious future threat to an incumbent.").

monopoly such that Facebook competes more vigorously among its own products—Facebook, Instagram, WhatsApp, and Messenger—than with actual competitors.

As demonstrated during a series of hearings held by the Subcommittee and as detailed in this Report,[8] the online platforms' dominance carries significant costs. It has diminished consumer choice, eroded innovation and entrepreneurship in the U.S. economy, weakened the vibrancy of the free and diverse press, and undermined Americans' privacy.

These concerns are shared by the majority of Americans. On September 24, 2020, Consumer Reports (CR) published a survey titled "Platform Perceptions: Consumer Attitudes on Competition and Fairness in Online Platforms."[9] Among its findings:

- 85% of Americans are concerned—either very concerned or somewhat concerned— about the amount of data online platforms store about them, and 81% are concerned that platforms are collecting and holding this data in order to build out more comprehensive consumer profiles.

- 58% are not confident that they are getting objective and unbiased search results when using an online platform to shop or search for information.

- 79% say Big Tech mergers and acquisitions unfairly undermine competition and consumer choice.[10]

- 60% support more government regulation of online platforms, and mandating interoperability features, to make it easier for users to switch from one platform to another without losing important data or connections.

b. Facebook

Facebook has monopoly power in the market for social networking. Internal communications among the company's Chief Executive Officer, Mark Zuckerberg, and other senior executives indicate that Facebook acquired its competitive threats to maintain and expand its dominance. For example, a senior executive at the company described its acquisition strategy as a "land grab" to "shore up" Facebook's position,[11] while Facebook's CEO said that Facebook "can likely always just buy any

---

[8] *See infra* Section V.

[9] CONSUMER REPORTS, PLATFORM PERCEPTIONS: CONSUMER ATTITUDES ON COMPETITION AND FAIRNESS IN ONLINE PLATFORMS (2020), https://advocacy.consumerreports.org/wp-content/uploads/2020/09/FINAL-CR-survey-report.platform-perceptions-consumer-attitudes-.september-2020.pdf.

[10] *Id.*

[11] Production from Facebook, to H. Comm. on the Judiciary, FB-HJC-ACAL-00045388 (Feb. 18, 2014), https://judiciary.house.gov/uploadedfiles/0004538800045389.pdf ("[W]e are going to spend 5-10% of our market cap every

competitive startups,"[12] and agreed with one of the company's senior engineers that Instagram was a threat to Facebook.[13]

Facebook's monopoly power is firmly entrenched and unlikely to be eroded by competitive pressure from new entrants or existing firms. In 2012, the company described its network effects as a "flywheel" in an internal presentation prepared for Facebook at the direction of its Chief Financial Officer.[14] This presentation also said that Facebook's network effects get "stronger every day."[15]

More recent documents produced during the investigation by Facebook show that it has tipped the social networking market toward a monopoly, and now considers competition within its own family of products to be more considerable than competition from any other firm. These documents include an October 2018 memorandum by Thomas Cunningham, a senior data scientist and economist at Facebook,[16] for Mr. Zuckerberg and Javier Olivan, Facebook's Director of Growth.[17] Among other things, the Cunningham Memo found that the network effects of Facebook and its family of products are "very strong,"[18] and that there are strong tipping points in the social networking market that create competition for the market, rather than competition within the market.[19]

According to a former senior employee at Instagram who was involved in the preparation of this document for review by Mr. Zuckerberg and Mr. Olivan, the Cunningham Memo guided Facebook's growth strategy, particularly with regard to Instagram.[20] They explained:

> The question was how do we position Facebook and Instagram to not compete with each other. The concern was the Instagram would hit a tipping point . . . There was

---

couple years to shore up our position . . . I hate the word 'land grab' but I think that is the best convincing argument and we should own that.").

[12] Production from Facebook, to H. Comm. on the Judiciary, FB-HJC-ACAL-00067600 (Apr. 9, 2012), https://judiciary.house.gov/uploadedfiles/0006760000067601.pdf.

[13] *Id.*

[14] Production of Facebook, to Comm. on the Judiciary, FB-HJC-ACAL-00049006 (Apr. 18, 2012) ("Network effects make it very difficult to compete with us - In every country we've tipped we are still winning.") (on file with Comm.).

[15] *Id.*

[16] Production of Facebook, to Comm. on the Judiciary FB-HJC-ACAL-00111406 (Oct. 2018) (on file with Comm.) [hereinafter Cunningham Memo] ("Facebook has high reach and time-spent in most countries. User growth is tracking internet growth: global reach is roughly stable.").

[17] *Id.*

[18] Cunningham Memo at 11.

[19] *Id.* at 9.

[20] *Id.*

brutal in-fighting between Instagram and Facebook at the time. It was very tense. It was back when Kevin Systrom was still at the company. He wanted Instagram to grow naturally and as widely as possible. But Mark was clearly saying "do not compete with us." . . . It was collusion, but within an internal monopoly. If you own two social media utilities, they should not be allowed to shore each other up. It's unclear to me why this should not be illegal. You can collude by acquiring a company.[21]

Facebook has also maintained its monopoly through a series of anticompetitive business practices. The company used its data advantage to create superior market intelligence to identify nascent competitive threats and then acquire, copy, or kill these firms. Once dominant, Facebook selectively enforced its platform policies based on whether it perceived other companies as competitive threats. In doing so, it advantaged its own services while weakening other firms.

In the absence of competition, Facebook's quality has deteriorated over time, resulting in worse privacy protections for its users and a dramatic rise in misinformation on its platform.

c. Google

Google has a monopoly in the markets for general online search and search advertising. Google's dominance is protected by high entry barriers, including its click-and-query data and the extensive default positions that Google has obtained across most of the world's devices and browsers. A significant number of entities—spanning major public corporations, small businesses, and entrepreneurs—depend on Google for traffic, and no alternate search engine serves as a substitute.

Google maintained its monopoly over general search through a series of anticompetitive tactics. These include an aggressive campaign to undermine vertical search providers, which Google viewed as a significant threat. Documents show that Google used its search monopoly to misappropriate content from third parties and to boost Google's own inferior vertical offerings, while imposing search penalties to demote third-party vertical providers. Since capturing a monopoly over general search, Google has steadily proliferated its search results page with ads and with Google's own content, while also blurring the distinction between paid ads and organic results. As a result of these tactics, Google appears to be siphoning off traffic from the rest of the web, while entities seeking to reach users must pay Google steadily increasing sums for ads. Numerous market participants analogized Google to a gatekeeper that is extorting users for access to its critical distribution channel, even as its search page shows users less relevant results.

A second way Google has maintained its monopoly over general search has been through a series of anticompetitive contracts. After purchasing the Android operating system in 2005, Google used contractual restrictions and exclusivity provisions to extend Google's search monopoly from

---

[21] Interview with Former Instagram Employee (Oct. 2, 2020).

desktop to mobile. Documents show that Google required smartphone manufacturers to pre-install and give default status to Google's own apps, impeding competitors in search as well as in other app markets. As search activity now migrates from mobile to voice, third-party interviews suggest Google is again looking for ways to maintain its monopoly over search access points through a similar set of practices.

Since capturing the market for online search, Google has extended into a variety of other lines of business. Today Google is ubiquitous across the digital economy, serving as the infrastructure for core products and services online. Through Chrome, Google now owns the world's most popular browser—a critical gateway to the internet that it has used to both protect and promote its other lines of business. Through Google Maps, Google now captures over 80% of the market for navigation mapping service—a key input over which Google consolidated control through an anticompetitive acquisition and which it now leverages to advance its position in search and advertising. And through Google Cloud, Google has another core platform in which it is now heavily investing through acquisitions, positioning itself to dominate the "Internet of Things," the next wave of surveillance technologies.

Internal communications also reveal that Google exploits information asymmetries and closely tracks real-time data across markets, which—given Google's scale—provide it with near-perfect market intelligence. In certain instances, Google has covertly set up programs to more closely track its potential and actual competitors, including through projects like Android Lockbox.

Each of its services provides Google with a trove of user data, reinforcing its dominance across markets and driving greater monetization through online ads. Through linking these services together, Google increasingly functions as an ecosystem of interlocking monopolies.

d. Amazon

Amazon has significant and durable market power in the U.S. online retail market. This conclusion is based on the significant record that Subcommittee staff collected and reviewed, including testimonials from third-party sellers, brand manufacturers, publishers, former employees, and other market participants, as well as Amazon's internal documents. Although Amazon is frequently described as controlling about 40% of U.S. online retail sales, this market share is likely understated, and estimates of about 50% or higher are more credible.

As the dominant marketplace in the United States for online shopping, Amazon's market power is at its height in its dealings with third-party sellers. The platform has monopoly power over many small- and medium-sized businesses that do not have a viable alternative to Amazon for reaching online consumers. Amazon has 2.3 million active third-party sellers on its marketplace worldwide, and a recent survey estimates that about 37% of them—about 850,000 sellers—rely on Amazon as their sole source of income.[22]

Amazon achieved its current dominant position, in part, through acquiring its competitors, including Diapers.com and Zappos. It has also acquired companies that operate in adjacent markets, adding customer data to its stockpile and further shoring up its competitive moats. This strategy has entrenched and expanded Amazon's market power in e-commerce, as well as in other markets. The company's control over, and reach across, its many business lines enables it to self-preference and disadvantage competitors in ways that undermine free and fair competition. As a result of Amazon's dominance, other businesses are frequently beholden to Amazon for their success.

Amazon has engaged in extensive anticompetitive conduct in its treatment of third-party sellers. Publicly, Amazon describes third-party sellers as "partners." But internal documents show that, behind closed doors, the company refers to them as "internal competitors." Amazon's dual role as an operator of its marketplace that hosts third-party sellers, and a seller in that same marketplace, creates an inherent conflict of interest. This conflict incentivizes Amazon to exploit its access to competing sellers' data and information, among other anticompetitive conduct.

Voice assistant ecosystems are an emerging market with a high propensity for lock-in and self-preferencing. Amazon has expanded Alexa's ecosystem quickly through acquisitions of complementary and competing technologies, and by selling its Alexa-enabled smart speakers at deep discounts. The company's early leadership in this market is leading to the collection of highly sensitive consumer data, which Amazon can use to promote its other business, including e-commerce and Prime Video.

Finally, Amazon Web Services (AWS) provides critical infrastructure for many businesses with which Amazon competes. This creates the potential for a conflict of interest where cloud customers are forced to consider patronizing a competitor, as opposed to selecting the best technology for their business.

e. Apple

Apple has significant and durable market power in the mobile operating system market. Apple's dominance in this market, where it controls the iOS mobile operating system that runs on Apple mobile devices, has enabled it to control all software distribution to iOS devices. As a result, Apple exerts monopoly power in the mobile app store market, controlling access to more than 100 million iPhones and iPads in the U.S.

---

[22] JUNGLESCOUT, THE STATE OF THE AMAZON SELLER 2020 4 (2020), https://www.junglescout.com/wp-content/uploads/2020/02/State-of-the-Seller-Survey.pdf.

Apple's mobile ecosystem has produced significant benefits to app developers and consumers. Launched in 2008, the App Store revolutionized software distribution on mobile devices, reducing barriers to entry for app developers and increasing the choices available to consumers. Despite this, Apple leverages its control of iOS and the App Store to create and enforce barriers to competition and discriminate against and exclude rivals while preferencing its own offerings. Apple also uses its power to exploit app developers through misappropriation of competitively sensitive information and to charge app developers supra-competitive prices within the App Store. Apple has maintained its dominance due to the presence of network effects, high barriers to entry, and high switching costs in the mobile operating system market.

Apple is primarily a hardware company that derives most of its revenue from sales of devices and accessories. However, as the market for products like the iPhone have matured, Apple has pivoted to rely increasingly on sales of its applications and services, as well as collecting commissions and fees in the App Store. In the absence of competition, Apple's monopoly power over software distribution to iOS devices has resulted in harms to competitors and competition, reducing quality and innovation among app developers, and increasing prices and reducing choices for consumers.

f.   Effects of Market Power

The Subcommittee also examined the effects of market power in digital markets on the free and diverse press, innovation, privacy and data, and other relevant matters summarized below for ease of reference.

As part of this process, the Subcommittee received testimony and submissions showing that the dominance of some online platforms has contributed to the decline of trustworthy sources of news, which is essential to our democracy.[23] In several submissions, news publishers raised concerns about the "significant and growing asymmetry of power" between dominant platforms and news organizations, as well as the effect of this dominance on the production and availability of trustworthy sources of news. Other publishers said that they are "increasingly beholden" to these firms, and in particular, to Google and Facebook.[24] Google and Facebook have an outsized influence over the distribution and monetization of trustworthy sources of news online,[25] undermining the quality and

_____

[23] Free and Diverse Press Hearing at 1–3 (statement of David Pitofsky, Gen. Counsel, News Corp).

[24] Submission from Source 53 to H. Comm. on the Judiciary, 7 (Oct. 14, 2019) (on file with Comm.) Although Apple News and Apple News Plus are increasingly popular news aggregators, most market participants that the Subcommittee received evidence from during the investigation do not view it as a critical intermediary for online news at this time. Some publishers raised competition concerns about the tying of payment inside Apple's news product. Others, however, did raise concern about Apple News and Apple News Plus, noting that it is "not creating any original journalism itself" and competes "against publishers' news products . . . for subscription revenues."

[25] Submission of Source 52 to H. Comm. on the Judiciary, 12 (Oct. 30, 2019) (on file with Comm.).

availability of high-quality sources of journalism.[26] This concern is underscored by the COVID-19 pandemic, which has laid bare the importance of preserving a vibrant free press in both local and national markets.

The rise of market power online has also materially weakened innovation and entrepreneurship in the U.S. economy.[27] Some venture capitalists, for example, report that there is an innovation "kill zone" that insulates dominant platforms from competitive pressure simply because investors do not view new entrants as worthwhile investments.[28] Other investors have said that they avoid funding entrepreneurs and other companies that compete directly or indirectly with dominant firms in the digital economy.[29] In an interview with Subcommittee staff, a prominent venture capital investor explained that due to these factors, there is a strong economic incentive for other firms to avoid head-on competition with dominant firms.[30]

Additionally, in the absence of adequate privacy guardrails in the United States, the persistent collection and misuse of consumer data is an indicator of market power online.[31] Online platforms rarely charge consumers a monetary price—products appear to be "free" but are monetized through people's attention or with their data.[32] In the absence of genuine competitive threats, dominant firms offer fewer privacy protections than they otherwise would, and the quality of these services has deteriorated over time. As a result, consumers are forced to either use a service with poor privacy safeguards or forego the service altogether.[33]

---

[26] Free and Diverse Press Hearing at 3 (statement of David Chavern, President and CEO, News Media Alliance) ("In effect, a couple of dominant tech platforms are acting as regulators of the digital news industry.").

[27] Innovation and Entrepreneurship Hearing at 1 (statement of Timothy Wu, Julius Silver Professor of Law, Columbia Law School); Data and Privacy Hearing at 1–3 (statement of Jason Furman, Professor of the Practice of Economic Policy, Harvard Kennedy School).

[28] Raghuram Rajan, Sai Krishna Kamepalli & Luigi Zingales, *Kill Zone* (Becker Friedman Institute Working Paper No. 2020-19), https://ssrn.com/abstract=3555915.

[29] *See generally* United States Department of Justice Antitrust Division Public Workshop on Venture Capital and Antitrust (Feb. 12, 2020) [hereinafter Venture Capital and Antitrust Workshop], https://www.justice.gov/atr/page/file/1255851/download; CHICAGO BOOTH STIGLER CTR. FOR THE STUDY OF ECON. & STATE, STIGLER CMTE. ON DIG. PLATFORMS 9 (2019) [hereinafter Stigler Report].

[30] *See* Interview with Source 146 (May 28, 2020).

[31] Howard A. Shelanski, *Information, Innovation, and Competition Policy for the Internet,* 161 U. PA. L. REV. 1663, 1689 (2013) ("One measure of a platform's market power is the extent to which it can engage in [privacy exploitation] without some benefit to consumers that offsets their reduced privacy and still retain users.").

[32] Data and Privacy Hearing at 3 (statement of Jason Furman, Professor of the Practice of Economic Policy, Harvard Kennedy School); Data and Privacy Hearing at 4-5 (statement of Tommaso Valletti, Professor of Economics, Imperial College Business School).

[33] DIG. COMPETITION EXPERT PANEL, UNLOCKING DIGITAL COMPETITION 43 (2019) ("[T]he misuse of consumer data and harm to privacy is arguably an indicator of low quality caused by a lack of competition,") [hereinafter Dig. Competition Expert Panel Report]; Dina Srinivasan, *The Antitrust Case Against Facebook: A Monopolist's Journey Towards Pervasive Surveillance in Spite of Consumers' Preference for Privacy*, 16 BERKELEY BUS. L.J. 39, 88 (2019) ("Consumers effectively face a singular choice—use Facebook and submit to the quality and stipulations of Facebook's product or forgo all use of the only social network.").

Finally, the market power of the dominant platforms risks undermining both political and economic liberties. Subcommittee staff encountered a prevalence of fear among market participants that depend on the dominant platforms, many of whom expressed unease that the success of their business and their economic livelihood depend on what they viewed as the platforms' unaccountable and arbitrary power. Additionally, courts and enforcers have found the dominant platforms to engage in recidivism, repeatedly violating laws and court orders. This pattern of behavior raises questions about whether these firms view themselves as above the law, or whether they simply treat lawbreaking as a cost of business. Lastly, the growth in the platforms' market power has coincided with an increase in their influence over the policymaking process. Through a combination of direct lobbying and funding think tanks and academics, the dominant platforms have expanded their sphere of influence, further shaping how they are governed and regulated.

3. Recommendations

As part of the investigation of competition in digital markets, the Subcommittee conducted a thorough examination of the adequacy of current laws and enforcement levels. This included receiving submissions from experts on antitrust and competition policy who were selected on a careful, bipartisan basis to ensure the representation of a diverse range of views on these matters. The Subcommittee also received other submissions from leading experts—including Executive Vice President Margrethe Vestager of the European Commission and Chair Rod Sims of the Australian Competition and Consumer Commission—to inform this inquiry. Most recently, on October 1, 2020, the Subcommittee held an oversight hearing on "Proposals to Strengthen the Antitrust Laws and Restore Competition Online" to examine potential solutions to concerns identified during the investigation to further inform the Report's recommendations.

Based on this oversight activity, Subcommittee Chairman Cicilline requested that staff provide a menu of reforms to Members of the Subcommittee for purposes of potential legislative activity during the remainder of the 116th Congress and thereafter. As he noted in remarks to the American Antitrust Institute in June 2019:

> [I]t is Congress' responsibility to conduct oversight of our antitrust laws and competition system to ensure that they are properly working and to enact changes when they are not. While I do not have any preconceived ideas about what the right answer is, as Chairman of the Antitrust Subcommittee, I intend to carry out that responsibility with the sense of urgency and serious deliberation that it demands.[34]

---

[34] David N. Cicilline, Chairman, Subcomm. on Antitrust, Commercial and Admin. Law of the H. Comm. on the Judiciary, Keynote Address at American Antitrust Institute's 20th Annual Policy Conference (June 20, 2019), https://cicilline.house.gov/press-release/cicilline-delivers-keynote-address-american-antitrust-institute%E2%80%99s-20th-annual-policy.

In response to this request, Subcommittee staff identified a broad set of reforms for further examination by the Members of the Subcommittee for purposes of crafting legislative responses to the findings of this Report. These reforms include proposals to: (1) address anticompetitive conduct in digital markets; (2) strengthen merger and monopolization enforcement; and (3) improve the sound administration of the antitrust laws through other reforms. We intend these recommendations to serve as a complement to vigorous antitrust enforcement. Consistent with the views expressed by Chairman Nadler and Subcommittee Chairman Cicilline in the Foreword to this Report, we view these recommendations as complements, and not substitutes, to forceful antitrust enforcement.

For ease of reference, these recommendations for further examination are summarized below.

a. Restoring Competition in the Digital Economy

- Structural separations and prohibitions of certain dominant platforms from operating in adjacent lines of business;

- Nondiscrimination requirements, prohibiting dominant platforms from engaging in self-preferencing, and requiring them to offer equal terms for equal products and services;

- Interoperability and data portability, requiring dominant platforms to make their services compatible with various networks and to make content and information easily portable between them;

- Presumptive prohibition against future mergers and acquisitions by the dominant platforms;

- Safe harbor for news publishers in order to safeguard a free and diverse press; and

- Prohibitions on abuses of superior bargaining power, proscribing dominant platforms from engaging in contracting practices that derive from their dominant market position, and requiring due process protections for individuals and businesses dependent on the dominant platforms.

b. Strengthening the Antitrust Laws

- Reasserting the anti-monopoly goals of the antitrust laws and their centrality to ensuring a healthy and vibrant democracy;

- Strengthening Section 7 of the Clayton Act, including through restoring presumptions and bright-line rules, restoring the incipiency standard and protecting nascent competitors, and strengthening the law on vertical mergers;

- Strengthening Section 2 of the Sherman Act, including by introducing a prohibition on abuse of dominance and clarifying prohibitions on monopoly leveraging, predatory pricing, denial of essential facilities, refusals to deal, tying, and anticompetitive self-preferencing and product design; and

- Taking additional measures to strengthen overall enforcement, including through overriding problematic precedents in the case law.

c. Reviving Antitrust Enforcement

- Restoring robust congressional oversight of the antitrust laws and their enforcement;

- Restoring the federal antitrust agencies to full strength, by triggering civil penalties and other relief for "unfair methods of competition" rules, requiring the Federal Trade Commission to engage in regular data collection on concentration, enhancing public transparency and accountability of the agencies, requiring regular merger retrospectives, codifying stricter prohibitions on the revolving door, and increasing the budgets of the FTC and the Antitrust Division; and

- Strengthening private enforcement, through eliminating obstacles such as forced arbitration clauses, limits on class action formation, judicially created standards constraining what constitutes an antitrust injury, and unduly high pleading standards.

II.   THE INVESTIGATION OF COMPETITION IN DIGITAL MARKETS

A. Requests for Information and Submissions

1. First-Party Requests for Information

On September 13, 2019, the Committee sent bipartisan requests for information (RFIs) to each of the four investigated platforms: Alphabet,[35] Amazon, Apple, and Facebook. For each company, the RFI asked for a comprehensive set of information about each of the company's products and services. In addition, the RFI asked the company to submit communications among high-level executives relating to various potentially anticompetitive acquisitions and conduct. The Committee requested that the platforms respond to the RFIs by October 14, 2019.

---

[35] In 2015, Google reorganized under a new name and parent company, Alphabet, separated various businesses, and placed Sundar Pichai as chief executive of Google. Larry Page, chief executive of Google, became head of Alphabet with Sergey Brin. *See* Conor Dougherty, *Google to Reorganize as Alphabet to Keep Its Lead as an Innovator*, N.Y. TIMES (Aug. 10, 2015), https://www.nytimes.com/2015/08/11/technology/google-alphabet-restructuring.html.

a. Alphabet

The Committee's RFI to Alphabet, the parent company of Google, asked for information necessary to understand how the company operates and its role in the digital marketplace.[36] For example, in Request A, the RFI asked for detailed financial statements and a description of Alphabet's relevant products and services, including Google Ads, Google Search, YouTube, and Waze. In addition, the RFI asked for information helpful for determining whether Alphabet has monopoly power for any of its products or services, including for each product or service: (i) a list of Alphabet's top ten competitors; and (ii) internal or external analyses of Alphabet's market share relative to its competitors. Request A also asked for copies of documents and information that Alphabet had submitted to any U.S. or international antitrust enforcement agency for antitrust investigations that took place in any of those agencies within the past decade.[37]

Request B asked for all communications from high-level executives, including former CEO Larry Page and current CEO Sundar Pichai, relating to a number of Alphabet's key acquisitions and potentially anticompetitive conduct, most of which have been widely reported in the news.[38] The RFI asked for communications, including, but not limited to, discussions relating to the deal rationale and any competitive threat posed by the acquired company for the following acquisitions: Google/Android in 2005, Google/YouTube in 2006, Google/DoubleClick in 2007, Google/AdMob in 2009, and Google's acquisition of a minority stake in Vevo in 2013. Request B of the Alphabet RFI also requested executive communications relating to certain categories of potential anticompetitive conduct.[39]

In response to this request, Alphabet produced 1,135,398 documents, including strategy memoranda, presentations, and materials produced in prior investigations. Although Google produced a significant amount of material, Subcommittee staff did not view this volume as a proxy for quality.

---

[36] Letter from Hon. Jerrold Nadler, Chairman, H. Comm. on the Judiciary, Hon. Doug Collins, Ranking Member, H. Comm on the Judiciary, Hon. David N. Cicilline, Chairman, Subcomm. on Antitrust, Commercial and Admin. Law of the H. Comm. on the Judiciary, Hon. F. James Sensenbrenner, Ranking Member, Subcomm. on Antitrust, Commercial and Admin. Law of the H. Comm. on the Judiciary to Larry Page, Chief Executive Officer, Alphabet (Sept. 13, 2019) [hereinafter Committee Request for Information, Alphabet] https://judiciary.house.gov/sites/democrats.judiciary.house.gov/files/documents/alphabet%20inc.%20rfi%20-%20signed%20(003).pdf.

[37] *Id.* at 1–4.

[38] The Alphabet RFI defines the term "Relevant Executives" as Larry Page, Sergey Brin, Ruth Porat, David Drummond, Eric Schmidt, Sundar Pichai, Susan Wojcicki, Philipp Schindler, Prabhakar Raghavan, Thomas Kurian, Hiroshi Lockheimer, Rishi Chandra, Keith Enright, and Kent Walker. *See id.* at 4.

[39] *Id.* at 4–9.

b. Amazon

The Committee's RFI to Amazon asked for similar types of information helpful for understanding the competitive dynamics of the digital marketplace and the company's role.[40] For example, in Request A, the RFI asked for detailed financial statements and a description of Amazon's relevant products and services, including Alexa, Amazon Marketplace, Amazon Prime, and Amazon Web Services (AWS). In addition, the RFI asked for information helpful for determining whether Amazon has monopoly power for any of its products or services, including for each product or service: (i) a list of Amazon's top ten competitors; and (ii) internal or external analyses of Amazon's market share relative to its competitors. Request A also asked for copies of documents and information that Amazon had submitted to any U.S. or international antitrust enforcement agency for antitrust investigations that took place in any of those agencies within the past decade.[41]

Request B asked for all communications from high-level executives, including CEO Jeff Bezos and Jay Carney, Senior Vice President for Global Corporate Affairs, relating to a number of Amazon's key acquisitions and potentially anticompetitive conduct, most of which have been widely reported in the news.[42] The RFI asked for communications, including, but not limited to, discussions relating to the deal rationale and any competitive threat posed by the acquired company for the following acquisitions: Amazon/Audible in 2008, Amazon/Zappos in 2009, Amazon/Quidsi (Diapers.com) in 2010[43], Amazon/Whole Foods in 2017, and Amazon/Ring in 2018. Request B of the Amazon RFI also requested executive communications relating to certain categories of potential anticompetitive conduct.[44]

In response to the Committee's requests, Amazon produced 24,299 documents, including internal emails among the company's senior executives, memoranda, presentations, and other materials.

---

[40] Letter from Hon. Jerrold Nadler, Chairman, H. Comm. on the Judiciary, Hon. Doug Collins, Ranking Member, H. Comm on the Judiciary, Hon. David N. Cicilline, Chairman, Subcomm. on Antitrust, Commercial and Admin. Law of the H. Comm. on the Judiciary, Hon. F. James Sensenbrenner, Ranking Member, Subcomm. on Antitrust, Commercial and Admin. Law of the H. Comm. on the Judiciary to Jeff Bezos, Chief Executive Officer, Amazon (Sept. 13, 2019) [hereinafter Committee Request for Information, Amazon] https://judiciary.house.gov/sites/democrats.judiciary.house.gov/files/documents/amazon%20rfi%20-%20signed.pdf.

[41] *Id.* at 1–3.

[42] The Amazon RFI defines the term "Relevant Executives" as Jeff Bezos, Jeff Wilke, Andy Jassy, Jeff Blackburn, Dave Limp, Brian Olsavsky, David Zapolsky, and Jay Carney. *See id.* at 3.

[43] Amazon acquired "Quidsi, the e-commerce company that runs Diapers.com" in 2010. Claire Cain Miller, *Amazon Has a Reported Deal to Buy Parent of Diapers.com*, N.Y. TIMES (Nov. 7, 2010), https://www.nytimes.com/2010/11/08/technology/08amazon.html.

[44] Committee Request for Information, Amazon at 3–7.

c. Apple

The Committee's RFI to Apple also asked for information helpful for understanding the company's role in the digital marketplace. For example, in Request A, the RFI asked for detailed financial statements and a description of Apple's relevant products and services, including the iPhone, App Store, and Apple Pay.[45] In addition, the RFI asked for information helpful for determining whether Apple has monopoly power for any of its products or services, including for each product or service: (i) a list of Apple's top ten competitors; and (ii) internal or external analyses of Apple's market share relative to its competitors. Request A also asked for copies of documents and information that Apple had submitted to any U.S. or international antitrust enforcement agency for antitrust investigations that took place in any of those agencies within the past decade.[46]

Request B asked for all communications from high-level executives, including CEO Tim Cook and Eddy Cue, Senior Vice President of Internet Software and Services, relating to potentially anticompetitive conduct, most of which has been widely reported in the news.[47] The RFI asked for communications, including, but not limited to, discussions relating to certain categories of potentially anticompetitive conduct.[48]

In response to the Committee's requests, Apple produced 2,246 documents. These documents include internal communications among the company's senior executives describing governance of the App Store, as well as the company's internal deliberations and strategy responding to recent controversies.

d. Facebook

The Committee's RFI to Facebook also asked for information helpful for understanding how the company operates and its role in the digital marketplace.[49] For example, in Request A, the RFI

---

[45] Letter from Hon. Jerrold Nadler, Chairman, H. Comm. on the Judiciary, Hon. Doug Collins, Ranking Member, H. Comm on the Judiciary, Hon. David N. Cicilline, Chairman, Subcomm. on Antitrust, Commercial and Admin. Law of the H. Comm. on the Judiciary, Hon. F. James Sensenbrenner, Ranking Member, Subcomm. on Antitrust, Commercial and Admin. Law of the H. Comm. on the Judiciary to Tim Cook, Chief Executive Officer, Apple (Sept. 13, 2019) [hereinafter Committee Request for Information, Apple]
https://judiciary.house.gov/sites/democrats.judiciary.house.gov/files/documents/apple%20rfi%20-%20signed.pdf.

[46] *Id.* at 1–3.

[47] The Apple RFI defines the term "Relevant Executives" as Tim Cook, Katherine Adams, Eddy Cue, Philip Schiller, Johny Srouji, Dan Riccio, Jonathan Ive, Craig Frederighi, Luca Maestri, Jeff Williams, Steve Dowling, Tor Myhren, Lucas Maestri, and Jane Horvath. *See id.* at 3.

[48] *Id.* at 3–6.

[49] Letter from Hon. Jerrold Nadler, Chairman, H. Comm. on the Judiciary, Hon. Doug Collins, Ranking Member, H. Comm on the Judiciary, Hon. David N. Cicilline, Chairman, Subcomm. on Antitrust, Commercial and Admin. Law of the H. Comm. on the Judiciary, Hon. F. James Sensenbrenner, Ranking Member, Subcomm. on Antitrust, Commercial and Admin. Law of the H. Comm. on the Judiciary to Mark Zuckerberg, Chief Executive Officer, Facebook (Sept. 13, 2019)

asked for detailed financial statements and a description of Facebook's relevant products and services, including Facebook, Instagram, and WhatsApp. In addition, the RFI asked for information helpful for determining whether Facebook has monopoly power for any of its products or services, including for each product or service: (i) a list of Facebook's top ten competitors; and (ii) internal or external analyses of Facebook's market share relative to its competitors. Request A also asked for copies of documents and information that Facebook had submitted to any U.S. or international antitrust enforcement agency for antitrust investigations that took place in any of those agencies within the past decade.[50]

Request B asked for all communications from high-level executives, including Founder and CEO Mark Zuckerberg and Sheryl Sandberg, Chief Operating Officer, relating to a number of Facebook's key acquisitions and potentially anticompetitive conduct, most of which have been widely reported in the news.[51] The RFI asked for communications, including, but not limited to, discussions relating to the deal rationale and any competitive threat posed by the acquired company for the following acquisitions: Facebook/Instagram in 2012, Facebook/Onavo in 2013, and Facebook/WhatsApp in 2014. Request B of the Facebook RFI also requested executive communications relating to certain categories of potentially anticompetitive conduct.[52]

In response to the Committee's requests, Facebook produced 41,442 documents, including documents produced in response to prior investigations into Facebook's acquisitions and into whether it had abused its dominance. Facebook also produced 83,804 documents in connection with litigation in an ongoing matter. Among other items, these documents include internal communications among the company's senior executives describing Facebook's acquisition and overall competition strategy. In response to supplemental requests by Subcommittee staff, Facebook produced internal market data over a multi-year period, as well as a memorandum prepared by a senior data scientist and economist at the company related to competition among Facebook's family of products and other social apps.

2. Process for Obtaining Responses to First-Party Requests

After sending the RFIs, Subcommittee staff invested considerable time and resources in making themselves available for calls with the platforms to answer any questions the platforms had about responding to the requests, on a nearly weekly basis from October 2019 through March 2020. On these calls, staff addressed a range of issues, including clarifying the meaning and intent of language in the

---

[hereinafter Committee Request for Information, Facebook]
https://judiciary.house.gov/sites/democrats.judiciary.house.gov/files/documents/facebook%20rfi%20-%20signed.pdf.

[50] *See id.* at 1–2.

[51] The Facebook RFI defines the term "Relevant Executives" as Mark Zuckerberg, Sheryl Sandberg, Jennifer Newstead, Javier Olivan, Chris Cox, Mike Schroepfer, David Wehner, Colin Stretch, Will Cathcart, Adam Mosseri, Stan Chudnovsky, Fidji Simo, Chris Daniels, Erin Egan, and Kevin Martin. *See id.* at 2–3.

[52] *See id.* at 2–5.

request; maintaining the confidentiality of sensitive business information; and, where appropriate, narrowing requests in an effort to balance the Committee's need for relevant information against the platforms' burden of production. Each of the investigated platforms failed to meet the October 14, 2019 deadline, citing various difficulties.

On December 4, 2019, nearly three months after the deadline for submitting the RFI responses, the Committee sent a letter to the platforms' CEOs pointing out their failure to comply. The Committee stated its expectation that the platforms would complete production by December 18, 2019 for Request A and January 2, 2020 for Request B, to avoid the need to invoke other processes and procedures to obtain the requested materials.[53]

After the platforms failed to meet the revised deadlines, in early February 2020, staff asked for the companies' outside counsel to attend in-person meetings to discuss the substantial gaps in production that remained, and to identify ways to address any obstacles the platforms identified to filling those gaps. Despite the Committee's best efforts to address those obstacles—and allowing substantial time for the platforms to navigate delays relating to the COVID-19 pandemic—staff again had to reach out to the platforms regarding the deficiency of their responses. On June 9, 2020, in a final effort to avoid resorting to issuing subpoenas to the platforms to compel the production of documents and information, staff requested that the platforms voluntarily provide information responsive to a reduced list of targeted requests by June 22, 2020.

3. Third-party Requests for Information

As part of the investigation, the Subcommittee collected a large amount of information from market participants, including customers and competitors of Amazon, Apple, Facebook, and Google. Staff also received information and analysis from other third parties, including academics, former antitrust government officials, public interest organizations, and trade associations.

a. Market Participants

In September, the Committee sent a request for information to over 80 market participants. The RFI asked the recipient to voluntarily provide information regarding the state of competition in the digital marketplace for various products and services, including number and identity of market participants, market shares, and barriers to entry. These third-party RFIs also asked for a description of any conduct by Amazon, Apple, Facebook, or Google that raises competition concerns, and the impact of such conduct on the recipient's business. The Committee also sought to gather information through

---

[53] *See e.g.*, Letter from Hon. Jerrold Nadler, Chairman, H. Comm. on the Judiciary, Hon. Doug Collins, Ranking Member, H. Comm on the Judiciary, Hon. David N. Cicilline, Chairman, Subcomm. on Antitrust, Commercial and Admin. Law of the H. Comm. on the Judiciary, Hon. F. James Sensenbrenner, Ranking Member, Subcomm. on Antitrust, Commercial and Admin. Law of the H. Comm. on the Judiciary to Mark Zuckerberg, Chief Executive Officer, Facebook (Dec. 4, 2019) (on file with House Comm. on the Judiciary).

these RFIs regarding broader questions based on the recipient's experience in the digital marketplace, including (i) whether market participants are able to compete on the merits of their goods and services; (ii) the adequacy of antitrust enforcement relating to merger review and anticompetitive conduct; (iii) the adequacy of current antitrust law to address anticompetitive mergers and anticompetitive conduct; and (iv) suggestions for improving enforcement of antitrust law and making changes to antitrust law itself, statutory or otherwise.

On January 7, 2020, the Committee sent a second round of RFIs to 29 market participants. These RFI recipients consisted of additional businesses and individuals that staff had identified during the first half of the investigation as likely to have relevant information and an interest in sharing that information with the Committee. These RFIs asked for similar information to the September RFIs and provided staff with additional valuable information and insights into the functioning and challenges of operating in the digital marketplace.

Unfortunately, some market participants did not respond to substantive inquiries due to fear of economic retaliation. These market participants explained that their business and livelihoods rely on one or more of the digital platforms. One response stated, "Unfortunately, [the CEO] is not able to be more public at this time out of concern for retribution to his business," adding, "I am pretty certain we are not the only ones that are afraid of going public."[54] Another business that ultimately declined to participate in the investigation expressed similar concerns, stating, "We really appreciate you reaching out to us and are certainly considering going on the record with our story. . . . Given how powerful Google is and their past actions, we are also quite frankly worried about retaliation."[55] Stacy Mitchell, Co-Director of the Institute for Local Self-Reliance, similarly testified that many businesses have a fear of speaking out about Amazon, stating, "I spend a lot of time interviewing and talking with independent retailers, manufacturers of all sizes. Many of them are very much afraid of speaking out publicly because they fear retaliation."[56]

---

[54] Email from Source 685 to Hon. Jerrold Nadler, Chairman, H. Comm. on the Judiciary, Hon. Doug Collins, Ranking Member, H. Comm on the Judiciary, Hon. David N. Cicilline, Chairman, Subcomm. on Antitrust, Commercial and Admin. Law of the H. Comm. on the Judiciary, Hon. F. James Sensenbrenner, Ranking Member, Subcomm. on Antitrust, Commercial and Admin. Law of the H. Comm. on the Judiciary (July 11, 2020) (on file with H. Comm. on the Judiciary).

[55] Email from Source 147 to Hon. Jerrold Nadler, Chairman, H. Comm. on the Judiciary, Hon. Doug Collins, Ranking Member, H. Comm on the Judiciary, Hon. David N. Cicilline, Chairman, Subcomm. on Antitrust, Commercial and Admin. Law of the H. Comm. on the Judiciary, Hon. F. James Sensenbrenner, Ranking Member, Subcomm. on Antitrust, Commercial and Admin. Law of the H. Comm. on the Judiciary (July 15, 2019) (on file with H. Comm. on the Judiciary).

[56] *Online Platforms and Market Power, Part 2: Innovation and Entrepreneurship: Hearing Before the Subcomm. on Antitrust, Commercial and Admin. Law of the H. Comm. on the Judiciary,* 116th Cong. 250 (2019) (Stacy F. Mitchell, Co-Director, Institute for Local Self-Reliance),) [hereinafter Innovation and Entrepreneurship Hearing] https://docs.house.gov/meetings/JU/JU05/20190716/109793/HHRG-116-JU05-Wstate-MitchellS-20190716.pdf.

b. Antitrust Experts

The Committee's final round of outreach to third parties involved sending letters on March 13, 2020, soliciting insights and analysis from several dozen antitrust experts who were identified on a bipartisan basis and whose submissions represent a diverse range of experience and perspectives. In support of the investigation's objective to assess the adequacy of existing antitrust laws, competition policies, and current enforcement levels, the Committee invited submissions on three main topics. The first topic covered the adequacy of existing laws—case law and statutes—that prohibit monopolization and monopolistic conduct. The second topic similarly dealt with the adequacy of existing law, but focused on its sufficiency to address anticompetitive mergers and acquisitions, including vertical and conglomerate mergers, serial acquisitions, data acquisitions, and strategic acquisitions of potential competitors. Third, the Committee sought feedback on whether the institutional structure of antitrust enforcement is adequate to promote the robust enforcement of the antitrust laws, including current levels of appropriations to the antitrust agencies, existing agency authorities, and congressional oversight of enforcement.

c. Additional Outreach and Submissions

In addition to sending the RFIs in September and January, Subcommittee staff engaged in extensive outreach to additional third parties based on public reports and non-public information gathered throughout the investigation, suggesting that such entities had relevant information.

Subcommittee staff also received submissions from numerous individuals and businesses throughout the course of the investigation. These submissions came from a wide range of sources and in a variety of forms. For example, an anonymous source sent thumb drives to the Committee's main office in the Rayburn House Office Building. Other examples included former or current employees submitting tips to the Subcommittee's investigation email address, or through the form for anonymous submissions posted on the Subcommittee's investigation website.

4. Antitrust Agencies Requests for Information

As part of the Committee's September 2019 efforts to gather information, the Committee also sent requests for information to the Federal Trade Commission and the Department of Justice. In part, the Committee sought this information to carry out its function as the principal oversight authority for the Department of Justice, including its component agencies, its personnel, and its law enforcement activities.[57] Similarly, the Committee's jurisdiction extends to the FTC's antitrust-related work, and to administrative practice and procedure, including at the FTC.[58] The Committee's RFIs requested

---

[57] *Government Oversight*, U.S. HOUSE OF REPRESENTATIVES JUDICIARY COMMITTEE, https://judiciary.house.gov/issues/government-oversight/.

[58] RULES OF THE HOUSE OF REPRESENTATIVES, 116th Cong., lst Sess., Rule X, cl. (1)(1)(2) (2019), http://clerk.house.gov/legislative/house-rules.pdf.

documents relating to the agencies' decisions to open or close investigations into potential violations of antitrust law in digital markets, decisions to challenge mergers or conduct in federal district court or in administrative action, and decisions to forego litigation in favor of a settlement agreement.[59] Senior officials from the FTC and the Antitrust Division also provided several briefings to Members of the Subcommittee and staff in response to the requests of the Subcommittee Chairman and Ranking Member. These briefings served as an opportunity for Members to obtain information and updates about the current state of antitrust law and enforcement in digital markets.

B.   Hearings

On June 11, 2019, the Subcommittee held part one of its series of investigation hearings titled "Online Platforms and Market Power, Part 1: The Free and Diverse Press." At this hearing, the Subcommittee heard testimony from the following Majority witnesses: David Chavern, President of the News Media Alliance; Gene Kimmelman, President and CEO of Public Knowledge; Sally Hubbard, Director of Enforcement Strategy at Open Markets Institute (OMI); and Matthew Schruers, Vice President for Law and Policy at Computer and Communications Industry Association (CCIA). The Minority witnesses were David Pitofsky, General Counsel for News Corp; and Kevin Riley, Editor of the *Atlanta-Journal Constitution*.[60]

On July 16, 2019, the Subcommittee held its second hearing, a two-paneled hearing titled "Online Platforms and Market Power, Part 2: Innovation and Entrepreneurship." On the first panel, the Subcommittee heard testimony from the following: Adam Cohen, Director of Economic Policy at Google; Nate Sutton, Associate General Counsel, Competition, at Amazon; Matt Perault, Head of Global Policy Development at Facebook; and Kyle Andeer, Vice President and Corporate Law and Chief Compliance Officer at Apple. On the second panel, the Subcommittee heard testimony from the following Majority witnesses: Timothy Wu, Julius Silver Professor of Law, Science and Technology at Columbia Law School; Fiona Scott Morton, Theodore Nierenberg Professor of Economics at Yale University School of Management; and Stacy Mitchell, Co-Director of the Institute for Local Self-Reliance. On the second panel, the Minority witnesses were Maureen Ohlhausen, Partner at Baker Botts and former Commissioner and Acting Chairwoman of the Federal Trade Commission; Morgan Reed, Executive Director of The App Association; and Carl Szabo, Vice President and General Counsel at NetChoice.[61]

---

[59] Subcommittee staff recognizes that publication of these documents could cause competitive injury to firms that cooperated with prior investigations or in ongoing investigations. Where possible, this Report summarizes or draws conclusions from these sources without reproducing them.

[60] *Online Platforms and Market Power, Part 1: The Free and Diverse Press: Hearing Before the Subcomm. on Antitrust, Commercial and Admin. Law of the H. Comm. on the Judiciary*, 116th Cong. (2019) [hereinafter Free and Diverse Press Hearing] https://judiciary.house.gov/legislation/hearings/online-platforms-and-market-power-part-1-free-and-diverse-press.

[61] *Online Platforms and Market Power, Part 2: Innovation and Entrepreneurship: Hearing Before the Subcomm. on Antitrust, Commercial and Admin. Law of the H. Comm. on the Judiciary*, 116th Cong. (2019) [hereinafter Innovation and Entrepreneurship Hearing] https://judiciary.house.gov/legislation/hearings/online-platforms-and-market-power-part-2-innovation-and-entrepreneurship.

On October 18, 2019, the Subcommittee held its third hearing titled "Online Platforms and Market Power, Part 3: The Role of Data and Privacy in Competition." At this hearing, the Subcommittee heard testimony from the following Majority witnesses: the Honorable Rohit Chopra, Commissioner at the Federal Trade Commission; Dr. Jason Furman, Professor of the Practice of Economic Policy at Harvard Kennedy School and former Chairman of the Council of Economic Advisers (CEA); and Dr. Tommaso Valletti, Professor of Economics and Head of the Department of Economics & Public Policy at Imperial College Business School and former Chief Competition Economist of the European Commission's Directorate General for Competition (DG-Comp). The Minority witness at the hearing was Dr. Roslyn Layton, Visiting Scholar at the American Enterprise Institute.[62]

On November 13, 2019, the Subcommittee held its fourth hearing titled "Online Platforms and Market Power, Part 4: Perspectives of the Antitrust Agencies." At this hearing, the Subcommittee heard testimony from the following witnesses: the Honorable Makan Delrahim, Assistant Attorney General for the Antitrust Division at the Department of Justice; and the Honorable Joseph J. Simons, Chairman of the Federal Trade Commission.[63]

On January 17, 2020, the Subcommittee held its fifth hearing titled "Field Hearing: Online Platforms and Market Power, Part 5: Competitors in the Digital Economy." At this hearing, which took place in the congressional district of Subcommittee Vice Chairman Joe Neguse (D-CO) at the University of Colorado School of Law, the Subcommittee heard testimony from the following Majority witnesses: Patrick Spence, Chief Executive Officer of Sonos; David Barnett, Founder and Chief Executive Officer of PopSockets; and Kirsten Daru, Vice President and General Counsel at Tile. The Minority witness at the hearing was David Heinemeier Hansson, Founder and Chief Technology Officer of Basecamp.[64]

On July 29, 2020, the Subcommittee held its sixth hearing titled "Online Platforms and Market Power, Part 6: Examining the Dominance of Amazon, Apple, Facebook, and Google." At this hearing, the Subcommittee heard testimony from the following witnesses: Jeff Bezos, Chief Executive Officer

---

[62] *Online Platforms and Market Power, Part 3: The Role of Data and Privacy in Competition: Hearing Before the Subcomm. on Antitrust, Commercial and Admin. Law of the H. Comm. on the Judiciary*, 116th Cong. (2019) [hereinafter Data and Privacy Hearing] https://judiciary.house.gov/calendar/eventsingle.aspx?EventID=2248.

[63] *Online Platforms and Market Power, Part 4: Perspectives of the Antitrust Agencies: Hearing Before the Subcomm. on Antitrust, Commercial and Admin. Law of the H. Comm. on the Judiciary*, 116th Cong. (2019) [hereinafter Antitrust Agencies Hearing] https://judiciary.house.gov/calendar/eventsingle.aspx?EventID=2287.

[64] *Online Platforms and Market Power, Part 5: Competitors in the Digital Economy: Hearing Before the Subcomm. on Antitrust, Commercial and Admin. Law of the H. Comm. on the Judiciary*, 116th Cong. (2020) [hereinafter Competitors Hearing] https://judiciary.house.gov/calendar/eventsingle.aspx?EventID=2386.

at Amazon; Sundar Pichai, Chief Executive Officer at Alphabet and Google; Tim Cook, Chief Executive Officer at Apple; and Mark Zuckerberg, Chief Executive Officer at Facebook.[65]

On October 1, 2020, the Subcommittee held its seventh hearing titled "Proposals to Strengthen the Antitrust Laws and Restore Competition Online." The Majority witnesses at the hearing included: William Baer, Visiting Fellow, Brookings Institution, and former Associate Attorney General, Department of Justice; Zephyr Teachout, Associate Professor of Law, Fordham University School of Law; Michael Kades, Director of Markets and Competition Policy, Washington Center for Equitable Growth; Sabeel Rahman, Associate Professor of Law, Brooklyn Law School and President, Demos; and Sally Hubbard, Director of Enforcement Strategy, Open Markets Institute. The Minority witnesses at the hearing were Christopher Yoo, John H. Chestnut Professor of Law, Communication, and Information Science, University of Pennsylvania Carey Law School; and Rachel Bovard, Senior Director of Policy, Conservative Partnership Institute; and Tad Lipsky, Antonin Scalia Law School, George Mason University.[66]

C.   Roundtables

In addition to holding public hearings, the Subcommittee also held a series of bipartisan roundtables for Members of the Subcommittee and staff to provide Members with an opportunity to conduct further oversight of (1) the state of competition and problems in digital markets; (2) whether dominant firms have engaged in anticompetitive conduct; and (3) if antitrust laws, competition policies, and current enforcement levels are adequate to address these issues. In total, the Subcommittee held twelve briefings and roundtables in Washington, DC; four roundtables in Boulder, CO; and a virtual roundtable with stakeholders from Rhode Island and elsewhere in New England.[67]

The Subcommittee hosted multiple briefings and roundtables with experts on the digital economy on a range of topics. Experts included state antitrust enforcers, former officials from the Antitrust Division of the Department of Justice and the Federal Trade Commission, former technology industry executives, small business owners, representatives from the news industry, entrepreneurs, antitrust scholars, representatives from civil society, and representatives from libraries.

The briefings and roundtables covered a broad array of topics related to competition in the digital marketplace. These topics included:

---

[65] *Online Platforms and Market Power, Part 6: Examining the Dominance of Amazon, Apple, Facebook, and Google: Hearing Before the Subcomm. on Antitrust, Commercial and Admin. Law of the H. Comm. on the Judiciary*, 116th Cong. (2020) [hereinafter CEO Hearing] https://judiciary.house.gov/calendar/eventsingle.aspx?EventID=3113.

[66] *Online Platforms and Market Power, Part 7: Proposals to Strengthen the Antitrust Laws and Restore Competition Online: Hearing Before the Subcomm. on Antitrust, Commercial and Admin. Law of the H. Comm. on the Judiciary*, 116th Cong. (2020) [hereinafter Remedies Hearing] https://judiciary.house.gov/calendar/eventsingle.aspx?EventID=3367.

[67] This roundtable was originally scheduled to take place physically as a field hearing in Providence, Rhode Island, but was held virtually due to the COVID-19 pandemic.

- The effect that small algorithm changes by dominant platforms can have on small businesses that rely on the platform;

- The data advantages that dominant online platform companies have over smaller competitors and startups, and how those data advantages can reinforce dominance and serve as a barrier to entry;

- The effect of dominant online platform company power and practices on a free and diverse press and the local newsgathering and reporting;

- The impact of dominant online platform company power and practices on investment in startups by venture capital firms;

- The fear of economic retaliation by dominant platforms against smaller companies that raise concerns about anticompetitive conduct in the digital marketplace;

- Other features of digital markets—including, but not limited to, network effects, economies of scale and scope, and barriers to entry—that make them prone to high concentration and monopolization;

- Enforcement of the antitrust laws; and

- Modernization of antitrust statutes and competition policy.

Additionally, the Subcommittee held briefings also allowed representatives from Google, Amazon, Facebook, and Apple to make their own presentations to Subcommittee staff and to answer questions and provide details regarding their companies' business practices, structures, and strategies in the marketplace.

D.   Prior Investigations

The Subcommittee's current review of competition in the digital marketplace continues a long oversight tradition. Over many decades, the House Judiciary Committee and its antitrust subcommittee have conducted careful, fact-based inquiries into industrial sectors showing signs of undue concentration and anticompetitive conduct. As a 1951 report from the then-named Subcommittee on the Study of Monopoly Power described its mandate, "It is the province of this subcommittee to investigate factors which tend to eliminate competition, strengthen monopolies, injure small business, or promote undue concentration of economic power; to ascertain the facts, and to make recommendations based on those findings."[68]

The Subcommittee followed the same process "to ascertain the facts" in this investigation. It has included hearings with industry and government witnesses, consultations with subject-matter experts, and a careful—and at times painstaking—review of large volumes of evidence provided by industry participants and regulators. Recognizing that antitrust investigations are by their nature fact-dependent, teams of investigators invested significant resources to study the structure of the relevant markets and the important firms in those markets.[69]

The purpose of these exercises was not to supersede the activities of antitrust enforcers such as the Federal Trade Commission (FTC) and the Department of Justice (DOJ), but to compile the Committee's own record about current market conditions; to assess how antitrust laws and principles are being applied in the current business environment; and to determine whether revised laws, or new laws, or better enforcement are needed to protect competition.

While the Committee's investigations were not intended to interfere with the enforcement activities of antitrust enforcers or regulators, they often conducted inquiries into the same sectors and issues that DOJ, the FTC, the Federal Communications Commission (FCC), and other agencies with authority over competition policy or enforcement were also examining. As Members and staff of the Committee charged with the "protection of trade and commerce against unlawful restraints and monopolies,"[70] these investigators exercised their legislative authority to probe any aspect of antitrust that they deemed warranted attention.

These investigations were guided by the principle that "[h]istory has proven that the most conducive environment for innovation and new product availability is a competitive market,"[71] and that a "free competitive economy" is an important American value.[72] It was a value that had been formally embedded in our economy and society by the Sherman Act of 1890, "the peculiarly American

---

[68] *Aluminum: Report of the Subcomm. on Study of Monopoly Power of the H. Comm. on the Judiciary*, 82d Cong., H. REP. NO. 255, 2 (1st Sess. 1951).

[69] *See, e.g.*, *The Ocean Freight Industry: Report of the Antitrust Subcomm. of the H. Comm. on the Judiciary*, 87th Cong., H. Rep. No. 1419, 2 (2d Sess. 1962) [hereinafter *1962 Ocean Freight Industry Report*] (describing how Subcommittee staff spent more than nine months examining "tens of thousands of documents in the files of over 50 ocean-freight conferences" and other materials).

[70] RULES OF THE HOUSE OF REPRESENTATIVES, 116th Cong., lst Sess., Rule X, cl. (1)(1)(16) (2019), http://clerk.house.gov/legislative/house-rules.pdf.

[71] *Antitrust Reform Act of 1992, H. Comm. on the Judiciary*, H. REP. NO. 102-850, 15 (1992) [hereinafter Antitrust Reform Act of 1992].

[72] *The Mobilization Program: Report of the Subcomm. on Study of Monopoly Power of the H. Comm. on the Judiciary*, 82d Cong., H. REP. NO. 1217, at 1 (1st Sess. 1951) [hereinafter *1951* Mobilization Program Report].

charter of economic freedom."[73] In a 1958 report on the airline industry, the then-named Antitrust Subcommittee explained that Americans' social and political freedoms depended on "opportunity for market access and market rivalries in a private-enterprise economy."[74] The "freedom of entry into any industry or field of endeavor," a 1962 Subcommittee report explained, is a cornerstone of U.S. antitrust policy that has "encouraged extensive individual proprietorship . . . and has made our free enterprise system great and strong."[75] A 1992 Committee report recommended restrictions on the monopolistic Regional Bell Operating Companies (RBOCs) "[f]or the sake of the democratic economic and political values which depend on the preservation of free markets."[76]

In some cases, antitrust investigations exposed antitrust problems that the Committee concluded required attention from regulators. For example, a 1958 Antitrust Subcommittee report on the rapidly growing domestic airline industry exposed the behind-the-scenes anticompetitive campaign that incumbent air carriers and their advocacy group, the Air Transport Association of America (ATA), had been waging to prevent the Civil Aeronautics Board (CAB) from approving market entry by new air carriers (known at the time as "nonskeds").[77] The Committee found the conduct of the ATA so egregious that it recommended an investigation by the DOJ Antitrust Division.[78] As for international air transportation, the report concluded that Pan American's dominance in the market was the "result of its use of devices to foreclose competition in order to secure and maintain control over markets in which it does business," and recommended that the CAB undertake a broad investigation of the company.[79]

In other cases, the Committee investigated matters that were currently under review by antitrust enforcers. In a 1957 report on the broadcast television industry, which was quickly reshaping Americans' consumption of news and entertainment, the then-named Antitrust Subcommittee described the anticompetitive tactics CBS and NBC were using to promote their own content at the expense of independent content producers.[80] According to the report, networks were improperly using their power as vertical distributors of content to extract financial concessions from independent competitors seeking to place their programming on network affiliates.[81] There was also evidence that

---

[73] *Id.* at 2.

[74] *The Airlines Industry: Report of the Antitrust Subcomm. of the H. Comm. on the Judiciary*, 85th Cong., H. REP. NO. 1328, at 1 (2d Sess. 1958) [hereinafter 1958 Airlines Industry Report].

[75] 1962 Ocean Freight Industry Report at 394.

[76] *Antitrust Reform Act of 1992, H. Comm. on the Judiciary*, H. REP. NO. 102-850, 10 (1992) [hereinafter Antitrust Reform Act of 1992].

[77] Airlines Industry Report at 268–69.

[78] *Id.* at 272.

[79] *Id.* at 278.

[80] *The Television Broadcasting Industry: Report of the Antitrust Subcomm. of the Comm. on the Judiciary*, 85th Cong., H. REP. NO. 607, at 143 (1st Sess. 1957).

[81] *Id.*

the networks were using their substantial power with advertisers to unfairly favor their own content.[82] After praising the DOJ Antitrust Division's "alertness to vindicate the competitive dictates of the antitrust laws," the Subcommittee urged the Division to press its investigation into this conduct with "vigor and dispatch."[83]

In the case of the Committee's inquiry into the RBOCs' conduct in the aftermath of the 1984 breakup of AT&T, we concluded that federal courts and regulators were not adequately protecting competition in the telecommunications marketplace and that new legislation was necessary. A 1992 Committee report reviewed the long, troubled history of attempts by DOJ and the FCC[84] to check the monopolistic power of AT&T, culminating the in the famous Modified Final Judgment (the "MFJ") that Judge Harold Greene approved in August 1982 to break up the company.[85] But even after the MFJ, the report found, the FCC had failed to prevent the RBOCs from using their local monopolies to commit a number of anticompetitive violations, "many eerily reminiscent of pre-divestiture Bell System abuses."[86] We were also critical of the DOJ's actions to water down the MFJ's procompetitive line-of-business restrictions on the RBOCs. Describing the massive lobbying campaign that the RBOCs were waging to enter the business lines the MFJ had opened up to competitors, we observed, "The thousands upon thousands of competitive enterprises now thriving in information service, telecommunications equipment, and long distance markets face the prospect of their future prosperity being decided by the self-interested designs of a monopoly with 'bottleneck' control over the local telephone exchange on which they all depend."[87] In light of the antitrust agencies' demonstrated failure to protect competition, the Committee approved legislation that would codify the MFJ's line-of-business restrictions into law.[88]

Finally, in these prior investigations, the Committee has not hesitated to recommend that antitrust authorities further investigate suspicious conduct. After examining the conduct of the Air Transport Association of America, the industry group representing the established passenger airline

---

[82] *Id.*

[83] *Id.*

[84] Antitrust Reform Act of 1992 at 39 ("The FCC, while claiming boldly to be a forum where complaints about monopolistic practices would be received and vigorously pursued had, instead, become a regulatory 'graveyard' for telecommunications competition policy, characterized by inaction and equivocation.")

[85] *Id.* at 45.

[86] *Id.* at 51.

[87] Antitrust Reform Act of 1992 at 10. The report explained that the RBOCs' bottleneck, in antitrust terminology, functioned as an "essential facility," which gave them "an inherent ability and – for activities in which they are engaged themselves – a natural incentive to impede competition in lines of business dependent upon that essential facility." *Id.* at 13.

[88] H.R. 5096 (102nd Congress); H.R. 3626 (103rd Congress); *see Antitrust and Communications Reform Act of 1994, H. Comm. on the Judiciary*, H. Rep. No. 103-559, Pt. II at 25 (1994) ("The Judiciary Committee has resolved that the Government not lose its nerve once again and allow an industry born in monopoly to be reborn in monopoly.") The pro-competitive policies proposed in this legislation later became law, in modified form, as part of the Telecommunications Act of 1996. P.L. 104-104, 110 Stat. 56, §§271-6 (codified at 47 U.S.C., §§ 271-76).

carriers in the 1950s, the Antitrust Subcommittee recommended that the Antitrust Division of the Department of Justice further investigate the "serious antitrust problems" it had identified.[89]

III.   BACKGROUND

A. Overview of Competition in Digital Markets

1. The Role of Competition Online

At a fundamental level, competition has been a key engine of economic activity in the United States,[90] resulting in the "pioneering of entire industries that, in time, come to employ millions and generate trillions."[91] This is especially true in the digital economy. As in other industries, competition in digital markets incentivizes incumbent firms and new entrants to build new technologies and improve business processes.[92] It spurs capital investment and incentivizes firms to improve the quality of their offerings.[93] In its absence, incumbent firms lack incentive to invest in research and development.[94] This in turn slows the rate of innovation across industry.[95] Disruptive new products or services are replaced with slow, incremental alterations[96] "designed to protect [incumbent firms']

---

[89] Airlines Industry Report at 272.

[90] Innovation and Entrepreneurship Hearing at 1 (statement of Tim Wu, Julius Silver Prof. of Law, Columbia Univ. School of Law).

[91] *Id.* at 1; Roger McNamee, Co-Founder and Managing Director, Elevation Partners, Remarks at United States Dep't of Justice Antitrust Div. Public Workshop on Venture Capital and Antitrust 34 (Feb. 12, 2020), https://www.justice.gov/atr/page/file/1255851/download ("[T]here is a case that antitrust has in fact been a major catalysis of growth in every wave of technology.").

[92] Antitrust Agencies Hearing at 8 (statement of Makan Delrahim, Ass't Att'y Gen., U.S. Dep't of Justice Antitrust Div.) ("Competition also promotes improvements and upgrades to the quality and functionality of existing offerings."); Jeffrey A. Rosen, Deputy Att'y Gen., U.S. Dep't of Justice, Speech at the Free State Foundation's 12th Annual Telecom Policy Conference (Mar. 10, 2020), https://www.justice.gov/opa/speech/deputy-attorney-general-jeffrey-rosen-speaks-free-state-foundations-12th-annual-telecom; Giulio Federico, Fiona Scott Morton & Carl Shapiro, *Antitrust and Innovation: Welcoming and Protecting Disruption* 1 (Nat'l Bureau of Econ. Res. Working Paper No. 26005, June 2019), https://www.nber.org/papers/w26005.pdf.

[93] Innovation and Entrepreneurship Hearing at 4 (statement of Maureen K. Ohlhausen, Partner, Baker Botts L.L.P.) ("Antitrust law's focus on protecting the competitive process does not mean that it cannot reach many of the competitive concerns. . . [that] may include price effects, reductions in quality, and impacts on innovation, as well as the ability of a dominant player to acquire and neutralize a nascent competitor."); Innovation and Entrepreneurship Hearing at 2 (statement of Fiona Scott Morton, Theodore Nierenberg Prof. of Econs., Yale Sch. of Mgmt.) ("The harms from insufficient competition appear in prices that are higher than competitive prices, quality that is lower than competitive quality, and less innovation than consumers would benefit from in competitive markets.").

[94] Innovation and Entrepreneurship Hearing at 2 (statement of Fiona Scott Morton, Theodore Nierenberg Prof. of Econs, Yale School of Mgmt.).

[95] *See generally* Jeffrey A. Rosen, Deputy Att'y Gen., U.S. Dep't of Justice, Speech at the Free State Foundation's 12th Annual Telecom Policy Conference (Mar. 10, 2020), https://www.justice.gov/opa/speech/deputy-attorney-general-jeffrey-rosen-speaks-free-state-foundations-12th-annual-telecom. (referencing research by economist Kenneth Arrow.).

[96] Data and Privacy Hearing at 3 (statement of Jason Furman, Prof. of the Practice of Econ. Pol'y, Harvard Kennedy School).

existing revenue streams."[97] Slowly but surely, venture capitalists lose the incentive to invest in new entrants willing to challenge the dominance of incumbent firms through direct competition.[98] What we are left with are so-called "kill zones"— the near-complete absence of competition.

The benefits of robust competition in the digital economy goes beyond innovation and productivity. It can also spur firms to compete along other dimensions such as privacy and data protection. As a general matter, inadequate competition not only leads to higher prices and less innovation in many cases, but it can also reduce the quality of goods and services.[99] Given that many digital products do not charge consumers directly for services, these firms often compete on quality.[100] Along these lines, lack of competition can result in eroded privacy and data protection.[101] Growing evidence indicates that a lack of competition goes hand in hand with just such quality degradation.[102]

2. Market Structure

a. Winner-Take-All Markets

Certain features of digital markets—such as network effects, switching costs, the self-reinforcing advantages of data, and increasing returns to scale—make them prone to winner-take-all economics.[103] As a result, many technology markets "tip" in favor of one or two large companies,[104] shifting the "the competitive process from competition *in* the market to

---

[97] Innovation and Entrepreneurship Hearing at 4 (statement of Tim Wu, Julius Silver Prof. of Law, Columbia Univ. School of Law).

[98] Innovation and Entrepreneurship Hearing at 2 (statement of Fiona Scott Morton, Theodore Nierenberg Prof. of Econs., Yale Sch. of Mgmt.). *See also* Sai Krishna Kamepalli, Raghuram Rajan & Luigi Zingales, *Kill Zone* (Univ. of Chicago, Becker Friedman Inst. for Econ. Working Paper No. 2020-19, Apr. 2020), https://ssrn.com/abstract=3555915.

[99] Data and Privacy Hearing at 4 (statement of Tommaso Valletti, Prof. of Econs., Imperial College Bus. Sch.) ("Quality, choice, and innovation are also important aspects for competition and for consumer welfare."); Innovation and Entrepreneurship Hearing at 2–4 (statement of Maureen K. Ohlhausen, Partner, Baker Botts L.L.P.).

[100] *Id.* at 3 (statement of Rohit Chopra, Comm'r, Fed. Trade Comm'n) ("These services do have a price, and you are paying for them with your data."); Data and Privacy Hearing at 3 (statement of Jason Furman, Prof. of the Practice of Econ. Pol'y, Harvard Kennedy School) ("Consumers may think they are receiving 'free' products but they are paying a price for these products in a number of ways.").

[101] Innovation and Entrepreneurship Hearing at 4 (statement of Maureen K. Ohlhausen, Partner, Baker Botts L.L.P.); Data and Privacy Hearing at 3–4 (statement of Jason Furman, Prof. of the Practice of Econ. Pol'y, Harvard Kennedy School); Data and Privacy Hearing at 1 (statement of George Slover, Justin Brookman & Jonathan Schwantes) ("[A] dominant platform can disregard the interests of consumers in protecting their privacy, and design their platform to maximize its ability to monitor, monetize, and manipulate our personal interactions as consumers and as citizens.").

[102] Data and Privacy Hearing at 5 (statement of Tommaso Valletti, Prof. of Econs., Imperial College Bus. Sch.).

[103] Data and Privacy Hearing at 2 (statement of Jason Furman, Prof. of the Practice of Econ. Pol'y, Harvard Kennedy School) (Other anticompetitive practices in digital markets—such as product design, self-preferencing, and anti-competitive contracting, among others—may also contribute to barriers that impede entry by rivals or new firms. While these issues are also present in other markets, they are much more pronounced in digital markets.)

[104] *Id.*

competition *for* the market."[105] In turn, high barriers to entry may diminish the ability of new firms to challenge incumbent firms, further undermining the competitive process and protecting the dominance of existing firms.[106] As the United Kingdom's Competition and Markets Authority explains:

> [I]f potential competitors face substantial barriers to entry and expansion, such that the market is no longer properly contestable, then a high market share can translate into market power, giving the platform the opportunity to increase prices, reduce quality or leverage market power to undermine competition in potentially competitive markets and deny innovative rivals the chance to bring new services to market.[107]

b. Market Concentration

Consistent with winner-take-all dynamics, the digital economy is highly concentrated.[108] A number of key markets online—such as social media, general online search, and online advertising— are dominated by just one or two firms.[109] In some instances, this concentration is the result of a high volume of acquisitions by the dominant digital platforms. Together, the largest technology firms have acquired hundreds of companies in the last ten years.[110] Antitrust enforcers in the United States did not block any of these transactions,[111] many of which eliminated actual or potential competitors.[112] In some instances these acquisitions enabled the dominant firm to neutralize a competitive threat; in other instances, the dominant firm shut down or discontinued the underlying product entirely—transactions aptly described as "killer acquisitions."[113]

---

[105] Stigler Report at 29, 35.

[106] Data and Privacy Hearing at 2–3 (statement of Jason Furman, Prof. of the Practice of Econ. Pol'y, Harvard Kennedy School).

[107] COMPETITION & MKTS. AUTH., ONLINE PLATFORMS AND DIGITAL ADVERTISING, MARKET STUDY FINAL REPORT 10–11 (2020) [hereinafter Competition & Mkts. Auth. Report].

[108] Data and Privacy Hearing at 1 (statement of Jason Furman, Prof. of the Practice of Econ. Pol'y, Harvard Kennedy School).

[109] *Id.* at 2; Innovation and Entrepreneurship Hearing at 3 (statement of Tim Wu, Julius Silver Prof. of Law, Columbia Univ. School of Law).

[110] Tim Wu & Stuart A. Thompson, *The Roots of Big Tech Run Disturbingly Deep*, N.Y. TIMES (June 7, 2019), https://www.nytimes.com/interactive/2019/06/07/opinion/google-facebook-mergers-acquisitions-antitrust.html; *see* *"Visualizing Tech Giants' Billion-Dollar Acquisitions,"* CB INSIGHTS (May 5, 2020) https://perma.cc/KJD9-HT3Z.

[111] Although several transactions, including Google's acquisition of ITA in 2010, were subject to settlements, U.S. antitrust enforcers did not attempt to prevent the consummation of these transactions.

[112] Tim Wu & Stuart A. Thompson, *The Roots of Big Tech Run Disturbingly Deep*, N.Y. TIMES (June 7, 2019), https://www.nytimes.com/interactive/2019/06/07/opinion/google-facebook-mergers-acquisitions-antitrust.html; Carl Shapiro, *Antitrust in a Time of Populism*, 61 INT'L J. INDUS. ORG. 714, 739–40 (2018), https://faculty.haas.berkeley.edu/shapiro/antitrustpopulism.pdf.

[113] Colleen Cunningham, Florian Ederer & Song Ma, *Killer Acquisitions* at 1 (Yale Sch. of Mgmt. Working Paper, Apr. 2020), https://ssrn.com/abstract=3241707 (describing the practice whereby "an incumbent firm may acquire an innovative target and terminate the development of the target's innovations to preempt future competition."). *See also* C. Scott

Evidence also suggests that the venture capital industry, which plays a critical role in funding innovative startups, contributes to market consolidation by encouraging startups to exit via a sale to an incumbent firm.[114] As initial public offerings (IPOs) have become more expensive and time-consuming in recent decades, venture capitalists have shown a preference for realizing their investments through acquisitions rather than through public markets.[115]

c. The Role of Online Platforms as Gatekeepers

As Amazon, Apple, Facebook, and Google have captured control over key channels of distribution, they have come to function as gatekeepers. A large swath of businesses across the U.S. economy now depend on these gatekeepers to access users and markets. In interviews with Subcommittee staff, numerous businesses described how dominant platforms exploit this gatekeeper power to dictate terms and extract concessions that third parties would not consent to in a competitive market.[116] According to these companies, these types of concessions and demands carry significant economic harm but are "the cost of doing business" given the lack of options.

Their role as gatekeepers also gives the dominant platforms outsized power to control the fates of other businesses. Reflecting this fact, several major publicly owned firms that rely on the dominant platforms have noted in investor statements that this dependent relationship creates an inherent risk to their businesses.[117] For example, Lyft, a ride-sharing company, has cited its use of Amazon's cloud services and Google Maps as a potential risk to its business model.[118] As Lyft stated in a filing, "Some of our competitors or technology partners may take actions which disrupt the interoperability of our platform with their own products or services."[119] Pinterest, a photo-sharing service, likewise noted in a financial filing that changes to Google's search algorithm may harm Pinterest. As it noted, Pinterest's "ability to maintain and increase the number of visitors directed to our service from search engines is not within our control. Search engines, such as Google, may modify their search algorithms and

---

Hemphill & Tim Wu, *Nascent Competitors*, 168 U. PA. L. REV. (forthcoming 2020) (manuscript at 2), https://perma.cc/62HH-34ZL ("A nascent competitor is a firm whose prospective innovation represents a serious future threat to an incumbent.").

[114] Mark Lemley & Andrew McCreary, *Exit Strategy* at 24–45 (Stanford Law & Economics Olin Working Paper No. 542, Jan. 2020), https://ssrn.com/abstract=3506919.

[115] *Id.*

[116] *See infra* Section V.

[117] Gerrit De Vynck, *The Power of Google and Amazon Looms Over Tech IPOs*, BLOOMBERG (July 1, 2019), https://www.bloomberg.com/news/articles/2019-07-01/google-s-and-amazon-s-power-looms-over-procession-of-tech-ipos (noting that 17 of 22 initial public offerings by technology companies cited online platforms as competitors or risks to their businesses).

[118] *Id.*

[119] *Id.*

policies or enforce those policies in ways that are detrimental to us."[120] In submissions and interviews with Subcommittee staff, many companies reiterated the general concern that a single act or decision by one of the dominant platforms could wreck their businesses.

Since the dominant platforms in many cases have also integrated into adjacent lines of business, these firms operate both as key intermediaries for third-party companies as well as direct competitors to them. Numerous entrepreneurs, small businesses, and major companies told Subcommittee staff that the dominant platforms' dual role raises significant competition concerns.[121] In recent years, significant reporting has documented how the dominant platforms can exploit this dual role, through data exploitation,[122] self-preferencing,[123] appropriation of key technologies,[124] and abrupt changes to a platform's policies.[125] The Subcommittee's investigation uncovered numerous examples of this exploitative conduct, suggesting that these are increasingly systemic, rather than isolated, business practices.

3. Barriers to Entry

a. Network Effects

Digital markets tend to be characterized by strong network effects, making them prone to concentration and monopolization.[126] There are two types of network effects: direct and indirect. In markets with direct network effects, the more people who use a product or service, the more valuable that product or service becomes to other users.[127] By contrast, indirect network effects arise when

---

[120] *Id.*

[121] *See infra* Section V.

[122] *See* Press Release, Eur. Comm'n, Antitrust: Commission opens investigation into possible anti-competitive conduct of Amazon (July 17, 2019), https://ec.europa.eu/commission/presscorner/detail/en/IP_19_4291 ("Based on the Commission's preliminary fact-finding, Amazon appears to use competitively sensitive information – about marketplace sellers, their products and transactions on the marketplace.").

[123] Tripp Mickle, *Apple Dominates App Store Search Results, Thwarting Competitors*, WALL ST. J. (July 23, 2019), https://www.wsj.com/articles/apple-dominates-app-store-search-results-thwarting-competitors-11563897221.

[124] Jack Nicas & Daisuke Wakabayashi, *Sonos, Squeezed by the Tech Giants, Sues Google*, N.Y. TIMES (Jan. 7, 2020), https://www.nytimes.com/2020/01/07/technology/sonos-sues-google.html.

[125] Reed Albergotti, *Apple says recent changes to operating system improve user privacy, but some lawmakers see them as an effort to edge out its rivals*, WASH. POST (Nov. 26, 2019), https://www.washingtonpost.com/technology/2019/11/26/apple-emphasizes-user-privacy-lawmakers-see-it-an-effort-edge-out-its-rivals/; Jason Del Rey, *An Amazon revolt could be brewing as the tech giant exerts more control over brands*, Vox: RECODE (Nov. 29, 2018), https://www.vox.com/2018/11/29/18023132/amazon-brand-policy-changes-marketplace-control-one-vendor.

[126] JAY SHAMBAUGH, RYAN NUNN, AUDREY BREITWISER & PATRICK LIU, BROOKINGS INST., THE STATE OF COMPETITION AND DYNAMISM: FACTS ABOUT CONCENTRATION, START-UPS, AND RELATED POLICIES, 10 (June 2018), https://www.brookings.edu/wp-content/uploads/2018/06/ES_THP_20180611_CompetitionFacts_20180611.pdf.

[127] *See* Luigi Zingales & Guy Rolnik, *A Way To Own Your Social-Media Data*, N.Y. TIMES (June 30, 2017), https://www.nytimes.com/2017/06/30/opinion/social-data-google-facebook-europe.html.

greater use of a product or service forms a new type of standard and increases the incentive for third parties to invest in developing compatible technologies, which in turn reinforces the popularity of the original product or service with users.[128]

Online platforms display strong network effects because they connect disparate market segments. For example, online commerce platforms like Amazon connect buyers and sellers. Just as with social networks, the value of Amazon marketplace increases as more users—both sellers and buyers—engage with the platform.[129] Similarly, the value of online platforms that facilitate advertising, such as Google, increases with the number of users, as advertisers gain access to a larger consumer base and therefore to a larger trove of consumer data.[130]

Similarly, social networks like Facebook exhibit powerful direct network effects because they become more valuable as more users engage with the network—no person wants to be on a social network without other users.[131] Meanwhile, once a firm captures a network it can become extremely difficult to dislodge or replace. As Mark Zuckerberg explained to then-CFO David Ebersman the benefits that would accrue to Facebook from acquiring Instagram:

> [T]here are network effects around social products and a finite number of different social mechanics to invent. Once someone wins at a specific mechanic, it's difficult for others to supplant them without doing something different. It's possible someone beats Instagram by building something that is better to the point that they get network migration, but this is harder as long as Instagram keeps running as a product.[132]

Strong network effects serve as a powerful barrier to entry for new firms to enter a market and displace the incumbent.[133] When combined with other entry barriers such as restrictions on consumers or businesses easily switching services, network effects all but ensure not just market concentration but durable market power.[134]

b. Switching Costs

Switching costs present another barrier for potential market entrants. In many cases, large technology firms can maintain market power in part because it is not easy for users to switch away

---

[128] Maurice E. Stucke & Allen P. Grunes, Big Data and Competition Policy 163 (2016).

[129] *Id.*

[130] *Id.*

[131] Stigler Report at 38.

[132] Production of Facebook, to H. Comm. on the Judiciary, FB-HJC-ACAL-00063222 (Feb. 27, 2012), https://judiciary.house.gov/uploadedfiles/0006322000063223.pdf.

[133] *See* Stigler Report at 40.

[134] *See* Dig. Competition Expert Panel Report at 35.

from the incumbent's technology. A market exhibits "lock-in" when switching costs are sufficiently high that users stay with an incumbent firm rather than switch to a firm whose product or service they would prefer.[135] Over time, lock-in tends to reduce competition, deter market entry, and may even worsen data privacy.[136]

High switching costs are a central feature of digital search and social media platforms, such as Google and Facebook, where users contribute data to the platform but may not be able to migrate that data to a competing platform. For example, a user may upload a variety of data to Facebook, including photos and personal information, but may not be able to easily download that data and move it to another social media site; instead, the user would have to start from scratch, re-uploading her photos and re-entering her personal information to the new platform.[137] An online seller who has generated hundreds of product reviews and ratings on Amazon may face a similar challenge when considering migrating to a different platform. Other significant factors that contribute to switching costs in digital markets include anticompetitive contracting terms, default settings, product design that favor dominant platforms.[138]

c. Data

The accumulation of data can serve as another powerful barrier to entry for firms in the digital economy. Data allows companies to target advertising with scalpel-like precision, improve services and products through a better understanding of user engagement and preferences, and more quickly identify and exploit new business opportunities.[139]

Much like a network effect, data-rich accumulation is self-reinforcing. Companies with superior access to data can use that data to better target users or improve product quality, drawing more users and, in turn, generating more data—an advantageous feedback loop.[140] In short, new users and greater engagement brings in more data, which enables firms to improve user experiences and develop

---

[135] MAURICE E. STUCKE & ALLEN P. GRUNES, BIG DATA AND COMPETITION POLICY 159 (2016).

[136] *Id.*

[137] Data and Privacy Hearing at 3 (statement of Dina Srinivasan, Fellow, Yale Thurman Arnold Project).

[138] Dig. Competition Expert Panel Report at 36. Unlike the European Union, which provides internet users with a right to data portability, the U.S. does not have any law requiring online platforms to make data portable. Platforms like Google and Facebook are therefore largely uninhibited in imposing switching costs for users, hurting competition in the process. Allen St. John, *Europe's GDPR Brings Data Portability to U.S. Consumers*, CONSUMER. REPS. (May 25, 2018), https://www.consumerreports.org/privacy/gdpr-brings-data-portability-to-us-consumers; *see* Chris Dixon, *The Interoperability of Social Networks*, BUS. INSIDER (Nov. 10, 2010), https://www.businessinsider.com/the-interoperability-of-social-networks-2011-2; Josh Constine, *Friend Portability Is the Must-Have Facebook Regulation*, TECHCRUNCH (May 12, 2019), https://technologycrunch.com/2019/05/12/friends-wherever.

[139] Dig. Competition Expert Panel Report at 23.

[140] Maurice E. Stucke, *Should We Be Concerned About Data-opolies?*, 2 GEO. L. TECH. REV. 275, 323 (2018) (discussing the dynamics of data-driven network effects).

new products—in turn capturing more data.[141] While data is non-rivalrous—meaning that one party's use does not prevent or diminish use by another—firms may nonetheless exclude rivals from using their data through technical restrictions and legal contracts.[142] These exclusionary tactics can close off markets and shield incumbents from competition.[143]

In addition to serving as a barrier to entry, superior access to data can enable and exacerbate anticompetitive conduct in digital markets. This is particularly true when a dominant platform operates as both a marketplace for third-party goods as well as a seller of its own products on that same marketplace.[144] Through this dual role, a dominant platform can mine commercially valuable information from third-party businesses to benefit its own competing products.[145] Additionally, a dominant platform can use its market power to extract more data from users, undermining their privacy.[146]

Persistent data collection can also create information asymmetries and grant firms access to non-public information that gives them a significant competitive edge. These insights include information on user behavior as well as on broader usage trends that enable the dominant platforms to track nascent competitive threats. In an interview with Subcommittee staff, a senior executive at a social media company referred to this ability as akin to having "a spy camera on the production floor" of a competitive threat.[147] Roger McNamee, the Co-Founder of Elevation Partners, has noted that the dominant platforms' role as digital infrastructure gives them both leverage and insights that other competitors lack:

> Essentially, the interplay of Google's dominant position in … infrastructure elements [such as] ad tech infrastructure, Chrome browser, [and Nest] … collectively provide leverage over other market participants, which include not just startups, but also advertisers, and other would-be competitors. And the key thing is, it's not just about Google's infrastructure. When you add in Gmail, Search, Maps, apps, and all the other things that Google does so well … [t]hey provide further levels of user lock-in—further

---

[141] MAURICE E. STUCKE & ALLEN P. GRUNES, BIG DATA AND COMPETITION POLICY 36–50 (2016); PATRICK BARWISE & LEO WATKINS, *The Evolution of Digital Dominance: How and Why We Got to GAFA, in* DIGITAL DOMINANT: THE POWER OF GOOGLE, AMAZON, FACEBOOK, AND APPLE 28–29 (2018), http://www.lse.ac.uk/law/Assets/Documents/orla-lynskey/orla-3.pdf.

[142] MAURICE E. STUCKE & ALLEN P. GRUNES, BIG DATA AND COMPETITION POLICY 23–34 (2016).

[143] *Id.* at 34 (2016).

[144] JACQUES CRÉMER, YVES-ALEXANDRE DE MONJOYE & HEIKE SCWHEITZER, EUR. COMM'N, COMPETITION POLICY FOR THE DIGITAL ERA 66–67 (2019) [hereinafter Eur. Comm'n Competition Report].

[145] *Id.* at 66.

[146] *See* Dina Srinivasan, *The Antitrust Case Against Facebook: A Monopolist's Journey Towards Pervasive Surveillance in Spite of Consumers' Preference for Privacy*, 16 BERKELEY BUS. L.J. 39, 70 (2019); Data and Privacy Hearing at 1 (statement of Dina Srinivasan, Fellow, Yale Thurman Arnold Project).

[147] Interview with Source 247 (June 4, 2020).

43

protective modes that really limit the opportunity of competitors and even, frankly, suppliers and advertisers, to do the things that they should be able to do in a freely competitive economy.[148]

This significant data advantage also enables dominant platforms to identify and acquire rivals early in their lifecycle. Leading economists and antitrust experts have expressed concern that serial acquisitions of nascent competitors by large technology firms have stifled competition and innovation.[149] This acquisition strategy exploits dominant firms' information advantages in order to acquire rapidly growing companies just before those companies become true threats.[150] Lacking access to this same information or failing to appreciate its significance, enforcers may fail to identify these acquisitions as anticompetitive. This is more likely when the dominant platform buys a nascent threat before it has fully developed into a rival.

In a briefing before Members of the Subcommittee, Jonathan Sallet, former Deputy Assistant Attorney General at the Antitrust Division, explained that data-driven acquisitions of nascent or potential rivals can significantly undermine competition while systematically evading antitrust scrutiny.[151] One reason is that upstart competitors are often data-rich but cash-poor, a combination that is unlikely under a price-centric framework to trigger antitrust scrutiny if the acquisition is priced below the relevant threshold for merger review.[152] For example, had Microsoft sought to exploit its monopoly power in the market for personal computer operating systems by *acquiring* Netscape— rather than by foreclosing it—it is unlikely that antitrust enforcers would have taken action. He noted that this the type of acquisition can tip the market in favor of a dominant firm, having the same ultimate effect as monopolistic conduct but escaping the antitrust enforcement that monopolistic conduct has triggered in the past.[153]

---

[148] Roger McNamee, Co-Founder and Managing Dir., Elevation Partners, Remarks at U.S. Dep't of Justice Antitrust Div. Public Workshop on Venture Capital and Antitrust 30 (Feb. 12, 2020), https://www.justice.gov/atr/page/file/1255851/download.

[149] *See, e.g.*, Stigler Report at 74, 87.

[150] *See* Maurice E. Stucke, *Should We Be Concerned About Data-opolies?*, 2 GEO. L. TECH. REV. 275, 309 (2018) (discussing the growing concern with "kill zone" tactics and the chilling effect on "entrepreneurism and autonomy").

[151] Briefing by Jonathan Sallet, Deputy Ass't Att'y Gen., U.S. Dep't of Justice, Antitrust Div. (July 11, 2020).

[152] Colleen Cunningham, Florian Ederer & Song Ma, *Killer Acquisitions* at 53 (Yale Sch. of Mgmt. Working Paper, Apr. 2020), https://ssrn.com/abstract=3241707 (finding that killer acquisitions "routinely avoid regulatory scrutiny" because they "disproportionately occur just below [HSR] thresholds for antitrust scrutiny").

[153] Jonathan Sallet, *Competitive Edge: Five Building Blocks For Antitrust Success: The Forthcoming FTC Competition Report*, WASH. CTR. FOR EQUITABLE GROWTH (Oct. 1, 2019), https://equitablegrowth.org/competitive-edge-five-building-blocks-for-antitrust-success-the-forthcoming-ftc-competition-report/.

d. Economies of Scale and Scope

Increasing returns to scale are another feature of technology markets that make them prone to tip towards concentration and monopolization.[154] In markets with increasing returns to scale, as sales increase, average unit cost decreases.[155] Because entry into these markets requires significant up-front costs, the market favors firms that are already large, making it difficult for new firms to enter the market and challenge large incumbents.[156]

Likewise, a dominant firm that enjoys economies of scope can extend its reach across adjacent markets through an expansive ecosystem of its own products while incurring relatively low cost.[157] For example, if a firm has sufficient technical expertise or access to consumer data, the cost of applying this resource into a new market is relatively low.

Businesses that specialize in providing information, such as Google, frequently benefit from increasing returns to scale.[158] These businesses require high upfront fixed costs, but then may scale with relatively low increases in cost. For example, "Google can update Google Calendar for 100 million users with similar fixed expenses as would be needed for only a fraction of such users."[159] Facebook is another company that benefits from increasing returns to scale.[160] Although building the Facebook platform required a large upfront investment, the platform was able to grow exponentially with relatively little increase in costs. With the benefit of increasing returns to scale, Facebook was able to grow from one million users in 2004, the year of its founding, to more than 350 million users in only five years.[161]

Recent economic evidence indicates that economies of scale achieved through data collection allow platforms to get more out of consumers than consumers get out of platforms.[162] In exchange for "free" services, users provide valuable *social* data—information that may also shed light about other people's behavior—in addition to their own *personal* information. For instance, a person's location

---

[154] Innovation and Entrepreneurship Hearing at 81 (Fiona Scott Morton, Theodore Nierenberg Prof. of Econs., Yale Sch. of Mgmt.); Dig. Competition Expert Panel Report at 32; Stigler Report at 13; *see also* JAY SHAMBAUGH, RYAN NUNN, AUDREY BREITWIESER & PATRICK LIU, THE BROOKINGS INST., THE STATE OF COMPETITION AND DYNAMISM: FACTS ABOUT CONCENTRATION, START-UPS, AND RELATED POLICIES 10 (June 2018), https://www.brookings.edu/wp-content/uploads/2018/06/ES_THP_20180611_CompetitionFacts_20180611.pdf

[155] Stigler Report at 36.

[156] Dig. Competition Expert Panel Report at 32.

[157] *Id.*

[158] Stigler Report at 37.

[159] *Id.*

[160] *Id.*

[161] *Id.* at 36–37.

[162] *See generally* Dirk Bergemann, Alessandro Bonatti & Tan Gan, *The Economics of Social Data* (Cowles Foundation Discussion Paper No. 2203R Sept. 2019), https://ssrn.com/abstract=3459796.

history using Google Maps reveals valuable and sensitive information about others as well—such as traffic patterns and other data. According to Professors Dirk Bergemann, Alessandro Bonatti, and Tan Gan, the creation of this "data externality" means that, for firms like Google, Amazon, and Facebook, "the cost of acquiring … individual data can be substantially below the value of the information to the platform."[163] In other words, notwithstanding claims that services such as Google's Search or Maps products or Facebook are "free" or have immeasurable economic value to consumers,[164] the social data gathered through these services may exceed their economic value to consumers.

B.   Effects of Platform Market Power

1. Innovation and Entrepreneurship

Competition is a critical source of innovation, business dynamism, entrepreneurship, and the "launching of new industries."[165] Vigorously contested markets have been a critical competitive asset for the United States over the past century.[166] While large firms with significant resources may invest in research and development for new products and services, competition forces companies to "run faster" in order to offer improved products and services.[167] Without competitive pressure, some level of innovation may still occur, but at a slower, iterative pace than would be present under competitive market conditions.[168]

In recent decades, however, there has been a sharp decline in new business formation as well as early-stage startup funding.[169] The number of new technology firms in the digital economy has declined,[170] while the entrepreneurship rate—the share of startups and young firms in the industry as a

---

[163] *Id.* at 4.

[164] *See, e.g.*, Erik Brynjolfsson & Avinash Collis, *How Should We Measure the Digital Economy?*, HARV. BUS. REV. (Nov.–Dec. 2019), https://hbr.org/2019/11/how-should-we-measure-the-digital-economy.

[165] Innovation and Entrepreneurship Hearing at 1 (statement of Tim Wu, Julius Silver Prof. of Law, Columbia Univ. School of Law).

[166] *Id.*

[167] Stigler Report at 74.

[168] Innovation and Entrepreneurship Hearing at 1 (statement of Tim Wu, Julius Silver Prof. of Law, Columbia Univ. School of Law).

[169] This is trend is also present in the broader U.S. economy as well. *See, e.g.*, Ufuk Akcigit & Sina T. Ates, *Knowledge in the Hands of the Best, Not the Rest: The Decline of U.S. Business Dynamism*, VOXEU (July 4, 2019), https://voxeu.org/article/decline-us-business-dynamism.

[170] IAN HATHWAY, EWING MARION KAUFFMAN FOUND., TECH STARTS: HIGH-TECHNOLOGY BUSINESS FORMATION AND JOB CREATION IN THE UNITED STATES 5 (2013), https://www.kauffman.org/-/media/kauffman_org/research-reports-and-covers/2013/08/bdstechnologystartsreport.pdf.

whole—has also fallen significantly in this market.[171] Unsurprisingly, there has also been a sharp reduction in early-stage funding for technology startups.[172]

The rates of entrepreneurship and job creation have also declined over this period. The entrepreneurship rate—defined as the "share of startups and young firms" in the industry as a whole— fell from 60% in 1982 to a low of 38% as of 2011.[173] As entry slows, the average age of technology firms has skewed older.[174] Job creation in the high-technology sector has likewise slowed considerably.[175] In 2000, the job creation rate in the high-technology sector was approaching 20% year-over-year. Within a decade, the rate had halved to about 10%.[176] Although the job creation rate in the high-technology sector has fallen substantially since the early 2000s, the job destruction rate in 2011 was roughly unchanged from 2000.[177] As a result, in 2011 the rate of job destruction in the high-technology sector was higher than the rate of job creation, a reversal from the year 2000, when the job-creation rate far outpaced the job-destruction rate.[178]

In line with this trend, there is mounting evidence that the dominance of online platforms has materially weakened innovation and entrepreneurship in the U.S. economy.[179] Some venture capitalists, for example, report that they avoid funding entrepreneurs and other companies that compete directly with dominant firms in the digital economy.[180]

Often referred to as an innovation "kill zone," this trend may insulate powerful incumbent firms from competitive pressure simply because venture capitalists do not view new entrants as good

---

[171] *Id.*

[172] The number of technology startup financings fell from above 10,000 startup financings in 2015 to just above 6,000 in 2018. In 2014, startups closed 4,255 deals in which they raised seed money from investors. By 2018, however, that figure had dropped by nearly a half, to 2,206. Gené Teare, *Decade in Review: Trends in Seed- and Early-Stage Funding*, TECHCRUNCH (Mar. 13, 2019), https://technologycrunch.com/2019/03/16/decade-in-review-trends-in-seed-and-early-stage-funding. *See also American Technology Giants Are Making Life Tough for Startups*, THE ECONOMIST (June 2, 2018), https://www.economist.com/business/2018/06/02/american-technology-giants-are-making-life-tough-for-startups.

[173] John Haltiwanger, et al., *Declining Business Dynamism in the U.S. High-Technology Sector* at 8, EWING MARION KAUFFMAN FOUND. (Feb. 2014), https://www.kauffman.org/-/media/kauffman_org/research-reports-and-covers/2014/02/declining_business_dynamism_in_us_high_technology_sector.pdf.

[174] *Id.*

[175] *Id.*

[176] *Id.* at 4.

[177] *Id.* at 5.

[178] *Id.* at 4.

[179] Innovation and Entrepreneurship Hearing at 1 (statement of Tim Wu, Julius Silver Prof. of Law, Columbia Univ. School of Law); Data and Privacy Hearing at 1–3 (statement of Jason Furman, Prof. of the Practice of Econ. Pol'y, Harvard Kennedy School).

[180] *See generally* Venture Capital and Antitrust Workshop; Stigler Report at 9.

investments.[181] Albert Wenger, the managing partner of Union Square Ventures, commented that the "scale of these companies and their impact on what can be funded, and what can succeed, is massive."[182] Paul Arnold, an early-stage investor and founder of Switch Ventures, commented at the Justice Department's recent workshop on the intersection between venture capital and antitrust law that he considers markets dominated by large platforms to be kill zones.[183] He explained:

> [T]here's an incredibly, concentrated market share because of the economies of scale or because of network effects, it's a really hard barrier to overcome. And sometimes there's an answer and often, that will kill things. And I think that that's my view, that's my, sort of, lived experience as a venture investor, but I think it's a common view of a lot of venture investors.[184]

In the same vein, Mr. Arnold said in a submission to the Subcommittee that:

> Venture capitalists are less likely to fund startups that compete against monopolies' core products … As a startup investor, I see this often. For example, I will meet yet another founder who wants to disrupt Microsoft's LinkedIn. They will have a clever plan to build a better professional social network. I always pass on the investment. It is nearly impossible to overcome the monopoly LinkedIn enjoys. It is but one example of an innovation kill zone.[185]

> For example, the entrenched power of firms with weak privacy protections has created a kill zone around the market for products that enhance privacy online .[186] To the extent that a firm successfully offers a service to give people tools to control their privacy, "Google or Facebook are going to want to pull that back as fast as they possibly can. They don't want you aggressively limiting their extremely valuable information collection."[187]

Other prominent venture capitalists, such as Roger McNamee, the Co-Founder of Elevation Partners, have commented that these trends harm more than just startups. The advantage of dominant

---

[181] Raghuram Rajan, Sai Krishna Kamepalli & Luigi Zingales, *Kill Zone* (Becker Friedman Institute Working Paper No. 2020-19 2020), https://ssrn.com/abstract=3555915.

[182] Asher Schechter, *Google and Facebook's "Kill Zone": "We've Taken the Focus Off of Rewarding Genius and Innovation to Rewarding Capital and Scale,"* PROMARKET (May 25, 2018), https://promarket.org/2018/05/25/google-facebooks-kill-zone-weve-taken-focus-off-rewarding-genius-innovation-rewarding-capital-scale/.

[183] Venture Capital and Antitrust Workshop Transcript at 24 (statement of Paul Arnold, Founder and Partner, Switch Partners).

[184] *Id.*

[185] Submission from Paul Arnold, General Partner, Switch Ventures, to H. Comm. on the Judiciary, 2 (Sept. 3, 2020) (on file with Comm.).

[186] Venture Capital and Antitrust Workshop Transcript at 24 (Paul Arnold, Founder and Partner, Switch Partners).

[187] *Id.*

firms online—access to competitively significant sources of data, network effects, intellectual property, and excess capital—are "a barrier to a wide range of activities, not just startups, but actually a lot of other market participants."[188]

Merger activity may be another contributor to reduced venture capital investment of startups. In a recent study, several leading economists and researchers at the University of Chicago—Raghuram G. Rajan, Luigi Zingales, and Sai Krishna Kamepalli—found that major acquisitions by larger firms in sectors of the digital economy led to significantly less investment in startups in this same sector.[189] As they note, in the wake of an acquisition by Facebook or Google, investments in startups in the same space "drop by over 40% and the number of deals falls by over 20% in the three years following an acquisition."[190]

The threat of entry from a large platform has had significant effects on other firms' incentives to innovate,[191] while the actual entry of the larger online platform can result in less innovation and an additional increase in prices.[192] During the investigation, Subcommittee staff interviewed a prominent venture capital investor in the cloud marketplace who explained that this power imbalance creates a strong economic incentive for other firms to avoid head-on competition. As he noted:

> I think of Amazon as the sun. It is useful but also dangerous. If you're far enough away you can bask. If you get too close you'll get incinerated. So, you have to be far enough from Amazon and be doing something that they wouldn't do. If you're a net consumer of Amazon's infrastructure, like Uber, then you're okay. As long as Amazon doesn't want to get into ridesharing. But it's hard to predict what Amazon wants to get into. If they were going to stop at retail and computing, you're safe. But you can't know.[193]

As discussed in this Report, other behavior by dominant firms—such as cloning the products of new entrants—may also undermine the likelihood that new entrants will be able to compete directly or that early adopters will switch to a new entrant's product, lowering the valuation of these companies as well as their profitability.[194]

---

[188] *Id.* at 29 (statement of Roger McNamee, Co-Founder and Managing Dir., Elevation Partners).

[189] Raghuram Rajan, Sai Krishna Kamepalli & Luigi Zingales, *Kill Zone* at 5 (Becker Friedman Institute Working Paper No. 2020-19, 2020), https://ssrn.com/abstract=3555915.

[190] *Id.*

[191] *See* Wen Wen & Feng Zhu, *Threat of Platform-Owner Entry and Complementor Responses: Evidence from the Mobile App Market*, 40 STRATEGIC MGMT. J. 1336 (2019); Feng Zhu & Qihong Liu, *Competing with Complementors: An Empirical Look at Amazon.com*, 39 STRATEGIC MGMT. J. 2618 (2018).

[192] *Id.*

[193] Interview with Source 146 (May 28, 2020).

[194] Raghuram Rajan, Sai Krishna Kamepalli & Luigi Zingales, *Kill Zone* at 5 (Becker Friedman Institute Working Paper No. 2020-19, 2020), https://ssrn.com/abstract=3555915.

In July 2019, the Subcommittee held a hearing to examine the effects of market power on innovation and entrepreneurship. There, a panel of experts noted that the lack of competitive pressure in the U.S. economy has reduced innovation and business formation, while also allowing dominant firms to control innovation.[195] Professor Tim Wu of Columbia Law School, a pioneer in internet policy, said that there is:

> no question as to whether there were barriers to entry and whether the tech economies have, in fact, become a very difficult place for people to get started . . . the decline in the number of startups, almost unthinkable in the United States, which has always had a comparative advantage in being the place where startups will get their start.[196]

Professor Fiona Scott Morton of the Yale University School of Management reinforced this concept in her testimony, noting that insufficient competition has given dominant firms the ability to channel innovation in the direction they prefer "rather than being creatively spread across directions chosen by entrants."[197]

In addition to innovation harms in the digital marketplace, Stacy Mitchell, the Co-Director of the Institute for Local Self Reliance, explained that entrepreneurism among locally owned businesses has also suffered as a result of this power. As she noted, "Local businesses are disappearing and, with them, a pathway to the middle class. Producers are struggling to invest in new products and grow their companies. New business formation is down to historic lows."[198]

At the Subcommittee's field hearing, senior executives representing different businesses across the economic spectrum offered similar testimony about the effects of market power on innovation and entrepreneurship. Patrick Spence, the CEO of Sonos, testified that the lack of fair competition diminishes innovation, particularly for firms that cannot afford to sell products at a loss.[199] He explained:

---

[195] Innovation and Entrepreneurship Hearing at 81 (Fiona Scott Morton, Theodore Nierenberg Professor of Economics, Yale Sch. of Mgmt.).

[196] Innovation and Entrepreneurship Hearing at 74 (Tim Wu, Julius Silver Professor of Law, Columbia University School of Law).

[197] Innovation and Entrepreneurship Hearing at 81 (Fiona Scott Morton, Theodore Nierenberg Prof. of Econs, Yale Sch. of Mgmt.); Data and Privacy Hearing at 3 (statement of Jason Furman, Prof. of the Practice of Econ. Pol'y, Harvard Kennedy School) (Professor Jason Furman of the Harvard Kennedy School, the former Chairman of the Council on Economic Advisers, similarly testified at another hearing that the lack of competition online is that "major platforms have reduced incentives to innovate and incumbents have distorted incentives to make more incremental improvements that can be incorporated into the dominant platforms rather than more paradigmatic changes that could challenge these platforms.").

[198] Innovation and Entrepreneurship Hearing at 187 (Stacy Mitchell, Co-Director, Inst. for Local Self-Reliance).

[199] Competitors Hearing at 7 (statement of Patrick Spence, CEO, Sonos, Inc.).

These companies have gone so far as demanding that we suppress our inventions in order to work with them. The most recent example of this is Google's refusal to allow us to use multiple voice assistants on our product simultaneously. . . . I think the whole spirit of trying to encourage small companies, encourage new innovations and new startups is at risk, given how dominant these companies are.[200]

Furthermore, the ability of a dominant firm to extract economic concessions from smaller companies that rely on it to reach the market can also depress innovation. David Barnett, the CEO and Founder of PopSockets, testified at the field hearing that Amazon required his company "to pay almost two million in marketing dollars in order to remove illegal product from the Amazon marketplace."[201] In response to questions from Representative Ken Buck (R-CO) on the effect of this policy on innovation, Mr. Barnett testified that this money could have been used to double the number of employees dedicated to developing innovative products at the company.[202]

2. Privacy and Data Protection

The persistent collection and misuse of consumer data is an indicator of market power in the digital economy.[203] Traditionally, market power has been defined as the ability to raise prices without a loss to demand, such as fewer sales or customers.[204] Scholars and market participants have noted that even as online platforms rarely charge consumers a monetary price—products appear to be "free" but are monetized through people's attention or with their data[205]—traditional assessments of market power are more difficult to apply to digital markets.[206]

The best evidence of platform market power therefore is not prices charged but rather the degree to which platforms have eroded consumer privacy without prompting a response from the market.[207]

---

[200] *Id.*

[201] Competitors Hearing at 3 (statement of David Barnett, Founder and CEO, PopSockets LLC).

[202] Competitors Hearing at 57 (David Barnett, Founder and CEO, PopSockets LLC).

[203] Howard A. Shelanski, *Information, Innovation, and Competition Policy for the Internet,* 161 U. PA. L. REV. 1663, 1689 (2013) ("One measure of a platform's market power is the extent to which it can engage in [privacy exploitation] without some benefit to consumers that offsets their reduced privacy and still retain users.").

[204] W. KIP VISCUSI ET AL., ECONOMICS OF REGULATION AND ANTITRUST 164 (3d ed. 2000).

[205] Data and Privacy Hearing at 3 (statement of Jason Furman, Prof. of the Practice of Econ. Pol'y, Harvard Kennedy School); Data and Privacy Hearing at 5 (statement of Tommaso Valletti, Prof. of Econs., Imperial College Bus. Sch.).

[206] Howard A. Shelanski, *Information, Innovation, and Competition Policy for the Internet,* 161 U. PA. L. REV. 1663, 1687 (2013) ("While increased competition, at least on its own, will not always cause firms to better use or protect customer information, any competitive effects analysis that misses these two nonprice dimensions of platform market performance will be incomplete and could be biased toward underenforcement.").

[207] *See, e.g.,* Makan Delrahim, Assistant Attorney General, U.S. Dep't of Justice Antitrust Div., Remarks for the Antitrust New Frontiers Conference (June 11, 2019), https://www.justice.gov/opa/speech/assistant-attorney-general-makan-delrahim-delivers-remarks-antitrust-new-frontiers ("It is well-settled, however, that competition has price and non-price

As scholars have noted, a platform's ability to maintain strong networks while degrading user privacy can reasonably be considered equivalent to a monopolist's decision to increase prices or reduce product quality.[208] A firm's dominance can enable it to abuse consumers' privacy without losing customers.[209] In the absence of genuine competitive threats, a firm offers fewer privacy protections than it otherwise would. In the process, it extracts more data, further entrenching its dominance.[210] When paired with the tendency toward winner-take-all outcomes, consumers are forced to either use a service with poor privacy safeguards or forego the service altogether.[211] As the United Kingdom's Competition and Markets Authority observes, "The collection and use of personal data by Google and Facebook for personalised advertising, in many cases with no or limited controls available to consumers, is another indication that these platforms do not face a strong enough competitive constraint."[212]

Given the increasingly critical role platforms play in mediating access to everyday goods and services, users are also far more likely to surrender more information than to cease using the service entirely.[213] Without adequate competition, firms are able to collect more data than a competitive market would allow,[214] further entrenching their market power while diminishing privacy in the process.[215]

---

dimensions."); Maurice E. Stucke & Ariel Ezrachi, *When Competition Fails to Optimize Quality: A Look at Search Engines*, 18 YALE J.L. & TECH. 70, 103 (2016); ELEONORA OCELLO & CRISTINA SJOODIN, EUR. COMM'N, COMPETITION MERGER BRIEF: MICROSOFT/LINKEDIN: BIG DATA AND CONGLOMERATE EFFECTS IN TECH MARKETS 5 (2017), http://ec.europa.eu/competition/publications/cmb/2017/kdal17001enn.pdf.

[208] Dina Srinivasan, *The Antitrust Case Against Facebook: A Monopolist's Journey Towards Pervasive Surveillance in Spite of Consumers' Preference for Privacy*, 16 BERKELEY BUS. L.J. 39, 44 (2019) ("Facebook is a monopolist, and what Facebook extracts overtly from consumers today, from a quality perspective, is a direct function of Facebook's monopoly power."); *see also* Katharine Kemp, *Concealed Data Practices and Competition Law: Why Privacy Matters* (UNSW Law Research Paper No. 19-53, 2019), https://papers.ssrn.com/sol3/papers.cfm?abstract_id=3432769; OECD, BIG DATA: BRINGING COMPETITION POLICY TO THE DIGITAL ERA (2016), https://one.oecd.org/document/DAF/COMP(2016)14/en/pdf.

[209] Data and Privacy Hearing at 5 (statement of Tommaso Valletti, Prof. of Econs., Imperial College Bus. Sch.); Dig. Competition Expert Panel Report at 42–45.

[210] David N. Cicilline & Terrell McSweeny, *Competition Is at the Heart of Facebook's Privacy Problem*, WIRED (Apr. 24, 2018), https://www.wired.com/story/competition-is-at-the-heart-of-facebooks-privacy-problem.

[211] Dig. Competition Expert Panel Report at 43 ("[T]he misuse of consumer data and harm to privacy is arguably an indicator of low quality caused by a lack of competition."); Dina Srinivasan, *The Antitrust Case Against Facebook: A Monopolist's Journey Towards Pervasive Surveillance in Spite of Consumers' Preference for Privacy*, 16 BERKELEY BUS. L.J. 39, 40 (2019) ("Consumers effectively face a singular choice—use Facebook and submit to the quality and stipulations of Facebook's product or forgo all use of the only social network.").

[212] Competition & Mkts. Auth. Report at 318.

[213] Giuseppe Colangelo & Mariateresa Maggiolino, *Data Protection in Attention Markets: Protecting Privacy through Competition?*, 8 J. OF EUR. COMPETITION L. & PRACTICE 363, 365 (2017).

[214] Data and Privacy Hearing at 4 (statement of Dina Srinivasan, Fellow, Yale Thurman Arnold Project); Innovation and Entrepreneurship Hearing at 82 (Fiona Scott Morton, Theodore Nierenberg Prof. of Econs., Yale Sch. of Mgmt.).

[215] Data and Privacy Hearing at 2 (statement of Jason Furman, Prof. of the Practice of Econ. Pol'y, Harvard Kennedy School); Data and Privacy Hearing at 5 (statement of Tommaso Valletti, Prof. of Econs., Imperial College Bus. Sch.); Dig. Competition Expert Panel Report at 4 ("It can be harder for new companies to enter or scale up."); Giuseppe Colangelo & Mariateresa Maggiolino, *Data Protection in Attention Markets: Protecting Privacy through Competition?*, 8 J. OF EUR.

Because persistent data collection online is often concealed,[216] it is more difficult to compare privacy costs across different products and services.[217] Consumers are largely unaware of firms' data collection practices, which are presented in dense and lengthy disclosures.[218] The use of manipulative design interfaces has also become a pervasive tool "to increase the likelihood of users consenting to tracking."[219] These behavioral nudges—referred to as dark patterns—are commonly used in online tracking and advertising markets to enhance a firm's market power and "maximize a company's ability to extract revenue from its users."[220] And in e-commerce, Jamie Luguri and Lior Strahilevitz observe that dark patterns "are harming consumers by convincing them to surrender cash or personal data in deals that do not reflect consumers' actual preferences and may not serve their interests. There appears to be a substantial market failure where dark patterns are concerned—what is good for ecommerce profits is bad for consumers."[221]

More recently, as remote work became commonplace during the COVID-19 pandemic, Google attempted to manipulate users into using its Google Meet videoconferencing tool instead of upstart competitor Zoom. As Zoom emerged as the market leader during the early stages of the pandemic, Google introduced a new widget for Meet inside Gmail. A similar message could be found inside Google Calendar, which prompted users to "Add Google Meet video conferencing" to their appointments. "For people with the Zoom Video Communications Inc. extension on their Chrome browsers, the prompt sits directly above the option to: 'Make it a Zoom Meeting.'"[222]

COMPETITION L. & PRACTICE 363, 365 (2017) ("Similarly, in such a market, a dominant firm could abuse its power to exclude a rival producing privacy-friendly goods that consumer would otherwise prefer."); Stigler Report at 67 ("When facing a zero-money price, and when quality is difficult to observe, consumers are not receiving salient signals about the social value of their consumption because the price they believe they face does not reflect the economics of the transaction, and they are ignorant of those numbers.").

[216] Data and Privacy Hearing at 4-5 (statement of Tommaso Valletti, Prof. of Econs., Imperial College Bus. Sch.).

[217] Maurice E. Stucke, *Should We Be Concerned About Data-opolies?*, 2 GEO. L. TECH. REV. 275, 311 (2018).

[218] *See, e.g.*, Paul Hitlin & Lee Rainie, *Facebook Algorithms and Personal Data*, PEW RES. CTR. (Jan. 16. 2019), https://www.pewinternet.org/2019/01/16/facebook-algorithms-and-personal-data/. *See* AUSTL. COMPETITION & CONSUMER COMM'N, DIG. PLATFORMS INQUIRY FINAL REPORT 11 (2019) [hereinafter Austl. Competition & Consumer Comm'n Report]; Ryan Calo & Alex Rosenblat, *The Taking Economy: Uber, Information, and Power*, 117 COLUM. L. REV. 1623 (2017); Dina Srinivasan, *The Antitrust Case Against Facebook: A Monopolist's Journey Towards Pervasive Surveillance in Spite of Consumers' Preference for Privacy*, 16 BERKELEY BUS. L.J. 39, 41 (2019) ("[A]ccepting Facebook's policies in order to use its service means accepting broad-scale commercial surveillance.").

[219] Arvind Narayanan, Arunesh Mathur, Marshini Chetty & Mihir Kshirsagar, *Dark Patterns: Past, Present, and Future*, 18(2) ACM QUEUE 67, 77 (2020) https://queue.acm.org/detail.cfm?id=3400901.

[220] *Id.* at 77 (2020); NORWEGIAN CONSUMER COUNCIL, DECEIVED BY DESIGN (June 27, 2018) (describing the use of "dark patterns"), https://fil.forbrukerradet.no/wp-content/uploads/2018/06/2018-06-27-deceived-by-design-final.pdf.

[221] Jamie Luguri & Lior Strahilevitz, *Shining a Light on Dark Patterns* at 29 (Univ. of Chicago Public Law Working Paper No. 719, 2019), https://papers.ssrn.com/sol3/papers.cfm?abstract_id=3431205.

[222] Mark Bergen, *Google Really Wants You to Try Its New Video Tool*, BLOOMBERG (May 19, 2020), https://www.bloomberg.com/news/newsletters/2020-05-19/google-really-wants-you-to-try-its-new-video-tool.

To the extent that consumers are aware of data collection practices, it is often in the wake of scandals involving large-scale data breaches or privacy incidents such as Cambridge Analytica.[223] As Dina Srinivasan notes, "Today, nuances in privacy terms are relegated to investigative journalists to discover and explain. When the media does report on them—as they did around Google's practice of letting employees and contractors read Gmail users' emails—consumers often switch to a competitor that offers a better product or service."[224] The opacity of data collection and use contributes to consumer confusion and the misperception that consumers do not care about their privacy—the so-called privacy paradox—simply because they use services that have become essential.[225]

While insufficient competition can lead to reduced quality in many markets, the loss of quality due to monopolization—and in turn, privacy and data protection—is even more pronounced in digital markets because product quality is often the "relevant locus of competition."[226] Without transparency or effective choice, dominant firms may impose terms of service with weak privacy protection that are designed to restrict consumer choice,[227] creating a race to the bottom.[228] As David Heinemeier Hansson, the Co-Founder and Chief Technology Officer of Basecamp,[229] explained in his testimony before the Subcommittee:

> When businesses do not have to account for the negative externalities they cause, it's a race to the bottom. The industrial-scale exploitation of privacy online is much the same. Facebook and Google have built comprehensive dossiers on almost everyone, and they can sell incredibly targeted advertisement on that basis. When Facebook knows you're pregnant, or worse, thinks it knows when you're pregnant, they can target ads for baby clothes or strollers with striking efficiency. But doing so represents an inherent violation of the receiver's privacy. Every ad targeted using personal information

---

[223] Dig. Competition Expert Panel Report at 45; David N. Cicilline & Terrell McSweeny, *Competition Is at the Heart of Facebook's Privacy Problem*, WIRED (Apr. 24, 2018), https://www.wired.com/story/competition-is-at-the-heart-of-facebooks-privacy-problem.

[224] Data and Privacy Hearing at 4 (statement of Dina Srinivasan, Fellow, Yale Thurman Arnold Project).

[225] Brooke Auxier, et al., *Americans and Privacy: Concerned, Confused and Feeling Lack of Control Over Their Personal Information*, PEW RES. CTR. (Nov. 15 2019), https://www.pewresearch.org/internet/2019/11/15/americans-and-privacy-concerned-confused-and-feeling-lack-of-control-over-their-personal-information/; Daniel J. Solove, *The Myth of the Privacy Paradox*, 89 GEO. WASH. L. REV. (forthcoming 2021).

[226] Data and Privacy Hearing at 4 (statement of Tommaso Valletti, Prof. of Econs., Imperial College Bus. Sch.).

[227] *Id.*

[228] Competitors Hearing at 11 (statement of David Heinemeier Hansson, Co-Founder and CTO, Basecamp); Dig. Competition Expert Panel Report at 6 ("[W]ell-functioning competitive digital markets have the potential to develop new solutions and increased choice for consumers, where privacy and quality of service can be differentiating factors."); Howard A. Shelanski, *Information, Innovation, and Competition Policy for the Internet*, 161 U. PA. L. REV. 1663, 1691 (2013) ("Competition, however, may drive platforms to adopt and adhere to stronger privacy policies, making it worthwhile for a platform to advertise such policies to consumers in order to differentiate itself from its competitors.").

[229] Basecamp is an internet software firm based in Chicago, Illinois, that sells project-management and team-collaboration tools. Competitors Hearing at 2 (statement of David Heinemeier Hansson, Co-Founder and CTO, Basecamp).

gathered without explicit, informed consent is at some level a violation of privacy. And Facebook and Google are profiting immensely by selling these violations to advertisers. Advertisers who may well feel that purchasing these violations go against their ethics, but see no choice to compete without participating.[230]

In addition to creating a race to the bottom, this same dynamic can also prevent new firms from offering products with strong privacy protections or reduce the incentive of new entrants or rivals to compete directly.[231] Roger McNamee, the Co-Founder and Managing Director of Elevation Partners has also explained that to the extent there is direct competition between a firm with a privacy-centric business model, such as DuckDuckGo's search engine, they can "still have trouble applying different business models once they're not compatible with the business models that have made the Internet platforms so successful."[232]

Conversely, without adequate safeguards in place, measures that appear to improve privacy for consumers may also have anticompetitive effects. Kirsten Daru, Chief Privacy Officer and General Counsel of Tile, told the Subcommittee: "Apple has used the concept of privacy as a shield by making changes in the name of privacy that at the same time give it a competitive advantage."[233] In particular, she testified at the Subcommittee's field hearing:

> Apple has attempted to justify its own collection of sensitive information and disparate treatment of competitors because FindMy is 'part of the OS,' as well as due to a need for enhanced consumer privacy. But the changes don't meaningfully improve or enhance privacy of third-party app developers.[234]

Ram Shriram, a prominent investor who is a founding board member of Google, noted that "[p]rivacy does impact how you think about dominance, for example, in a market because Google and Apple both eliminated third-party cookies, which then makes your data a little more private. But it ironically will hurt the young companies that are trying to build digital advertising businesses while improving user privacy.[235]

The Subcommittee held several hearings during the investigation that examined the role of competition and privacy online.

---

[230] Competitors Hearing at 11 (statement of David Heinemeier Hansson, Co-Founder and CTO, Basecamp).

[231] Data and Privacy Hearing at 3–4 (statement of Dina Srinivasan, Fellow, Yale Thurman Arnold Project); Venture Capital and Antitrust Workshop at 24 (Paul Arnold, Founder and Partner, Switch Partners).

[232] Venture Capital and Antitrust Workshop at 30 (statement of Roger McNamee, Co-Founder and Managing Dir., Elevation Partners).

[233] Competitors Hearing at 3 (response to Questions for the Record of Kirsten Daru, Vice Pres. and Gen. Counsel, Tile).

[234] Competitors Hearing at 2 (statement of Kirsten Daru, Vice Pres.and Gen. Counsel, Tile).

[235] Venture Capital and Antitrust Workshop at 36 (Ram Shriram, Managing Partner, Sherpalo Ventures LLC).

In September 2016, the Subcommittee held a hearing on the role of data and privacy in competition. There, Federal Trade Commissioner Rohit Chopra testified that dominant firms have the ability to impose "complex and draconian" terms of service that can change suddenly "to collect and use data more expansively and more intensely."[236] As he noted, this behavior is the equivalent of a price hike that would be difficult to impose unilaterally in a competitive marketplace.[237] Without sufficient competition, however, "companies can focus on blocking new entrants and limiting choice to protect their dominance and pricing power."[238] Tommaso Valletti, the former Chief Competition Economist for the European Commission, noted that it is "self-evident that data is key to digital platforms, and that some applications imply real-time knowledge of consumer behaviour as well as cross linkages across apps that only very few digital players have access to."[239] And finally, Jason Furman, the former Chairman of the Council of Economic Advisers and an author of the "Unlocking Digital Competition" report, said that "the misuse of consumer data and harm to privacy is arguably an indicator of low quality caused by a lack of competition."[240]

At the Subcommittee's oversight hearing in November 2019, Makan Delrahim, the Assistant Attorney General of the Justice Department's Antitrust Division, testified that because privacy is a dimension of quality, protecting competition "can have an impact on privacy and data protection."[241] And finally, Maureen Ohlhausen, the former Acting Chair of the FTC, echoed this point at the Subcommittee's hearing on innovation and entrepreneurship, noting that quality reductions online could "include factors such as reduced features, restricted consumer choice, or lessened control over privacy."[242]

Leading international antitrust enforcers offered similar testimony before the Subcommittee. Margrethe Vestager, the European Union's Competition Commissioner, testified that due to the Commission's finding that data protection is an important dimension of competition that could be undermined by certain merger activity, the Commission "has … integrated, where appropriate, data protection as a quality parameter for the assessment of merger cases."[243] Similarly, Rod Sims, the Chair of the Australian Competition and Consumer Commission, told the Subcommittee that the ACCC's "Digital Platforms Inquiry" report recommends "[u]pdating Australia's merger law to

---

[236] Data and Privacy Hearing at 3 (statement of Rohit Chopra, Comm'r, Fed. Trade Comm'n).

[237] *Id.*

[238] *Id.*

[239] Data and Privacy Hearing at 2 (statement of Tommaso Valletti, Prof. of Econs., Imperial College Bus. Sch.).

[240] Dig. Competition Expert Panel Report at 43.

[241] Antitrust Agencies Hearing at 15 (statement of Makan Delahim, Assistant Attorney General, United States Dep't of Justice Antitrust Div.).

[242] Innovation and Entrepreneurship Hearing at 4 n.14 (statement of Maureen K. Ohlhausen, Partner, Baker Botts, L.L.P.).

[243] Data and Privacy Hearing at 4 (statement of Margrethe Vestager, then-Eur. Comm'r for Competition).

incorporate … the nature and significance of assets, including data and technology, acquired through a merger."[244]

3. The Free and Diverse Press

A free and diverse press is essential to a vibrant democracy. Whether exposing corruption in government, informing citizens, or holding power to account, independent journalism sustains our democracy by facilitating public discourse.

Since 2006, newspaper advertising revenue, which is critical for funding high-quality journalism, fell by over 50%.[245] Despite significant growth in online traffic among the nation's leading newspapers,[246] print and digital newsrooms across the country are laying off reporters or folding altogether.[247] As a result, communities throughout the United States are increasingly going without sources for local news. The emergence of platform gatekeepers—and the market power wielded by these firms—has contributed to the decline of trustworthy sources of news.[248]

a. Journalism in Decline

Since 2006, the news industry has been in economic freefall, primarily due to a massive decrease in advertising revenue. Both print and broadcast news organizations rely heavily on advertising revenue to support their operations, and as the market has shifted to digital platforms, news organizations have seen the value of their advertising space plummet steeply.[249] For newspapers, advertising has declined from $49 billion in 2006 to $16.5 billion in 2017.[250] This decrease has been felt by national and local news sources alike. As total annual advertising revenues have fallen over

---

[244] *Id.* at 8 (statement of Rod Sims, Chair, Austl. Competition & Consumer Comm'n).

[245] Noah Smith, Opinion, *Goodbye, Newspapers. Hello, Bad Government.*, BLOOMBERG (June 1, 2018), https://www.bloomberg.com/opinion/articles/2018-06-01/goodbye-newspapers-hello-bad-government.

[246] Free and Diverse Press Hearing at 2 (statement of David Chavern, President and CEO, News Media Alliance).

[247] Douglas McLennan & Jack Miles, Opinion, *A Once Unimaginable Scenario: No More Newspapers*, WASH. POST: THE WORLDPOST (Mar. 21, 2018), https://www.washingtonpost.com/news/theworldpost/wp/2018/03/21/newspapers/?utm_term=.c1b57c9efcd7.

[248] Free and Diverse Press Hearing at 2–3 (statement of David Pitofsky, Gen. Counsel, News Corp).

[249] eMarketer estimates that Google's and Facebook's U.S. ad revenues will be $39.58 billion and $31.43 billion, respectively, in 2020. eMarketer, *Google Ad Revenues to Drop for the First Time* (June 23, 2020). According to BIA, local TV and radio station ad revenues (counting both their OTA and much more limited digital revenues) will total $31.3 billion this year. *See* BIA Advisory Services, *BIA Revises Local Radio Advertising Estimates Down to $12.8B in 2020 Due to Pandemic* (June 25, 2020); BIA Advisory Services, *BIA Lowers 2020 Local Television Station Advertising Revenue Forecast to $18.5B* (May 21, 2020).

[250] Michael Barthel, *Despite Subscription Surges for Largest U.S. Newspapers, Circulation and Revenue Fall for Industry Overall*, PEW RES. CTR.: FACTTANK (June 1, 2017), https://www.pewresearch.org/fact-tank/2017/06/01/circulation-and-revenue-fall-for-newspaper-industry; *Newspapers Fact Sheet*, PEW RES. CTR. (June 13, 2018), https://www.journalism.org/fact-sheet/newspapers.

62% across the industry since 2008, one major national newspaper told the Subcommittee that its annual advertising revenue has fallen 48% over that period.[251] Additionally, ethnic news outlets have suffered from the shift from broadcast and print ads to digital ads.[252] Regarding television and radio broadcast news, the National Association of Broadcasters told the Subcommittee, "[T]his year, the U.S. advertising revenue of a single company—Google—are projected to exceed the *combined* ad revenue of *all* TV and radio stations in the country by over $8 billion."[253]

While the decline of advertising revenue has most severely affected local news publishers, prominent digital publishers have also been affected. In January 2019, Buzzfeed announced layoffs of 220 employees, about 15% of its workforce, due to advertising losses.[254] Jonah Peretti, the Chief Executive Officer of BuzzFeed, commented prior to the layoffs that consolidation of digital publishers into a single large digital media company may be the only path forward for profitability, suggesting that publishers' lack of bargaining power in negotiations with online platforms is the central obstacle to long-term survival.[255]

Despite a recent boost in the number of digital subscriptions and the level of online traffic for the top newspapers in the United States, these increases did not offset losses in online advertising or circulation in the industry overall.[256] As one news publisher told the Subcommittee, "For the vast majority of news publishers, digital subscription revenues remain a minor revenue stream and do not appear to be on a path to replace the decline in print subscriptions."[257] Over the past two decades, hundreds of local news publishers have been acquired or gone bankrupt.[258] In some cases, private

---

[251] Submission from Source 220, to H. Comm. on the Judiciary, 7 (Oct. 14, 2019) (on file with Comm.).

[252] *See* PENELOPE MUSE ABERNATHY, UNIV. N.C. SCH. OF MEDIA AND JOURNALISM, NEWS DESERTS AND GHOST NEWSPAPERS: WILL LOCAL NEWS SURVIVE 45 (2020), https://www.usnewsdeserts.com/wp-content/uploads/2020/06/2020_News_Deserts_and_Ghost_Newspapers.pdf.

[253] Submission from Nat'l Ass'n of Broads., to H. Comm. on the Judiciary, 2 (Oct. 14, 2019), http://www.nab.org/documents/newsRoom/pdfs/09220_HJC_Local_Journalism_At_Risk_Submission.pdf.

[254] Oliver Darcy & Tom Kludt, *Media Industry Loses About 1,000 Jobs as Layoffs Hit News Organizations*, CNN (Jan. 24, 2019), https://edition.cnn.com/2019/01/24/media/media-layoffs-buzzfeed-huffpost-gannett/index.html; Edmund Lee, *Founder's Big Idea to Revive BuzzFeed's Fortunes? A Merger with Rivals*, N.Y. TIMES (Nov. 19, 2018), https://www.nytimes.com/2018/11/19/business/media/buzzfeed-jonah-peretti-mergers.html.

[255] Edmund Lee, *Founder's Big Idea to Revive BuzzFeed's Fortunes? A Merger with Rivals*, N.Y. TIMES (Nov. 19, 2018), https://www.nytimes.com/2018/11/19/business/media/buzzfeed-jonah-peretti-mergers.html.

[256] Michael Barthel, *Despite Subscription Surges for Largest U.S. Newspapers, Circulation and Revenue Fall for Industry Overall*, PEW RES. CTR.: FACTTANK (June 1, 2017), https://www.pewresearch.org/fact-tank/2017/06/01/circulation-and-revenue-fall-for-newspaper-industry/; *Newspapers Fact Sheet,* PEW RES. CTR (July 9, 2019), https://www.journalism.org/fact-sheet/newspapers; David Chavern, Opinion, *Protect the News From Google and Facebook*, WALL ST. J. (Feb. 25, 2018), https://www.wsj.com/articles/protect-the-news-from-google-and-facebook-1519594942.

[257] Submission from Source 220, to H. Comm. on the Judiciary, 7 (Oct. 14, 2019) (on file with Comm.).

[258] PENELOPE MUSE ABERNATHY, UNIV. N.C. SCH. OF MEDIA AND JOURNALISM, THE EXPANDING NEWS DESERT 33 (2018), https://www.cislm.org/wp-content/uploads/2018/10/The-Expanding-News-Desert-10_14-Web.pdf.

equity firms and hedge funds have purchased major regional chains and newspapers, resulting in mass layoffs of journalists and increased debt burdens for publishers.[259]

In recent years, news consumption has largely shifted to a model of content aggregation, through which platforms consolidate content from multiple news sources.[260] In submissions to the Subcommittee and public statements, publishers across the spectrum say they have little choice but to participate in content aggregation, particularly those run by dominant platforms because the aggregators' "use of news publishers' content does send substantial traffic to news publishers."[261] But this can also prevent traffic from flowing to newspapers. As some publishers have noted, news aggregators package and present content to users using attention-grabbing quotes from high points of stories, which can make it unnecessary for the user to click through to the publisher's website.[262] As these publishers noted, this dynamic forces news organizations to effectively compete with their own content, lowering the potential revenue from user traffic to news organizations' websites.[263]

As a result of falling revenues, newspapers and broadcast stations are steadily losing the ability to financially support their newsrooms, which are costly to maintain but provide immense value to their communities.[264] A robust local newsroom requires the financial freedom to support in-depth, sometimes years-long reporting, as well as the ability to hire and retain journalists with expertise in fundamentally local issues, such as coverage of state government.[265]

The societal value of local news is significant. As noted by the National Association of Broadcasters, local broadcast stations provide on-the-air programming which is "rooted in localism and the public interest" offering content which "[is] still free to the public and accessible to all Americans."[266] Kevin Riley, the editor of *The Atlanta Journal-Constitution*, similarly testified before the Subcommittee that "it would be impossible to even put a cost estimate on the work" of local journalists.[267]

---

[259] Alex Shephard, *Finance Is Killing the News*, NEW REPUBLIC (Apr. 18, 2018), https://newrepublic.com/article/148022/finance-killing-news.

[260] Lesley Chiou & Catherine Tucker, *Content Aggregation by Platforms: The Case of the News Media* (NBER Working Paper No. 21404, 2015), https://www.nber.org/papers/w21404.pdf.

[261] NEWS MEDIA ALLIANCE, HOW GOOGLE ABUSES ITS POSITION AS A MARKET DOMINANT PLATFORM TO STRONG-ARM NEWS PUBLISHERS AND HURT JOURNALISM 2 (2020), http://www.newsmediaalliance.org/wp-content/uploads/2020/06/Final-Alliance-White-Paper-June-18-2020.pdf.

[262] *Id.* at 12.

[263] *Id.* at 12–14 (2020).

[264] Submission from the Nat'l Association of Broads, to H. Comm. on the Judiciary, 9 (Sept. 2, 2020), http://www.nab.org/documents/newsRoom/pdfs/09220_HJC_Local_Journalism_At_Risk_Submission.pdf.

[265] Free and Diverse Press Hearing at 3–4 (statement of Kevin Riley, Editor, The Atlanta Journal-Constitution).

[266] Submission from the Nat'l Association of Broads, to H. Comm. on the Judiciary, 1 (Sept. 2, 2020), http://www.nab.org/documents/newsRoom/pdfs/09220_HJC_Local_Journalism_At_Risk_Submission.pdf.

[267] Free and Diverse Press Hearing at 2 (statement of Kevin Riley, Editor, The Atlanta Journal-Constitution).

The COVID-19 pandemic has particularly highlighted the importance of local news sources. Despite taking major revenue losses,[268] local journalists have provided valuable reporting on the transmission of the novel coronavirus, particularly for underserved and vulnerable communities.[269] For example, PBS New Mexico provided an in-depth focus on the effects of the coronavirus on Native Americans "dealing with scarce resources as they respond to novel coronavirus outbreaks on tribal lands."[270] Apart from serving their communities, local news stories bring national attention to these critical issues.[271] In addition to news coverage, the National Association of Broadcasters aired public-service announcements in response to the pandemic "more than 765,000 times for an estimated ad value of more than $156,500,000," a number which "do[es] not include the likely much greater number of other coronavirus-related PSAs" aired by local television and radio stations across the United States.[272]

To run a new operation, broadcast stations must be able to sustain "the basic costs of running a station, including engineering, sales, [and] programming" costs, and must make significant capital expenditures in equipment, such as satellite trucks.[273] These expenses must be satisfied before broadcast stations can invest in improvements to keep pace with changing technologies, "including ultra-high definition programming, better emergency alerting, mobile services, interactivity, hyper-local content and more."[274]

The costs of news production add up. From 2003 to 2013, these costs "accounted for nearly 24 percent of TV stations' total expenses (and nearly 26 percent of the total expenses of ABC/CBS/Fox/NBC stations)."[275] In light of the expenses associated with producing high-quality journalism, declining revenue has major implications for the maintenance—let alone enrichment—of quality news production.

---

[268] Sara Fischer & Margaret Harding McGill, *Coronavirus Sends Local News Into Crisis,* Axios (Mar. 21, 2020), https://www.axios.com/coronavirus-local-news-853e96fa-51aa-43cc-a990-eb48cc896b17.html.

[269] Mark Glaser, *6 Ways Local News Makes a Crucial Impact Covering COVID-19*, Knight Found. (Apr. 20, 2020), https://knightfoundation.org/articles/6-ways-local-news-makes-a-crucial-impact-covering-covid-19/.

[270] *COVID-19 Response from Native Tribes*, New Mexico PBS (Mar. 30, 2020), https://www.newmexicopbs.org/productions/newmexicoinfocus/covid-19-response-from-native-tribes/.

[271] *See, e.g.*, Bill Chappell, *Coronavirus Cases Spike In Navajo Nation, Where Water Service Is Often Scarce*, NPR (Mar. 26, 2020), https://www.npr.org/sections/coronavirus-live-updates/2020/03/26/822037719/coronavirus-cases-spike-in-navajo-nation-where-water-service-is-often-scarce.

[272] Submission from the Nat'l Ass'n of Broads., to H. Comm. on the Judiciary, 2 (Sept. 2, 2020), http://www.nab.org/documents/newsRoom/pdfs/09220_HJC_Local_Journalism_At_Risk_Submission.pdf.

[273] *Id.* at 4, 7 n.16.

[274] *Id.* at 7.

[275] *Id.* at 4 (citing NAB Television Financial Reports 2004–19)

Budget cuts have also led to a dramatic number of newsroom job losses. This decline has been primarily driven by a reduction in newspaper employees, who have seen employment fall by half over a recent eight-year period, from 71,000 in 2008 to 35,000 in 2019.[276] In 2019 alone, 7,800 media industry employees were laid off.[277] The Bureau of Labor Statistics estimates that the total employment of reporters, correspondents, and broadcast news analysts will continue to decline by about 11% between 2019 and 2029.[278]

Researchers at the University of North Carolina School of Media and Journalism found that the United States has lost nearly 1,800 newspapers since 2004 either to closure or merger, 70% of which were in metropolitan areas.[279] As a result, the majority of counties in America no longer have more than one publisher of local news, and 200 without any paper.[280] At the Subcommittee's hearing on online platforms' effects on a free and diverse press, Mr. Riley described this new media landscape characterized by digital platform dominance and disappearing local newspapers:

> We produce journalism that is distinguished by its depth, accuracy and originality. That costs money and is expensive, but if the system works correctly, it also makes money that the paper uses to investigate and develop the next story or cover the next local event. If others repackage our journalism and make money off it, yet none of that money makes its way back to the local paper, then it makes breaking that next story or exposing the next scandal more challenging. If that cycle continues indefinitely, quality local journalism will slowly wither and eventually cease to exist.[281]

This cycle has a profoundly negative effect on American democracy and civic life. Communities without quality local news coverage have lower rates of voter turnout.[282] Government

---

[276] Elizabeth Grieco, *U.S. newspapers have shed half of their newsroom employees since 2008*, PEW RES. CTR: FACTTANK (Apr. 20, 2020), https://www.pewresearch.org/fact-tank/2020/04/20/u-s-newsroom-employment-has-dropped-by-a-quarter-since-2008/.

[277] Benjamin Goggin, *7,800 People Lost Their Media Jobs in a 2019 Landslide,* BUS. INSIDER (Dec. 10, 2019), https://www.businessinsider.com/2019-media-layoffs-job-cuts-at-buzzfeed-huffpost-vice-details-2019-2#spin-media-group-29-jobs-september-and-january-18.

[278] *Occupational Outlook Handbook: Reporters, Correspondents, and Broadcast News Analysts*, U.S. DEP'T OF LABOR: BUR. OF LABOR STATS. (last modified Apr. 12, 2019), https://www.bls.gov/ooh/media-and-communication/reporters-correspondents-and-broadcast-news-analysts.htm.

[279] PENELOPE MUSE ABERNATHY, UNIV. N.C. SCH. OF MEDIA AND JOURNALISM, THE EXPANDING NEWS DESERT 10-11 (2018), https://www.cislm.org/wp-content/uploads/2018/10/The-Expanding-News-Desert-10_14-Web.pdf.

[280] *Id.* at 8, 10.

[281] Free and Diverse Press Hearing at 3 (statement of Kevin Riley, Editor, The Atlanta Journal-Constitution)

[282] Matthew Gentzkow, et al., *The Effects of Newspaper Entry and Exit on Electoral Politics*, 101 AM. ECON. REV. 2980 (2011) ("We find that newspapers have a robust positive effect on political participation, with one additional newspaper increasing both presidential and congressional turnout by approximately 0.3 percentage points.").

corruption may go unchecked, leaving communities vulnerable to serious mismanagement.[283] Relatedly, these communities see local government spending increase.[284] Towns without robust local news coverage also exhibit lower levels of social cohesion, undermining a sense of belonging in a community.[285] As fewer publishers operate in local markets, local news is supplanted by aggregation of national coverage, reducing residents' knowledge of local happenings and events, and generally leaving them less connected to their communities.[286]

Compounding this problem, the gap created by the loss of trustworthy and credible news sources has been increasingly filled by false and misleading information. Once communities lack a local newspaper source, people tend to get their local news from social media. As local news dies, it is filled by unchecked information, some of which can spread quickly and can have severe consequences.

b. The Effect of Market Power on Journalism

During the Subcommittee's investigation, news publishers raised concerns about the "significant and growing asymmetry of power" between dominant online platforms and news publishers, as well as the effect of this dominance on the production and availability of trustworthy sources of news. In interviews, submissions, and testimony before the Subcommittee, publishers with distinct business models and distribution strategies said they are "increasingly beholden" to these firms, and in particular, Google and Facebook.[287] As a result, several dominant firms have an outsized influence over the distribution and monetization of trustworthy sources of news online,[288] undermining the availability of high-quality sources of journalism.[289]

---

[283] Mary Ellen Klas, *Less Local News Means Less Democracy*, NIEMAN REPORTS (Sept. 20, 2019), https://niemanreports.org/articles/less-local-news-means-less-democracy/.

[284] Noah Smith, Opinion, *Goodbye Newspapers. Hello, Bad Government*, BLOOMBERG (June 1, 2018), https://www.bloomberg.com/opinion/articles/2018-06-01/goodbye-newspapers-hello-bad-government ("[T]he authors show that without local newspapers, local governments tend to engage in more inefficient or dubious financing arrangements.").

[285] Amy Mitchell, et al., *Civic Engagement Strongly Tied to Local News Habits*, PEW RES. CTR. (Nov. 3, 2016), https://www.journalism.org/2016/11/03/civic-engagement-strongly-tied-to-local-news-habits.

[286] Danny Hayes & Jennifer L. Lawless, *As Local News Goes, So Goes Citizen Engagement: Media, Knowledge, and Participation in U.S. House Elections*, 77 J. POL. 447, 447 (2014).

[287] Submission from Source 220, to H. Comm. on the Judiciary, 7 (Oct. 14, 2019) (on file with Comm.). Although Apple News and Apple News Plus are increasingly popular news aggregators, most market participants interviewed by Subcommittee staff do not view it as a critical intermediary for online news at this time, although some publishers raised concerns about the tying of payments inside Apple's news product.

[288] Submission of Source 955, to H. Comm. on the Judiciary, 12 (Oct. 30, 2019) (on file with Comm.).

[289] Free and Diverse Press Hearing at 3 (statement of David Chavern, President and CEO, News Media Alliance) ("In effect, a couple of dominant tech platforms are acting as regulators of the digital news industry.").

i. Distribution of News Online

Several dominant platforms function as intermediaries to news online. Due to their outsized role as digital gateways to news, a change to one of these firm's algorithm can significantly affect the online referrals to news publishers,[290] directly affecting their advertising revenue.[291] One news publisher stated in its submission to the Subcommittee that it and other news organizations "depend on a few big tech platforms to help them distribute their journalism to consumers."[292]

In submissions to the Subcommittee, several news publishers noted that the dominance of Google and Facebook allows them to "pick winners" online by adjusting visibility and traffic.[293] For example, an update to Google's search algorithm in June 2019 decreased a major news publisher's online traffic "by close to 50%" even as their referrals from other sources—such as their home page and apps—grew during the same period.[294] As they noted, a "smaller business would have been crushed" by this decline.[295]

Similarly, news organizations were negatively affected when, in January 2018, Facebook adjusted its News Feed algorithm to prioritize content based on audience engagement.[296] According to an internet analytics firm, these changes significantly affected the visibility of news content on Facebook, resulting in a 33% decrease in referral traffic from Facebook to news publishers' sites.[297] As one publisher noted in its submission to the Subcommittee, this change "was made without notice, consultation or warning to the market, [leading] to significant disruption for a range of businesses."[298] Nicholas Thompson, the Editor-in-Chief of *Wired* magazine, and *Wired* contributing editor Fred Vogelstein described the relationship between publishers and Facebook as being "sharecroppers on Facebook's massive industrial farm," writing that:

---

[290] *See, e.g.*, Submission of Source 140, to H. Comm. on the Judiciary, 2 (Oct. 15, 2019) (on file with Comm.) ("Facebook's decision, announced in June 2016, to make significant changes to its algorithm to [favor] content from friends and family, which was made without notice, consultation or warning to the market, and which led to significant disruption for a range of businesses.").

[291] Submission of Source 114, to H. Comm. on the Judiciary, 12 (Oct. 2, 2019) (on file with Comm.); Data and Privacy Hearing at 6 (statement of Rod Sims, Chair, Austl. Competition & Consumer Comm'n).

[292] Submission of Source 220, to H. Comm. on the Judiciary, 3 (Mar. 10, 2020) (on file with Comm.).

[293] Submission of Source 955, to H. Comm. on the Judiciary, 12 (Oct. 15, 2019) (on file with Comm.).

[294] *Id.* at 17.

[295] *Id.*

[296] Adam Mosseri, *Bringing People Closer Together*, FACEBOOK: NEWSROOM (Jan. 11, 2018), https://newsroom.fb.com/news/2018/01/news-feed-fyi-bringing-people-closer-together.

[297] *How Much Have Facebook Algorithm Changes Impacted Publishers?*, MARKETING CHARTS (Apr. 4, 2019), https://www.marketingcharts.com/digital/social-media-107974.

[298] Submission from Source 140, to H. Comm. on the Judiciary, 2 (Oct. 15, 2019) (on file with Comm.).

Even at the best of times, meetings between Facebook and media executives can feel like unhappy family gatherings. The two sides are inextricably bound together, but they don't like each other all that much. . . . And then there's the simple, deep fear and mistrust that Facebook inspires. Every publisher knows that, at best, they are sharecroppers on Facebook's massive industrial farm. The social network is roughly 200 times more valuable than the *Times*. And journalists know that the man who owns the farm has the leverage. ***If Facebook wanted to, it could quietly turn any number of dials that would harm a publisher—by manipulating its traffic, its ad network, or its readers.***[299]

The Subcommittee has also received evidence that the dominance of several online platforms has created a significant imbalance of bargaining power. In several submissions, news publishers note that dominant firms can impose unilateral terms on publishers, such as take-it-or-leave-it revenue sharing agreements.[300] A prominent publisher described this relationship as platforms having a "finger on the scales" with the ability to suppress publishers that do not "appease platforms' business terms."[301]

During the Subcommittee's hearing on the effects of market power on journalism,[302] several witnesses also testified about the lack of equal bargaining power between news publishers and dominant platforms.[303] At the Subcommittee's hearing on market power and the free and diverse press, Sally Hubbard, Director of Enforcement Strategy at the Open Markets Institute, testified that the lack of competition online has led to diminished bargaining power among news publishers. Consequently, in response to changing terms and algorithmic treatment by platforms, "publishers have little choice but to adapt and accommodate regardless of how the changes may negatively affect their own profitability."[304] David Chavern, President of the News Media Alliance, similarly testified that publishers have a "collective action problem," stating that "no news organization on its own can stand up to the platforms. The risk of demotion or exclusion from the platforms is simply too great."[305]

---

[299] Nicholas Thompson & Fred Vogelstein, *Inside the Two Years That Shook Facebook—and the World*, WIRED (Feb. 12, 2018), https://www.wired.com/story/inside-facebook-mark-zuckerberg-2-years-of-hell/ (emphasis added).

[300] *See, e.g.*, Submission of Source 140, to H. Comm. on the Judiciary, 2 (Oct. 15, 2019) (on file with Comm.) ("Apple's decision to tie all payments made through iOS apps to its own payment system, which takes a 30% share of any contributions and subscriptions made to news [publishers] through news apps downloaded from the Apple store.").

[301] Submission of Source 114, to H. Comm. on the Judiciary, 12 (Oct. 2, 2019) (on file with Comm.).

[302] Free and Diverse Press Hearing.

[303] Data and Privacy Hearing at 4 (statement of Rod Sims, Chair, Austl. Competition & Consumer Comm'n) (testifying that the power of dominant platforms "creates an imbalance of bargaining power between digital platforms and news media businesses, meaning that agreements they reach are likely much different to those that would be reached in a competitive market.").

[304] Free and Diverse Press Hearing at 8 (statement of Sally Hubbard, Dir. of Enforcement Strategy, Open Mkts. Inst.).

[305] Free and Diverse Press Hearing at 5 (statement of David Chavern, Pres., News Media Alliance).

In June 2020, the News Media Alliance published a white paper examining the relationship between news publishers and Google based on interviews with its members over the course of more than a year.[306] As it notes, "Google has exercised control over news publishers to force them into several relationships that benefit Google at the publishers' expense."[307] In the context of Google's placement of news on accelerated mobile pages (AMP)—a format for displaying web pages on mobile devices—publishers raised concerns that "Google effectively gave news publishers little choice but to adopt it," requiring the creation of parallel websites "that are hosted, stored and served from Google's servers rather than their own."[308]

While this format has benefits in terms of loading information quickly on mobile devices, publishers argue that these benefits "could have been achieved through means that did not so significantly increase Google's power over publishers or so favor its ability to collect data to foster its market domination."[309] And when a publisher attempts to avoid this cost by moving its content behind a paywall, its rise in subscriptions was offset by declines in traffic from Google and other platforms.[310] Referring to this tradeoff as a "Hobson's choice," the News Media Alliance explained:

> Newspapers such as *The Wall Street Journal* employ a highly customized paywall on their websites, significantly varying the number of free articles that a user is permitted to read before being asked to subscribe to the newspaper. This flexibility is highly beneficial, allowing them to maximize engagement and increase subscriptions. For AMP articles, however, Google restricts the paywall options. Unless publishers rebuild their paywall options and their meters for AMP, they can only provide *all* of their content for free or *none* of their content for free. The only other option is to use Subscribe with Google, which has many benefits for Google and downsides for news publishers.[311] Accordingly, unless they invest in building another and separate paywall, news publishers who do not want to use Subscribe with Google have a *de facto* all-or-nothing choice regarding the imposition of a paywall, which lowers subscriber conversion rates.[312]

---

[306] NEWS MEDIA ALLIANCE, HOW GOOGLE ABUSES ITS POSITION AS A MARKET DOMINANT PLATFORM TO STRONG-ARM NEWS PUBLISHERS AND HURT JOURNALISM (2020), http://www.newsmediaalliance.org/wp-content/uploads/2020/06/Final-Alliance-White-Paper-June-18-2020.pdf.

[307] *Id.* at 1.

[308] *Id.* at 5.

[309] *Id.* at 7.

[310] *Id.* at 6.

[311] *Id.* at 8 n.14 ("These include the following: (1) Google gets the subscriber data; (2) the user must use Google Wallet or Google Pay, instead of providing its credit card to the news publisher and establishing a direct relationship with the publisher; and (3) Google takes a 5-15% cut. *See* Nushin Rashidian, George Civeris, Pete Brown, *Platforms and Publishers: The End of an Era,* COLUM. JOURNALISM REV. (Nov. 22, 2019), https://www.cjr.org/tow_center_reports/platforms-and-publishers-end-of-an-era.php.")).

[312] *Id.* at 8.

Google has responded to this concern by noting that AMP does not prevent publishers from placing ads on AMP pages, but restricting the number of ads "leads to improved page load times, increased site traffic, superior ad engagement, and thus typically increases advertising revenue overall."[313] Google also said in its responses to Subcommittee Chairman Cicilline's questions for the record that it "does not privilege publishers who use AMP over publishers that adopt non-Google technical solutions that would also guarantee fast-loading pages."[314]

Finally, because news is often accessed online through channels other than the original publication—including search results, voice assistants, social platforms, or news aggregators—journalism has increasingly become "atomized" or removed from its source and placed alongside other content.[315] In the context of audio news, one market participant noted that aggregating different news sources can create a bad experience for users.[316] The aggregation of different news sources without editorial oversight can also cause reputational harm to news publishers, such as when highly credible reporting appears alongside an opinion-based news source.[317]

Indirectly, the atomization of news may increase the likelihood that people are exposed to disinformation or untrustworthy sources of news online. When online news is disintermediated from its source, people generally have more difficulty discerning the credibility of reporting online. This process may also "foster ambivalence about the quality and nature of content that garners users' attention," particularly among young people.[318]

For example, during the Subcommittee's sixth hearing, Subcommittee Chairman David N. Cicilline presented Facebook CEO Mark Zuckerberg with evidence of a Breitbart video that claimed

---

[313] Submission from Google Australia Pty. Ltd., to Austl. Competition & Consumer Comm'n, at 45–46 (Feb. 18, 2019), https://www.accc.gov.au/system/files/Google%20%28February%202019%29.PDF. *But see* Austl. Competition & Consumer Comm'n Report at 240 ("[T]here is a broader issue about the extent to which Google, by way of AMP, retains users within its ecosystem and reduces monetisation opportunities for media businesses outside of AMP. That is, rather than directing users to the websites of media businesses, AMP's design encourages users to stay within the Google ecosystem. As a result, media businesses are less likely to monetise content on their own properties, either through advertising or subscription revenue.").

[314] Innovation and Entrepreneurship Hearing at 27 (response to Questions for the Record of Adam Cohen, Dir. of Econ. Pol'y, Google LLC).

[315] Austl. Competition & Consumer Comm'n at 297 (describing atomization as "the process by which news is 'decoupled from its source' and consumed on a 'story-by-story basis."). Free and Diverse Press Hearing at 3 (statement of David Chavern, Pres., News Media Alliance) ("These tech giants use secret, unpredictable algorithms to determine how and even whether content is delivered to readers. They scrape news organizations' content and use it to their own ends, without permission or remuneration for the companies that generated the content in the first place. They also suppress news organizations' brands, control their data, and refuse to recognize and support quality journalism.").

[316] Submission of Source 114, to H. Comm. on the Judiciary, 12 (Oct. 2, 2019) (on file with Comm.);

[317] Interview with Source 114 (Oct. 2, 2019).

[318] Submission of Source 140, to H. Comm. on the Judiciary, 2 (Oct. 15, 2019) (on file with Comm.).

that "you don't need a mask and hydroxychloroquine is a cure for COVID."[319] As he noted, within the first five hours of this video being posted, it had nearly "20 million views and over 100,000 comments before Facebook acted to remove it."[320] Mr. Zuckerberg responded that "a lot of people shared that, and we did take it down because it violate[d] our policies."[321] In response, Chairman Cicilline asked if "20 million people saw it over the period of five hours . . . doesn't that suggest, Mr. Zuckerberg, that your platform is so big that, even with the right policies in place, you can't contain deadly content?"[322] Mr. Zuckerberg responded by claiming that Facebook has a "relatively good track record of finding and taking down lots of false content."[323]

Moreover, because there is not meaningful competition, dominant firms face little financial consequence when misinformation and propaganda are promoted online.[324] Platforms that are dependent on online advertising have an incentive to prioritize content that is addictive or exploitative to increase engagement on the platform.[325] And the reliance on platforms by advertisers has generally diminished their ability to push for improvements in content standards. As a news publisher explained in a submission to the Subcommittee:

> As advertisers have become more reliant on dominant search and social platforms to reach potential consumers, they have lost any leverage to demand change in the policies or practices of the platforms. In the era of newspapers, television, radio, or indeed direct sales of digital advertising online, there was a connection between advertising and the content it funds, creating a high degree of accountability for both parties in that transaction. This maintained high content standards, and enabled advertisers to demand or pursue change from publishers whose content standards fell. While many high-quality publishers continue to operate stringent policies in relation to the digital advertising that they permit to appear within their services, in a world of programmatic

---

[319] CEO Hearing Transcript at 143 (Rep. David N. Cicilline, Chairman, Subcomm. on Antitrust, Commercial and Admin. Law of the H. Comm. on the Judiciary).

[320] *Id.*

[321] *Id.* (Mark Zuckerberg, CEO, Facebook).

[322] *Id. at 143-144* (Rep. David N. Cicilline, Chairman, Subcomm. on Antitrust, Commercial and Admin. Law of the H. Comm. on the Judiciary).

[323] *Id.* at 144 (statement of Mark Zuckerberg, CEO, Facebook).

[324] Free and Diverse Press Hearing at 8 (statement of Sally Hubbard, Dir. of Enforcement Strategy, Open Mkts. Inst.); Charlie Warzel, Opinion, *Facebook Can't Be Reformed*, N.Y. TIMES (July 1, 2020), https://www.nytimes.com/2020/07/01/opinion/facebook-zuckerberg.html.

[325] Conversely, the decline of trustworthy sources of news due to rising market power and declining ad revenue has also contributed to this harm. Competition & Mkts Auth. Report at 9 ("[C]oncerns relating to online platforms funded by digital advertising can lead to wider social, political and cultural harm through the decline of authoritative and reliable news media, the resultant spread of 'fake news' and the decline of the local press which is often a significant force in sustaining communities.").

audience trading that self-regulated compact between advertisers and platform does not exist.[326]

During the Subcommittee's sixth hearing, Representative Jamie Raskin (D-MD) raised this concern. As he noted, in July 2020, Facebook faced an advertiser boycott by hundreds of companies.[327] This effort, which has been spearheaded by the Stop Hate for Profit campaign, a coalition of civil rights groups organizing in protest of "the rapid spread of hate messages online, the presence of boogaloo and other right-wing extremist groups trying to infiltrate and disrupt Black Lives Matter protests and the fact that alt-right racists and anti-Semitic content flourishes on Facebook."[328]

As a result of this campaign, more than a thousand major companies—including Disney, Coca-Cola, and General Motors—announced that they would pull $7 billion in advertisements on Facebook as part of the Stop Hate for Profit boycott.[329] But as Representative Raskin pointed out during the hearing Facebook does not "seem to be that moved by their campaign."[330]

Representative Pramila Jayapal (D-WA) also noted during the hearing that Mr. Zuckerberg reportedly told Facebook's employees at an internal meeting that the company is "not gonna change our policies or approach on anything because of a threat to a small percent of our revenue, or to any percent of our revenue."[331] During that meeting, Mr. Zuckerberg reportedly acknowledged that the boycott "hurts us reputationally," but said that the company was insulated from threats by large advertisers due to advertising revenue from small businesses.[332] In response to this report, Ms. Jayapal asked Mr. Zuckerberg whether Facebook is "so big that you don't care how you're impacted by a major boycott of 1,100 advertisers?"[333] Mr. Zuckerberg responded that "[o]f course we care. But we're

---

[326] Submission of Source 140, to H. Comm. on the Judiciary, 5 (Oct. 15, 2019) (on file with Comm.).

[327] CEO Hearing Transcript at 57 (Rep. Jamie Raskin, Member, Subcomm. on Antitrust, Commercial and Admin. Law of the H. Comm. on the Judiciary).

[328] *Id.* Stop Hate for Profit was established by the Anti-Defamation League, the NAACP, Color of Change, and other civil rights groups in the wake of the May 2020 police killing of George Floyd, an unarmed black man, in Minneapolis and the ensuing national protests. Shirin Ghaffary & Rebecca Heilweil, *Why Facebook Is "The Front Line in Fighting Hate Today,"* RECODE (July 15, 2020), https://www.vox.com/recode/2020/7/15/21325728/facebook-stop-hate-for-profit-campaign-jonathan-greenblatt-anti-defamation-league.

[329] Steven Levy, *Facebook Has More to Learn From the Ad Boycott*, WIRED (Aug. 6, 2020), https://www.wired.com/story/rashad-robinson-facebook-ad-boycott/.

[330] CEO Hearing Transcript at 57 (statement of Rep. Jamie Raskin, Subcomm. on Antitrust, Commercial and Admin. Law of the H. Comm. on the Judiciary).

[331] *Id.* (statement of Mark Zuckerberg, CEO, Facebook).

[332] *Id.*

[333] *Id.* at 216 (question of Rep. Pramila Jayapal, Subcomm. on Antitrust, Commercial and Admin. Law of the H. Comm. on the Judiciary).

also not going to set our content policies because of advertisers. I think that that would be the wrong thing for us to do."[334]

Since then, the civil rights groups have said that although Facebook made some changes in response to the boycott—such as the creation of a position within the company dedicated to overseeing civil rights and algorithmic bias—it ultimately has not made meaningful changes at scale, and "lags competitors in working systematically to address hate and bigotry on their platform."[335]

The group organized further action in September 2020, when it called for companies and public figures to stop posting on Instagram beginning September 16th.[336] This protest, aimed again at Facebook's treatment of hate groups, was spurred by the police shooting of Jacob Blake in Kenosha, Wisconsin.[337] In the aftermath, Facebook failed to remove a group promoting the coalescence of an armed militia in the streets of Kenosha, despite numerous users reporting the page.[338] Mr. Zuckerberg called this failure an "operational mistake."[339]

ii. Monetization

The rise of market power online has severely affected the monetization of news, diminishing the ability of publishers to deliver valuable reporting.[340]

The digital advertising market is highly concentrated, with Google and Facebook controlling the majority of the online advertising market in the United States,[341] and capturing nearly all of the its

---

[334] *Id.* at 216 (statement of Mark Zuckerberg, CEO, Facebook).

[335] *Statement from Stop Hate For Profit on July 2020 Ad Pause Success and #StopHateForProfit Campaign*, STOP HATE FOR PROFIT (July 30, 2020), https://www.stophateforprofit.org/.

[336] Donie O'Sullivan, *Group That Led Facebook Boycott Is Back With New Action*, CNN BUSINESS (Sept. 14, 2020), https://www.cnn.com/2020/09/14/tech/facebook-boycott-return/index.html.

[337] *Id.*

[338] Brian Fung, *Facebook CEO Admits 'Operational Mistake' In Failure To Remove Kenosha Militia Page*, CNN BUSINESS (Sept. 4, 2020), https://www.cnn.com/2020/08/28/tech/zuckerberg-kenosha-page/index.html.

[339] *Id.*

[340] *See, e.g.*, Austl. Competition & Consumer Comm'n Report at 7; David Chavern, Opinion, *Protect the News from Google and Facebook*, WALL ST. J. (Feb. 25, 2018), https://www.wsj.com/articles/protect-the-news-from-google-and-facebook-1519594942; *infra* section II.C.3.

[341] *See e.g.*, Hamza Shaban, *Digital Advertising To Surpass Print and TV for the First Time, Report Says*, WASH. POST: TECH. (Feb. 20, 2019), https://www.washingtonpost.com/technology/2019/02/20/digital-advertising-surpass-print-tv-first-time-report-says/.

growth in recent years.[342] Although Amazon has grown its digital advertising business to become the third largest competitor in the market,[343] it still accounts for a relative small percentage.[344]

News publishers have raised concerns that this significant level of concentration in the online advertising market—commonly referred to as the digital ad duopoly—has harmed the quality and availability of journalism.[345] They note that as a result of this dominance, there has been a significant decline in advertising revenue to news publishers,[346] undermining publishers' ability to deliver valuable reporting, and "siphon[ing] revenue away from news organizations."[347]

Jason Kint, the CEO of Digital Content Next, a trade association that represents both digital and traditional news publishers, notes that there is "a clear correlation between layoffs and buyouts with the growth in market share for the duopoly—Google and Facebook."[348] David Chavern, the President and CEO of the News Media Alliance, has likewise said that "[t]he problem is that today's internet distribution systems distort the flow of economic value derived from good reporting."[349] The effects of this revenue decline are most severe at the local level, where the decimation of local news sources is giving rise to local news deserts.[350]

Other news publishers have expressed concerns about the dual role of platforms as both intermediaries and platforms for people's attention.[351] By keeping people inside a "walled garden," platforms can monetize their attention through ads, creating a strong economic incentive to minimize

[342] Sarah Sluis, *Digital Ad Market Soars To $88 Billion, Facebook And Google Contribute 90% Of Growth*, AD EXCHANGER (May 10, 2018), https://adexchanger.com/online-advertising/digital-ad-market-soars-to-88-billion-facebook-and-google-contribute-90-of-growth.

[343] Jean Baptiste Su, *Amazon Is Now The #3 Digital Ad Platform In The U.S. Behind Google And Facebook, Says eMarketer*, FORBES (Sept. 20, 2018), https://www.forbes.com/sites/jeanbaptiste/2018/09/20/amazon-is-now-the-3-digital-ad-platform-in-the-u-s-behind-google-and-facebook-says-emarketer/#333342de3926.

[344] *Id.*

[345] *See, e.g.*, Shannon Bond, *Google and Facebook Build Digital Ad Duopoly*, FIN. TIMES (Mar. 14, 2017), https://www.ft.com/content/30c81d12-08c8-11e7-97d1-5e720a26771b; John Diaz, Opinion, *How Google and Facebook Suppress the News*, S.F. CHRON. (Apr. 5, 2019), https://www.sfchronicle.com/opinion/diaz/article/How-Google-and-Facebook-suppress-the-news-13745431.php.

[346] Data and Privacy Hearing at 5 (statement of Rod Sims, Chair, Austl. Competition & Consumer Comm'n); Free and Diverse Press Hearing at 3 (statement of David Pitofsky, General Counsel, News Corp).

[347] Free and Diverse Press Hearing at 3 (statement of David Chavern, Pres., News Media Alliance).

[348] Daniel Funke, *What's Behind the Recent Media Bloodbath? The Dominance of Google and Facebook*, POYNTER (June 14, 2017), https://www.poynter.org/business-work/2017/whats-behind-the-recent-media-bloodbath-the-dominance-of-google-and-facebook.

[349] David Chavern, Opinion, *How Antitrust Undermines Press Freedom*, WALL ST. J. (July 9, 2017), https://www.wsj.com/articles/how-antitrust-undermines-press-freedom-1499638532.

[350] PENELOPE MUSE ABERNATHY, UNIV. N.C. SCH. OF MEDIA AND JOURNALISM, THE EXPANDING NEWS DESERT 33 (2018), https://www.cislm.org/wp-content/uploads/2018/10/The-Expanding-News-Desert-10_14-Web.pdf.

[351] Submission of Source 140, to H. Comm. on the Judiciary, 11 (Oct. 15, 2019) (on file with Comm.); Submission of Source 114, to H. Comm. on the Judiciary, 13 (Oct. 2, 2019) (on file with Comm.).

outbound referrals that lead to a decline in users' attention and engagement. In turn, this diminishes the incentives of publishers to invest in high-quality journalism.[352] David Pitofsky, the General Counsel of NewsCorp, described this as a free-riding problem in his testimony before the Subcommittee, explaining that platforms:

> [D]eploy our highly engaging news content to target our audiences, then turn around and sell that audience engagement to the same advertisers news publishers are trying to serve. Dominant platforms take the overwhelming majority of advertising revenue without making any investment in the production of the news, all while foreswearing any responsibility for its quality and accuracy. As a result, one of the pillars of the news industry's business model, advertising revenue, is crumbling.[353]

c. International Scrutiny

Several of the concerns regarding the distribution and monetization of news through platform intermediaries were raised as part of a comprehensive inquiry by the Australian Competition and Consumer Commission (ACCC). Over the span of several years, the Commission collected evidence from more than a hundred market participants and organizations as part of its review. Following its publication of a Preliminary Report in December 2018 and an Issues Paper in February 2018, the ACCC issued an extensive Final Report spanning more than 600 pages and including submissions from more than 100 market participants.[354]

Among its findings, the ACCC concluded that Facebook and Google have significant and durable market power over the distribution of news online.[355] As the ACCC noted, "Google and Facebook are the gateways to online news media for many consumers," accounting for a significant amount of referral traffic to news publishers' websites.[356] As a result, news publishers are reliant on these platforms for reaching people online, which affects publishers' ability to monetize journalism, particularly on formats such as Google's Accelerated Mobile Pages (AMP).[357]

---

[352] Competition & Mkts Auth. Report at 319.

[353] Free and Diverse Press Hearing at 2 (statement of David Pitofsky, Gen. Counsel, News Corp).

[354] Press Release, Austl. Competition & Consumer Comm'n, Holistic, Dynamic Reforms Needed to Address Dominance of Digital Platforms (July 26, 2019), https://www.accc.gov.au/media-release/holistic-dynamic-reforms-needed-to-address-dominance-of-digital-platforms.

[355] Austl. Competition & Consumer Comm'n Report at 226.

[356] *Id.* at 296.

[357] *Id.* at 206, 247 (concluding that AMP is a "must have" product for publishers).

The ACCC made 23 recommendations to address concerns across a broad range of issues, including antitrust, privacy, and consumer protection.[358] Within the context of addressing the effects of market power on the news industry—particularly as it relates to the imbalance of bargaining power between platforms and publishers—the Commission recommended developing "a code of conduct to govern the relationship between media businesses and digital platforms [which] seeks, among other things, to address this imbalance."[359]

On July 31, 2020, the Commission released a draft code to address a "fundamental bargaining power imbalance" between news publishers and dominant platforms that has led to "news media businesses accepting less favourable terms for the inclusion of news on digital platform services than they would otherwise agree to in response to a request by the Australian government."[360]

Under this code, Facebook, Google, and other platforms with significant bargaining power designated by Australia's Treasurer must negotiate with covered news publishers "in good faith over all issues relevant to news on digital platform services."[361] News publishers may negotiate either individually or collectively over a three-month period, allowing local and rural publishers "to negotiate from a stronger position than negotiating individually."[362]

If publishers are unable to reach an agreement during the mediated negotiation period, they may bring the dispute to compulsory arbitration. As part of this process, the arbitrator must consider the parties' final offers covering: (1) the benefits of news content to the platform; (2) the costs of producing news by the publisher; and (3) whether a payment model would unduly burden the commercial interests of the platform.[363] The arbitrator must choose one of the parties' proposals, encouraging both parties to make reasonable offers.[364]

Facebook and Google have responded to the draft code by warning that they may no longer display news on their respective platforms in Australia. Despite an "unprecedented surge in audiences

---

[358] Press Release, Austl. Competition & Consumer Comm'n, ACCC Commences Inquiry Into Digital Platforms (Dec. 4, 2017), https://www.accc.gov.au/media-release/accc-commences-inquiry-into-digital-platforms.

[359] Austl. Competition & Consumer Comm'n Report at 245.

[360] AUSTL. COMPETITION & CONSUMER COMM'N, DRAFT NEWS MEDIA BARGAINING CODE, https://www.accc.gov.au/focus-areas/digital-platforms/draft-news-media-bargaining-code (last visited on Sept. 27, 2020).

[361] AUSTL. COMPETITION & CONSUMER COMM'N, Q&As: DRAFT NEWS MEDIA AND DIGITAL PLATFORMS MANDATORY BARGAINING CODE 7 (July 2020), https://www.accc.gov.au/system/files/DPB%20-%20Draft%20news%20media%20and%20digital%20platforms%20mandatory%20bargaining%20code%20Q%26As.pdf.

[362] *Id.* at 6.

[363] *Id.* at 9.

[364] *Id.*

for news websites and TV news,"[365] Google claims that the draft code does not reflect the "more than $200 million in value that Google provides to publishers each year by sending people to their websites."[366] Facebook described the draft code as "unprecedented in its reach," notwithstanding similar proposals in other countries, including France,[367] as well as the United States.[368]

In response to Google's threat to boycott journalism in Australia, ACCC Chair Rod Sims said that Google's statement contained "misinformation" about the draft code, asserting that the draft code responds to "a significant bargaining power imbalance between Australian news media businesses and Google and Facebook."[369] Australia's Treasurer, Josh Frydenberg, similarly said that the country would not "respond to coercion or heavy-handed threats wherever they come from."[370]

4. Political and Economic Liberty

During the investigation, the Subcommittee examined the effects of market power on political and economic liberty. Concerns about the democratic effects of private monopolies trace back to the foundational antitrust statutes, where lawmakers worried that monopolies were "a menace to republican institutions themselves."[371] The Subcommittee's examination of these matters follows a long tradition of congressional attention to this issue.[372]

---

[365] Amanda Meade, *News Corp To Suspend Print Editions Of 60 Local Newspapers As Advertising Revenue Slumps*, THE GUARDIAN (Mar. 31, 2020), https://www.theguardian.com/media/2020/apr/01/news-corp-to-suspend-print-editions-of-60-local-newspapers-as-advertising-revenue-slumps.

[366] *Update To Our Open Letter to Australians*, GOOGLE, https://about.google/google-in-australia/an-open-letter/.

[367] Natasha Lomas, *France's Competition Watchdog Orders Google To Pay For News Reuse*, TECHCRUNCH (Apr. 9, 2020), https://techcrunch.com/2020/04/09/frances-competition-watchdog-orders-google-to-pay-for-news-reuse/.

[368] Ashley Cullins, *National Association of Broadcasters Warns Congress Tech Giants Could Kill Local Journalism*, HOLLYWOOD REPORTER (Sept. 3, 2020), https://www.hollywoodreporter.com/thr-esq/national-association-of-broadcasters-warns-congress-tech-giants-could-kill-local-journalism.

[369] Naaman Zhou, *Google's Open Letter To Australians About News Code Contains 'Misinformation', ACCC Says*, THE GUARDIAN (Aug. 17, 2020), https://www.theguardian.com/technology/2020/aug/17/google-open-letter-australia-news-media-bargaining-code-free-services-risk-contains-misinformation-accc-says.

[370] Jamie Smyth & Alex Barker, *Battle Lines Drawn As Australia Takes On Big Tech Over Paying For News*, FIN. TIMES (Sept. 2, 2020), https://www.ft.com/content/0834d986-eece-4e66-ac55-f62e1331f7f7.

[371] 21 CONG. REC. 3146 (1890) (statement of Sen. Hoar).

[372] *Id.* at 2459 (statement of Sen Sherman); *see* 95 CONG. REC. 11486 (statement of Rep. Celler) ("[B]usiness concentration is politically dangerous, leading inevitably to increasing Government control"); also 96 CONG. REC. 16,452 (1950) (statement of Rep. Kefauver) ("the history of what has taken place in other nations where mergers and concentrations have placed economic control in the hands of a very few people is too clear to pass over easily. A point is eventually reached, and we are rapidly reaching that point in this country, where the public steps in to take over when concentration and monopoly gain too much power. The taking over by the public through its government always follows one or two methods and has one or two political results. It either results in a Fascist state or the nationalization of industries and thereafter a Socialist or Communist state.")

Based on interviews and submissions from market participants, along with other evidence examined by the Subcommittee, there are several ways in which the market power of the dominant platforms affects political and economic power.

First, the Subcommittee encountered a prevalence of fear among market participants who depend on the dominant platforms. Repeatedly, market participants expressed deep concern that speaking about the dominant platforms' business practices—even confidentially without attribution—would lead a platform to retaliate against them, with severe financial repercussions. The source of this fear was twofold. Some firms were so dependent on the platform that even potentially risking retaliation caused alarm. Others had previously seen a platform retaliate against someone for raising public concerns about their business practices and wanted to avoid the same fate.

Several market participants told the Subcommittee that they "live in fear" of the platforms. One said, "It would be commercial suicide to be in Amazon's crosshairs . . . If Amazon saw us criticizing, I have no doubt they would remove our access and destroy our business."[373] Another told the Subcommittee, "Given how powerful Google is and their past actions, we are also quite frankly worried about retaliation."[374] An attorney representing app developers said they "fear retaliation by Apple" and are "worried that their private communications are being monitored, so they won't speak out against abusive and discriminatory behavior."[375]

Market participants also expressed unease about the success of their business and their economic livelihood depending on the decision-making of the platforms. A single tweak of an algorithm, intentional or not, could cause significant costs if not financial disaster—with little recourse. Market participants routinely characterized the platforms as having arbitrary and unaccountable power—the same forms of undue power that antitrust laws were designed to prevent. As Senator John Sherman (R-OH) explained, antitrust was essential to preserve liberty "at the foundation of the equality of all rights and privileges" because concentrations of power outside of democratic institutions were a "kingly prerogative, inconsistent with our form of government."[376]

Additionally, courts and regulators have found that several of the dominant platforms have engaged in recidivism. For example, Facebook settled charges brought in 2012 by the Federal Trade Commission (FTC) that it had "deceived consumers by telling them they could keep their information on Facebook private, and then repeatedly allowing it to be shared and made public."[377] As part of this

---

[373] Interview with Source 636 (Mar. 11, 2020)

[374] Submission from Source 147 (on file with Comm.).

[375] Submission from Source 88 (on file with Comm.).

[376] 21 Cong. Rec. 2457 (1890) (statement of Sen. Sherman).

[377] Press Release, Federal Trade Comm'n, Facebook Settles FTC Charges That It Deceived Consumers By Failing To Keep Privacy Promises (Nov. 29, 2011) (proposed settlement), https://www.ftc.gov/news-events/press-releases/2011/11/facebook-settles-ftc-charges-it-deceived-consumers-failing-keep.

settlement, Facebook agreed to abide by an administrative order requiring that Facebook not misrepresent its privacy protections.[378] Seven years later, the FTC concluded that Facebook had almost immediately begun violating that order following its adoption.[379] Ruling on the FTC's subsequent settlement with Facebook, District Court Judge Timothy Kelley wrote that "the unscrupulous way in which the United States alleges Facebook violated both the law and the administrative order is stunning."[380] The FTC has similarly sanctioned Google on several occasions for privacy violations.[381] In 2010, Apple settled charges it had conspired to fix employees' wages.[382] Two years later, Apple was found guilty of orchestrating a price-fixing conspiracy.[383] In that case, the presiding judge stated that the record "demonstrated a blatant and aggressive disregard" by Apple "for the requirements of the law," noting that the conduct "included Apple lawyers and its highest level executives."[384]

Lastly, the growth in the platforms' market power has coincided with an increase in their influence over the policymaking process. Over the past decade, the dominant online platforms have significantly increased their lobbying activity,[385] which tends to create a feedback loop for large companies. More money spent on lobbying may deliver higher equity returns and market share,[386] which, in turn, may spur more lobbying.

---

[378] *Id.*

[379] United States v. Facebook, Inc., No. CV 19-2184 (TJK), 2020 WL 1975785, *4 (D.D.C. Apr. 23, 2020) ("The United States now alleges that Facebook violated the 2012 Order by "subvert[ing] users privacy choices to serve its own business interests" in several ways, starting almost immediately after agreeing to comply with the 2012.").

[380] *Id.* at *1.

[381] Press Release, Federal Trade Comm'n, FTC, Google and YouTube Will Pay Record $170 Million for Alleged Violations of Children's Privacy Law (Sept. 4, 2019), https://www.ftc.gov/news-events/press-releases/2019/09/google-youtube-will-pay-record-170-million-alleged-violations.

[382] Press Release, Dep't of Justice, Justice Department Requires Six High Tech Companies to Stop Entering into Anticompetitive Employee Solicitation Agreements (Sept. 24, 2010), https://www.justice.gov/opa/pr/justice-department-requires-six-high-tech-companies-stop-entering-anticompetitive-employee.

[383] United States v. Apple Inc., 952 F. Supp. 2d 638, 644 (S.D.N.Y. 2013), aff'd, 791 F.3d 290 (2d Cir. 2015).

[384] August 27, 2013 Hr'g Tr. at 17:1-6, United States v. Apple, Inc. et al., (S.D.N.Y 2012) (No. 12-cv-2826). During the investigation, the Subcommittee also encountered instances in which the platforms did not appear fully committed to telling lawmakers the truth, including one incident in which members of the Subcommittee were forced to question whether Amazon had committed perjury. Letter from U.S. Rep. Jerrold Nadler, Chairman, H. Comm. on the Judiciary, et al., to Jeff Bezos, CEO, Amazon.com, Inc. (May 1, 2020), https://judiciary.house.gov/uploadedfiles/2020-05-01_letter_to_amazon_ceo_bezos.pdf.

[385] *See e.g.*, Spencer Soper et al., *Amazon's Jeff Bezos Can't Beat Washington, So He's Joining It: The Influence Game*, BLOOMBERG, (Feb. 14, 2018), https://www.bloomberg.com/graphics/2018-amazon-lobbying/. This is a trend for the industry. The total reported lobbying expenditures by digital platforms increased from $1,190,000 a year in 1998, to $74,285,000 in 2019 as the industry consolidated and gained market power. LOBBYING SPENDING DATABASE, CTR. FOR RESPONSIVE POLITICS, https://www.opensecrets.org/lobby/top.php?indexType=i&showYear=2019 (last visited on Sept. 27, 2020).

[386] *See* J.H. Kim, *Corporate Lobbying Revisited*, 10 BUS. AND POL, 1 (2008) (analyzing lobbying's effect on equity returns); Brian Shaffer et al., *Firm Level Performance Implications of Nonmarket Actions*, 39 BUS. AND SOC. 126 (2000) (analyzing lobbying's effect on market share).

Outside of traditionally reported and regulated lobbying, firms with market power and dispensable income fund think tanks and nonprofit advocacy groups to steer policy discussion. For example, Facebook, Google, and Amazon reportedly donated significant amounts to the American Enterprise Institute (AEI), which, in turn, has argued that antitrust critiques of the big platforms are "astonishingly weak."[387] More recently, Google and Amazon have contributed significant funding to the Global Antitrust Institute at the George Mason University's Antonin Scalia School of Law, which advocates against antitrust scrutiny of the dominant platforms.[388] By funding academics and advocacy groups, the dominant platforms can expand their sphere of influence, further shaping how they are governed and regulated.

At several hearings, Members of the Subcommittee noted that the outsized political influence of dominant firms has adverse effects on the democratic process. At the Subcommittee's field hearing in Colorado, Representative Ken Buck (R-CO) asked each of the witnesses about this issue.[389] As Rep. Buck noted, the dominant platforms are generally well represented in the policymaking process:

> Part of what we are dealing with here is the reality that [dominant firms] walk into our offices and they tell us their side of the story and we very rarely hear the other side of the story, and somehow part of this solution has to be that public policymakers elected, appointed, have to have access to that kind of information. So I thank you for being here and I also would encourage you to make sure that, you know, we are accessible. We are trying our best to make sure that we continue to create the environment for your kinds of companies.[390]

During the Subcommittee's sixth hearing, Subcommittee Chairman David Cicilline (D-RI) noted the democratic stakes of the Subcommittee's work. He said, "Because concentrated economic power also leads to concentrated political power, this investigation also goes to the heart of whether we, as a people, govern ourselves, or whether we let ourselves be governed by private monopolies."[391]

---

[387] Andrew Perez and Tim Zelina, *Facebook, Google, Amazon are ramping up their secretive influence campaigns in D.C.*, FAST COMPANY (Oct. 31, 2019), https://www.fastcompany.com/90424503/facebook-google-amazon-are-ramping-up-their-secretive-influence-campaigns-in-dc.

[388] Daisuke Wakabayashi, *Big Tech Funds a Think Tank Pushing for Fewer Rules. For Big Tech.*, N.Y. TIMES (July 24, 2020), https://www.nytimes.com/2020/07/24/technology/global-antitrust-institute-google-amazon-qualcomm.html.

[389] Competitors Hearing at 57.

[390] *Id.*

[391] CEO Hearing Transcript at 7 (statement of Rep. David N. Cicilline, Chairman, Subcomm. on Antitrust, Commercial and Admin Law).

IV.   MARKETS INVESTIGATED

A. Online Search

Online search engines enable users to retrieve webpages and information stored on the Internet. After a user enters a query into the search engine, the search provider returns a list of webpages and information that are relevant to the search term entered.

There are two types of search engines: horizontal and vertical. Horizontal search engines are designed to retrieve a comprehensive list of general search results. Vertical search engines are designed to retrieve a narrower category of content, such as photo images (e.g., Dreamstime) or travel (e.g., Expedia). The majority of general search engines monetize the service through selling ad placements rather than charging search users a monetary price. The overwhelmingly dominant provider of general online search is Google, which captures around 81% of all general search queries in the U.S. on desktop and 94% on mobile. Other search providers include Bing, which captures 6% of the market, Yahoo (3%), and DuckDuckGo (1%).[392]

---

[392] *Search Engine Market Share United States of America: Sept. 2019–Sept. 2020*, STATCOUNTER, http://gs.statcounter.com/search-engine-market-share/all/united-states-of-america (last visited Oct. 3, 2020).

U.S. Desktop and Mobile Search Market Share[393]

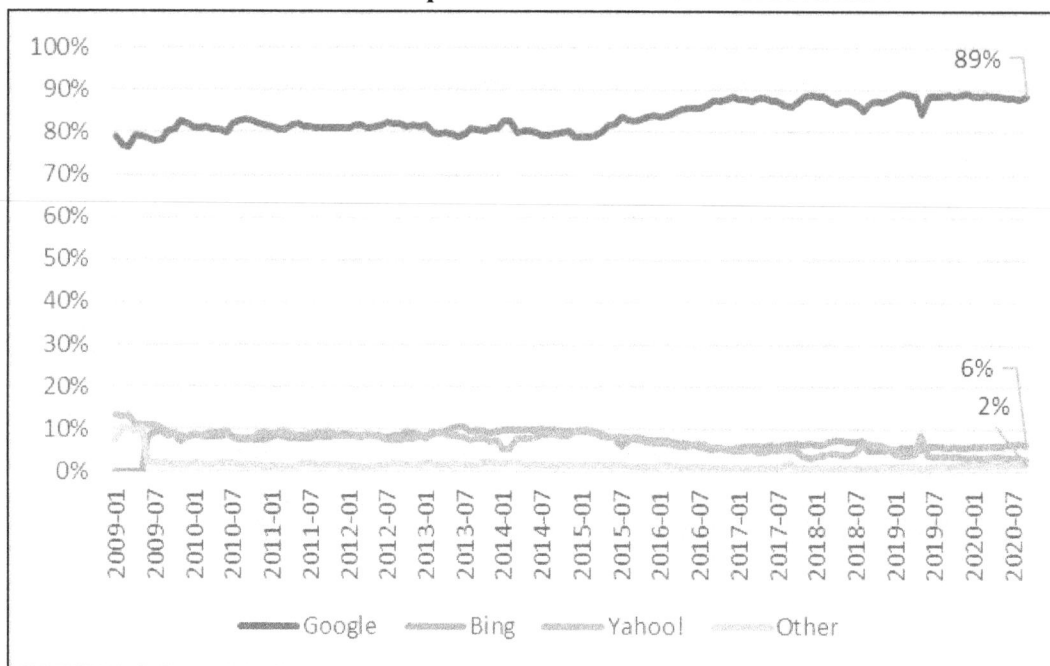

Online search is comprised of three distinct activities. First, an engine must "crawl" the Internet by using an automated bot to collect copies of all of the webpages it can find. Once a crawler has recorded all of this material, it must be collated and organized into an "index," or a map of the Internet that can be searched in real-time. Indexing organizes the information into the formats and databases required for the querying function. When a user enters a query into the search engine, the engine draws from the index to pull a list of responsive websites, ordered in terms of relevance. The relevance, in turn, is determined by the search algorithm applied by the search engine. A search engine can function only if it has access to an index, and an index can exist only once web pages have been crawled and collated into a repository.[394] Indexing has high fixed costs and requires significant server storage and compute power.[395] The ability to invest heavily in computing power and storage yields a significant advantage.[396]

---

[393] Prepared by the Subcomm. based on *Desktop & Mobile Search Engine Market Share United States Of America January 2009 to September 2020,* STATCOUNTER https://gs.statcounter.com/search-engine-market-share/desktop-mobile/united-states-of-america/#monthly-200901-202009 Other category includes AOL, Ask Jeeves, DuckDuckGo, MSN, Webcrawler, Windows Live, AVG Search, Baidu, Comcast, Babylon, Dogpile, Earthlink, Norton Safe Search, YANDEX RU. *Id.*

[394] Submission from Source 531, to H. Comm. on the Judiciary, Source 531-000017 (Nov. 21, 2011) (on file with Comm.) (According to one market participant, "[t]he greatest challenges in building a search index are finding the URLs for documents stored on the Web and then being able to parse the best URLs and documents to include in the index. Overcoming these challenges requires massive amounts of data on user interactions with websites to discover new URLs and then filter down to the 5% of known URLs [the search engine] uses to determine which documents to index, and how frequently these documents should be refreshed.").

[395] Submission from Source 531, to H. Comm. on the Judiciary, Source 531-000016–19 (July 26, 2011) (on file with Comm).

[396] Submission from Source 209, to H. Comm. on the Judiciary, Source 209-000537–38 (Aug. 24, 2009) (on file with Comm.) ("Comprehensiveness, freshness, and responsiveness are all directly related to the amount of computing power and

78

Several online search features tilt the market towards the dominant incumbent and make entry by new market participants difficult. First, web crawling is costly and strongly favors first-movers.[397] In a submission to the Subcommittee, one expert described how Google's early efforts have locked in its dominance.[398] In particular, Google was the first company to crawl the entirety of the Internet, a feat motivated in part due to its PageRank algorithm, which used links between pages to identify the most relevant webpages for specific topics and queries. Unlike most search engine algorithms at the time, the quality of PageRank results improved with more webpages, incentivizing Google to crawl a greater portion of the web.

The web has grown exponentially over the last two decades,[399] which means the cost of crawling the entire Internet has increased too, despite advances in crawling technology. Today several major webpage owners block all but a select few crawlers, in part because being constantly crawled by a large number of bots can hike costs for owners and lead their webpages to crash. The one crawler that nearly all webpages will allow is Google's "Googlebot," as disappearing from Google's index would lead most webpages to suffer dramatic drops in traffic and revenue.[400] Any new search engine crawler, by contrast, would likely be blocked by major webpage owners unless that search engine was driving significant traffic to webpages—which a search engine cannot do until it has crawled enough webpages.[401]

The high cost of maintaining a fresh index and the decision by many large webpages to block most crawlers significantly limits new search engine entrants. In 2018, Findx—a privacy-oriented search engine that had attempted to build its own index—shut down its crawler, citing the impossibility of building a comprehensive search index when many large websites only permit crawlers from

---

storage capacity brought to bear on the problem of crawling and indexing the web. It would therefore be implausible to attribute Google's massive search advantage to superior technology. Rather, the main driver of search performance is scale. Scale is driven primarily by the level of financial investment in search infrastructure.").

[397] *See, e.g.*, Submission from Source 534, to H. Comm. on the Judiciary, 1 (Oct. 14, 2019) (on file with Comm.) ("[The Company] does not own its own search index and is not planning to invest into building an own index because of the high investment costs."; Google Search (Shopping) Commission Decision (non-confidential version), European Commission 66 (June 27, 2017); Submission from Source 481, to H. Comm. on the Judiciary ("Bing and Google each spend hundreds of millions of dollars a year crawling and indexing the deep Web. It costs so much that even big companies like Yahoo and Ask are giving up general crawling and indexing. Therefore, it seems silly to compete on crawling and, besides, we do not have the money to do so.").

[398] Submission from Zack Maril, to H. Comm. on the Judiciary (Sept. 30, 2019) (on file with Comm.).

[399] *Total Number of Websites*, INTERNET LIVE STATS, https://www.internetlivestats.com/total-number-of-websites (last visited Oct. 3, 2020) (In 2000, the Internet had around 17,000 websites; today, it has more than 1.8 billion. Internet Live Stats, Total Number of Websites.).

[400] Submission from Submission from Zack Maril, to H. Comm. on the Judiciary (Sept. 30, 2019) (on file with Comm.); *see also* Submission from Source 481, to H. Comm on the Judiciary (Feb. 20, 2020) (on file with Comm.); Innovation and Entrepreneurship Hearing at 2 (statement of Megan Gray, Chief Counsel and Policy Advocate, DuckDuckGo).

[401] Submission from Submission from Zack Maril, to H. Comm. on the Judiciary (Sept. 30, 2019) (on file with Comm.).

Google and Bing.[402] Today the only English-language search engines that maintain their own comprehensive webpage index are Google and Bing.[403] Other search engines—including Yahoo and DuckDuckGo—must purchase access to the index from Google and/or Bing through syndication agreements that provide syndicated search engines with access to search results and search advertising.[404] While Yahoo previously maintained an independent index, it entered a deal with Microsoft in 2009 to integrate search technologies—a move driven by the two firms' belief that combining was necessary to provide a real alternative to Google.[405]

A second major competitive advantage enjoyed by search engine incumbents is their access to voluminous click-and-query data. This data, which tracks what users searched for and how they interacted with the search results, benefits search engines in several key ways.[406] First, search engines rely on click-and-query data to guide their search index's upkeep, as this data helps identify which webpages are most relevant and should be most regularly updated in the index.[407] Second, click-and-query-data is used to refine the search algorithm and the relevance of search results, as past user interactions improve the algorithm's ability to predict future interactions.[408] In particular, data on "tail"

---

[402] Findx, *Game over* (Sept. 21, 2019), https://web.archive.org/web/20190921180535/https://privacore.github.io ("Many large websites like LinkedIn, Yelp, Quora, Github, Facebook and others only allow certain specific crawlers like Google and Bing to include their webpages in a search engine index. . . . That meant that the Findx search index was incomplete and was not able to return results that were likely both relevant and good quality. When you compare any independent search engine's results to Google for example, they have no chance to be as relevant or complete because many large websites refuse to allow any other search engine to include their pages."); Submission from Source 407, to H. Comm. on the Judiciary, Source 407-000024 (Nov. 21, 2011) (on file with Comm.); Competition & Mkts. Auth. Report at 91.

[403] Competition & Mkts. Auth. Report at 89.

[404] Innovation and Entrepreneurship Hearing at 3 (statement of Megan Gray, Gen. Counsel and Pol'y Advocate, DuckDuckGo) (noting that alternatives to serving ads through Google or Microsoft, such as only showing product ads from Amazon or travel ads from Booking.com, as "not sufficiently lucrative to cover the costs of purchasing organic links," which means "an aspiring search engine start-up today (and in the foreseeable future) cannot avoid the need to sign a search syndication contract.").

[405] Submission from Source 209 to H. Comm. on the Judiciary, Source 209-0000346 (Aug. 24, 2009) (on file with Comm.).

[406] Competition & Mkts. Auth. Report at 11–12.

[407] Submission from Source 26, to H. Comm. on the Judiciary, Source 26-000016 (Nov. 21, 2011) (on file with Comm.) ("Queries are a critical component of the user data necessary to identify and rank URLs and documents for inclusion in a search index. Fewer queries mean fewer opportunities to identify relevant URLs and documents, which ultimately means a smaller usable search index."); rep-000026 (Nov. 21, 2011) ("Index freshness also is an important factor in the quality of a search engine's result . . . A [] survey found that a lack of freshness was a significant driver of dissatisfaction among users searching in the Entertainment and News categories.").

[408] *Id.* at Source 531-000015 ("The more user queries the search engine handles, the more data it obtains to improve the relevance of the search results it serves."); Source 531-000060 ("The secret to successful algorithmic search matching algorithms is user feedback . . . Ultimately this feedback helps the engine improve core relevance and other experience factors—driving higher engagement."); Innovation and Entrepreneurship Hearing at 3 (statement of Megan Gray, Gen. Counsel and Pol'y Advocate, DuckDuckGo) ("Another barrier facing a start-up search engine is that it needs data, such as the most commonly clicked links for a particular query, in order to produce a useful ranking of organic links, i.e., what organic link is first, second, etc."); Submission from Source 209, to H. Comm. on the Judiciary, Source 209-0000346–52 (Aug. 24, 2009) (on file with Comm.) ("Increased search traffic brings more indications of user intent, facilitating more experimentation and allowing a search platform to generate more relevant natural and paid search results."); *see also*

(or rare) queries enable a search engine to offer relevant results across a higher set of potential queries—improving the overall quality of the search engine—and Google's internal documents show that the company recognizes its long-tail advantage.[409] And third, increased query scale increases advertiser engagement rates, given that more user queries generally translate to more advertisement clicks, generating greater revenue for advertisers.[410]

Overall there are significant advantages to scale in click-and-query data, though the marginal benefit of additional data on tail queries is higher than the marginal benefit of additional data on "head" (or relatively common) queries.[411] Some market participants also stated that the benefits of scale diminish once a search engine reaches a certain size.[412] The benefits of scale create a feedback loop, where access to greater click-and-query data improves search quality, which drives more usage and generates additional click-and-query data.

A third barrier to competition in general online search is that Google has established extensive default positions across both browsers and mobile devices. Among desktop browsers, Google enjoys default placement in Chrome (which captures 51% of the U.S. market), Safari (31%), and Firefox (5%)—or 87% of the browser market.[413] Meanwhile, Microsoft's Edge, which captures 4% of the desktop browser market, sets Bing as its search default, leaving little opening for independent search engines.[414] In mobile, Google Search is primarily the default on Android and on Apple's iOS mobile operating system—together Android and iOS account for over 99% of smartphones in the United

---

Schaefer, M, Sapi, G and Lorincz, S (2018); He, D, Kannan, A, Liu, TY, McAfee, RP, Qin, T and Rao, JM, '*Scale Effects in Web Search*', *International Conference on Web and Internet Economics*, 294–310 (2017).

[409] Production of Google, to H. Comm. on the Judiciary , GOOG-HJC-03815864 (Apr. 23, 2010) ("Google leads competitors. . . Our long-tail precision is why users continue to come to Google. Users may try the bells and whistles of Bing and other competitors, but Google still produces the results. As soon as this ceases to be the case, our business is in jeopardy."); Competition & Mkts. Auth. Report Appendix I, at 15 (finding "that around 1% of Google 'tail' search events are for queries which are seen by Bing," whereas "31% of Bing 'tail' search events are for queries which are seen by Google." Furthermore, "0.8% of Google's 'tail' distinct queries are seen by Bing, whereas 30% of Bing's 'tail' distinct queries are seen by Google."); *see also* Submission from Source 209, to H. Comm. on the Judiciary, Source 209-0000528 at Source 209-0000532 (Feb. 17, 2011) (on file with Comm.) ("[W]ithout strong tail performance, a horizontal search engine cannot compete against Google."); *id.* at Source 209-0000535–36 ("[P]oor search engine performance in the tail means overall weak search engine performance.").

[410] *See, e.g.*, Submission from Source 531, to H. Comm. on the Judiciary, Source 531-000056 (July 11, 2011) (on file with Comm.) (stating that query scale increases advertiser engagement, since at scale the platform "makes better matches, has higher value generation").

[411] *See* Competition & Mkts. Auth. Report Appendix I at 18.

[412] Submission from Source 531, to H. Comm. on the Judiciary, Source 531-000874 (May 5, 2011) (on file with Comm.) ("As a platform gains more and more scale, the associated benefits begin to taper off such that eventually additional scale provides only modest returns."); Source 531-000025 (Nov. 21, 2011) (on file with Comm.) ("Above 30 billion documents, user satisfaction improves rapidly with increased index size; above 90 billion documents, it still continues to improve albeit at a slower rate.").

[413] Innovation and Entrepreneurship Hearing at 5 (statement of Megan Gray, Gen. Counsel and Pol'y Advocate, DuckDuckGo).

[414] *Id.*

States.[415] This default position provides Google with a significant advantage over other search engines, given users' tendency to stick with the default choice presented. Moreover, market participants identified several ways Google dissuades even those users who do attempt to switch default search engines on Chrome.[416]

Google won itself default placement across the mobile and desktop ecosystem through both integration and contractual arrangements. By owning Android, the world's most popular mobile operating system, Google ensured that Google Search remained dominant even as mobile replaced desktop as the critical entry point to the Internet. Documents submitted to the Subcommittee show that at certain key moments, Google conditioned access to the Google Play Store on making Google Search the default search engine, a requirement that gave Google a significant advantage over competing search engines.[417] Through revenue-sharing agreements amounting to billions of dollars in annual payments, Google also established default positions on Apple's Safari browser (on both desktop and mobile) and Mozilla's Firefox.[418]

In public statements, Google has downplayed the significance of default placement, claiming that "competition is just a click away."[419] However, Google's internal documents show that when Google was still jostling for search market share, Google executives closely tracked search defaults on Microsoft's Internet Explorer and expressed concern that non-Google defaults could impede Google Search.[420] In an internal presentation about Internet Explorer's default search selection, Google recommended that users be given an initial opportunity to select a search engine and that browsers minimize the steps required to change the default search engine.[421] These discussions—along with the steep sums Google pays Apple and various browsers for default search placement—further highlight the competitive significance of default positions.

Independent search engines told the Subcommittee that because they are not set as the default search engine on popular browsers, they face significant business challenges. As a result, DuckDuckGo said it was compelled to invest in browser technology, including creating its own

---

[415] *Mobile Operating System Market Share in United States Of America – September 2020*, STATCOUNTER, https://gs.statcounter.com/os-market-share/mobile/united-states-of-america (last visited Oct. 3, 2020).

[416] Submission from Source 534, to H. Comm. on the Judiciary, 1 (Oct. 14, 2019) (on file with Comm.).

[417] *See infra* Section V.

[418] Innovation and Entrepreneurship Hearing at 12 (response to Questions for the Record of Kyle Andeer, Vice Pres., Corp. Law, Apple, Inc.).

[419] *See, e.g.*, Adam Kovacevich, *Google's approach to competition*, GOOGLE PUBLIC POLICY BLOG (May 8, 2009), https://publicpolicy.googleblog.com/2009/05/googles-approach-to-competition.html.

[420] *See, e.g.*, Production of Google, to H. Comm. on the Judiciary, GOOG-HJC-01196214 (May 31, 2005) (on file with Comm.).

[421] Production of Google, to H. Comm. on the Judiciary, GOOG-HJC-01680749 (February 16, 2006) (on file with Comm.) (identifying several recommendations, including, "[f]ewest clicks required to change default, which promotes search innovation by facilitating the user's ability to switch.").

browser for Android and iOS and various browser extensions.[422] It noted, however, that "the same default placement challenges exist in the browser market, just one level up – with the device makers requiring millions or billions of dollars to become a default browser on a device."[423]

A fourth challenge facing upstart search engines is the growing number of features and services that a general search provider must offer to be competitive with Google. Through the mid-2000s, a general search engine could compete through providing organic links alone. Since Google and Bing now incorporate information boxes and various specialized services directly onto their general search results page, a market entrant would similarly need to provide a broader set of search features and services. One market participant told the Subcommittee that this set of "mandatory high-quality search features" includes maps, local business answers, news, images, videos, definitions, and "quick answers."[424] Delivering this variety of features requires access to various sources of data, raising the overall costs of entry.

Vertical search providers differ from horizontal search engines in several ways. By offering specialized search focused on a particular topic or activity, they fulfill a separate role and require distinct tools and expertise. The necessary inputs vary by search vertical. Flight search, for example, requires access to flight software and data, whereas certain local search providers rely on user-generated content such as reviews. Many vertical providers use structured data feeds that pull from third-party databases, rather than from a general index.

A significant challenge for vertical providers is reaching users. Although they serve distinct needs, most vertical search providers still depend on horizontal search engines—and specifically on Google—to reach users.[425] In submissions to the Subcommittee, even some of the largest and most well-known verticals stated that they depend on Google for up to 80–95% of their traffic.[426] Since Google now also provides vertical search services, it has the incentive and ability to use its dominance in horizontal search to disfavor vertical providers that compete with its own vertical search services. Internal documents from Google show that it has used its dominance in general search to closely track traffic to competing verticals, demanding that certain verticals permit Google to scrape their user-generated content and demote several verticals. Several market participants told the Subcommittee that Google's preferential treatment of its own verticals, as well as its direct listing of information in the

---

[422] Innovation and Entrepreneurship Hearing at 5 (statement of Megan Gray, Gen. Counsel and Pol'y Advocate, DuckDuckGo).

[423] *Id.* at 5–6.

[424] *Id.* at 1.

[425] Submission from Source 564, to H. Comm. on the Judiciary, 5 (Nov. 12, 2019) (on file with Comm.) ("The most important source of traffic for local search services are general search websites").

[426] Submission from Source 564, to H. Comm. on the Judiciary, 5 (Nov. 12, 2019) (on file with Comm.); Submission from Source 115, to H. Comm. on the Judiciary, 19 (Dec. 27, 2019) (on file with Comm.); Submission from Source 887, to H. Comm. on the Judiciary, 3 (Oct. 28, 2019) (on file with Comm.); Submission from Foundem, to H. Comm. on the Judiciary, 9 (Dec. 12, 2016) (on file with Comm.).

"OneBox" that appears at the top of Google search results, has the net effect of diverting traffic from competing verticals and jeopardizing the health and viability of their business.[427]

Google's internal documents and submissions from third-party market participants suggest that verticals are both a complement to horizontal search as well as a competitive threat to it. One market participant explained that while vertical search providers can increase demand for horizontal search engines in the short-term, they can divert traffic from horizontal search providers in the long-term, as the growing popularity of a vertical may lead users to navigate to it directly.[428] Diverting traffic from general search providers, in turn, would deprive them of both advertiser revenue as well as valuable click-and-query data. Given these dynamics, a dominant horizontal search provider that also enters vertical search faces a significant conflict of interest that can skew search results to the detriment of third-party businesses and users alike.

B.   Online Commerce

Online commerce, also known as e-commerce, is the activity of buying or selling products or services using the Internet.[429] E-commerce transactions take place through a variety of channels, including online marketplaces like Amazon Marketplace, where a wide variety of brands and products from different sellers are sold in one place, or a business's direct to consumer website like Nike.com. In 2019, the U.S. Census Bureau estimated e-commerce retail sales to be about $600 billion,[430] compared to just under $33 billion in 2001.[431] As the COVID-19 pandemic pushes more American shoppers online, e-commerce growth has exploded.[432] This is particularly true for online marketplaces,

---

[427] Submission from Source 564, to H. Comm. on the Judiciary, 5 (Nov. 12, 2019) (on file with Comm.); Submission from Source 115, to H. Comm. on the Judiciary, 19 (Dec. 27, 2019) (on file with Comm.); Submission from Source 887, to H. Comm. on the Judiciary, 3 (Oct. 28, 2019) (on file with Comm.); Submission from Foundem, to H. Comm. on the Judiciary, 9 (Dec. 12, 2016) (on file with Comm.).

[428] Submission from Source 407, to H. Comm. on the Judiciary, Source 407-000071 (Nov. 12, 2019) (on file with Comm.).

[429] Press Release, U.S. Dep't of Commerce, U.S. Census Bur., Retail E-Commerce Sales in Fourth Quarter 2001 Were $10.0 Billion, Up 13.1 Percent from Fourth Quarter 2000, Census Bureau Reports (Feb. 20, 2002), https://www2.census.gov/retail/releases/historical/ecomm/01q4.pdf (defining e-commerce as "sales of goods and services where an order is placed by the buyer or price and terms of sale are negotiated over an Internet, extranet, Electronic Data Interchange (EDI) network, electronic mail, or other comparable online system. Payment may or may not be made online.").

[430] Press Release, U.S. Dep't of Commerce, U.S. Census Bur., Quarterly Retail E-Commerce Sales 4th Quarter 2019, https://www2.census.gov/retail/releases/historical/ecomm/19q4.pdf.

[431] Press Release, U.S. Dep't of Commerce, U.S. Census Bur., Retail E-Commerce Sales in Fourth Quarter 2001 Were $10.0 Billion, Up 13.1 Percent from Fourth Quarter 2000, Census Bureau Reports (Feb. 20, 2002). https://www2.census.gov/retail/releases/historical/ecomm/01q4.pdf.

[432] Gayle Kesten, *As Online Prices Increase, Consumers' Purchasing Power Declines*, ADOBE: RETAIL (July 13, 2020), https://blog.adobe.com/en/2020/07/13/as-online-prices-increase-consumers-purchasing-power-declines.html#gs.dv6lwa ("[T]otal online spending of $73 billion in June marked a 76.2 percent increase year-over-year."); *see also* ANDREW LIPSMAN, EMARKETER, US ECOMMERCE BY CATEGORY 2020: HOW THE PANDEMIC IS RESHAPING THE PRODUCT CATEGORY LANDSCAPE (July 22, 2020), https://www.emarketer.com/content/us-ecommerce-by-category-2020 ("US ecommerce sales

where sales for essential items like groceries, masks, and electronics for home offices increased sharply in the wake of the pandemic.[433]

An online marketplace's most basic function is to serve as a platform that connects buyers and sellers. Marketplaces include product listings from a variety of sellers. Some online marketplaces, such as Amazon and eBay, aim to be fully integrated, multi-category e-commerce sites. Other marketplaces, however, operate as vertical, single-category sites, such as Newegg.com, for computer hardware and consumer electronics. The primary customers of e-commerce marketplaces are customers looking to buy an item or service online, and businesses looking to sell goods or services to customers online. Because of this, a successful marketplace must be attractive to consumers and third-party sellers.

The consumer-facing side of the marketplace allows users to search for and purchase products. Most online marketplaces offer features that enable users to compare competing products based on details like their price, popularity, and customer satisfaction reviews. Amazon is by far the largest marketplace.[434] Other marketplaces that are popular with consumers include eBay, Walmart, and Wayfair.[435]

Online marketplaces also serve third-party sellers. Third-party sellers have needs that are distinct from consumers visiting the marketplace to make a purchase. The seller-facing side of the business consists of providing third-party sellers with a platform to list their products for consumers to purchase. Often, the marketplace will supply vendors with services such as inventory tracking and pricing recommendations. Online marketplaces usually offer additional paid services to third-party sellers such as advertising and fulfillment services, consisting of warehousing, packing, and shipping.

The businesses that own and operate e-commerce marketplaces may host only independent, third-party seller listings, or list their own items for sale alongside third-party sellers. Amazon Marketplace is an example of the latter, in that customers view Amazon Retail offers for its own

---

will surge 18.0% to $709.78 billion, while brick-and-mortar retail sales will experience a historically significant decline of 14.0% to $4.184 trillion.").

[433] FEEDVISOR, 2020 Q4 TRENDS AND PROJECTIONS: THE DIGITAL REVOLUTION OF RETAIL AND E-MARKETPLACES at 2–3, 5 (2020) (showing that Grocery and Gourmet sales on Amazon and Walmart were up 91% and 46% over the months of March and April 2020, respectively, compared to February); s*ee also* Giselle Abramovich, *How COVID-19 is Impacting Online Shopping Behavior*, ADOBE: COVID-19 (Mar. 26, 2020), https://blog.adobe.com/en/2020/03/26/how-covid-19-is-impacting-online-shopping-behavior.html#gs.dv63z7 (reporting that after the COVID-19 outbreak, "purchases for cold, cough & flu products increased 198%, while online purchases for pain relievers increased 152%").

[434] *See, e.g.*, ANDREW LIPSMAN, EMARKETER, TOP 10 US ECOMMERCE COMPANIES 2020 (Mar. 10, 2020), https://www.emarketer.com/content/top-10-us-ecommerce-companies-2020 (forecasting Amazon's e-commerce market share for 2020 at 38.7%, compared to second-place Walmart at 5.3% and third-place eBay at 4.7%); *see also* Production of Amazon, to H. Comm. on the Judiciary, AMAZON_HJC_00061156 (Oct. 30, 2019) (on file with Comm.) (showing that Amazon.com was about five times larger than eBay in 2018, its next closest marketplace competitor at the time).

[435] ANDREW LIPSMAN, EMARKETER, TOP 10 US ECOMMERCE COMPANIES 2020 (Mar. 10, 2020), https://www.emarketer.com/content/top-10-us-ecommerce-companies-2020.

private-label brands, such as AmazonBasics,[436] alongside independent, third-party seller offers. Amazon Retail also acts as a reseller of brand-name items, purchasing items like Levi's jeans from a wholesaler, and then reselling them on the marketplace. In these circumstances, third-party sellers are both customers and competitors of online marketplaces.

Marketplace operators benefit financially from the sale of services to third-party sellers and consumers.[437] On the seller-facing side of their business, marketplaces usually take a cut of third-party sales and charge fees for sales-related services like fulfillment, payment, and advertising. If the marketplace operators also sell products on their own platforms, they make money like a typical retailer from the difference between the wholesale and retail price. Marketplaces may also make money from fees paid by customers to participate in membership programs. For example, Amazon offers Amazon Prime for $119 per year as a paid membership program that provides customers with benefits such as unlimited free shipping on eligible items and digital streaming video.[438] Other revenue sources for marketplaces may include credit card and gift card services that are tied to the platform.[439]

A few large companies dominate the e-commerce industry, and Amazon is the clear leader among them. The market research company eMarketer estimates that Amazon is about eight times larger than eBay and Walmart in terms of market share.[440] Other metrics further demonstrate Amazon's role as a gatekeeper for e-commerce. Amazon is the most-visited website globally for e-commerce and shopping,[441] and recent analyses suggest that over 60% of all online product searches in the U.S. begin on Amazon.com.[442]

Amazon's dominance in e-commerce extends to its role as a marketplace operator and its relationship with sellers. Because of its size and scale, no other marketplace comes close to providing

---

[436] Production of Amazon, to H. Comm. on the Judiciary, 1 (Oct. 14, 2019) (on file with Comm.) ("AmazonBasics is an Amazon private brand that launched in 2009. The brand offers a number of products, including electronics accessories, luggage, and office products.").

[437] *See, e.g.*, Amazon.com, Inc., Quarterly Report (Form 10-Q) 18 (July 31, 2020), http://d18rn0p25nwr6d.cloudfront.net/CIK-0001018724/a77b5839-99b8-4851-8f37-0b012f9292b9.pdf (showing net sales for third-party seller services increased from $23 billion in the first six months of 2019 to $32 billion in the first six months of 2020).

[438] Production of Amazon, to H. Comm. on the Judiciary, 1–2 (Oct. 14, 2019) (on file with Comm.).

[439] *See, e.g.*, Amazon.com, Inc., Annual Report (Form 10-K) 23, 47 (Jan. 31, 2017), https://www.sec.gov/Archives/edgar/data/1018724/000101872417000011/amzn-20161231x10k.htm.

[440] ANDREW LIPSMAN, EMARKETER, TOP 10 US ECOMMERCE COMPANIES 2020 (Mar. 10, 2020), https://www.emarketer.com/content/top-10-us-ecommerce-companies-2020.

[441] *Worldwide E-Commerce and Shopping Category Performance*, SIMILARWEB (July 2020), https://pro.similarweb.com/#/industry/overview/E-commerce_and_Shopping/999/1m/?webSource=Total (showing that Amazon had 2.6 billion visits compared to 940.8 million for eBay in July 2020).

[442] Lucy Koch, *Looking for a New Product? You Probably Searched Amazon*, EMARKETER (Mar. 31, 2019), https://www.emarketer.com/content/looking-for-a-new-product-you-probably-searched-amazon (last visited Oct. 3, 2020) (citing FEEDVISOR, THE 2019 AMAZON CONSUMER BEHAVIOR REPORT 14 (2019)); *see also* WUNDERMAN THOMPSON COMMERCE, THE FUTURE SHOPPER REPORT 2020, 11 (2020) (on file with Comm.).

sellers with access to such a large pool of buyers, as well as sales-related services. There are over 112 million Prime members in the United States—about 44% of the adult population. The number of Prime members has doubled since reaching 50 million members in 2015, with Amazon projecting additional growth.[443] Amazon.com has 2.3 million active sellers on its marketplace worldwide.[444] In comparison, Amazon's closest e-commerce competitor, Walmart, has roughly 54,000 sellers on its marketplace.[445] In general, the more sellers a platform has, the more buyers it can attract and vice versa.[446] According to a competing online marketplace, sellers feel forced to be on Amazon because that is where the buyers are.[447]

If current trends continue, no company is likely to pose a threat to Amazon's dominance in the near or distant future. Although some alternatives to Amazon have experienced growth during the pandemic, there is still a massive gap between the market leader and its competitors.[448] Several factors privilege Amazon as the dominant e-commerce marketplace, and also make entry or expansion by a challenger unlikely. While some of these barriers to entry are inherent to e-commerce—such as economies of scale and network effects—others result from Amazon's anticompetitive conduct. As discussed elsewhere in the Report, Amazon's acquisition strategy and many of its business practices were successfully designed to protect and expand its market power. An Amazon executive referred to some of these tactics as the company's "Big Moats," and suggested "doubl[ing] down" on them in a business strategy document.[449] Similarly, in 2018, an investment analyst report expressed skepticism

---

[443] Press Release, Consumer Intelligence Research Partners, LLC, U.S. Amazon Prime Members – Slow, Steady Growth (Jan. 16, 2020), https://files.constantcontact.com/150f9af2201/9f9e47b4-0d66-4366-ad76-552ae3daa4f0.pdf (last visited Oct. 3, 2020); see Todd Bishop, *Amazon Tops 150M Paid Prime Subscribers Globally After Record Quarter for Membership Program*, GEEKWIRE (Jan. 30, 2020) https://www.geekwire.com/2020/breaking-amazon-tops-150m-paid-prime-members-globally-record-quarter/; Parkev Tatevosian, *Will Amazon Prime Reach 200 Million Members by the End of 2020?*, MOTLEY FOOL (July 18, 2020), https://www.fool.com/investing/2020/07/18/will-amazon-prime-reach-200-million-members-by-the.aspx (noting a 29% increase in Amazon's revenue in the second quarter of 2020 versus the same quarter in 2019, primarily as a result of COVID-19).

[444] *Number of Sellers on Amazon Marketplace*, MARKETPLACE PULSE, https://www.marketplacepulse.com/amazon/number-of-sellers (last visited Oct. 3, 2020).

[445] *Walmart's Fulfillment Service for Sellers Not Seeing Adoption*, MARKETPLACE PULSE, (Sept. 1, 2020), https://www.marketplacepulse.com/articles/walmarts-fulfillment-service-for-sellers-not-seeing-adoption.

[446] Stigler Report at 38 (describing indirect, multi-sided network effects in e-commerce, noting that "in ecommerce platforms, which intermediate trade between sellers and buyers, a buyer does not directly benefit from the presence of other buyers but does benefit from the presence of more sellers—who are in turn attracted by the presence of the buyers.").

[447] Submission from Source 718, to H. Comm. on the Judiciary, 5 (Oct. 14, 2019) (on file with Comm.).

[448] ANDREW LIPSMAN, EMARKETER, TOP 10 US ECOMMERCE COMPANIES 2020 (Mar. 10, 2020), https://www.emarketer.com/content/top-10-us-ecommerce-companies-2020 (illustrating that although Walmart's increased share of the U.S. retail e-commerce market will allow it to overtake eBay for second place, it will remain a distant second to Amazon).

[449] Production of Amazon, to H. Comm. on the Judiciary, AMAZON_HJC_00068510 (Sep. 8, 2010) (on file with Comm.).

about Walmart's ability to challenge Amazon, commenting, "[W]e are concerned Amazon's Prime membership program is fortifying an impenetrable moat around its customers."[450]

C. Social Networks and Social Media

Social media products and services include social networking, messaging, and media platforms designed to engage people by facilitating sharing, creating, and communicating content and information online.[451] Although the boundaries of the social media market are imprecise,[452] social media platforms generally allow users on their networks to interact with people or groups they know, display content through linear feeds, or otherwise add socially layered functionality for services online, usually through a mobile app. In response to the Committee's requests for information, several market participants said they view social media as driven by networks, while many social media products and services include common functionalities, such as public profiles, curated feeds, followers, messaging, and other use cases.[453] Others focus on certain aspects of public and private communications.[454]

A principal feature of social media platforms is that they typically offer their services for a zero monetary price to the platform's users.[455] The platform develops a service it hopes will attract a critical mass of users to then attract advertisers to the platform.[456] Some social media companies offer additional services to users for a price or allow users to pay for additional functionality. For example, LinkedIn Premium provides users with an option to pay for additional features, such as their network and in-app messaging insights.[457]

---

[450] *See* Lydia Ramsey Pflanzer, *Walmart's talks with an insurance giant could be part of an assault on Amazon Prime*, BUS. INSIDER (Apr. 3, 2018), https://www.businessinsider.com/morgan-stanley-why-walmart-could-bid-on-humana-2018-4.

[451] Competition & Mkts. Auth. Report at 53.

[452] Jan H. Kietzmann, Kristopher Hermkens, Ian P. McCarthy & Bruno S. Silvestre, *Social Media? Get Serious! Understanding the Functional Building Blocks of Social Media*, 54 BUS. HORIZONS 241 (2011), http://summit.sfu.ca/system/files/iritems1/18103/2011_social_media_bh.pdf.

[453] Submission from Source 247, to H. Comm. on the Judiciary, Source 247-0000000006 (Oct. 23, 2019) (on file with Comm.); Competition & Mkts. Auth. Report at 53.

[454] Submission from Source 471, to H. Comm. on the Judiciary, 4 (Oct. 15, 2019) (on file with Comm.) ("[T]here are a number of other competitors who focus on different or additional aspects of public and private communication. For example, some competitors focus on sharing and expression though images and other media (e.g., Instagram, YouTube, and Pinterest). Some companies focus more on private communications (e.g., WhatsApp, Snap (for the most part), Facebook, Signal, and Telegram). Other companies focus on communications about specific topics (e.g., Discord for gaming and Slack for workplace communications).").

[455] Submission from Source 164, to H. Comm. on the Judiciary, Source 164-000015 (Oct. 28, 2019) (on file with Comm.) (describing how online advertising requires building an ad product, a sales team to sell that product, the engineering and product capacity to target and measure the effectiveness of those ads.).

[456] FIONA M. SCOTT & DAVID C. DINIELLI, OMIDYAR NETWORK, ROADMAP FOR AN ANTITRUST CASE AGAINST FACEBOOK 3 (June 2020), https://www.omidyar.com/wp-content/uploads/2020/06/Roadmap-for-an-Antitrust-Case-Against-Facebook.pdf.

[457] LINKEDIN PREMIUM, https://premium.linkedin.com/ (last visited Oct. 3, 2020).

Social media platforms with a larger network of users are more likely to attract users and advertisers.[458] In a briefing to Subcommittee members and staff, Brad Smith, the President of Microsoft, described this value:

> You don't always need to have a proven business model to attract capital. You just need an idea that will get a lot of users. And then people assume you'll find a way to turn that usage into a business model that will produce revenue. That's been very important for the US. It distinguishes us and allows venture funding. There's something magical about 100 million active monthly users (MAU) in the United States. At that level a company becomes a force unto themselves. If you see a company acquire another company that's in the same product market and is on the path to reach 100 million MAU, that's more likely to raise a competitive concern. Historically, I think regulators were slow to notice that issue.[459]

As another market participant describes it, "attracting a critical mass of users is essential to delivering a viable social network, as there is no reason for users to start using a social network if there is no one there with whom they can connect."[460]

Social media companies may also focus on attracting particular types or groups of consumers to differentiate themselves from larger companies.[461] Many of the top-ranking apps on iOS are complementary to popular social media applications. For example, Dazz Cam, a vintage-inspired photo-editing app used with TikTok, was popular in the U.S. in 2020.[462] Similarly, Lens is a popular iOS app that allows users to browse, like, and comment on photos and videos on Instagram using the Apple Watch.[463]

---

[458] Production from Facebook, to H. Comm. on the Judiciary, FB_HJC_ACAL_00059100 (Apr. 6, 2012) (on file with Comm.) ("Advertising is a scale thing, it wasn't until we reached 350 million users did we become interesting to big brands.").

[459] Briefing with Brad Smith, President, Microsoft, in Washington, D.C. (June 23, 2020).

[460] Submission from Source 164, to H. Comm. on the Judiciary, Source 164-000014 (Oct. 28, 2019) (on file with Comm.). *But see* Bundeskartellamt, B6-22/16, Case Summary, *Facebook, Exploitative business terms pursuant to Section 19(1) GWB for inadequate* data processing, 8 (Feb. 15, 2019), https://www.bundeskartellamt.de/SharedDocs/Entscheidung/EN/Fallberichte/Missbrauchsaufsicht/2019/B6-22-16.pdf?__blob=publicationFile&v=4 ("At least as far as the services affected in this case are concerned, it is not sufficient to have a 'critical mass' of users or technical, financial and personal expertise in order to be able to enter neighbouring markets and be as successful as on the original market. As the example of Google+ has shown, a service cannot expect to have the same reach when providing a different type of service, due to strong direct network effects.").

[461] Competition & Mkts. Auth. Report at 115.

[462] Michelle Santiago Cortes, *These Are the TikTok Editing Apps You've Been Seeing on Your 'For You' Page*, REFINERY29 (Mar. 25, 2020, 5:00 PM), https://www.refinery29.com/en-us/tik-tok-editing-apps (last visited Oct. 3, 2020).

[463] Zac Hall, *Lens Is a Modern and Feature-Packed Instagram App for Apple Watch that Works Without the iPhone*, 9TO5MAC (Apr. 24, 2019, 12:28 PM), https://9to5mac.com/2019/04/24/lens-instagram-for-apple-watch/ (last visited Oct. 3, 2020).

Due to network effects in the social media market, new entrants may choose to begin as a complement by relying on the incumbent platform's application programming interfaces (APIs) such as Facebook's Open Graph or Twitter's search API.[464] However, because incumbent platforms control access to these APIs and can foreclose access to a complementary app that is successful or gaining users,[465] some market participants view relying on these platforms to reach users as a constant business risk.[466] One market participant noted that in addition to harming their business, these actions also "restrict users' ability to multi-home and increase barriers to entry, including network effects and switching costs."[467]

Given Facebook's dominance, the primary way for new entrants to compete is to attract a subgroup or niche.[468] One market participant explained, "competitors may be limited to niche strategies that do not challenge the incumbent directly. For example, Facebook (including Instagram) is by far the most popular social networking platform. Although there are several competitors, such as LinkedIn, and fast-growing new entrants, such as TikTok, most or all employ niche strategies to varying degrees, and most have far less user engagement, attention, and data and a smaller share of advertising revenue than Facebook."[469]

1. Social Networks are Distinguishable from Social Media

While a broad view of the social media market is useful for considering the wider landscape for social data and online advertising,[470] it is important to focus on the actual use, demand, and substitutability of social products when examining competition among social platforms online.[471] The

---

[464] FIONA M. SCOTT & DAVID C. DINIELLI, OMIDYAR NETWORK, ROADMAP FOR AN ANTITRUST CASE AGAINST FACEBOOK 22 (June 2020), https://www.omidyar.com/wp-content/uploads/2020/06/Roadmap-for-an-Antitrust-Case-Against-Facebook.pdf.

[465] Id. at 22–25; Submission from Source 471, to H. Comm. on the Judiciary, 8 (Oct. 15, 2019) (on file with Comm.) ("In or around 2010, [Source 471] restricted the access of our API by some third-party developers because we had significant concerns regarding some third-party developers use of [Source 471]'s private data. In order to protect private data, [Source 471] determined such changes were necessary to ensure that these data were not used improperly.").

[466] Submission from Source 164, to H. Comm. on the Judiciary, Source 164-00023 (Oct. 28, 2019) (on file with Comm.); Submission from Source 471, to H. Comm. on the Judiciary, 10 (Oct. 15, 2019) (on file with Comm.) ("[Our company's] business would be affected if other social networking networks were to disallow cross-posting . . . to their platforms or discontinue APIs central to the functionality of our products or services.").

[467] Submission from Source 471, to H. Comm. on the Judiciary, 10 (Oct. 15, 2019) (on file with Comm.).

[468] FIONA M. SCOTT & DAVID C. DINIELLI, OMIDYAR NETWORK, ROADMAP FOR AN ANTITRUST CASE AGAINST FACEBOOK 16 (June 2020), https://www.omidyar.com/wp-content/uploads/2020/06/Roadmap-for-an-Antitrust-Case-Against-Facebook.pdf.

[469] Submission from Source 407, to H. Comm. on the Judiciary, 4 (Nov. 1, 2019); Competition & Mkts. Auth. Report at 55 ("Differentiation can incentivise consumers to access multiple platforms, allowing for the co-existence of platforms.").

[470] Submission from Source 164, to H. Comm. on the Judiciary, Source-32-000014 (Oct. 28, 2019) (on file with Comm.) (discussing how they see "social media sites" as competitors for ads even though they don't think they are in that market.).

[471] See United States v. Microsoft Corp., 253 F.3d 34, 51–52 (D.C. Cir. 2001) ("the relevant market must include all products 'reasonably interchangeable by consumers for the same purposes.'") (quoting United States v. Du Pont & Co., 351

critical distinction between social networking and social media markets is how people use the platform. As Germany's Federal Cartel Office (Bundeskartellamt) and the United Kingdom's Competition and Markets Authority (CMA) have noted, the specific demand for social networks "is fundamentally different from the demand for other social media."[472]

Social network platforms facilitate their users finding, interacting, and networking with other people they already know online, and by providing a "rich social experience" through features on their products.[473] People regularly use social network platforms to exchange "experiences, opinions and contents among specific contacts which the users define based on identity."[474]

In contrast, social media platforms principally facilitate the distribution and consumption of content. Much of the content on YouTube, for example, can be enjoyed by users with a wide range of relationships to the person posting, including by strangers.[475] Similarly, TikTok describes itself as a "global platform for users to express their ideas by sharing videos with a broader community."[476] In light of this distinction, the CMA concluded that YouTube is focused on offering content and does not compete with Facebook, facilitating communication and sharing content among groups of friends who choose each other and enjoy content in large part because of those relationships.[477]

In sum, social networking sites have a robust social graph, whereas content-centric sites do not.[478] Although users can share videos or stream events on Facebook and YouTube in similar ways, there is a fundamental difference between sharing a video among a person's social network on Facebook, Instagram, or WhatsApp—such as a child's first steps—and broadcasting it publicly on

---

U.S. 377, 395 (1956)); *see also* Competition & Mkts. Auth. Report at 117–18 ("the closeness of competition between different platforms depends on the degree to which consumers consider them substitutes, rather than the extent to which they share common functionalities.").

[472] Competition & Mkts. Auth. Report at 54 (citing Bundeskartellamt (Feb. 6, 2019), B6-22/16, para. 249, https://www.bundeskartellamt.de/SharedDocs/Entscheidung/EN/Entscheidungen/Missbrauchsaufsicht/2019/B6-22-16.pdf?__blob=publicationFile&v=5).

[473] *Id.*

[474] *Id.*

[475] FIONA M. SCOTT & DAVID C. DINIELLI, OMIDYAR NETWORK, ROADMAP FOR AN ANTITRUST CASE AGAINST FACEBOOK 6 (June 2020), https://www.omidyar.com/wp-content/uploads/2020/06/Roadmap-for-an-Antitrust-Case-Against-Facebook.pdf.

[476] Letter from Michael Beckerman, Vice Pres., Head of U.S. Public Pol'y, TikTok, to Hon. David Cicilline, Chairman, Subcomm. on Antitrust, Commercial and Admin. Law of the H. Comm. on the Judiciary, Hon. F. James Sensenbrenner, Ranking Member, Subcomm. on Antitrust, Commercial and Admin. Law of the H. Comm. on the Judiciary, Hon. Jerrold Nadler, Chairman, H. Comm. on the Judiciary, Hon. Jim Jordan, Ranking Member, H. Comm. on the Judiciary (July 29 2020) at 1, https://docs.house.gov/meetings/JU/JU05/20200729/110883/HHRG-116-JU05-20200729-SD005.pdf.

[477] FIONA M. SCOTT & DAVID C. DINIELLI, OMIDYAR NETWORK, ROADMAP FOR AN ANTITRUST CASE AGAINST FACEBOOK 6 (June 2020), https://www.omidyar.com/wp-content/uploads/2020/06/Roadmap-for-an-Antitrust-Case-Against-Facebook.pdf.

[478] THOMAS CUNNINGHAM, POSSIBLE END STATES FOR THE FAMILY OF APPS (2018) (on file with Comm.) (discussing social networking platforms with comparable and orthogonal social graphs.).

YouTube. While people may spend significant time on both YouTube and Facebook,[479] these firms provide distinct services to their users, and including both in the same market would be inconsistent with how users engage with each platform.

2. Market Concentration

Social platforms that are within a broad definition of social media include YouTube, Facebook and its family of products—Instagram, Messenger, and WhatsApp—as well as TikTok, Twitter, LinkedIn, Pinterest, Reddit, and Tumblr.[480] According to Facebook's internal market data, YouTube and Facebook's family of products were by far the most popular social media sites by Monthly Active Persons (MAP) as of December 2019.[481]

Social Media Companies by Monthly Active Persons (MAP) in Millions[482]

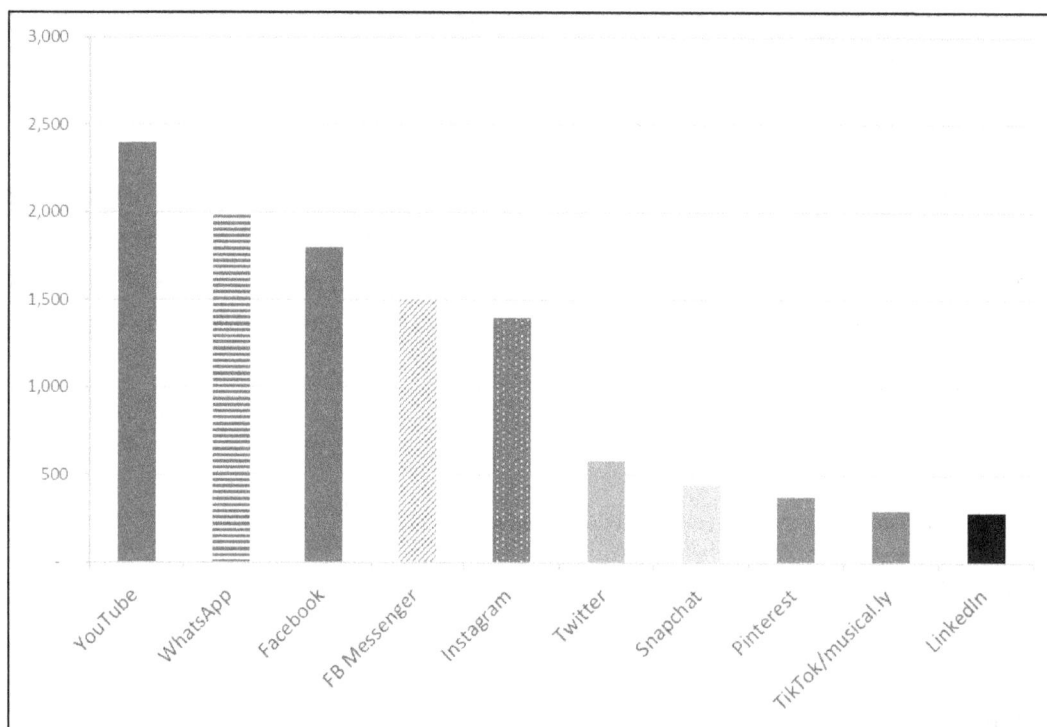

---

[479] *Average Time Spent Daily on Social Media (Latest 2020 Data)*, BROADBAND SEARCH, https://www.broadbandsearch.net/blog/average-daily-time-on-social-media#post-navigation-4 (last visited Oct. 3, 2020).

[480] Competition & Mkts. Auth. Report at 115 n.140 (indicating that there are several other smaller firms that conform to this definition of social media but lack a significant user base).

[481] Production of Facebook, to H. Comm. on the Judiciary, FB-HJC-00086585 (Jan. 2020) (on file with Comm.).

[482] Prepared by the Subcomm. based Production of Facebook, to H. Comm. on the Judiciary, FB-HJC-00086585 (Jan. 2020) (on file with Comm.). (metrics collected by Facebook).

The social network marketplace is highly concentrated. Facebook (1.8 billion users) and its family of products—WhatsApp (2.0 billion users), Instagram (1.4 billion users)— have significantly more users and time spent on its platform than its closest competitors, Snapchat (443 million users) or Twitter (582 million users).[483] TikTok is growing quickly and is often referenced as evidence that the social media landscape is competitive.[484] Although it meets the broad definition of social media as a social app for distributing and consuming video content, TikTok is not a social network.

D.   Mobile App Stores

Mobile application stores (app stores) are digital stores that enable software developers to distribute software applications (apps) to mobile device users.[485] A mobile app is a standardized piece of software optimized for use on a mobile device. Users can install this software to access digital content or services, share content, play games, or make transactions for physical goods and services. Apps are configured to run on a device's operating system as "native apps." These apps may be pre-installed on a mobile device as a component of the operating system or by the device manufacturer, downloaded from an app store, or loaded directly from the web using a browser—a process referred to as sideloading. Software developers upload apps and updates to app stores, and mobile device users can then install apps by downloading them from the app store to their device.

App stores include free and paid apps that charge a fee. In addition to allowing users to install apps, app stores enable users to search, browse, and find reviews for apps, as well as remove apps from their devices.[486] The leading app stores also offer tools and services to support developers to building apps for the app store.[487] App stores have rules that govern the types of apps permitted in the app store, conduct of app developers, how users pay for apps, the distribution of revenue between the app and the app store, and other details regarding the relationship between the app store operator and the app developers that distribute apps through the store.[488]

---

[483] THOMAS CUNNINGHAM, POSSIBLE END STATES FOR THE FAMILY OF APPS (2018) (on file with Comm.) (discussing social networking platforms with comparable and orthogonal social graphs.).

[484] *See* Alex Sherman, *TikTok reveals detailed user numbers for the first time*, CNBC (Aug. 24, 2020), https://www.cnbc.com/2020/08/24/tiktok-reveals-us-global-user-growth-numbers-for-first-time.html.

[485] *See e.g.*, Letter from Apple to H. Comm. on the Judiciary, HJC_APPLE_000003 (Oct. 14, 2019) (on file with Comm.); Letter from Executive at Source 736, to Members of the Subcomm. on Antitrust, Commercial and Admin. Law of the H. Comm. on the Judiciary, 4 (Oct. 31, 2019) (on file with Comm.); BRICS COMPETITION, INNOVATION, LAW & POL'Y CTR, DIGITAL ERA COMPETITION: A BRICS VIEW 347 (2019), http://bricscompetition.org/upload/iblock/6a1/brics%20book%20full.pdf.

[486] Neth. Auth. for Consumers & Mkts. Study at 20.

[487] NETH. AUTH. FOR CONSUMERS & MKTS. MARKET STUDY INTO MOBILE APP STORES 20 (2019), https://www.acm.nl/sites/default/files/documents/market-study-into-mobile-app-stores.pdf [hereinafter Neth. Auth. for Consumers & Mkts Study].

[488] *See Apple App Store Review Guidelines*, APPLE, https://developer.apple.com/app-store/review/guidelines/#legal; *Apple Developer Program License Agreement*, APPLE, https://developer.apple.com/services-account/agreement/XV2A27GUJ6/content/pdf; *Google Play Developer Policy Center*, GOOGLE,

App stores provide mobile device users with a sense of trust and security that the apps they install from an app store have been reviewed, will not harm the user's mobile device, will function as intended, and will not violate user privacy.[489] App stores also reduce customer acquisition costs for app developers by allowing developers to reach an extraordinarily large consumer base—every mobile device user in the U.S. is addressable by developing for the Apple App Store and the Google Play Store. By reducing the costs of app developers, app stores help make software applications more affordable for consumers.[490]

Deloitte has explained that app stores provide developers with various benefits, including providing a consistent interface and experience for users on a mobile operating system, a secure platform for apps, storage systems for hosting apps and managing downloads and updates, and billing and payment management systems that can reduce overhead for developers.[491] Apple and Google also provide developers with software-development tools to create, test, and publish apps; technical support and analytics tools; and tutorials.[492]

The mobile operating system on a device determines which app stores the user can access. The provider of the mobile operating system determines which app stores may be pre-installed on devices running the operating system, and whether and how additional app stores may be installed. As discussed elsewhere in the Report, both Apple and Google have durable and persistent market power in the mobile operating system market; iOS and Android run on more than 99% of mobile devices in the U.S. and globally.[493] There are high switching costs in the mobile operating system market and high barriers to entry. Due their dominance in the mobile operating system market, Apple and Google have the power to dictate the terms and extent of competition for distributing software on to mobile devices running their respective mobile operating systems.[494]

---

https://play.google.com/about/developer-content-policy/; *Google Play Developer Distribution Agreement*, GOOGLE, https://play.google.com/intl/ALL_us/about/developer-distribution-agreement.html .

[489] *See* CEO Hearing Transcript at 3 (response to Questions for the Record of Tim Cook, CEO, Apple, Inc.) https://docs.house.gov/meetings/JU/JU05/20200729/110883/HHRG-116-JU05-20200729-QFR054.pdf; *See also* JOHN BERGMAYER, PUBLIC KNOWLEDGE, TENDING THE GARDEN: HOW TO ENSURE THAT APP STORES PUT USERS FIRST 1, 5, 18 (2020), https://www.publicknowledge.org/wp-content/uploads/2020/06/Tending_the_Garden.pdf.

[490] Production of Apple, to H. Comm. on the Judiciary, HJC_APPLE_000003 (Oct. 14, 2019) (on file with Comm.); Neth. Auth. for Consumers & Mkts. Study at 108.

[491] DELOITTE, THE APP ECONOMY IN THE UNITED STATES 8 (2018), https://www.ftc.gov/system/files/documents/public_comments/2018/08/ftc-2018-0048-d-0121-155299.pdf

[492] Neth. Auth. for Consumers & Mkts. Study at 29.

[493] *Id.* at 15.

[494] *See* Data and Privacy Hearing at 15 (statement of Maurice E. Stucke, Prof. of Law, Univ. of Tennessee, and Ariel Ezrachi, Slaughter and May Prof. of Competition Law, Univ. of Oxford, Fellow, Pembroke Coll., Dir., Oxford Ctr. For Competition Law and Pol'y), https://docs.house.gov/meetings/JU/JU05/20191018/110098/HHRG-116-JU05-20191018-SD010.pdf.

The Google Play Store is the primary app store installed on all Android devices. The Apple App Store is the only app store available on iOS devices.[495] Apps are not interoperable between operating systems—native apps developed for iOS only work on iOS devices, and native apps developed for Android only work on Android devices.[496] The App Store and the Play Store do not compete against one another. Android users cannot access the Apple App Store, and iOS users cannot access the Google Play Store, so the dominance of the Play Store is not constrained by the App Store and vice versa.[497]

Statista reports that in the first quarter of 2020 there were approximately 2.56 million apps available in the Google Play Store and 1.847 million apps available in Apple's App Store.[498] Apple's App Store is the only means to distribute software on iOS devices.[499] The Google Play Store is the dominant app store on Android devices; however, Google does permit users to sideload alternative app stores. Some Android device partners, such as Samsung, pre-install their own app stores on their devices.[500] Leading alternative Android app stores include Amazon's Appstore, Aptoide, F-Droid, and the Samsung Galaxy Store.[501] App developers who want to reach the entire addressable market of U.S. or global smartphone users must have an app in both the App Store and the Play Store.[502] Apple and Google also determine the terms and conditions app developers must agree to in order to distribute software through the App Store and Play Store, respectively. As a result, app developers and industry observers agree that Apple and Google control the app distribution market on mobile devices.[503]

---

[495] Neth. Auth. for Consumers & Mkts. Study at 4, 21.

[496] *See* Interview with Source 407 (Sept. 10, 2020); Interview with Source 143 (Aug. 27, 2020); Neth. Auth. for Consumers & Mkts. Study at 51–52, 67, 73.

[497] *See* Press Release, Eur. Comm'n, Antitrust: Commission Fines Google €4.34 Billion for Illegal Practices Regarding Android Mobile Devices to Strengthen Dominance of Google's Search Engine (July 18, 2018) https://ec.europa.eu/commission/presscorner/detail/en/IP_18_4581; Letter from Executive at Source 181, to Members of the Subcomm. on Antitrust, Commercial and Admin. Law, 4 (Oct. 31, 2019) (on file with Comm.); Submission from Source 301, to H. Comm. on the Judiciary, 5, 7 (Oct. 15, 2019) (on file with Comm).

[498] *Number of Apps Available in Leading App Stores as of 1st Quarter* 2020, STATISTA, (https://www.statista.com/statistics/276623/number-of-apps-available-in-leading-app-stores/ .

[499] Neth. Auth. for Consumers & Mkts. Study at 50; Interview with Source 766 (July 2, 2020).

[500] Neth. Auth. for Consumers & Mkts. Study at 50. *See* Press Release, Eur. Comm'n, Antitrust: Commission Fines Google €4.34 Billion for Illegal Practices Regarding Android Mobile Devices to Strengthen Dominance of Google's Search Engine (July 18, 2018), https://ec.europa.eu/commission/presscorner/detail/en/IP_18_4581 (explaining that worldwide, excluding China, "the Play Store accounts for more than 90% apps downloaded on Android devices").

[501] Joe Hindy, *10 Best Third Party App Stores for Android and Other Options Too*, Android Authority (Aug. 28, 2020), https://www.androidauthority.com/best-app-stores-936652/.

[502] Neth. Auth. for Consumers & Mkts. Study at 15.

[503] *See e.g.*, Interview with Source 143 (Aug. 27, 2020); Production of Facebook, to H. Comm. on the Judiciary, FB-HJC-ACAL-00045377 (Feb. 14, 2014) (on file with Comm.) (demonstrating that Facebook COO Sheryl Sandberg explained to Facebook's Board of Directors that Apple and Google's positions as dominant mobile operating system and app store operators posted a "significant strategic threat" to Facebook's business and adding another popular mobile app to Facebook's suite of apps "would make it more difficult for operating system providers to exclude the Company's mobile applications from mobile platforms."); Letter from Executive at Source 181, to Members of the Subcomm. on Antitrust, Commercial and Admin. Law, 4 (Oct. 31, 2019) (on file with Comm.); Kara Swisher, *Is It Finally Hammer Time for Apple*

There is no method for a third-party app store to challenge the App Store on iOS devices. Apple CEO Tim Cook told the Subcommittee that Apple has no plans to open iOS to alternative app stores.[504] For a third-party app store to successfully challenge the Play Store, consumers must be able to install the app store and the store must have popular apps that users want. As with mobile operating systems, network effects create momentum so that as more consumers install software from the app store, more developers will build apps for the app store, increasing the value of the app store for users and attracting more consumers. Once users have migrated to a large platform—such as an operating system and its app store, it is difficult for smaller competitors to attract users and app developers.[505]

The United Kingdom's Competition and Markets Authority observed that "almost all mobile app downloads are made through the App Store, on iOS devices, or Google Play, on Android devices."[506] Alternatives app distribution methods such as third-party app stores, gaming platforms, or sideloading are often irrelevant to the mobile applications market, not always practical options for users, have significant disadvantages compared to the pre-installed app stores, and offer only limited functionality.[507]

Web sites and web apps are not competitively significant alternatives to the dominant app stores on iOS and Android devices for distributing software to mobile devices. Apps provide a deeper, richer user experience and can provide additional functionality by accessing features within the mobile device's hardware and operating system, such as a camera or location services.[508] Web apps and browsers are also reliant on the device being connected to the Internet. Native apps can continue to work even when a device loses access to the Internet.[509] Apple's App Store Review Guidelines

---

and Its App Store, N.Y. TIMES (June 19, 2020), https://www.nytimes.com/2020/06/19/opinion/apple-app-store-hey.html?referringSource=articleShare.

[504] CEO Hearing at 3 (response to Questions for the Record of Tim Cook, CEO, Apple, Inc.).

[505] Data and Privacy Hearing at 5 (statement of Maurice E. Stucke, Prof. of Law, Univ. of Tennessee, and Ariel Ezrachi, Slaughter and May Prof. of Competition Law, Univ. of Oxford, Fellow, Pembroke Coll., Dir., Oxford Ctr. For Competition Law and Pol'y).

[506] Competition & Mkts. Auth. Report at 29; *see also* Japan Fair Trade Commission, Press Release, Report Regarding Trade Practices on Digital Platforms: Business-to-Business Transactions on Online Retail Platform and App Store 24–25 (Oct. 2019), https://www.jftc.go.jp/en/pressreleases/yearly-2019/October/191031Report.pdf (explaining that consumers rely on pre-installed app stores to install apps, so developers believe they "have no choice but to use the app store services" to reach consumers).

[507] *See* Production of Facebook, to H. Comm. on the Judiciary, FB-HJC-ACAL-00068877 (Feb. 21, 2012) (on file with Comm.) ("Native apps will dominate over mobile-web for a long time (maybe forever) and we cannot prop up HTML-5 / are not strong enough to lead a shift - The mobile OS makers have a strong incentive in native apps performing better / working better than the web? so theory / what is possible aside, native apps will work better & be better experiences than the mobile web."); Neth. Auth. for Consumers & Mkts. Study at 42–51, 69.

[508] *See* Letter from Executive at Source 181, to Members of the Subcomm. on Antitrust, Commercial and Admin. Law of the H. Comm. on the Judiciary, 1 (Oct. 31, 2019) (on file with Comm.); Neth. Auth. for Consumers & Mkts. Study at 59, 81.

[509] *See* Interview with Source 88 (May 12, 2020).

differentiates apps from websites, explaining that apps submitted to the App store "should include features, content and [user interface] that elevate [the app] beyond a repackaged website."[510] Curation and centralized review of apps is an advantage touted by app store operators. Apple CEO Tim Cook explained to the Subcommittee that on iOS devices, Apple's control of software installation through the App Store ensures downloaded apps "meet our high standards for privacy, performance, and security," which is important for maintaining user trust.[511] Additionally, distributing software via app stores lowers customer acquisition costs for software developers.[512]

Consumers do access content on their mobile devices via the open Internet. However, mobile apps are the primary way users access content and services on mobile devices and have become integral in Americans' daily lives for basic communication, business transactions, entertainment, and news. In the U.S., nearly 90% of time users spend online on mobile devices occurs in apps.[513] Software distribution via web apps or through a website accessible on a browser is not a competitively significant alternative to distributing apps through the dominant app store on a mobile device and does not discipline the market power of the dominant app stores controlled by Apple and Google.

Similarly, the ability for consumers to sideload apps—installing apps without using an app store—does not discipline the dominance of Apple and Google in the mobile app store market. Apple does not permit users to sideload apps on iOS devices, and few consumers have the technical savvy to "jailbreak" an iOS device to sideload apps.[514] Google does permit sideloading on Android devices, but developers find that given the option, consumers prefer to install apps from app stores and few opt for sideloading.[515] Google has created significant friction for sideloading apps to Android devices. One developer explained to Subcommittee staff that sideloading entails a complicated twenty-step process, and users encounter multiple security warnings designed to discourage sideloading.[516] Additionally, software developers that have left the Play Store to distribute software to Android users via sideloading have experienced precipitous declines in downloads and revenue and report problems updating their

[510] *App Store Review Guidelines, § 4.2*, APPLE, https://developer.apple.com/app-store/review/guidelines/#design (last visited Oct. 4, 2020).

[511] CEO Hearing at 3 (response to Questions for the Record of Tim Cook, CEO, Apple, Inc.).

[512] *See* Production of Apple, to H. Comm. on the Judiciary, HJC_APPLE_000003 (Oct. 14, 2019) (on file with Comm.); Neth. Auth. for Consumers & Mkts. Study at 102.

[513] COMSCORE, 2019 REPORT GLOBAL STATE OF MOBILE 7 (2019); *see also* Letter from Executive at Source 181, to Members of the Subcomm. on Antitrust, Commercial and Admin. Law of the H. Comm. on the Judiciary, 1 (Oct. 31, 2019) (on file with Comm.); Submission from Source 301, to H. Comm. on the Judiciary, 7 (Oct. 15, 2019) (on file with Comm.).

[514] Neth. Auth. for Consumers & Mkts. Study at 45–46; Submission from Source 736, to H. Comm. on the Judiciary, Source 736-00000166 (July 1, 2019).

[515] Interview with Source 59 (May 13, 2020).

[516] Interview with Source 83 (June 30, 2020).

apps.[517] Thus, the option for sideloading apps on mobile devices does not discipline the market power of dominant app stores.

There are no competitive constraints on the power Apple and Google have over the software distribution marketplace on their mobile ecosystems. The core benefit of mobile app stores—centralizing and curating software distribution—also gives Apple and Google control over which apps users discover and can install.[518] As the gateways to the primary way users access content and services on mobile devices, the App Store and the Play Store can extract revenue from and exercise control over everything users do on their devices.[519] This dominance enable Apple and Google to establish terms and conditions app developers have to comply with, leaving developers with the choice of complying or losing access consumers. The terms and conditions app stores impose include requirements regarding app functionality, content, interactions with consumers, collection and distribution of revenue between the app and app store.[520]

Mobile app stores charge app developers commissions on sales of paid apps through the app store. Apple and Google, along with other mobile app stores on Android devices, charge a 30% commission when users install the app.[521] Apple established its 30% commission on paid apps in 2009 with the introduction of the App Store, and that rate has become the industry standard.[522]

Apple and Google have both developed mechanisms for collecting payments from users for purchases within applications—these transactions are called in-app purchases (IAP). Apple and Google both charge developers a standard 30% for IAP.[523] In collecting IAP, Apple and Google collect user personal and payment information, process the payment, and then remit the payment to the app developer, minus a processing fee or commission.[524] Developers selling digital content through their

---

[517] See Neth. Auth. for Consumers & Mkts. Study at 48; JOHN BERGMAYER, PUBLIC KNOWLEDGE, TENDING THE GARDEN: HOW TO ENSURE THAT APP STORES PUT USERS FIRST 44 (June 2020), https://www.publicknowledge.org/wp-content/uploads/2020/06/Tending_the_Garden.pdf; Interview with Source 83 (June 30, 2020).

[518] See JOHN BERGMAYER, PUBLIC KNOWLEDGE, TENDING THE GARDEN: HOW TO ENSURE THAT APP STORES PUT USERS FIRST 19 (2020), https://www.publicknowledge.org/wp-content/uploads/2020/06/Tending_the_Garden.pdf.

[519] See id. at 7, 19.

[520] See Neth. Auth. for Consumers & Mkts. Study at 3, 15.

[521] See ANALYSIS GROUP, APPLE'S APP STORE AND OTHER DIGITAL MARKETPLACES: A COMPARISON OF COMMISSION RATES 4–6 (July 22, 2020), https://www.analysisgroup.com/globalassets/insights/publishing/apples_app_store_and_other_digital_marketplaces_a_comparison_of_commission_rates.pdf.

[522] See id. at 4.

[523] See Neth. Auth. for Consumers & Mkts. Study at 23, 29, 86, 89.

[524] See e.g., Letter from Executive at Source 181, to Members of the Subcomm. on Antitrust, Commercial and Admin. Law of the H. Comm. on the Judiciary, 3, 5–6 (Oct. 31, 2019) (on file with Comm.); Submission from Source 736, to H. Comm. on the Judiciary, Source 736-00000009 (on file with Comm.); Submission from Source 304, to H. Comm. on the Judiciary, 7–8 (Sept. 3, 2020); see also Reed Albergotti & Tony Romm, Tinder and Fortnite criticize Apple for its 'App Store

apps on iOS and Android devices are required to use the app store operator's IAP.[525] For subscription services, like news apps or streaming media, the commission is 15% for the second year and thereafter.[526] IAP systems provide mobile device users with convenience by allowing consumers to make transactions in their apps and only enter their payment details a single time, and protects user privacy by limiting sharing of sensitive financial information.[527] However, developers have noted that lack of competition in pricing by app stores, particularly given the scale the App Store and Play Store have achieved since introducing their standard commission rates for paid apps and in-app purchases, demonstrates the lack of competition in the software distribution market on both the iOS and Android ecosystems.[528] Developers have also said that the 30% commissions charged by app stores have led them to increase prices for consumers and diminished innovation by software developers.[529]

Apple and Google also develop and distribute apps that directly compete against third-party developers in their app stores.[530] This dynamic, coupled with the fact that App Store and Play Store are dominant distribution channels and can exert gatekeeper power over their platforms, has the potential to distort competition, lead to discrimination and higher entry barriers for third-party developers, and result in the app store operator self-preferencing its own apps, harming consumers and competition.[531]

New app stores face high barriers to entry. It is unlikely that a third strong mobile app ecosystem can emerge. To offer a new mobile app store that is compelling to consumers, the app store must have a built-in customer base to attract developers to build apps for the store and must have popular apps to attract customers. Before the introduction of the App Store, third-party apps were not a central component of the user experience on mobile devices. New entrants, such as Apple, could disrupt the mobile device and operating system market by offering superior handset design, user interface, and first-party applications. Now, third-party apps are critical to the success of any mobile ecosystem. Millions of apps are developed for iOS and Android, and leading device manufacturers have built their device ecosystems around those operating systems. As a result, it is unlikely that a new

---

monopoly', WASH. POST (June 16, 2020), https://www.washingtonpost.com/technology/2020/06/16/apple-antitrust-european-commission/.

[525] *See* Neth. Auth. for Consumers & Mkts. Study at 29.

[526] *Id.* at 29.

[527] *Id.* at 7.

[528] *See* Interview with Source 83 (June 30, 2020); Competitors Hearing at 8 (statement of David Heinemeier Hansson, CTO, Basecamp).

[529] *See* Letter from Executive at Source 181 to Members of the Subcomm. on Antitrust, Commercial and Admin. Law of the H. Comm. on the Judiciary, 9–10 (Oct. 31, 2019) (on file with Comm.) (internal citations omitted); Submission from Source 736, Source 736-00000236 (Oct. 23, 2019) (on file with Comm).

[530] Japan Fair Trade Comm'n, Press Release, Report Regarding Trade Practices on Digital Platforms: Business-to-Business Transactions on Online Retail Platform and App Store 21 (Oct. 2019), https://www.jftc.go.jp/en/pressreleases/yearly-2019/October/191031Report.pdf.

[531] *See e.g.*, Neth. Auth. for Consumers & Mkts. Study at 22, 31–32, 69, 89–90, 95–99.

mobile operating system entrant can disrupt the current market dynamics.[532] Because of the control that Apple and Google exert over software distribution on their mobile ecosystems and the unlikelihood of entry by a new competitive mobile operating system, it is unlikely that a new, competitive app store will be able to successfully challenge the existing, dominant app store operators.

E. Mobile Operating Systems

A mobile operating system (OS) provides a mobile device with its underlying functionality, such as user interface, motion commands, button controls, and facilitates the operation of the device's features, such as the microphone, camera, and GPS. The mobile OS is the interface between the mobile device hardware, such as the smartphone handset or tablet, and the applications that run on the device, like email or streaming apps. The mobile OS is pre-installed on mobile devices; an alternative mobile OS cannot be installed or substituted. The characteristics of the mobile OS determine aspects of the mobile device's performance and functionality, including the app stores and apps that can run on the device. The mobile OS also determines which company's ecosystem of products and services the device is integrated with.[533]

Google's Android and Apple's iOS are the two dominant mobile operating systems.[534] Combined, they run on more than 99% of all smartphones in the world.[535] The third-largest mobile operating system is KaiOS, which runs on feature phones (i.e., non-smartphone mobile devices).[536] Apple's mobile devices run on Apple's proprietary iOS operating system, while other leading handset manufacturers, such as Samsung, LG, and Motorola, run on Android.[537] iOS is not available on non-Apple devices.

---

[532] Dig. Competition Expert Panel Report at 29–30.

[533] *See* Steven Böhm, Fabian Adam & Wendy Colleen Farrell, *Impact of the Mobile Operating System on Smartphone Buying Decisions: A Conjoint-Based Empirical Analysis*, MOBILE WEB AND INTELLIGENT INFORMATION SYSTEMS 198 (Muhammad Younas, Irfan Awan & Massimo Mecella eds., 2015), https://doi.org/10.1007/978-3-319-23144-0_18.

[534] *See* GSMA INTEL., GLOBAL MOBILE TRENDS 2020: NEW DECADE, NEW INDUSTRY?, 6, 26 (2019), https://data.gsmaintelligence.com/api-web/v2/research-file-download?id=47743151&file=2863-071119-GMT-2019.pdf.

[535] Neth. Auth. for Consumers & Mkts. Study at 15; *see also* Dig. Competition Expert Panel Report at 29 ("However market shares are measured, Google (Android) and Apple (iOS) have a global duopoly over mobile phone operating systems."); Michael Muchmore, *Android vs. iOS: Which Mobile OS Is Best?*, PC MAG (Aug. 11, 2020), https://www.pcmag.com/comparisons/android-vs-ios-which-mobile-os-is-best ("[W]e're locked in a duopoly when it comes to mobile operating system choice").

[536] *A Short History of KaiOS*, KAIOS, https://developer.kaiostech.com/introduction/history (last visited Oct. 4, 2020); Stephen Shankland, *Mozilla helps modernize feature phones powered by Firefox tech*, CNET (Mar. 11, 2020), https://www.cnet.com/news/mozilla-helps-modernize-feature-phones-powered-by-firefox-tech/.

[537] *See* Production of Apple, to H. Comm. on the Judiciary, HJC_APPLE_000021 (Oct. 14, 2019) (on file with Comm.) ("Many smartphone brands around the world compete with iPhone on the basis of price, performance, features, and design. These smartphones generally incorporate Google's Android operating system.").

Mobile OS Market Share Worldwide[538]

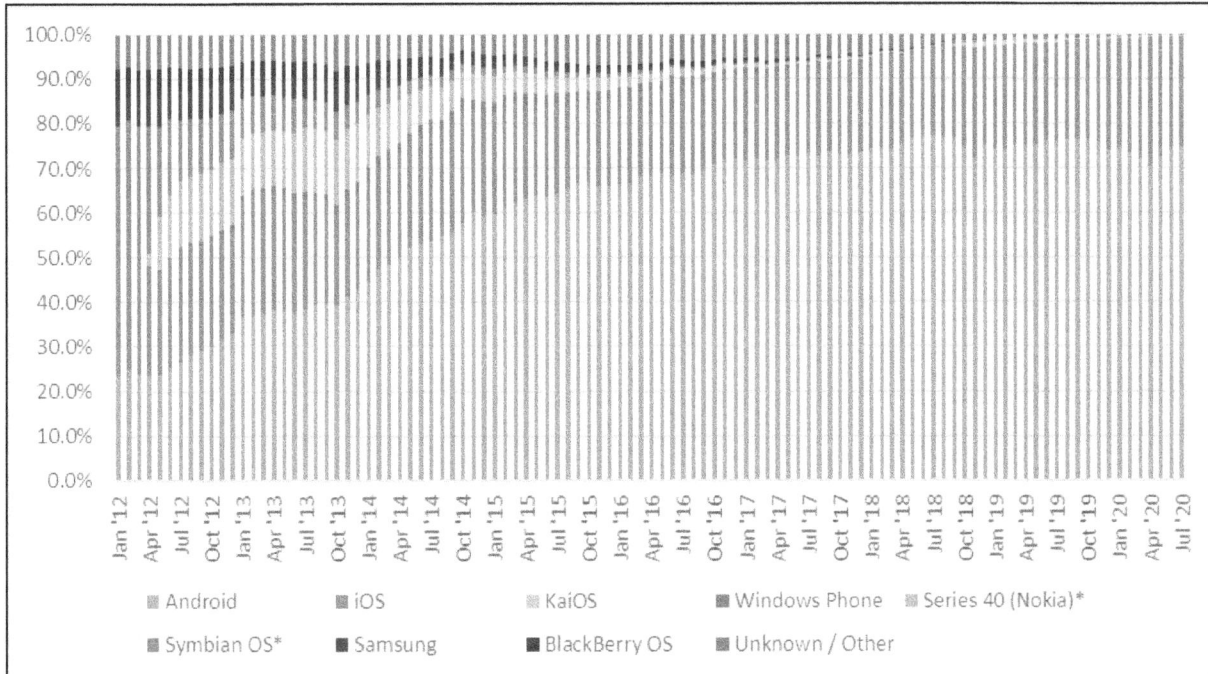

Over the past decade, once-strong competitors have exited the mobile OS market and Google and Apple have built dominant positions that are durable and persistent.[539] While there are other

---

[538] Prepared by the Subcomm. based on Felix Richter, *The Smartphone Market: The Smartphone Duopoly*, STATISTA (July 27, 2020), https://www.statista.com/chart/3268/smartphone-os-market-share/ (citing *Mobile Operating System Market Share Worldwide*, STATCOUNTER GLOBALSTATS. StatCounter which "calculates the data based on more than 1.7 billion page views per month worldwide. StatCounter defines a mobile device as a pocket-sized computing device. As a result, tablets are not included . . . Nokia devices (including some S40 devices) had been grouped largely under Symbian OS.").

[539] *See* Felix Richter, *The Smartphone Market: The Smartphone Duopoly*, STATISTA (July 27, 2020), https://www.statista.com/chart/3268/smartphone-os-market-share/ ("Having started out as a multi-platform market, the smartphone landscape has effectively turned into a duopoly in recent years, after Apple's iOS and Google's Android crowded out any other platform including Microsoft's Windows Phone, BlackBerry OS and Samsung's mobile operating system called Bada."); Data and Privacy Hearing at 7 (statement of Maurice E. Stucke, Prof. of Law, Univ. of Tennessee, and Ariel Ezrachi, Slaughter and May Prof. of Competition Law, Univ. of Oxford, Fellow, Pembroke Coll., Dir., Oxford Ctr. For Competition Law and Pol'y) ("The mobile operating system market went from multiple competitors in 2010 (with Google and Apple collectively accounting for 39 percent of unit sales), to a duopoly eight years later."); Matthew Feld, *Microsoft Is Finally Killing Off the Windows Phone*, The TELEGRAPH (Oct. 9, 2017), https://www.telegraph.co.uk/technology/2017/10/09/microsoft-finally-killing-windows-phone/; Arjun Kharpal, *TCL Launches New $549 Smartphone Under BlackBerry's Banner, Featuring Android Software*, CNBC (Feb. 25, 2017), https://www.cnbc.com/2017/02/25/blackberry-keyone-launch-physical-keyboard-android-specs-price.html); Jack Schofield, *Can I Buy a Phone that Doesn't Use Anything from Google or Apple?*, THE GUARDIAN (July 4, 2019), https://www.theguardian.com/technology/askjack/2019/jul/04/can-i-buy-a-phone-that-does-not-use-anything-from-google-or-apple.

101

mobile OSs—such as Tizen, Sailfish OS, and Ubuntu Touch—those OSs make up less than 1% of the global mobile OS market.[540]

Market Share of Mobile Operating Systems in the U.S.[541]

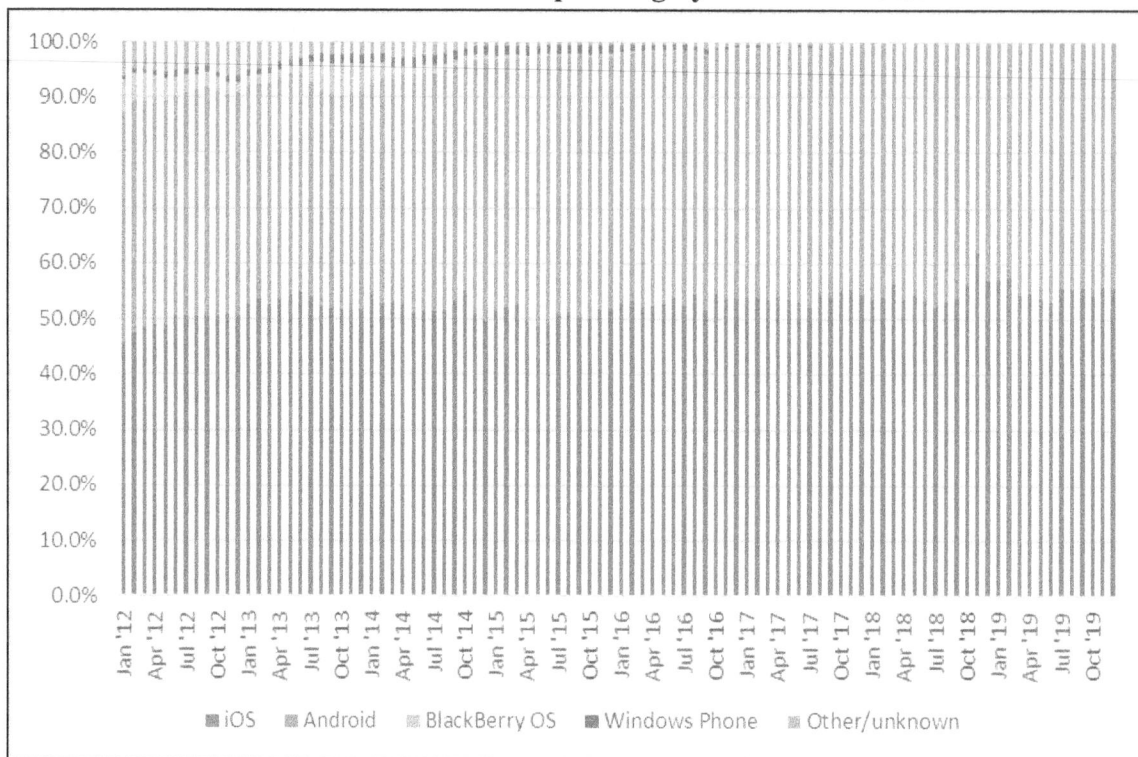

Although both Google Android and Apple iOS both have dominant positions in the mobile OS market, high switching costs and a lack of on-device competition mean that neither firm's market power is disciplined by the presence of the other. The European Commission's investigation into Google's Android platform found that because iOS is not available on non-Apple devices, it cannot constrain Google's dominance in the mobile OS market.[542] Conversely, Android is not available on Apple devices and does not constrain Apple's dominant position and conduct on Apple mobile devices. An investment research firm recently noted that switching costs were high for Apple users because iOS is not available on non-Apple devices.[543]

---

[540] *See, e.g.*, Simon O'Dea, *Market Share of Mobile Operating Systems in the United States from January 2012 to December 2019*, STATISTA (Feb. 27, 2020), https://www.statista.com/statistics/272700/market-share-held-by-mobile-operating-systems-in-the-us-since-2009/.

[541] Prepared by Subcomm. based on S. O'Dea, *Market share of mobile operating systems in the United States from January 2012 to December 2019*, STATISTA (Feb. 27, 2020), https://www.statista.com/statistics/272700/market-share-held-by-mobile-operating-systems-in-the-us-since-2009/ (citing *Mobile Operating System Market Share in United States Of America*, STATCOUNTER).

[542] Press Release, Eur. Comm'n, Antitrust: Commission Fines Google €4.34 Billion for Illegal Practices Regarding Android Mobile Devices to Strengthen Dominance of Google's Search Engine (July 18, 2018) https://ec.europa.eu/commission/presscorner/detail/en/IP_18_4581.

[543] MORNINGSTAR EQUITY ANALYST REPORT, APPLE INC 1 (Aug. 6, 2020) (on file with Comm.).

There are significant barriers to switching between the dominant mobile operating systems. As a general matter, consumers rarely switch mobile operating systems. SellCell's 2019 survey found that more than 90% of users with iPhones tend to stick with Apple when they replace their current device.[544] In 2018, Consumer Intelligence Research Partners reported that more than 85% of iOS users who purchased a new device purchased another iOS device, and more than 90% of Android users who bought a new device purchased a new Android device.[545] A 2017 study from Morgan Stanley found that 92% of iPhone owners intending to buy a new mobile device planned to buy another iPhone.[546] Mobile carriers—a main retail distribution channel for mobile devices—agreed that it is rare for customers to switch from one mobile OS because once customers are used to the mobile OS they generally do not switch.[547] App developers also said in interviews with Subcommittee staff that they observed minimal customer switching between iOS and Android.[548]

In addition to the cost of buying a new mobile device, consumers encounter other costs to switch to a new operating system. Android and iOS have different operating concepts, user interface designs, and setting and configuration options. As a result, instead of switching operating systems, "users pick one, learn it, invest in apps and storage, and stick with it."[549]

Other barriers to switching include the loss of compatibility with other smart devices designed to work in conjunction with the mobile device and its OS, the hassle of porting data from one OS to another, re-installing apps and configuring settings, and learning an unfamiliar user interface.[550] Apple's co-founder and former CEO Steve Jobs advocated this approach, noting Apple should "[t]ie

---

[544] *iPhone vs. Android – Cell Phone Brand Loyalty Survey 2019*, SELLCELL (Aug. 20, 2019), https://www.sellcell.com/blog/iphone-vs-android-cell-phone-brand-loyalty-survey-2019/; *see also* MORNINGSTAR EQUITY ANALYST REPORT, APPLE INC. 2 (Aug. 6, 2020) ("Recent survey data shows that iPhone customers are not even contemplating switching brands today. In a December 2018 survey by Kantar, 90% of U.S.-based iPhone users said they planned to remain loyal to future Apple devices.") (on file with Comm.).

[545] Press Release, Consumer Intel. Research Partners, LLC, Mobile Operating System Loyalty: High and Steady, (Mar. 8, 2018), http://files.constantcontact.com/150f9af2201/4bca9a19-a8b0-46bd-95bd-85740ff3fb5d.pdf.

[546] Martin Armstrong, *Most iPhone Users Never Look Back*, STATISTA (May 22, 2017), https://www.statista.com/chart/9496/most-iphone-users-never-look-back/.

[547] Interview with Source 72 (June 23, 2020).

[548] Interview with Source 83 (June 30, 2020).

[549] Press Release, Consumer Intel. Research Partners, LLC, Mobile Operating System Loyalty: High and Steady (Mar. 8, 2018), http://files.constantcontact.com/150f9af2201/4bca9a19-a8b0-46bd-95bd-85740ff3fb5d.pdf.

[550] *See* Neth. Auth. for Consumers & Mkts. Study at 55–56; Press Release, Eur. Comm'n, Antitrust: Commission Fines Google €4.34 Billion for Illegal Practices Regarding Android Mobile Devices to Strengthen Dominance of Google's Search Engine (July 18, 2018), https://ec.europa.eu/commission/presscorner/detail/en/IP_18_4581; *see also iPhone vs. Android – Cell Phone Brand Loyalty Survey 2019*, SELLCELL (Aug. 20, 2019), https://www.sellcell.com/blog/iphone-vs-android-cell-phone-brand-loyalty-survey-2019/ (finding "21% of iPhone users might be tempted to switch if they weren't too tied into the Apple Ecosystem or it wasn't so much hassle changing operating system from iOS to Android" and "13% of Samsung users might be tempted to switch if they weren't too tied into the Google/Android Ecosystem or it wasn't so much hassle changing operating system").

all of our products together, so we further lock customers into our ecosystem."[551] Recently, Morningstar observed that people using Apple's other products such as the Apple Watch and AirPods "lose significant functionality when paired with a smartphone other than the iPhone," locking iPhone users into the iOS ecosystem.[552] Competition regulators in the Netherlands explained that this strategy creates "path dependency" for consumers. Although mobile devices have a limited lifespan and consumers might be expected to "break the lock-in cycle" when it is time to upgrade to a new device, consumers often have software, data and files, and other hardware and accessories that are only compatible with one product ecosystem, making it unlikely they switch to a non-compatible mobile device.[553]

There are significant entry barriers in the mobile operating system market. One former mobile OS competitor observed that its experience showed that it was doubtful that a new, competitive mobile OS will emerge in the U.S.[554] Another former mobile OS provider explained that it exited the market after concluding "the market for mobile operating systems was too established for a new entry."[555] To compete, a new OS must offer a superior product packaged in an attractive handset, as well as a fully realized suite of apps and compatible devices comparable to what Apple and Google (and Google's hardware partners) currently offer. Industry experts have testified before the Subcommittee that the "reality is that it would be very difficult for a new mobile phone operating system today" to compete with Apple and Google, "even if it offered better features."[556] Investment analysts agree, noting it is likely Android and iOS "will continue to power nearly every smartphone around the world in the long run."[557]

The mobile OS market is also characterized by strong network effects. In short, a new mobile OS must have a sufficiently large user base to attract app developers to build apps to run on the OS An OS with an insufficient number of users and developers is unlikely to receive support from mobile

---

[551] Don Reisinger, *Steve Jobs wanted to 'further lock customers' into Apple's 'ecosystem'*, CNET (Apr. 2, 2014), https://www.cnet.com/news/steve-jobs-wanted-to-further-lock-customers-into-apples-ecosystem/.

[552] MORNINGSTAR EQUITY ANALYST REPORT, APPLE INC 2 (Aug. 6, 2020) (on file with Comm.).

[553] Neth. Auth. for Consumers & Mkts. Study at 21, 55–56.

[554] Interview with Source 407 (Sept. 10, 2020).

[555] Submission from Source 385, to H. Comm. on the Judiciary, 2 (Sept. 18, 2020) (on file with Comm).

[556] Data and Privacy Hearing at 8 (statement of Maurice E. Stucke, Prof. of Law, Univ. of Tennessee, and Ariel Ezrachi, Slaughter and May Prof. of Competition Law, Univ. of Oxford, Fellow, Pembroke Coll., Dir., Oxford Ctr. For Competition Law and Pol'y); *see also* Richard Trenholm, *Elegant Ubuntu Touch OS Impresses for Phones and Tablets (Hands-On)*, CNET (Feb. 28, 2013), https://www.cnet.com/reviews/ubuntu-touch-preview/; Adrian Covert, *The Ubuntu Smartphone (Which No One Will Use) Is a Glimpse of the Future*, CNN BUS. (Jan. 2, 2013), https://money.cnn.com/2013/01/02/technology/mobile/ubuntu-smartphone-linux/ (explaining success in the mobile market required more than merely building a superior OS to Android or iOS, it also requires a robust app ecosystem).

[557] MORNINGSTAR EQUITY ANALYST REPORT, APPLE INC 3 (Aug. 6, 2020) (on file with Comm.).

device manufacturers that will install the OS on their devices, or mobile network operators that will support those devices on their networks.[558]

The most important factor that developers consider before building apps for an OS is the install base of the OS—how many users have devices running the OS that can install the app. Developers will not build apps for an OS with few users.[559] This reinforces the power of dominant mobile operating systems. The more consumers use the OS, the more developers will build apps for the OS, increasing the value of the OS for users and attracting more consumers.[560] Consumers are unlikely to purchase a device with an OS that cannot run the most popular apps and lacks a robust app ecosystem comparable to what is offered by iOS and Android. Due to the dominance of Apple and Google in the mobile OS and app store markets, "there is little incentive for app developers to go the trouble and expense of ensuring their apps work on any smaller rival operating systems," because the user base would be too small.[561]

Additionally, the third-party app ecosystem advantages of iOS and Android make new market entry unlikely. The U.K.'s Competition and Markets Authority explained, before the iPhone, third-party apps were not part of the mobile experience. As a result, new entrants like Apple could enter the market and compete by offering a superior product. But now, there are "millions of apps that have been written for Apple's iOS and Google's Android, making it hard for a new entrant mobile operating system to offer a competitive and attractive product."[562] The European Commission (E.C.) has similarly observed that strong network effects have created high entry barriers in the mobile OS market.[563]

Over the past decade, several large technology companies have attempted and failed to leverage their large user bases to compete against Apple and Google in the mobile OS market.[564] Facebook and Amazon both tried to enter the market with variants of Google's Android OS. Both companies quickly exited the market because consumers were mostly content accessing Facebook and Amazon content through apps on iOS and Android devices.[565] Technology reviewers also expressed disappointment

---

[558] Interview with Source 407 (Sept. 10, 2020).

[559] *Id.*

[560] MORNINGSTAR EQUITY ANALYST REPORT, APPLE INC 3 (Aug. 1, 2020) (on file with Comm.).

[561] Dig. Competition Expert Panel Report at 29.

[562] *Id.* at 40.

[563] *See* Press Release, Eur. Comm'n, Antitrust: Commission Fines Google €4.34 Billion for Illegal Practices Regarding Android Mobile Devices to Strengthen Dominance of Google's Search Engine (July 18, 2018) https://ec.europa.eu/commission/presscorner/detail/en/IP_18_4581.

[564] *See* GSMA INTEL., GLOBAL MOBILE TRENDS 2020: NEW DECADE, NEW INDUSTRY? 26 (2019), https://data.gsmaintelligence.com/api-web/v2/research-file-download?id=47743151&file=2863-071119-GMT-2019.pdf; Interview with Source 83 (June 30, 2020).

[565] *See* Ryan Mac, *What Amazon Can Learn from The Failed Facebook Phone*, FORBES (Jun. 17, 2014), https://www.forbes.com/sites/ryanmac/2014/06/17/what-amazon-can-learn-from-the-failed-facebook-

that Amazon's Fire Phone did not offer the same extensive library of apps and services as iOS or Android devices.[566]

Companies like Mozilla and Alibaba have also attempted to enter the mobile OS market. Mozilla unveiled its Firefox OS in 2013 and exited the market altogether by 2016.[567] In 2012, Chinese tech giant Alibaba developed a mobile OS called Aliyun for the Chinese market. However, Acer, Alibaba's hardware partner, abruptly canceled its collaboration with Alibaba before the launch of Acer's device running the OS[568]

Over the past decade, once-competitive mobile operating systems like Nokia, BlackBerry, and Microsoft struggled to survive as Apple and Google grew more dominant, eventually exiting the marketplace altogether. BlackBerry—once a leading mobile OS developer—now licenses the BlackBerry name to TCL to market TCL's smartphones. TCL's BlackBerry phones run on Android.[569] In the last quarter of 2016, Windows devices accounted for less than half of one-percent of new smartphone sales.[570] In 2017 Microsoft abandoned its mobile OS business, and by that time more than 99% of all new smartphones were running on iOS or Android and market observers expressed no

phone/#7f7d402f47de; Roger Cheng, *Here's Why the Facebook Phone Flopped*, CNET (May 8, 2013), https://www.cnet.com/news/heres-why-the-facebook-phone-flopped/; Marcus Wohlsen, *The Amazon Fire Phone Was Always Going to Fail*, WIRED (Jan. 6, 2015), https://www.wired.com/2015/01/amazon-fire-phone-always-going-fail/; Austin Carr, *The Inside Story of Jeff Bezos' Fire Phone Debacle*, FAST CO. (Jan. 6, 2015), https://www.fastcompany.com/3039887/under-fire.

[566] *See* Austin Carr, *The Inside Story of Jeff Bezos' Fire Phone Debacle*, FAST CO. (Jan. 6, 2015), https://www.fastcompany.com/3039887/under-fire.

[567] *See* J. Sullivan, *Firefox OS: Looking Ahead*, MOZILLA BLOG (Jan. 6, 2014), https://blog.mozilla.org/blog/2014/01/06/firefox-os-looking-ahead/; Ingrid Lunden, *Mozilla Will Stop Developing And Selling Firefox OS Smartphones*, TECHCRUNCH (Dec. 8, 2015), https://techcrunch.com/2015/12/08/mozilla-will-stop-developing-and-selling-firefox-os-smartphones/; Chris Hoffman, *Mozilla Is Stopping All Commercial Development on Firefox OS*, PC WORLD (Sept. 28, 2016), https://www.pcworld.com/article/3124563/mozilla-is-stopping-all-commercial-development-on-firefox-os.html.

[568] *See* Don Reisinger, *Acer Taps Alibaba's Aliyun OS for New Smartphone*, CNET (Sept. 12, 2012), https://www.cnet.com/news/acer-taps-alibabas-aliyun-os-for-new-smartphone/; Edward Moyer, *Alibaba: Google Just Plain Wrong About Our OS*, CNET (Sept. 15, 2012), https://www.cnet.com/news/alibaba-google-just-plain-wrong-about-our-os/ ; Roger Cheng, *Alibaba: Google Forces Acer to Drop Our New Mobile OS*, CNET (Sept. 13, 2012), https://www.cnet.com/news/alibaba-google-forced-acer-to-drop-our-new-mobile-os/; T.C. Sottek, *Acer Cancels Phone Launch with Alibaba, Allegedly in Response to Threats from Google*, THE VERGE (Sept. 13, 2012), https://www.theverge.com/2012/9/13/3328690/acer-google-alibaba-phone; Dieter Bohn, *Google Explains Why It Stopped Acer's Aliyun Smartphone Launch (Updated)*, THE VERGE (Sept. 14, 2012), https://www.theverge.com/2012/9/14/3335204/google-statement-acer-smartphone-launch-aliyun-android; Jon Brodkin, *Google Blocked Acer's Rival Phone to Prevent Android "Fragmentation"*, ARS TECHNICA (Sept. 14, 2012), https://arstechnica.com/gadgets/2012/09/google-blocked-acers-rival-phone-to-prevent-android-fragmentation/.

[569] *See* Arjun Kharpal, *TCL Launches New $549 Smartphone Under BlackBerry's Banner, Featuring Android Software*, CNBC (Feb. 27, 2017), https://www.cnbc.com/2017/02/25/blackberry-keyone-launch-physical-keyboard-android-specs-price.html.

[570] *See* Press Release, GARTNER Gartner Says Worldwide Sales of Smartphones Grew 7 Percent in the Fourth Quarter of 2016 (Feb. 15, 2017), https://www.gartner.com/en/newsroom/press-releases/2017-02-15-gartner-says-worldwide-sales-of-smartphones-grew-7-percent-in-the-fourth-quarter-of-2016).

confidence that new competition would emerge.[571] One key factor leading to Microsoft's withdrawal from the mobile marketplace was that developers were reluctant to develop apps for a third mobile operating system when already building apps for iOS and Android.[572] These market dynamics remain in place today.

F. Digital Mapping

Digital mapping provides users with virtual maps of the physical world. There are two sets of customers for mapping services: consumers, who use map products for navigation, and businesses, who use underlying mapping libraries and design tools to produce customized maps. With the proliferation of smart devices, digital mapping has become a critical resource for users and businesses alike.

The essential input for both types of services is a digital-map database. Mapping data can be gathered in a few ways, including through the collection of imagery from satellites and streets, the tracking of global positioning system (GPS) traces, and the collation of public domain mapping data. Building a digital map database is costly and time-intensive, requiring significant investment in mapping technologies and data collection.[573] The leading provider of digital mapping data is Google. Smaller providers include HERE and TomTom, as well as open-source providers like OpenStreetMap (OSM).[574] Waze, which developed navigable maps by relying on driver-generated live maps and crowd-sourced updates, was an additional mapping provider purchased by Google in June 2013.

Consumer-facing providers of mapping services license map databases and layer search and traffic technologies atop of the map data. Consumers use these search and traffic tools either through a standalone turn-by-turn navigation service that licenses the underlying data—like MapQuest or Bing Maps—or through a vertically integrated provider, like Google Maps, Waze, or Apple Maps.[575] The

---

[571] Tom Warren, *Windows Phone Dies Today*, THE VERGE (July 11, 2017), https://www.theverge.com/2017/7/11/15952654/microsoft-windows-phone-end-of-support; *see also* Press Release, Gartner, Gartner Says Worldwide Sales of Smartphones Grew 7 Percent in the Fourth Quarter of 2016 (Feb. 15, 2017), https://www.gartner.com/en/newsroom/press-releases/2017-02-15-gartner-says-worldwide-sales-of-smartphones-grew-7-percent-in-the-fourth-quarter-of-2016; James Vincent, *99.6 Percent of New Smartphones Run on Android or iOS*, THE VERGE (Feb. 16, 2017), https://www.theverge.com/2017/2/16/14634656/android-ios-market-share-blackberry-2016.

[572] Dig. Competition Expert Panel Report at 40.

[573] Innovation and Entrepreneurship Hearing at 6 (response to Questions for the Record by Kyle Andeer, Vice Pres., Corp. Law, Apple, Inc.); Production of Google, to H. Comm. on the Judiciary, GOOG-HJC-04208423 (on file with Comm.) (showing that prior to being acquired by Google, a Waze presentation stated, "There are very few companies in the world that are making navigable maps, and the process is very expensive."); Submission from Source 531, to H. Comm. on the Judiciary, Source 531-000628 (on file with Comm.).

[574] Submission from Source 531, to H. Comm. on the Judiciary, Source 531-000628 (on file with Comm.).

[575] Although Apple Maps licensed U.S. mapping data from TomTom upon launching in 2012, in 2015 it began developing its own map database by deploying cars with cameras and sensors to collect images and mapping data that it could combine with anonymized iPhone data to create an independent underlying base map. Lauren Goode, *The Biggest Apple Maps Change Is One You Can't See*, WIRED (Jan. 31, 2020), https://www.wired.com/story/apple-maps-redesign/.

dominant providers of consumer mapping applications are Google Maps and Google-owned Waze, followed by Apple Maps and MapQuest.[576] Google and Apple set their mapping products as the default options on Android and iOS products—their respective devices—which also enables them to maintain and expand their market position.

These providers of consumer mapping services generally do not charge users a monetary fee. Instead, they monetize maps through selling location-based advertisements, or by subsidizing consumer-facing mapping with enterprise contracts or other lines of business. Although data on the value of the consumer-facing digital mapping industry is not publicly available, analysts have estimated that Google Maps earned Google around $2.95 billion in revenue last year and that the standalone product is worth up to $60 billion.[577]

Business-facing providers serve map design tools and mapping libraries required to produce customized maps. The leading providers of business-to-business mapping software are Google, HERE, Mapbox, and TomTom, followed by Apple Maps, Bing, ESRI, Comtech, and Telenav.[578] Some of these providers operate in more specialized markets. For example, HERE and TomTom primarily serve automotive customers, while ESRI provides desktop GIS software used by governments and spatial analysts.[579]

Market participants cite several factors that privilege dominant digital map incumbents and impede entry. First is the capacity of dominant firms to invest heavily in creating mapping databases and technology without needing to turn a profit. For example, prior to its acquisition by Google, Waze executives observed that Google Maps had "disrupted the market" primarily through "financial disruption," namely that it had "unlimited funds" and was giving away Google Maps to users for free.[580] Startups seeking to enter this market yet lacking the financial cushion that permits them to incur losses while developing the product will be at a relative disadvantage.

Another factor is that incumbents that are integrated can collect relevant map and location data from across complementary lines of business, feeding this data back into mapping. For example, one market participant noted that Google "collects an unparalleled amount of data used in digital mapping

---

[576] Submission from Source 572, to H. Comm. on the Judiciary, 1 (Oct. 29, 2019) (on file with Comm) ("For vehicle navigation, and excluding OEM-provided in-console automotive systems, Google's Waze and Google Maps are currently the most used consumer apps by a wide margin."); Submission from Source 333, to H. Comm. on the Judiciary, 2 (Oct. 21, 2019) (on file with Comm.).

[577] Daniel Schaal, *Google Maps Poised to Be an $11 Billion Business in 4 Years*, SKIFT (Aug. 30, 2019), https://skift.com/2019/08/30/google-maps-poised-to-be-an-11-billion-business-in-4-years/; ROSS SANDLER, BARCLAYS, ALPHABET INC., STEADY COMPOUNDER, WITH PLENTY OF INNOVATION AHEAD 20 (Mar. 28, 2017) (on file with Comm.).

[578] Submission from Source 572, to H. Comm. on the Judiciary, 1 (Oct. 29, 2019) (on file with Comm).

[579] *Id.*

[580] Production of Google, to H. Comm. on the Judiciary, GOOG-HJC-04209630 (Nov. 2012) (on file with Comm.)

from users of its dominant search engine and Android smartphone OS."[581] Another market participant stated that Google's dominant position in search and advertising incentivizes businesses to closely monitor and maintain the accuracy of their information in Google's systems, "leading to a dynamic by which Google enjoys a free, crowdsource effort to improve and maintain their data's quality," thereby improving the quality of Google Maps.[582] Firms without concurrent positions in web search and the smartphone market are comparatively disadvantaged.

A third factor is the superior distribution that integrated firms in maps-adjacent lines of business can provide their own mapping product at the expense of third-party mapping products. Google gives Google Maps default placement on its Android devices, while Apple does the same with Apple Maps on iOS devices. Together, Android and iOS account for 99% of the smartphone operating systems in the United States.[583]

Market participants explained that the default placement of Google Maps on Android devices also disadvantages third-party mapping providers technologically. If a developer chooses a third-party mapping provider when building an app, downloading that app on Android would involve downloading both the app features and the mapping functionality. Choosing to develop the app with Google Maps, by contrast, would reduce the app's file size on Android, as Google Maps is already on the device.

Lastly, incumbents benefited from a lack of prohibitions on collecting location data—an advantage that startups today lack given the passage of new data restrictions that limit the development of digital mapping technology. Notably, many of these rules came into existence following public outrage prompted by Google Street View. By the time these rules were implemented, Google had already mapped out most of the planet.

Except for Apple's independent mapping database, there has been no recent entry in the market for underlying mapping data. Similarly, the list of leading providers of consumer mapping services and business-to-business services has mostly been unchanged since 2013.

G.   Cloud Computing

Cloud computing refers to the service that enables remote storage and software programs on demand through the Internet. Prior to cloud computing, data was stored locally on a computer's hard

---

[581] Submission from Source 531, to H. Comm. on the Judiciary, Source 531-000624 (on file with Comm); Production of Google, H. Comm. on the Judiciary, GOOG-HJC-04211078 (July 24, 2013) (on file with Comm.) (Google made a similar observation in July 2013. In a letter responding to the FTC's request for information relating to its acquisition of Waze, Google wrote, "Apple has access to as much or more US GPS traffic data than Google does, with tens of millions of Apple iOS users potentially providing Apple with real-time traffic speed and flow information throughout the country.").

[582] Submission from Source 572, to H. Comm. on the Judiciary, 3 (Oct. 29, 2019) (on file with Comm).

[583] Neth. Auth. for Consumers & Mkts. Study at 15.

drive, in a local server room, or remote data center where companies managed all of the I.T. services.[584] Today, companies can essentially rent "network access to a shared pool of configurable computing resources . . . [including] networks, servers, storage, applications and services."[585] As a result of the convenience and cost savings associated with the ability to scale up or down on demand, cloud computing has grown into one of the technology sector's largest and most lucrative businesses.[586] It has enabled the growth of enterprise businesses such as Netflix, Airbnb, Lyft, Slack, and the Weather Channel, as well as new startups that are not yet household names.

Cloud computing is a critical input to many of the digital markets the Subcommittee investigated, providing infrastructure for online commerce, social media and networking, digital advertising, voice assistants, and digital mapping—technologies that benefit from dynamic storage and computational power. In a future with smart homes, autonomous vehicles and artificial intelligence applications in nearly every sector from agriculture to healthcare, understanding the dynamics of the cloud market place becomes critical. These ground-breaking technologies work because they can access and analyze massive amounts of data in real time, companies looking to innovate in these spaces will struggle to rely solely on traditional I.T. and will likely turn to public cloud vendors. The testimony of Morgan Reed on behalf of ACT, the App Association, illustrates how important "continuous cloud access [is] to create custom software solutions that adapt quickly and rival the products and services of larger SaaS companies."[587]

Cloud computing service models vary by vendor, and new models are being developed continually. The Subcommittee's investigation focused on the dynamics between the three models most referenced and defined by the National Institute of Standards and Technology.

---

[584] *See generally* HEIDI M. PETERS, CONG. RESEARCH SERV., R45847, THE DEPARTMENT OF DEFENSE'S JEDI CLOUD PROGRAM (2019).

[585] *See* NAT'L INST. OF STANDARDS AND TECH, THE NIST DEFINITION OF CLOUD COMPUTING 2 (Sept. 2011), https://nvlpubs.nist.gov/nistpubs/Legacy/SP/nistspecialpublication800-145.pdf.

[586] MARKET SHARE ANALYSIS; IAAS AND IUS, WORLDWIDE (July 5, 2019); Production of Amazon, to H. Comm. on the Judiciary, AMAZON-HJC-00219352 (on file with Comm.).

[587] Innovation and Entrepreneurship Hearing at 7 (statement of Morgan Reed, Pres., ACT | The App Ass'n).

Cloud Computing Services[588]

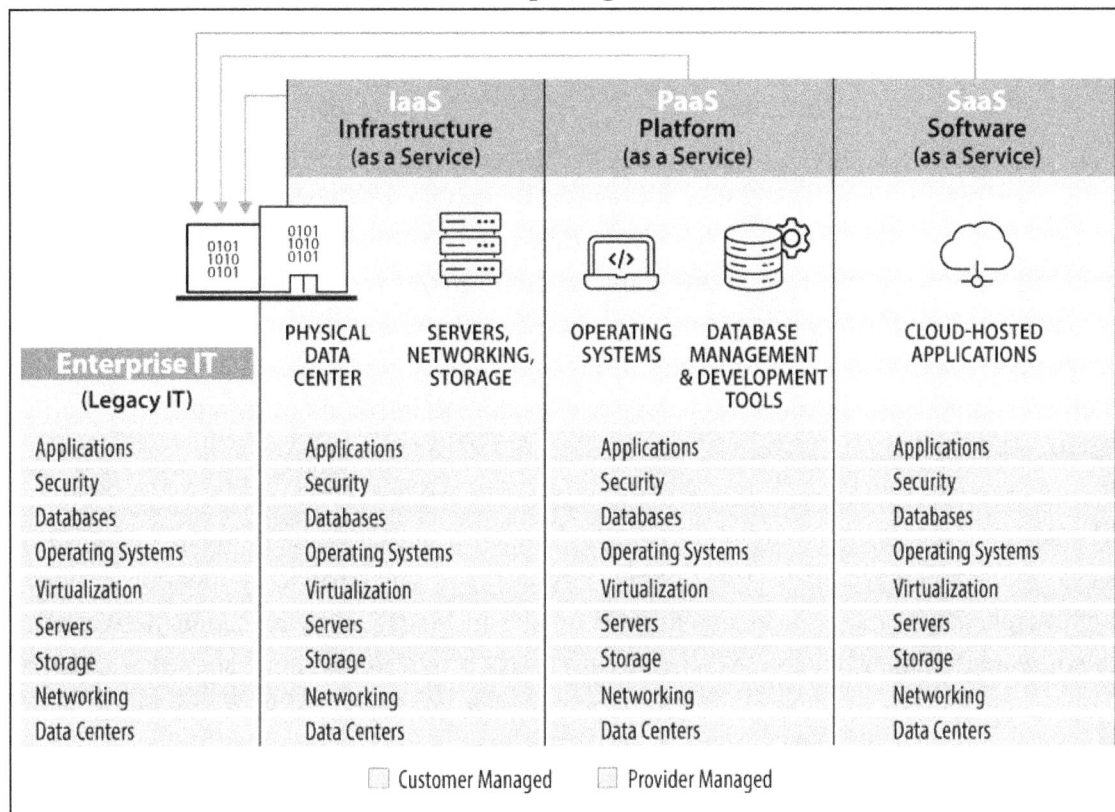

Enterprise IT (Legacy IT)	IaaS Infrastructure (as a Service)		PaaS Platform (as a Service)		SaaS Software (as a Service)
	PHYSICAL DATA CENTER	SERVERS, NETWORKING, STORAGE	OPERATING SYSTEMS	DATABASE MANAGEMENT & DEVELOPMENT TOOLS	CLOUD-HOSTED APPLICATIONS
Applications	Applications		Applications		Applications
Security	Security		Security		Security
Databases	Databases		Databases		Databases
Operating Systems	Operating Systems		Operating Systems		Operating Systems
Virtualization	Virtualization		Virtualization		Virtualization
Servers	Servers		Servers		Servers
Storage	Storage		Storage		Storage
Networking	Networking		Networking		Networking
Data Centers	Data Centers		Data Centers		Data Centers

☐ Customer Managed   ☐ Provider Managed

In the Software as a Service (SaaS) model, the user accesses applications from various client devices "through either a thin client interface, such as a web browser, or a program interface."[589] Common examples include Google Docs, Slack, and Mailchimp. In the Platform as a Service (PaaS) model, the user, most often a cloud application developer, builds new applications by accessing programming languages, libraries, services and tools supported by the cloud provider.[590] Common PaaS tools include AWS Elastic Beanstalk, Google App Engine and Salesforce's Heroku. In the Infrastructure as a Service (IaaS) model, the user, most often an engineer, can deploy and run software, which can include operating systems and applications while the cloud provider provisions fundamental computing resources including processing, storage, and network applications.[591] Common IaaS tools include Amazon Elastic Compute Cloud (EC2), Google Compute Engine, and Microsoft Azure.[592]

---

[588] Prepared by the Subcomm. based on data from Nat'l Inst. of Standards and Tech.

[589] NAT'L INST. OF STANDARDS AND TECH., THE NIST DEFINITION OF CLOUD COMPUTING 2 (Sept. 2011), https://nvlpubs.nist.gov/nistpubs/Legacy/SP/nistspecialpublication800-145.pdf.

[590] *Id.* at 2.

[591] *Id.* at 3.

[592] HEIDI M. PETERS, CONG. RESEARCH SERV., R45847, THE DEPARTMENT OF DEFENSE'S JEDI CLOUD PROGRAM 1 (2019).

SaaS, PaaS, and IaaS can be deployed through several different models.[593] Subcommittee staff focused primarily on the market for public cloud services in which the cloud provider provisions infrastructure for open use by the general public. The infrastructure resides on the premise of the cloud provider.[594]

To review market dynamics, Subcommittee staff examined two types of cloud service providers. The first are infrastructure providers. Amazon Web Services (AWS), Microsoft Azure and Google Cloud Platform (GCP) are the most common domestic infrastructure providers. They offer customers IaaS, PaaS and SaaS offerings through their customer consoles or portals, but are distinct in their ability to offer IaaS at scale. This Report refers to them as infrastructure providers. They also operate online marketplaces for third-party software vendors to list cloud offerings that integrate with their infrastructure services.

The second are third-party software vendors, sometimes referred to as Independent Software Vendors (ISVs). Companies such as Salesforce, MariaDB, and The Apache Foundation provide operating systems, databases, security and applications. Third-party software can be delivered as a packaged software or managed service. When a third party provides packaged software, it can be installed onto a customer's existing cloud infrastructure. The packaged software can be listed on the infrastructure provider's marketplace or through a third-party vendor's website.

When third-party software is sold as a managed service, the customer pays a subscription based on the amount of services used, and the third-party software vendor manages all the underlying infrastructure.[595] In this scenario, the software has become a cloud offering sold "as-a-service." The underlying infrastructure can be owned and managed by the third-party software vendor or the third-party software vendor may have contracts with an infrastructure provider, and in some cases the software vendor uses a combination of owned and rented servers. For example, Salesforce's Heroku—a PaaS product—is built using AWS IaaS offerings.[596] When a company purchases a Heroku license, Salesforce's use of AWS is included in the price. In the case that a PaaS or SaaS offering uses its own infrastructure, it is likely it will need to be able to integrate with products managed by the infrastructure providers as it grows, and to expand to new regions it will need to contract with infrastructure providers.[597]

---

[593] NAT'L INST. OF STANDARDS AND TECH., THE NIST DEFINITION OF CLOUD COMPUTING 3 (Sept. 2011).

[594] *Id.*

[595] *Id.*

[596] *See e.g.*, Kelly Cochran, *Simplify Your Customer Engagement with AWS and Salesforce Heroku*, AWS PARTNER NETWORK (APN) BLOG (June 9, 2017), https://aws.amazon.com/blogs/apn/simplify-your-customer-engagement-with-aws-and-salesforce-heroku/.

[597] Mark Innes, *Salesforce is live on AWS Cloud Infrastructure in Australia*, SALESFORCE BLOG (Oct. 17, 2017), https://www.salesforce.com/au/blog/2017/10/salesforce-is-live-on-aws-cloud-infrastructure-in-australia.html. For example, for many years Salesforce.com's CRM ran on self-managed infrastructure but when the company expanded to Australia in 2007, they entered into a contract with AWS.

In 2018, public cloud services, including IaaS, PaaS, SaaS and management services, accounted for $182.4 billion of the overall $3.7 trillion information technology (I.T.) infrastructure spending worldwide—less than 1%.[598] Despite being a small fraction of I.T. spending, Gartner projects the market size of the cloud services industry to increase at nearly three times the rate of overall I.T. services through 2022, to reach $331 billion.[599] AWS is the market leader, capturing approximately 24% of the U.S. spend on cloud computing in 2018.[600]

Amazon—the leading cloud platform—is dominant in the cloud market due to the concentration of the IaaS market.[601] According to Gartner, "the worldwide IaaS market grew 31.3% in 2018 to total $32.4 billion, up from $24.7 billion in 2017."[602] As seen in the chart below, AWS is the unquestioned leader in the cloud computing infrastructure market, with triple the market share of Microsoft. Alibaba, Google, and Microsoft are growing at the fastest rates—rates double that of Amazon. Gartner expects the IaaS Worldwide Public Cloud Service Revenue to grow faster than any other set of services, and to be worth $76.6 billion in 2022.[603]

---

[598] Letter from David Zapolsky, Gen. Counsel, Amazon.com, Inc., to Hon. David N. Cicilline, Chairman, Subcomm. on Antitrust, Commercial and Admin. Law of the H. Comm. on the Judiciary, 6 (July 26, 2019) (on file with Comm.).

[599] Press Release, Gartner, Gartner Says Global IT Spending to Reach $3.7 Trillion in 2018 (July 29, 2019), https://www.gartner.com/en/newsroom/press-releases/2019-07-29-gartner-says-worldwide-iaas-public-cloud-services-market-grew-31point3-percent-in-2018.

[600] Letter from David Zapolsky, Gen. Counsel, Amazon.com, Inc., to Hon. David N. Cicilline, Chairman, Subcomm. on Antitrust, Commercial and Admin. Law of the H. Comm. on the Judiciary, 6 (July 26, 2019) (on file with Comm.).

[601] Submission from Source 170 to H. Comm. on the Judiciary, 6 (Nov. 21, 2011) (on file with Comm.).

[602] Press Release, Gartner, Gartner Forecasts Worldwide Public Cloud Revenue to Grow 17.5 Percent in 2019 (Apr. 2, 2019), https://www.gartner.com/en/newsroom/press-releases/2019-07-29-gartner-says-worldwide-iaas-public-cloud-services-market-grew-31point3-percent-in-2018.

[603] *Id.*

IaaS Worldwide Public Cloud Services Revenue (Millions of US Dollars)[604]

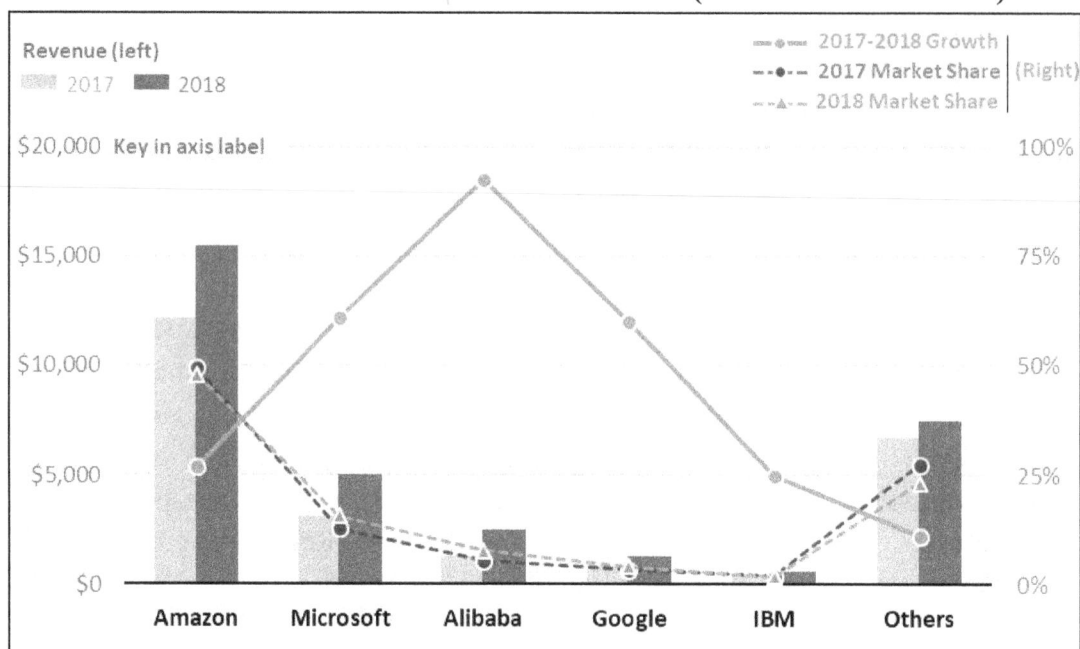

Industry reports suggest that the cloud computing market is consolidating around three providers domestically—AWS, Microsoft Azure and Google Cloud Platform.[605]

Market leaders benefit from early mover advantage coupled with network effects and high switching costs that lock-in customers. AWS pioneered cloud computing, launching officially in March 2006 with Simple Storage Service (S3) and Elastic Compute Cloud (EC2), two fundamental IaaS offerings.[606] Microsoft announced Azure in October 2008 along with core services that made up the "Azure Services Platform."[607] Google's first public cloud service, App Engine, a PaaS offering, was released in 2008.[608] Google's Compute Engine, an AWS Elastic Compute Cloud and Microsoft Azure Virtual Machines competitor, went live as a preview in June 2012.[609]

---

[604] Prepared by Subcomm. based on Press Release, Gartner, Gartner Forecasts Worldwide Public Cloud Revenue to Grow 17.5 Percent in 2019 (Apr. 2, 2019), https://www.gartner.com/en/newsroom/press-releases/2019-07-29-gartner-says-worldwide-iaas-public-cloud-services-market-grew-31point3-percent-in-2018.

[605] Production of Amazon, to H. Comm. on the Judiciary, AMAZON-HJC-00219350 (July 5, 2019) (on file with Comm).

[606] *What's New*, AMAZON (Oct. 4, 2006) https://aws.amazon.com/about-aws/whats-new/2006/.

[607] Press Release, Microsoft, Microsoft Unveils Windows Azure at Professional Developers Conference (Oct. 27, 2008), https://news.microsoft.com/2008/10/27/microsoft-unveils-windows-azure-at-professional-developers-conference/#IP8XlBTCMpvORgaV.97.

[608] Paul McDonald, *Introducing Google App Engine + our new blog*, GOOGLE DEVELOPER BLOG (Apr. 7, 2008), http://googleappengine.blogspot.com/2008/04/introducing-google-app-engine-our-new.html.

[609] Ryan Lawler, *Google Launches Computer Engine to Take on Amazon Web Services*, TECHCRUNCH (June 28, 2012), https://techcrunch.com/2012/06/28/google-compute-engine/.

A 2010 Google strategy document predicted that the cloud computing market would concentrate. An internal document titled "Where Industry is Headed in 5 Years," stated that there would be some concentration in the market within five years, with cloud service providers consisting of Google, Amazon, Microsoft, and a hybrid of Cisco and VMWare.[610] According to this document, each company would offer cloud-based apps and other tools.[611] Later, in a 2018 strategy document, Google emphasized the importance of first-mover advantage in the space, writing "AWS and Azure have had more years to gain customers, and cloud customers typically grow [in] scale over time; in contrast" reiterating the tendency for cloud customers to choose a single vendor as their primary cloud service provider.[612] In a roundtable held by Subcommittee Chairman Cicilline, Mark Tracy, the CEO of Cloudacronomics, described these concerns:

> We pull down terabytes of data, and they have to upload it to the cloud to improve farmers practices. The two cloud providers are AWS and Azure. Since so many businesses and so much value can be extracted by improving health and data, this concentration of cloud services is a concern.[613]

As seen in the figure below, IaaS prices have decreased over time, with the three dominant U.S. providers able to price their services at less than $30/GB RAM according to a 2018 RBC Capital Markets report.[614] Market participants reference economies of scale and a focus on increasing revenue from PaaS and SaaS offerings, as opposed to IaaS offerings, as an explanation for this trend. IaaS vendors benefit from economies of scale both with regards to the size of the datacenters and the ability to operate multiple datacenters across the globe. To enter the market and reach the economies of scale needed to compete with the incumbents, infrastructure providers must invest significant capital and be able to offer competitive prices to lure customers.

---

[610] Production of Google, to H. Comm. on the Judiciary, GOOG-HJC-01777633 (on file with Comm.).

[611] *Id.*

[612] *Id.* at GOOG-HJC-04167638–66 (June 3, 2019).

[613] Rhode Island Roundtable (Mar. 17, 2020) (statement of Mark Tracy, CEO, Cloudacronomics) (on file with Comm.).

[614] Production of Amazon, to H. Comm. on the Judiciary, AMAZON-HJC-00183326 (Dec. 4, 2018) (on file with Comm.) (showing a 2018 RBC Capital Markets Report which analyzed the cost of IaaS across five usage scenarios: Standard, High Compute, High Memory, High Storage, High Input/Output (I/O) and three workload sizes, small, medium and large, to create 15 cases.).

Average Monthly Costs Per GB RAM Across 15 Use Cases[615]

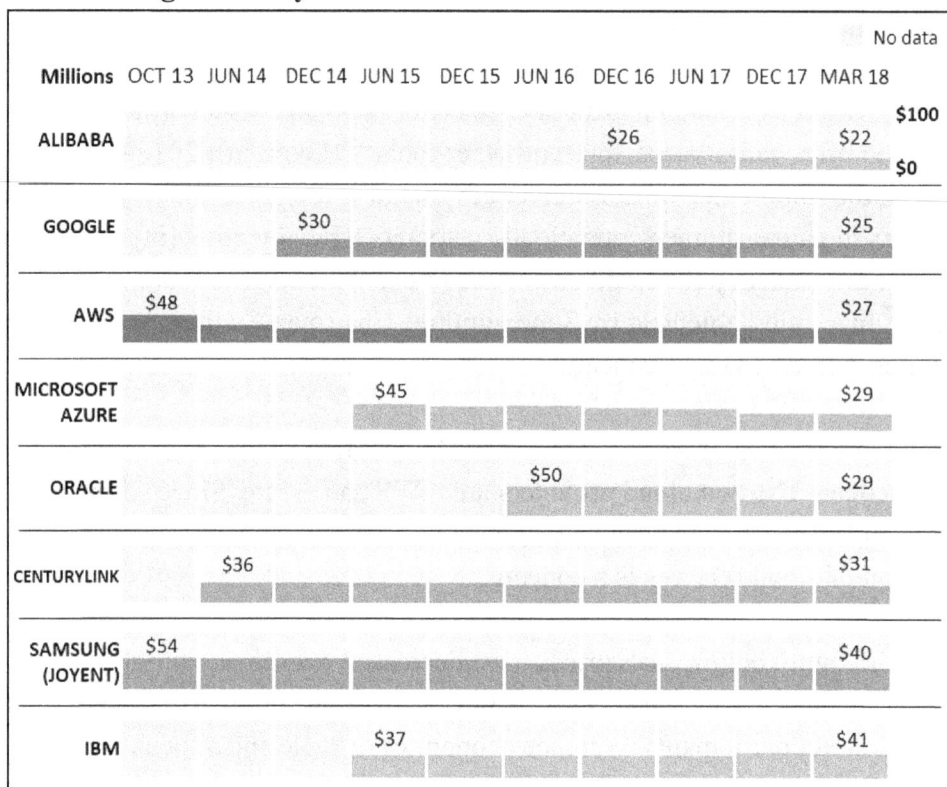

Millions	OCT 13	JUN 14	DEC 14	JUN 15	DEC 15	JUN 16	DEC 16	JUN 17	DEC 17	MAR 18	No data
ALIBABA							$26			$22	$100 / $0
GOOGLE			$30							$25	
AWS	$48									$27	
MICROSOFT AZURE				$45						$29	
ORACLE						$50				$29	
CENTURYLINK		$36								$31	
SAMSUNG (JOYENT)	$54									$40	
IBM				$37						$41	

The "cloud" is a system of cables connected to a wide network of data centers—all underground, under water or in large industrial buildings. Building data centers in dozens of regions worldwide costs billions of dollars.[616] Market participants described the investment as "bigger than building a cellular network" and only "for countries and major companies."[617]

Two additional inputs that can provide a barrier to becoming a leading infrastructure provider are compliance certifications and reputation. Federal Risk and Authorization Management Program (FedRAMP) authorization is required for any service that holds U.S. federal data.[618] The

---

[615] Prepared by Subcomm. based Production of Amazon, to H. Comm. on the Judiciary, AMAZON-HJC-00183326 (Dec. 4, 2018) (on file with Comm.) (2018 RBC Capital Markets Report which analyzed the cost of IaaS across five usage scenarios: Standard, High Compute, High Memory, High Storage, High Input/Output (I/O) and three workload sizes, small, medium and large, to create 15 cases.).

[616] Submission from Source 170, to H. Comm. on the Judiciary, 8 (Nov. 21, 2011) (on file with Comm.).

[617] Interview with Source 144 (April 17, 2020).

[618] OFF. OF MGMT. & BUDGET, EXEC. OFF. OF THE PRESIDENT, SECURITY AUTHORIZATION OF INFORMATION SYSTEMS IN CLOUD COMPUTING ENVIRONMENTS (2011), https://www.fedramp.gov/assets/resources/documents/FedRAMP_Policy_Memo.pdf.

FedRAMP authorization process can be resource and time intensive as vendors have to undergo a process of technical and security reviews and audits.[619]

When a customer chooses to use cloud computing they must trust that their data will be secure and available to access quickly. The leading cloud infrastructure providers are major technology companies that handled massive amounts of data and run large technical operations before offering managed services. Market participants have shared with Subcommittee staff that a smaller company attempting to enter the IaaS market to contest these firms must convince large customers that they can provide a reliable service that is compliant with industry-specific regulations.[620]

Market participants and industry reports highlight that IaaS offerings have become commoditized. To compete, infrastructure providers must offer a range of PaaS and SaaS services to attract users and developers to their platform.[621] First-party PaaS and SaaS offerings are made available in the infrastructure provider's console. As of this Report, AWS, Azure and GCP all list over 100 first-party cloud offerings.[622] Each cloud infrastructure provider has taken their own approach to building its platform, but all involve acquisitions, in-house software development, and the use of open-source software. Google and Azure have also relied on their company's existing products—Microsoft leveraging its Office 360 Suite and Google leveraging its collection of APIs.[623]

In the case that a new entrant can overcome this entry barrier, it must also invest substantial resources to overcome network effects within the market. Infrastructure providers benefit from network effects—the more customers on a platform, the more third parties build services that integrate well with that platform leading to more services to attract customers. Amazon, Microsoft, and Google all have hundreds of products listed in their third-party marketplace, while Amazon lists 9,250.[624] In interviews with Subcommittee staff, third-party software vendors said that they had little choice but to integrate their products with the incumbents, most notably, AWS.

Cloud infrastructure providers also need to ensure that the knowledge and expertise of their platform's technology are available to their customers. To achieve this, cloud infrastructure providers launch partner networks that include consulting firms trained to help enterprise customers move to the

---

[619] *Get Authorized: Joint Authorization Board*, FEDRAMP, https://www.fedramp.gov/jab-authorization/ (last visited on Sept. 26, 2020).

[620] Interview with Source 407 (Sept. 10, 2020).

[621] Submission from Source 264, to H. Comm. on the Judiciary, 58 (Nov. 21, 2011) (on file with Comm.).

[622] *AWS Marketplace*, AMAZON https://aws.amazon.com/marketplace (last visited on Oct. 4 2020); *Find solutions to support innovation*, MICROSOFT AZURE https://azure.microsoft.com/en-us/marketplace/ (last visited on Oct. 4, 2020); GOOGLE CLOUD PLATFORM, https://console.cloud.google.com/marketplace (last visited on Oct. 4, 2020).

[623] Submission from Source 170, to H. Comm. on the Judiciary (Nov. 21, 2011) (on file with Comm.); Production of Google, to H. Comm. on the Judiciary, GOOG-HJC-02456801 (2010) (on file with Comm.).

[624] *AWS Marketplace*, AMAZON https://aws.amazon.com/marketplace (last visited on Oct. 4, 2020).

public cloud, such as AWS Partner Network (APN) Consulting Partners,[625] and Microsoft Solution Providers.[626] Cloud infrastructure providers also offer trainings and exams to certify members of the workforce as proficient in various uses of their technology. Additionally, infrastructure providers have programs to support third-party software vendors working to integrate with the infrastructure provider's cloud.

Many market participants interviewed by Subcommittee staff believe that surpassing the incumbents in the market will be challenging because of the potential for vendor lock-in. Other evidence reviewed by Subcommittee staff bolsters this concern, suggesting that lock-in exists because switching costs for cloud computing customers are high.[627]

Subcommittee staff has identified several common techniques infrastructure providers use to initially lock-in customers, including contract terms, free tier offerings, and egress fees. The first is long-term contracts. In several responses to the Committee's requests for information, third parties explained they have contracts lasting from 3-to-5 years with the infrastructure providers.

Another common technique is using free tier products, where each cloud platform offers a free tier of services ranging from always free to trial offers.[628] Market participants suggest that while the free tier products vary slightly among the major firms, they are relatively similar. When a customer's free trial expires, it is faced with switching to another provider or starting to pay for service. Switching requires an investment of time and resources in the adapting to the new service provider, as well as possibly paying egress fees to the prior vendor. As a result, customers may decline to switch at the conclusion of free trials.

Whether a customer begins using cloud on free tier products or not, once they have substantially built and migrated to a platform, they face high switching costs in the form of fees to move the data, along with the technical and labor costs associated with switching the data. When a company moves data into the cloud from hard drives or private servers, they are often charged ingress fees, which are generally low or free.[629] When a company, however, chooses to move data to another infrastructure provider, they are charged an egress fee. Egress fees vary slightly by company and region.

---

[625] *Partners*, AMAZON, https://aws.amazon.com/partners/ (last visited on Sept. 26, 2020).

[626] *Solution Providers*, MICROSOFT, https://www.microsoft.com/en-us/solution-providers/home (last visited on Oct. 4, 2020).

[627] Production of Google, to H. Comm. on the Judiciary, GOOG-HJC-04215099 (Dec. 31, 2018) (on file with Comm.).

[628] *See, e.g.*, *AWS Free Tier*, AMAZON, https://aws.amazon.com/free/ (last visited on Oct. 4, 2020).

[629] *All Network Pricing*, GOOGLE CLOUD, https://cloud.google.com/vpc/network-pricing (last visited on Oct. 4, 2020).

Market participants explain that egress fees are often not transparent and are sometimes charged even when data is not leaving the datacenter.[630] One market participant said that these fees "can create significant financial barriers to migrating away from particular cloud storage providers."[631]

Additionally, when a customer decides to move any of its operations to a different infrastructure provider, it often must overcome technical design challenges. Several market participants spoke to the challenges of finding cloud developers that know the underlying technology of multiple cloud infrastructures as a barrier to both switching, either from one cloud to another or to setup multi-cloud operations. As one third party describes, "businesses often have to calibrate a complex set of technical frameworks, settings, and customized interfaces to adapt their business to the potentially unique way the cloud storage provider has chosen to operate their service."[632] For example, in an investor statement in 2020, Snap explained:

> [T]he vast majority of our computing [runs] on Google Cloud and AWS, and our systems are not fully redundant on the two platforms. Any transition of the cloud services currently provided by either Google Cloud or AWS to the other platform or to another cloud provider would be difficult to implement and will cause us to incur significant time and expense.[633]

When asked about lock-in, many market participants discussed how in response to the rise of a few dominant platforms in the cloud market, new strategies have emerged to increase portability between vendors and allow customers to use multiple clouds. Market participants note, however, that today interoperability is a challenge, and it is unclear how cooperative dominant cloud infrastructure providers will be in supporting partnerships and standards to facilitate these strategies. Given the current trends towards concentration in the cloud infrastructure market, further scrutiny of the role standards play towards decreasing switching costs and enabling portability and interoperability is warranted.

Finally, Subcommittee staff interviewed market participants about related competition concerns facing third-party software vendors. Many third-party software vendors compete with first-party products listed in the infrastructure provider's console. Market participants explain that these competitive offerings are often the first products customers see because they are displayed within the customer's existing console in a format that makes it easier for users to add to their existing cloud

---

[630] Interview with Source 465 (May 27, 2020).

[631] Submission from Source 264, to H. Comm. on the Judiciary, 6 (Nov. 21, 2011) (on file with Comm.).

[632] *Id.* at 5.

[633] Snap Inc., Annual Report (Form 10-K) 11 (Dec. 31, 2019), http://d18rn0p25nwr6d.cloudfront.net/CIK-0001564408/0cfebc98-816e-44ac-8351-5067b4f88f0c.pdf.

stack, seamlessly including the product in their billing and licenses and with minimal technical set-up.[634]

As a result, it is difficult for customers to compare prices and features included in the offerings when they are not listed side-by-side. Although third-party vendors can sell their service directly to consumers through their own websites, many smaller cloud vendors use the marketplaces of the dominant infrastructure providers to reach customers, which require fees and are subject to competition concerns that are similar to other marketplaces examined by Subcommittee staff during the investigation. Market participants have raised concerns that cloud infrastructure providers can preference their own offerings, or offer these products with exceedingly steep discounts, making it difficult for third-party software vendors with fewer products to compete.[635]

Significantly, because the leading infrastructure providers have access to competitively significant data in the marketplace, they have insight into usage metrics regarding any managed service that runs on their infrastructure.[636] Market participants told the Subcommittee that they have concerns that this data can be used by infrastructure providers to make decisions regarding which types of software to acquire or replicate to offer through their first-party console.[637]

H.   Voice Assistant

Voice assistants act as a user interface that enables exchanges between computing devices through a person's voice.[638] Today users can ask their electronic devices to play the morning news or start a conference call.[639] When combined with smart speakers, voice assistants can become a gateway to the internet, and also be used to connect other "smart" devices, such as lighting, thermostats, security monitors, and even kitchen appliances.[640] While voice assistants began as mobile phone apps, they have become integrated into other devices, including cars and homes.[641]

---

[634] *Getting Started*, AMAZON WEB SERVICES, https://docs.aws.amazon.com/awsaccountbilling/latest/aboutv2/billing-getting-started.html (last visited on Oct. 4, 2020).

[635] Submission from Source 170, to H. Comm. on the Judiciary, 7 (Oct. 18, 2019) (on file with Comm.).

[636] Innovation and Entrepreneurship Hearing at 93 (response to Questions for the Record of Adam Cohen, Dir. of Econ. Pol'y, Google LLC), 44–45 (response to Questions for the Record of Nate Sutton, Assoc. Gen. Counsel, Amazon.com, Inc.).

[637] *See* Alistair Barr, *Amazon Finds Startup Investments in the 'Cloud,'* REUTERS (Nov. 9, 2011), http://www.reuters.com/article/amazon-cloud-idUSN1E7A727Q20111109.

[638] Submission from Source 301, to H. Comm. on the Judiciary, Source 301-00000080 at 2 (Oct. 15, 2019) (on file with. Comm.).

[639] Submission from Source 918, to H. Comm. on the Judiciary, 2 (Nov. 4, 2019) (on file with. Comm.).

[640] Submission from Source 918, to H. Comm. on the Judiciary, Source 918-0002029 (Nov. 4, 2019) (on file with Comm.).

[641] Submission from Source 711, to H. Comm. on the Judiciary, Source 711-00000080 at 13 (Oct. 15, 2019) (on file with. Comm.).

There are two types of voice assistants on the market: general and specialized. General voice assistants—such as Siri, Alexa, and Google Assistant—can respond to queries and interact with a range of applications. Specialized voice assistants focus on specific verticals—such as healthcare or banking—where there is a limited vocabulary universe and more specific responses.[642] For example, Snips, a privacy-centric voice assistant owned by Sonos, specializes in commands for playing music on smart speakers.[643]

Today, voice assistants interact with humans by receiving specific requests and sending feedback through a voice response. The first step is to deliver the "wake word"—such as "hey, Siri" on iPhones—designed to activate the system. Once activated, a voice assistant can execute a command, which triggers a voice application.[644]

Voice Assistant Ecosystem[645]

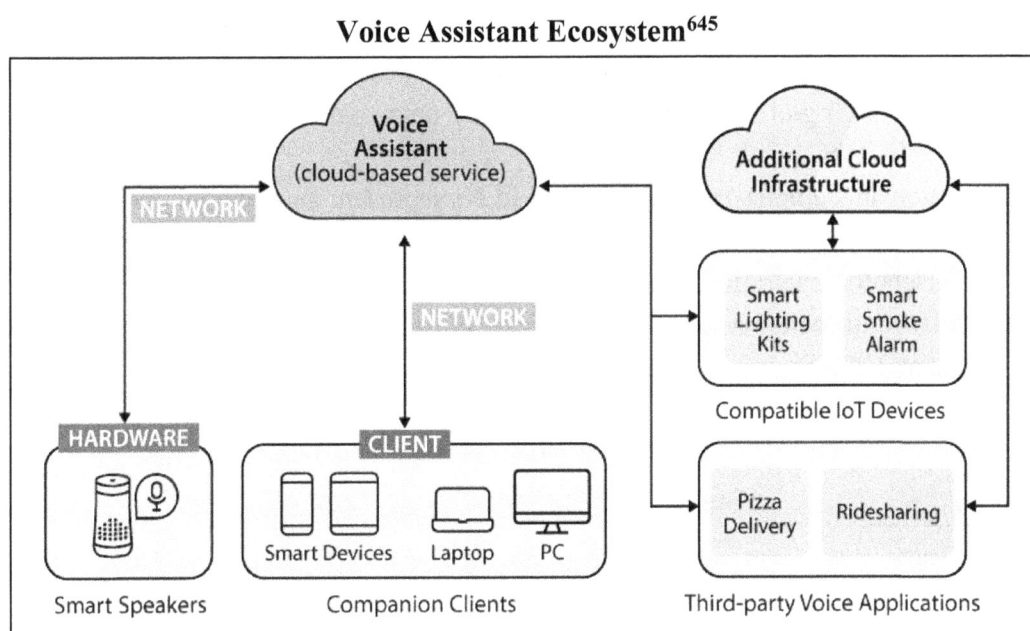

Although there are multiple types of voice assistants within the ecosystem, Subcommittee staff focused primarily on voice assistant platform vendors and third-party hardware manufacturers, including smart speaker manufactures and Internet of Things (IoT) compatible device manufactures. The business model for these two groups varies. A Voice assistant platform vendors can monitize its platform by using its ecosystem to drive revenue to complementry lines of business such as e-

---

[642] *Id.*

[643] Thomas Ricker, *Sonos buys Snips, a privacy-focused voice assistant*, THE VERGE (Nov. 21, 2019), https://www.theverge.com/2019/11/21/20975607/sonos-buys-snips-ai-voice-assistant-privacy.

[644] Hyunji Chung, Jungheum Park & Sangjin Lee, *Digital Forensic Approaches for Amazon Alexa Ecosystem*, DFRWS (2017), https://arxiv.org/ftp/arxiv/papers/1707/1707.08696.pdf

[645] Prepared by the Subcomm. based on Hyunji Chung, Jungheum Park & Sangjin Lee, *Digital Forensic Approaches for Amazon Alexa Ecosystem*, DFRWS (2017), https://arxiv.org/ftp/arxiv/papers/1707/1707.08696.pdf

commerce, search or entertainment.[646] It can also charge voice-application developers to be the recommended application for a specific command.[647] As they become widely adopted, stores on voice assitant platforms—such as the "Alexa Skills Store"—can offer premium content and collect revenue share on payments.[648] Third-party hardware manufactures generate income by selling hardware, and in some cases, by offering subscription services such as home monitoring.[649]

Voice assistants have grown in popularity over recent years due to technological advancements in natural language processing. Although the market is nascent, market participants and industry experts view voice-enabled devices as an opportunity to lock consumers into information ecosystems. The smartphone and smart speaker are the two main portals for voice assistants. Apple and Google lead in the smartphone market, and Amazon leads in the smart speaker market.[650] According to one consulting firm, of the 1.1 billion shipments of virtual assistants in 2019, Apple's Siri (35%) has the highest market share globally, followed by Google Assistant (9%) and Amazon Alexa (4%).[651] Although a significant share of shipments is attributed to Microsoft Cortana (22%) because of the popularity of Windows PCs globally, Cortana is generally not considered a voice assistant platform.[652]

Market participants emphasize that smart speakers represent an essential "hub" or gateway for smart homes and are driving voice-assistant adoption.[653] Smart speakers are estimated to currently have 35% U.S. household penetration, which is predicted to grow to 75% by 2025.[654] As of January 2019, Amazon had a significant lead in the U.S. market at 61.1%, followed by Google at 23.8%, Apple at 2.7%, and Sonos at 2.2%.[655]

---

[646] Production from Google, to H. Comm. on the Judiciary, GOOG-HJC-04257931 (Mar. 9, 2017) (on file with Comm.).

[647] *Id.*

[648] *Id.*

[649] Alison DeNisco Rayome, *How to Monetize Your IoT Project*, TECHREPUBLIC (June 20, 2018), https://www.techrepublic.com/article/6-steps-to-monetizing-your-iot-project/.

[650] Submission from Source 918, to H. Comm. on the Judiciary, Source 918-0002763 (Nov. 4, 2019) (on file with Comm.).

[651] Press Release, Futuresource Consulting, Virtual Assistants to Exceed 2.5 Billion Shipments in 2023 (Dec. 18, 2019) https://www.futuresource-consulting.com/press-release/consumer-electronics-press/virtual-assistants-to-exceed-25-billion-shipments-in-2023/.

[652] *Id.* Mary Jo Foley, *Microsoft CEO Nadella makes it official: Cortana is an app, not a standalone assistant*, ZDNET (Jan. 18, 2019), https://www.zdnet.com/article/microsoft-ceo-nadella-makes-it-official-cortana-is-an-app-not-a-standalone-assistant/.

[653] Production from Google, to H. Comm. on the Judiciary, GOOG-HJC-04258666 (Jan. 28, 2019) (on file with Comm.) ("Speakers still going to be very important. [company] cited stats that suggested that only 20% of their "smart home" customers are new to the category. And it's fair to say that many/most of these existing smart home customers started with sound.").

[654] *See generally* Submission from Source 918, to H. Comm. on the Judiciary (Nov. 4, 2019) (on file with Comm.).

[655] *Id.* at 7.

A voice assistant platform vendor can expand its ecosystem by adding IoT devices and voice applications. Both IoT devices and voice applications can be first-party—owned by the voice assistant platform vendor—or third-party, if the vendor has set up services to allow for manufacturers to create voice assistant-enabled devices. Amazon's Alexa ecosystem, measured in terms of compatible IoT devices and voice applications, is the largest of the three primary ecosystems. In 2017, voice assistants made their first serious moves beyond smart speakers into other product categories.[656] The voice assistant-compatible device market is vast and includes kitchen appliances, security cameras, and even trash cans.[657]

Market participants suggest there are several barriers to entry to compete with general voice assistant platforms. These include overcoming the network effects early entrants have benefited from, including financial investment in hardware, software and infrastructure, and the ability to sell voice assistant-enabled devices at a discount.

Like many platform-based businesses, the voice assistant market benefits from network effects. The more users on a platform, the more third-party devices and applications become available, attracting more users to the platform. [658] These network effects for voice assistant platforms are amplified by machine learning and artificial intelligence (AI). Improvements in Natural Language Processing (NLP) and AI are expected to improve the quality of voice assistants and contribute to wider adoption.[659] Voice assistant technology improves at a faster rate when there are more users providing the voice samples needed to train AI. In testimony to the Subcommittee, Professors Maurice Stucke and Ariel Ezrachi describe this a "Learning-by-Doing." As they note:

> Learning–by–doing network effect is not limited to online searches, but will be present in any environment in which algorithms evolve and adapt based on experience, such, for example, the development of voice recognition or other instances based on machine learning.[660]

---

[656] Submission from Source 918, to H. Comm. on the Judiciary, Source 918-0002024 (Nov. 4, 2019) (on file with Comm.).

[657] *See, e.g.*, Christopher Mims, *All Ears: Always-On Listening Devices Could Soon Be Everywhere*, WALL ST. J. (July 12, 2018), https://www.wsj.com/articles/all-ears-always-on-listening-devices-could-soon-be-everywhere-1531411250.

[658] Submission of Source 918, to H. Comm. on the Judiciary, Source 918-0002025 at 12 (Oct. 15, 2019) (on file with Comm.).

[659] Submission of Source 711, to H. Comm. on the Judiciary, Source 711-00000080 at 12 (Oct. 15, 2019) (on file with Comm.).

[660] Data and Privacy Hearing at 6-7 (statement of Maurice E. Stucke, Prof. of Law, Univ. of Tennessee, and Ariel Ezrachi, Slaughter and May Prof. of Competition Law, Univ. of Oxford, Fellow, Pembroke Coll., Dir., Oxford Ctr. For Competition Law and Pol'y).

The scale of users generating data is arguably the most important asset in terms of AI.[661] The incumbents have access to large data sets that—when combined with machine learning and AI—position them to benefit from economies of scope in the smart home.[662]

Competing as a voice assistant platform also requires significant financial resources. A firm must make significant investments to design and train a voice assistant, as well as acquiring the physical infrastructure: hardware and cloud computing. Additionally, incumbents have also acquired various firms that specialize in voice recognition and natural language processing, a functionality that is used in their voice assistants. For example, both Apple and Amazon acquired companies to develop their core voice recognition technologies, and every incumbent has continually invested in AI startups to improve their voice assistant ecosystem.[663]

Currently, voice assistant software is built on cloud computing infrastructure. In the case of Amazon Alexa and Google Assistant, the voice assistant platforms also own the underlying cloud infrastructure, AWS, and GCP, respectively. Market participants note that advancements in voice assistant ecosystems are beginning to rely on edge computing technology, which brings the computation and data storage closer to the device and is a technology in which the incumbent cloud market leaders have a head start.[664]

Market participants have also raised concerns about incumbent firms offering voice-enabled hardware—specifically hubs such as smart speakers—to both collect large amounts of personal user data and strengthen other lines of business. At the Subcommittee's field hearing, Sonos CEO Patrick Spence explained:

> Google and Amazon have flooded the market with dramatically price-subsidized products. Indeed, they make no pretense of the fact that the products themselves are money losers and they routinely give them away at steep discounts, even for free. It is difficult to predict the impact that voice assistants will have on search and e-commerce, but voice activated speakers have the potential to dramatically alter the way that consumers interact with the internet. We believe that Google and Amazon have been willing to forgo profits in smart speakers for this reason, in addition to their ability to monetize the valuable household data that these products vacuum up. And if voice purchasing and voice search do become the next big thing, they will own the market because their strategy is succeeding. Those two companies now control roughly 85% of

---

[661] Submission of Source 918, to H. Comm. on the Judiciary, Source 918-0002763 at 12 (Oct. 15, 2019) (on file with Comm.).

[662] Submission of Source 918, to H. Comm. on the Judiciary, 37 (Sept. 1, 2019) (on file with Comm.).

[663] *See, e.g., How Big Tech Is Battling To Own the $49B Voice Market*, CBINSIGHTS (Feb. 13, 2019), https://www.cbinsights.com/research/facebook-amazon-microsoft-google-apple-voice/.

[664] FUTURE TODAY INST., 2020 TECH TRENDS REPORT (2020), https://futuretodayinstitute.com/2020-tech-trends/.

the U.S. smart speaker market . . . It's not because their hardware businesses are profitable in and of themselves.[665]

As the voice assistant market expands, it may be difficult for users to switch between platforms. Because voice assistant platforms are not always interoperable, users would incur costs to purchase one or more new devices. Moreover, voice assistant technology is designed to learn its user's preferences over time. These preferences range from settings like billing information and default services for responding to music commands, to more advanced learning like past voice commands and shopping history. As a voice assistant improves its "understanding" of its user, it may increase the costs associated with switching to another platform. As one market participant noted in a submission to the Subcommittee, "the user may become more dependent on that particular voice assistant and be far less likely to use a rival voice assistant that has not yet 'caught up' with the user's preferences."[666]

The design of most voice assistants—specifically on screenless devices—amplifies the ability of voice assistant platforms to favor their services as a default or as a response with limited choice.[667] This dynamic makes it easier for popular voice assistants to favor their first-party services.

There is also a significant potential for misuse of data to harm competition or consumers. Similar to other platforms, such as cloud and operating systems, voice assistant platforms collect and store users' interactions with the voice assistant.[668] During the investigation, several companies shared concerns that voice assistant platforms would be able to use this vantage to glean competitive insights from third-party voice applications or smart appliances that are performing well. As a result, platforms could use that data to acquire competitive threats or integrate their features into the company's product.

Privacy and data experts have also commented that the smart home ecosystem is some of the most sensitive data that can be collected.[669] Voice assistant platforms not only record voice interactions, they receive information about the skills used—"whether a light is on or off. Or, if a customer links Alexa to a third-party calendar skill, Alexa may receive information about the events on the customer's calendar."[670] This raises significant concerns regarding whether a person has provided consent to data collection. Voice assistants not only collect information on the primary user, but also people in their environment, including children.

---

[665] Competitors Hearing at 3 (statement of Patrick Spence, CEO, Sonos, Inc.).

[666] Submission of Source 711, to H. Comm. on the Judiciary, Source 711-00000080 at 20 (Oct. 15, 2019) (on file with Comm.).

[667] *Id.* at 17.

[668] Innovation and Entrepreneurship Hearing at 86–87 (response to Questions for the Record of Adam Cohen, Dir. of Econ. Policy, Google LLC).

[669] *See generally* SHOSHANA ZUBOFF, THE AGE OF SURVEILLANCE CAPITALISM (2019).

[670] Innovation and Entrepreneurship Hearing at 40 (response to Questions for the Record of Nate Sutton, Assoc. Gen. Counsel, Amazon.com, Inc.).

Finally, leaders in the voice assistant ecosystem set the rules for third parties. To make a voice assistant enabled device, market participants must comply with voice assistant platform vendor specifications. As Mr. Spence of Sonos noted in his testimony before the Subcommittee:

> To gain access to their platforms and integrate with their services, these companies issue all manner of take-it-or-leave-it demands, from early and technically detailed access to our product roadmaps, to proprietary business data, including sales forecasts, to waivers of essential contractual rights.[671]

The Subcommittee also heard from multiple voice assistant developers that have struggled to gain access to key functionality needed to build their applications, such as the unprocessed user commands.[672] While still developing, the voice assistant market shows early signs of market concentration.

I.   Web Browsers

A web browser is software that retrieves and displays pages from the Internet. People often use browsers to navigate to and spend time on websites and to search the web. Most other activities online, whether it is on a mobile phone or a television screen, are made possible through a browser.[673]

Behind every browser is a "browser engine," also known as a layout engine or rendering engine. A browser engine is the central software component of a web browser, transforming content hosted on web servers into a graphic depiction that people can interact with. Browsers interpret control codes within web pages, which indicate the structure of the data, such as the beginning and end of an item, and the way to present it to the user, such as headings, paragraphs, lists, or embedded images. The browser engine takes this code to "draw the web page" on the user's screen and noting which parts of it are interactive. The non-engine components of the browser typically include the menus, toolbars, and other user-facing features, which are layered over top of the engine.[674]

Browsers abide by standards to ensure that anyone can properly use features within a website on any browser. For example, standards such as CSS and XML help ensure that a website functions the same in every browser.[675] Web browser standards organizations include the World Wide Web

---

[671] Competitors Hearing at 4 (2020) (statement of Patrick Spence, CEO, Sonos, Inc.).

[672] Submission of Source 301, to H. Comm. on the Judiciary, Source 301-00000080 at 23 (Oct. 15, 2019) (on file with Comm.).

[673] Submission from Source 385, to H. Comm. on the Judiciary, 3 (Oct. 11, 2019) (on file with. Comm.).

[674] *Id.* at 4.

[675] *Standards*, W3C, https://www.w3.org/standards/ (last visited on Sept. 26, 2020).

Consortium (W3C), Web Hypertext Application Technology Working Group (WHATWG), and Internet Engineering Task Force (IETF). Through these organizations, stakeholders work in partnership to ensure that browser engines and web pages are interoperable.[676] W3C has become one of the most important organizations for browser standards. W3C standards undergo a rigorous review process prior to implementation.[677]

Browser vendors monetize their access to users, usually through search royalties. For example, whenever someone types a search query into the search bar on Firefox, Google records that action, and the Mozilla corporation receives a royalty.[678] Browsers also bring in ad revenues. For example, Brave sells advertisers the option to run desktop notification ads to users who choose to see ads.[679]

The browser market is highly concentrated. Google's Chrome browser and Apple's Safari control roughly 80% of the browser market.[680] As of August 2020, Chrome is the leader in the U.S. desktop browser market with 58.6% of the market share, followed by Safari (15.8%), Edge (8.76%), Firefox (7.6%), and Internet Explorer (5.36%).[681] On mobile devices, Safari (55.5%) and Chrome (37.4%) have significant leads on their rivals, such as Samsung Internet (5.01%), Firefox (0.77%), and Opera (0.44%).[682] Additionally, the browser market has concentrated around three browser engines, Gecko, WebKit and Blink, used in Firefox, Apple's Safari, and Google's Chrome, respectively.[683]

Google's hold on the browser market extends beyond Chrome. Google releases the code base used to make the Chrome browser as the free, open-source project Chromium.[684] Chromium is used in: Microsoft's Edge browser, Amazon's Silk browser, Opera and other browser that are often referred to as "Chromium-based."[685] Similarly, Apple extends its power by mandating that all browser applications on the iPhone use Apple's browser engine, WebKit.[686]

---

[676] Submission from Source 993, to H. Comm. on the Judiciary (Oct. 11, 2019) (on file with. Comm.).

[677] *Process for 2020*, W3C, https://www.w3.org/wiki/Process2020 (last visited on Sept. 26, 2020).

[678] Innovation and Entrepreneurship Hearing at 42 (response to Questions for the Record of Adam Cohen, Dir. of Econ. Pol'y, Google LLC).

[679] *Expand your business with Brave Ads*, BRAVE, https://brave.com/brave-ads-waitlist/ (last visited on Sept. 26, 2020).

[680] *U.S. Browser Market Share*, STATCOUNTER https://gs.statcounter.com/browser-market-share/all/united-states-of-america (last visited on Sept. 26, 2020).

[681] *U.S. Desktop Market Share*, STATCOUNTER https://gs.statcounter.com/browser-market-share/desktop/united-states-of-america (last visited on Sept. 26, 2020).

[682] *U.S. Mobile Market Share*, STATCOUNTER, https://gs.statcounter.com/browser-market-share/mobile/united-states-of-america (last visited on Sept. 26, 2020).

[683] Submission from Source 993, to H. Comm. on the Judiciary, 5 (Oct. 11, 2019) (on file with. Comm.).

[684] THE CHROMIUM PROJECTS, https://www.chromium.org/.

[685] Submission from Source 993, to H. Comm. on the Judiciary, 3 (Oct. 11, 2019) (on file with. Comm.).

[686] Innovation and Entrepreneurship Hearing at 1–2 (response to Questions for the Record of Kyle Andeer, Vice Pres., Corp. Law, Apple, Inc.).

Browser competition has also led to the creation of a browser extension submarket. A browser extension adds additional features to a web browser including user interface modifications, and ad blocking. They can also provide for niche browser customization and experimentation of new functionality before it is implemented into the main browser functionality.[687] Popular add-ons include ad blockers, LastPass, and Grammarly.[688]

Competition in this market is important to promoting innovation online. In a submission to the Subcommittee, a market participant explained:

> Competing browser engines push each other for innovations in raw performance in several respects, including faster rendering, greater reliability, and a number of other technical improvements; this competition is qualitatively different from, and greater than, competition over just the browser product.[689]

Browser diversity is also important for ensuring an open internet and reduces the risk that web developers will build sites optimized for the leading engine as opposed to web standards.[690] Moreover, as developers work on advancing browser engine technology, they create technologies that can improve the overall internet ecosystem. For example, Rust is a programming language that Mozilla engineers developed while writing the Servo layout technology for browser engines.[691] Developers use Rust for other applications today, including gaming, operating systems, and other new software applications.[692] There is a general concern that without vibrant competition this form of innovation will suffer, discouraging the development of new browser engine technology.[693]

Browsers protect their dominance through default settings, which create a barrier to entry.[694] Defaults exist in both desktop and mobile markets. Although users can set different browsers more easily for desktop computers than on mobile devices, "settings can impact the stickiness over time," such as when a software update overrides a user's preference, requiring them to take "complex steps to restore their browser choice."[695] In some cases, consumers are unable to delete the preloaded browser.

---

[687] Interview with Source 27 (June 29, 2020).

[688] Tyler Lacoma, *The best Google Chrome extensions*, DIGITALTRENDS (Apr. 4, 2020), https://www.digitaltrends.com/computing/best-google-chrome-extensions/.

[689] Submission from Source 993, to H. Comm. on the Judiciary, 5 (Oct. 11, 2019) (on file with. Comm.).

[690] *Id.*

[691] *Rust language*, MOZILLA RESEARCH, https://research.mozilla.org/rust/ (last visited on Sept. 26, 2020).

[692] *Id.*

[693] Interview with Source 481 (July 2, 2020)

[694] Submission from Source 993, to H. Comm. on the Judiciary, 10-11 (Oct. 11, 2019) (on file with. Comm.); Submission from Source 269, to H. Comm. on the Judiciary, 2-3 (July 23, 2019) (on file with. Comm.).

[695] Submission from Source 993, to H. Comm. on the Judiciary, 10 (Oct. 11, 2019) (on file with. Comm.).

For example, on Apple iOS devices and Facebook's Oculus, users are unable to delete the preloaded browser. Some popular mobile applications can preset webpage links to a predetermined browser, such as the Apple Mail App (Safari) and the Search widget on an Android device (Chrome).[696]

J. Digital Advertising

There are two principal form of digital advertising: search advertising and display advertising. Search advertising refers to digital ads on desktop or mobile search engines, such as the Google.com homepage, displayed via "search ad tech" alongside search engine results. Search advertising is often bought and sold via real-time bidding (RTB) auctions among advertisers, where advertisers set the prices they are willing to pay for a specific keyword in a query.[697] Display advertising refers to the delivery of digital ad content to ad space on websites and mobile apps, which is referred to as "inventory." Like search advertising, buying and selling display ads often involves real-time bidding.[698]

Within display advertising there are two separate "ad tech" markets that Subcommittee staff reviewed during the investigation: first-party and third-party. "First-party" platforms refer to companies such as Facebook, Twitter, and Snap which sell ad space on their own platforms directly to advertisers. Google also uses first-party ad tech to sell display ads on its own properties, most notably YouTube. Third-party display ad tech platforms are run by intermediary vendors and facilitate the transaction between third-party advertisers, such as the local dry cleaner or a Fortune 500 company, and third-party publishers, such as *The Washington Post* or a blog.[699] Third-party ad tech providers include Google, Flashtalking, Sizmek (owned by Amazon), and the Trade Desk among others.[700]

Software in display ads is "programmatic," meaning that specialized software automates the buying and selling of digital ads. Market participants explain that this automated approach provides greater liquidity, better return-on-investment metrics, more precise ad targeting, and lower transaction costs. One major drawback, however, is that this process lacks transparency.[701] Google, specifically, "does not disclose to the publishers on the other ends of these trades what their space ultimately sold for and how much Google keeps as its share."[702] As another market participant told Subcommittee staff

---

[696] *Id.* at 5; Submission from Source 269, to H. Comm. on the Judiciary, 2 (July 23, 2019) (on file with. Comm.).

[697] Submission from Source 465, to H. Comm. on the Judiciary, 6 (June 3, 2019) (on file with Comm.).

[698] *Id.*

[699] *Id.* at 5.

[700] Competition & Mkts. Auth. Report at 266.

[701] Dina Srinivasan, *Why Google Dominates Advertising Markets*, 24 STAN. TECH. L. REV. (forthcoming 2020) (manuscript at 7–8), https://papers.ssrn.com/sol3/papers.cfm?abstract_id=3500919

[702] *Id.* at 8.

, Google could make the process "more transparent," but given Google's financial stake in maintaining secrecy, "there is no incentive to."[703]

The Ad-Tech Suite[704]

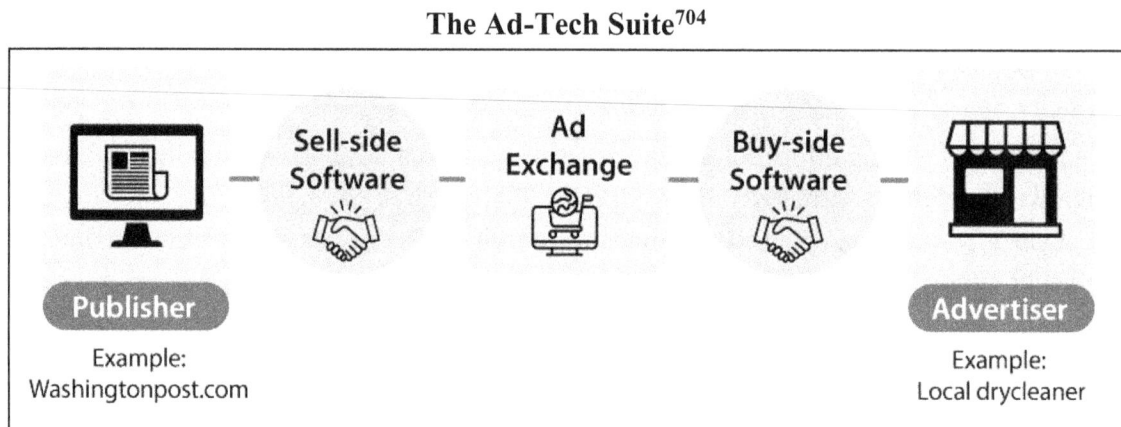

Ad exchanges refer to the "ad trafficking system that connects advertisers looking to buy inventory with publishers selling inventory."[705] Sales on ad exchanges occur primarily through (1) open real-time bidding auctions, (2) closed real-time bidding auctions, or (3) programmatic direct deals.[706]

Sell-side software includes publisher ad servers.[707] The primary function of a publisher ad server is to fill ad space on a publisher's website that is personalized to the interests of a specific website viewer.[708] Sell-side software also includes ad networks which aggregate ad inventory from many different publishers and divide that inventory based on user characteristics—such as age or location. Ad networks sell the pool of inventory through ad exchanges or demand-side platforms (DSPs).[709]

Buy-side software includes advertiser ad servers, software that stores, maintains, and delivers digital ads to the available inventory. Ad servers facilitate the programmatic process that makes instantaneous decisions about which ads to display on which websites to which users and helps executes to display the ad on that site. Ad servers collect and report data, such as ad impressions and

---

[703] Interview with Source 004 (Apr. 23, 2020).

[704] Prepared by Subcomm. based on Dina Srinivasan, *Why Google Dominates Advertising Markets*, 23 STAN. TECH. L. REV. 15 (forthcoming 2020), https://papers.ssrn.com/sol3/papers.cfm?abstract_id=3500919.

[705] Submission from Source 465, to H. Comm. on the Judiciary, 9 (June 3, 2019) (on file with Comm.).

[706] *Id.*

[707] Competition & Mkts. Auth. Report at 263.

[708] Submission from Source 465, to H. Comm. on the Judiciary, 8 (June 3, 2019) (on file with Comm.).

[709] *Id.* at 9.

clicks, for advertisers to monitor ad performance and track conversion metrics.[710] Buy-side software also includes demand-side platforms, software that allows advertisers to buy advertising inventory from a range of publishers. Demand-side platforms use data to create targeted ad audiences and engage in purchasing and bidding.[711]

The ad tech suite also includes analytics tools that allow advertisers and publishers to measure ad campaign efficiency, including consumers' interactions with an ad. Similarly, data management platforms (DMPs) aggregate and store consumer data from various sources and process the data for analysis. Advertisers and publishers use data management platforms to track, partition, and target consumer audiences across websites.[712]

Over the last decade, the digital advertising market has experienced double-digit year-over-year growth. The market, however, has become increasingly concentrated since the advent of programmatic trading. In 2017, *Business Insider* reported that Google and Facebook accounted for 99% of year-over-year growth in U.S. digital advertising revenue.[713] Today, advertisers and publishers alike have few options when deciding how to buy and sell online ad space.[714]

Market participants suggest this concentration likely exists in part due to high barriers to entry. Google and Facebook both have a significant lead in the market due to their significant collection of behavioral data online, which can be used in targeted advertising. Additionally, Google and Facebook do not provide access to this unique data in open data exchanges. Advertisers' only access to this information is indirect—through engagement with Google and Facebook's ad tech.[715]

Amazon's advertising business is starting to obtain a portion of the U.S. year-over-year digital advertising revenue growth.[716] Amazon has been able to enter the market because it has its own trove of user data—namely, competitively significant first-party data related to retail searches and purchases. Moreover, Amazon's 50% penetration across U.S. households and its reach with high-income customers are likely to help drive its ad revenue growth.[717] While Amazon can leverage its ecosystem to overcome some of the barriers to entry in ad tech, the recent U.K. Competition and Markets

---

[710] Competition & Mkts. Auth. Report at 263.

[711] Submission from Source 888, to H. Comm. on the Judiciary, 8 (June 3, 2019) (on file with Comm.).

[712] *Id.* at 10.

[713] Alex Heath, *Facebook and Google Completely Dominate the Digital Ad Industry*, BUSINESS INSIDER. (Apr 26, 2017), https://www.businessinsider.com/facebook-and-google-dominate-ad-industry-with-a-combined-99-of-growth-2017-4.

[714] Dina Srinivasan, *Why Google Dominates Advertising Markets*, 23 STAN. TECH. L. REV. 4-5 (forthcoming 2020), https://papers.ssrn.com/sol3/papers.cfm?abstract_id=3500919.

[715] *Id.* at 92.

[716] Kiri Masters, *What's Driving Amazon's $10 Billion Advertising Business*, FORBES (July 26, 2019), https://www.forbes.com/sites/kirimasters/2019/07/26/whats-driving-amazons-10bn-advertising-business/#4cc9c84aa043.

[717] *Id.*

Authority report found that, as of today, Amazon's ad tech likely only has advantages in the retail sector.[718]

V. DOMINANT ONLINE PLATFORMS

A. Facebook

1. Overview

Founded in 2004 by Mark Zuckerberg, Eduardo Saverin, Chris Hughes, and Dustin Moskowitz,[719] Facebook is the largest social networking platform in the world. Its business operates around five primary product offerings, including: (1) Facebook, a social network platform; (2) Instagram, a social network app for photos and videos; (3) Messenger, a cross-platform messaging app for Facebook users; (4) WhatsApp, a cross-platform messaging app; and (5) Oculus, a virtual reality gaming system.

Facebook reported in July 2020 that its platform includes 1.79 billion daily active users (DAUs),[720] 2.7 billion monthly active users (MAUs),[721] and an average revenue per user (ARPU) of $7.05.[722] Last year, Facebook's businesses collected about $70 billion in revenue—a 27% increase from the prior year—earning about $24 billion in income from its operations.[723] Facebook reported that its family of products—including Facebook, Instagram, Messenger, and WhatsApp—includes 2.47 billion daily active people (DAP),[724] 3.14 billion monthly active people (MAP), and a family average revenue per person (ARPP) of $6.10.[725]

In addition to the Subcommittee's investigation of Facebook's monopoly power, state and federal antitrust authorities are investigating Facebook for potential violations of the U.S. antitrust laws. In July 2019, Facebook disclosed that the Federal Trade Commission (FTC) had opened an

---

[718] Competition & Mkts. Auth. Report at 282.

[719] STEVEN LEVY, FACEBOOK: THE INSIDE STORY 65–69 (2020).

[720] Facebook Inc., Quarterly Report (Form 10-Q) 29 (July 31, 2020), https://investor.fb.com/financials/sec-filings-details/default.aspx?FilingId=14302237.

[721] *Id.* at 30.

[722] *Id.* at 32.

[723] *Id.* at 35. *See generally* Howard A. Shelanski & J. Gregory Sidak, *Antitrust Divestiture in Network Industries*, 68 U. CHI. L. REV. 1, 6 (2001) ("High profit margins might appear to be the benign and necessary recovery of legitimate investment returns in a Schumpeterian framework, but they might represent exploitation of customer lock-in and monopoly power when viewed through the lens of network economics.").

[724] Facebook Inc., Quarterly Report (Form 10-Q) 25 (July 31, 2020), https://investor.fb.com/financials/sec-filings-details/default.aspx?FilingId=14302237.

[725] *Id.* at 35.

antitrust investigation of Facebook in June 2019.[726] Facebook also disclosed that in July 2019 the Department of Justice announced that it would begin an antitrust review of market-leading online platforms.[727] In September 2019, New York Attorney General Letitia James announced that she joined with eight other attorneys general to lead a multistate investigation of Facebook, Inc.[728] In October 2019, Attorney General James reported that the investigation into Facebook grew to include 47 attorneys general.[729]

2. Social Networking

a. Market Power

Facebook has monopoly power in the market for social networking.[730] According to internal documents produced by Facebook to the Committee, it has high reach, time-spent, and significantly more users than its rivals in this market. Despite significant changes in the market—such as the advent of mobile devices, applications, and operating systems—Facebook has held an unassailable position in the social network market for nearly a decade, demonstrating its monopoly power.[731]

Facebook's monopoly power is firmly entrenched and unlikely to be eroded by competitive pressure from new entrants or existing firms. Documents produced during the investigation by Facebook, including communications among its senior executives on market strategy, as well as a memorandum by a senior data scientist and economist at Facebook,[732] support the conclusion that Facebook's monopoly is insulated from competitive threats. The social network market has high entry barriers—including strong network effects, high switching costs, and Facebook's significant data

---

[726] Facebook Inc., Quarterly Report (Form 10-Q) 42 (July 24, 2019), https://investor.fb.com/financials/sec-filings-details/default.aspx?FilingId=13550646.

[727] *Id.* at 53.

[728] Press Release, N.Y. Attorney General, AG James Investigating Facebook For Possible Antitrust Violations (Sept. 6, 2009), https://ag.ny.gov/press-release/2019/ag-james-investigating-facebook-possible-antitrust-violations.

[729] Press Release, N.Y. Attorney General, Attorney General James Gives Update On Facebook Antitrust Investigation (Oct. 22, 2019), https://ag.ny.gov/press-release/2019/attorney-general-james-gives-update-facebook-antitrust-investigation.

[730] Facebook has argued to other antitrust enforcement bodies that limiting the product market to social networks at the exclusion of other markets, such as user attention, "would be artificial and would not reflect the competitive realities," and that "competitive pressures to which Facebook reacts are global in nature." *See, e.g.,* Production of Facebook, to H. Comm. on the Judiciary, FB-HJC-ACAL-00012074 (2016) (White Paper on Relevant Markets and Lack of Dominance for Federal Cartel Office) (on file with Comm.).

[731] Fiona M. Scott Morton & David C. Dinielli, *Roadmap for an Antitrust Case Against Facebook*, OMIDYAR NETWORK (June 2020), https://www.omidyar.com/wp-content/uploads/2020/06/Roadmap-for-an-Antitrust-Case-Against-Facebook.pdf.

[732] Production of Facebook, to H. Comm. on the Judiciary, FB-HJC-ACAL-00111406 (Oct. 2018) (on file with Comm.) [hereinafter Cunningham Memo] ("Facebook has high reach and time-spent in most countries. User growth is tracking internet growth: global reach is roughly stable.").

advantage—that discourage direct competition by other firms to offer new products and services.[733] Facebook has also maintained and expanded its dominance through a series of acquisitions of companies it viewed as competitive threats, and selectively excluded competitors from using its platform to insulate itself from competitive pressure. Together, these factors have tipped the social networking market toward a monopoly.[734]

Several antitrust enforcement agencies have examined Facebook's monopoly in recent years and reached similar conclusions. In July 2020, the United Kingdom's Competition and Markets Authority (CMA) found that Facebook is dominant in the markets for social networks and digital display ads, and that its market power "derives in large part from strong network effects stemming from its large network of connected users and the limited interoperability it allows to other social media platforms."[735] In July 2019, Germany's Federal Cartel Office (Bundeskartellamt) found that "Facebook is the dominant company in the market for social networks," and that in Germany's social network market, "Facebook achieves a user-based market share of more than 90%."[736] And in June 2019, the Australian Competition & Consumer Commission (ACCC) found that "Facebook has substantial market power in a number of markets and that this market power is unlikely to erode in the short to medium terms."[737]

Facebook's responses to the Committee's requests for information claimed that it competes in a "rapidly evolving and dynamic marketplace in which competition is vigorous," citing Twitter, Snapchat, Pinterest, and TikTok as examples of competition Facebook faces for "every product and

---

[733] Instead of competing directly with Facebook, such as Google attempted but failed to do with Google+, other social platforms provide niche products with social graphs that are orthogonal to Facebook's graph. *See id.* at 4; FB-HJC-ACAL-00111394 ("Linkedin, and Nextdoor coexist in the US with similar userbases but orthogonal graphs: Facebook connects friends and family, LinkedIn connects coworkers, Nextdoor connects neighbors.").

[734] *See* Bundeskartellamt, B6-22/16, Case Summary, *Facebook, Exploitative business terms pursuant to Section 19(1) GWB for inadequate* data processing, 8 (Feb. 15, 2019) ("The facts that competitors can be seen to exit the market and that there is a downward trend in the user-based market shares of the remaining competitors strongly indicate a market tipping process which will result in Facebook.com becoming a monopolist."), https://www.bundeskartellamt.de/SharedDocs/Entscheidung/EN/Fallberichte/Missbrauchsaufsicht/2019/B6-22-16.pdf?__blob=publicationFile&v=4.

[735] Competition & Mkts. Auth. Report at 26.

[736] In addition to Facebook's high market share, the Bundeskartellamt also found that Facebook has market power based on other measures, including its "access to competitively relevant data, economies of scale based on network effects, the behaviour of users who can use several different services or only one service and the power of innovation-driven competitive pressure were seen as relevant factors of market power." Press Release, Bundeskartellamt, Bundeskartellamt prohibits Facebook from combining user data from different sources 4 (Feb. 7, 2019), https://www.bundeskartellamt.de/SharedDocs/Publikation/EN/Pressemitteilungen/2019/07_02_2019_Facebook_FAQs.pdf?__blob=publicationFile&v=6. The Bundeskartellamt also noted that in terms of assessing market share by time spent on the network, "the Facebook group would have a combined market share far beyond the market dominance threshold pursuant to Section 18(4) GWB, even if YouTube, Snapchat, Twitter, WhatsApp, and Instagram were included in the relevant market." *Id.* at 6.

[737] Austl. Competition & Consumer Comm'n Report at 9; 78 (adopting a broader view on Facebook's product market to include Twitter and Snapchat).

service" that it offers.[738] According to Facebook, its users "have many choices and can leave Facebook if they're not happy,"[739] allowing people to quickly abandon it. The ability of users to "explore the myriad other options available . . . creates strong competition for every product and service Facebook offers, as well as pressure to develop new products to attract and retain users."[740]

In response to other antitrust inquiries, Facebook said that it competes for users' attention broadly.[741] In a 2016 white paper prepared in response to an investigation by Germany's Federal Cartel Office, Facebook stated that it "faces intense competition for user attention and engagement at every level," listing companies as diverse as Candy Crush and Clash of the Clans—popular mobile gaming apps—along with YouTube, Twitter, Pinterest, Snapchat and others as competitors for users' attention.[742] Facebook similarly submitted to the ACCC that if the company does not compete vigorously, users will go to other "platforms, websites, apps, and other services—not just social media services—that compete for their attention."[743] In an interview conducted by Subcommittee staff, a former employee explained that as a product manager at Facebook "your only job is to get an extra minute. It's immoral. They don't ask where it's coming from. They can monetize a minute of activity at a certain rate. So the only metric is getting another minute."[744]

Facebook describes a diverse list of other firms as competitive substitutes for Facebook, including Microsoft's Bing, a search engine; Yelp, a publisher of crowd-sourced business reviews; and BuzzFeed, a digital news publisher.[745] According to Facebook, these firms exert competitive pressure on Facebook in the market for users' attention.[746] Most recently, in response to an inquiry by the United Kingdom's Competition and Markets Authority, Facebook calculated its market share as "time captured by Facebook as a percentage of total user time spent on the internet, including social media, dating, news and search platforms."[747] Based on these measures, Facebook concluded that it lacks monopoly power.

---

[738] Production of Facebook, to H. Comm. on the Judiciary, FB-HJC-ACAL-APP0004 (Oct. 14, 2019); Innovation and Entrepreneurship Hearing at 1 (statement of Matt Perault, Dir. of Public Pol'y, Facebook), https://docs.house.gov/meetings/JU/JU05/20190716/109793/HHRG-116-JU05-Wstate-PeraultM-20190716.pdf.

[739] Innovation and Entrepreneurship Hearing at 1 (response to Questions for the Record of Matt Perault, Dir. of Public Pol'y, Facebook).

[740] *Id.*

[741] *See, e.g.*, Production of Facebook, to H. Comm. on the Judiciary, FB-HJC-ACAL-00012074 (2016) (on file with Comm.).

[742] *Id.*

[743] FACEBOOK, FACEBOOK'S RESPONSE TO THE DIGITAL PLATFORMS INQUIRY FOR AUSTRALIAN COMPETITION AND CONSUMER COMMISSION 25 (Sept. 12, 2019), https://fbnewsroomus.files.wordpress.com/2019/09/facebook-submission-to-treasury-on-digital-platforms-inquiry.pdf.

[744] Interview with Former Instagram Employee (Oct. 2, 2020).

[745] *Id.*

[746] *Id.*

[747] Competition & Mkts. Auth. Report at 121 n.152.

Facebook's position that it lacks monopoly power and competes in a dynamic market is not supported by the documents it produced to the Committee during the investigation. Instead, Facebook's internal business metrics show that Facebook wields monopoly power. In response to a supplemental information request by Subcommittee staff,[748] Facebook produced industry updates prepared in the ordinary course of business by Facebook's Market Strategy team.[749] It has described these reports as both "internal competitive metrics" and as a "competitive survey regularly prepared for Facebook's management team [that] tracks a variable set of competitors not by specific products or features, but by the degree of user attention and engagement that they command in terms of monthly active users ('MAU') and daily active users ('DAU')."[750]

Facebook's industry updates were shared internally with senior executives, including Mark Zuckerberg, Facebook's CEO.[751] Facebook used data collected through Onavo, a virtual private network (VPN) app, to provide detailed competitive insights into the usage and engagement of other firms.[752] Facebook also relied on this data in response to inquiries by the European Commission and the Bundeskartellamt,[753] as well as to prepare detailed internal reports on market strategy.[754]

i. Usage and Reach

Facebook has monopoly power in the social networking market. Based on its internal documents, Facebook and its family of products—Facebook, Instagram, Messenger, and WhatsApp—control a significant share of users and high reach in the social networking market.[755] Facebook's family of products includes three of the seven most popular mobile apps in the United States by monthly active persons, reach, and percentage of daily and monthly active persons.[756]

---

[748] Subcommittee staff made a supplemental request after identifying Facebook's industry updates during the review of documents produced in response to the Committee's September 2019 request for information.

[749] Production of Facebook, to H. Comm. on the Judiciary, FB-HJC-ACAL-000025 (Mar. 5, 2020) (on file with Comm.).

[750] Id. at *FB*-HJC-ACAL-00012074, FB-HJC-ACAL-00012090 (2016) (on file with Comm.).

[751] Id. at FB-HJC-ACAL-00054944 (Apr. 27, 2012) (on file with Comm.).

[752] Although it does not include data from users of Apple's iMessage, which is relevant for purposes of usage on WhatsApp and Messenger, Facebook's documents note that iMessage's growth is limited by the adoption of iPhones, whereas Facebook's products can be used across different devices. *See generally* Cunningham Memo at 15.

[753] Production of Facebook, to H. Comm. on the Judiciary, FB-HJC-ACAL-00012090 (2016) (on file with Comm.).

[754] Cunningham Memo at 9 (citing data from MINT, another name used for Onavo within Facebook).

[755] Id. at 2, 16 ("Facebook has high reach and time-spent in most countries. User growth is tracking internet growth: global reach is roughly stable.").

[756] Production of Facebook, to Comm. on the Judiciary, 38 (Jan. 2020) (Monthly Update for December 2019) (based on Facebook's internal calibrations of App Annie data) (on file with Comm.). According to Facebook, monthly active persons (MAP) is "based on the activity of users who visited at least one of Facebook, Instagram, Messenger, and WhatsApp (collectively, our 'Family' of products) during the applicable period of measurement." *See* Facebook Inc., Quarterly Report (Form 10-Q) 29 (Apr. 30, 2020), http://d18rn0p25nwr6d.cloudfront.net/CIK-0001326801/bfe31518-2e18-48fb-8d98-5e8b07d94b2a.pdf-.

136

As a standalone product, the Facebook app had *the third highest reach* of all mobile apps,[757] with 200.3 million users in the United States, reaching 74% of smartphone users as of December 2019.[758] Facebook Messenger had the *fourth highest reach*, with 183.6 million monthly active persons, reaching 54.1% of U.S. smartphone users.[759] Finally, Instagram had the *sixth highest reach,* with 119.2 million users, reaching 35.3% of smartphone users.[760] In contrast, Snapchat, the mobile app with the seventh highest reach, had 106.5 million users in the United States, reaching 31.4% of smartphone users.[761]

Facebook's maintenance of these high market shares over a long time period demonstrates its monopoly power.[762] From September 2017 to September 2018, Facebook reached more than 75% of users internationally with at or near 100% market penetration in nine of the twenty most populous countries in the world.[763] In the United States, Facebook alone reached more than 75% of internet users during this period, while Messenger and Instagram both achieved significant reach as well.[764] According to a white paper prepared by a senior data scientist and economist at Facebook, the Facebook app has high reach in most countries, and its growth is in line with that of the Internet, whereas Instagram and WhatsApp are still growing "very rapidly."[765] For Instagram, "there appear to be *no* countries in which growth has hit a ceiling."[766]

Facebook's family of products are more immersive of users' attention.[767] According to Facebook's internal market data, its users spend significantly more time on its family of products than

---

[757] Interview with Former Instagram Employee (Oct. 2, 2020) ("Reach is closer to market penetration [than usage and engagement]. It applies to the number of internet users we think are in that country, how many use a Facebook Family app and have taken one meaningful action. What people forget is that Facebook believes its total addressable market being anyone that has access to the internet.").

[758] Production of Facebook, to Comm. on the Judiciary, 38 (Jan. 2020) (Monthly Update for December 2019) (on file with Comm.); Production of Facebook, to Comm. on the Judiciary, 32 (Oct. 2019) (Monthly Update for September 2019) (based on Facebook's internal calibrations of App Annie data) (on file with Comm.).

[759] *Id.*

[760] *Id.*

[761] *Id.*

[762] *See generally* Fiona M. Scott Morton & David C. Dinielli, *Roadmap for an Antitrust Case Against Facebook*, OMIDYAR NETWORK 11 (June 2020).

[763] Cunningham Memo at 2.

[764] *Id.*

[765] *Id.* at 12.

[766] *Id.* at 16. (emphasis added).

[767] *Id.* ("Facebook has high reach and time-spent in most countries. User growth is tracking internet growth: global reach is roughly stable.").

on competing services. For example, social media users spent more time on Facebook (48.6 minutes) than on Snapchat (21 minutes) or Twitter (21.6 minutes) in 2018.[768]

Since at least 2012, Facebook's documents show that Facebook believed it controlled a high share of the social networking market.[769] In a presentation prepared for Sheryl Sandberg, Facebook's Chief Operating Officer, to deliver at a large telecommunications firm, Facebook said that it controlled "95% of all social media" in the United States in terms of monthly minutes of use—as compared to Twitter, Tumblr, Myspace, and all other social media—and noted that the "industry consolidates as it matures."[770]

Facebook Investor Presentation[771]

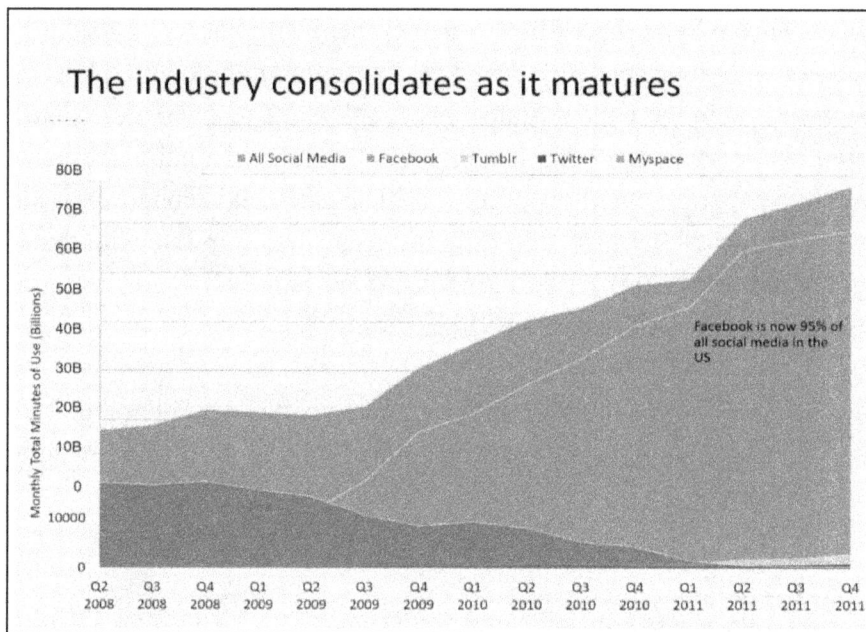

A 2012 investor presentation prepared for Facebook described it as having an "enduring competitive advantage" similar to other historically dominant firms.[772] According to this document, which was reviewed and edited by Facebook's Chief Financial Officer to present to investors,[773] Facebook had nearly 100% market penetration among 25-34 year-olds in the United States.[774] It also

---

[768] Production of Facebook, to H. Comm. on the Judiciary, FB-HJC-ACAL-00086798 (Aug. 22, 2020) (Monthly Update for August 2018) (on file with Comm.).

[769] Id. at FB-HJC-ACAL-00057113; FB-HJC-ACAL-00049006 (Jan. 28, 2012) (on file with Comm.).

[770] Id. at FB-HJC-ACAL-00057113, https://judiciary.house.gov/uploadedfiles/00057113_picture.pdf.

[771] Prepared by Subcommmittee based on id.

[772] Id. at FB-HJC-ACAL-00049006 (Apr. 30, 2012) (on file with Comm.).

[773] Id. at FB-HJC-ACAL-00064320 (Apr. 18, 2012).

[774] Id. at FB-HJC-ACAL-00049006 (Apr. 30, 2012).

had more than 85% penetration in certain countries.[775] As noted in the presentation, "In every country we've tipped, we have maintained that penetration."[776] This point was underscored by a suggestion in the presentation that within a decade, it would be doubtful that entrepreneurs could compete with Facebook.[777]

At the Subcommittee's sixth hearing, Representative Joe Neguse (D-CO) asked Mr. Zuckerberg about Facebook's monopoly power.[778] As Mr. Neguse noted, based on this evidence, "most folks would concede Facebook was a monopoly as early as 2012."[779] Since then, he added that Facebook's strategy has been to "protect what I describe as a monopoly" by acquiring, copying, or eliminating its competitors.[780] Mr. Zuckerberg responded by characterizing the social networking market as "a very large space."[781] However, Facebook did not corroborate this claim through the evidence it produced during the investigation.

Lastly, after reviewing relevant market data and documents provided during the investigation, the Subcommittee found that there are distinct, relevant markets for social networking and social media. Facebook proposes that online services with social functions, such as YouTube, are social networks that compete in the same product market as Facebook and its other products for user attention.[782] For example, in a white paper submission, Facebook compares its News Feed, which includes a stream of posts and videos uploaded by users, as similar to the content feed that users encounter on YouTube.[783] However, longstanding antitrust doctrine describes relevant product markets as those that are "reasonably interchangeable by consumers for the same purposes."[784] Although YouTube is a dominant social app, it is primarily used to consume video content online. It does not provide the core functionality of Facebook or its family of products, such as Pages, Marketplace, or limited sharing within a person's network.

---

[775] *Id.*

[776] *Id.*

[777] *Id.* ("Imagine 10 years from now . . . [a] [l]ocal TV show asking an entrepreneur how he can hope to compete with Facebook.").

[778] CEO Hearing Transcript at 85 (question of Rep. Joe Neguse (D-CO), Vice Chairman, Subcomm. on Antitrust, Commercial and Admin. Law).

[779] *Id.* at 86.

[780] *Id.*

[781] *Id.* (statement of Mark Zuckerberg, CEO, Facebook).

[782] FACEBOOK, SUBMISSION TO AUSTL. COMPETITION AND CONSUMER COMM'N 13 (Sept. 12, 2019), https://assets.publishing.service.gov.uk/media/5e8c827ae90e070774c61fdb/Facebook_response_to_interim_report_with_co ver_letter.pdf.

[783] Production of Facebook, to H. Comm. on the Judiciary, FB-HJC-ACAL-00012074 (2016) (on file with Comm.).

[784] *See* United States v. Microsoft Corp., 253 F.3d 34, 51–52 (D.C. Cir. 2001); *see also* Competition & Mkts. Auth. Report at 117–18 ("[T]he closeness of competition between different platforms depends on the degree to which consumers consider them substitutes, rather than the extent to which they share common functionalities.").

The United Kingdom's Competition and Markets Authority reached a similar conclusion, finding that YouTube is primarily a market for consuming video content rather than a market for communication.[785] As it noted, "consumers seem to access YouTube for particularly distinctive reasons . . . YouTube does not currently appear to compete closely with Facebook's platforms, despite its comparable reach and levels of consumer engagement."[786] Internal documents produced to the United Kingdom bolstered this finding, indicating "that the most common reasons consumers in the UK access YouTube are for entertainment and to view 'how-to' videos on the platform."[787]

ii. Barriers to Entry

Facebook's persistently high market share is not contestable due to high barriers to entry that discourage competition. These barriers to entry include its strong network effects, high switching costs for consumers, and data advantages.

1) Network Effects

Facebook's significant reach among users, and high levels of engagement, create very strong network effects.[788]

As a result, Facebook has tipped the market in its favor,[789] primarily facing competitive pressure from within its *own* family of products—such as through Instagram competing with Facebook or WhatsApp competing with Messenger—rather than actual competition from other firms in the market.[790] This finding is supported by Facebook's documents and internal analysis. These include a

---

[785] Competition & Mkts. Auth. Report at 126 ("[T]here are particularly important differences between YouTube, which most consumers use for video streaming, and platforms such as those of Facebook, which focus more on consumer needs related to social networking.").

[786] *Id.* at 127.

[787] *Id.*

[788] *See* United States v. Microsoft Corp., 84 F. Supp. 2d 9, 20 (D.D.C. 1999) ("A positive network effect is a phenomenon by which the attractiveness of a product increases with the number of people using it."). Conversely, a negative or reverse network effect exists when the attractiveness of a product decreases as less people use it, which can tip the market in favor of another firm if there are low entry barriers. Dig. Competition Expert Panel Report at 35.

[789] *See generally* Fiona M. Scott Morton & David C. Dinielli, *Roadmap for an Antitrust Case Against Facebook*, OMIDYAR NETWORK 18 (June 2020), https://www.omidyar.com/wp-content/uploads/2020/06/Roadmap-for-an-Antitrust-Case-Against-Facebook.pdf.

[790] *See, e.g.*, Cunningham Memo at 7 ("Messenger and WhatsApp clearly compete for time-spent."). While Facebook's overall penetration and network effects are high in the United States and across many other large countries, Facebook appears to have intermediate reach in some countries due to differing levels of adoption among users of certain ages. *Id.* at 12 ("In Japan and South Korea Facebook has significantly higher penetration among youth than among elderly. The role of an intergenerational social network is partly filled by other apps (LINE and Kakao).").

memorandum on Facebook's family of products prepared in October 2018 by Thomas Cunningham, a senior data scientist and economist,[791] as well as communications among senior executives.[792]

Mr. Cunningham's 2018 memorandum on "Possible End States for the Family of Apps" is an analysis of user trends among Facebook's products and other competitors.[793] It is based on the company's Onavo data from September 2017 to September 2018.[794] It was prepared for review by Facebook's senior executives, including Mr. Zuckerberg and Mr. Olivan, Facebook's Director of Growth.[795] The Subcommittee's staff interviewed a former senior employee at the company who attended meetings preparing the document for presentation to Mr. Zuckerberg and Mr. Olivan. The former employee noted that "this specific working group—and Tom Cunningham's work in particular—was guiding Mark's views" on the company's growth strategy.[796] The former employee explained the purpose of the Cunningham Memo:

> The question was how do we position Facebook and Instagram to not compete with each other. The concern was that Instagram would hit a tipping point . . . There was brutal in-fighting between Instagram and Facebook at the time. It was very tense. It was back when Kevin Systrom was still at the company. He wanted Instagram to grow naturally and as widely as possible. But Mark was clearly saying "do not compete with us." . . . It was collusion, but within an internal monopoly. If you own two social media utilities, they should not be allowed to shore each other up. It's unclear to me why this should not be illegal. You can collude by acquiring competitors and forbidding competition.[797]

The Cunningham Memo characterized the network effects of Facebook, WhatsApp, and Messenger are "very strong."[798] The memorandum notes that social apps have tipping points such that "either everyone uses them, or no-one uses them."[799] Importantly, it distinguishes between apps with a

---

[791] Subcommittee staff requested the 2018 memorandum prepared by Tom Cunningham on July 1, 2020 in response to earlier reporting about the memorandum. *See* Alex Heath, *Facebook Secret Research Warned of 'Tipping Point' Threat to Core App*, THE INFORMATION (July 23, 2020), https://www.theinformation.com/articles/facebook-secret-research-warned-of-tipping-point-threat-to-core-app. Subcommittee staff appreciates that Facebook cooperated with this supplemental request.

[792] Production of Facebook, to H. Comm. on the Judiciary, FB-HJC-ACAL-00063222 (Feb. 27, 2012), https://judiciary.house.gov/uploadedfiles/0006322000063223.pdf.

[793] Cunningham Memo at 1, 3.

[794] During this period, Facebook referred to data derived from Onavo as MINT data.

[795] Interview with Former Instagram Employee (Oct. 2, 2020).

[796] *Id.*

[797] *Id.*

[798] Cunningham Memo at 11.

[799] *Id.* at 9.

social graph that are used for broadcast sharing and messaging—Facebook, Instagram, Messenger, WhatsApp, and Snapchat—and social apps for music or video consumption, such as YouTube or Spotify.[800] In contrast, non-social apps "can exist along a continuum of adoption."[801]

Network effects and tipping points are particularly strong in messaging apps. Because WhatsApp and other regional messaging apps have bimodal distribution of reach in countries—an all-or-nothing reach at above 90% or below 10%—messaging tends toward consolidation and market tipping.[802] Most countries have a single messaging app or protocol because they cannot support multiple messaging apps."[803] As a result of this dynamic, there are "tradeoffs in time-spent between Messenger and WhatsApp,"[804] demonstrating "very strong tipping points."[805]

Facebook already has high reach in many countries,[806] including the United States, so a primary concern addressed in Mr. Cunningham's "Possible End States" memorandum is whether cross-app sharing among Facebook's family of products poses a competitive threat to its flagship product, the Facebook app.[807] While the Cunningham Memo concluded that it is unclear whether Instagram and Facebook can coexist, it is much less concerned with Facebook's user loss due to cannibalization by Instagram than with market tipping (i.e., Instagram tipping the market in its favor and Facebook rapidly losing value due to negative or reverse network effects). It notes:

> The most important concern should be network effects, not within-user cannibalization. We have reviewed many studies which estimate cannibalization among apps for individual users, all of which find positive incrementality across the family: i.e. when a user increases their use of one app, they tend to decrease their use of other apps, but the

---

[800] To underscore this point, the Cunningham Memo does not characterize YouTube as a direct competitor, noting that YouTube would only be a danger if it "becomes more social." Cunningham Memo at 16.

[801] *Id.* at 9.

[802] *Id.* at 10, 14 ("Most countries have a single messaging app with 70%+ daily reach. The most common app is WhatsApp. Others include Messenger, LINE, and Kakotalk.").

[803] *Id.* at 3.

[804] *Id.*

[805] *Id.* at 12 ("WhatsApp does very well when it is the market-leader (in many Latin American countries WhatsApp has nearly 90% daily reach and users spend 60 minutes/day), this suggests that it would be worth a substantial investment to try to push WhatsApp over its tipping point in other countries."). An exception to this trend appears to be where a messaging app exists as part of a social network—such as messaging services on Snapchat—but these apps operate with reduced reach. Another exception is in markets with high penetration by Apple's iPhone, but this growth is limited by adoption of iPhones since iMessage is its native app. *Id.* at 15.

[806] *Id.* at 16 ("Facebook has high reach and time-spent in most countries. User growth is tracking internet growth: global reach is roughly stable. DAP is showing weakness in developed countries and especially teens.").

[807] The Cunningham Memo refers to Facebook's flagship product as "Facebook-Blue" or "Blue" as a reference to the app's color. *Id.* at 15. There is overlap and cross-use among Facebook's products in the United States. While 40% of Instagram users' friends are also their friends on Facebook, only 12% of Facebook users' friends are "reciprocal follows" on Instagram. *Id.* at 9.

total family effect is positive. This should not be surprising - it is unlikely that any of our apps are perfect substitutes for an individual user. However a serious concern is network effects: when you use an app less, that makes it less appealing to other people, and at certain times and places those effects could be very large.[808]

As a result of this dynamic, even though there may be several social apps that exist in an ecosystem, they are unlikely to gain traction among users once a firm has tipped the market in their favor or is otherwise dominant. As the study notes, while mobile phone users tend to use five different social maps in a month, they only use "1.5 messaging apps and 1 social app, out of 10 total apps per day."[809]

Facebook's executives—including Mr. Zuckerberg—have extensively discussed the role of network effects and tipping points as part of the company's acquisition strategy and overall competitive outlook. For example, Mr. Zuckerberg told the company's Chief Financial Officer in 2012 that network effects and winner-take-all markets were a motivating factor in acquiring competitive threats like Instagram. He said:

> [T]here are network effects around social products and a finite number of different social mechanics to invent. Once someone wins at a specific mechanic, it's difficult for others to supplant them without doing something different. It's possible someone beats Instagram by building something that is better to the point that they get network migration, but this is harder as long as Instagram keeps running as a product . . . one way of looking at this is that what we're really buying is time. Even if some new competitors springs[sic] up, buying Instagram now . . . will give us a year or more to integrate their dynamics before anyone can get close to their scale again. Within that time, if we incorporate the social mechanics they were using, those new products won't get much traction since we'll already have their mechanics deployed at scale.[810]

Mr. Zuckerberg also stressed the competitive significance of having a first-mover advantage in terms of network effects prior to acquiring WhatsApp.[811] In the context of market strategies for Messenger competing with WhatsApp, Mr. Zuckerberg told the company's growth and product management teams that "being first is how you build a brand and a network effect."[812] He also told

---

[808] *Id.* at 9.

[809] *Id.* at 6. A recent investor report similarly noted that although "many users access more than one social network per day, it does not appear to be at the cost of declining users or user engagements within the Facebook ecosystem." MORNINGSTAR EQUITY ANALYST REPORT, FACEBOOK INC 3 (Aug. 3, 2020) (on file with Comm.).

[810] Production of Facebook, to H. Comm. on the Judiciary, FB-HJC-ACAL-00063222 (Feb. 28, 2012), https://judiciary.house.gov/uploadedfiles/0006322000063223.pdf.

[811] *Id.* at FB-HJC-ACAL-00046826–34 (Dec. 13, 2013) (on file with Comm.).

[812] *Id.*

them that Facebook has "an opportunity to do this at scale, but that opportunity won't last forever. I doubt we have even a year before WhatsApp starts moving in this direction."[813]

In 2012, the company described its network effects as a "flywheel" in an internal presentation prepared for Facebook at the direction of its Chief Financial Officer.[814] This presentation also said that Facebook's network effects get "stronger every day."[815] Around that time, prominent investors similarly noted that the social networking market had "extreme network effects," making it "increasingly hard to see a materially successful new entrant, even with all of Google's resources."[816]

2) Switching Costs

In addition to the competitive insulation resulting from strong network effects, Facebook is also unlikely to face direct competition from other firms or new entrants due to the high costs for users to switch from Facebook to a competing social network.[817]

Other social network platforms are not interoperable with Facebook. Facebook users invest significant time building their networks on Facebook. This investment includes uploading and curating photos, engaging with their friends, other users, and businesses, and otherwise interacting with their social graph.[818] To switch to another platform, Facebook users have to rebuild their social graph elsewhere. In the process, they lose access to their data—including photos, posts, and other content—

---

[813] *Id.*

[814] Production of Facebook, to H. Comm. on the Judiciary, FB-HJC-ACAL-00049006 (Apr. 18, 2012) ("Network effects make it very difficult to compete with us - In every country we've tipped we are still winning.") (on file with Comm.).

[815] *Id.*

[816] Production of Facebook, to H. Comm. on the Judiciary, FB-HJC-ACAL-00086834–38 (Apr. 3, 2012) (Citi Summary of Investment Outlook) (on file with Comm.). Comscore noted in 2012 that "Facebook has proven to be a dominant global force in social networking that shows no immediate signs of slowing down." According to Comscore, Facebook was the "third largest web property in the world . . . and accounted for approximately 3 in every 4 minutes spent on social networking sites and 1 in every 7 minutes spent online around the world." Production of Facebook, to H. Comm. on the Judiciary, FB-HJC-ACAL-00051905 (Mar. 12, 2012) (Comscore 2012 Report) (on file with Comm.).

[817] Fiona M. Scott Morton & David C. Dinielli, *Roadmap for an Antitrust Case Against Facebook*, OMIDYAR NETWORK 11 (June 2020) ("A very significant reason that Facebook has market power is that a user cannot change platforms and expect to be able to stay in contact with her friends. Because Facebook has a near monopoly, the vast majority of the people with whom they want to exchange feeds are likely on Facebook already. The switching cost for any one user is therefore enormous.").

[818] Production of Facebook, to H. Comm. on the Judiciary, FB-HJC-ACAL-00045349 (Feb. 15, 2014) (on file with Comm.).

along with other elements of their social graph.[819] They also have to learn how to use a new service and rebuild their network.[820] As a result, Facebook's users are effectively "locked in" to its platform.[821]

Facebook's internal documents and communications reveal that Facebook employees recognize that high switching costs insulate Facebook from competition. In 2014, Facebook's Chief Financial Officer told the company's director of growth that investors like this quality about Facebook and "the idea is that after you have invested hours and hours in your friend graph or interest graph or follower graph, you are less likely to leave for a new or different service that offers similar functionality."[822] Similarly, an internal survey prepared for Facebook's senior management team about Google+ explained that "[p]eople who are big fans of G+ are having a hard time convincing their friends to participate because . . . switching costs would be high due to friend density on Facebook."[823] And in 2012, the company indicated that people's significant time investment on Facebook building their identity and connections on the platform increased the company's "stickiness."[824]

In contrast to its public statements, Facebook has not done enough to facilitate data portability for its consumers. Facebook offers a tool called "Download Your Information," which provides users with a limited ability to download their data and upload it elsewhere. But in practice, this tool is unusable for switching purposes given that it allows users to do little other than move their photos from Facebook to Google Photos. Another barrier for switching associated with this tool is that Facebook's users can only download their data in PDF or .zip format. The result is that, while Facebook publicly claims to support data portability,[825] its users seldom leave Facebook due to the challenges of migrating their data. An interview with a former employee at the company reinforces this conclusion. As the former employee noted, this tool is behind a series of menu, explaining:

> If you hide something behind more than one menu, no one sees it and they know it. Then they advertise features that they don't expect anyone to find or use. They say: "It's data portable, you can send it to Google drive?" But who cares? They've just done it to

---

[819] *See, e.g.*, Nicole Nguyen, *If You Created A Spotify Account With Facebook, It Is Forever Tied To Facebook*, BUZZFEED (Oct. 3, 2018), https://www.buzzfeednews.com/article/nicolenguyen/disconnect-facebook-account-from-spotify.

[820] *See, e.g.*, Danny Crichton, *Why no one really quits Google or Facebook*, TECHCRUNCH (Feb. 4, 2019) ("I have 2,000 contacts on Facebook Messenger — am I just supposed to text them all to use Signal from now on? Am I supposed to completely relearn a new photos app, when I am habituated to the taps required from years of practice on Instagram?"), https://techcrunch.com/2019/02/04/why-no-one-really-quits-google-or-facebook/; United States v. Microsoft Corp., 84 F. Supp. 2d 9, 15 (D.D.C. 1999) (noting that switching costs include "the effort of learning to use the new system, the cost of acquiring a new set of compatible applications, and the work of replacing files and documents that were associated with the old applications.").

[821] *See generally* Austl. Competition & Consumer Comm'n Report at 99; Dig. Competition Expert Panel Report at 42.

[822] Production of Facebook, to H. Comm. on the Judiciary, FB-HJC-ACAL-00045349 (Feb. 15, 2014) (on file with Comm.).

[823] *Id.* at FB-HJC-ACAL-00048755–57 (Dec. 14, 2011).

[824] *Id.* at FB-HJC-ACAL-00049006 (Apr. 18, 2012).

[825] *See, e.g.*, DATA TRANSFER PROJECT, https://datatransferproject.dev/ (last visited on Sept. 28, 2020).

generate talking points. They are not allowing you to export your social graph, which is actually valuable.[826]

Leaving Facebook may create additional costs in other key respects. Switching from Facebook may degrade a person's other social apps that integrate with Facebook's Platform APIs. For example, Spotify users who signed up with Facebook "can't disconnect it."[827] To leave Facebook, they must set up a new account on Spotify.[828] In the process, they lose access to their playlists, listening history, social graph of other friends on Spotify, and their other data on the app.[829]

People who leave Facebook may also lose access to popular features on Facebook that, due to its scale and network effects, are not available on other social apps (e.g., events, marketplace, and groups).[830] For example, a church may actively maintain a Facebook page for its parishioners and not on other social apps. Furthermore, some Facebook users who believe they are switching from the company's platform may nevertheless continue using its family of products, such as Instagram or WhatsApp.[831] As the United Kingdom's Competition and Markets Authority noted, this reinforces Facebook's market power.[832]

In response to the concern about switching costs, Facebook replied that its users have meaningful choices and alternatives to Facebook.[833] Additionally, Facebook notes that its users have been able to download their data since 2010.[834] The company describes its users' ability to download their data as a "robust portability tool."[835] However, in March 2019, Mr. Zuckerberg explained that a

---

[826] Interview with Former Instagram Employee (Oct. 2, 2020).

[827] SPOTIFY, *Facebook Login Help*, https://support.spotify.com/us/article/using-spotify-with-facebook/.

[828] *Id.*

[829] Spotify users can manually attempt to recreate playlists or request that Spotify transfer their data, but this is not intuitive. Samantha Cole, *How to Unlink Spotify from Your Facebook Account*, VICE (Dec. 21, 2018), https://www.vice.com/en_us/article/wj3anm/how-to-unlink-spotify-from-your-facebook-account.

[830] *See* Cunningham Memo at 3.

[831] *See, e.g.*, Tiffany Hsu, *For Many Facebook Users, a 'Last Straw' That Led Them to Quit*, N.Y. TIMES (Mar. 21, 2018), https://www.nytimes.com/2018/03/21/technology/users-abandon-facebook.html#:~:text=In%20the%20wake%20of%20the,easy%20as%20pressing%20%E2%80%9Cdelete.%E2%80%9D ("The Cambridge Analytica scandal led her to remove the Facebook app from her phone . . . But she is keeping the messaging function open for professional purposes and will continue using Instagram.").

[832] Competition & Mkts. Auth. Report at 179, 256.

[833] Innovation and Entrepreneurship Hearing at 1 (response to Questions for the Record of Matt Perault, Dir. of Public Pol'y, Facebook).

[834] Erin Egan, *Charting a Way Forward*, FACEBOOK 6 (Sept. 2019), https://about.fb.com/wp-content/uploads/2020/02/data-portability-privacy-white-paper.pdf.

[835] *Id.*

Facebook user's ability to download their data is not "[t]rue data portability."[836] Instead, he said its users should be able to sign into other services in "the way people use our platform to sign into an app."[837]

Currently, Facebook's users lack the ability to port their social networks to a different platform. To switch social networking platforms, a Facebook user can import their contacts from their mobile devices, such as email addresses or phone numbers, to build a network on a different platform. But importing contacts is not a substitute for a person's social graph and, as the CMA concluded, this method is likely limited to a person's close friends.[838] In recognition of this, Javier Olivan, Facebook's Director of Growth, told the company's senior management team that information from a person's address book on their mobile device is "incomplete" because people typically only store limited information in their contacts (e.g., a person's first name, last name, and their phone number).[839] In contrast, Facebook users "have a much richer profile—which creates a much richer experience (we have data that shows how . . . profile pictures make for better / more functional [user interfaces]."[840]

3) Access to Data

Facebook has a significant data advantage in the social networking market. While data may be non-rivalrous—meaning users can provide the same piece of data to more than one platform—it creates another entry barrier, reinforcing Facebook's monopoly power.

Subcommittee staff conducted interviews with market participants that described Facebook as having nearly perfect market intelligence. Facebook's data dominance creates self-reinforcing advantages through two types of "feedback loops."[841] First, by virtue of its significant number of users, Facebook has access to and collects more user data than its competitors.[842] And second, Facebook uses this data to create a more targeted user experience, which in turn attracts more users and leads those users to spend more time on the platform.[843] In contrast, smaller platforms with less access to data must compete by providing a different user experience with less targeting capacity. Facebook's data advantage is thus compounded over time, cementing Facebook's market position and making it even more difficult for new platforms to provide a competitive user experience.

---

[836] Mark Zuckerberg, *The Internet Needs New Rules*, WASH. POST (Mar. 29, 2019), https://www.washingtonpost.com/opinions/mark-zuckerberg-the-internet-needs-new-rules-lets-start-in-these-four-areas/2019/03/29/9e6f0504-521a-11e9-a3f7-78b7525a8d5f_story.html.

[837] *Id.*

[838] Competition & Mkts. Auth. Report at 137.

[839] Production of Facebook, to H. Comm. on the Judiciary, FB-HJC-ACAL-00045364 (Feb. 4, 2014) (on file with Comm.).

[840] *Id.*

[841] Dig. Competition Expert Panel Report at 33.

[842] Competition & Mkts. Auth. Report at 143–44.

[843] *Id.*

Facebook's data advantages also provide a monetization feedback loop. Revenue generated through targeted advertising to existing users can be reinvested into the platform, thereby attracting more users. Facebook's ability to provide targeted advertising is highly valuable to advertisers and allows Facebook to monetize its service. Meanwhile, smaller entrants are less attractive to advertisers since "no de novo entrant [has] access to anywhere near the volume or quality of data" as Facebook.[844] As with its user feedback loop, Facebook's monetization feedback loop creates a runaway virtuous circle that serves as a powerful barrier to entry.

Facebook's data also enables it to act as a gatekeeper because Facebook can exclude other firms from accessing its users' data.[845] Beginning in 2010, Facebook's Open Graph provided other companies with the ability to scale through its user base by interconnecting with Facebook's platform. Some companies benefited immensely from this relationship, experiencing significant user growth from Open Graph and in-app signups through Facebook Connect, now called Facebook Login.[846] Around that time, investors commented that Open Graph gave some companies "monstrous growth," referring to it as "steroids for startups."[847] For example, documents produced by Facebook indicate that it was the top referrer of traffic to Spotify, driving 7 million people "to install Spotify in the month after [Facebook] launched Open Graph."[848] At one point, nearly all of Spotify's growth originated from Facebook, while Pinterest "grew to 10 million users faster than any standalone site in the history of the Internet."[849]

Conversely, interconnecting with the Facebook Platform also gave the company the ability to prioritize access to its social graph—effectively picking winners and losers online.[850] These tools also gave Facebook advanced data insights into other companies' growth and usage trends. For example, a daily report on metrics for Facebook Login included daily and monthly active users for companies interconnecting with Facebook, referral traffic, and daily clicks, among other metrics. As this report

---

[844] Fiona M. Scott Morton & David C. Dinielli, *Roadmap for an Antitrust Case Against Facebook*, OMIDYAR NETWORK 18 (June 2020), https://www.omidyar.com/wp-content/uploads/2020/06/Roadmap-for-an-Antitrust-Case-Against-Facebook.pdf.

[845] *See, e.g.*, MAURICE STUCKE & ALLEN GRUNES, BIG DATA AND COMPETITION POLICY 46 (2017).

[846] Also referred to as Facebook login, Facebook Connect allowed its users to connect their Facebook identity—their profile, friends, and other data—to other social apps through Facebook's APIs. The company explained in 2008 that "[w]ith Facebook Connect, users can bring their real identity information with them wherever they go on the Web, including: basic profile information, profile picture, name, friends, photos, events, groups, and more." Dave Morin, *Announcing Facebook Connect*, FACEBOOK (Mar. 9, 2008), https://developers.facebook.com/blog/post/2008/05/09/announcing-facebook-connect/.

[847] Ben Popper, *Startup steroids: Pinterest feels the burn of Facebook's Open Graph*, THE VERGE (May 3, 2012), https://www.theverge.com/2012/5/3/2993999/pinterest-burn-facebook-open-graph-startup-steroids.

[848] Production of Facebook, to H. Comm. on the Judiciary, FB-HJC-ACAL-00049471 (Script of Keynote for Mobile World Congress (on file with Comm.).

[849] *Id.*

[850] *See, e.g.*, MAURICE STUCKE & ALLEN GRUNES, BIG DATA AND COMPETITION POLICY 46 (2017).

noted, 8.3 million distinct sites used Facebook Connect on a monthly basis in March 2012.[851] Facebook was also able to exclude others from accessing this data.[852] As the United Kingdom's Competition and Markets Authority observed, "the inability of smaller platforms and publishers to access user data creates a significant barrier to entry."[853]

b. Relevant Acquisitions

i. Overview

Since its founding in 2004, Facebook has acquired at least 63 companies.[854] The majority of these acquisitions have involved software firms, such as Instagram, WhatsApp, Face.com, Atlas, LiveWire, and Onavo.[855] Facebook has also acquired several virtual reality and hardware companies, such as Oculus.[856] More recently, the company has acquired several niche social apps,[857] a blockchain platform,[858] Oculus game developers,[859] and a prominent GIF-making and sharing company.[860]

Facebook's internal documents indicate that the company acquired firms it viewed as competitive threats to protect and expand its dominance in the social networking market. As discussed earlier in this Report, Facebook's senior executives described the company's mergers and acquisitions strategy in 2014 as a "land grab" to "shore up our position."[861] In 2012, Mr. Zuckerberg told

---

[851] Production of Facebook, to H. Comm. on the Judiciary, FB_FTC_CID_00364078–147 (Mar. 24, 2012) (Email on Daily Metrics Report) (on file with Comm.).

[852] *See* Stigler Report at 43.

[853] Competition & Mkts. Auth. Report at 15.

[854] *See* Aoife White, *Facebook Told by U.K. Watchdog to Monitor Giphy Independence*, BLOOMBERG (Aug. 10, 2020), https://www.bloomberg.com/news/articles/2020-08-10/facebook-told-by-u-k-watchdog-to-monitor-giphy-independence.

[855] *Id.*; BERKELEY, THE ACQUISITION TAKEOVER BY THE 5 TECH GIANTS, http://people.ischool.berkeley.edu/~neha01mittal/infoviz/dashboard/ (last visited on Sept. 28, 2020).

[856] *See, e.g.*, Josh Constine, *Facebook's $2 Billion Acquisition Of Oculus Closes, Now Official*, TECHCRUNCH (July 21, 2014), https://techcrunch.com/2014/07/21/facebooks-acquisition-of-oculus-closes-now-official/.

[857] *See, e.g.*, Jacob Kastrenakes, *Facebook is shutting down a teen app it bought eight months ago*, THE VERGE (July 2, 2018), https://www.theverge.com/2018/7/2/17528896/facebook-tbh-moves-hello-shut-down-low-usage.

[858] Stan Schroeder, *Facebook acquires team behind blockchain startup Chainspace*, MASHABLE (Dec. 5, 2019), https://mashable.com/article/facebook-acquires-blockchain-team-chainspace/.

[859] Dean Takahashi, *Facebook acquires Lone Echo VR game maker Ready At Dawn*, VENTURE BEAT (June 22, 2020), https://venturebeat.com/2020/06/22/facebook-acquires-lone-echo-vr-game-maker-ready-at-dawn/; Lucas Matney, *Facebook acquires the VR game studio behind one of the Rift's best titles*, TECHCRUNCH (Feb. 25, 2020), https://techcrunch.com/2020/02/25/facebook-acquires-the-vr-game-studio-behind-one-of-the-rifts-best-games/.

[860] Chaim Gartenberg, *Facebook is buying Giphy and integrating it with Instagram*, THE VERGE (May 15, 2020), https://www.theverge.com/2020/5/15/21259965/facebook-giphy-gif-acquisition-buy-instagram-integration-cost.

[861] Production of Facebook, to H. Comm. on the Judiciary, FB-HJC-ACAL-00045388 (Feb. 18, 2014), https://judiciary.house.gov/uploadedfiles/0004538800045389.pdf ("[W]e are going to spend 5-10% of our market cap every couple years to shore up our position . . . I hate the word 'land grab' but I think that is the best convincing argument and we should own that."). Mr. Wehner is currently Facebook's Chief Financial Officer. He replaced David Ebersman, Facebook's

149

Facebook's former Chief Financial Officer that the purpose of acquiring nascent competitors like Instagram was to neutralize competitive threats and to maintain Facebook's position. Documents show that when Facebook acquired WhatsApp, Mr. Zuckerberg and other senior executives and data scientists viewed WhatsApp as a potential threat to Facebook Messenger, as well as an opportunity to further entrench Facebook's dominance. Facebook used critical acquisitions to increase the adoption of its social graph and expand its reach in markets. Finally, Facebook's serial acquisitions reflect the company's interest in purchasing firms that had the potential to develop into rivals before they could fully mature into strong competitive threats.[862]

ii. Instagram

Instagram was founded in February 2010 by Kevin Systrom and Mike Krieger.[863] Originally launched as Burbn, a location-sharing social app,[864] the company released Instagram as a photo-sharing app for Apple iPhones in October 2010,[865] and released its app in the Google Play Store on April 3, 2012.[866]

On April 9, 2012, Facebook proposed its acquisition of Instagram for approximately $1 billion.[867] Facebook formally acquired Instagram in August 2012.[868] The Federal Trade Commission (FTC) opened an investigation into the acquisition but closed it in August 2012 without taking

---

former Chief Financial Officer, in June 2014. David Cohen, *Facebook CFO David Ebersman Leaving Company; David Wehner To Assume Post June 1*, ADWEEK (Apr. 23, 2014), https://www.adweek.com/digital/cfo-david-ebersman-leaving-david-wehner/.

[862] Austl. Competition & Consumer Comm'n Report at 81 ("While any of these acquisitions may not have amounted to a substantial lessening of competition, there appears to be a pattern of Facebook acquiring businesses in related markets which may or may not evolve into potential competitors, which has the effect of entrenching its market power.").

[863] Production of Facebook, to H. Comm. on the Judiciary, FB-HJC-ACAL-00087590 (July 19, 2011) (Valuation of Burbn, Inc. as of May 31, 2011) (on file with Comm. on the Judiciary).

[864] *Id.*

[865] MG Siegler, *Instagram Launches With The Hope Of Igniting Communication Through Images*, TECHCRUNCH (Oct. 6, 2010), https://techcrunch.com/2010/10/06/instagram-launch/. The company received $500,000 in seed funding in March 2010 from Baseline Ventures and Andreesen Horowitz. It later received $7 million in another round of financing in December 2010 primarily from Benchmark Capital and Baseline Ventures. Production of Facebook, to H. Comm. on the Judiciary, FB-HJC-ACAL-00101426 (Dec. 5, 2011) (Instagram Financial History and Projections) (on file with Comm.).

[866] Production of Facebook, to H. Comm. on the Judiciary, FB-HJC-ACAL-00106124 (Apr. 13, 2012) (Instagram Chat Log) (on file with Comm.); *see also* Matt Burns, *Instagram's User Count Now at 40 Million, Saw 10 Million New Users in Last 10 Days*, TECHCRUNCH (Apr. 13, 2012), https://techcrunch.com/2012/04/13/instagrams-user-count-now-at-40-million-saw-10-million-new-users-in-last-10-days/.

[867] The transaction's value was approximately $300 million in cash and roughly $700 million in shares of Facebook at the time of the transaction. Due to changes in the company's value following the launch of its IPO, the final transaction value was worth about $300 million in cash and $460 million in Facebook stock. *See* Facebook Inc., Quarterly Report (Form 10-Q) 9 (Sept. 30, 2012), https://www.sec.gov/Archives/edgar/data/1326801/000132680112000006/fb-9302012x10q.htm.

[868] Facebook Inc., Annual Report (Form 10-K) 5 (Dec. 31, 2012), https://www.sec.gov/Archives/edgar/data/1326801/000132680113000003/fb-12312012x10k.htm.

action.[869] According to the FTC, "Upon further review of this matter, it now appears that no further action is warranted by the Commission at this time."[870] The letter added that its closing of the investigation "is not to be construed as a determination that a violation may not have occurred . . . . The Commission reserves the right to take such further action as the public interest may require."[871]

In the context of reports that Facebook was planning to integrate Whatsapp, Instagram and Facebook Messenger,[872] and concerns about the company's motives for doing so,[873] a former employee of Instagram explained the ease with which Facebook and Instagram came together—and could potentially be pulled apart. They explained:

> Why can't Facebook fork the backend of the product? Facebook makes an odd argument that they use the same system. But you can just copy and paste code, make a copy of the system, and give it to the new company. If you can put them together, you can pull them apart. Facebook can always pull out the data that Instagram would not need. They spent the last year pushing the two products together, it just simply doesn't make sense that they can't work back to where they were in 2019. It's not like building a skyscraper and then suddenly needing to knock the building down again. They can just roll back the changes they've been making over the past year and you'd have two different apps again. It's not about the pipeline. It's an intangible object. You can just copy and paste. Right now, they have a switch inside the app. They could just change something from true to false and it would work. It's not building a skyscraper; it's turning something on and off.[874]

According to Facebook's internal documents, Facebook acquired Instagram to neutralize a nascent competitive threat. In 2012, Mark Zuckerberg wrote to several Facebook executives citing concerns that Instagram posed a risk to Facebook. In February 2012, he said to David Ebersman, Facebook's Chief Financial Officer, that he had "been thinking about . . . how much [Facebook] should be willing to pay to acquire mobile app companies like Instagram . . . that are building networks that

[869] Letter from April Tabor, Acting Sec. of the Fed. Trade Comm'n, to Thomas Barnett (Aug. 22, 2012), https://www.ftc.gov/sites/default/files/documents/closing_letters/facebook-inc./instagram-inc./120822barnettfacebookcltr.pdf.

[870] *Id.*

[871] *Id.*

[872] *See, e.g.*, Mike Isaac, *Zuckerberg Plans to Integrate WhatsApp, Instagram and Facebook Messenger*, N.Y. TIMES (Jan. 25, 2019), https://www.nytimes.com/2019/01/25/technology/facebook-instagram-whatsapp-messenger.html?auth=login-facebook.

[873] *See, e.g.*, Makena Kelly, *Facebook's messaging merger leaves lawmakers questioning the company's power*, THE VERGE (Jan. 28, 2019), https://www.theverge.com/2019/1/28/18200658/facebook-messenger-instagram-whatsapp-google-congress-markey-blumenthal-schatz-william-barr-doj-ftc.

[874] Email from Former Instagram Employee (Oct. 4, 2020).

are competitive with our own."[875] Mr. Zuckerberg told Mr. Ebersman that these "businesses are nascent but the networks are established, the brands are already meaningful and if they grow to a large scale they could be very disruptive to us."[876]

In response, Mr. Ebersman asked Mr. Zuckerberg whether the goals of the acquisition would be to: (1) neutralize a potential competitor; (2) acquire talent; or (3) integrate Instagram's product with Facebook's to improve its service.[877] Mr. Zuckerberg replied that a purpose of the transaction would be to neutralize Instagram, saying that the goals of the deal were "a combination of (1) and (3)." He explained:

> One thing that may make (1) more reasonable here is that there are network effects around social products and a finite number of different social mechanics to invent. Once someone wins at a specific mechanic, it's difficult for others to supplant them without doing something different. It's possible someone beats Instagram by building something that is better to the point that they get network migration, but this is harder as long as Instagram keeps running as a product.[878]

Mr. Zuckerberg wrote that acquiring Instagram would allow Facebook to integrate the product to improve its service. But, he added, that "in reality we already know these companies' social dynamics and will integrate them over the next 12-24 months anyway."[879] He explained:

> By a combination of (1) and (3), one way of looking at this is that *what we're really buying is time*. Even if some new competitors springs[sic] up, buying Instagram, Path, Foursquare, etc [sic] now will give us a year or more to integrate their dynamics before anyone can get close to their scale again. Within that time, if we incorporate the social mechanics they were using, those new products won't get much traction since we'll already have their mechanics deployed at scale.[880]

In March 2012, Mr. Zuckerberg told Mike Schroepfer, Facebook's Chief Technology Officer,[881] that acquiring Instagram would provide the company with "[i]nsurance" for Facebook's

---

[875] Production of Facebook, to H. Comm. on the Judiciary, FB-HJC-ACAL-00063220–23 (Feb. 27, 2012) (on file with Comm.).

[876] *Id.*

[877] *Id.*

[878] *Id.*

[879] *Id.*

[880] *Id.* (emphasis added).

[881] Mr. Schroepfer was Facebook's Vice President of Engineering at the time of the Instagram acquisition. He was elevated to chief technology officer in March 2013. *See* Tomio Geron, *Facebook Names Mike Schroepfer CTO*, FORBES (Mar. 15, 2013), https://www.forbes.com/sites/tomiogeron/2013/03/15/facebook-names-mike-schroepfer-cto/#1a88880b20e3.

main product.[882] Mr. Schroepfer agreed, responding that "not losing strategic position in photos is worth a lot of money."[883] He added that the "biggest risk" would be if Facebook were to "kill" Instagram "by not investing in the company and thereby opening a window for a new entrant."[884]

In a message to another Facebook employee on April 5, 2012, Mr. Zuckerberg said that "Instagram can hurt us meaningfully without becoming a huge business."[885] In contrast, he did not view other smaller firms, such as Pinterest and Foursquare, as comparable competitive threats.[886] As he noted, if these companies "become big we'll just regret not doing them . . . Or we can buy them then, or build them along the way."[887] In an all-hands meeting the following day, Mr. Zuckerberg responded to a question about Instagram's rapid growth by saying that "we need to dig ourselves out of a hole." [888] He also told employees at the company that Instagram is "growing really quickly" and that it would be "tough to dislodge them."[889]

Following the announcement of the transaction, Mr. Zuckerberg said internally that Facebook "can likely always just buy any competitive startups," and agreed with one of the company's senior engineers that Instagram was a "threat" to Facebook.[890] Mr. Zuckerberg concluded that "[o]ne thing about startups though is you can often acquire them."[891]

At the Subcommittee's sixth hearing, Judiciary Committee Chairman Jerrold Nadler (D-NY) asked Mr. Zuckerberg about his characterization of Instagram as a competitive threat prior to the acquisition.[892] In response, Mr. Zuckerberg said that Facebook has always viewed Instagram as "both a

---

[882] Production of Facebook, to H. Comm. on the Judiciary, FB-HJC-ACAL-00063184–85 (Mar. 9, 2012), https://judiciary.house.gov/uploadedfiles/0006318000063197.pdf. These documents are consistent with reporting. Following the acquisition, Gregor Hochmuth, an Instagram engineer, was reportedly told by employees on the Facebook Camera team that "our job was to kill you guys." Following the acquisition, Instagram's employees were also reportedly told by Facebook's growth team "Instagram wouldn't get any help adding users unless they could determine, through data, that the product wasn't competitive with Facebook." SARAH FRIER, NO FILTER 90 (2020).

[883] Id. at FB-HJC-ACAL-00063180, https://judiciary.house.gov/uploadedfiles/0006318000063197.pdf.

[884] Id. at FB-HJC-ACAL-00063184–85, https://judiciary.house.gov/uploadedfiles/0006318000063197.pdf.

[885] Id. at FB-HJC-ACAL-00063319, https://judiciary.house.gov/uploadedfiles/0006331600063321.pdf.

[886] Id. at FB-HJC-ACAL-00063319-00063320 (Apr. 5, 2012), https://judiciary.house.gov/uploadedfiles/0006331600063321.pdf.

[887] Id.

[888] Id. at FB-HJC-ACAL-00047340 (Apr. 6, 2012) (on file with Comm.).

[889] Id.

[890] Id. at FB-HJC-ACAL-00067600 (Apr. 9, 2012), https://judiciary.house.gov/uploadedfiles/0006760000067601.pdf.

[891] Id. at FB-HJC-ACAL-00063341 (Apr. 9, 2012), https://judiciary.house.gov/uploadedfiles/0006334000063341.pdf

[892] CEO Hearing Transcript at 43 (question of Rep. Jerrold Nadler (D-NY), Chairman, H. Comm. on the Judiciary).

competitor and as a complement to our services."[893] He added that at the time of the transaction, Instagram was a competitor in mobile photos and camera apps.[894]

Chairman Nadler also asked that if this "was an illegal merger at the time of the transaction, why shouldn't Instagram now be broken off into a separate company?"[895] In response, Mr. Zuckerberg said that "with hindsight, it probably looks obvious that Instagram would have reached the scale that it has today."[896] But he elaborated:

> It was not a guarantee that Instagram was going to succeed. The acquisition has done wildly well, largely because not just of the founders' talent but because we invested heavily in building up the infrastructure and promoting it and working on security and working on a lot of things around this, and I think that this has been an American success story.[897]

This response, however, is not consistent with many of the documents Facebook provided to the Subcommittee.[898]

Instagram was growing significantly at the time of the transaction. In December 2011, with only 13 employees, Instagram already had 14 million users.[899] Instagram's internal financial history and projections noted that it did not plan to charge for its app or for downloading filters due to its "rapid user growth" and "implied network value."[900] Instagram's internal market projections showed the company growing to nearly 20 million users by January 2012 with a 22% monthly growth rate.[901] By March 31, 2012, Instagram had 30.2 million users and a 17% user growth rate.[902] After releasing its

---

[893] *Id.* at 44 (statement of Mark Zuckerberg, CEO, Facebook).

[894] *Id.* (statement of Mark Zuckerberg, CEO, Facebook).

[894] *Id.*

[895] *Id.* at 45 (question of Rep. Jerrold Nadler (D-NY), Chairman, H. Comm. on the Judiciary).

[896] *Id.* at 46 (statement of Mark Zuckerberg, CEO, Facebook).

[897] *Id.* (statement of Mark Zuckerberg, CEO, Facebook).

[898] *Id.* at 46 (statement of the Hon. Jerrold Nadler, Chairman, H. Comm. on the Judiciary) ("Facebook, by Mr. Zuckerberg's own admission and by the documents we have from the time, Facebook saw Instagram as a threat that could potentially syphon business away from Facebook. And so, rather than compete with it, Facebook bought it. This is exactly the type of anticompetitive acquisition that the antitrust laws were designed to prevent. This should never have happened in the first place. It should never have been permitted to happen, and it cannot happen again.").

[899] Production of Facebook, to H. Comm. on the Judiciary, FB-HJC-ACAL-00101426 (Dec. 5, 2011) (Instagram Financial History and Projections) (on file with Comm.).

[900] *Id.*

[901] *Id.* at FB-HJC-ACAL-00101473 (Dec. 5, 2011) (Instagram Budget) (on file with Comm.).

[902] *Id.* at FB-HJC-ACAL-0110268 (2012) (Instagram Growth and Projections).

app in the Google Play Store on April 3, 2012, Instagram added ten million users within ten days,[903] growing to nearly 50 million users by April 30, 2012,[904] and 100 million users by the time the acquisition closed in August 2012.[905]

Instagram's growth also appeared to be sustainable. In an email between senior executives at both companies on April 16, 2012, Instagram's head of business operations said that Instagram has not had difficulties with scaling or cloud storage availability, noting that "[s]caling has been really easy" despite the need to "keep adding machine capacity."[906] They also noted that user uptake on Android devices exceeded the company's expectations, but did not raise concerns about their ability to scale in response to this demand.[907]

Facebook's support of Instagram's growth after acquiring it is overstated. Before acquiring Instagram, Mr. Zuckerberg said that Facebook should "invest a few more engineers in it" but let Instagram "run relatively independently."[908] Prior to being acquired, Instagram's internal projections showed the company gaining nearly 88 million users by January 2013,[909] and that its growth trajectory would not be significantly affected by the transaction.[910]

iii. WhatsApp

1) Overview

WhatsApp was founded in February 2009 by Jan Koum and Brian Acton.[911] Originally designed to allow users to provide temporary updates to their contacts,[912] WhatsApp is a cross-

---

[903] *Id.* at FB-HJC-ACAL-00106124 (Apr. 13, 2012) (Instagram Chat Log).

[904] *Id.* at FB-HJC-ACAL-00106131 (Apr. 30, 2012).

[905] Facebook Inc., Annual Report (Form 10-K) 5 (Dec. 31, 2012), https://www.sec.gov/Archives/edgar/data/1326801/000132680113000003/fb-12312012x10k.htm.

[906] Production of Facebook, to H. Comm. on the Judiciary, FB-HJC-ACAL-00110279 (Apr. 16, 2012) (Instagram's Growth Projections) (on file with Comm); *see generally* SARAH FRIER, NO FILTER (2020) ("Every hour, Instagram seemed to grow faster. D'Angelo eventually helped the company transition to renting server space from Amazon Web Services instead of buying their own.").

[907] Production of Facebook, to H. Comm. on the Judiciary, FB-HJC-ACAL-00110279 (Apr. 16, 2012) (Instagram's Growth Projections) (on file with Comm).

[908] *Id.* at FB-HJC-ACAL-00063184-00063185 (Mar. 9, 2012), https://judiciary.house.gov/uploadedfiles/0006318000063197.pdf.

[909] *Id.* at FB-HJC-ACAL-0110268 (2012) (Instagram's Growth Projections) (on file with Comm).

[910] *Id.*

[911] STEVEN LEVY, FACEBOOK: THE INSIDE STORY 317–18 (2020).

[912] *Id.* at 319.

platform messaging and calling service.[913] Unlike traditional text and multimedia messages sent over a cellular network at the time, WhatsApp messages and calls do not require a cellular connection, and are transmitted by an internet connection.[914] A main distinction between Facebook Messenger and WhatsApp is the network that people are able to communicate with on each messaging service. A Facebook user can only send messages to other Facebook users on the Messenger app, whereas a WhatsApp user can send messages to other people based on contacts on their mobile device.[915]

Until 2016, WhatsApp monetized its service through subscriptions for a nominal fee after the first year of use.[916] Around that time, WhatsApp was the only messaging app that competed using this business model.[917] Importantly, WhatsApp's founders strongly opposed an advertisement-based business model. In June 2012, they wrote that "when advertising is involved **you the user** are the product," explaining:

> Advertising isn't just the disruption of aesthetics, the insults to your intelligence and the interruption of your train of thought. At every company that sells ads, a significant portion of their engineering team spends their day tuning data mining, writing better code to collect all your personal data, upgrading the servers that hold all the data and making sure it's all being logged and collated and sliced and packaged and shipped out.[918]

WhatsApp also maintained robust privacy policies. In its June 2012 privacy policy, WhatsApp stated that it does not collect names, emails, location data, or the contents of messages sent through WhatsApp.[919] According to its policy, "WhatsApp is currently ad-free and we hope to keep it that way forever."[920]

---

[913] Letter from Reginald Brown and Jon Yarowsky to H. Comm. on the Judiciary (Oct. 14, 2019), FB-AJC-ACAL-APP00003.

[914] *Id.* Although WhatsApp originally charged a subscription fee after the first year of use, it removed fees in January 2016. *See also* WHATSAPP, *Making WhatsApp free and more useful* (Jan. 18, 2016), https://blog.whatsapp.com/making-whatsapp-free-and-more-useful.

[915] Production of Facebook, to H. Comm. on the Judiciary, FB-HJC-ACAL-00042171 (2014) (on file with Comm.).

[916] STEVEN LEVY, FACEBOOK: THE INSIDE STORY 320 (2020) ("'We were building a communication service,' says Acton. 'You pay forty bucks a month to Verizon for their service, I figured a dollar a year was enough for a messaging service.'").

[917] Production of Facebook, to H. Comm. on the Judiciary, FB-HJC-ACAL-00042157 (2014) (on file with Comm.) ("To the best of WhatsApp's knowledge, Threema is the only other provider that has adopted a model based on usage fees. In contrast to WhatsApp's subscription model, users of Threema pay a one-time fee for a life-time service.").

[918] WHATSAPP, *Why we don't sell ads* (June 18, 2012) ("Advertising has us chasing cars and clothes, working jobs we hate so we can buy shit we don't need."), https://blog.whatsapp.com/why-we-don-t-sell-ads.

[919] WHATSAPP, *Privacy Notice* (July 7, 2012), https://www.whatsapp.com/legal?doc=privacy-policy&version=20120707.

[920] *Id.*

2) Acquisition Review

On February 19, 2014, Facebook announced its proposed acquisition of WhatsApp for approximately $16 billion at the time of the announcement.[921] Following the transaction, WhatsApp's co-founder wrote that the company would "remain autonomous and operate independently" from Facebook, and that "nothing" will change for users because there "would have been no partnership between our two companies if we had to compromise on the core principles that will always define our company, our vision and our product."[922] Mr. Zuckerberg said that "[w]e are absolutely not going to change plans around WhatsApp and the way it uses user data."[923]

The Federal Trade Commission opened an initial investigation into the proposed transaction on March 13, 2014. On April 10, 2014, the FTC's Director of the Bureau of Consumer Protection sent a letter advising the companies that WhatsApp "must continue to honor" its privacy data security commitments to its users, and that "a failure to keep promises made about privacy constitutes a deceptive practice under section 5 of the FTC Act."[924] The Commission did not initiate a full-phase investigation into the acquisition.

In September 2014, the European Commission initiated a review of Facebook's proposed acquisition of WhatsApp.[925] At the time of the transaction, Facebook calculated that the combined share of Facebook Messenger and WhatsApp in February 2014 was approximately 36% of the European Economic Area (EEA) market.[926] In a filing in support of the transaction, Facebook told the European Commission that multi-homing—the use of multiple apps with similar features—was a key characteristic of the messaging market, saying that "approximately 70% of consumers use at least two, and 43% use at least three, communications apps in parallel."[927] Facebook characterized the WhatsApp

---

[921] The transaction included $4 billion in cash and approximately $12 billion of Facebook shares. FACEBOOK, *Facebook to Acquire WhatsApp* (Feb. 19, 2014), https://about.fb.com/news/2014/02/facebook-to-acquire-whatsapp/ (last visited on Sept. 28, 2020). The final value of WhatsApp exceeded $21 billion due to changes in the value of Facebook's stock during the transaction and due to the addition of granting $3 billion in Facebook shares following the closing of the transaction. Sarah Frier, *Facebook $22 Billion WhatsApp Deal Buys $10 Million in Sales,* BLOOMBERG (Oct. 29, 2014), https://www.bloomberg.com/news/articles/2014-10-28/facebook-s-22-billion-whatsapp-deal-buys-10-million-in-sales.

[922] WHATSAPP, FACEBOOK (Feb. 19, 2014) ("Here's what will change for you, our users: nothing."), https://blog.whatsapp.com/facebook.

[923] Jessica Guynn, *Mark Zuckerberg: WhatsApp worth even more than $19 billion*, L.A. TIMES (Feb. 24, 2014), https://www.latimes.com/business/la-xpm-2014-feb-24-la-fi-tn-mark-zuckerberg-whatsapp-worth-even-more-than-19-billion-20140224-story.html.

[924] Letter from Jessica Rich, Dir., Bur. of Consumer Protection of the Fed. Trade Comm'n, to Erin Egan, Chief Privacy Officer, Facebook & Anne Hoge, Gen. Counsel, WhatsApp 1–2 (Apr. 10, 2014), https://www.ftc.gov/system/files/documents/public_statements/297701/140410facebookwhatappltr.pdf.

[925] Facebook noticed the proposed transaction to the European Commission on August 29, 2014. Press Release, Eur. Comm'n, Mergers: Commission approves acquisition of WhatsApp by Facebook (Oct. 3, 2014), https://ec.europa.eu/commission/presscorner/detail/en/IP_14_1088.

[926] Production of Facebook, to H. Comm. on the Judiciary, FB-HJC-ACAL-00042161 (on file with Comm.).

[927] *Id.* at FB-HJC-ACAL-00042160.

product market as being distinct from the social networking market because WhatsApp "does not offer social features," and represented that it had "no plans to make changes to WhatsApp's current strategy" after closing the proposed acquisition.[928]

On October 3, 2014, the European Commission approved the proposed transaction, finding that "Facebook Messenger and WhatsApp are not close competitors and that consumers would continue to have a wide choice of alternative consumer communications apps after the transaction."[929] Although the European Commission noted that the messaging apps are characterized by network effects, it concluded that Facebook would "continue to face sufficient competition after the merger."[930] The Commission acknowledged that there is overlap between social networking and messaging apps. As it noted, the distinction between these apps is "becoming blurred and each of these services adopts traditional functionalities of the other." [931] However, the Commission concluded that social networking services generally provide more social features than messaging apps—such as commenting on or "liking" other users' posts and photos—whereas messaging apps had more limited functionality that is focused on real-time communication.[932]

In 2016, the European Commission fined Facebook after it concluded that Facebook provided "incorrect or misleading information" during the Commission's review of the transaction.[933] In its Statement of Objections to Facebook, the Commission concluded that Facebook provided misleading evidence on whether the company could match its users' accounts with those of WhatsApp's users.[934] In August 2016, WhatsApp had updated its policies to allow the linking of Facebook user identities with WhatsApp user phone numbers.[935] As discussed below, Facebook intended to create this functionality at the time of the transaction.[936]

Documents obtained by the Subcommittee indicate that Facebook acquired WhatsApp to expand its dominance. Prior to acquiring WhatsApp, Facebook viewed the acquisition as providing an opportunity to expand its reach in countries with intermediate levels of penetration.[937] Facebook's

---

[928] *Id.* at FB-HJC-ACAL-00042173.

[929] Press Release, Eur. Comm'n, Mergers: Commission approves acquisition of WhatsApp by Facebook (Oct. 3, 2014), https://ec.europa.eu/commission/presscorner/detail/en/IP_14_1088.

[930] *Id.*

[931] Facebook/WhatsApp Android (Case M.7217) Commission Decision No. 139/2004 [2014], para. 52, https://ec.europa.eu/competition/mergers/cases/decisions/m7217_20141003_20310_3962132_EN.pdf.

[932] *Id.* at para. 54.

[933] Press Release, Eur. Comm'n, Mergers: Commission fines Facebook €110 million for providing misleading information about WhatsApp takeover (May 18, 2017), https://ec.europa.eu/commission/presscorner/detail/en/IP_17_1369.

[934] *Id.*

[935] *Id.*

[936] Production of Facebook, to H. Comm. on the Judiciary, FB-HJC-ACAL-00045364 (Feb. 4, 2014) (on file with Comm.).

[937] *Id.*

internal documents at the time of the transaction reveal that WhatsApp had already tipped markets in its favor where it had high penetration.[938]

In an internal email to Facebook's management team, Facebook Director of Growth Javier Olivan wrote that WhatsApp had higher levels of reach and usage than Facebook in countries that it had penetrated. For example, based on Facebook's internal data, WhatsApp reached 99.9% of the smartphone population in Spain, or as Mr. Olivan described it, "literally everyone."[939] By purchasing WhatsApp, Mr. Olivan suggested that they could "grow Facebook even further" by exposing new users to Facebook.[940] Additionally, by bundling free services with WhatsApp and Facebook's other services, the transaction could serve as another mechanism to expand Facebook's reach among WhatsApp users.[941] Mr. Zuckerberg responded supportively, saying that "I really agree with this analysis."[942]

In an email to David Ebersman, Facebook's Chief Financial Officer, Mr. Olivan wrote that WhatsApp's "reach amongst smartphone users is actually bigger than ours . . . we have close to 100% overlap, our user-base being a subset of theirs."[943] He explained that "in markets where they do well, they literally reach 100% of smartphone users—which is a big part of the population."[944] In the company's internal documents describing the transaction rationale, there was a heavy emphasis on WhatsApp's growth and usage—450 million users, a clear path to a billion users, and adding one million new users every day with no marketing—and expanding Facebook's social graph to phones.[945] Prior to the acquisition, Mr. Zuckerberg had requested a list of all mobile apps with more than 100 million daily and monthly active users globally.[946] Facebook's data showed that WhatsApp had the second most daily active users and fourth most monthly active users of any freestanding mobile app.[947]

Finally, a week after announcing the transaction, David Wehner, then-Vice President of Corporate Finance and Business Planning at Facebook, said to Mr. Ebersman that "we are going to spend 5-10% of our market cap every couple years to shore up our position."[948] Mr. Wehner said that

---

[938] *See, e.g., id.*

[939] *Id.*

[940] *Id.*

[941] *Id.*

[942] *Id.* at FB-HJC-ACAL-00045363.

[943] Production of Facebook, to H. Comm. on the Judiciary, FB-HJC-ACAL-00045388 (Feb. 18, 2014), https://judiciary.house.gov/uploadedfiles/0004538800045389.pdf.

[944] *Id.*

[945] *Id.* at FB-HJC-ACAL-00045379–87 (Feb. 19, 2014) (on file with Comm.).

[946] *Id.*

[947] *Id.*

[948] *Id.* at FB-HJC-ACAL-00045388 (Feb. 18, 2014), https://judiciary.house.gov/uploadedfiles/0004538800045389.pdf.

"I hate the word 'land grab' but I think that is the best convincing argument and we should own that."[949]

Other documents indicate that Facebook viewed WhatsApp as a maverick competitor. In December 2013, Mr. Zuckerberg sent an email to Facebook's management team on competitive issues facing the company. In this email, he called attention to a feature that WhatsApp had implemented on its platform, and warned that Facebook should move quickly:

> I want to call out two competitive near term issues we face. The first is WhatsApp adding a feature like this for public figures . . . If the space is going to move in this direction, being the leader and establishing the brand and network effects matters a lot. This alone should encourage us to consider this soon. . . . When the world shifts like this, being first is how you build a brand and network effect. We have an opportunity to do this at scale, but that opportunity won't last forever. I doubt we even have a year before WhatsApp starts moving in this direction.[950]

Facebook's documents also indicate that the company monitored WhatsApp closely to determine whether it was a threat to the Messenger app. Prior to consummating the merger, Facebook's data scientists used Onavo data to model WhatsApp's engagement and reach to determine whether it was "killing Facebook Messenger,"[951] as well as how its usage trends compared to Snapchat.[952]

c. Conduct

In addition to protecting and expanding its dominance by acquiring firms that Facebook identified as competitive threats over the past decade, Facebook abused its monopoly power to harm competition in the social networking market. Facebook used its data advantage to create superior market intelligence to identify nascent competitive threats and then acquire, copy, or kill these firms. Once dominant, Facebook selectively enforced its platform policies based on whether it perceived other companies as competitive threats. In doing so, it advantaged its own services while weakening other firms.

i. Facebook's Use of Non-Public Data to Identify Competitive Threats

Prior to Facebook's acquisition of Instagram, Facebook used internal data to track the growth of Instagram and other popular apps. While this data was probative for companies that interconnected

---

[949] Id.

[950] Id. at, FB-HJC-ACAL-00046826–34 (Dec. 13, 2013) (on file with Comm.).

[951] Id. at FB-HJC-ACAL-00014564–74 (Mar. 27, 2014).

[952] Id. at FB-HJC-ACAL-00014575.

with Facebook through Open Graph, it was incomplete for studying mobile app usage trends across the entire mobile ecosystem. In April 2012, Facebook's Director of Growth Javier Olivan emailed Mr. Zuckerberg and Facebook Chief Product Officer Chris Cox, about improving Facebook's "competitive research."[953] He said that "getting our data in great shape is going to require effort."[954] Although the company had made "some good progress" using data from Comscore, a data analytics and measurement firm, Mr. Olivan said that with a significant investment, Facebook could build its own custom panel for mobile data that would "allow us to get 10x better at understanding" the mobile ecosystem:

> I keep seeing the same suspects (instagram, pinterest, …) [sic] both on our competitive radar / platform strategy as wins . . . I think having the exact data about their users [sic] engagement, value they derive from [Facebook] . . . would help us make more bold decisions on whether they are friends or foes. Back to your thread about "copying" vs. "innovating" we could also use this info to inspire our next moves.[955]

Mr. Zuckerberg responded: "Yeah, let's do it. We can find some time periodically during my weekly reviews to go over this stuff."[956]

A year later, on October 14, 2013, Facebook acquired Onavo, a virtual private network (VPN), for $115 million and other consideration.[957] In an email to Facebook's board, Facebook's Vice President and Deputy General Counsel said the purpose of the acquisition was to "enhance our analytics related to cross-app user engagement data, as well as user behavior and market trends, and also to improve advertising effectiveness through demand data and audience targeting in the long term."[958] Importantly, Facebook planned to place the incoming Onavo employees, including its cofounder, Guy Rosen, under Facebook's Growth team reporting to Javier Olivan.[959]

Facebook's acquisition of Onavo provided the company with the ability to track potential competitors through non-public, real-time data about engagement, usage, and how much time people spend on apps. Following this acquisition, Facebook used Onavo data as an "early bird warning

---

[953] *Id.* at FB-HJC-ACAL-00068928 (Apr. 3, 2012).

[954] *Id.*

[955] *Id.*

[956] *Id.* at FB-HJC-ACAL-00068929.

[957] Hayley Tsukayama, *Facebook acquires Israeli start-up Onavo to bolster data compression and mobile tech*, WASH. POST (Oct. 14, 2013), https://blogs.wsj.com/digits/2013/10/14/facebook-deal-gives-it-office-in-israel/.

[958] Production of Facebook, to H. Comm. on the Judiciary, FB-HJC-ACAL-00072168 (Oct. 9, 2013) (on file with Comm.).

[959] *Id.*

system,"[960] identifying fast-growing apps that could potentially threaten Facebook's market position or enable it to protect and expand its dominance. For instance, days prior to Facebook's acquisition of WhatsApp in 2014, Facebook senior executives provided Mark Zuckerberg with a list of all mobile apps with greater than 90 million monthly active users—WhatsApp, one of the only top mobile apps not owned at the time by either Facebook or Google, was fourth on the list.[961]

In August 2018, Apple removed Onavo from its app store following reporting that Facebook was using the app to track users and other apps.[962] An Apple spokesperson said the company intended to make "it explicitly clear that apps should not collect information about which other apps are installed on a user's device for the purposes of analytics or advertising/marketing and must make it clear what user data will be collected and how it will be used."[963] In January 2019, Apple removed Facebook's functional successor to Onavo, the Facebook Research app, following reports by *TechCrunch* that Facebook paid "teenagers and adults to download the Research app and give it root access to network traffic in what may be a violation of Apple policy so the social network can decrypt and analyze their phone activity."[964]

Most recently, Facebook acquired Giphy, a platform for sharing GIFs online and through messaging apps, for $400 million in May 2020.[965] As several reporters have noted, this transaction would give Facebook competitive insights into other messaging apps. One commenter said, "While you may successfully block trackers like the Facebook ad pixel following you around online, or even delete your Facebook account, the majority of us wouldn't suspect we're being monitored when we're sending funny images to friends."[966]

---

[960] Betsy Morris & Deepa Seetharaman, *The New Copycats: How Facebook Squashes Competition From Startups*, WALL ST. J. (Aug. 9, 2017), https://www.wsj.com/articles/the-new-copycats-how-facebook-squashes-competition-from-startups-1502293444.

[961] Production of Facebook, to H. Comm. on the Judiciary, FB-HJC-ACAL-00045412-14 (Feb. 16, 2014), https://judiciary.house.gov/uploadedfiles/0004541200045414.pdf.

[962] Deepa Seetharaman, *Facebook Removes Data-Security App From Apple Store*, WALL ST. J. (Aug. 22, 2018), https://www.wsj.com/articles/facebook-to-remove-data-security-app-from-apple-store-1534975340.

[963] Taylor Hatmaker, *Apple removed Facebook's Onavo from the App Store for gatherine app data*, TECHCRUNCH (Aug. 22, 2018), https://techcrunch.com/2018/08/22/apple-facebook-onavo/.

[964] Josh Constine, *Facebook pays teens to install VPN that spies on them*, TECHCRUNCH (Jan. 29, 2019), https://techcrunch.com/2019/01/29/facebook-project-atlas/; Josh Constine, *Apple bans Facebook's Research app that paid users for data*, TECHCRUNCH (Jan. 30, 2019), https://techcrunch.com/2019/01/30/apple-bans-facebook-vpn/.

[965] Kurt Wagner & Sarah Frier, *Facebook Buys Animated Image Library Giphy for $400 Million*, BLOOMBERG (May 15, 2020), https://www.bloomberg.com/news/articles/2020-05-15/facebook-buys-animated-image-library-giphy-to-boost-messaging; *see, e.g.*, @VivekxK, TWITTER (May 15, 2020, 11:43 AM), https://twitter.com/VivekxK/status/1261321201210626048.

[966] Owen Williams, *How Facebook Could Use Giphy to Collect Your Data*, ONEZERO (May 15, 2020), https://onezero.medium.com/how-facebook-could-use-giphy-to-collect-your-data-70824aa2647b.

ii. Facebook's Strategy to Acquire, Copy, or Kill Competitors

Facebook's internal documents indicate that once it identified a competitive threat, it attempted to buy or crush them by cloning their product features or foreclosing them from Facebook's social graph. Facebook took these steps to harm competitors and insulate Facebook from competition, not just to grow or offer better products and services.

In a March 2012 email to other senior executives at Facebook, Mr. Zuckerberg wrote that cloning other apps could help Facebook move faster by "building out more of the social use cases ourselves and prevent our competitors from getting footholds."[967] Other senior employees at Facebook agreed with this strategy. Sheryl Sandberg, Facebook's Chief Operating Officer, said that "it is better to do more and move faster, especially if that means you don't have competitors build products that takes some of our users." Sam Lessin, Facebook's Product Management Director added, "I would love to be far more aggressive and nimble in copying competitors. . . Let's 'copy' (aka super-set) Pinterest!"[968] Another senior executive responded, "I've been thinking about why we haven't moved faster on Roger and Snap . . . I'm increasingly concerned as I watch startups siphon our graph and create awesome new experiences faster than we can."[969]

Prior to its acquisition of Instagram in 2012, Facebook's senior executives had identified Instagram as a growing threat. Mr. Zuckerberg told employees at an internal meeting that the "bad news is that [Instagram is] growing really quickly, they have a lot of momentum, and it's going to be tough to dislodge them."[970] One engineer wrote in an internal company chat that "Instagram is eating our lunch. We should've owned this space but we're already losing quite badly."[971] In response, another engineer asked, "Isn't that why we're building an Instagram clone?" referencing Facebook's development of Facebook Camera, a standalone photo app.[972]

During negotiations to acquire Instagram, Mr. Zuckerberg referenced Facebook's development of a similar app to Kevin Systrom, Instagram's Chief Executive Officer.[973] In messages between Mr. Zuckerberg and Mr. Systrom, Mr. Systrom said that it was difficult to evaluate the transaction independently of reports that Facebook was developing a similar product. He told Mr. Zuckerberg that

---

[967] Production of Facebook, to H. Comm. on the Judiciary, FB-HJC-ACAL-00053511–16 (Mar. 30, 2012) (on file with Comm.).

[968] *Id.*

[969] *Id.* at FB-HJC-ACAL-00067549 (Apr. 3, 2012).

[970] *Id.* at FB-HJC-ACAL-00047340 (Apr. 6, 2012).

[971] *Id.* at FB-HJC-ACAL-00063367 (Jan. 26, 2012), https://judiciary.house.gov/uploadedfiles/0006336700063373.pdf.

[972] Josh Constine, *FB launches Facebook Camera—An Instagram-Style Photo Filtering, Sharing, Viewing iOS App*, TECHCRUNCH (May 24, 2012), https://techcrunch.com/2012/05/24/facebook-camera/.

[973] Production of Facebook, to H. Comm. on the Judiciary, FB-HJC-ACAL-00091648–50 (Mar. 20, 2012) (on file with Comm.).

he "wouldn't feel nearly as strongly [about the acquisition] if independently you weren't building a mobile photos app that makes people choose which engine to use."[974] Similarly, Mr. Zuckerberg suggested that refusing to enter into a partnership with Facebook, including an acquisition, would have consequences for Instagram, referencing the product Facebook was developing at the time:

> At some point soon, you'll need to figure out how you actually want to work with us. This can be an acquisition, through a close relationship with Open Graph, through an arms length relationship using our traditional APIs, or perhaps not at all. . . Of course, at the same time we're developing our own photos strategy, so how we engage now will determine how much we're partners vs. competitors down the line—and I'd like to make sure we decide that thoughtfully as well.[975]

In an earlier conversation with Matt Cohler, an Instagram investor and former senior Facebook adviser, Mr. Systrom asked whether Mr. Zuckerberg would "go into destroy mode if I say no" to being acquired, saying that the companies "have overlap in features."[976] Mr. Cohler responded "probably" and that Mr. Zuckerberg would "conclude that it's best to crush [I]nstagram."[977]

Facebook's approach towards rival social networking app Snapchat is another case study in how Facebook enters "destroy mode" when its market position is threatened. In 2013, as the company was growing rapidly, Snapchat co-founder Evan Spiegel turned down an offer from Mr. Zuckerberg to acquire the company for $3 billion.[978] Thereafter, Instagram—owned by Facebook—introduced the Instagram Stories feature, which allows users to post content that is available for only 24 hours, and which was "nearly identical to the central feed in Snapchat, which [was] also called Stories."[979]

Less than a year after its introduction, Instagram Stories had more daily active users (200 million) than Snapchat Stories (161 million).[980] By 2018, Instagram Stories had doubled the number of

---

[974] *Id.*

[975] *Id.*

[976] *Id.* at FB-AJC-ACAL-0010438 (Feb. 13, 2012), https://judiciary.house.gov/uploadedfiles/0010143800101441.pdf.

[977] *Id.*

[978] Evelyn Rusli & Douglas MacMillan, *Messaging Service Snapchat Spurned $3 Billion Facebook Bid*, WALL ST. J. (Nov. 13, 2013), https://www.wsj.com/articles/messaging-service-snapchat-spurned-facebook-bid-1384376628.

[979] Casey Newton, *Instagram's new stories are a near-perfect copy of Snapchat stories*, THE VERGE (Aug. 2, 2016), https://www.theverge.com/2016/8/2/12348354/instagram-stories-announced-snapchat-kevin-systrom-interview.

[980] Kaya Yurieff, *Instagram's Snapchat clone is more popular than Snapchat*, CNN BUS. (Apr. 13, 2017), https://money.cnn.com/2017/04/13/technology/instagram-stories-snapchat/index.html.

Snapchat Stories daily users.[981] When discussing Instagram's decision to clone the Snapchat feature, Instagram VP of Product Kevin Weil remarked: "This is the way the tech industry works."[982]

In another example, Facebook executives approached Houseparty, a social networking app,[983] about a potential acquisition. Houseparty's founders turned down Facebook's offer, and released the product they referred to as "the internet's living room."[984] Shortly thereafter, Facebook announced that its Messenger app would become a "virtual living room."[985] Houseparty's active user base fell by half between 2017 and 2018.[986]

At the Subcommittee's sixth hearing, Representative Henry C. "Hank" Johnson, Jr. (D-GA) asked Mr. Zuckerberg about Facebook's use of data to identify competitive threats. Rep. Johnson noted that "over nearly a decade, Mr. Zuckerberg, you led a sustained effort to surveil smaller competitors to benefit Facebook. These were steps taken to abuse data, to harm competitors, and to shield Facebook from competition."[987] He asked Mr. Zuckerberg whether Facebook used Onavo data to purchase WhatsApp. Mr. Zuckerberg responded:

> I think every company engages in research to understand what their customers are enjoying so they can learn and make their products better. And that's what we were trying to do. That is what our analytics team was doing. And I think, in general, that allowed us to make our services better for people to be able to connect in a whole lot of different ways, which is our goal. . . . [Onavo] was one of the signals that we had about WhatsApp's trajectory, but we didn't need it. Without a doubt, it was pretty clear that WhatsApp was a great product.[988]

[981] *Id.*

[982] Josh Constine, *Instagram on copying Snapchat: "This is the way the tech industry works,"* TECHCRUNCH (May 16, 2017), https://techcrunch.com/2017/05/16/to-clone-or-not-to-clone/.

[983] Betsy Morris & Deepa Seetharaman, *The New Copycats: How Facebook Squashes Competition From Startups,* WALL ST. J. (Aug. 9, 2017), https://www.wsj.com/articles/the-new-copycats-how-facebook-squashes-competition-from-startups-1502293444.

[984] *Id.*

[985] *Id.*

[986] Mansoor Iqbal, *Houseparty Revenue and Usage Statistics* (2020) (June 23, 2020), https://www.businessofapps.com/data/houseparty-statistics/.

[987] CEO Hearing Transcript at 149–50 (question of Rep. Henry C. "Hank" Johnson, Jr. (D-GA), Chairman, Subcomm. on Courts & Intellectual Property, H. Comm. on the Judiciary).

[988] *Id.* (statement of Mark Zuckerberg, CEO, Facebook).

iii. Facebook Weaponized Access to its Platform

Internal communications by Facebook's senior executives and interviews with former employees at the company indicate that Facebook selectively enforced its platform policies based on whether it perceived other companies as competitive threats.

Facebook developed the Facebook Platform to connect other applications to Facebook's social graph. In an interview in 2007, Mr. Zuckerberg described the goals of the Facebook Platform as making "Facebook into something of an operating system so you can run full applications."[989] A year later, in an email to senior executives at Facebook, Mr. Zuckerberg described Facebook Platform as key to the company's long term success:

> Platform is key to our strategy because we believe that there will be a lot of different social applications and ways that people communicate and share information, and we believe we can't develop all of them ourselves. Therefore, even though it's a challenge for us to get this right, it's important for us to focus on it because the company that defines this social platform will be in the best position to offer the most good ways for people to communicate and succeed in the long term.[990]

Over the next few years, Facebook recognized that access to its social graph provided other applications with a tool for significant growth. In exchange, Facebook hosted content that kept users engaged on its social graph, and considered other ways to monetize this relationship, such as through revenue sharing or advertisements.

By 2012, however, Facebook's senior executives realized that apps could use the Facebook Platform to build products that were competitive with Facebook and "siphon our users."[991] Mike Vernal, Facebook's Vice President of Product and Engineer, described this dynamic to Doug Purdy, Facebook's Director of Product Management:

> When we started Facebook Platform, we were small and wanted to make sure we were an essential part of the fabric of the Internet. We've done that—**we're now the biggest service on earth**. When we were small, apps helped drive our ubiquity. **Now that we are big, (many) apps are looking to siphon off our users to competitive services**. We

---

[989] David Kirkpatrick, *Facebook's plan to hook up the world*, CNNMONEY (May 29, 2007), https://money.cnn.com/2007/05/24/technology/facebook.fortune/.

[990] Production of Facebook, to H. Comm. on the Judiciary, FB_FTC_CID_00072185–88 (Feb. 14, 2008) (on file with Comm.).

[991] *Id.* at FB_FTC_CID_00072020–23 (Feb. 14, 2013) (emphasis added).

need to be more thoughtful about what integrations we allow and we need to make sure that we have sustainable, long-term value exchanges.[992]

In another conversation between Sam Lessin, Facebook's Director of Product Engagement, and other executives, Facebook's senior employees agreed that competitive apps used Facebook Platform to "steal our engagement" and "could be viewed as replacing Facebook functionality," adding that they planned to raise this concern with Mr. Zuckerberg.[993] Mr. Lessin raised these concerns with Mr. Zuckerberg in October 2012. In response, Mr. Zuckerberg agreed with this conclusion:

> Reading your responses, I do think you are right . . . I would be more comfortable with competition if I thought we knew better how to leverage our scale asset (and if scale weren't becoming cheaper and cheaper to achieve every day). What I think is that we should effectively not be helping our competitors more / much more than how they could get help from elsewhere in the market. They can acquire users in ways other than us so obviously we shouldn't be failing to take their money when they will just give it to someone else and get the same outcome. I do, however, again think that we want as much control here as we can get. I agree we shouldn't help our competitors whenever possible. **I think the right solution here is to just be a lot stricter about enforcing our policies and identifying companies as competitors.**[994]

Recognizing that some social apps had grown too popular and could compete with Facebook's family of products, Facebook cut off their access to Facebook's social graph.[995]

In 2013, Facebook claimed that the short-form video app Vine, a video-sharing app that Twitter acquired in 2012, "replicated Facebook's core News Feed functionality."[996] In response, Facebook cut off Vine's access to Facebook APIs.[997] In doing so, "Facebook was able to degrade consumers'

---

[992] *Id.*

[993] *Id.* at FB_FTC_CID_0008058182 (Sept. 15, 2012).

[994] *Id.* at FB_FTC_CID_00491746–63 (Oct. 27, 2012) (emphasis added); (Elena Botella, *Facebook Earns $132.80 From Your Data per Year*, SLATE (Nov. 15, 2019), https://slate.com/technology/2019/11/facebook-six4three-pikinis-lawsuit-emails-data.html.

[995] Olivia Solon & Cyrus Farivar, *Mark Zuckerberg Leveraged Facebook User Data to Fight Rivals and Help Friends, Leaked Documents Show*, NBC NEWS (Apr. 16, 2019), https://www.nbcnews.com/tech/social-media/mark-zuckerberg-leveraged-facebook-user-data-fight-rivals-help-friends-n994706.

[996] Innovation and Entrepreneurship Hearing at 3 (response to Questions for the Record of Matt Perault, Dir. of Public Pol'y, Facebook), https://docs.house.gov/meetings/JU/JU05/20190716/109793/HHRG-116-JU05-20190716-SD039.pdf.

[997] Rachel Kraus, *Mark Zuckerberg gave the order to kneecap Vine, emails show*, MASHABLE (Dec. 5, 2018), https://mashable.com/article/mark-zuckerberg-helped-thwart-vine/.

experience of Vine and reduce the platform's competitive threat."[998] Twitter shut down Vine in 2016.[999]

Facebook's actions in the wake of Cambridge Analytica, raise concerns about pretextual anticompetitive enforcement in the name of privacy. In 2019, Facebook cut off marketing firm Stackla's access to its APIs "due to data scraping, which violates [Facebook's] policies."[1000] Damien Mahoney, the Chief Executive Officer of Stackla, denied these allegations.[1001] In an interview with the Subcommittee, Mr. Mahoney explained the economic harm of the company's foreclosure from the Facebook Platform:

> What we went through with Facebook was company altering, and if not for the resolve of our team and board, would have destroyed it. We had to lay off half our team. We made huge investments in the company in the previous 12 months, having raised $4m to increase our sales capacity by 160% and other functions in the business, then this occurred. It was a critical blow that almost forced us to close the doors. We were approaching 75 employees and 30% growth after 8 long years of toil. Now we have 26 employees, declining revenue and ongoing collateral damage that we continue to sink time and money into. While we try and stabilize, and get the company back to a position of growth, it's a long way off as we continue, to this very day, deal with the after-effects. The fact this all resulted from a single erroneous and factually incorrect news article, combined with zero consultation from Facebook prior to their damaging actions, remains baffling and completely unfair.[1002]

Around that time, Facebook became aware of MessageMe, a fast-growing app that used Facebook graph data to support its "Find Friends" feature. Recognizing that MessageMe could compete with Facebook Messenger, Facebook's then-director of platform partnerships cut off the app's access to Facebook's Graph API.[1003]

---

[998] Competition & Mkts. Auth. Report at at 141.

[999] Casey Newton, *Why Vine died*, THE VERGE (Oct. 28, 2016), https://www.theverge.com/2016/10/28/13456208/why-vine-died-twitter-shutdown.

[1000] Innovation and Entrepreneurship Hearing at 3 (statement of Matt Perault, Dir. of Public Pol'y, Facebook), https://docs.house.gov/meetings/JU/JU05/20190716/109793/HHRG-116-JU05-Wstate-PeraultM-20190716.pdf.

[1001] Rob Price, *Facebook is reviewing hundreds of its official 'Facebook Marketing Partners' over Instagram data-scraping issues*, BUSINESS INSIDER (Aug. 23, 2019), https://www.businessinsider.com/facebook-review-all-marketing-partners-instagram-data-scraping-2019-8.

[1002] Interview with Damien Mahoney, CEO, Stackla (Apr. 14, 2020).

[1003] Olivia Solon & Cyrus Farivar, *Mark Zuckerberg Leveraged Facebook User Data to Fight Rivals and Help Friends, Leaked Documents Show*, NBC NEWS (Apr. 16, 2019), https://www.nbcnews.com/tech/social-media/mark-zuckerberg-leveraged-facebook-user-data-fight-rivals-help-friends-n994706.

In a submission to the Subcommittee, a former Facebook employee who handled platform management at the company said that Facebook unevenly enforced its platform policies based on the degree of another firm's competition with Facebook and whether it could extract concessions from other firms. According to this former employee, Facebook was primarily concerned with whether a company was "a competitive threat," and it "was biasing its enforcement actions against [firms] they saw as competitors."[1004] In a submission to the Subcommittee, the former Facebook employee provided an example:

> [I]n one Facebook Messages conversation involving the CEO, Mr. Zuckerberg, and various executives in mid-2012, Mr. Zuckerberg expressed concern about an app called Ark that was accessing large amounts of user data in a way that could enable showing user content to people who didn't have permission to see the content. An investigation was conducted, and it was determined that Ark was violating Facebook's platform policies regarding the use of data from friends of Facebook users. Ultimately, leadership decided to terminate Ark's access to Facebook's APIs and ban Ark from the platform for six months. This was a harsh punishment relative to other developers conducting similar activity—indeed, Mr. Zuckerberg had been informed on the thread that "tons" of other apps were acquiring data the same way and there was not further investigation or action taken against those apps. Other apps that had been accused of violating data policies similarly had been treated much more leniently. **It seemed clear that leadership imposed the more severe punishment against Ark because Mr. Zuckerberg viewed Ark as competitive with Facebook, as Facebook was exploring an acquisition of Ark at the same time as it was being investigated for policy violations.**[1005]

In contrast to punishing rivals, according to the former employee and other market participants interviewed by the Subcommittee, Facebook used "whitelists" to give preferential treatment to friends of the company.[1006] For example, in a report published by NBC, Facebook gave Amazon extended API access because Amazon was spending money on advertising and partnering with Facebook on the launch of its Fire smartphone. Facebook's Director of Business Development asked, "Remind me, why did we allow them to do this? Do we receive any cut of purchases?" In response, a Facebook employee who worked with Facebook's "strategic partners" responded, "No, but Amazon is an advertiser and supporting this with advertisement . . . and working with us on deeper integrations for the Fire."[1007]

[1004] Interview with Former Facebook Employee (Jan. 14, 2020).

[1005] Submission from Former Facebook Employee, to H. Comm. on the Judiciary, 2 (Apr. 2, 2020) (on file with Comm.).

[1006] *Id.*

[1007] Olivia Solon & Cyrus Farivar, *Mark Zuckerberg Leveraged Facebook User Data to Fight Rivals and Help Friends, Leaked Documents Show*, NBC NEWS (Apr. 16, 2019), https://www.nbcnews.com/tech/social-media/mark-zuckerberg-leveraged-facebook-user-data-fight-rivals-help-friends-n994706.

In response to these concerns, Facebook told the Subcommittee that it "does not restrict access to its Platform APIs simply because an app competes with a Facebook product or service; but Facebook will restrict apps that violate its policies."[1008] This is, however, inconsistent with the company's internal communications and other evidence examined by the Subcommittee during the investigation.

3. Digital Advertising

a. Overview

Facebook monetizes its platform through the sales of digital advertising.[1009] Facebook garnered over $70 billion in revenue in 2019, a nearly 27% increase from 2018.[1010] It generates this revenue predominately from selling advertisement placements.

Facebook has monopoly power in online advertising in the social networking market.[1011] Notwithstanding Google's dominance, Facebook also has a significant share of revenue and growth in online advertising with many market participants referring to them as duopolies in this broad market. Some market participants interviewed by the Subcommittee consider Facebook "unavoidable" or "must have" due to the reach and scale of its platform. In particular, some businesses consider Facebook's identity product—its ability to persistently track users online and offline conduct to serve tailored ads—as a unique feature.[1012] For example, at the Subcommittee's fifth hearing, David Heinemeier Hansson, the Chief Technology Officer and Cofounder of Basecamp, testified that the nature of Facebook's targeted advertising makes it difficult to replace, saying:

> At Basecamp, we ultimately ended up swearing off the use of targeted advertisement based on the exploitation of personal data. Facebook's record of protecting people's privacy, and gathering their consent in the exploitation of their data for advertisement purposes, is atrocious, and we decided that we wanted no part of it. But choosing to opt out of targeted advertisement on the internet is like competing with one arm behind your back. It is very clear why most companies feel compelled to do this kind of advertisement, even if it's a violation of their ethics. If their competitors are doing it, they're at a significant disadvantage if they don't. And the same is true for us. We have

---

[1008] Innovation and Entrepreneurship Hearing at 3 (response to Questions for the Record of Matt Perault, Dir. of Public Pol'y, Facebook).

[1009] *Transcript of Mark Zuckerberg's Senate hearing*, WASH. POST (Apr. 10, 2018) ("'Senator, we run ads,' Zuckerberg replied."), https://www.washingtonpost.com/news/the-switch/wp/2018/04/10/transcript-of-mark-zuckerbergs-senate-hearing.

[1010] *Id.*

[1011] Competition & Mkts. Auth. Report at 211.

[1012] Competitors Hearing at 10 (statement of David Heinemeier Hansson, Chief Technology Officer and Cofounder, Basecamp).

undoubtedly given up growth to competitors because we've refrained from pursuing targeted ads.[1013]

Facebook's advantages in terms of access to data and its reach contribute to its ability to earn higher revenue per user than other firms in the social networking market.[1014] Facebook reported an average revenue per user (ARPU) of $7.05 worldwide and $36.49 in the United States and Canada in July 2020.[1015] It has also averaged significant annual growth—26% on average over the past five years.[1016] In contrast, its closest competitor, Snap, reported in July 2020 that its ARPU "remained flat" at $1.91 worldwide and $3.48 in North America.[1017] A recent investment report underscored this point, noting that Facebook enjoys a significant economic moat illustrated by the inability of Snap and other firms to meaningfully challenge its dominance.[1018] As a result, entry or success by other firms is unlikely:

> With more users and usage time than any other social network, Facebook provides the largest audience and the most valuable data for social network online advertising. Facebook's ad revenue per user is growing, demonstrating the value that advertisers see in working with the firm . . . Facebook has also expanded its user base in the growing mobile market, which positively affected the network effect as it became more valuable to advertisers, and resulted in more ad revenue growth. The main drivers behind growth in online advertising have been growths in the mobile ad market and the video ad format. Most Facebook users are now accessing Facebook and its apps via mobile devices.[1019]

Facebook's internal documents reinforce this finding. In a presentation prepared to deliver to investors ahead of the company's initial public offering, Facebook characterized its advertising product as having a significant advantage over the industry average in accuracy and narrowly targeted campaigns due to its reach, engagement, and using people's "real identity—people as their real

---

[1013] *Id.*

[1014] Competition & Mkts. Auth. Report at 211.

[1015] FACEBOOK, FACEBOOK Q2 2020 RESULTS (July 31, 2020), https://s21.q4cdn.com/399680738/files/doc_financials/2020/q2/Q2-2020-FB-Earnings-Presentation.pdf.

[1016] MORNINGSTAR EQUITY ANALYST REPORT, FACEBOOK INC 2 (Aug. 3, 2020) ("The value of such data and advertisers' willingness to use it is demonstrated by the 26% average annual growth of Facebook's average ad revenue per user, or ARPU, during the past five years, which we view as indicative of the price that advertisers pay Facebook for ad placement. During the same period, Facebook's monthly average users have grown 12% annually.") (on file with Comm.).

[1017] Snap, Inc., Quarterly Report (Form 10-Q) 25, 27 (June 30, 2020), https://d18rn0p25nwr6d.cloudfront.net/CIK-0001564408/9aacfdca-55a1-4928-9a31-c2462d2386c0.pdf.

[1018] MORNINGSTAR EQUITY ANALYST REPORT, FACEBOOK INC 1–2 (Aug. 3, 2020) (on file with Comm.).

[1019] *Id.*

selves."[1020] In comparison to television broadcasters, the company noted that in the United States, "everyday on Facebook is like the season finale of American idol—the most popular show on TV—times two."[1021]

These findings are also consistent with those of Australian,[1022] British,[1023] French,[1024] and German antitrust authorities, which conducted an extensive examination of Facebook's market power in the social networking market and in digital advertising. For example, the United Kingdom's Competition and Markets Authority (CMA) found in July 2020 that Facebook and Instagram generated over half of display advertising revenues in 2019" in the United Kingdom, which it found to be a relevant market.[1025] In contrast to other firms in the same market, Facebook's lead was significantly larger than its closes competitor, YouTube, which "earned between 5 and 10%."[1026] In June 2019, the Australian Competition and Consumer Commission (ACCC) found that Facebook has "substantial market power in the supply of display advertising in Australia."[1027] Similar to the CMA's findings, the ACCC concluded that the share of the display advertising market controlled by Facebook and Instagram is significant—more than half—and growing, while the rest of the market is highly fragmented.[1028]

b. Relevant Acquisitions

On February 27, 2013, Facebook executed an agreement to purchase Atlas, an advertiser-side platform to manage and measure ad performance, from Microsoft for $100 million.[1029] At the time of the transaction, Atlas captured data to track conversions—when a specific action is taken in response to an ad, such as making a purchase—through clicks and impressions.[1030] In other words, if someone saw a BestBuy ad, Atlas enabled serving the ad, recording the user seeing the ad via a browser identifier, and recorded the impression as well as if the person clicked on the ad. Later, if the same user

---

[1020] Production of Facebook, to H. Comm. on the Judiciary, FB-HJC-ACAL-00054106. (Apr. 9, 2012) (on file with Comm.).

[1021] *Id.*

[1022] Competition & Mkts. Auth. Report at 9.

[1023] *Id.* at 11–12, 211.

[1024] French Autorité de la Concurrence & Bundeskartellamt, Competition Law and Data (2016), https://www.bundeskartellamt.de/SharedDocs/Publikation/DE/Berichte/Big%20Data%20Papier.pdf;jsessionid=D86CD9D1 3899F2590F84E82092187858.2_cid362?__blob=publicationFile&v=2.

[1025] Competition & Mkts. Auth. Report at 10.

[1026] *Id.*

[1027] Austl. Competition & Consumer Comm'n Report at 97.

[1028] *Id.*

[1029] Production of Facebook, to H. Comm. on the Judiciary, FB-HJC-ACAL-00043659 (Mar. 2013) (on file with Comm.).

[1030] *Id.*

bought the item from BestBuy.com, Atlas recognized the user through their browser and would record the conversion if the user purchased the item advertised.

Prior to the acquisition, Amin Zoufonoun, Facebook's Vice President for Corporate Development, described the "primary thesis" of the acquisition to Sherly Sandberg as giving Facebook "immediate scale to retarget, provide premium insights, do look-alike modeling, prove and measure efficacy of [Facebook] as a marketing medium, [and] enhance custom audiences and associated revenue."[1031] Facebook's primary strategic rationale for integrating Atlas into its ad product was to improve its ability to measure ad performance and use identity-based targeting through Facebook Identity—its unique identifier for Facebook users across all browsers and devices—to serve highly targeted ads.[1032] Facebook described the value of Facebook Identity as its ability to "target *people* across browsers and devices" and to "activate offline data to enrich online targeting," among other features.[1033] The company believed that its "unique data" and "unique reach and engagement (across devices and platforms)" would boost its value to advertisers.[1034]

Facebook also noted in its summary of the deal at the time of the transaction that the major opportunities of the transaction were (1) to become the "buy-side desktop tool that media planners fire up first thing in the day;" and (2) to acquire "a deep installed base of pixels which we can immediately turn on to power conversion tracking and attribution of ads across offerings."[1035]

Absent the transaction, Facebook raised concerns that Google's "lead in this market may become insurmountable" and limit Facebook's ads in other ways.[1036] The company also raised concerns that Facebook's Custom Audiences tool would not be able "to scale beyond click-oriented advertisers."[1037] Among other potential risks of the deal, such as rebuilding the product on Facebook's ad stack, the company identified "[m]anaging perceptions around privacy" as an area of concern.[1038]

[1031] *Id.* at FB-HJC-ACAL-00043509 (Oct. 18, 2012) (internal punctuation omitted).

[1032] *Id.* at FB-HJC-ACAL-00043660.

[1033] *Id.* at FB-HJC-ACAL-00043680 (emphasis in original).

[1034] *Id.* at FB-HJC-ACAL-00043705.

[1035] *Id.* at FB-HJC-ACAL-00043710.

[1036] *Id.* at FB-HJC-ACAL-00043660.

[1037] *Id.* at FB-HJC-ACAL-00043697.

[1038] *Id.* at FB-HJC-ACAL-00043658.

B.   Google

1. Overview

Google was launched in 1998 as a general online search engine.[1039] Founded by Larry Page and Sergey Brin, the corporation got its start by serving users web results in response to online queries. Google's key innovation was its PageRank algorithm, which ranked the relevance of a webpage by assessing how many other webpages linked to it.[1040] In contrast with the technology used by rival search engines, PageRank enabled Google to improve the quality of its search results even as the web rapidly grew. While Google had entered a crowded field, by 2000 it had become the world's largest search engine.[1041] Later that year Google launched AdWords, an online advertising service that let businesses purchase keywords advertising to appear on Google's search results page—an offering that would evolve to became the heart of Google's business model.[1042]

Today Google is ubiquitous across the digital economy, serving as the infrastructure for core products and services online. It has grown and maintained its search engine dominance, such that "Googling" something is now synonymous with online search itself. The company is now also the largest provider of digital advertising, a leading web browser, a dominant mobile operating system, and a major provider of digital mapping, email, cloud computing, and voice assistant services, alongside dozens of other offerings. Nine of Google's products—Android, Chrome, Gmail, Google Search, Google Drive, Google Maps, Google Photos, Google Play Store, and YouTube—have more than a billion users each.[1043] Each of these services provides Google with a trove of user data, reinforcing its dominance across markets and driving greater monetization through online ads.

In several markets Google established its position through acquisition, buying up successful technologies that other businesses had developed. In a span of 20 years, Google purchased well over 260 companies—a figure that likely understates the full breadth of Google's acquisitions, given that many of the firm's purchases have gone unreported.[1044] Documents collected by the Subcommittee

---

[1039] Google Inc., Registration Statement (Form S-1) 1 (Apr. 29, 2004), https://www.sec.gov/Archives/edgar/data/1288776/000119312504073639/ds1.htm.

[1040] *Id.* at 65 ("PageRank is a query-independent technique for determining the importance of web pages by looking at the link structure of the web.").

[1041] Press Release, Google Launches World's Largest Search Engine, Google (June 26, 2000), http://googlepress.blogspot.com/2000/06/google-launches-worlds-largest-search.html (stating that Google had indexed over 1 billion webpages).

[1042] Press Release, Google Launches Self-Service Advertising Program, Google (Oct. 23, 2000), http://googlepress.blogspot.com/2000/10/google-launches-self-service.html.

[1043] Harry McCracken, *How Google Photos joined the billion-user club*, FAST CO. (July 24, 2019), https://www.fastcompany.com/90380618/how-google-photos-joined-the-billion-user-club.

[1044] *See infra* Appendix; Leena Rao, *Google Spent Nearly $2 Billion on 79 Acquisitions in 2011*, TECHCRUNCH (Jan. 27, 2012), https://techcrunch.com/2012/01/27/google-spent-nearly-2-billion-on-79-acquisitions-in-2011/ ("As of Q3, Google

reveal that executives recognized as early as 2006 that Google's "tremendous cash resources" could be deployed to help execute Google's "strategic plan."[1045]

Google is now one of the world's largest corporations. For 2019, Google reported total revenues of $160.7 billion—up 45% from 2017—and more than $33 billion in net income.[1046] Although Google has diversified its offerings, it generates the vast majority of its money through digital ads, which accounted for over 83% of Google's revenues in 2019.[1047] Search advertising, in particular, is critical to Google, accounting for approximately 61% of its total sales.[1048] In recent months Google reported a drop in ad revenue due to pandemic-related cuts in spending, though the company partly made up for the decline through revenue growth in Google Cloud, Google Play, and YouTube.[1049] Google has enjoyed strong and steady profits, with profit margins greater than 20% for nine out of the last 10 years, close to three times larger than the average for a U.S. firm.[1050] Financial analysts predict that Google is well positioned to maintain its dominance, noting that "Alphabet has established unusually deep competitive moats around its business."[1051]

In 2015 Google underwent a reorganization, introducing Alphabet as a parent company under which Google would reside as a wholly owned subsidiary.[1052] Alphabet also houses the company's non-search ventures, such as Calico, the biotech company focused on longevity, and Waymo, which develops self-driving cars.[1053] In December 2019, Page and Brin stepped down from their management

---

had spent over $1.4 billion on 55 acquisitions for the year. Google ended 2011 spending $1.9 billion (including cash and stock) on completing 79 acquisitions during the entirety of the year.").

[1045] Production of Google, to H. Comm. on the Judiciary, GOOG-HJC-04232284 at 2 (Sept. 25, 2006) (on file with Comm.) (stating that Google viewed transactions as falling into three categories: (1) bolt-on; (2) outside existing efforts; and (3) around existing efforts).

[1046] Alphabet Inc., Annual Report (Form 10-K) 26–30 (Feb. 3., 2020), https://www.sec.gov/Archives/edgar/data/1652044/000165204420000008/goog10-k2019.htm.

[1047] *Id.* at 30.

[1048] *Id.*

[1049] Alphabet Inc., Quarterly Report (Form 10-Q) (June 30, 2020) https://abc.xyz/investor/static/pdf/20200731_alphabet_10Q.pdf?cache=f16f989; *Alphabet Q2 Earnings Call* (July 30, 2020), https://abc.xyz/investor/static/pdf/2020_Q2_Earnings_Transcript.pdf?cache=6bfce23.

[1050] Alphabet Inc., Quarterly Report (Form 10-K) (2009–2019)

[1051] Marc S.F. Mahaney, *Digging For Buried Treasure – The Google Maps Opportunity*, ROYAL BANK OF CANADA 2 (Sept. 23, 2019) (on file with Comm.).

[1052] Letter from Larry Page, CEO, Alphabet, and Sundar Pichai, CEO, Google (2015), https://abc.xyz/investor/founders-letters/2015/index.html#2015-larry-alphabet-letter.

[1053] *Id.*

roles at Alphabet, though they remain on the board and together control approximately 51.3% of the voting power.[1054] Sundar Pichai now serves as the CEO of both Google and Alphabet.[1055]

For years Google has been the subject of antitrust investigations and enforcement actions around the world. From 2011 to 2013, the Federal Trade Commission investigated Google's role in search and advertising markets, culminating in a staff recommendation to file a complaint against Google—although the Commission ultimately decided not to do so. At various points over the last decade, Mississippi, Missouri, and Texas have each separately investigated Google for antitrust violations, and, in September 2019, attorneys general from 50 U.S. states and territories announced that they were opening a fresh antitrust inquiry into the search and advertising giant.[1056] The Department of Justice has also been investigating Google since the summer of 2019, and recent news reports state that a lawsuit may be imminent.[1057] These ongoing U.S. investigations follow multiple antitrust inquiries worldwide, as well as antitrust-related penalties levied on Google by the European Commission, France, India, and Russia.[1058]

2. Search

a. Market Power

Google overwhelmingly dominates the market for general online search. Publicly available data suggest the firm captures over 87% of U.S. search and over 92% of queries worldwide.[1059] Despite

---

[1054] Alphabet Inc., Quarterly Report (Form 10-Q) 60 (June 30, 2020) https://abc.xyz/investor/static/pdf/20200731_alphabet_10Q.pdf?cache=f16f989 ("The concentration of our stock ownership limits our stockholders' ability to influence corporate matters… Through their stock ownership, Larry and Sergey have significant influence over all matters requiring stockholder approval, including the election of directors and significant corporate transactions, such as a merger or other sale of our company or our assets, for the foreseeable future.").

[1055] Letter from Larry Page, CEO, Alphabet, and Sundar Pichai, CEO, Google (2015), https://abc.xyz/investor/founders-letters/2015/index.html#2015-larry-alphabet-letter.

[1056] Tony Romm, *50 US states and territories announce broad antitrust investigation of Google*, WASH. POST (Sept. 9, 2019), https://www.washingtonpost.com/technology/2019/09/09/states-us-territories-announce-broad-antitrust-investigation-google/.

[1057] Alphabet Inc., Annual Report (Form 10-Q) (July 30, 2020), https://abc.xyz/investor/static/pdf/20200731_alphabet_10Q.pdf?cache=f16f989; Leah Nylen, *Trump administration to launch antitrust suit against Google as soon as next week*, POLITICO (Oct. 2, 2020), https://www.politico.com/news/2020/10/02/trump-doj-google-antitrust-lawsuit-425617.

[1058] Aditya Kalra and Aditi Shah, *Exclusive: Google faces antitrust case in India over payments app – sources*, REUTERS (May 27, 2020), https://www.reuters.com/article/us-india-google-antitrust-exclusive/exclusive-google-faces-antitrust-case-in-india-over-pagos-app-sources-idUSKBN2331G3; Thomas Grove, *Russia Fines Google $6.75 Million in Antitrust Case*, WALL ST. J. (Aug. 11, 2016), https://www.wsj.com/articles/russia-fines-google-6-75-million-in-antitrust-case-1470920410; Charles Riley and Ivana Kottasová, *Europe hits Google with a third, $1.7 billion antitrust fine*, CNN (Mar. 20, 2019), https://www.cnn.com/2019/03/20/tech/google-eu-antitrust/index.html; Natasha Lomas, *France slaps Google with $166M antitrust fine for opaque and inconsistent ad rules*, TECHCRUNCH (Dec. 20, 2019) https://techcrunch.com/2019/12/20/france-slaps-google-with-166m-antitrust-fine-for-opaque-and-inconsistent-ad-rules/.

[1059] *Search Engine Market Share Worldwide*, STATCOUNTER, https://gs.statcounter.com/search-engine-market-share (last visited Sept. 29, 2020).

notable changes in the market—such as the switch from desktop to mobile—Google has maintained this dominance for more than a decade, a period during which its lead over its most significant competitors has only increased.[1060] Over that time, Google benefited from economies of scale and the self-reinforcing advantages of data, as well as from aggressive business tactics that Google wielded at key moments to thwart competition. The combined result is that Google now enjoys durable monopoly power in the market for general online search.

Several factors render Google's power in online search generally immune to competition or threat of entry. General online search strongly favors scale due to (1) the high fixed costs of servers needed for crawling and indexing the entire web, and (2) the self-reinforcing advantages of click-and-query data, which let a search engine constantly improve the relevance of search results. Even an upstart that was able to secure the necessary capital to invest heavily in computing infrastructure would find itself at a considerable disadvantage given that Google's search algorithm has been refined through trillions upon trillions of queries.[1061] Meanwhile, steps that website owners take to block non-Google crawlers has rendered the task of creating an independent comprehensive index extremely challenging, if not effectively impossible.

Even search engines that choose to syndicate their search results rather than create their own index and algorithm face major obstacles. This is primarily because Google—through both integration and contractual agreements—has established itself as the default search provider on 87% of desktop browsers and the vast majority of mobile devices. Specifically, Google used its search dominance to promote the use of its Chrome browser on laptops, personal computers, and workstations, which sets Google Search as its default. For mobile devices, Google imposed a set of restrictive contractual terms effectively requiring manufacturers of devices that used its Android operating system to pre-install both Chrome and Google Search. Additionally, Google pays Apple an undisclosed amount, estimated

---

[1060] Enforcers and courts have held that Google dominates the market for online search in various cases stretching back over a decade. *See, e.g.*, Press Release, U.S. Dep't of Justice, Yahoo! Inc. and Google Inc. Abandon Their Advertising Agreement (Nov. 5, 2008), https://www.justice.gov/archive/opa/pr/2008/November/08-at-981.html ("The Department's investigation revealed that Internet search advertising and Internet search syndication are each relevant antitrust markets and that Google is by far the largest provider of such services, with shares of more than 70 percent in both markets."); Press Release, U.S. Dep't of Justice, Statement of the Department of Justice Antitrust Division on Its Decision to Close Its Investigation of the Internet Search and Paid Search Advertising Agreement Between Microsoft Corporation and Yahoo! Inc. (Feb. 18, 2010), https://www.justice.gov/opa/pr/statement-department-justice-antitrust-division-its-decision-close-its-investigation-internet ("The proposed transaction will combine the back-end search and paid search advertising technology of both parties. U.S. market participants express support for the transaction and believe that combining the parties' technology would be likely to increase competition by creating a more viable competitive alternative to Google, the firm that now dominates these markets."); Author's Guild v. Google, No. 05 Civ. 8136 (DC), 2011 WL 986049, *12 (S.D.N.Y. Mar. 22, 2011) (recognizing "Google's market power in the online search market").

[1061] *See* Innovation and Entrepreneurship Hearing at 1 (response to Questions for the Record of Adam Cohen, Dir. of Econ. Pol'y, Google LLC) ("Google Search responds to trillions of user queries from around the world every year."); *see also* MAURICE E. STUCKE & ALLEN P. GRUNES, BIG DATA AND COMPETITION POLICY 12.10 (2016) ("Entry barriers into the search engine market are already high. Microsoft reportedly invested in 2010 'more than $4.5 billion into developing its algorithm and building the physical capacity necessary to operate Bing.").

to be $12 billion per year, to secure the search default across iOS devices.[1062] In general, users tend to stick with the default presented.[1063] Moreover, Google takes steps to hamper and dissuade even those users that do attempt to switch search engines on Chrome.[1064] Combined, Google's conduct significantly impedes other search providers from reaching users at scale—and further expands and entrenches Google's dominance.

In submissions to the Committee, Google states that Google Search "operates in a highly competitive environment," facing a "vast array of competitors" in general online search, including Bing, DuckDuckGo, and Yahoo!.[1065] Google also claims that for any given search query, Google competes against a "wide range of companies," including Amazon, eBay, Kayak, and Yelp.[1066] Google argues that this broader set of competitors means that public estimates of its share of general online search "do not capture the full extent of Google's competition in search."[1067]

Despite these statements, Google failed to provide the Subcommittee with contemporary market share data that would corroborate its claims. In response to the Committee's written request for market share data, combined with several follow-ups from Subcommittee staff, Google stated that the company "doesn't maintain information in the normal course of business about market share in its products."[1068] After the Subcommittee identified communications where Google executives had discussed regularly tracking search market share data and further developing internal tools for doing so, Google told the Subcommittee that this data is either no longer collected or no longer used for examining site traffic.[1069] It added, "[W]hile Google may have examined certain 'shares' of usage,

---

[1062] Lisa Marie Segarra, *Google to Pay Apple $12 Billion to Remain Safari's Default Search Engine in 2019: Report*, FORTUNE (Sept. 29, 2018), https://fortune.com/2018/09/29/google-apple-safari-search-engine/.

[1063] Competition & Mkts. Auth. Report at 194.

[1064] *See, e.g.*, Submission from Source 481 to H. Comm. on the Judiciary (Jan. 30, 2020) (on file with Comm.).

[1065] Production of Google, to H. Comm. on the Judiciary, A-11 (Nov. 22, 2019) (on file with Comm.).

[1066] *Id.*; *see also* Innovation and Entrepreneurship Hearing at 6 (statement of Adam Cohen, Dir. of Econ. Pol'y, Google LLC). Although the specialized search providers that Google lists as competitors may, in some instances, compete with Google for queries, "[t]he competition between Google and vertical search engines" is "to some extent asymmetrical. From a user's point of view, a generalist search engine that fully covers a given vertical can be a complete substitute for the vertical search engine, while the reverse is not generally true. Consequently, Google imposes more significant competitive constraints on a vertical search engine than vice versa." *See* Submission from Source 209, to H. Comm. on the Judiciary, Source 209-0000540 (Feb. 17, 2011) (on file with Comm.).

[1067] Production of Google, to H. Comm. on the Judiciary, A-11 (Nov. 22, 2019) (on file with Comm.). In certain regards, Google's argument echoes the claim Microsoft made when it contested the district court's decision to exclude "middleware" from its definition of the relevant market. The court found that although it was true that middleware could "usurp the operating system's platform function and might eventually take over other operating system functions," it was also true that no middleware product "could now, or would soon, expose enough APIs to serve as a platform for popular applications, much less take over all operating system functions." United States v. Microsoft Corp., 253 F.3d 34, 53-54 (D.C.C. 2001). Similarly, although certain vertical search providers could under certain circumstances "usurp" the horizontal provider's platform function, no vertical provider does or would soon serve this function.

[1068] Meeting with Google (Feb. 10, 2020).

[1069] Production of Google, to H. Comm. on the Judiciary, GOOG-HJC-01967913 (Jan. 27, 2007) (on file with Comm.) ("Each quarter we gather comprehensive search and market share data even though we NOT share it with the board

clicks, queries, or traffic in limited and incomplete data sets over time, we do not believe any of this constitutes 'market share' analysis."[1070]

Market share information that Google did provide from over a decade ago reveals that Google viewed itself as a leader in general search as early as 2007. One slide deck tracking search query volume and revenues stated that "[c]ontinued leadership in search underpins the whole business."[1071] In 2009, a top executive circulated market share analysis documenting that Google captured 71.5% of general search in the United States, followed by Yahoo with 17%, and Bing with 7.5%.[1072] And in 2010, one Google employee observed, "Google leads competitors. This is our bread-and-butter. Our long-tail precision is why users continue to come to Google. Users may try the bells and whistles of Bing and other competitors, but Google still produces the best results."[1073] Noting that Bing was "making clear, significant progress" on "bringing the two search engines closer to parity," the employee stated it was "critical to redouble our efforts to maintain our lead."[1074]

The Subcommittee has not seen any compelling evidence to suggest that Google's dominance over the last decade has diminished; to the contrary, there is compelling evidence that Google has only strengthened and solidified what was already a leading market position. For example, in 2009 Microsoft and Yahoo!—Google's closest competitors—entered an agreement to integrate their search platforms, an effort to team up to tackle Google's dominance.[1075] A decade later, the two collectively have a lower share of the general search market than they did at the time of their deal, whereas Google's share has increased.[1076] As of 2016, Google employees were calculating that Bing had suffered a 30% year-over-year decline in query volume and that Bing's revenue per million impressions (RPM) was "70-77% lower" than Google's own U.S. search RPM.[1077] More recently, the United Kingdom's Competition and Markets Authority found that Google's index of the web is

---

anymore. I am pleased to say that we've finally turned the corner on getting decent data of our own rather than ComScore....Next steps include further work on internal sources such as the toolbar and AFC referrals which we believe will give us more data to model and help us adjust for the biases of external sources."); GOOG-HJC-01529590 (Oct. 11, 2011) (listing "internal US search share metrics" for Q2 2011); Email from Google to Committee Staff (Apr. 16, 2020) (on file with Comm.).

[1070] Email from Google to Committee Staff (Apr. 16, 2020) (on file with Comm.).

[1071] Production of Google, to H. Comm. on the Judiciary, GOOG-HJC-04231168 at 2 (on file with Comm.).

[1072] Production of Google, to H. Comm. on the Judiciary, GOOG-HJC-01207063 (Oct. 27, 2009) (on file with Comm.) (attachment to email from Marissa Mayer).

[1073] Production of Google, to H. Comm. on the Judiciary, GOOG-HJC-03815864 (Apr. 23, 2010) (on file with Comm.).

[1074] *Id.*

[1075] Submission from Source 209, to H. Comm. on the Judiciary, Source 209-0000346 at 351–52 (Aug. 24, 2009) (on file with Comm.).

[1076] *Search Engine Market Share Worldwide*, STATCOUNTER, https://gs.statcounter.com/search-engine-market-share (last visited Sept. 29, 2020).

[1077] Production of Google, to H. Comm. on the Judiciary, GOOG-HJC-04259758–59 (Apr. 20, 2016) (on file with Comm.).

anywhere from three- to five-times the size of Bing's.[1078] Furthermore, the fact that no new general search entrant over the last decade has ever accounted for more than 1% of all U.S. searches in any given year further confirms that Google's monopoly power is durable and its lead insurmountable.[1079]

Google's claim that it "operates in a highly competitive environment" is also at odds with the lived reality of market participants. Numerous companies—spanning major public corporations, small businesses, and upstart entrepreneurs—told the Subcommittee that they overwhelmingly depend on Google for traffic, and that no alternate search engine even remotely approaches serving as a substitute. For example, J&J Smith, a printer repair shop based in Rhode Island, stated, "Google is our lifeblood."[1080] Foundem, a UK-based comparison shopping search provider, has noted that Google's "overwhelming global dominance" of horizontal search creates for most websites an "uncomfortable but unavoidable reliance on Google."[1081] Many other companies described their dependence on Google in similar terms.

Furthermore, some of the same specialized search providers that Google identifies as competitors stated that their own businesses heavily rely on Google, in some cases for up to 80% of traffic on both desktop and mobile devices.[1082] One specialized search provider wrote that Google's business practices "have a very material effect on [our] business, but due to Google's monopoly power in search, there is nowhere else for [us] to turn for additional search traffic. The company is beholden to how Google decides to structure its search results page and algorithm."[1083] Another told the Subcommittee, "From [our] perspective, there are no adequate substitutes for Google,"[1084] and, "[T]hanks to its monopoly in general internet search, Google has become the gatekeeper for vertical search rivals."[1085] One specialized search provider said that 97.6% of its traffic comes from Google; another said that Google accounted for such an outsized share of traffic that "we don't even track non-Google sources."[1086]

At the Subcommittee's field hearing in January 2020, David Heinemeier Hansson, chief technology officer and co-founder of Basecamp, testified that Google increasingly functions as "the

---

[1078] Competition & Mkts. Auth. Report at 89.

[1079] Submission from Source 115, to H. Comm. on the Judiciary, 6 (Oct. 22, 2019) (on file with Comm.).

[1080] Interview with J&J Smith (Aug. 24, 2020).

[1081] Submission from Foundem, to H. Comm. on the Judiciary, 4 (Jan. 21, 2018) (on file with Comm.).

[1082] Submission from Source 564, to H. Comm. on the Judiciary, 5 (Nov. 13, 2019) (on file with Comm.); Submission from Source 3, to H. Comm. on the Judiciary, 34 (Nov. 22, 2019) (on file with Comm.).

[1083] Submission from Source 887, to H. Comm. on the Judiciary, 4 (Oct. 28, 2019) (on file with Comm.).

[1084] Submission from Source 626, to H. Comm. on the Judiciary, 2 (Oct. 15, 2019) (on file with Comm.).

[1085] Submission from Source 972, to H. Comm. on the Judiciary, 10 (Dec. 9, 2019) (on file with Comm.).

[1086] Interview with Source 147 (June 26, 2019).

front door of the internet."[1087] He noted, "[Google is] the start page for millions. It's a form of navigation around the internet. People these days rarely bother to remember the specific internet address of a company they want to do business with, they just google it."[1088] Commenting on the stark asymmetry in the general search market, Hansson stated that Yahoo, Bing, and DuckDuckGo all "could drop [Basecamp] from their listings tomorrow and we'd barely notice," but "[w]e lose our listing in Google and we may go out of business."[1089]

Google obtained default placement across the mobile and desktop ecosystem through both integration and contractual arrangements. Through owning Android, the world's dominant mobile operating system, Google was able to ensure that Google Search remained dominant even as mobile replaced desktop as the critical entry point to the Internet. As discussed elsewhere in the Report, documents submitted to the Subcommittee show that, at certain key moments, Google conditioned access to the Google Play Store on exclusively pre-installing Google Search, a requirement that gave Google a significant advantage over competing search engines. Through revenue-sharing agreements amounting to billions of dollars in annual payments, Google also established default positions on Apple's Safari browser (on both desktop and mobile) and on Mozilla's Firefox.[1090]

In public statements Google has downplayed the significance of default placement, claiming that "competition is just a click away."[1091] However Google's internal documents show that, at a time when Google was still jostling for search market share, Google executives closely tracked search defaults on Microsoft's Internet Explorer and expressed concern that non-Google defaults could impede Google Search.[1092] In an internal presentation about Internet Explorer's default search selection, Google recommended that users be given an initial opportunity to select a search engine and that browsers minimize the steps required to change the default search provider.[1093] These discussions, as well as the steep sums Google pays Apple and various browsers for default search placement, further highlight the competitive significance of default positions.

[1087] Competitors Hearing at 3 (statement of David Heinemeier Hansson, Chief Technology Officer and Cofounder, Basecamp).

[1088] *Id.*

[1089] *Id.*

[1090] Innovation and Entrepreneurship Hearing at 12 (response to Questions for the record by Kyle Andeer, Vice President, Corporate Law, Apple, Inc.).

[1091] *See, e.g.*, Adam Kovacevich, *Google's approach to competition*, GOOGLE PUBLIC POL'Y BLOG (May 8, 2009), https://publicpolicy.googleblog.com/2009/05/googles-approach-to-competition.html.

[1092] *See, e.g.*, Production of Google, to H. Comm. on the Judiciary, GOOG-HJC-01196214 (May 3, 2005) (on file with Comm.).

[1093] Production of Google, to H. Comm. on the Judiciary, GOOG-HJC-01680749 (2006) (on file with Comm.) (identifying several recommendations, including "Fewest clicks required to change default, which promotes search innovation by facilitating the user's ability to switch.").

Independent search engines told the Subcommittee that the lack of defaults available to them creates significant business challenges. DuckDuckGo said this lack of options compelled it to invest in browser technology, including the creation of its own browser for Android and iOS and various browser extensions.[1094] It noted, however, that "the same default placement challenges exist in the browser market, just one level up – with the device makers requiring millions or billions of dollars to become a default browser on a device."[1095]

Lastly, the Subcommittee's findings are consistent with conclusions reached by several enforcement bodies that recently have investigated Google's market dominance. For example, in July 2020 the United Kingdom's Competition and Markets Authority found that "Google has significant market power in the general search sector," a position maintained through "three key barriers to entry: economies of scale in developing a web index; access to click-and-query data at scale; and Google's extensive default positions."[1096] In July 2019, the Australian Competition and Consumer Commission (ACCC) found that Google has "substantial market power in supplying general search services," and that it is "likely to retain its dominant share of the market at least in the short- to medium-term."[1097] And in two separate enforcement actions in 2017 and 2018, the European Commission found that Google possessed market power in the market for online general search.[1098] While each of these enforcers focused on their respective national and regional markets, Google has failed to identify any factors that would compel the Subcommittee to reach a different conclusion for the U.S. market.

b.   Conduct

i.   Google Leverages Dominance Through Data Misappropriation and Self-Preferencing

When Google launched in 1998, the search listings it delivered were "ten blue links," or a set of organic results that guided users off Google's webpage to locate relevant information. In the years

---

[1094] Innovation and Entrepreneurship Hearing at 5 (statement of Megan Gray, Gen. Counsel and Pol'y Advocate, DuckDuckGo).

[1095] *Id.* at 5.

[1096] Competition & Mkts. Auth. Report at 73.

[1097] Austl. Competition & Consumer Comm'n Report at 58.

[1098] *Google Search (Shopping)* (Case AT.39740) Comm'n Decision of 27/6/2017 [2017], para. 271, https://ec.europa.eu/competition/antitrust/cases/dec_docs/39740/39740_14996_3.pdf [hereinafter Google Search (Shopping) Comm'n Decision] ("The Commission concludes that Google holds a dominant position in each national market for general search services since 2008, apart from in the Czech Republic, where Google holds a dominant position since 2011."); *Google Android* (Case AT.40099) Comm'n Decision of 18/7/2018 [2018], paras. 439, https://ec.europa.eu/competition/antitrust/cases/dec_docs/40099/40099_9993_3.pdf [hereinafter "Google Android Comm'n Decision"] ("[T]he Commission concludes that Google holds a dominant position in the following relevant markets since 2011: . . . (3) each national market for general search services in the EEA.").

since, Google, as well as Bing, has evolved to displaying blue links alongside a variety of Google's own content as well as "information boxes" that list responses directly on the search results page.

While this model may, in certain instances, provide users with direct information more quickly, documents collected by the Subcommittee show that Google built some of these features through aggressive tactics that exploited its search dominance. Google's conduct helped maintain its monopoly in online search and search advertising, while dissuading investment in nascent competitors, undermining innovation, and harming users and businesses alike.

According to internal documents, Google executives recognized as early as 2005 that specialized—or "vertical"—search engines could pose a threat to Google's long-term dominance. That year one program manager wrote:

[W]hat is the real threat if we don't execute on verticals?
(a) loss of traffic from google.com because folks search elsewhere for some queries
(b) related revenue loss for high spend verticals like travel
(c) missing [opportunity] if someone else creates the platform to build verticals
(d) if one of our big competitors builds a constellation of high quality verticals, we are hurt badly[1099]

Google's apprehension about vertical search providers persisted. For example, a 2006 strategy memo identifying challenges asked, "How do we deal with the problem of 'proliferating verticals?'"[1100] Another message noted, "Vertical search is of tremendous strategic importance to Google. Otherwise the risk is that Google is the go-to place for finding information only in the cases where there is sufficiently low monetization potential that no niche vertical search competitor has filled the space with a better alternative."[1101] In short, Google executives feared that vertical search providers would build direct relationships with users, thereby bypassing Google Search and diverting traffic, valuable data, and ad revenue. While vertical search providers were complements to Google in the short term, Google recognized their potential for disintermediating Google and therefore viewed them as a major competitive threat. The fact that several of these verticals specialized in commercial queries that were among the most valuable for Google further raised the stakes.[1102]

Documents show that Google developed a multi-pronged strategy to thwart the threat. Two of these tactics included: (1) misappropriating third-party content, and (2) privileging Google's own services while demoting those of third parties. Through these practices, Google exploited its dominance to weaken potential rivals and boost its search advertising revenue.

[1099] Production of Google, to H. Comm. on the Judiciary, GOOG-HJC-04137557 (Nov. 29, 2005) (on file with Comm.).

[1100] *Id.* at GOOG-HJC-01099230 (Oct. 20, 2006).

[1101] *Id.* at GOOG-HJC-03815865. (Apr. 23, 2010).

[1102] *Id.* at GOOG-HJC-04276684–87 (Sept. 21, 2012).

1) Misappropriating Third-Party Content

In the years following 2005, Google invested in building out its own vertical services. Documents reveal that Google partly did so through lifting content directly from third-party providers to bootstrap Google's own vertical services. In the process, Google leveraged its search dominance—demanding that third parties permit Google to take their content, or else be removed from Google's search results entirely.

For example, after identifying local search as a "particularly important" vertical to develop, Google built Google Local, which licensed content from local providers, including Yelp.[1103] In 2010 Google rolled out a service directly competing with Yelp, even as Google continued to license Yelp's content—prompting Yelp's CEO to request that Google immediately remove Yelp's proprietary content from Google's own service.[1104] At a time when Google Local was failing to gain momentum, Google told Yelp that the only way to have its content removed from Google's competing product was to be removed from Google's general results entirely.[1105] Yelp relied so heavily on Google for user traffic that the company could not afford to be delisted—a fact that Google likely knew.[1106] In short, Google weaponized its search dominance, demanding that Yelp surrender valuable content to Google's competing product or else risk heavy losses in traffic and revenue.

Evidence gathered by the Subcommittee identifies additional instances in which Google has intercepted traffic from third-party websites by forcibly scraping their content and placing it directly on Google's own site. For example, a submission from entrepreneur Brian Warner described how he built

---

[1103] *Id.* at GOOG-HJC-03665122–26 (Apr. 24, 2007) (internal Google discussion noting the strength of Yelp's local product) ("[T]here is nothing else 'yelp like' in our current lineup," and also noting that "[Yelp's CEO] just contacted the account manager here and asked that their contract be revised so that they could cancel it immediately if we launch reviews, that doesn't mean that they would do it, but clearly this is a big deal to them.").

[1104] *Id.* at GOOG-HJC-03249494 (Aug. 10, 2010) ("Given that this App directly competes with the Yelp App and offers little value to Yelp we cannot allow Google to continue leveraging our content in this way. We've communicated to Patrick and Carter that your team needs to remove our content within the next week. Since you already communicated to me that it would be un-Googley to not remove our content when requested, I'm confident your team will do the right thing.").

[1105] *See, e.g., id.* at GOOG-HJC-03255279 (Oct. 28, 2010) ("[I] want to tell you that my feelings are really hurt by the 'local is a failure' stuff that Nikesh has been lobbing around"); GOOG-HJC-03790807–08 (Apr. 24, 2007) ("[W]e are still waiting to be removed from Places (while remaining in organic and local merge results), which you initially agreed to (but more recently pulled away from)."); GOOG-HJC-01234494–96 (Aug. 10, 2011) ("I was surprised to find that by opting out of Google's local product, Yelp was automatically opted out of portions of Google's search results. Carter Maslan and John Hanke last year said they couldn't/wouldn't remove Yelp content from Google's local product because local was powered by the same index as web search, sounds like this was never really the case."); *see id.* ("To be able to reference Yelp's content in the parts of search results we discussed, our local service needs to be at least aware of the existence of Yelp pages. Since we stopped using any crawled Yelp pages for our local services in response to your request, this currently isn't possible. That said, I think that the approach we discussed, with Google making limited use of Yelp data in the ways you described, is a constructive way to get a comprehensive view for our users.").

[1106] *See, e.g., id.* at GOOG-HJC-03664462 (Apr. 23, 2007) ("78% of their uniques come from google. if they are acquired, i [sic] would assume that they wouldn't turn us off.").

a database from scratch and developed it into a sustainable and growing business—only to watch Google lift his content and sink his traffic.[1107] Warner, the founder of Celebrity Net Worth, told the Subcommittee that in 2012 the content he had initially developed as a side-project had such high demand that Warner was able to quit his day job and hire 12 staff members. In 2014 Google contacted Warner to ask if he would provide Google with an API that would display his webpage's content in an "answer box" that would appear directly on Google's search results page. Warner declined, observing that handing over his company's "most valuable asset" would "cause a catastrophic drop in traffic."[1108] Within two years, Google began populating its answer boxes with Celebrity Net Worth's content anyway—displaying net worth results for each of the 25,000+ celebrities from Warner's database directly on Google's search results page.[1109]

Combined with changes that pushed Warner's webpage from the top of organic listings to the middle of the second page, Google's scraping caused traffic to Celebrity Net Worth to drop by 50% overnight.[1110] Warner wrote, "With the flip of a switch, Google turned our original content into its own content. And with that move, Google would keep the searcher within its walled garden indefinitely. That is far more valuable to Google than taking a small cut of our AdSense revenue."[1111] Today Celebrity Net Worth's traffic is down 80% from 2014, and—due to the resulting drop in revenue—Warner has had to lay off half of his staff.[1112]

In a submission to the Subcommittee, lyrics site Genius described similar misappropriation by Google. Genius noted that it has invested "a decade and millions of dollars" developing a lyrics repository that relies on user-generated content as well as partnerships with songwriters.[1113] For years, however, Google has copied lyrics from Genius's website and displayed them in information boxes that it places at the top of its search results page.[1114] Although Genius shared with Google evidence showing that the platform was scraping lyrics directly from Genius, Google for two years "did nothing to address the issue."[1115] It was only after the *Wall Street Journal* published Genius's claims that Google responded, taking steps to remove the evidence that Google had copied the lyrics but leaving the lyrics in place.[1116] Google later announced that it would attribute lyrics placed in the information

---

[1107] *See generally* Innovation and Entrepreneurship Hearing (statement of Brian Warner, Founder, Celeb. Net Worth).

[1108] *Id.* at 4.

[1109] *Id.* Because Warner had added several conjured celebrities to his site to gauge whether Google was scraping his content or lifting it from elsewhere, he was able to determine that Google was sourcing its answers directly from Celebrity Net Worth.

[1110] *Id.* at 5.

[1111] *Id.*

[1112] *Id.*

[1113] Innovation and Entrepreneurship Hearing at 1 (statement from Ben Gross, Chief Strategy Officer, Genius).

[1114] *Id.* at 2.

[1115] *Id.*

[1116] *Id.*

box to the underlying content provider. "This would be encouraging," Genius wrote, "except for the fact that all of the lyrics we flagged for Google as featuring our watermark—and thus clearly copied from Genius—are currently attributed to another company."[1117]

At the Subcommittee's hearing on July 29, 2020, multiple members questioned Mr. Pichai about Google's misappropriation of third-party content. Subcommittee Chairman David Cicilline (D-RI) recounted Google's scraping of Celebrity Net Worth, asking, "[W]hy does Google steal content from honest businesses?"[1118] Mr. Pichai responded that he "disagree[d] with that categorization." Representative Ken Buck (R-CO) followed up by noting that Genius seemed to have collected clear evidence of Google's misappropriation:

> When Genius suspected this corporate theft was occurring, the company incorporated a digital watermark in its lyrics that spelled out red-handed in Morse code. Google's lyric boxes contained the watermark showing that your company stole what you couldn't or didn't want to produce yourself. After Google executives stated that they were investigating this problematic behavior, Genius created another experiment to determine the scope of the misappropriation. It turns out that, out of 271 songs where the watermark was applied, 43 percent showed clear evidence of matching. Your company, which advertises itself as a doorway to freedom, took advantage of this small company, all but extinguishing Genius' freedom to compete."[1119]

Mr. Pichai responded that Google "license[s] content from other companies," and that this issue was "a dispute between Genius and other companies in terms of where the source of the content is."[1120] In its response to Questions for the Record from the Subcommittee, Google also stated that it now gives webpage owners the ability to exclude certain content from appearing in information boxes on Google's search results page.[1121] However, multiple webpage publishers stated that, in practice, this option fails to mitigate the harm given that Google will continue to source and display content from others, thereby still intercepting traffic and displacing organic listings. One publisher described Google's claim to give webpage owners more control as "an empty offering."[1122]

[1117] *Id.*

[1118] CEO Hearing Transcript at 36 (question of Rep. David N. Cicilline (D-RI), Chairman, Subcomm. on Antitrust, Commercial and Admin Law).

[1119] *Id.* at 48–49 (Rep. Ken Buck (R-CO), Member, Subcomm. on Antitrust, Commercial and Admin. Law).

[1120] *Id.* at 49.

[1121] Innovation and Entrepreneurship Hearing at 8 (response to Questions for the Record of Adam Cohen, Dir. of Econ. Pol'y, Google LLC) (Sept. 13, 2019).

[1122] Interview with Source 489 (Sept. 19, 2020).

In an interview with Subcommittee staff, one webpage owner stated that he felt deceived by Google's decision to use its crawling advantages to misappropriate third-party content. The webpage owner said:

> A major violation occurred when Google used robotic information scraped by its crawler to create content of its own which is displayed in the search result page. We never would have created sitemaps for Google if those were the terms. Google wouldn't have had sitemaps from every website on earth feeding it content if those were the terms from the beginning. They would have been forced to create a new system in order to convince sites to comply or a new search service would have been born that had different options.[1123]

Google's practice of misappropriating third-party content to bootstrap its own rival search services and to keep users on Google's own webpage is further evidence of its monopoly power and an example of how Google has abused that power. Google seized value from third-party businesses without their consent. These businesses had no effective choice but to allow Google's misappropriation to continue, given Google's search dominance. In this way, Google leveraged its search dominance to misappropriate third-party content, free-riding on others' investments and innovations.

2) Self-Preferencing

Evidence shows that once Google built out its vertical offerings, it introduced various changes that had the effect of privileging Google's own inferior services while demoting competitors' offerings. This conduct has undermined the vertical search providers that Google viewed as a threat. It has also boosted Google's ad revenue by keeping users on Google's domains for longer and by compelling demoted firms to pay Google more ad fees to reach users.

In 2007 Google introduced "Universal Search," which presented users with search results that integrated Google's various specialized search services, including Google Images, Google Local, and Google News.[1124] Universal Search was designed to improve users' search experience, as well as to increase traffic to Google's own offerings—even when those offerings weren't the best or most relevant for users.[1125] Google's documents suggest that shortly after launching Universal Search, traffic

---

[1123] *Id.*

[1124] Production of Google, to H. Comm. on the Judiciary, GOOG-HJC-01230600 (Dec. 8, 2004) (on file with Comm.) ("Googlers have long argued for some type of 'universal' search that integrates all of Google's indices, including those that contain different media, like Images, and those that contain structured data, like Local and Froogle"); GOOG-HJC-03815864–65 (Apr. 23, 2010) (noting that universal search marked a shift to "increase our ability to provide new types of media in search results").

[1125] *Id.* at GOOG-HJC-02734893 (Dec. 15, 2006) (introducing Universal Search to help solve the problem that "Google search user experience has been internally and externally perceived as stagnant for the last 7 years").

to Google's own vertical services increased.[1126] Even early in its conception, Google executives were exploring how Universal Search could be used to show a "results page promo" to "bootstrap traffic" to Google's other products.[1127]

When Google launched Universal Search, it gave prominent placement to Google's vertical content over superior, more relevant competitors' products. Google's documents show that Google adjusted its search algorithm to automatically elevate the ranking of some of Google's services above those offered by rivals.[1128] These perks are generally not available to competing verticals, placing them at an instant disadvantage.[1129] Given that the likelihood that a user will click on a listing sharply declines with each drop in placement, traffic to rivals demoted by Google has fallen significantly.[1130] The effect is magnified on mobile search, where the small screen means fewer results are displayed on the first page of results.[1131]

In a submission to the Subcommittee, one vertical search provider described the practical effects of Google's discriminatory treatment:

> When the Local OneBox appears on the page, links to [the company's] website with highly relevant [results] get pushed down the page into the lower section for organic search results. This demotion puts [the company] at a competitive disadvantage relative to Google's local search results and jeopardizes the health of [our] business—and this problem is further exacerbated in the growing mobile context where links to [our] website may be pushed off the small screen or the first page of search results altogether. In evaluating options to reduce this harm, [the company] has reached out to Google to explore whether [we] or [our] providers' listings on [our] website could be included in

---

[1126] *Id.* at GOOG-HJC-03804474 (May 23, 2007) (on file with Comm.) (noting "large increases in absolute coverage for all five purposes," including a 4.5% increase in News and 4% increase in Local Search").

[1127] *Id.* at GOOG-HJC-01230599 (Dec. 8, 2004) (on file with Comm). ("Including some of Urs ideas around promoting the Labs property on the Google.com results pages for some subset of users ("New! Try your search on the next version of Google"). Urs main concern was that Lab gets limited traffic, and the set of users is not representative of Google's user base. He didn't mind the idea of a Labs launch in principle, but he suggested we show a results page promo for some small percentage of users to bootstrap traffic to the property with a more diverse set of users.").

[1128] *See, e.g., id.* at GOOG-HJC-01081099 (Oct. 11, 2007) ("We added a "cooccurring sites" signal to bias ourselves towards triggering when a local-oriented aggregator site (i.e. Citysearch) shows up in the web results.").

[1129] Submission from Source 564, to H. Comm. on the Judiciary, 9 (Nov. 13, 2020) (on file with Comm.).

[1130] Matt Southern, *Over 25% of People Click the First Google Search Result*, SEARCHENGINEJOURNAL (July 14, 2020) https://www.searchenginejournal.com/google-first-page-clicks/374516/#close.

[1131] *Why Page 2 of Google Search Results Is the Best Place to Hide a Dead Body*, DIG. SYNOPSIS (Oct. 29, 2019) https://digitalsynopsis.com/tools/google-serp-design/ (stating that the first organic result on the first search engine results page receives around 32.5% of overall click-based traffic, the second result receives around 17.6%, and the seventh receives 3.5%).

Google's local search results, but Google has either refused outright or taken no steps to allow such inclusion.[1132]

A submission from another vertical search provider stated that once Google began automatically placing its own competing service at the top of its search results page, the vertical provider's organic search traffic fell by approximately 20%.[1133] The vertical provider observed that Google's service is worse for users—showing higher prices and fewer choices than Google's competitors.[1134] However, Google continues to give its service top placement, occupying close to 100% of the above-the-fold mobile search results page and around 25% of desktop.[1135]

Additional market participants echoed the view that Google's self-preferencing comes at the expense of users. One search provider stated that Google prohibits it from displaying live prices on Google's results page, even as Google's own competing service is permitted to do so. Stating that there was no pro-competitive justification for this differential treatment, the firm also noted that Google's limits on rival vertical search providers likely prevents consumers from seeing the cheapest or best-valued prices.[1136]

In addition to placing its vertical offerings at the top of the search results page, Google has also actively demoted certain rivals through imposing algorithmic penalties. For example, in 2007 and in 2011 Google launched an algorithm that demoted sites that Google considered "low quality."[1137] Among the websites especially hit were comparison shopping providers, which enable users to compare product offers from multiple merchant websites.[1138] In a submission to the Subcommittee, one publisher stated that Google's algorithmic penalty caused search leads and revenues to its website to fall by 85%.[1139] Kelkoo, previously a leading comparison shopping site, explained that Google's demotion set off a "cyclic trend" whereby a reduction in traffic leads to fewer consumers, which leads

---

[1132] Submission from Source 887, to H. Comm. on the Judiciary, 4 (Oct. 28, 2019) (on file with Comm.).

[1133] Submission from Source 925, to H. Comm on the Judiciary, 11 (Nov. 4, 2019) (on file with Comm.).

[1134] *Id.*

[1135] *Id.* at 9.

[1136] Submission from Source 3, to H. Comm. on the Judiciary, 32 (Oct. 29, 2019) (on file with Comm.).

[1137] Amit Singhal & Matt Cutts, *Finding more high-quality sites in search*, GOOGLE: OFFICIAL BLOG (Feb. 24, 2011), https://googleblog.blogspot.com/2011/02/finding-more-high-quality-sites-in.html (defining "low-quality sites" as those that are "low-value add for users, copy content from other websites or sites that are just not very useful" and defining "high-quality sites" as "sites with original content and information such as research, in-depth reports, thoughtful analysis and so on").

[1138] Production of Google, to H. Comm. on the Judiciary, GOOG-HJC- 00090248-49 (Jan 27, 2011) (on file with Comm.).

[1139] Submission from Kelkoo, to H. Comm. on the Judiciary, Kelkoo-0032 at 6 (Nov. 4, 2019) (on file with Comm.).

to fewer listings and less revenue, which leads to reduced investment—which, in turn, contributes to a further decline in traffic, a "network effect in reverse."[1140]

In external messaging, Google justified the algorithmic penalties it imposed on third-party sites as a response to users' desire to see less "low quality" sites in their search results.[1141] However, Google did not subject its own vertical sites to the same algorithmic demotion, even though Google's vertical services aggregated and copied content from around the web—just like the third-party sites that Google had demoted.[1142] Indeed, Google's documents reveal that employees knew Google's own vertical sites would likely fit the demotion criteria that Google applied to other sites. When one employee suggested that Google index its comparison shopping site, Froogle, another responded that it was unlikely Froogle would get crawled "without special treatment," noting, "We'd probably have to provide a lot of special treatment to this content in order to have it be crawled, indexed, and rank well."[1143]

Despite the fact that Google's own comparison shopping service was of such low quality that Google's product team couldn't even get it indexed, Google continued to give Froogle top placement on its search results page, listing its results in the OneBox, a display box that Google populates with information on its search results page.[1144] Bill Brougher, a product manager, acknowledged that Google was privileging low-quality content, writing:

> Our algorithms specifically look for pages like [Froogle's] to either demote or remove from our index, and there are active projects to improve the integration into web search. The bigger problem these projects have is to improve their own result quality. For instance with Froogle, the onebox trigger is now very good and relevant, but the three results we show from Froogle in that onebox generally rate very low in our search quality evaluation. It is often the same with Local.[1145]

[1140] Submission from Kelkoo, to H. Comm. on the Judiciary, Kelkoo-0006 at 6 (Nov. 4, 2019) (on file with Comm.); Kelkoo-0044 at 19 (Nov. 4, 2019).

[1141] Production of Google, to H. Comm. on the Judiciary, GOOG-HJC-00632668 (on file with Comm.).

[1142] *Id.* at GOOG-HJC-02507422 (Apr. 4, 2006) (on file with Comm.) ("Keep in mind that, as we discussed, most of the information that is on pages that we create is aggregated from various sources, and those sources often have that material online already. Because of this, the search quality team has some concerns as to if/when this Google-created content will be indexed. And once it is indexed, it is unlikely to appear high in the search results.").

[1143] *Id.*

[1144] *Id.*

[1145] *Id.*; *see also* GOOG-HJC-03201904 (Mar. 22, 2006) (on file with Comm.) ("Generally we like to have the destination page in the index, not the aggregated pages. So if our local pages are lists of links to other pages, its [sic] more important that we have the other pages in the index. In addition, our pages would probably not rank well because of this.").

Another Google team member replied: "Yes, you're right that the Onebox result items often stink."[1146] A few years later, a Google employee again acknowledged that if Google ranked its own content according to the same criteria that it applied to competitors, "it will never rank."[1147]

In an interview with Subcommittee staff, one vertical site stated that Google had not only demoted the firm but had at least one instance removed it from Google's index entirely.[1148] The search provider stated that after Google purchased its rival, Google demoted the provider in search rankings while vaulting those of its rival.[1149] The search provider observed that Google's demotions sometimes followed favorable press that highlighted the search provider's popularity with users. "There was an article that came out in the press that painted [us] in a positive light and quoted an executive noting that [we are] the top result when a user searches [for a particular search term]. The next day, Google de-indexed [us] for [that search term]."[1150]

In July, the *Wall Street Journal* reported that Google also gives preferential treatment to YouTube.[1151] Tests conducted by the *Journal* found that searching Google for videos delivered YouTube in results much more prominently than competing video providers, even when competitor videos had more engagement. Reflecting interviews with those familiar with the matter, the piece stated that Google engineers:

> [M]ade changes that effectively preference YouTube over other video sources. Google executives in recent years made decisions to prioritize YouTube on the first page of search results, in part to drive traffic to YouTube rather than to competitors, and also to give YouTube more leverage in business deals with content providers seeking traffic for their videos." [1152]

In response to Questions for the Record from Subcommittee Chairman David Cicilline (D-RI), the company denied that Google Search is designed to favor YouTube. Although Google stated that it

---

[1146] Production of Google, to H. Comm. on the Judiciary, GOOG-HJC-02507420 (Apr. 5, 2006) (on file with Comm.).

[1147] *Id.* at GOOG-HJC-01069289 (May 6, 2009) (on file with Comm.) ("From a principal perspective it would be good if we could actually just crawl our product pages and then have the rank organically. Problem is that today if we crawl it will never rank.").

[1148] Interview with Source 147 (June 2019).

[1149] *Id.*

[1150] *Id.*

[1151] Sam Schechner, Kristen Grind & John West, *Searching for Video? Google Pushes YouTube Over Rivals*, WALL ST. J. (July 14, 2020), https://www.wsj.com/articles/google-steers-users-to-youtube-over-rivals-11594745232.

[1152] *Id.*

disagreed with the methodology used by the *Journal*, Google did not provide the Subcommittee with any data or internal reports that would support its claim.[1153]

Numerous market participants noted that Google's favoring of its own sites and demoting those of third parties has effectively increased their cost of distribution. Since demoted sites can generally only recover traffic through advertising on Google, the platform "essentially requires competitors to pay for their websites to appear above Google's own links," according to one market participant.[1154] Another business recalled that in 2016 Google demoted one of its vertical offerings, citing a policy of diversifying content.[1155] The firm stated that once it was penalized in organic rankings, it "could not get an appropriate customer service response for months" and ultimately "had to increase [marketing spend on Google] to regain lost traffic—a win-win for Google but a loss for [our business] and its users."[1156]

Meanwhile, Google's own competing vertical "is always listed at the top" of search results.[1157] The incident highlights how demoting rivals can enrich Google in two ways: first, through diverting greater traffic and business to its own products; and second, through earning ad revenues from the penalized sites that are subsequently scrambling to recover their search placement. When demoting firms that Google views as actual or potential competitive threats, Google is effectively raising rivals' costs.

Another firm noted that demoted vertical providers that go on to buy ads on Google not only feed revenue to a potential or actual competitor in specialized search, but also risk handing Google more commercially sensitive information. The market participant wrote:

> Google thus deceptively siphons internet traffic away from its vertical competitors in online travel and forces them to pay more for [search engine monetization] and [] Ads in order to get meaningful placement on Google's [search engine results page]. Importantly, Google also requires its vertical competitors to provide their inventory feed to populate the ads, allowing Google to appropriate vertical service providers' valuable inventory data.[1158]

A significant number of the website publishers that the Subcommittee interviewed noted the outsized effect that a single algorithmic change by Google can have on their business. Brian Warner,

---

[1153] Innovation and Entrepreneurship Hearing at 13 (response to Questions for the Record of Adam Cohen, Dir. of Econ. Pol'y, Google LLC).

[1154] Submission from Source 3, to H. Comm. on the Judiciary, 32 (Oct. 29, 2019) (on file with Comm.).

[1155] Submission from Source 972, to H. Comm. on the Judiciary, 9 (Dec. 9, 2019) (on file with Comm.).

[1156] *Id.*

[1157] *Id.*

[1158] Submission from Source 115, to H. Comm. on the Judiciary, 16 (Oct. 22, 2019) (on file with Comm.).

Celebrity Net Worth founder, stated, "All website owners live in constant fear of Google's algorithm updates. Without explanation or recourse, Google can deliver a fatal blow to a website's search ranking visibility."[1159] Foundem, the UK-based comparison shopping site, wrote, "An unjustified Google search penalty, whether imposed anticompetitively or in error, has the power to cause grave and irreparable harm to virtually any online business."[1160]

3) Threatening Innovation and the Open Internet

Through misappropriating third-party content and giving preferential treatment to its own vertical sites, Google abused its gatekeeper power over online search to coerce vertical websites to surrender valuable data and to leverage its search dominance into adjacent markets. Google's conduct both thwarted competition and diminished the incentive of vertical providers to invest in new and innovative offerings.

In an interview with the Subcommittee, one market participant observed that Google's conduct has sapped investment, as "investors don't want to invest in companies that are producing content that relies on Google traffic," resulting in "less capital invested in companies reliant on traffic from Google."[1161] The website noted that Google's business practices have also skewed the website's own investment decisions, leading it to allocate the vast majority of its revenue to creating "news-like temporary content" rather than "evergreen content."[1162] It added, "If we could trust that Google was not engaging in unfair search practices, we would be producing different content."[1163]

A vertical provider, meanwhile, said that Google's conduct had held the firm's growth "at bay" and risks reducing innovation over the long term, as providers whose growth is capped by Google may be more reluctant to invest and expand.[1164] It added:

Competitors are not the only ones who have a reduced incentive to innovate as a result of Google's conduct. The anticompetitive effects reduce Google's own incentives to improve the quality of its services, because it does not need to compete on the merits with rival services.[1165]

[1159] Submission from Celebrity Net Worth, to H. Comm. on the Judiciary, 10 (Oct. 14, 2019) (on file with Comm.).

[1160] Submission from Foundem, to H. Comm. on the Judiciary, 42 (Oct. 22, 2019) (on file with Comm.). Foundem was the lead complainant in the European Commission's antitrust investigation and case on Google Shopping.

[1161] Interview with Source 507 (July 10, 2019).

[1162] *Id.*

[1163] *Id.*

[1164] Submission from Source 564, to H. Comm. on the Judiciary, 4 (Nov. 13, 2019) (on file with Comm.).

[1165] *Id.*

To illustrate this point, Yelp offers a contrast between its own efforts to maintain high quality user reviews and Google's efforts. It states that of the approximately 150 million user reviews submitted to Yelp since 2005, Yelp has displayed only 72% of them to users, while flagging 21% as "not recommended."[1166] Yelp cites investment research noting that Google, by contrast, does not invest in curating its reviews: "25% of Google's reviews have zero characters and are simply Netflix-style one-click star ratings from which the user can derive few, if any, insights about trustworthiness of the submission."[1167]

Several market participants told the Subcommittee that Google's business practices in online search have already foreclosed opportunity. In a submission, Celebrity Net Worth founder Brian Warner wrote:

> It is my view that Google has removed essentially all of the oxygen from the open internet ecosystem. There is no longer any incentive or even basic opportunity to innovate as I did back in 2008. If someone came to me with an idea for a website or a web service today, I would tell them to run. Run as far away from the web as possible. Launch a lawn care business or a dog grooming business—something Google can't take away as soon as he or she is thriving.[1168]

More broadly, market participants expressed concern that Google has evolved from a "turnstile" to the rest of the web to a "walled garden" that increasingly keeps users within its sites.[1169] Many observers have noted that when Google filed its initial public offering, Google co-founder Larry Page identified the company's mission as the following: "We want you to come to Google and quickly find what you want…We want you to get you out of Google and to the right place as fast as possible."[1170] In recent years, however, studies have shown that more than half of all queries on Google either terminate on Google or result in a click to Google's own properties—a share that is growing over time.[1171] In July, *The Markup* published results showing that Google allocated 41% of the first search results page on mobile devices to Google's own content."[1172]

[1166] PIPERJAFFRAY, INTRODUCING REVIEW GROWTH FOR YELP VS. GOOGLE PLUS, (Apr. 16, 2014) (on file with Comm.).

[1167] *Id.*

[1168] Innovation and Entrepreneurship Hearing at 6 (statement from Brian Warner, Founder, Celeb. Net Worth).

[1169] *See, e.g.,* Submission from Source 972, to H. Comm. on the Judiciary, 9 (Dec. 9, 2019) (on file with Comm.). ("As opposed to cataloguing the internet and sending travelers to the most relevant websites, Google is instead creating a walled garden, using its place at the top of the internet funnel to ensure that the majority of users transact on Google's own pages and products.").

[1170] Google Inc., Registration Statement, (Form S-1) B-6 (2004), https://www.sec.gov/Archives/edgar/data/1288776/000119312504139655/ds1a.htm .

[1171] Rand Fishkin, *Less Than Half of All Google Searches Now Result in a Click*, SPARKTORO (Aug. 13, 2019), https://sparktoro.com/blog/less-than-half-of-google-searches-now-result-in-a-click/.

[1172] Adrianne Jeffries & Leon Yin, *Google's Top Search Result? Surprise! It's Google*, THE MARKUP (July 28, 2020), https://themarkup.org/google-the-giant/2020/07/28/google-search-results-prioritize-google-products-over-competitors.

On several occasions over the course of the investigation, Subcommittee Chairman David Cicilline (D-RI) asked Google about this trend.[1173] At the Subcommittee's July 16, 2019 hearing, Google's Director of Economic Policy, Adam Cohen, stated that Google's goal is "to provide users information as quickly and efficiently as possible," adding that he was "not familiar" with studies showing that a majority of queries now terminate on Google.[1174] In its July 26, 2019 response to a follow-up letter from Chairman Cicilline, Google wrote that it strives to "give users the most relevant, highest quality information as quickly as possible," a goal that Google claims is "[c]onsistent with Mr. Page's comments in 2004."[1175] When asked whether it was true that less than 50% of all searches on Google resulted in clicks to non-Google websites, Google responded that it "has long sent large amounts of traffic to other sites."[1176] In response to the Subcommittee's request for query metrics that would document the underlying trends, however, Google did not produce the relevant data.[1177]

Several enforcement bodies have examined these business practices. Between 2011 and 2013, the Federal Trade Commission pursued an inquiry into Google's data misappropriation and self-preferencing, among other conduct. Staff at the Bureau of Competition concluded that "the natural and probable effect" of Google's misappropriation was "to diminish the incentives of vertical websites to invest in, and to develop, new and innovative content."[1178] On Google's self-preferencing, staff concluded that Google's conduct had "resulted in anticompetitive effects,"[1179] but that Google had offered "strong procompetitive justifications."[1180] In 2017, the European Commission concluded that Google's self-preferencing in comparison shopping services constituted an illegal abuse of dominance and ordered Google to implement a remedy of "equal treatment."[1181] The European Commission stated

---

[1173] *See, e.g.*, Innovation and Entrepreneurship Hearing at 38–40 (response to Questions for the Record of Adam Cohen, Dir. of Econ. Pol'y, Google LLC); CEO Hearing Transcript at 1 (response to Questions for the Record from Sundar Pichai, Chief Executive Officer, Alphabet Inc.).

[1174] Innovation and Entrepreneurship Hearing at 38–40 (response to Questions for the Record of Adam Cohen, Dir. of Econ. Pol'y, Google LLC) , https://docs.house.gov/meetings/JU/JU05/20190716/109793/HHRG-116-JU05-20190716-SD030.pdf; Innovation and Entrepreneurship Hearing at 42 (Adam Cohen, Dir. of Econ. Pol'y, Google LLC).

[1175] Letter from Kent Walker, Senior Vice Pres., Global Affairs & Chief Legal Officer, Google, to Hon. David N. Cicillin (D-RI), Chairman, Subcomm. on Antitrust, Commercial and Admin. Law of the H. Comm. on the Judiciary, 1 (July 26, 2019).

[1176] *Id.* at 2.

[1177] In a September 2020 response to Chairman Cicilline on this same question, Google disputed Fishkin's analysis of the data. Google wrote "The fact that a user does not click on a link on a Google Search results page does not mean that the user has been "kept" on Google properties. Searches on Google may result in zero website clicks for many reasons, which is not discernable without directly asking the user why they did not click a link." CEO Hearing at A-2 (response to Questions for the Record of Sundar Pichai, CEO, Alphabet Inc.).

[1178] FED. TRADE COMM'N, THE FTC REPORT ON GOOGLE'S BUSINESS PRACTICES iii (Aug. 8, 2012), in WALL ST. J. (Mar. 24, 2015), http://graphics.wsj.com/google-ftc-report/.

[1179] *Id.* at 80.

[1180] *Id.* at 86.

[1181] Google Search (Shopping) Comm'n Decision at para. 671.

that Google had not "provided verifiable evidence to prove that its conduct is indispensable" to any procompetitive effects.[1182]

ii. Google Increased Prices for Market Access and Degraded Search Quality

In 2000, Google launched AdWords, which allowed advertisers to pay for keyword-based ads that would appear to the right of Google's search results.[1183] In the years since, Google has changed the display of the ads on its search engine results page in several ways, most notably by (1) increasing the number of ads placed above organic search results, and (2) blurring the distinction between how ads and organic listings are presented on Google's search results page. These changes have effectively raised the price that businesses must pay to access users through Google. Market participants told the Subcommittee that Google's conduct has undermined competition, misled consumers, and degraded the overall quality of Google's search results—all while enabling Google to further exploit its monopoly over general online search.

Google's clear dominance in online search also gives it significant control over the search advertising market. Publicly available data suggests Google captured around 73% of the search advertising market in 2019.[1184] Submissions from market participants show that many firms spend the vast majority of their ad budgets on Google. For example, one major vertical provider spent significantly more than half of its total ad spend on Google each year from 2016 to 2019, with the second top provider receiving less than 15%.[1185] Public reporting suggests that, as of 2019, Google had increased the price of search ads by about 5% per year, exceeding the U.S. inflation rate at that time of 1.6%.[1186]

Several market participants told Subcommittee staff that their ad spend on Google has increased largely because Google has made it more difficult for businesses to obtain organic traffic. Partly this follows from Google's preferencing of its own products, which compels demoted firms to pay Google for ad placement as a way to regain visibility. Another notable factor has been Google's decision to increase the number of ads posted above organic search results.

[1182] Summary of Google Search (Shopping) Comm'n Decision at O.J. C 9/13, para. 26 (Dec. 1, 2018), https://eur-lex.europa.eu/legal-content/EN/TXT/PDF/?uri=CELEX:52018XC0112(01)&from=EN.

[1183] Press Release, Google, *Google Launches Self-Service Advertising Program* (Oct. 23, 2000), http://googlepress.blogspot.com/2000/10/google-launches-self-service.html.

[1184] Submission from Source 115, to H. Comm. on the Judiciary, 6 (Oct. 22, 2019) (on file with Comm.) (citing Megan Graham, *Amazon Is Eating into Google's Most Important Business: Search Advertising,* CNBC (Oct. 15, 2019), https://www.cnbc.com/2019/10/15/amazon-is-eating-into-googles-dominance-in-search-ads.html).

[1185] Submission from Source 3, to H. Comm. on the Judiciary, 8 (Oct. 29, 2019) (on file with Comm.).

[1186] Alistair Barr & Garrit De Vynck, *Airlines, Hotels and Other Brands Are Tired of Paying Google for Their Own Names,* BLOOMBERG (Mar. 9, 2019); *see also* Mark Irvine, *Average Cost per Click by Country: Where in the World Are the Highest CPCs?,* WORDSTREAM BLOG (Nov. 8, 2018) https://www.wordstream.com/blog/ws/2015/07/06/average-cost-per-click (showing that the cost-per-click that Google charges search advertisers in the United States is notably higher than the rate it charges in countries where Google faces more competition).

Prior to 2016, Google's design of its search results page placed 8 ads to the right of organic search listings and 3 ads above them.[1187] Google's internal communications show that, as of 2011, rates of user engagement with right hand side ads was declining.[1188] Since Google made money from search ads only when users clicked on them, less user engagement meant those ads were becoming less valuable to Google. In February 2011, Sridhar Ramaswamy, senior vice president of ads at Google, noted that "users are no longer looking at the [right hand side ads]," and stated that Google either needed to "retrain people to look there by putting really good stuff there," or "live with the fact that users are going to stop looking there."[1189] By August 2011, a team at Google known as "Project Manhattan" was working on a redesign of Google's desktop search results page that focused on reducing or eliminating right hand side ads.[1190]

In 2016, Google rolled out the redesigned page, which eliminated the right hand side ads while adding a fourth ad above organic listings and 3 at the bottom of the page.[1191] The practical effect of adding a fourth ad at the top of the search results page was to push organic listings further down, requiring users to scroll down further before reaching a non-paid result. According to *Bloomberg*, when Google tested the addition of a fourth ad, some employees objected on the grounds that the fourth ad would be of lower quality than the first organic result, but Google altered the search results page anyway.[1192]

Google's decision to monetize a fourth ad at the expense of an organic listing fits a broader pattern of steps taken by Google to rank search results based on what is best for Google, rather than what is best for search users—be it preferencing its own vertical sites or allocating more space for ads. Several market participants noted that Google could afford to make these changes only once it had achieved a dominant position in the market for general search and search advertising.[1193] Now that Google is "unconstrained by competitors," one market participant noted, it "consistently reserves the

---

[1187] Dr. Peter J. Meyers, *Four Ads on Top: The Wait Is Over*, Moz (Feb. 19, 2016), https://moz.com/blog/four-ads-on-top-the-wait-is-over.

[1188] Production of Google, to H. Comm. on the Judiciary, GOOG-HJC-02981172–73 (Aug. 12, 2011) (on file with Comm.) ("RHS CTR has been steadily dropping over time to today's level…For the best ads on the RHS, some indication that CTR is lower than quality would suggest it should be"); GOOG-HJC-02983169-93 (Aug. 12, 2011) (stating that RHS is 16.5% of search revenue, 26% of queries have a RHS ad, and "Opportunity is accelerating due to declining RhsCTR").

[1189] *Id.* at GOOG-HJC-02983830 (Feb. 16, 2011).

[1190] *Id.* at GOOG-HJC-00482674–76 (Aug. 18, 2011).

[1191] Matt McGee, *Confirmed: Google To Stop Showing Ads On Right Side Of Desktop Search Results Worldwide*, Search Engine Land (Feb. 19, 2016), https://searchengineland.com/google-no-ads-right-side-of-desktop-search-results-242997.

[1192] Gerrit De Vynck, *Google Search Upgrades Make It Harder for Websites to Win Traffic*, Bloomberg (July 13, 2020) https://www.bloomberg.com/news/articles/2020-07-13/how-google-search-changes-make-it-more-expensive-to-win-traffic.

[1193] *See, e.g.*, Submission from Source 972, to H. Comm. on the Judiciary, 14 (Dec. 9, 2019) (on file with Comm.); Submission from Source 115, to H. Comm. on the Judiciary, 10 (Oct. 22, 2019) (on file with Comm.); Submission from Source 3, to H. Comm. on the Judiciary, 34 (Oct. 29, 2019) (on file with Comm.); Competitors Hearing at 3 (statement of David Heinemeier Hansson, Chief Technology Officer and Cofounder, Basecamp).

top of the [search engine results page] for its own vertical products or advertisements paid for through search engine marketing, pushing its rivals' organic results to the bottom, regardless of how relevant or useful they might be."[1194]

Internal data shown by one market participant to the Subcommittee demonstrates that "organic search listings have been pushed down over time, and 'click-throughs' (clicking to visit a site) on the first organic results have decreased by two-thirds over the past 3 years."[1195] The market participant's analysis also shows that the first organic listing on mobile now appears on the bottom of the third search results screen, which "effectively forces advertising customers to bid for a paid advertisement listing if they want their service or product to meaningfully reach consumers in a mobile search."[1196]

Google Search on Desktop Ad Placement[1197]

[1194] Submission from Source 972, to H. Comm. on the Judiciary,14 (Dec. 9, 2019) (on file with Comm.).

[1195] Submission from Source 3, to H. Comm. on the Judiciary, 33 (Oct. 29, 2019) (on file with Comm.).

[1196] *Id.*

[1197] Prepared by the Subcomm.

Google Search on Mobile Phone[1198]

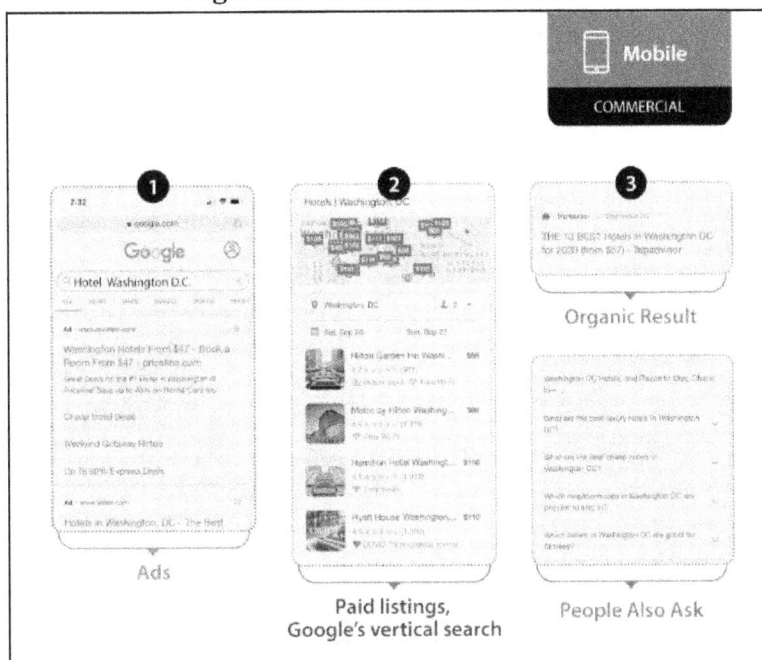

[1198] Prepared by the Subcomm.

Google Search on Desktop[1199]

[1199] Prepared by the Subcomm.

Google Search on Mobile Phone[1200]

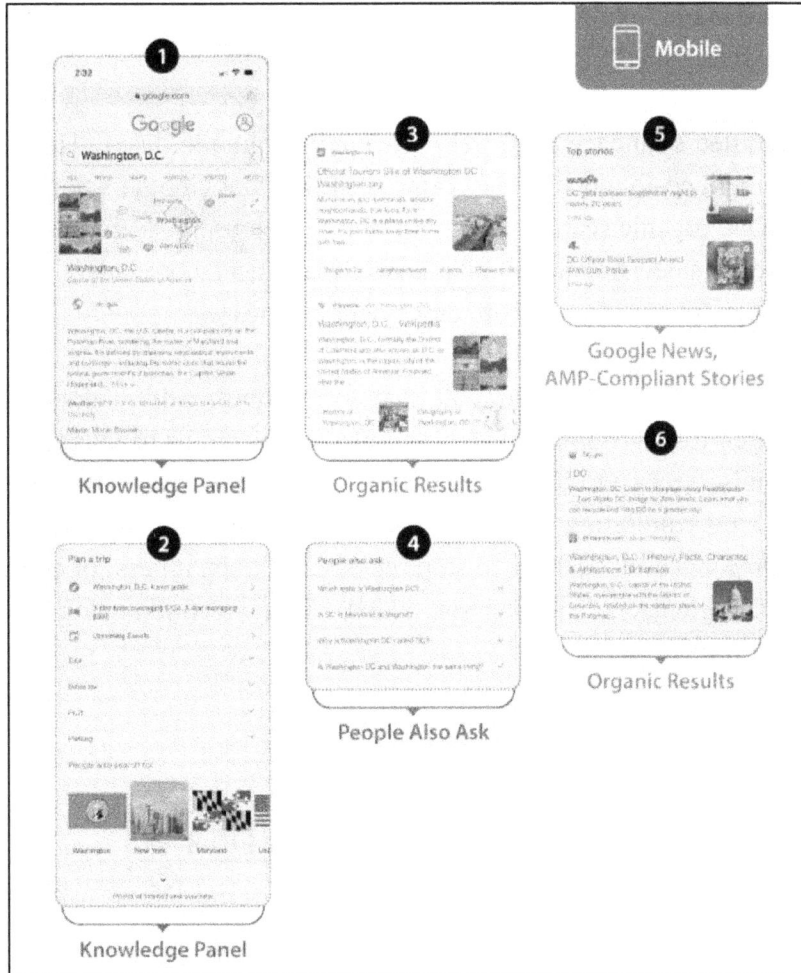

One result of these changes is that users click less on organic search results. As Google has reduced the share of top real estate that it devotes to organic listings, studies show that organic click-through as a share of all click-through plus zero-click searches has fallen.[1201] According to analysis by Rand Fishkin, the trend is especially pronounced in mobile, where organic click-through rates fell by more than 30% between January 2016 and June 2019, while paid click-through rates over that same period more than tripled.[1202]

For businesses that depend on Google to reach users, these trends amount to a toll hike, as traffic that firms could previously draw through organic listings is now increasingly pay-for-play. Instead of competing for users by offering high quality webpages and services that should lead to

---

[1200] Prepared by the Subcomm.

[1201] Rand Fishkin, *Less than Half of Google Searches Now Result in a Click*, SPARKTORO (Aug. 13, 2019) https://sparktoro.com/blog/less-than-half-of-google-searches-now-result-in-a-click/.

[1202] *Id.* (showing organic fell from 41.1% in January 2016 to 26.68% in June 2019, a period over which paid click-through rates increased from 3.29% to 11.38%.).

better organic search listings, these businesses must now compete for users based on how much money they pay Google. Several market participants analogized Google to a gatekeeper that is extorting users for access to its critical distribution channel.

At the Subcommittee's January 2020 field hearing in Colorado, David Heinemeier Hansson, chief technology officer and co-founder of Basecamp, testified that Google's decision to increase the number of ads listed above organic search results has hurt search users.[1203] Expanding on his criticism, Hansson stated that Google's decision to sell ad placement against a company's brand names is another way that Google extracts revenue from dependent businesses.

Hansson said, "Google uses this monopoly to extort businesses like ours to pay for the privilege that consumers who search for our trademarked brand name can find us because if we don't they will sell our brand name as misdirection to our competitors."[1204] He noted that while Google purports to recognize trademark law by prohibiting the use of trademark terms in ad copy, Google "puts the onus of enforcement on victims and does nothing to stop repeat offenders, unless, of course, the trademark terms are belonging to Google itself."[1205] Hansson added, "You will find no competitor ads for any of Google's own important properties."[1206]

Basecamp's Ad[1207]

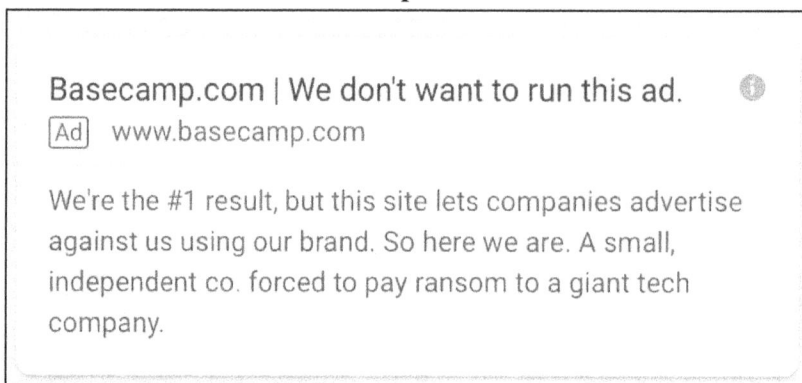

Basecamp.com | We don't want to run this ad.
[Ad]   www.basecamp.com

We're the #1 result, but this site lets companies advertise against us using our brand. So here we are. A small, independent co. forced to pay ransom to a giant tech company.

Other market participants generally echoed these views in submissions to the Subcommittee. One wrote that Google "effectively forces its advertising customers to pay for the ability to reach

---

[1203] Competitors Hearing Transcript at 62 (statement of David Heinemeier Hansson, Chief Technology Officer and Cofounder, Basecamp) ("Today, if a consumer goes to Google on their mobile device and search [sic] for Basecamp, the first thing that they will find is whoever bought that trademark term, which is usually one of our competitors. Ergo, consumers are not finding what they are looking for . . . . They are being presented with an ad and that is the tollbooth that [Google is] erecting.")

[1204] *Id.* at 23.

[1205] *Id.*

[1206] *Id.*

[1207] Jason Fried (@jasonfried), TWITTER (Sep. 3, 2019, 4:39 PM), https://twitter.com/jasonfried/status/1168986962704982016?lang=en.

consumers who are searching specifically for the customer's brand."[1208] The business added, "Facing no remotely comparable advertising and search engine alternative, Google has the ability to charge potentially inflated prices for its advertising services by forcing customers to increase their bids in order to receive a more favorable position."[1209]

A second factor that several third parties cited as contributing to both higher ad prices and the degradation of search for users is Google's effort over the years to blur the distinction between organic listings and paid ads.

Google's Ad Shading and Labeling: 2007–2013[1210]

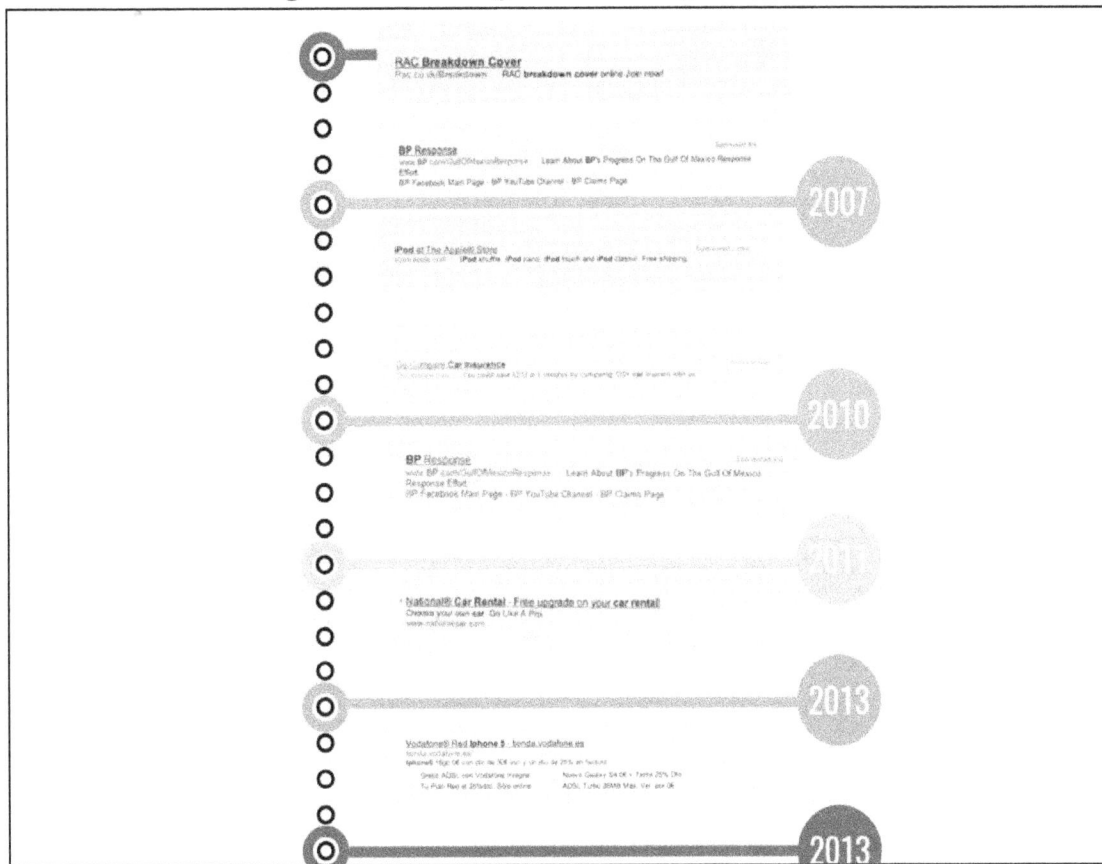

The diagram above depicts Google's practice between 2007 and 2013 of labeling its paid ads with a shaded background. As shown below, in 2013 Google abandoned the shaded background and instead inserted a small yellow square that states "Ad." Since 2016, Google has made various changes that make ads more subtle, culminating in a label that renders the overall appearance of paid ads much more similar to organic listings. Market participants have noted that Google also neglects to label some

---

[1208] Submission from Source 3, to H. Comm. on the Judiciary, 32 (Oct. 29, 2019) (on file with Comm.).

[1209] *Id.*

[1210] Ginny Marvin, *A Visual History of Google Ad Labeling in Search Results,* SEARCH ENGINE LAND, (Jan. 28, 2020). https://searchengineland.com/search-ad-labeling-history-google-bing-254332.

paid ads entirely, particularly those that appear in Google's vertical search offerings, such as listings for hotels that appear alongside maps.[1211]

Google's Ad Shading and Labeling: 2013–2019[1212]

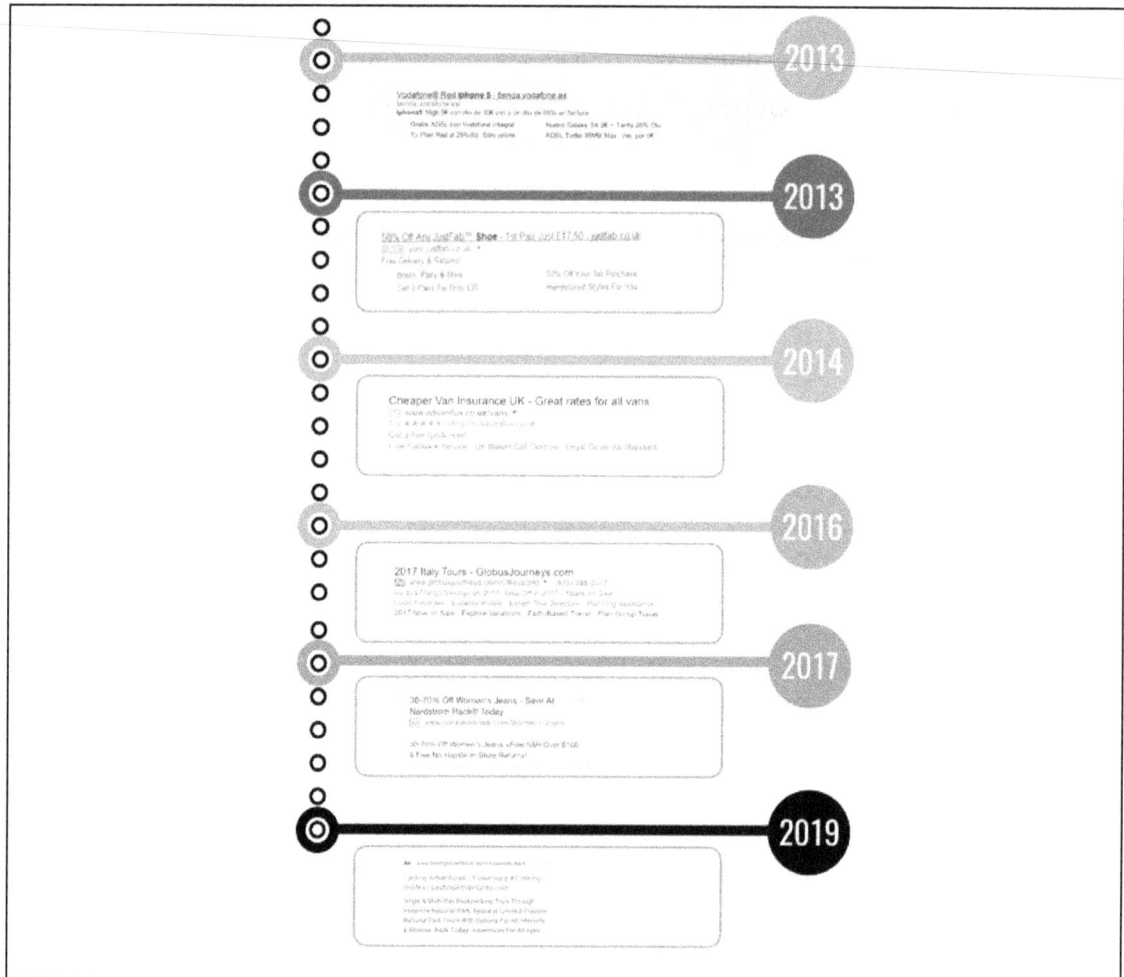

The natural result of Google's decision to blur the distinction between paid ads and organic listings is that users click on more ads and less organic search results. This misleading practice has likely contributed to the growth of paid click-through rates on Google. One study found that over 59% of consumers were not aware of the difference between organic results and paid ads on Google, and that one third of those who did recognize paid ads said they would deliberately avoid clicking on them.[1213] The Federal Trade Commission has recognized that search engines that fail to "prominently

---

[1211] Google Hotel Ads, https://ads.google.com/hotels/ (offering paid listings to hotels, but neglecting to designate these listings as "ads" on the search results page).

[1212] Ginny Marvin, *A Visual History of Google Ad Labeling in Search Results,* SEARCH ENGINE LAND, (Jan. 28, 2020). https://searchengineland.com/search-ad-labeling-history-google-bing-254332.

[1213] Mark Jones, *Two-thirds of people don't know the difference between Google paid and organic search results,* MARKETING TECH NEWS (Sept. 6, 2018) https://marketingtechnews.net/news/2018/sep/06/two-thirds-people-dont-know-difference-between-google-paid-and-organic-search-results/.

distinguish" paid ads from organic listings could be liable for deceiving consumers under Section 5 of the FTC Act.[1214]

Making ads less conspicuous makes it more likely that users will unwittingly click on them. Market participants note that like Google's decision to increase the number and prominence of paid ads, Google's decision to blur the distinction between paid listings and organic results deceives consumers and compels businesses to purchase ads from Google in order to be located by users.[1215]

In submissions and interviews with Subcommittee staff, businesses noted that higher advertising costs come at the expense of investments in innovation and consumer benefits.[1216] One vertical search provider stated:

> If the search market were fair, the internet would have four times more content on it, dramatically improving the web for consumers. Google's gatekeeper power allows it to show more advertisements for search queries with higher commercial intent. . . . The harm to consumers is not necessarily a lack of content, but a lack of quality content (requiring money to produce).[1217]

At the Subcommittee's January 2020 field hearing, Hansson testified that Google's conduct, which harms business customers and users alike, is enabled by its dominance:

> Google's monopoly on internet search must be broken up for the sake of a fair marketplace. Google would never be able to get away with such a user-hostile design as showing a full-page ad for something other than what you were searching for, if it had real competition. They would never have been able to establish their monopoly if this had been the design from the get-go. These are the monopoly spoils of complete domination.[1218]

At the Subcommittee's sixth hearing, Subcommittee Chairman David Cicilline (D-RI) noted that Google's search results page now features more ads and more of Google's own sites and asked

---

[1214] Letter from Mary K. Engle, Assoc. Dir. for Advert. Practices, Fed. Trade Comm'n (June 24, 2013), https://www.ftc.gov/sites/default/files/attachments/press-releases/ftc-consumer-protection-staff-updates-agencys-guidance-search-engine-industryon-need-distinguish/130625searchenginegeneralletter.pdf.

[1215] Submission from Source 115, to H. Comm. on the Judiciary, 10-12 (Oct 22, 2019) (on file with Comm.); Submission from Source 972, to H. Comm. on the Judiciary, 21 (Dec. 9, 2019) (on file with Comm.); Submission from Source 3, to H. Comm. on the Judiciary (Oct. 29, 2019) (on file with Comm.).

[1216] Submission from Source 3, to H. Comm. on the Judiciary 32 (Oct. 29, 2019) (on file with Comm.).

[1217] Interview with Source 507 (July 10, 2019).

[1218] Competitors Hearing at 7 (statement of David Heinemeier Hansson, Chief Technology Officer and Cofounder, Basecamp).

Google CEO Sundar Pichai whether this trend highlights a misalignment of Google's incentives.[1219] He asked, "Isn't there a fundamental conflict of interest between serving users who want to access the best and most relevant information and Google's business model, which incentivizes Google to sell ads and keep users on Google's own sites?"[1220] In response Mr. Pichai stated that Google has "always focused on providing users the most relevant information," and stated that Google shows ads "only for a small subset of queries where the intent from users is highly commercial."[1221] However, Mr. Pichai did not explain why the percentage of queries for which Google shows ads would implicate whether or not Google's business model compromises the integrity of its search results. Google also failed to produce data that would enable the Subcommittee to make an independent assessment of Pichai's assertion.

3. Digital Advertisements

   a. Overview and Dominance

Google makes the vast majority of its revenue through selling advertising placement across the internet. In 2019, Google's ad revenue accounted for approximately 83.3% of Alphabet's overall sales.[1222] Google is a prominent player in both search advertising and digital display advertising, and it captures over 50% of the market across the ad tech stack, or the set of intermediaries that advertisers and publishers must use to buy, sell, and place ads. Specifically, Google runs the leading ad exchange, while also running buy-side and sell-side intermediary platforms trade on the exchange.[1223]

Internationally, antitrust enforcers are currently investigating Google's dominance in digital advertising, including the United Kingdom's Competition and Markets Authority (CMA),[1224] and the Australian Competition and Consumer Commission (ACCC).[1225] In July 2020, the CMA concluded

---

[1219] CEO Hearing Transcript at 37 (question of Rep. David N. Cicilline (D-RI), Chairman, Subcomm. on Antitrust, Commercial and Admin. Law); Production of Google, to H. Comm. on the Judiciary, GOOG-HJC-01099375 (Mar. 30, 2012) (on file with Comm.); Sergey Brin & Larry Page, *The Anatomy of a Large-Scale Hypertextual Search Engine*, http://infolab.stanford.edu/~backrub/google.html (expressing reservations about an ad-based business model, noting that "the goals of the advertising business model do not always correspond to providing quality search to users," and given the conflicting motives that a search engine might face between serving users the most relevant information and selling more ads, arguing that "advertising funded search engines will be inherently biased towards the advertisers and away from the needs of the consumers.").

[1220] CEO Hearing Transcript at 37 (question of Rep. David N. Cicilline (D-RI), Chairman, Subcomm. on Antitrust, Commercial and Admin. Law).

[1221] *Id.* (statement of Sundar Pichai, CEO, Alphabet Inc.); Production of Google, to H. Comm. on the Judiciary, GOOG-HJC-01099375 (Mar. 30, 2012) (on file with Comm.).

[1222] Alphabet Inc., Annual Report (Form 10-K) 10 (Feb. 3, 2020), https://www.sec.gov/Archives/edgar/data/1652044/000165204420000008/goog10-k2019.htm.

[1223] Commission and Mks Auth. Report at 10.

[1224] *Id.*

[1225] *See generally* Austl. Competition & Consumer Comm'n Report.

that Google has "significant market power" in search advertising, and that its market power had enabled it to charge prices 30-40% higher than those set by Bing.[1226] In September 2020, the Senate Judiciary Committee held a hearing on the effects of Google's dominance in digital ads, where members expressed bipartisan concern that Google's market power across the ad tech stack was enabling anticompetitive conduct and harming publishers and advertisers alike.[1227] Lastly, public reports note that both the Justice Department and several states attorney generals are investigating Google's market power and conduct in digital ads, with reports that a lawsuit may be imminent.[1228] In light of the extensive attention already given to this issue, a comprehensive examination of the digital advertising market is beyond the scope of this Report.

Market participants and Google's documents suggest that Google is likely to maintain its lead in search and display advertising due to high entry barriers. Most critically, as other sections of this Report found, Google can mine its ecosystem—including Search, Chrome, Android, and Maps—to combine a unique set of user data points and build troves of online behavioral data that drive its ad business. Furthermore, its dominance across markets increasingly enables Google to set the terms of commerce. One third party described:

> Google is now not only a seller and broker of digital advertising across the Internet, but they now also control significant portions of the web browsers, operating systems, and platforms upon which these digital ads are delivered. This gives Google the ability to single-handedly shift an entire ecosystem in nearly any direction they decide, based simply on their scale. Google can then use its dominance to demand a higher share of ad revenues from buyers and sellers, and there is little leverage available to counteract this position in a negotiation.[1229]

One key factor that market participants and industry experts cite when accounting for why Google is likely to maintain its dominance in digital ads is its conflict of interest. With a sizable share in the ad exchange market, ad intermediary market, and as a leading supplier of ad space, Google simultaneously acts on behalf of publishers and advertisers, while also trading for itself—a set of conflicting interests that market participants say enable Google to favor itself and create significant information asymmetries from which Google benefits.[1230] At the Subcommittee's sixth hearing,

---

[1226] Commission and Mks Auth. Report at 211.

[1227] *Stacking the Tech: Has Google Harmed Competition in Online Advertising? Hearing Before S. Subcomm. on Antitrust and Consumer Rights of the S. Comm. on the Judiciary*, 116th Cong. (2019).

[1228] Sara Forden and David McLaughlin, *DOJ Scrutinizes Google Advertising, Search in Antitrust Probe*, BLOOMBERG (Aug. 8, 2019), https://www.bloomberg.com/news/articles/2019-08-08/doj-scrutinizes-google-advertising-search-in-antitrust-probe.

[1229] Submission from Source 688, to H. Comm. on the Judiciary, 2 (Oct. 24, 2019) (on file with Comm.).

[1230] Dina Srinivasan, *Why Google Dominates Advertising Markets*, 24 STAN. TECH. L. REV. 10-11 (forthcoming 2020) (on file with Comm.).

Congresswoman Jayapal (D-WA) questioned Google CEO Sundar Pichai about this conflict of interest:

> So [Google is] running the marketplace, it's acting on the buy side, and it's acting on the sell side at the same time, which is a major conflict of interest. It allows you to set rates very low as a buyer of ad space from newspapers, depriving them of their ad revenue, and then also to sell high to small businesses who are very dependent on advertising on your platform. It sounds a bit like a stock market, except, unlike a stock market, there's no regulation on your ad exchange market.[1231]

Mr. Pichai responded by citing the sums that Google has paid to publishers, describing it as a "low-margin business" for Google that it pursues "because we want to help support publishers."[1232] Google's overall margins have averaged over 20% for nine of the last ten years.[1233]

b. Merger Activity

Google came to control a sizable market share across the ad tech stack through acquisitions. Google acquired DoubleClick in 2007 for $3.1 billion.[1234] At the time of the acquisition, *The New York Times* described DoubleClick as a "Nasdaq-like exchange for online ads," and Google's own early description of DoubleClick describes it as "a stock exchange," such as "the NYSE."[1235] Google purchased DoubleClick to enter the display advertising market, a segment that Google's internal documented calculated at around $4.3 billion in 2006—and an area where Google at the time noted it "has no meaningful presence."[1236] A presentation from July 2006 stated "Build a Self-Reinforcing Online Ads Ecosystem," noting that acquiring DoubleClick or Atlas could create these "self-reinforcing benefits" for Google's ecosystem.[1237] The slide asked, "[I]s there some framework we have to demonstrate the synergies/inter-relationships from owning all these pieces?"[1238] Nine months later Google announced its bid to buy DoubleClick.

When reviewing the deal, the Federal Trade Commission assessed both horizontal and non-horizontal theories of harm, and noted that prior to announcing the acquisition, Google had been

---

[1231] CEO Hearing Transcript at 169 (Rep. Pramila Jayapal, Member, Subcomm. on Antitrust, Commercial and Admin Law).

[1232] *Id.* at 170.

[1233] Data compiled by Cong. Research Serv. (on file with Comm.).

[1234] Louise Story & Miguel Helft, *Google Buys DoubleClick for $3.1* Billion, N.Y. TIMES (Apr. 14, 2007), https://www.nytimes.com/2007/04/14/technology/14DoubleClick.html.

[1235] *Id. See also The DoubleClick Ad Exchange,* GOOGLE, https://static.googleusercontent.com/media/www.google.com/en//adexchange/AdExchangeOverview.pdf.

[1236] Submission from Google, to H. Comm. on the Judiciary, GOOG-HJC-04189346 (July 26, 2006) (on file with Comm.).

[1237] *Id.* at GOOG-HJC-04189347.

[1238] *Id.*

planning to enter the market and compete against DoubleClick directly.[1239] Ultimately the Commission concluded that the display advertising market was highly competitive, and therefore the loss of Google's potential entry would not be competitively significant.[1240] Examining the potential effects of the deal on privacy, the FTC said it found no evidence that competition between Google and DoubleClick affected their respective privacy policies.[1241] In December 2007 the FTC approved the acquisition.[1242]

In 2010 Google acquired AdMob, the leading mobile ad network at the time. In the FTC's approval of the merger it stated that "the combination of the two leading mobile advertising networks raised serious antitrust issues," but that these concerns were "overshadowed by recent developments in the market, most notably a move by Apple Computer Inc. – the maker of the iPhone – to launch its own, competing mobile ad network."[1243] The Commission's assumption that Apple would continue to build its presence in the mobile ad market prompted it to approve the deal.[1244] In the coming years, however, Apple's product never fully took off and in 2016 Apple abandoned the effort completely.[1245]

In 2011 Google also acquired AdMeld, a leading supply side platform.[1246] The Justice Department's Antitrust Division investigated the acquisition and concluded that the deal was "unlikely to cause consumer harm."[1247]

c. Conduct

i. Combination of Data

When Google purchased DoubleClick, it told Congress and the FTC that it would not combine the data collected on internet users via DoubleClick with the data collected throughout Google's

---

[1239] Press Release, Federal Trade Commission Closes Google/DoubleClick Investigation, Fed. Trade Comm'n (Dec. 20, 2007), https://www.ftc.gov/news-events/press-releases/2007/12/federal-trade-commission-closes-googledoubleclick-investigation.

[1240] *Id.*

[1241] *Id.*

[1242] Id.

[1243] Press Release, FTC Closes its Investigation of Google AdMob Deal, Fed. Trade Comm'n (May 21, 2010), https://www.ftc.gov/news-events/press-releases/2010/05/ftc-closes-its-investigation-google-admob-deal.

[1244] *Id.*

[1245] *About the iAd App Network Shutdown*, APPLE DEVELOPER (Dec. 31, 2016), https://developer.apple.com/support/iad/ (last visited on Oct. 4, 2020).

[1246] Press Release, *FTC Closes its Investigation of Google AdMob Deal,* Fed. Trade Comm'n (May 21, 2010), https://www.ftc.gov/news-events/press-releases/2010/05/ftc-closes-its-investigation-google-admob-deal.

[1247] Press Release, Statement of the Department of Justice's Antitrust Division on Its Decision to Close Its Investigation of Google Inc.'s Acquisition of Admeld Inc., Department of Justice (Dec. 2, 2011) https://www.justice.gov/opa/pr/statement-department-justices-antitrust-division-its-decision-close-its-investigation-google.

ecosystem.[1248] In 2016, however, Google reversed this commitment, and subsequently combined DoubleClick data with personal information collected through other Google services—effectively combining information from a user's personal identity with their location on Google Maps, information from Gmail, and their search history, along with information from numerous other Google products. At the Subcommittee's sixth hearing, Representative Val Demings (FL-D) asked Mr. Pichai about his direct involvement in the decision to renege on Google's commitment to lawmakers:

> When Google proposed the merger[,] alarm bells were raised about the access to data Google would have, specifically the ability to connect to users' personal identity with their browsing activity. Google, however, committed to Congress and to the antitrust enforcers that the deal would not reduce user privacy. Google's chief legal adviser testified before the Senate Antitrust Subcommittee that Google wouldn't be able to merge this data even if it wanted to, given contractual restrictions. But in June of 2016, Google went ahead and merged its data anyway, effectively destroying anonymity on the internet . . . Did you sign off on this decision to combine the sets of data with—that Google had told Congress would be kept separate?[1249]

Sundar Pichai confirmed that he approved the deal, claiming that "Today [we] make it very easy for users to be in control of their data."[1250] Rep. Demings also noted that at the time of the transaction, DoubleClick executives had noted that Google's founders were concerned that combining the data in this way—through a cross-site cookie—would lead to a privacy backlash. She stated:

> So, in 2007, Google's founders feared making this change because they knew it would upset their users, but in 2016, Google didn't seem to care. Mr. Pichai, isn't it true that what changed between 2007 and 2016 is that Google gained enormous market power. So. While Google had to care about user privacy in 2007. It no longer had to in 2016? Would you agree that what changed was Google gained enormous market power?[1251]

She closed by noting she was concerned that Google's "bait-and-switch" was "part of a broader pattern where Google buys up companies for the purposes of surveilling Americans, and because of

---

[1248] Dina Srinivasan, *Why Google Dominates Advertising Markets*, 24 STAN. TECH. L. REV. 24 (forthcoming 2020) (on file with Comm.).

[1249] CEO Hearing Transcript at 73-74 (Rep. Val Demings (D-FL), Member, Subcomm. on Antitrust, Commercial and Admin Law).

[1250] *Id.* at 75.

[1251] *Id.* at 74-75

Google's dominance users have no choice but to surrender."[1252] In recent months, Google's reversal on this commitment has become salient for enforcers now assessing Google's bid to purchase FitBit.[1253]

ii. Other Areas of Concern

While a comprehensive examination of this market is beyond the scope of this Report, the Subcommittee heard from numerous market participants about a set of alleged practices by Google that invite investigation. These include:

- Depriving advertisers and publishers of key market and pricing information and maintaining market opacity;

- Leveraging its market power in search advertising to compel advertisers to use Google's products in the display market;

- Leveraging control over YouTube to foreclose competition in digital video ad serving, in part by excluding rival ad servers from having access to YouTube;

- Inhibiting interoperability between Google's ad platforms and non-Google ad platforms; and

- Using its search dominance to impose standards like AMP that, by further depriving publishers of user data, benefit Google's ad business.

4. Android and Google Play Store

a. Android

i. Overview

Android is a dominant mobile operating system, running on approximately 75% of the world's mobile devices.[1254] In the United States, the only alternative to Android is Apple's iOS. Android

---

[1252] *Id.* at 75.

[1253] CEO Hearing at 32 (response to Questions for the Record of Sundar Pichai, CEO, Alphabet Inc.), https://docs.house.gov/meetings/JU/JU05/20200729/110883/HHRG-116-JU05-20200729-QFR051-U1.pdf.

[1254] Felix Richter, *The Smartphone Market: The Smartphone Duopoly*, STATISTA (July 27, 2020), https://www.statista.com/chart/3268/smartphone-os-market-share/ (citing *Mobile Operating System Market Share Worldwide*, STATCOUNTER GLOBALSTATS).

captures about 47% of the U.S. mobile operating system market, and Apple captures about 52% of it.[1255]

Google acquired Android in July 2005 for an estimated $50 million.[1256] Since then, Google has purchased a set of technologies to strengthen its mobile ecosystem, including both software and hardware.[1257] Notably, Google purchased Motorola Mobility in 2011 for $12.5 billion, the largest acquisition in Google's history.[1258]

Google describes Android as "a free, open-source mobile operating system" that is available to anyone to download and modify on a royalty-free basis.[1259] Indeed, Android is unique in that Google does not generally monetize its operating system through selling proprietary hardware or demanding licensing fees. In practice, however, smartphone manufacturers that seek to use Android must sign Google's licensing agreements, as Google limits the functionality of non-licensed usage. Only through Google's licensing agreements can smartphone manufacturers access Google's proprietary apps, such as Gmail, YouTube, Chrome, Google Maps, and Google Play Store.[1260] In return, Google requires that certain apps must be pre-installed and must receive prominent placement on mobile devices.[1261] Device manufacturers must also enter an agreement that prevents them from customizing Android,[1262] and

---

[1255] S. O'Dea, *Market share of mobile operating systems in the United States from January 2012 to December 2019*, STATISTA (Feb. 27, 2020), https://www.statista.com/statistics/272700/market-share-held-by-mobile-operating-systems-in-the-us-since-2009/, (citing *Mobile Operating System Market Share in United States Of America*, STATCOUNTER GLOBALSTATS).

[1256] Farhad Manjoo, *A Murky Road Ahead for Android, Despite Market Dominance* (May 27, 2015), https://www.nytimes.com/2015/05/28/technology/personaltech/a-murky-road-ahead-for-android-despite-market-dominance.html.

[1257] *See infra* Appendix.

[1258] *Google Buys Motorola Mobility For $12.5B, Says "Android Will Stay Open,"* TECHCRUNCH (Aug. 15, 2011), https://techcrunch.com/2011/08/15/breaking-google-buys-motorola-for-12-5-billion/ (reporting that Google purchased Motorola primarily to protect the Android ecosystem from patent litigation). In 2014, Google sold Motorola to Lenovo. *Facts about Google's acquisition of Motorola*, GOOGLE, https://www.google.com/press/motorola/) (lasted visited Oct. 4, 2020).

[1259] Production of Google, to H. Comm. on the Judiciary, A-6 (Nov. 22, 2019) (on file with Comm.) Android is managed by the Open Handset Alliance, a group of more than eighty hardware, software, and mobile network operators, including Samsung, LG, HTC, and Lenovo. *See Members*, OPEN HANDSET ALLIANCE, https://www.openhandsetalliance.com/oha_members.html (last visited Oct. 4, 2020); *Licenses*, ANDROID OPEN SOURCE PROJECT, https://source.android.com/setup/start/licenses (last visited Oct. 4, 2020) (stating that the Android source code is freely available for use under an open-source license).

[1260] *See* Google Android Comm'n Decision at paras. 160–63.

[1261] Production of Google, to H. Comm. on the Judiciary, GOOG-HJC-02393308 (Mar. 11, 2011) (on file with Comm.) (The Mobile Application Distribution Agreement (MADA) is an agreement that specifies which apps Google requires hardware manufactures to pre-install and where on the phone the apps should be placed.).

[1262] Production of Google, to H. Comm. on the Judiciary, GOOG-HJC-02393318 (Feb. 25, 2011) (Google's Antifragmentation Agreement ("AFA")).

from building an Android fork that would make the version of Android running on a device incompatible with apps built for the Android ecosystem.[1263]

The Subcommittee's investigation revealed that Google has used Android to entrench and extend its dominance in a host of ways that undermine competition. These include: (1) using contractual restrictions and exclusivity provisions to extend Google's search monopoly from desktop to mobile and to favor its own applications; and (2) devising Android Lockbox, a covert effort to track real-time data on the usage and engagement of third-party apps, some of which were Google's competitors. Additionally, Google's Play Store now functions as a gatekeeper, which Google is increasingly using to hike fees and favor its own apps. Overall, Android's business practices reveal how Google has maintained its search dominance through relying on various contractual restrictions that blocked competition and through exploiting information asymmetries, rather than by competing on the merits.

ii. Using Contracts to Extend Google's Search Monopoly and Self-Preference

Early communications within Google show that it began investing in the mobile ecosystem because it recognized that the rise of smartphone usage threatened to disintermediate Google Search. Since losing its monopoly on search would mean losing its valuable trove of user data, maintaining dominance over search access points was paramount.

To maintain its search dominance, Google invested in Android, which it recognized it could use to extend its search dominance onto mobile devices.[1264] Google required that any smartphone manufacturer seeking to license Android preinstall Google Search and Google Play Store, alongside a host of other rotating apps selected by Google.[1265] Google also offered mobile device manufacturers revenue-share agreements, under which smartphone manufacturers would receive a cut of the search advertising revenue that Google made from the use of Google's apps on their devices,[1266] as well as a cut of Play Store revenues.[1267] In return, however, manufacturers had to not only carry Google's apps, but also ensure that Google Search was the default *and* exclusive search app pre-installed on the manufacturers' devices. For example, one revenue share agreement reviewed by the Subcommittee stated that hardware manufacturers shall not "pre-install, install, or incorporate on any Covered Device

---

[1263] *Id.*; Google Android Comm'n Decision at paras. 170–71; *see also Device compatibility overview*, ANDROID DEVELOPERS, https://developer.android.com/guide/practices/compatibility (last visited Oct. 4, 2020). In 2017, Google released an alternative to its Antifragmentation Agreement called the Android Compatibility Commitment (ACC), which "would permit OEMs to manufacture incompatible Android devices for a third party that are marketed under a third-party brand." Google Android Comm'n Decision at paras. 170–71.

[1264] Production of Google, to H. Comm. on the Judiciary, GOOG-HJC-04216470 (May 2009) (on file with Comm.).

[1265] *Id.* at GOOG-HJC-02393308 (Mar. 11, 2011) (on file with Comm.) (The Mobile Application Distribution Agreement).

[1266] *Id.* at GOOG-HJC-00660371 (Apr. 11, 2011).

[1267] *Id.* at GOOG-HJC-04216470 (May 2009).

any application which is the same or substantially similar to a Google Search Client or the Google Search Services."[1268]

Documents show that Google executives knew that conditioning access to Android and to Google's suite of apps on the prominent placement of Google Search would disrupt existing partnerships between mobile network operators and rival search engines. For example, a 2009 slide deck stated that "[p]artners may have deals in place with other search providers," and noted that "T-Mobile and AT&T have closed deals with Yahoo…Verizon has tight relationship with MSFT re: search…Expect MSFT & Yahoo to aggressively pursue 'pre-load' deals on Android phones."[1269] Google's strategy of licensing Android for free to hardware partners and conditioning access to Google's must-have apps on favorable treatment for Google Search enabled Google to box out rivals in mobile search and other markets. Google's strategy was successful. These agreements, which were reached with the leading smartphone providers, solidified Google Search as the default search option on a majority of the world's smartphones.

As Android gained market share, its demands grew and hardened. The European Commission found that between 2009 and 2014, Google increased the number of pre-installed Google apps that it required from 12 to 30.[1270] Documents submitted to the Subcommittee also show that instructions to heavily push Google Search were coming from the company's top management. Summarizing a meeting with Sundar Pichai, then-Vice President of Product Development, Director of Engineering for Android Patrick Brady recalled, "His main feedback was . . . Search is sacred, must be front and center."[1271] He added, "Our proposal covers that through more prescriptive search placement requirements."[1272]

Google's licensing agreement gave Google the right to amend the list of apps it required device manufacturers to pre-install.[1273] Documents show that market participants expressed frustration at Google's ability to set the terms and also change them routinely. Explaining the situation, Mr. Brady wrote, "Some OEMs . . . do not like the idea of signing up to undefined requirements, but most of our partners are somewhat used to this as the [c]ompatibility requirements evolve with each release, and our [Google Mobile Services] suite expands (incl. mandatory apps) over time."[1274] When one hardware manufacturer attempted to secure additional rights, Google pushed back. In 2014, John Lagerling, Senior Director of Android Global Partnerships, responded to such an effort:

[1268] *Id.* at GOOG-HJC-00660364 (Apr. 11, 2011).

[1269] *Id.* at GOOG-HJC-04217467 (May 2009) (on file with Comm.).

[1270] Google Android Comm'n Decision at para. 182.

[1271] Production of Google, to H. Comm. on the Judiciary, GOOG-HJC-00050146 (May 23, 2013) (on file with Comm.).

[1272] *Id.*

[1273] *See* Google Android Comm'n Decision at para. 183.

[1274] *Id.* at GOOG-HJC-00050145 (May 23, 2013).

In your redlines on [the contract], you are suggesting [OEM] approves any new additions to GMS. This has never been the case in our past history[,] and I think it is the wrong message for [OEM] to send Google. We just spent some hours explaining . . . that one of the main reasons we do Android is in order to secure distribution of Google services.[1275]

Other smartphone manufacturers also attempted to resist Google's terms, noting that the requirements were crowding out placement for other apps while also taking up significant memory. For example, in 2014 one hardware manufacturer requested that Google "reduce the number of preloaded apps on the device . . . so that we don't clutter our products with apps that may not be necessary for the majority of users and we give them as much space as possible," adding that this would also "help us deal with complaints from governments, NGOs and end users."[1276] Forwarding the email to others at Google, Mr. Langerling noted that the manufacturer's grievance was "not about clutter but about system memory," adding that "[u]sers have been complaining to [the device maker] that [it] sells them a 16Gb phone and delivers something that only has 7-8Gb free."[1277]

Despite complaints that Android's pre-install conditions favored Google's products at the expense of user experience, Google maintained its requirements. Interviews with market participants suggest that Google's ability to set the terms of commerce hurt mobile device manufacturers as well as third-party developers, both of which had their own apps they were seeking to distribute. In a submission to the Subcommittee, one third party recalled being informed by a device manufacturer "that it could not provide home screen placement for our preloaded app due in part to contractual agreements to preload [Google's competing app]."[1278]

Market participants noted that pre-installation on devices can be critical for successful distribution. One developer explained that "integration into the initial device setup," in particular, can "meaningfully drive the acquisition of new users."[1279] Google's documents show that it recognized the importance of pre-installation, with one internal presentation stating that "activation and defaults are a known issue that we should explore, as OEM/carrier pre-installed apps are among the most used."[1280]

Documents also show that Google uses its leverage to push hardware manufacturers to privilege Google's products over the manufacturers' products. Discussing the agenda for an upcoming

---

[1275] *Id.* at GOOG-HJC-04300658 (Jan. 21, 2014).

[1276] *Id.* at GOOG-HJC-04308614 (Jan. 17, 2014).

[1277] *Id.*

[1278] Submission from Source 104, to H. Comm. on the Judiciary, Source 104--00000439 (Jan. 18, 2019) (on file with Comm.).

[1279] *Id.* at Source 104-00000437 (Jan. 8, 2019).

[1280] Production of Google, to H. Comm. on the Judiciary, GOOG-HJC-04200778 (May 25, 2017) (on file with Comm.).

meeting with a hardware manufacturer, one Google manager noted that the manufacturer should discourage the use of its email client for Gmail accounts, stating, "They should use Gmail native app."[1281] In a separate discussion in 2016, Google employees explained how Android Pay, a predecessor to Google Pay, would be given preferential treatment over the manufacturer's own mobile payment app.[1282] Recent reporting that Google is pressuring Samsung to promote Google apps over those offered by Samsung is consistent with the company's past conduct.[1283]

Lastly, Google appears to use its licensing agreements to deter mobile device manufacturers from collaborating with alternative mobile operating system providers. In 2012, for example, Acer, a hardware manufacturer, and Alibaba had planned to release a variant of Android, called Aliyun OS.[1284] Reporting suggests that Google threatened to terminate its partnership with Acer in retaliation, leading Acer to cancel the launch of devices running on the Aliyun OS.[1285] Google also requires hardware partners to agree that they will not run unsanctioned versions of Android on other hardware products, with the understanding that any manufacturer who violates this condition risks losing access to the Google Play Store and other popular apps across all of the manufacturer's devices.[1286]

After investigating Google's licensing agreements, the European Commission concluded in 2018 that Google's conduct had illegally benefited Google's own services while blocking the rise of rival operating systems.[1287] Although Google argued that users were free to download other apps and that Google's own apps were superior, the Commission determined that "users who find search and

---

[1281] *Id.* at GOOG-HJC-04204875 (Jan. 18, 2014).

[1282] *Id.* at GOOG-HJC-04299009 (Feb. 4, 2016) (discussing how the manufacture's mobile payment app would be placed inside of an apps folder while Google's mobile payment app would be placed more prominently outside the folder of Google apps).

[1283] *See, e.g.*, Mark Bergan & Sohee Kim, *Google in Talks to Take Over More Search Tasks on Samsung Phones*, BLOOMBERG (July 28, 2020), https://www.bloomberg.com/news/articles/2020-07-29/google-in-talks-to-take-over-more-search-tasks-on-samsung-phones; Paresh Dave & Hyunjoo Jin, *Samsung weighs dropping Bixby as Google dangles new mobile apps deal*, REUTERS (July 29, 2020), https://www.reuters.com/article/us-google-samsung/samsung-weighs-dropping-bixby-as-google-dangles-new-mobile-apps-deal-idUSKCN24U0TF.

[1284] *See, e.g.*, Dieter Bohn, *Google explains why it stopped Acer's Aliyun smartphone launch (updated)*, THE VERGE (Sept. 14, 2012), https://www.theverge.com/2012/9/14/3335204/google-statement-acer-smartphone-launch-aliyun-android; Roger Cheng, *Alibaba: Google forced Acer to drop our new mobile OS*, CNET (Sept. 13, 2012), https://www.cnet.com/news/alibaba-google-forced-acer-to-drop-our-new-mobile-os/; T.C. Sottek, *Acer cancels phone launch with Alibaba, allegedly in response to threats from Google*, THE VERGE (Sept. 13, 2012), https://www.theverge.com/2012/9/13/3328690/acer-google-alibaba-phone.

[1285] *Id.*

[1286] *See e.g.*, Janko Roettgers, *How Google kneecapped Amazon's smart TV efforts*, PROTOCOL (Mar. 11, 2020), https://www.protocol.com/google-android-amazon-fire-tv; James Brumley, *Google Just Made Sure It's Going to Win the Smart TV War*, MOTLEY FOOL (Mar. 20, 2020) https://www.fool.com/investing/2020/03/20/google-just-made-sure-its-going-to-win-the-smart-t.aspx.

[1287] Press Release, Eur. Comm'n, Antitrust: Commission fines Google €4.34 billion for illegal practices regarding Android mobile devices to strengthen dominance of Google's search engine (July 18, 2018), https://ec.europa.eu/commission/presscorner/detail/en/IP_18_4581.

browser apps pre-installed on their devices are likely to stick to these apps."[1288] Responding to Google's claims that its tying agreements were necessary in order for Google to be able to monetize its investment in Android, the European Commission stated:

> Google achieves billions of dollars in annual revenues with the Google Play Store alone, it collects a lot of data that is valuable to Google's search and advertising business from Android devices, and it would still have benefitted from a significant stream of revenue from search advertising without the restrictions.[1289]

iii. Accessing Real Time Market Data

The Subcommittee's investigation also revealed that Android gives Google unparalleled access to data on its users and developers. This includes information that Google can monetize through its ad business, as well as strategic intelligence that lets Google track emerging competitors and general business trends.

Android's dominance in the mobile operating system market enables it to extensively surveil its users. This surveillance is partly enabled through Google's technology. In key ways Google also uses its dominance and its integration across markets to increase the number of touch points from which it is constantly mining user data.

Google's documents show that it has used its leverage over hardware manufacturers to demand that they structure their devices in ways that facilitate Google's data collection efforts. Google's agreements with device manufacturers, for example, require that manufactures configure a "Client ID," which is a unique alphanumeric code incorporated in the smartphone that enables Google to combine metrics tracked via the hardware with all the other data Google collects on users.[1290] Additionally, Google's own documents also show that it has asked device manufacturers to use a Google Account as their identifier rather than a non-Google account—a way of ensuring that Google can capture a broader picture of its users.[1291] On the Play Store, meanwhile, Google does not permit users to download apps unless they have a Google Account, further funneling users into the Google ecosystem.[1292] Combined with location data, which Android also extensively collects, Google can build sophisticated user profiles reflecting a person's demographic, where they are, and where they go, as well as which apps they use at what time and for how long.[1293] These intimate user profiles, spanning billions of people,

---

[1288] *Id.*

[1289] *Id.*

[1290] Google Android Comm'n Decision at para. 187.

[1291] Production of Google, to H. Comm. on the Judiciary, GOOG-HJC-04204875 (Jan. 18, 2014) (on file with Comm.).

[1292] Innovation and Entrepreneurship Hearing at 76 (response to Questions for the Record of Adam Cohen, Dir. Of Econ Pol'y, Google LLC).

[1293] Production of Google, to H. Comm. on the Judiciary, GOOG-HJC-04198806-855

are a key source of Google's advantage in its ad business. In this way, Android's location data feeds into Google's dominance in ads.

Documents and information reviewed by Subcommittee staff also show that Google has used Android to closely monitor competing apps, data that amounts to near-perfect market intelligence. Since at least 2012, Google has collected installation metrics for third-party apps,[1294] which it combined with data analyzing search queries.[1295] These early documents outline the early stages of Google's "Lockbox," a project to collate data that provided Google with a range of competitor insights and market intelligence, ranging from an understanding of how installation of the Amazon app corresponded to a trend in Amazon shopping queries[1296] to a close tracking of trends relating to Candy Crush and Angry Birds.[1297]

While Lockbox began as a way to collect data on the installation of apps, Google quickly realized it could harness it to yield other insights as well. One document from 2013 identified a list of additional data points that the company desired, including "[m]ore signals (including uninstalls and device app mapping)" and "reliable and long term app usage data," for which the document noted Google Play Services could help.[1298] In short, Google began seeking out ways to collect specific usage data that enabled Google to track not just which apps a user has, but also how frequently they use the apps and for how long.

Documents obtained by the Subcommittee suggest that by 2015, Google's Lockbox data had succeeded in tracking more than just install rates.[1299] Google's internal reports show that Google was tracking in real-time the average number of days users were active on any particular app,[1300] as well as their "total time spent" in first- and third-party apps.[1301] Google subsequently used this data to benchmark the company's first-party apps against third-party apps, suggesting that Google was using Lockbox data to assess the relative strengths and weaknesses of its own offerings.[1302] Google's documents show how Lockbox furnishes Google with near-perfect market intelligence, which Google

---

(Jan. 13, 2017) (on file with Comm.).

[1294] *Id.* at GOOG-HJC-00055102 (Nov. 2013).

[1295] *Id.* at GOOG-HJC-02598471 (June 6, 2010).

[1296] *Id.* at GOOG-HJC-00055102 (Nov. 2013).

[1297] *Id.*

[1298] *Id.*

[1299] Alex Heath, Nick Bastone & Amir Efrati, *Internal Google Program Taps Data on Rival Android Apps*, THE INFO. (July 23, 2020), https://www.theinformation.com/articles/internal-google-program-taps-data-on-rival-android-apps.

[1300] Production of Google, to H. Comm. on the Judiciary, GOOG-HJC-04198806-55 (Jan. 13, 2017) (on file with Comm.).

[1301] *Id.* at GOOG-HJC-04198814 (Jan. 13, 2017).

[1302] *Id.* at GOOG-HJC-04198812. (Jan. 13, 2017).

has used to inform strategic moves and potential business transactions.[1303] Recent reporting by *The Information* documented how YouTube employees used Lockbox data to track TikTok usage in India as Google was developing and planning its own rival to TikTok.[1304]

During the Subcommittee's sixth hearing, Representative Joe Neguse (D-CO) asked Mr. Pichai about allegations that Google had used Android to surveil rival apps and develop competing products.[1305] Mr. Pichai responded, "Congressman, because we try to understand what's going on in [the] market and we are aware of, you know, popularity of apps," adding, "But, in general, the primary use for that data is to improve the health of Android."[1306]

In follow-up questions to Mr. Pichai, Google was asked to identify all acquisitions or product decisions that had been informed by data from Android Lockbox. Google's answer was not responsive to the question.[1307]

b. Play Store

The Play Store is the dominant app store on Android devices. Early documents reviewed by the Subcommittee show that Google chose for a single app store to control software distribution on the Android ecosystem, with one executive noting that "we would strongly prefer to have one Market that everyone focuses on."[1308]

Because Google's Play Store is the primary way that users install applications on Android devices, the Play Store effectively functions as a gatekeeper for software distribution on a majority of the world's mobile devices. The Subcommittee's investigation reveals that Google uses this gatekeeper power in several key ways.

First, Google uses its Play Store gatekeeper power to charge high fees to mobile developers. Amazon, Spotify, Netflix, Epic Games, and Tinder have all expressed public concerns about Google's app store fees, along with Apple.[1309] As a lawsuit recently filed by Epic Games stated, "Google has thus installed itself as an unavoidable middleman for app developers who wish to reach Android users and vice versa. Google uses this monopoly power to impose a tax that siphons monopoly profits for

---

[1303] *Id.* at GOOG-HJC-04199726. (Jan. 13, 2017).

[1304] Alex Heath, Nick Bastone & Amir Efrati, *Internal Google Program Taps Data on Rival Android Apps*, THE INFO. (July 23, 2020), https://www.theinformation.com/articles/internal-google-program-taps-data-on-rival-android-apps.

[1305] Jon Porter, *Google reportedly keeps tabs on usage of rival Android apps to develop competitors*, THE VERGE (July 24, 2020), https://www.theverge.com/2020/7/24/21336946/google-android-lockbox-data-rival-apps-antitrust-scrutiny.

[1306] CEO Hearing Transcript at 196 (statement of Sundar Pichai, CEO, Alphabet Inc.).

[1307] CEO Hearing at A-10 (response to Questions for the Record of Sundar Pichai, CEO, Alphabet Inc.).

[1308] Production of Google, to H. Comm. on the Judiciary, GOOG-HJC-04218465 (Nov. 26, 2009) (on file with Comm.).

[1309] *See infra* Section V.

itself every time an app developer transacts with a consumer for the sale of an app or in-app digital content."[1310]

Although Google doesn't block off all alternative channels for accessing apps—allowing, for example, both some app stores and side-loading—in practice, these options do not provide meaningful alternatives to the Google Play Store. In contrast, the dual dominance of the Play Store and the Android ecosystem enable Google to exert control and engage in conduct that harms competition by exploiting, excluding, and discriminating against rivals.

Google charges developers of paid apps a 30% commission for downloads from the Play Store.[1311] Google also charges developers a 30% fee for transactions within apps, or in-app purchases.[1312] According to documents obtained by the Subcommittee, from 2011 to 2015 revenue from the Play Store accounted for 85% of Google's total revenue from the Android operating system, hardware sales, and the Play Store."[1313]

Third-party apps can also avoid the Play Store's commissions and fees by directing consumers to sideload the app—that is install the app using a browser, outside of an app store. Rival app stores that are not pre-installed on the device, such as the Amazon Appstore, must be sideloaded. Although sideloading is technically an option for rival app stores and app developers, market participants explained that Google goes out of its way to make side-loading difficult. Epic's recent lawsuit against Google alleges:

> Google ensures that the Android process is technically complex, confusing and threatening, filled with dire warnings that scare most consumers into abandoning the lengthy process. For example, depending on the version of Android running on a mobile device, downloading and installing *Fortnite* on an Android device could take as many as 16 steps or more, including requiring the user to make changes to the device's default settings and manually granting various permissions while being warned that doing so is dangerous.[1314]

Additionally, Epic's complaint notes that when it attempted to work with LG, another Android device manufacturer, LG told Epic that it had a contract with Google "to block side downloading off

---

[1310] Complaint for Injunctive Relief at 2, Epic Games, Inc. v. Google LLC, No. 3:20-cv-05671 (N. D. Cal. Aug. 13, 2020).

[1311] *Play Console Help: Service* Fees, GOOGLE, https://support.google.com/googleplay/android-developer/answer/112622?hl=en (last visited Oct. 4, 2020).

[1312] *Transaction fees for merchants*, GOOGLE PAYMENTS HELP CENTER, https://support.google.com/paymentscenter/answer/7159343?hl=en#:~:text=The%20transaction%20fee%20for%20all,distribution%20partner%20and%20operating%20fees (last visited Oct. 4, 2020).

[1313] Production of Google, to H. Comm. on the Judiciary, GOOG-HJC-04217474 (on file with Comm.).

[1314] Complaint for Injunctive Relief at 7, Epic Games, Inc. v. Google LLC, No. 3:20-cv-05671 (N. D. Cal. Aug. 13, 2020).

Google Play Store this year."[1315] If a user is able to install the competing app store, Google blocks them "from offering basic functions, such as automatic updating of apps in the background, which is available for apps downloaded from the Google Play Store."[1316]

The Play Store's dominance over app distribution on Android devices has enabled Google to begin to require use of its in-app payment system (IAP). As a result, Google has become the middleman between app developers and their customers. This was not always the case. Market participants explain that Google has changed its stance and re-interpreted policies over time to require more app developers to use Google Pay. Beginning in 2014, for example, Google designated specific categories of applications—including mobile games—that would be required to use Google Play In-App Billing.[1317] Recently, however, several market participants have informed the Subcommittee that Google has begun insisting that a broader category of apps will be required to use Google IAP exclusively, no longer allowing the option of a third-party payment processor.[1318]

In interviews with Subcommittee staff, developers state that one way Google exercises its gatekeeper power over third-party app developers is through its arbitrary and unaccountable enforcement of Play Store policies. One developer that spoke with the Subcommittee described Google's Play Store policies as an "opaque system [that] threatens the ability of app developers to develop and compete in the market for consumers, who should ultimately determine which apps they use."[1319] Another developer explained, "When apps allegedly violate Google Play Store standards, Google does not ever explain how, other than to quote the policy above and attach pictures of the allegedly violating image. When the imagery does not fit the above definitions, app publishers such as [third party] are put in a position of having to guess how to apply these standards."[1320]

Developers also alleged that Google uses control over the Play Store to protect the dominance of its own services and stifle rivals. For example, Callsome, a mobile app that provided productive follow-up to phone calls or text messages, such as prompting a calendar entry or a reminder to text back, has sued Google and claimed it was banned from the Google Play store for "Ad Policy" violations only to later learn that a "fundamentally identical product" was able to stay and thrive in the

---

[1315] *Id.* at 28.

[1316] *Id.* at 7.

[1317] Innovation and Entrepreneurship Hearing at 85 (response to Questions for the Record of Adam Cohen, Dir. Of Econ Pol'y, Google LLC).

[1318] Submission from Source 736, to H. Comm. on the Judiciary (Sept. 25, 2020) (on file with Comm.).

[1319] Submission from Source 62 to H. Comm. on the Judiciary, 1 (July 31, 2020) (on file with Comm.)

[1320] Submission from Source 685, to H. Comm. on the Judiciary, 8 (Oct. 15, 2019) (on file with Comm.).

Play Store.[1321] Callsome believes it was banned because of its partnership with StartApp, which—at the time—was widely considered a nascent but rising rival to Google in the Russian search market.[1322]

Subcommittee staff also spoke with several market participants that said Google has abused its control of the Play Store by using rule violations as a pretext for retaliatory conduct. For example, one third party described how soon after it ceased using Google's AdMob, an in-app ads monetization tool,[1323] Google began sending the third-party notifications of policy violations related to content the third party had included in its app for years.[1324]

In response to questions from the Subcommittee, Google stated that it "only suspends apps from the Google Play Store if it finds the app in violation of Google Play Program Policies . . . or in violation of the Developer Distribution Agreement."[1325] Google also stated that it gives developers opportunities to address what they may view as incorrect enforcement decisions of Play Store policies, adding that a "developer can easily contact the Policy Support Team (Appeals) in order to challenge the enforcement decision or receive additional clarification on the infraction."[1326]

App developers, in contrast, said that challenging a Play Store decision was like navigating a black box. One third party explained that it, "tried for over a month through several channels to get a full explanation from Google of the problem and resolve it amicably. Google responded with silence, then roadblocks and runarounds."[1327] However, one third party told the Subcommittee:

> When apps allegedly violate Google Play Store standards, Google does not ever explain how, other than to quote the policy above and attach pictures of the allegedly violating image. When the imagery does not fit the above definitions, app publishers such as [third party] are put in a position of having to guess how to apply these standards.[1328]

In theory, one way that app developers could avoid Google's commissions and fees would be to negotiate with a mobile device manufacturer to have the app pre-installed on the device. In practice, however, Google's restrictive contracts with smartphone manufacturers have strictly limited—if not excluded—third-party apps from being pre-installed. In this way, Google's licensing agreements not

---

[1321] Submission from Callsome, to H. Comm. on the Judiciary, 3 (Apr. 28, 2020) (on file with Comm.).

[1322] *Id.* at 7.

[1323] *Google AdMob*, GOOGLE, https://admob.google.com/home/ (last visited Oct. 4 2020).

[1324] Submission from Source 685, to H. Comm. on the Judiciary (on file with Comm.).

[1325] Innovation and Entrepreneurship Hearing at 83 (response to Questions for the Record of Adam Cohen, Dir. Of Econ Pol'y, Google LLC).

[1326] *Id.* at 84.

[1327] Submission from Callsome, to H. Comm. on the Judiciary, 5 (Apr. 28, 2020) (on file with Comm.).

[1328] Submission from Source 685, to H. Comm. on the Judiciary, 12 (Oct. 15, 2019) (on file with Comm.).

only preclude the vast majority of third-party apps from being pre-installed, but they also funnel those apps into the Google Play Store, subject to Google's commissions and arbitrarily enforced policies.

5. Chrome

a. Overview

Google launched its web browser, Google Chrome, in 2008.[1329] Chrome makes a significant portion of its underlying code base available through the open-source Chromium Project,[1330] which has been used to build a series of "chromium-based" browsers such as Microsoft Edge and Opera.[1331] In 2010, Google introduced the Chrome web store, which enables users to access and install browser extensions, such as Easy Ad Blocker, Grammarly, and Netflix Party.[1332]

Prior to Chrome's launch, Internet Explorer, Firefox and Safari were the most popular browsers. Firefox leaned heavily on a partnership with Google Search, which documents show enabled Google to closely track Firefox's growth.[1333]

Chrome initially set itself apart by offering an address bar that also functioned as a Google search bar, and by enabling users to sign into the browser, offering a faster browsing experience compared to other browsers.[1334] Chrome was also integrated with other Google products. By signing into the browser, Chrome automatically signed users into Gmail, YouTube, and additional Google services when users visited those sites, while also allowing users to sync their bookmarks, passwords, and other browser settings.[1335] While automatic sign-in provided a more streamlined user experience, it also helped Google build more detailed user profiles by connecting activity data to the user's Google Account.[1336]

[1329] *Google Chrome: A New Take on the Browser*, GOOGLE PRESS (Sept. 2, 2008), http://googlepress.blogspot.com/2008/09/google-chrome-new-take-on-browser_02.html.

[1330] THE CHROMIUM PROJECTS, https://www.chromium.org/Home (last visited on Oct. 4, 2020).

[1331] Catalin Cimpanu, *All the Chromium-based browsers*, ZDNET (Jan. 29, 2019), https://www.zdnet.com/pictures/all-the-chromium-based-browsers/4/.

[1332] *An update on Chrome, the Web Store and Chrome OS*, CHROME BLOG (Dec. 7, 2010), https://chrome.googleblog.com/2010/12/update-on-chrome-web-store-and-chrome.html.

[1333] Submission from Google, to H. Comm. on the Judiciary, GOOG-HJC-00125917-29, GOOG-HJC-00125937 (April 25, 2005) (on file with Comm.).

[1334] Trefis Team, Great Speculations, *Rising Chrome Use Means Search Advertising Growth for Google*, FORBES (Aug. 23, 2012) https://www.forbes.com/sites/greatspeculations/2012/08/23/rising-chrome-use-means-search-advertising-growth-for-google/#579c604f2d66; MG Siegler, *Here It Is: Google's Kick-Ass Chrome Speed Test Video*, TECHCRUNCH (May 5, 2010) https://techcrunch.com/2010/05/05/google-chrome-video-test/.

[1335] *Turn sync on and off in Chrome,* GOOGLE CHROME HELP, https://support.google.com/chrome/answer/185277?co=GENIE.Platform%3DDesktop&hl=en (last visited on Oct. 4, 2020).

[1336] *Google Privacy Policy*, GOOGLE PRIVACY AND TERMS, https://policies.google.com/privacy (last visited on Oct. 4, 2020) ("When you're signed in, we also collect information that we store with your Google Account.").

In a 2019 presentation to the Justice Department's Antitrust Division, Google explained that it had launched Chrome as a defensive move to protect users' access to Google's products.[1337] Internally, however, Google frequently referred to Chrome as part of Google's growth strategy. For example, in 2010 one of Google's strategy documents listed Chrome as a driver of "significant value,"[1338] and Eric Schmidt gave a company-wide speech stating that the rise of cloud computing meant that the browser—the primary way users access cloud—would be increasingly critical to Google's success.[1339]

Perhaps most critically, Chrome serves as a way for Google to control the entry points for its core markets: online search and online advertising.[1340] Chrome uses Google Search as its default search engine, a default setting that market participants say Google makes difficult to change.[1341] Chrome also provides Google with another source of user data that the company can feed into its ad business to offer behavioral ads.[1342]

b. Market Power

Chrome became a leading web browser as early as 2012.[1343] In the U.S. market, Chrome captures an estimated 59% of desktop browser usage and 37% of mobile browser usage,[1344] while capturing and estimated 66% of overall browser usage worldwide.[1345]

[1337] Submission from Google, to H. Comm. on the Judiciary, GOOG-HJC-04214204 (Sept. 17, 2019) (on file with Comm.) ("Alternatives to IE (Firefox, Opera, Safari) proved unattractive: Google initially partnered with Mozilla, but Firefox had technical limitations and faced uncertain prospects, Apple launched Safari for Windows in 2007. If Firefox was displaced by Safari, Apple could further constrain user access to Google.").

[1338] Submission from Google, to H. Comm. on the Judiciary, GOOG-HJC-00005661 (on file with Comm.).

[1339] Submission from Google, to H. Comm. on the Judiciary, GOOG-HJC-00086891 (Jan. 24, 2011).

[1340] Competition & Mkts Auth. Report at 18-19.

[1341] Submission from Source 534, to H. Comm. on the Judiciary, 3 (Oct. 14, 2019) (on file with Comm.).

[1342] *Google Privacy Policy*, GOOGLE PRIVACY AND TERMS, https://policies.google.com/privacy (last visited on Sept. 29, 2020). ("We collect information to provide better services to all our users . . . which ads you'll find most useful . . . which YouTube videos you might like."); CEO Hearing Transcript at 73 (Sundar Pichai, Chief Executive Officer, Google). At the Subcommittee's sixth hearing, Committee Chairman Jerrold Nadler (D-NY) asked Google CEO Sundar Pichai to explain how Google uses data on browsing activity, asking "Does Google use that data for its own purposes, either in advertising or to develop and refine its algorithms?" Mr. Pichai responded that Google uses data "to improve our products and services for our users." *Id.*

[1343] *Id;* Trefis Team, Great Speculations, *Rising Chrome Use Means Search Advertising Growth for Google*, FORBES, (Aug. 23, 2012) https://www.forbes.com/sites/greatspeculations/2012/08/23/rising-chrome-use-means-search-advertising-growth-for-google/#579c604f2d66. (Forbes observed in 2012 that Google captured 67% of desktop searches across all browsers and 95% of shares conducted on Chrome. It noted, "This large discrepancy in search market share, depending on which browser is used, is one of the reasons why we think that the Chrome browser has helped increase Google's revenues.").

[1344] *Desktop Browser Market Share in the United States*, STATCOUNTER, https://gs.statcounter.com/browser-market-share/desktop/united-states-of-america.; *Mobile Browser Market Share in the United States*, STATCOUNTER, https://gs.statcounter.com/browser-market-share/mobile/united-states-of-america

[1345] *Browser Market Share*, STATCOUNTER, https://gs.statcounter.com/browser-market-share/all/united-states-of-america.

Several factors suggest that Google is likely to maintain its lead in the browser market. First, Google has established Chrome as the default browser on the majority of Android devices, which make up around 75% of smartphones globally.[1346] While Google does allow users to change default browsers on Android, in practice users rarely do. As the United Kingdom's Competition and Markets Authority recently found, even platforms that do provide users with options often end up using "defaults and choice architecture that make it difficult for consumers to exercise this choice."[1347]

Second, Chrome is likely to remain dominant because it benefits from network effects. Web developers design and build for the Chrome browser because it has the most users, and users, in turn, are drawn to Chrome because webpages work well on it. And third, Chrome is likely to maintain its lead because Google can leverage the popularity of its apps to favor Chrome. Specifically, Google's documents show that the company has focused on designing Chrome features to provide a better experience of apps like YouTube and Search, advantages that other browsers lack.

c. Conduct

Google used its search engine dominance and control over the Android operating system to grow its share of the web browser market and favor its other lines of business. Reciprocally, Chrome's dominance in the browser market gives it significant gatekeeper power over managing and monitoring users' browsing activity—power Google can wield to shape outcomes across markets for search, mobile operating systems, and digital advertising. These advantages across markets feed back into and reinforce one another, advantages that standalone browsers lack.

i. Exploiting Information Asymmetries

Even before it developed Chrome, Google's search business and popular web-based applications gave it unique insights into the browser market. Because Google.com is accessible through all browsers, Google Search usage data includes data on the browser where the search query began. Documents show that Google used search origination trends as early as 2004 to track Firefox's growth—and Internet Explorer's decline—in the browser market.[1348] Google's collection of Google Apps has also enabled it to monitor browser growth and performance. For example, in 2009 a Chrome team member explained:

> I've looked at the Gmail numbers a little—enough to know that we have per-browser breakdowns of performance already. In the Gmail case, it's quite clear which browsers are faster. There are a zillion numbers we collect, including Gmail startup times. I am

---

[1346] *Mobile operating systems' market share worldwide from January 2012 to July 2020,* STATISTA (July 2020), https://www.statista.com/statistics/272698/global-market-share-held-by-mobile-operating-systems-since-2009/.

[1347] Competition & Mkts Auth. Report at 149.

[1348] Production of Google, to H. Comm. on the Judiciary, GOOG-HJC-00126978-35 (November 2004) (on file with Comm.).

confident that the other Google Apps teams also have numbers. We could pull together a collection of 2-3 stats from each app, normalize the scores somehow, and produce a number.[1349]

This data from Google's adjacent lines of business helped the Chrome team track their performance against competitors. Most of Chrome's competitors then and now lack access to this type of data at Google's scale.

ii. Favoring Google's Products in Adjacent Markets

Through design choices and default settings, Google can use its dominance in any one market to favor its other lines of business. For example, when Chrome launched in 2008, Google Search was already the most popular search engine in the world.[1350] Shortly after releasing Chrome, Google began promoting the browser in the top corner of the Google.com homepage. The display was referred to internally as the "Google Chrome Promotion" and it was frequently discussed by Google's Chrome team within the company.[1351] Internet Explorer users that visited Google's home page would see the Google Chrome installation button in the top-right corner, as shown below:

Google Chrome Promotion on Google.com Homepage[1352]

[1349] Production of Google, to H. Comm. on the Judiciary, GOOG-HJC-04214714 (Jan. 4. 2009) (on file with Comm.).

[1350] Danny Sullivan, *Search Market Share 2008: Google Grew, Yahoo & Microsoft Dropped & Stabilized,* SEARCHENGINELAND (Jan. 26, 2009), https://searchengineland.com/search-market-share-2008-google-grew-yahoo-microsoft-dropped-stabilized-16310.

[1351] Production of Google, to H. Comm. on the Judiciary, GOOG-HJC-01465906 (Apr. 22, 2009) (on file with Comm.) ("We've been experimenting with some novel homepage promos for Chrome in preparation for the IE8 autoupgrade [sic]. Using 0.1% experiments, we found a few that performed very well. The promo on the homepage right now should be running for IE users only."); Production of Google, to H. Comm. on the Judiciary, GOOG-HJC-01164689 (Apr. 23, 2009) (on file with Comm.).

[1352] Christopher Williams, *Google Chrome takes second place from Firefox,* THE TELEGRAPH (Dec. 2, 2011), https://www.telegraph.co.uk/technology/news/8930759/Google-Chrome-takes-second-place-from-Firefox.html.

At the time, several Google employees expressed concerns internally that this promotion strategy was unfairly harnessing Google's search dominance to boost Chrome. In an email among Chrome employees in 2009, one employee wrote, "I find the very, very high-profile promotion of Google Chrome on Google.com quite frankly, startling."[1353] Senior executives at the company pushed to continue this strategy. For example, in 2009, Sundar Pichai, then-Vice President of Product Development, encouraged the Chrome team to "promote through Google.com" and to push users to set Chrome as their default browser.[1354]

This strategy drove significant growth to Chrome. In 2009, Director of Product Management Brian Rakowski informed his team that the promotion was "performing exceptionally well" and was "driving tremendous number of downloads."[1355] When Google halted the promotion, Chrome's growth rate dropped. In 2011, Chrome employees noted that "organic growth slowed a bit because our homepage promo was down for a couple of weeks."[1356]

Market participants view this behavior as an example of how Chrome does not compete on the merits. One firm stated, "Google has abused its dominant position in the search space to build up another dominant position in the browser space."[1357] In response to questions about this use of Google's search page, Google told the Subcommittee that these "promotional campaigns on Google.com on Internet Explorer have been run for over a decade."[1358]

Google has reinforced its market power in the browser market through its dominance in the mobile operating system market. Chrome is preinstalled on every mobile device that runs Google's Android operating system, and Android powers approximately 75% the world's mobile devices. Beginning in 2014, Google mandated that Chrome be pre-installed and prominently placed on all certified Android devices that had entered a Mobile Application Distribution Agreement (MADA), which grants smartphone manufactures access to Google's Play Store and other proprietary Google applications.[1359] During negotiations with Android manufactures for revenue share agreements, meanwhile, Google required that Chrome be set as the default browser.[1360]

[1353] Production of Google, to H. Comm. on the Judiciary, GOOG-HJC-01465903 (Apr. 22, 2009) (on file with Comm.) ("I find the very, very high profile promotion of Google Chrome on Google.com quite frankly, startling.").

[1354] Production of Google, to H. Comm. on the Judiciary, GOOG-HJC-04214743 (Apr. 03, 2009) (on file with Comm.).

[1355] Production of Google, to H. Comm. on the Judiciary, GOOG-HJC-01465906 (Apr. 22, 2009) (on file with Comm.).

[1356] Production of Google, to H. Comm. on the Judiciary, GOOG-HJC-04195391 (Mar. 4, 2011) ("[O]rganic growth slowed a bit because our homepage promo was down for a couple of weeks due to a change in the HPP system. It's back up now.").

[1357] Submission from Source 534, to H. Comm. on the Judiciary, 2 (Oct. 14, 2019) (on file with Comm.).

[1358] CEO Hearing at A-12 (response to Questions for the Record by Sundar Pichai, Chief Executive Officer, Google).

[1359] Production of Google, to H. Comm. on the Judiciary, GOOG-HJC-02393308 (Mar. 1, 2011) (on file with Comm.).

[1360] *See generally* Press Release, Eur. Comm'n, Antitrust: Commission Fines Google €4.34 Billion For Illegal Practices Regarding Android Mobile Devices To Strengthen Dominance Of Google's Search Engine (July 17, 2018), https://europa.eu/rapid/press-release_IP-18-4581_en.htm.

For the remaining portion of the global mobile phone market—Apple iOS—Google uses the popularity of its mobile applications to promote Chrome installations. Although Apple does not permit Chrome to be set as the default browser on an iPhone, Google provides users the option to use Chrome whenever a user selects a link within a Google application, such as Gmail or YouTube.[1361]

While Apple requires that Safari also be included as a choice,[1362] Google does not allow any other browser to be listed. If the user has not previously installed the Chrome browser, then the menu displays a "Get" button that prompts the user to install Google's browser.[1363]

Similarly, Google privileges its own line of businesses by setting Google Search as the default in Chrome. Although users can change this setting, the process is not intuitive and involves multiple steps, including:

1. At the top right, click More ⋮ ﹥ **Settings**.
2. Under "Search engine," click **Manage search engines**.
3. Find "Other search engines."
   - **Add**: To the right of "Other search engines," click **Add**. Fill out the text fields and click **Add**.
   - **Set as default**: To the right of the search engine, click More ⋮ ﹥ **Make default**.
   - **Edit**: To the right of the search engine, click More ⋮ ﹥ **Edit**.
   - **Delete**: To the right of the search engine, click More ⋮ ﹥ **Remove from list**.[1364]

One third party told the Subcommittee that in some cases, Google prompts users to change their default search engine back to Google Search even after they have switched:

> After a user installs the extension, Chrome is showing continuous warning prompts which ask users to restore their search settings back to Google. In user tests, we observe that most people are very confused about this prompt and often click "restore settings" even though they actually want to keep using [our search engine]. In many Chrome versions the button "restore settings" is even highlighted which makes it highly likely that users will click this button and thereby completely remove [our search engine] from

---

[1361] Submission from Source 269, to H. Comm on the Judiciary, 3 (July 23, 2019) (on file with Comm.).

[1362] *Id.*

[1363] *Id.*

[1364] *Set your default search engine*, GOOGLE CHROME HELP, https://support.google.com/chrome/answer/95426?co=GENIE.Platform%3DDesktop&hl=en (last visited Oct. 2, 2020).

their computers. We believe that we have already lost millions of users because of this prompt.[1365]

iii. Unilaterally Setting Standards

By virtue of its dominance in the browser market, Google can effectively set standards for the industry in two ways.

First, changes to Chrome's functionality create *de facto* standards. Market participants must adhere to these standards or risk their technology no longer being compatible with most websites. Market participants explain that Google will often build features quickly without using the standard-setting process or giving smaller browsers time to implement new features. Once web developers start building to these specifications, however, smaller browsers are under pressure to quickly implement these changes, often with little notice.[1366] If smaller browsers cannot keep up, users are flooded with "[b]rowser not supported" messages on webpages that have already built to Chrome's specifications.[1367] Several market participants told the Subcommittee that they felt "bullied" by this process.[1368]

Second, Google's has an outsized role in the formal stakeholder standards-making processes. As explained earlier in this Report, the World Wide Web Consortium (W3C) is one of the leading standards organizations in the browser market. Its stated mission is to be "open and collectively empowering."[1369] Other market participants believe that Google is significantly overrepresented in the W3C web platform incubator community group (WICG). They note that Google's employees comprise 106 members, more than eight times the number of employees from Microsoft, the next largest stakeholder represented. Most companies, meanwhile, have only one representative.[1370] One market participant said:

> Though standards bodies like the W3C give the impression of being a place where browser vendors collaborate to improve the web platform; in reality Google's monopoly position and aggressive rate of shipping non-standard features frequently reduce standards bodies to codifying web features and decisions Google has already made.[1371]

[1365] Submission from Source 534, to H. Comm. on the Judiciary, 3 (Oct. 14, 2019) (on file with Comm.).

[1366] Submission from Source 269, to H. Comm. on the Judiciary, (Jan. 2020) (on file with Comm.).

[1367] Martin Brinkmann, *The new Skype for Web does not work in Firefox or Opera*, GHACKS.NET (Mar. 08, 2019), https://www.ghacks.net/2019/03/08/the-new-skype-for-web-does-not-work-in-firefox-or-opera/.

[1368] Interview with Source 482 (July 2, 2020).

[1369] *W3C Mission*, W3C https://www.w3.org/Consortium/mission (last visited on Oct. 4, 2020).

[1370] Submission from Source 269, to H. Comm. on the Judiciary, 4 (July 23, 2019) (on file with Comm.).

[1371] Submission from Source 269, to H. Comm. on the Judiciary, (Apr. 1, 2020) (on file with Comm.).

Recent events underscore how Google's ad-based business model can prompt questions about whether the standards Google chooses to introduce are ultimately designed primarily to serve Google's interests. In January 2020, Google announced that it plans to phase out third-party cookies in Chrome within two years.[1372] Unlike other browsers that have limited cross-site tracking, Google's decision appears to be motivated by "trying to cut down on tracking without kneecapping revenue for websites."[1373]

Several observers have noted that this change would have the likely effect of reinforcing Google's power and harming rivals, shifting more advertisers toward Google.[1374] In particular market participants are concerned that while Google phases out third-party cookies needed by other digital advertising companies, Google can still rely on data collected throughout its ecosystem.

During the Subcommittee's sixth hearing Congressman Kelly Armstrong (R-ND) asked Mr. Pichai, "[D]o you have other ways of collecting it [data] through Gmail or consumer facing platforms?" Mr. Pichai responded, "[T]o the extent on the services where we provide ads and if users have consented to ads personalization, yes, we do have data."[1375]

6. Maps

a. Overview

Google dominates the market for digital maps with over a billion users.[1376] Between Google Maps and Waze—which Google also owns—the corporation captures an estimated 80% of the navigation app market.[1377] Financial analysts have described navigation maps as a "utility" that people cannot do without,[1378] and one bank estimated that if Google Maps were a standalone product its market capitalization would hit $61.5 billion.[1379]

[1372] Sarah Sluis, *Google Chrome Will Drop Third-Party Cookies in 2 Years*, AD EXCHANGER (Jan. 14, 2020), https://www.adexchanger.com/online-advertising/google-chrome-will-drop-third-party-cookies-in-2-years/.

[1373] Dieter Bohn, *Google to 'phase out' Third-party cookies in Chrome, but not for two years*, THE VERGE (Jan. 14, 2020), https://www.theverge.com/2020/1/14/21064698/google-third-party-cookies-chrome-two-years-privacy-safari-firefox.

[1374] Nick Bastone, *In Ironic Twist, Google's Pro-Privacy Move Boosted U.S. Antitrust Probe*, THE INFORMATION (Sept. 18, 2020), https://www.theinformation.com/articles/in-ironic-twist-googles-pro-privacy-move-boosted-u-s-antitrust-probe.

[1375] CEO Hearing Transcript at 125 (Sundar Pichai, Chief Executive Officer, Google).

[1376] Ethan Russell, *9 things to know about Google's maps data: Beyond the Map*, Google Cloud (Sept. 30, 2019), https://cloud.google.com/blog/products/maps-platform/9-things-know-about-googles-maps-data-beyond-map.

[1377] MARC S.F. MAHANEY, ROYAL BANK OF CANADA CAP. MKTS., ALPHABET INC.: DIGGING FOR BURIED TREASURE – THE GOOGLE MAPS OPPORTUNITY 5 (Sept. 23, 2019) (on file with Comm.).

[1378] *Id.*

[1379] Ross Sandler, BARCLAYS, ALPHABET INC., STEADY COMPOUNDER, WITH PLENTY OF INNOVATION AHEAD 20 (Mar. 28, 2017) (on file with Comm.).

Google Maps can be traced to a series of acquisitions. In September 2003, Google Labs launched "Search by Location," a feature that sought to filter search results based on a user's geographic location.[1380] Because Google lacked mapping data, however, the feature stalled.[1381] In October 2004, a few months after Google's IPO, Google acquired Where 2 Technologies, an Australian startup that created web-based dynamic maps.[1382] Google soon followed this acquisition with two additional purchases: Keyhole, a firm that used satellite images and aerial photos to create digital-mapping software, and ZipDash, a provider of real-time traffic information captured through GPS.[1383] In February 2005, Google launched Google Maps.[1384]

The following year, Google introduced Google Maps API, which enabled developers to use and build on top of its digital maps.[1385] In 2008, it launched "Ground Truth," a project devoted to assembling and refining underlying mapping data and images.[1386] This effort included Google Street View Cars, which drove around the country—and, eventually, the world—taking pictures of the surrounding buildings and landscapes, and delivering Google structured data that it could use to create digital maps.[1387] As part of Project Ground Truth, Google also obtained mapping information from satellite and aerial imagery, as well as from public databases.[1388]

A 2008 budget request for Ground Truth stated that the goal of the project was "long term independence from Tele Atlas and Navteq," two sources of mapping data that Google had been using at the time and that were owned by TomTom and Nokia, respectively.[1389] The presentation stated that achieving independence would take several years and requested a 5-7 year renewal of the Tele Atlas contract to help Google bridge "between now and completion of Google Truth initiatives."[1390]

[1380] Scarlett Pruitt, *Google Test Drives New Search Tool*, PC WORLD (Sept. 23, 2003), https://www.pcworld.com/article/112604/article.html.

[1381] Google Maps, ACQUIRED (Aug. 26, 2019), https://www.acquired.fm/episodes/google-maps.

[1382] *Id.*

[1383] *Google Acquires Keyhole*, WALL ST. J.: NEWS ROUNDUP (Oct. 27, 2004); Michael Bazeley, *Google acquires traffic info start-up ZipDash*, VENTUREBEAT (Mar. 30, 2005) https://venturebeat.com/2005/03/30/google-acquires-traffic-info-start-up-zipdash/#:~:text=According%20to%20the%20company's%20web,the%20GPS%20in%20their%20phones.

[1384] Elizabeth Reid, *A look back at 15 years of mapping the world*, THE KEYWORD (Feb. 6, 2020), https://blog.google/products/maps/look-back-15-years-mapping-world/.

[1385] *Id.*

[1386] Frederic Lardinois, *Google's Ground Truth Initiative for Building More Accurate Maps Now Covers 50 Countries*, TECHCRUNCH (Sept. 3, 2014), https://techcrunch.com/2014/09/03/googles-ground-truth-initiative-for-building-more-accurate-maps-now-covers-50-countries/.

[1387] Greg Miller, *The Huge, Unseen Operation Behind the Accuracy of Google Maps*, WIRED (Dec. 8, 2014), https://www.wired.com/2014/12/google-maps-ground-truth/ (As of December 2014, Google's "Street View cars ha[d] driven over 7 million miles, including 99 percent of the public roads in the U.S.").

[1388] *Id.*

[1389] Production of Google, to H. Comm. on the Judiciary, GOOG-HJC-03386002 (Dec. 6, 2007) (on file with Comm.).

[1390] *Id.*

Although Google Maps was not generating revenues, Google was investing in it heavily. Google's documents show that from 2008 to 2009, the company spent $32 million on the Street View program and $88.7 million on Ground Truth overall.[1391] When Google launched Google Maps in 2005, MapQuest had been the "king of Internet-based maps and driving directions," with Yahoo gearing up to heavily compete.[1392] By 2008, Google's internal documents show that Google was "#1 in Maps usage" as well as at the top in capturing online local search.[1393]

In 2009, Google introduced Google Maps for Mobile, a navigation service featuring turn-by-turn directions, live traffic updates, and automatic rerouting.[1394] Whereas market leaders TomTom and Garmin sold navigation services through subscriptions, Google was offering its service for free[1395]—a fact widely seen as disfavoring the incumbents, whose stock prices fell upon Google's announcement.[1396] As one analyst noted at the time, "If it's free and a good service, why would you pay for something you can get for free?"[1397]

As smartphones overtook personal navigation devices, Google Maps further eclipsed TomTom and Garmin.[1398] When asked in 2015 what had accounted for TomTom's decline, its CEO cited two factors: the 2008 economic crisis and the fact that "Google began offering navigation for free."[1399]

Some market participants at the time questioned whether Google was using its search dominance to give Google Maps a boost. In 2009, one publisher noted that "61% of visits to Google Maps came directly from Google," giving it an advantage over MapQuest.[1400] The publisher wrote,

---

[1391] *Id.* at GOOG-HJC-04211018 (Oct. 17, 2010).

[1392] Chris Gaither, *Overtaking MapQuest a Challenge for Yahoo*, L.A. TIMES (Jan. 10, 2005), https://www.latimes.com/archives/la-xpm-2005-jan-10-fi-maps10-story.html.

[1393] Production of Google, to H. Comm. on the Judiciary, GOOG-HJC-03610422 (Oct. 28, 2008) (on file with Comm.).

[1394] *Announcing Google Maps Navigation for Android 2.0*, GOOGLE OFFICIAL BLOG (Oct. 28, 2009), https://googleblog.blogspot.com/2009/10/announcing-google-maps-navigation-for.html.

[1395] Jenna Wortham & Miguel Helft, *Hurting Rivals, Google Unveils Free Phones GPS*, N.Y. TIMES (Oct. 28, 2009), https://www.nytimes.com/2009/10/29/technology/companies/29gps.html.

[1396] Arik Hesseldahl, *Garmin, TomTom Slash Prices Amid Google Threat*, BLOOMBERG (Dec. 8, 2009), https://www.bloomberg.com/news/articles/2009-12-08/garmin-tomtom-slash-prices-amid-google-threat (stating that upon Google's announcement, Garmin stock dropped around 16% and TomTom stock fell by around 29%).

[1397] Jenna Wortham & Miguel Helft, *Hurting Rivals, Google Unveils Free Phones GPS*, N.Y. Times (Oct. 28, 2009), https://www.nytimes.com/2009/10/29/technology/companies/29gps.html (internal quotation marks omitted).

[1398] Kevin J. O'Brien, *Smartphone Sales Taking Toll on G.P.S. Devices*, N.Y. TIMES (Nov. 14, 2010), https://www.nytimes.com/2010/11/15/technology/15iht-navigate.html.

[1399] Charles Arthur, *Navigating decline: what happened to TomTom?*, THE GUARDIAN (July 21, 2015), https://www.theguardian.com/business/2015/jul/21/navigating-decline-what-happened-to-tomtom-satnav.

[1400] Experian Marketing Services, *Google Maps Edges Closer to Mapquest*, EXPERIAN BLOG (Feb. 11, 2009), http://www.experian.com/blogs/marketing-forward/2009/02/11/google-maps-edges-closer-to-mapquest/.

"As long as Google dominates search, MapQuest will face a tough battle for visits."[1401] A few years later, Consumer Watchdog wrote a letter to the Antitrust Division noting that Google "was able to muscle its way to dominance by unfairly favoring its own service ahead of such competitors as Mapquest in its online search results."[1402]

In 2013, Google purchased Waze, an Israeli crowd-sourced mapping provider, for $1.3 billion.[1403] The acquisition solidified Google's dominance in turn-by-turn navigation, eliminating its only meaningful competitive threat.

While Google captured the navigation market through offering Google Maps for free, even as it generated no revenue, Google now monetizes both Waze and Google Maps through selling ads. In 2013 Google introduced a limited form of maps advertising, and in recent years it has expanded the program, allowing local businesses to purchase advertising on maps to maximize foot traffic.[1404] Research by Google shows that 76% of users who search for locations nearby end up visiting a related business within a day, and that 28% of those searches ultimately lead to a purchase.[1405] This high conversion rate leads analysts to believe that Google Maps alone could help drive between $1.9 billion and $3.7 billion of incremental revenue by 2021.[1406] Commenting on the value of Google Maps to the Google ecosystem, one analyst noted:

> [Google Maps'] user base has been impressive for years, crossing 1B a few years ago, but monetization is just getting started … Maps is the closest thing to a platform that Google has at the application layer, with three stakeholders in the ecosystem: 1) users; 2) publishers; and 3) advertisers. The importance of Maps to mobile, including both the advertising and transportation-on-demand spaces, is one of the biggest potential markets Google is servicing in the future.[1407]

[1401] *Id.*

[1402] Letter from John M. Simpson, Privacy Project Dir., Consumer Watchdog, to William J. Baer, U.S. Dep't of Justice, Ass't Att'y Gen., Antitrust Division (June 12, 2013), https://www.consumerwatchdog.org/resources/cltrdojwaze061213.pdf.

[1403] Brian McClendon, *Google Maps and Waze, outsmarting traffic together*, GOOGLE BLOG (June 11, 2013), https://googleblog.blogspot.com/2013/06/google-maps-and-waze-outsmarting.html; Vindu Goel, *Google Expands Its Boundaries, Buying Waze for $1 Billion*, N.Y. TIMES (June 11, 2013), https://bits.blogs.nytimes.com/2013/06/11/google-expands-its-boundaries-buying-waze-for-1-billion/.

[1404] MARC S.F. MAHANEY, ROYAL BANK OF CANADA CAP. MKTS., ALPHABET INC.: DIGGING FOR BURIED TREASURE – THE GOOGLE MAPS OPPORTUNITY 10–11 (Sept. 23, 2019) (on file with Comm.).

[1405] *How Mobile Search Connects Users to Stores*, THINK WITH GOOGLE (May 2016), https://www.thinkwithgoogle.com/marketing-strategies/app-and-mobile/mobile-search-trends-consumers-to-stores/.

[1406] *See, e.g.*, MARC S.F. MAHANEY, ROYAL BANK OF CANADA CAP. MKTS., ALPHABET INC.: DIGGING FOR BURIED TREASURE – THE GOOGLE MAPS OPPORTUNITY 20 (Sept. 23, 2019) (on file with Comm.).

[1407] ROSS SANDLER, BARCLAYS, ALPHABET INC., STEADY COMPOUNDER, WITH PLENTY OF INNOVATION AHEAD 20 (Mar. 28, 2017) (on file with Comm.).

b. Market Power

Google Maps is the dominant provider of mapping data and turn-by-turn navigation services. The company declined to provide the Committee with information about the market share captured by Google Maps.[1408] According to a third-party estimate, however, Google Maps combined with Waze captures 81% of the market for turn-by-turn navigation services.[1409] One market participant, meanwhile, estimated that Google Maps API captures over 90% of the business-to-business market.[1410]

Several developers stated that Google Maps introduced greater licensing restrictions as it gained a stronger market position. One noted that Google's control over what now serves as a key mapping technology has allowed Google to call all the shots.[1411] "We license Google Maps and it's essentially a contract of adhesion. It's full of restrictions and we aren't able to negotiate any changes," the developer said.[1412] The developer added that they have explored switching to alternative mapping providers, but that no other provider has the same geographic depth and coverage as Google Maps. "Other providers still value us and want to know how they can accommodate us," they said. "With Google, we just have to comply with all their restrictions."[1413]

Several factors suggest that Google Maps is well positioned to maintain its dominance. The high fixed costs of creating mapping data pose a significant barrier to entry. Apple, which recently built its mapping database from the ground up, told the Subcommittee that the effort required billions of dollars.[1414] Google, moreover, also benefits from an enormous lead in the tracking and processing of location data, as well as from the prevalence of tracking-enabled Android devices.[1415] Commenting on

---

[1408] Production of Google, to H. Comm. on the Judiciary, A-4 (Nov. 22, 2019) (on file with Comm.) ("Google Maps has a number of features, including maps, turn-by-turn navigation and directions, Street View, and information on local businesses (such as restaurants and services)and travel destinations (such as hotels and tourist spots) that are also offered by competitors. These competitors include Apple Maps, Bing Maps, TomTom, Yelp, TripAdvisor, Angie's List, and Facebook .... All of these competitors are widely used, with some having a strong presence on key platforms: for example, one report from 2015 estimated that iPhone users use Apple Maps three times more than Google Maps. However, we are not aware of any public market share estimates that reflect the frequency of multi-homing among users or that account for competitors like TripAdvisor, OpenTable, Yelp, or directory apps such as Yellow Pages that overlap with many of the features of Google Maps, which would reflect the full range of robust competition in maps that drives Google to continually invest and innovate in the Google Maps product.").

[1409] MARC S.F. MAHANEY, ROYAL BANK OF CANADA CAP. MKTS., ALPHABET INC.: DIGGING FOR BURIED TREASURE – THE GOOGLE MAPS OPPORTUNITY 4 (Sept. 23, 2019) (on file with Comm.).

[1410] Submission from Source 564, to H. Comm. on the Judiciary, 2 (Nov. 13, 2019) (on file with Comm.).

[1411] Interview with Source 703 (June 22, 2020).

[1412] *Id.*

[1413] *Id.*

[1414] Innovation and Entrepreneurship Hearing at 6 (response to Questions for the record from Kyle Andeer, Vice Pres., Corp. Law).

[1415] MARC S.F. MAHANEY, ROYAL BANK OF CANADA CAP. MKTS., ALPHABET INC.: DIGGING FOR BURIED TREASURE – THE GOOGLE MAPS OPPORTUNITY 10–11 (Sept. 23, 2019) (on file with Comm.).

its monetization potential, an analyst recently wrote that Google Maps has "reasonably sustainable moats."[1416]

Certain businesses have made public disclosures about their reliance on Google Maps. For example, in 2019, Uber disclosed that it relies on Google Maps for "the mapping function that is critical to the functionality" of its platform.[1417] It added, "We do not believe that an alternative mapping solution exists that can provide the global functionality that we require to offer our platform in all of the markets in which we operate."[1418] Uber disclosed that between January 1, 2016 through December 31, 2018, the company paid Google $58 million for use of Google Maps.[1419]

In a submission to the Subcommittee, one market participant who uses Google Maps to power its reservation system, website, and mobile app, stated that there are no alternatives to using Google Maps. It wrote, "Local businesses are most likely to use Google's tools to index their websites because Google controls the search engine space, which has the ability to deliver—or restrict—whether these websites appear in corresponding links in consumer search results."[1420] The market participant added that this dependence reinforces Google's market power, as it "provides Google with another opportunity to monetize companies' supply chains and leverage its pricing power over companies that need to promote their businesses and/or purchase ad space to grow."[1421] This business predicted that "the data advantages that Google incorporates into its tools will only grow with time, making it impossible for a new player to ever achieve the scale, user base, or database necessary to compete."[1422]

c. Merger Activity

Google has made several acquisitions related to digital mapping: Where2Technologies (2004); Keyhole (2004); Skybox (2011); and Waze (2013). Of these acquisitions, only Waze—for which Google paid $1.1 billion—was subject to an antitrust investigation. Although Google did not originally report the Waze transaction, both the Federal Trade Commission and the United Kingdom's Office of Fair Trading (OFT) reviewed the deal.[1423] Both enforcers initially approved the transaction but have

---

[1416] *Id.* at 1.

[1417] Uber Technologies, Inc., Registration Statement (Form S-1) 46 (Apr. 11, 2019), https://www.sec.gov/Archives/edgar/data/1543151/000119312519103850/d647752ds1.htm.

[1418] *Id.* It is unclear whether Uber pays Google for the underlying maps data or for the place search function, both of which are part of "Google Maps Core Services."

[1419] *Id.* at 254.

[1420] Submission from Source 333, to H. Comm. on the Judiciary, 5 (Oct. 21, 2019) (on file with Comm.).

[1421] *Id.*

[1422] *Id.*

[1423] Mark Bergen & Ben Brody, *Google's Waze Deal Is a Likely Target in FTC Antitrust Sweep*, BLOOMBERG (Feb. 14, 2020), https://www.bloomberg.com/news/articles/2020-02-14/google-s-waze-deal-is-a-likely-target-in-new-ftc-antitrust-sweep.

since revisited the decision. In 2019 the OFT commissioned a study reviewing its past merger cases, including Google/Waze, and the FTC is reportedly examining the Waze deal as part of its broader review of previous tech mergers.[1424]

Materials that the FTC produced to the Subcommittee suggest that the Commission's analysis of the Google/Waze deal was limited. A document from the FTC shows that the agency focused on assessing the quality of Waze's data and concluded that its maps were "not a Google maps replacement."[1425] It is unclear if or how closely the agency considered that Google was acquiring Waze not for its mapping features (which Google's own documents had suggested were inferior to Google's), but in order to eliminate an independent source of mapping data.[1426]

In acquiring Waze, Google bought out one of the few companies in the world making navigable maps while also providing turn-by-turn navigation service.[1427] Founded in Israel, Waze had entered the U.S. market by initially relying on public domain public data, which it refined through input from drivers.[1428] Waze's model has relied on user-generated maps, whereby drivers using Waze's app feed real-time data back into the app, and volunteer "editors" proactively fine-tune the maps by fixing street names, adding businesses, and making other updates. Waze's documents reveal that through 2012 the firm had prioritized achieving growth and attracting users over earning revenue, although it had begun to monetize its navigation app through location-based advertising.[1429]

Internal Waze presentations stated that its crowd-sourced data was one of the company's defining features. One presentation stated, "The DNA of the company is of a social network, and user generated, we are merely the stage, and not the performers."[1430] In a 2013 document, Waze identified its two main competitive advantages: first, the fact that Waze was a real-time map with fresh data, accounting for updates such as car accidents and road closures; and, second, that its business involved "zero cost."[1431]

Google's documents reveal that by 2012, Google Maps was the top provider of digital maps in desktop, mobile, and API,[1432] and it was closely tracking Waze's fast growth. One Google presentation

---

[1424] *Id.*

[1426] *Id.*

[1427] Production of Google, to H. Comm. on the Judiciary, GOOG-HJC-04208423 (June 2013) (on file with Comm.)

[1428] *Id.* at GOOG-HJC-04211080 (Jul 24, 2013) (citing the U.S. Census Bureau's TIGER mapping data as one source).

[1429] *Id.* at GOOG-HJC-04208066 (June 2013) (on file with Comm.) (Waze was "earning $250k in revenue in January 2013 and less than $1 million in revenue in 2012").

[1430] *Id.* at GOOG-HJC-04208423 (June 2013).

[1431] *Id.*

[1432] *Id.* at GOOG-HJC-04208281 (May 2012).

in 2012 noted that Waze was the most-downloaded app in the navigation category, and that it was seeing a 30% increase in daily downloads and averaging around 100,000 downloads a day.[1433] Google also honed in on the fact that Waze was the only other mapping provider that was vertically integrated across the full stack, spanning the provider, application, map, traffic, and search layers.[1434]

In an internal presentation, Google identified several strategic rationales for acquiring Waze.[1435] These included obtaining a "highly-engaged community of map contributors and expertise" in order to "nurture/grow communities," which Google said it struggled with; achieving a "scalable solution" for maintaining a fresh map with "real-time incident data"; using Waze as a "sandbox" to "test map/navigation features"; and acquiring a "highly-talented team" with "deep experience in maps."[1436] Google also ranked Waze poorly on several metrics, including the accuracy of its results in smaller cities and its limited map search capabilities.[1437] Commenting on Waze's mapping tiles, Google wrote, "[D]ata is missing and rendering is overly simple and missing detail."[1438] Meanwhile, Google described Waze's future financial projections as "highly speculative,"[1439] and noted that its purchase price of just under $1 billion was "expensive for a company with < $1 million in 2012 revenue."[1440]

In its correspondence with the FTC, Google stated that "there is no shortage of full-featured navigation alternatives for users," which it said reflected the "low (and continually decreasing) barriers to entry."[1441] Google emphasized Waze's entry, in particular, focusing on how Waze "spent far less than $20 million *for all purposes* in the two years preceding its US launch" and noting that it was able to enter the market using only public domain data.[1442]

In contrast, market participants viewed Google and Waze as close competitors in a "highly concentrated" market for navigable digital map databases and turn-by-turn navigation applications. Prior to the transaction, Waze had observed that it and Google were "the only vertically integrated stacks."[1443] One market participant told antitrust enforcers that it viewed Waze as "Google's closest competitor for real-time, updated [turn-by-turn] navigation services" and that Waze "was the digital-

[1433] *Id.* at GOOG-HJC-04208072 (Nov. 2012).

[1434] *Id.* at GOOG-HJC-04209632. (Nov. 2012).

[1435] *Id.* at GOOG-HJC-04208127 (May 2013)

[1436] *Id.*

[1437] *Id.* at GOOG-HJC-04208140 (May 2013).

[1438] *Id.*

[1439] *Id.* at GOOG-HJC-04213996 (June 2013).

[1440] *Id.* at GOOG-HJC-04208047. (June 2013).

[1441] *Id.* at GOOG-HJC-04211046 (July 24, 2013).

[1442] *Id.* at.GOOG-HJC-04211080 (July 24, 2013).

[1443] *Id.* at GOOG-HJC-04208696.

map competitor with the best opportunity to overcome Google's significant data and funding advantage."[1444]

Market participants cited a few reasons the transaction would undermine competition. First, they noted that barriers to entry in the market for turn-by-turn navigation providers were high, and that it would be difficult for new firms to enter. One market participant stated, "Navigable digital map databases contain far more information than maps and addresses. For example, Google's database includes a range of other information, including traffic, conditions and rerouting information, interior and exterior photographs, reviews, commentary from Google+ friends."[1445] And Waze, in particular, had a unique crowd-sourced model that would be difficult for other firms to replicate. Although Waze had secured a "first-mover advantage" and acquired a "critical mass of users," the group of self-selected volunteers who edited Waze's maps were "unlikely to fill such a role (without payment) for more than one set of mapping data."[1446] The market participant added, "Once those editors provide the benefit of their input into Waze they create a powerful map that passive Waze users will turn to as well given the lack of other real-time-updated maps of comparable quality. As a result, passive Waze users likely will have no incentive to multi-home."[1447]

Second, market participants pointed to the fact that Waze was the only firm meaningfully positioned to dislodge Google Maps because it—like Google—lacked financial pressures. One entrepreneur noted, "Google and Waze do not care how much it costs to keep the maps up-to-date. Google because it has a lot of money, and Waze because it relies on the community."[1448] One market participant stated:

> The acquisition would effectively lead to the elimination of Waze as a market disrupting force that would otherwise be capable of challenging the model adopted by Google's dominant Google Maps. In essence, Google's acquisition of Waze is defensive - seeking to remove a disruptive force from the market.[1449]

Several market participants and advocates who opposed the deal noted that Waze's own CEO, Noam Bardin, had recently stated that Waze was "the only reasonable competition" to Google Maps, which would suggest that Google may have been pursuing the acquisition in efforts to quash its most significant competitor.[1450]

[1444] Submission from Source 26, to H. Comm. on the Judiciary, Source 26-000622 (Sept. 21, 2013) (on file with Comm.).

[1445] *Id.*; Interview with Source 572 (Sept. 24, 2020).

[1446] Interview with Source 572 (Sept. 24, 2020).

[1447] *Id.*

[1448] *Id.*

[1449] *Id.*

Letter from John M. Simpson, Privacy Project Dir., Consumer Watchdog, to William J. Baer, U.S. Dep't of Justice, Ass't Att'y Gen., Antitrust Division (June 12, 2013), https://www.consumerwatchdog.org/resources/cltrdojwaze061213.pdf.

And third, market participants argued that the acquisition would give Google both the incentive and ability to foreclose rivals, including those apps that offer mobile navigation and social networking services. Seeking to mitigate this concern, Google's letter to the FTC emphasized the "numerous providers who license mapping, traffic, and incident" data for use in mobile apps.[1451]

Today, the Google Maps and Waze teams remain separate. Analysts have reported that Google has used Waze as a tool to "test and iterate on monetizing Navigation without disrupting its much larger Google Maps asset."[1452] One market participant stated, "Google has used Waze as an ads guinea pig,"[1453] noting that Waze has released efficacy reports of location-tailored ads, information that seems to have informed Google Maps' recent expansion of advertising.[1454]

Since completing the Waze acquisition, Google has reportedly come to capture 81% of the market for navigation mapping services.[1455] Despite Google's claims that entry barriers were low and alternate offerings abundant, no meaningful competitor has emerged since Google acquired Waze. Based on the materials the FTC provided to the Subcommittee, it is unclear whether the Commission fully assessed the barriers to entry. It instead appears the FTC primarily took a static view—focusing on the existing quality of Waze's maps—rather than assessing the dynamic effects of the acquisition.

d. Conduct

i. Raising Prices

For years, Google offered a free tier of the Maps API, incentivizing developers to build their apps with Google Maps. In 2018, however, Google Maps introduced a single "pay-as-you-go" pricing plan for the core mapping APIs.[1456] This shift dramatically reduced the number of free Maps API calls a firm could make—from 25,000 per day to around 930 per day.[1457] Developers stated that the change amounted to a price increase of 1,400%.[1458]

[1451] Production of Google, to H. Comm. on the Judiciary, GOOG-HJC-04211030 (July 24, 2013) (on file with Comm.). *See also* Interview with Source 572 (Sept. 24, 2020).

[1452] Marc S.F. Mahaney, *Digging For Buried Treasure – The Google Maps Opportunity*, ROYAL BANK OF CANADA 14 (Sept. 23, 2019) (on file with Comm.).]

[1453] Interview with Source 572 (Sept. 24, 2020).

[1454] *Id.*

[1455] MARC S.F. MAHANEY, ROYAL BANK OF CANADA CAP. MKTS., ALPHABET INC.: DIGGING FOR BURIED TREASURE – THE GOOGLE MAPS OPPORTUNITY 5 (Sept. 23, 2019) (on file with Comm.).

[1456] Jagmeet Singh, *Google Maps API Price Hike is Threatening the Future of Some Companies*, GADGETS 360 (Aug. 28, 2018), https://gadgets.ndtv.com/apps/features/google-maps-apis-new-pricing-impact-1907242.

[1457] *Id.*

[1458] Ishveena Singh, *Insane, shocking, outrageous: Developers react to changes in Google Maps API*, GEO AWESOMENESS (May 3, 2018), https://geoawesomeness.com/developers-up-in-arms-over-google-maps-api-insane-price-hike/ ("The Standard (no access to customer support) and Premium plans are being merged into one pay-as-you-go pricing plan. And

In a submission to the Subcommittee, one market participant said that Google instituted this price hike after "gaining dominance."[1459] Since becoming a Google Maps customer, the market participant's costs "have increased over 20x" and "there are no viable alternatives."[1460] Another developer stated that the 2018 pricing change "took our bill from $90/month in October to $20,000/month in December."[1461] The developer stated that it was able to subsequently reduce its bill through making a change that enabled the location-retrieval function to occur directly on a user's device—a change that gave Google "greater ability to identify and track" the device user.[1462]

Several developers expressed their frustrations publicly, noting that Google's decision to hike prices so sharply, and without giving developers significant notice, underscored its power to set the terms of commerce. One developer stated:

> I understand that Google wants to make this into a line of business. But it feels like they're taking advantage of us. They know that they're the best, and that no one else is even close. Instead of just giving us Maps for free or very cheap, in exchange for collecting all our usage data, they now feel they need to charge really high prices.[1463]

In effect, Google makes market participants pay twice to access Google Maps—first by giving Google their valuable usage data and then again by paying Google's volume-based fees for API calls.

ii. Tying

Business-facing mapping products usually consist of a core set of features to provide greater mapping functionality. For example, the "Google Maps Platform" offers developers traffic data and places data (also known as place search) as well as map data.[1464] Some developers choose to mix and match, using map data from one firm but places data from another. Google, however, prohibits

---

the new fee structure is not pretty. Google is raising its prices by more than 1,400%. Obviously, no direct comparison figures of old and new prices have been provided by Google, but that's the average surge that is being reported by developers.").

[1459] Submission from Source 564, to H. Comm. on the Judiciary, 2 (Nov. 13, 2019) (on file with Comm.).

[1460] *Id.* at 4.

[1461] Submission from Source 685, to H. Comm. on the Judiciary, 4 (Oct. 15, 2019) (on file with Comm.).

[1462] *Id.*

[1463] Jagmeet Singh, *Google Maps API Price Hike is Threatening the Future of Some Companies*, GADGETS 360 (Aug. 28, 2018), https://gadgets.ndtv.com/apps/features/google-maps-apis-new-pricing-impact-1907242.

[1464] *Google Maps Platform Terms of Service, 21. Definitions*, GOOGLE ("'Google Maps Content' means any content provided through the Service (whether created by Google or its third-party licensors), including map and terrain data, imagery, traffic data, and places data (including business listings)."), https://cloud.google.com/maps-platform/terms (last visited on Oct. 3, 2020).

developers from using any part of its mapping tools alongside any non-Google mapping features. Until April 2020, Google's Maps Platform Terms of Service included the following provision:

> (e) <u>No Use With Non-Google Maps</u>. Customer will not use the Google Maps Core Services in a Customer Application that contains a non-Google map. For example, Customer will not (i) display Places listings on a non-Google map, or (ii) display Street View imagery and non-Google maps in the same Customer Application.[1465]

In April 2020, Google amended the language slightly:

> (e) No Use With Non-Google Maps. To avoid quality issues and/or brand confusion, Customer will not use the Google Maps Core Services with or near a non-Google Map in a Customer Application. For example, Customer will not (i) display or use Places content on a non-Google map, (ii) display Street View imagery and non-Google maps on the same screen, or (iii) link a Google Map to non-Google Maps content or a non-Google map.[1466]

Both versions of this provision prohibit developers from using *any* component of the Google Maps Core Service with mapping services provided by non-Google firms. The April 2020 change to the terms of service is even more restrictive: it prohibits developers from even displaying any component of Google Maps "near" any other map. In practice, Google's contractual provision has led several major companies to switch entirely to Google's ecosystem, even in cases where they preferred mapping services from a non-Google provider, such as Mapbox.

Through interviews with market participants, the Subcommittee learned that Google now enforces this provision aggressively. According to one firm, Google closely tracks and pressures developers who use Google's place data in conjunction with mapping data from a non-Google firm, effectively forcing them to choose whether they will use all of Google's mapping services or none of them.[1467] One firm described Google's coercive tactics, stating, "It's a bigger player putting a gun to our head saying 'switch or else.'"[1468]

Because Google's monopoly in online search has furnished it with a trove of data, as well as a robust index, its place search feature is also seen by many market participants effectively as a must-have. One market participant that has lost business partnerships due to Google's coercive restrictions stated that Google is "using access to its dominant search products as leverage to intimidate businesses

---

[1465] *Id.* at 3.2.2(e).

[1466] *Id.*

[1467] Interview with Source 572 (Sept. 24, 2020).

[1468] Interview with Source 157 (Sept. 25, 2020).

out of working with other map providers."[1469] He noted that Google's conduct now threatens his firm's survival, saying, "This is existential for us."[1470]

Google was asked to identify and justify any limits it places on the ability of app developers who use the Google Maps Platform to use non-Google mapping services.[1471] Google responded that it does "restrict developers from incorporating Google Maps Core Services into an application that uses a non-Google map" in order to "prevent brand confusion and other negative user experiences."[1472] As described above, Google subsequently changed its terms of service to mirror its response to the Subcommittee's question. However, developers and mapping providers questioned Google's rationale, noting that developers were the ones best positioned to determine whether combining mapping services from multiple providers created a "negative user experience." One provider added, "The developers we partner with are extremely sophisticated. They're not confused."[1473]

Google has also used its dominance in mapping to acquire cloud computing customers for its Google Cloud Platform (GCP). Specifically, in 2018, Google implemented a change requiring all API calls to use a valid API key, which must be linked to a Google Cloud Platform account. All keyless calls to the Maps JavaScript API and Street View API trigger low-resolution maps that are watermarked with "for development purposes only."[1474] Developers who do not have a Google Cloud account, and therefore do not have an API key, are effectively locked out of Google Maps. Even if an application is built on a non-Google cloud platform, developers are forced to use GCP for the Maps API portion of their app.[1475] By one estimate, revenue from Google Cloud Platform has more than tripled since 2017, the year before Google began tying access to Google Maps to Google Cloud Platform.[1476]

iii. Self-Preferencing through Contractual Restrictions

Some developers told the Subcommittee that Google uses its control over digital mapping to favor its own products in other lines of business. Since Google provides mapping services but also

---

[1469] Interview with Source 572 (Sept. 24, 2020).

[1470] *Id.*

[1471] Innovation and Entrepreneurship Hearing at 29 (response to Questions for the Record of Adam Cohen, Dir. of Econ. Pol'y, Google LLC).

[1472] *Id.*

[1473] Interview with Source 572 (Sept. 24, 2020).

[1474] *Guide for Existing Users*, GOOGLE CLOUD, https://cloud.google.com/maps-platform/user-guide (last visited Oct. 3, 2020).

[1475] Daria Bulatovych, *Mapbox as a Worthy Alternative to Google Maps Price Hike*, YALANTIS, https://yalantis.com/blog/mapbox-maps-ready-mobile-apps/.

[1476] Larry Dignan, *Top cloud providers in 2020: AWS, Microsoft Azure, and Google Cloud, hybrid, SaaS players*, ZDNET (Oct. 1, 2020), https://www.zdnet.com/article/the-top-cloud-providers-of-2020-aws-microsoft-azure-google-cloud-hybrid-saas/.

offers non-mapping products that use mapping as an input, Google can selectively degrade access for third parties that rely on its mapping product to disfavor them as competitors to its non-mapping products. For example, market participants noted that Google has added various restrictions to the license agreement for Google Maps API—restrictions that apply to third-party developers but not to Google's own competing products.

One example is unequal rights to map caching. Map caching occurs when a server stores copies of map images that it can speedily distribute when next recalled. Without caching, a map is drawn each time it is requested, a much slower process.[1477] Although previous versions of the Google Maps API agreement permitted caching by developers, the recent versions prohibit caching of maps with limited exception.[1478] Third-party apps built on Google Maps API can no longer store a map cache. Market participants note, however, that Google's own products built on Google Maps—ranging from its local search service to its hotel finder—face no similar restrictions, enabling them to load faster than those run by third parties.

Commenting on the asymmetry, one market participant stated that Google's decision to deny third parties caching "denigrates the service that our maps can provide compared to Google's."[1479] They added, "[T]hat's why we can't create an app that provides directions as well as Google or we can't update a user's location as quickly as Google."[1480]

iv. Strategic Platform Mismanagement

Although Google's responses to the Subcommittees' questions about its conduct regarding Google Maps emphasized "quality" and "user experience,"[1481] public reporting has documented that Google Maps' listings are "overrun with millions of false business addresses and fake names."[1482] A fake listing can occur when a business creates a fake listing or when a fraudulent business hijacks the name of a legitimate business on Google Maps, diverting user calls or visits from the legitimate business to a fraudulent one. A survey of experts conducted by the *Wall Street Journal* estimated that

---

[1477] WHAT IS MAP CACHING?, ARCGIS ENTERPRISE, https://enterprise.arcgis.com/en/server/latest/publish-services/linux/what-is-map-caching-.htm (last visited Oct. 3, 2020).

[1478] *Places API Policies, Google Maps Platform*, GOOGLE, https://developers.google.com/places/web-service/policies (last visited Oct. 3, 2020) (stating "that you must not pre-fetch, index, store, or cache any Content except under the limited conditions stated in the terms.").

[1479] Interview with Source 521 (June 22, 2020).

[1480] *Id.*

[1481] Innovation and Entrepreneurship Hearing at 8 (response to Questions for the Record of Adam Cohen, Dir. of Econ. Pol'y, Google) (Sept. 13, 2019).

[1482] Rob Copeland & Katherine Bindley, *Millions of Business Listings on Google Maps Are Fake—and Google Profits*, WALL ST. J. (June 20, 2019), https://www.wsj.com/articles/google-maps-littered-with-fake-business-listings-harming-consumers-and-competitors-11561042283.

Google Maps hosts around 11 million falsely listed businesses on any given day.[1483] The same experts stated that "a majority" of the listings on Google Maps for businesses such as "contractors, electricians, towing and car repair services, movers and lawyers," as well as others, are not actually located at the location given by Google Maps.[1484]

These fake listings endanger consumer safety, giving rise to situations where users of Google Maps have unknowingly requested home repairs and other services from fraudulent providers, ultimately, paying inflated prices for shoddy work.[1485] The fraudulent listings also disadvantage legitimate businesses, both those whose listings have been hijacked as well as those whose own listings appear below those of sham businesses. Marketers have weaponized this problem to demand ransom payments from businesses under the threat of wiping out their listings through a flood of fake businesses. When the listing of one auto junkyard fell from the first to the second page of Google Maps results, the owner's income fell by half and pushed him to the edge of closing shop entirely.[1486]

Legitimate businesses hurt by fake listings say that contacting Google to report the situation generally fails to resolve the problem. In practice, the only ways legitimate businesses can shield themselves from fake listings is to buy ads from Google. Ad prices for categories that are most susceptible to ad fraud have increased more than 50% over the last two years.[1487]

The Subcommittee asked Google about this practice on several occasions. At the Subcommittee's July 16, 2019 hearing, Congresswoman Lucy McBath (D-GA) asked Adam Cohen, Google's director of economic policy, what steps Google was taking to identify and remove fraudulent listings on Google Maps.[1488] She added, "Is it a lack of competition in online search that allows Google to be so complacent by addressing this problem head on?"[1489] Mr. Cohen responded that he was "not familiar" with the relevant facts.[1490] In response to a follow-up letter sent by Chairman Cicilline, Google wrote that it has "no evidence" that the number of fake listings on Google Maps is around 10

[1483] *Id.*

[1484] *Id.*

[1485] *Id.* (reporting that a 67-year-old-woman contacted a local home repair service she found through Google, only to be serviced by a man who was pretending to be from the company she had hired. The man charged almost twice the cost of previous repairs and demanded a personal check or cash. The woman told the *Wall Street Journal*, "I'm at my house by myself with this guy. He could have knocked me over dead.").

[1486] *Id.*

[1487] *Id.*

[1488] Innovation and Entrepreneurship Hearing at 67 (question of Rep Lucy McBath (D-GA), Member, Subcomm. on Antitrust, Commercial and Admin. Law)

[1489] *Id.*

[1490] *Id.* (statement of Adam Cohen, Dir. of Econ. Pol'y, Google LLC).

million.[1491] Google stated that, as of July 2019, it had taken down more than 3 million fake business profiles and that it has "implemented strict policies and created tools that enable people to flag false content."[1492]

Both digital advertisement experts and individuals engaging in fraudulent activity believe that Google has turned a blind eye to the problem. According to the *Wall Street Journal*, one ad specialist who was invited by Google to help root out the problem left after concluding that Google "has obviously chosen not to solve the problem."[1493] A business owner who helps facilitate the fake listings says his activity leaves a "huge footprint" and yet Google is "just letting it happen." He added, "I know Google knows."[1494]

7. Cloud

Google Cloud Platform (GCP) is Google's suite of public cloud computing services that first launched in 2008.[1495] Today, Google Cloud is Alphabet's fastest growing line of business, with revenues in Q1 2020 hitting $2.78 billion, up 52% from $1.83 billion in Q1 2019.[1496] Documents provided to the Subcommittee make clear that the cloud market is a priority for the company.[1497] GCP is the third largest provider of IaaS services in the United States and has a year-over-year growth rate twice that of Amazon Web Services—the current market leader.[1498] Today, GCP boasts long term contracts with data intensive companies such as SNAP, Spotify and TikTok.[1499]

[1491] Letter from Kent Walker, Senior Vice Pres., Global Affairs and Legal Officer, Google to the Hon. David N. Cicilline, Chairman, Subcomm. on Antitrust, Commercial and Admin. Law (July 26, 2019), https://judiciary.house.gov/sites/democrats.judiciary.house.gov/files/documents/07.26.19%20-%20google%20response.pdf.

[1492] *Id.*

[1493] Rob Copeland & Katherine Bindley, *Millions of Business Listings on Google Maps Are Fake—and Google Profits*, WALL ST. J. (June 20, 2019), https://www.wsj.com/articles/google-maps-littered-with-fake-business-listings-harming-consumers-and-competitors-11561042283 (internal quotation marks omitted).

[1494] *Id.* (internal quotation marks omitted).

[1495] Michael Arrington. *Google Jumps Head First Into Web Services With Google App Engine*, TECHCRUNCH (Apr.8, 2008). https://techcrunch.com/2008/04/07/google-jumps-head-first-into-web-services-with-google-app-engine/ (reporting that GCP's first public cloud offering, App Engine, launched as a private preview for developers in April 2008).

[1496] Benjamin Pimentel, *Google just reported cloud revenue for the first time ever, showing that it's growing fast but nowhere close to Amazon Web Services*. BUS. INSIDER (Feb 3, 2020). https://www.businessinsider.com/google-cloud-revenue-first-time-thomas-kurian-2020-2.

[1497] Production of Google, to H. Comm. on the Judiciary, GOOG-HJC-04266215 (on file with Comm.).

[1498] GCP's position in the cloud market is explained in the cloud computing market overview section. *See infra* Section IV.

[1499] Snap Inc., Annual Report (Form 10-K) 11 (Feb 4, 2020) (indicating that Snap had committed to spend $2.0 billion with Google Cloud over five years beginning January 2017); Kevin McLaughlin and Amir Efrati, *TikTok Agreed to Buy More Than $800 Million in Cloud Services From Google*, THE INFO. (July 14, 2020), https://www.theinformation.com/articles/tiktok-agreed-to-buy-more-than-800-million-in-cloud-services-from-google (reporting that TikTok signed a three-year agreement with GCP in 2019, with a minimum commitment of $800 million over the time-period).

Subcommittee staff reviewed internal documents that outline Google's plans to invest significantly in acquisitions.[1500] To date, these acquisitions include Orbitera,[1501] Cask Data, Velostrata, and Elastifile among others.[1502] Most recently, Google purchased Looker for $2.6 billion to "add a new analytics tool for Google Cloud's customers."[1503] In some instances, Google acquired firms that were multi-cloud solutions but, after acquisition, Google made them compatible only with Google's cloud infrastructure, at times integrating them into first-party PaaS and SaaS offerings only available through the Google Cloud Portal.[1504]

According to interviews with market participants and Google's internal documents, Google employs two strategies that raise concerns about potential anticompetitive conduct. First, Google appears to leverage its dominant business lines, including popular APIs such as Google Search and Maps, along with machine learning services, to attract customers to its platform through discounts and free tier services.[1505] For example, according to internal strategy documents, in 2018 Google "launched a program with the Play team to provide GCP credits to game developers based on their Play Store spend, to increase focus on Play and incentivize migration to GCP."[1506] By harnessing Google's advantages in existing markets, GCP is undermining competition on the merits.

Second, Google's documents suggest the company is considering bundling its popular machine learning service with other services that Google is seeking to promote. One recent Google cloud pricing strategy document explains, "the question that we need to think about is whether we use our entry point with Big Query to get a customer to use all the services such as Data Proc, Data Flow, as a suite and give them a price break on the Analytics Suite because it will be much harder for them to migrate away from us if they use all the other services."[1507] The document goes on to describe potential

---

[1500] Production of Google, to H. Comm. on the Judiciary, GOOG-HJC-04266215 (on file with Comm.).

[1501] Nan Boden, *Orbitera joins the Google Cloud Platform team*, GOOGLE (Aug. 8, 2016), https://cloud.google.com/blog/products/gcp/orbitera-joins-the-google-cloud-platform-team (noting that GCP leveraged Orbitera technology to offer automated test drives and lead management, custom pricing and billing, cloud cost visibility and control, self-serve onboarding to be fully integrated into the GCP console).

[1502] Ingrid Lunden, *Google acquires Cask Data to beef up its tools for building and running big data analytics*, TECHCRUNCH (May 16, 2018), https://techcrunch.com/2018/05/16/google-acquires-cask-data-to-beef-up-its-tools-for-building-and-running-big-data-analytics/.

[1503] Lauren Feiner & Jordan Novet, *Google cloud boss Thomas Kurian makes his first big move -- buys Looker for $2.6 billion*, CNBC (June 6, 2019), https://www.cnbc.com/2019/06/06/google-buys-cloud-company-looker-for-2point6-billion.html.

[1504] Production of Google, to H. Comm. on the Judiciary, GOOG-HJC-04167298-381. (July 2, 2019) (on file with Comm.). *See, also*, Donna Goodison, *Google Cloud's New Alooma Migration Service Won't Accept New AWS, Microsoft Azure Customers*, CRN (Feb 20, 2019) https://www.crn.com/news/cloud/google-cloud-s-new-alooma-migration-service-won-t-accept-new-aws-microsoft-azure-customers.

[1505] Production of Google, to H. Comm. on the Judiciary, GOOG-HJC-02456801 (on file with Comm.). *See also*, GOOG-HJC-04214427 (Aug 4, 2016).

[1506] *Id.* at GOOG-HJC-04266213 (May 23, 2018) (on file with Comm.).

[1507] *Id.* at GOOG-HJC-04215099 (December 31, 2018).

discounts and ultimately a plan to have "a pricing model that makes it advantageous for customers to put 80% of their workload on GCP."[1508] As described elsewhere in this Report, absent interventions, the barriers to entry and network effects in this market mean there is a high potential for single-homing and an overall concentrated market.[1509] As Google grows in this space, regulators and enforcers should be watchful for potential anticompetitive conduct.

C.   Amazon

1. Overview

Amazon.com, Inc. was founded in 1994 as an online bookseller.[1510] Today, it is one of the largest companies in the world. Based in Seattle, Amazon is estimated to be the second-largest private employer in the United States, with over 500,000 employees.[1511] The company operates across a wide range of direct-to-consumer and business-to-business markets, including e-commerce, consumer electronics, television and film production, groceries, cloud services, book publishing, and logistics. Amazon went public in 1997 but did not post its first full-year profit until 2003.[1512] This is partly because Amazon's business strategy has generally focused on long-term growth over short-term profits.[1513] Amazon is currently one of the most valuable companies in the world, and its CEO, Jeff Bezos, is reported to be the wealthiest person in the world.[1514]

Amazon's Annual Revenue, Operating Expenses, and Profits[1515]

[1508] *Id.*

[1509] *See infra* Section IV.

[1510] Amazon.com, Inc., Annual Report (Form 10-K) 3 (Jan. 31, 2020), http://d18rn0p25nwr6d.cloudfront.net/CIK-0001018724/4d39f579-19d8-4119-b087-ee618abf82d6.pdf.

[1511] Press Release, Amazon, Amazon.com Announces Second Quarter Results 2 (July 30, 2020), https://s2.q4cdn.com/299287126/files/doc_financials/2020/q2/Q2-2020-Amazon-Earnings-Release.pdf; Charles Duhigg, *Is Amazon Unstoppable?*, THE NEW YORKER (Oct. 21, 2019), https://www.newyorker.com/magazine/2019/10/21/is-amazon-unstoppable.

[1512] Amazon.com, Inc., Annual Report (Form 10-K) 83–84 (Mar. 9, 2005), https://www.annualreports.com/HostedData/AnnualReportArchive/a/NASDAQ_AMZN_2004.pdf; Saul Hansell, *Amazon Reports First Full-Year Profit*, N.Y. TIMES (Jan. 28, 2004), https://www.nytimes.com/2004/01/28/business/technology-amazon-reports-first-full-year-profit.html.

[1513] *See, e.g.*, CEO Hearing at 3 (statement of Jeff Bezos, CEO, Amazon.com, Inc.) ("As I have said since my first shareholder letter in 1997, we make decisions based on the long-term value we create . . ."); Production of Amazon, to H. Comm. on the Judiciary, AMAZON-HJC-00035545 (July 14, 2010) (on file with Comm.) ("Membership programs are created with a long-term, company-wide perspective with the goal of increasing loyalty and cross-category shopping behavior. The programs do not optimize for short-term gain or profitability in a single category.").

[1514] *See, e.g.*, Annie Palmer, *Jeff Bezos is Now Worth More than $200 Billion*, CNBC (Aug. 26, 2020), https://www.cnbc.com/2020/08/26/amazon-ceo-jeff-bezos-worth-more-than-200-billion.html.

[1515] Prepared by Subcomm. based on Amazon.com, Inc., Annual Reports (Form 10-K) (1997–2019).

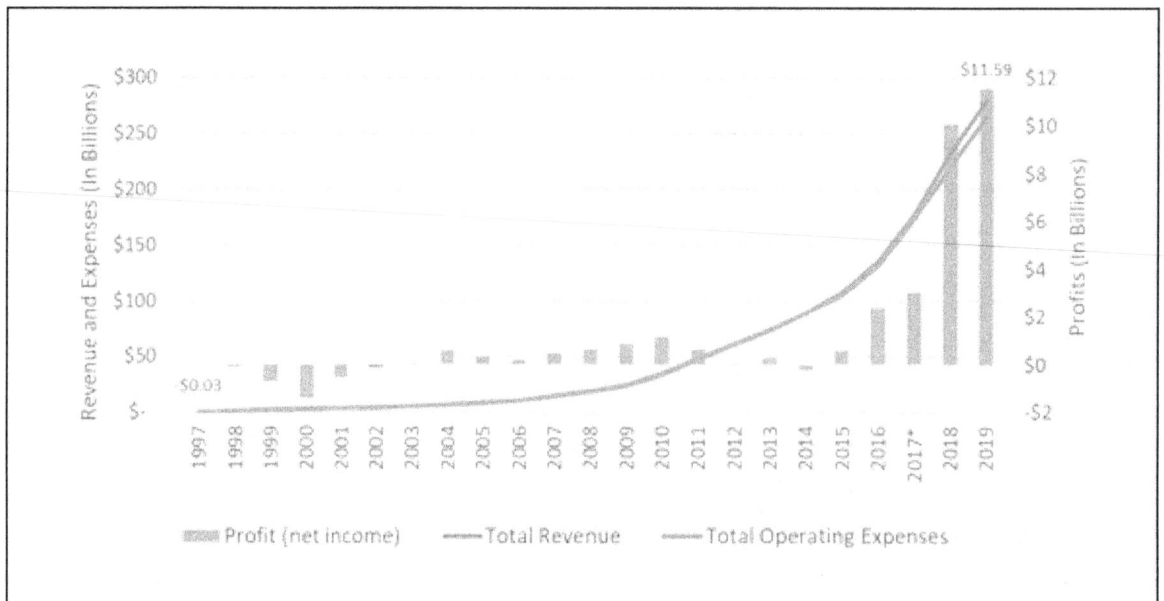

Profit (net income) ——— Total Revenue ——— Total Operating Expenses

Amazon reports financial information for three business segments: North America, International, and Amazon Web Services (AWS), Amazon's cloud services business.[1516] Despite the fact that Amazon is already so large that it dominates several important industries, it continues to report strong and steady growth—as well as increasing profits. For 2019, Amazon reported total revenue of about $280 billion, up 20% from the previous year, and a net income of over $11 billion.[1517] AWS's revenue increased 37% in 2019 to $35 billion.[1518] Retail operations continue to be the platform's largest source of revenue, but AWS is a key source of its overall profits.[1519] In 2019, Amazon's cloud business contributed over 60% of Amazon's total operating income, despite accounting for only 12.5% of its total revenue.[1520]

Sales on Amazon.com fall into one of two categories. First-party sales are those where Amazon retails its own private-label products or sources products wholesale from a vendor or manufacturer. Third-party sales, in contrast, refer to sales by independent merchants who sell through the Amazon Marketplace. When a consumer visits Amazon.com, Amazon's private-label products, such as AmazonBasics or its Kindle E-Readers, are listed for sale alongside independent merchants' offers.

[1516] Amazon.com, Inc., Annual Report (Form 10-K) 3 (Jan. 31, 2020), http://d18rn0p25nwr6d.cloudfront.net/CIK-0001018724/4d39f579-19d8-4119-b087-ee618abf82d6.pdf.

[1517] *Id.* at 18.

[1518] *Id.* at 24.

[1519] *Id.* at 3; *see also* Nathan Reiff, *How Amazon Makes Money*, INVESTOPEDIA (Aug. 12, 2020), https://www.investopedia.com/how-amazon-makes-money-4587523 ("Retail remains Amazon's primary source of revenue, with online and physical stores accounting for the biggest share.").

[1520] Amazon.com, Inc., Annual Report (Form 10-K) 24–25 (Jan. 31, 2020), http://d18rn0p25nwr6d.cloudfront.net/CIK-0001018724/4d39f579-19d8-4119-b087-ee618abf82d6.pdf.

One of the unique features about Amazon's e-commerce site is its fast and free shipping on an extremely broad selection of products. Amazon Prime Members can choose from over 100 million items that are available for free two-day delivery in the continental United States. Walmart, by contrast, has only single-digit millions of products eligible for free two-day shipping.[1521] In response to questions from the Subcommittee, Amazon represented that it offers approximately 158,000 private-label products across 45 in-house brands, not including some additional private-label products sold through Amazon Fresh.[1522] Amazon also hosts 2.3 million active third-party sellers from around the world,[1523] about 45 times more than the 52,000 third-party sellers that Walmart hosts on its marketplace.[1524] A recent survey estimated that about 37% of Amazon's third-party sellers, representing over 850,000 sellers, rely on Amazon as their sole source of income.[1525]

Amazon does not limit the number of sellers that can offer the same product for sale on its platform. Because of this, the same product may be sold by multiple sellers, as well as by Amazon. Each time a consumer clicks on a product, Amazon chooses a single seller from all the vendors offering that product to display as the featured offer in the "Buy Box."[1526] In its response to questions from the Subcommittee, Amazon stated that the featured merchant algorithm, also commonly referred to as the Buy Box algorithm, is designed to predict the offer that consumers would choose after comparing all the available offers in detail.[1527]

The *Amazon Buy Box Playbook*, a well-known guide for sellers, explains this in lay terms:

> When a shopper lands on a product detail page, Amazon chooses one seller whose details appear in the Buy Box—the white box on the right hand side of the page. When a customer clicks on the "Add to Cart" button, the sale goes to the seller in this box.[1528]

[1521] J.P. MORGAN, RETAIL VS. AMAZON: LIFE IN A POST COVID-19 WORLD (2020), https://markets.jpmorgan.com/research/email/-lbk68f4/Alp1kP9tQUPS29jlzW_bOg/GPS-3397412-0.

[1522] Innovation and Entrepreneurship Hearing at 3 (response to Questions for the Record of Nate Sutton, Assoc. Gen. Counsel, Competition, Amazon.com, Inc.).

[1523] *Number of Sellers on Amazon Marketplace*, MARKETPLACE PULSE, https://www.marketplacepulse.com/amazon/number-of-sellers (last visited Sept. 25, 2020); *see also* CEO Hearing at 5 (statement of Jeff Bezos, CEO, Amazon.com, Inc.) ("There are now 1.7 million small and medium-sized businesses around the world selling in Amazon's stores.").

[1524] *Number of Sellers on Amazon Marketplace*, MARKETPLACE PULSE, https://www.marketplacepulse.com/amazon/number-of-sellers (last visited on Oct. 5, 2020).

[1525] JUNGLESCOUT, THE STATE OF THE AMAZON SELLER 2020 4 (2020), https://www.junglescout.com/wp-content/uploads/2020/02/State-of-the-Seller-Survey.pdf.

[1526] Innovation and Entrepreneurship Hearing at 2 (response to Questions for the Record of Nate Sutton, Assoc. Gen. Counsel, Competition, Amazon.com, Inc.).

[1527] *Id.*

[1528] FEEDVISOR, THE AMAZON BUY BOX PLAYBOOK FOR SELLERS AND RETAILERS 4 (2020).

Industry experts estimate that about 80% of Amazon sales go through the Buy Box, and the percentage is even higher for mobile purchases.[1529] In response to a question from the Subcommittee, Amazon provided only high-level information about how it chooses which offer will win the Buy Box, stating that the algorithm considers criteria such as price, delivery speed and cost, Prime eligibility, and seller performance.[1530] Despite the importance of winning the Buy Box to sellers on its platform, only Amazon knows exactly how its featured merchant algorithm works.

As Amazon's e-commerce business has grown, it has also developed a significant logistics business providing fulfillment and delivery services to third-party sellers through its Fulfillment by Amazon (FBA) program. Nearly 85% of the top 10,000 Amazon Marketplace sellers reportedly rely on this program to fulfill and deliver their orders.[1531] Third-party sellers that use FBA keep their inventory in Amazon's fulfillment centers.[1532] After a consumer places an order online, Amazon does the picking, packing, and shipping, and provides customer service to complete the order.[1533] The figure below explains the different types of sellers on Amazon.com and the various modes of delivery and fulfillment they use.

Types of Sellers on Amazon and Shipping Options[1534]

[1529] *Id.* at 5.

[1530] CEO Hearing at 3 (response to Questions for the Record of Jeff Bezos, CEO, Amazon.com, Inc.).

[1531] *FBA Usage Among Amazon Marketplace Sellers*, MARKETPLACE PULSE, https://www.marketplacepulse.com/amazon/fulfillment-by-amazon-fba (last visited Oct. 5, 2020).

[1532] *Fulfillment by Amazon*, AMAZON, https://sell.amazon.com/fulfillment-by-amazon.html (last visited Sept. 28, 2020).

[1533] *Id.*

[1534] Prepared by the Subcomm. based on *Amazon 1P vs. 3P: What Are the Differences?*, FEEDVISOR, https://feedvisor.com/university/amazon-1p-vs-3p/ (last visited Sept. 24, 2020).

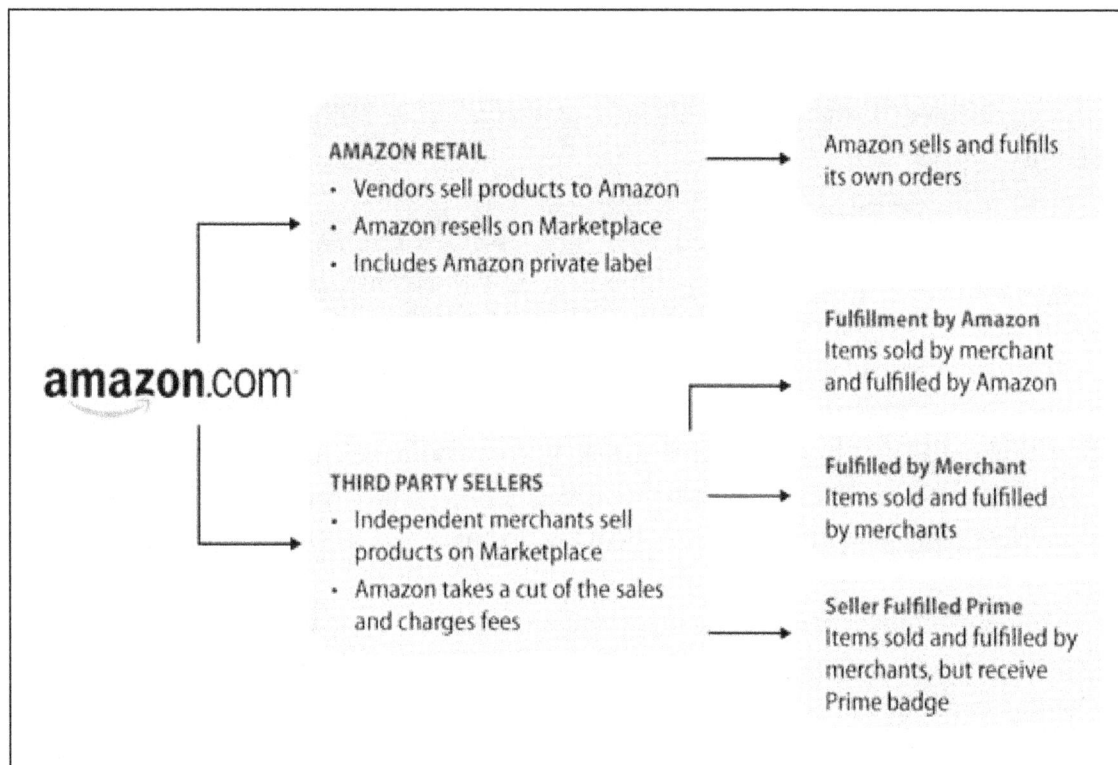

Amazon generates a significant amount of revenue from the fees that it charges third-party sellers. According to a recent SEC filing, net sales for services provided to third-party sellers increased from $23 billion in the first six months of 2019 to $32 billion over the same period in 2020—an increase of 39%.[1535] For the ability to sell a product on the platform, a seller might pay the company a monthly subscription fee, a high-volume listing fee, a referral fee on each item sold, and a closing fee on each item sold.[1536] Amazon charges additional fees for fulfillment and delivery services, as well as for advertising.[1537]

AWS, the company's cloud services business, offers digital infrastructure services to businesses that require increased computing infrastructure, such as increased capacity for servers to host or store data. Amazon is the dominant provider of infrastructure as a service. AWS accounts for close to half of all global spending on cloud infrastructure services and the business has three times the market share of Microsoft, its closest competitor.[1538] Cloud services are an essential and increasingly

[1535] Amazon.com, Inc., Quarterly Report (Form 10-Q) 18 (July 31, 2020), http://d18rn0p25nwr6d.cloudfront.net/CIK-0001018724/a77b5839-99b8-4851-8f37-0b012f9292b9.pdf.

[1536] *Selling on Amazon Fee Schedule*, AMAZON SELLER CENTRAL, https://sellercentral.amazon.com/gp/help/external/200336920 (last visited Sept. 25, 2020).

[1537] *Pricing Overview*, AMAZON SELLER CENTRAL (2020), https://sell.amazon.com/pricing.html (last visited Sept. 25, 2020); *see also* Production of Amazon, to H. Comm. on the Judiciary, 12 (Oct. 14, 2019) (on file with Comm.) (noting that advertising revenue is not included in seller services).

[1538] Press Release, Gartner, Gartner Says Worldwide IaaS Public Cloud Services Market Grew 31.3% in 2018 (July 29, 2019), https://www.gartner.com/en/newsroom/press-releases/2019-07-29-gartner-says-worldwide-iaas-public-cloud-

expensive line item for many companies. Given AWS's role as a dominant cloud provider, some of Amazon's competitors in other business lines often end up dependent on the platform. For example, Netflix, a competitor of Amazon Prime Video, paid AWS $500 million in 2018 to store its streaming video library.[1539]

While the pandemic has harmed many businesses, Amazon has experienced a surge in sales.[1540] The company's operating profit of $5.8 billion during the second quarter of 2020 significantly outperformed the -$1.5 billion to +$1.5 billion projection that Amazon had issued to investors.[1541] One analyst described the magnitude of Amazon's recent sales growth outperformance as a "paradigm-shifting update."[1542] In October 2020, Amazon's stock price was about $3,000, giving it a market valuation of about $1.5 trillion[1543]—greater than that of Walmart, Target, Salesforce, IBM, eBay, and Etsy combined.[1544] The company is consistently one of the highest-priced stocks on Wall Street,[1545] which is a clear indication investors expect Amazon to maintain and expand its market power.

The Subcommittee initiated its investigation of Amazon's market power and its role as a gatekeeper for digital markets in June 2019. Before and concurrent with the Subcommittee's investigation, many international and U.S. enforcement authorities also opened antitrust investigations into Amazon's business practices. Some of these investigations have led to Amazon making policy

---

services-market-grew-31point3-percent-in-2018; *see also* Letter from David Zapolsky, Gen. Counsel, Amazon.com, Inc., to Hon. David N. Cicilline (D-RI), Chairman, Subcomm. on Antitrust, Commercial and Admin. Law of H. Comm. on the Judiciary at 6 (July 26, 2019) (on file with Comm.).

[1539] Kevin McLaughlin, *Amazon's Cloud King: Inside the World of Andy Jassy*, THE INFO. (Jan. 23, 2019), https://www.theinformation.com/articles/amazons-cloud-king-inside-the-world-of-andy-jassy.

[1540] *See, e.g.*, Alana Semeuls, *Many Companies Won't Survive the Pandemic. Amazon Will Emerge Stronger Than Ever*, TIME (July 28, 2020), https://time.com/5870826/amazon-coronavirus-jeff-bezos-congress/ ("Consumer spending on Amazon between May and July was up 60% from the same time frame last year.").

[1541] MORNINGSTAR EQUITY ANALYST REPORT, AMAZON.COM INC. 6 (Aug. 27, 2020) (on file with Comm.); Press Release, Amazon, Amazon.com Announces First Quarter Results (Apr. 30, 2020), https://s2.q4cdn.com/299287126/files/doc_financials/2020/Q1/AMZN-Q1-2020-Earnings-Release.pdf.

[1542] MORNINGSTAR EQUITY ANALYST REPORT, AMAZON.COM INC. 6 (Aug. 27, 2020) (on file with Comm.).

[1543] *Amazon.com, Inc. Common Stock (AMZN)*, NASDAQ https://www.nasdaq.com/market-activity/stocks/amzn (last visited Oct. 3, 2020).

[1544] *See Walmart, Inc. Common Stock (WMT)*, NASDAQ https://www.nasdaq.com/market-activity/stocks/wmt (last visited Oct. 5, 2020) ($398 billion); *Target Corp. Common Stock (TGT)*, NASDAQ https://www.nasdaq.com/market-activity/stocks/tgt (last visited Oct. 5, 2020) ($79.6 billion); *Salesforce.com Inc. Common Stock (CRM)*, NASDAQ https://www.nasdaq.com/market-activity/stocks/crm (last visited Oct. 5, 2020) ($225.5 billion); *Int'l Bus. Machines Corp. Common Stock (IBM)*, NASDAQ https://www.nasdaq.com/market-activity/stocks/ibm (last visited Oct. 5, 2020) ($107 billion); *eBay, Inc. Common Stock (EBAY)*, NASDAQ https://www.nasdaq.com/market-activity/stocks/ebay (last visited Oct. 5, 2020) ($36.2 billion); *Etsy, Inc. Common Stock (ETSY)*, NASDAQ https://www.nasdaq.com/market-activity/stocks/etsy (last visited Oct. 3, 2020) ($16.7 billion).

[1545] *See, e.g.*, Gabe Alpert, *Top 5 Highest Priced Stocks in America*, INVESTOPEDIA (May 19, 2020), https://www.investopedia.com/financial-edge/0711/the-highest-priced-stocks-in-america.aspx.

changes.[1546] The European Commission began its in-depth antitrust investigation of Amazon on July 17, 2019.[1547] According to Executive Vice President Margrethe Vestager, the European Commission's investigation "focuses on the use by Amazon of accumulated, competitively sensitive information about marketplace sellers, their products and transactions on the Amazon marketplace, which may inform Amazon's retail business decisions."[1548] In the United States, the Federal Trade Commission (FTC) is investigating Amazon's past acquisition activity.[1549] The FTC is also reportedly investigating Amazon's treatment of third-party sellers and its cloud services business.[1550] Additionally, Amazon reportedly faces antitrust scrutiny by state attorneys general offices in California, Washington, and New York.[1551]

During the course of the investigation, Amazon displayed a lack of candor to the Subcommittee in response to questions about its business practices. As Chairman Nadler, Subcommittee Chairman Cicilline, and Ranking Member Sensenbrenner, along with other members of the Committee, wrote to Mr. Bezos in a bipartisan letter in May of this year, the Subcommittee was troubled that some of the "statements Amazon made to the Committee about the company's business practices appear to be misleading, and possibly criminally false or perjurious."[1552] In light of this concern, Subcommittee staff

---

[1546] *See, e.g.*, Data and Privacy Hearing at 3 (statement of Margrethe Vestager, Eur. Comm'r for Competition), https://docs.house.gov/meetings/JU/JU05/20191018/110098/HHRG-116-JU05-20191018-SD002.pdf ("[I]n 2017 we accepted commitments from Amazon not to introduce or enforce what are sometimes called 'most-favoured nation' clauses in the e-books market."); Press Release, Bundeskartellamt, Bundeskartellamt obtains far-reaching improvements in the terms of business for sellers on Amazon's online marketplaces (July 17, 2019), https://www.bundeskartellamt.de/SharedDocs/Meldung/EN/Pressemitteilungen/2019/17_07_2019_Amazon.html ("In response to the competition concerns expressed by the Bundeskartellamt, Amazon is amending its terms of business for sellers on Amazon's online marketplaces."); *Amazon online retailer: investigation into anti-competitive practices*, COMPETITION & MKTS. AUTH. (Oct. 1, 2013), https://www.gov.uk/cma-cases/amazon-online-retailer-investigation-into-anti-competitive-practices ("In light of [Amazon's] decision to remove the price parity policy and subsequent steps to implement that decision . . . the [Office of Fair Trading] has decided to close its investigation on administrative priority grounds.").

[1547] Press Release, Eur. Comm'n, Antitrust: Commission Opens Investigation into Possible Anti-competitive Conduct of Amazon (July 17, 2019), https://ec.europa.eu/commission/presscorner/detail/en/IP_19_4291.

[1548] CEO Hearing at 4 (statement of Margrethe Vestager, Eur. Comm'r for Competition).

[1549] Press Release, Fed. Trade Comm'n, FTC to Examine Past Acquisitions by Large Technology Companies (Feb. 11, 2020), https://www.ftc.gov/news-events/press-releases/2020/02/ftc-examine-past-acquisitions-large-technology-companies.

[1550] Jason Del Rey, *Amazon May Soon Face an Antitrust Probe. Here are 3 Questions the FTC is Asking About It.*, VOX: RECODE (June 4, 2019), https://www.vox.com/recode/2019/6/4/18651694/amazon-ftc-antitrust-investigation-prime; Dina Bass, David McLaughlin & Naomi Nix, *Amazon Faces Widening U.S. Antitrust Scrutiny in Cloud Business*, BLOOMBERG (Dec. 4, 2019), https://www.bloomberg.com/news/articles/2019-12-04/amazon-faces-widening-u-s-antitrust-scrutiny-in-cloud-business.

[1551] Tyler Sonnemaker, *Amazon is Reportedly Facing a New Antitrust Investigation into its Online Marketplace Led by the FTC and Attorneys General in New York and California*, BUS. INSIDER (Aug. 3, 2020), https://www.businessinsider.com/amazon-antitrust-probe-ftc-new-york-california-online-marketplace-2020-8; Karen Weise & David McCabe, *Amazon Said to Be Under Scrutiny in 2 States for Abuse of Power*, N.Y. TIMES (June 12, 2020), https://www.nytimes.com/2020/06/12/technology/state-inquiry-antitrust-amazon.html.

[1552] Bipartisan Letter from the Chairman, Ranking Member, and Members of H. Comm. on the Judiciary to Jeff Bezos, CEO, Amazon.com, Inc. (May 1, 2020), https://judiciary.house.gov/uploadedfiles/2020-05-01_letter_to_amazon_ceo_bezos.pdf.

views Amazon's other claims and representations with a degree of skepticism in instances where they conflict with credible sources, such as investigative reporting, interviews with market participants, or other evidence uncovered by Subcommittee staff during the investigation.

2. Amazon.com

a. Market Power

Amazon has significant and durable market power in the U.S. online retail market.[1553] The company's actual share of U.S. e-commerce is unknown outside of Amazon because it does not report the gross merchandise volume of third-party sales made on its marketplace. A frequently cited analysis by market research company eMarketer estimates that Amazon's share in this market is 38.7%.[1554] eMarketer's estimate, however, is likely understated because its definition of e-commerce is overly broad. For example, under eMarketer's approach to e-commerce, the Auto and Parts category includes online sales of cars.[1555] In contrast, marketing analytics company Jumpshot estimates that Amazon captures an average of 74% of digital transactions across a wide range of product categories.[1556] The Jumpshot analysis may overstate Amazon's share because it calculates market share as a percentage of transactions made on well-known market participants' websites, like Amazon, Walmart, and Target, but excludes small, online retailers.[1557] Based on the information Subcommittee staff gathered during its investigation, estimates that place Amazon's share of U.S. e-commerce at about 50% or higher are more credible than lower estimates of 30-40%.[1558]

[1553] *See generally* Dig. Competition Expert Panel Report at 30 (finding that recent financial indicators suggest Amazon's "dominan[ce] in a meaningfully distinct sector of online retail" will endure and that "investors are expecting it to retain its dominant position, and to earn significantly higher profits in future"); Stigler Report at 78 ("[T]he evidence thus far does suggest that current digital platforms face very little threat of entry . . . . [T]he key players in this industry remained the same over the last two technology waves, staying dominant through the shift to mobile and the rise of AI. In the past, dominant business found it difficult to navigate innovation or disruption waves. By contrast, Facebook, Google, Amazon, Apple, and even Microsoft were able to ride these waves without significant impact on market share or profit margins.").

[1554] ANDREW LIPSMAN, TOP 10 US ECOMMERCE COMPANIES 2020, EMARKETER (Mar. 10, 2020), https://www.emarketer.com/content/top-10-us-ecommerce-companies-2020.

[1555] Production of Amazon, to H. Comm. on the Judiciary, AMAZON-HJC-00206583 (2019) (on file with Comm.) (eMarketer Inc. – Global Ecommerce 2019 Report).

[1556] *See* Kimberly Collins, *Google + Amazon: Data on Market Share, Trends, Searches from Jumpshot*, SEARCH ENGINE WATCH (Aug. 1, 2019), https://www.searchenginewatch.com/2019/08/01/amazon-google-market-share/.

[1557] *See id.*

[1558] *See* Submission from Source 11, to H. Comm. on the Judiciary, 2 (Oct. 14, 2019) (on file with Comm.) ("Amazon has amassed at least a 50% share of the ecommerce market and continues to expand, both its market share and the breadth of its offerings."); PYMNTS.COM, WALMART VS. AMAZON, WHOLE PAYCHECK TRACKER: BATTLE FOR THE DIGITAL FIRST CONSUMER 6 (2020), https://securecdn.pymnts.com/wp-content/uploads/2020/09/Amazon-Walmart-Whole-Paycheck-092020.pdf (estimating Amazon's market share at 51.2% in Q1 2020 and 44.4% in Q2 2020, but noting U.S. e-commerce increased by 44% over the same period, and that "[f]or Amazon to drop only 7 percent in total eCommerce share with that kind of overall increase is actually quite an achievement.").

In a number of key product categories, ranging from household essentials to sports, fitness and outdoors, Amazon is reported to account for well over 50% of online sales.[1559] The platform also has significant market power over the entire book industry, including sales, distribution, and publishing. In the U.S. market, Amazon accounts for over half of all print book sales and over 80% of e-book sales.[1560]

Amazon is the dominant online marketplace. It reportedly controls about 65% to 70% of all U.S. online marketplace sales.[1561] The platform's market power is at its height in its dealings with third-party sellers, as well as many of its suppliers, which Amazon refers to as vendors. Increasingly, Amazon is also gaining market power in certain business-to-business (B2B) online markets through Amazon Business, its B2B marketplace.[1562]

In response to the Committee's requests for information, Amazon claims that "estimates of total retail share are the most appropriate and relevant method of estimating" Amazon's market share.[1563] This approach is inconsistent with evidence gathered by Subcommittee staff, conventional antitrust analysis of relevant product markets, and common sense. In a recent investigation, for example, the FTC concluded that a "relevant market may be divided by channel of sale, resulting in separate markets for brick-and-mortar sales and online sales."[1564] Illustrating the extent of Amazon's overly broad approach to identifying the relevant market and its top competitors, in response to the

[1559] *See, e.g.*, Kimberly Collins, *Google + Amazon: Data on Market Share, Trends, Searches from Jumpshot*, SEARCH ENGINE WATCH (Aug. 1, 2019), https://www.searchenginewatch.com/2019/08/01/amazon-google-market-share/; *see also* J.P. MORGAN REPORT: RETAIL VS. AMAZON: LIFE IN A POST COVID-19 WORLD 13 (Amazon's market share of online sales of Books & Magazines is 75%).

[1560] *See, e.g.*, Ben Evans, *What's Amazon market share?*, BENEDICT EVANS https://www.ben-evans.com/benedictevans/2019/12/amazons-market-share19#:~:text=Amazon%20has%2050%25%20or%20more,it%20has%20over%2050%25 ("Amazon has 50% or more of the US print book market"); Submission from Source 17, to H. Comm. on the Judiciary, 33 (Nov. 14, 2019) (on file with Comm.) ("Amazon accounts for roughly 83 percent of all e-book sales, about 90 percent of online print sales, and about 90 percent of digital audiobook sales."); Dig. Competition Expert Panel Report at 30 ("In the e-book market, Amazon was reported in February 2017 to account for around 88% of total annual unit sales.").

[1561] Submission from Top Shelf Brands, to H. Comm. on the Judiciary, 26 (Oct. 26, 2019) (on file with Comm.) (citing DIGITAL COMMERCE 360, 2019 ONLINE MARKETPLACES REPORT).

[1562] *See* MARKETPLACE PULSE, MARKETPLACES YEAR IN REVIEW 48 (2019), https://cdn.marketplacepulse.com/misc/marketplaces-year-in-review-2019.pdf ("Amazon's 'business-to-business', or B2B, marketplace is gaining market share faster than its retail operation."); Phone Interview with Nat'l Ass'n of Wholesaler-Distributors (Sept. 3, 2020); STACY MITCHELL & OLIVIA LAVECCHIA, REPORT: AMAZON'S NEXT FRONTIER: YOUR CITY'S PURCHASING 4 (2018), https://ilsr.org/amazon-and-local-government-purchasing/ ("Amazon is leveraging its growing relationship with local governments to induce more businesses to join its Marketplace.").

[1563] Production of Amazon, to H. Comm. on the Judiciary, 3 (Oct. 14, 2019).

[1564] *See* Complaint at 4, In the Matter of Edgewell Personal Care Co.& Harry's Inc., No. 9390 (F.T.C. Feb. 2, 2020), https://www.ftc.gov/system/files/documents/cases/public_p3_complaint_-_edgewell-harrys.pdf.

Committee's request for "A list of the Company's top ten competitors," Amazon identified 1,700 companies, including Eero (a company Amazon owns), a discount surgical supply distributor, and a beef jerky company.[1565]

Amazon also included single-category companies in response to the Committee's request for a list of Amazon's top ten competitors. Yet documents produced by Amazon suggest that even in its early days it did not view such retailers as direct competitors. For instance, a recap of an Amazon marketing presentation identified one of its key points as: "No direct competitors, closest competitors would be what you refer to as category driven i.e. Best Buy, Barnes and Noble...etc."[1566]

Regardless of the precise boundaries of e-commerce or online marketplaces, the sum of evidence that Subcommittee staff examined demonstrates that Amazon functions as a gatekeeper for e-commerce. Amazon is the most-visited website in the world for e-commerce and shopping.[1567] In a submission to the Committee, an e-commerce market participant said that "many of the 64% of American households that have Prime memberships are effectively locked into Amazon for their online shopping."[1568] Meanwhile, recent market analysis suggests that over 60% of all online product searches in the U.S. begin on Amazon.com.[1569]

At the Subcommittee's hearing on innovation and entrepreneurship, Stacy Mitchell, the Co-Director of the Institute for Local Self-Reliance, described one independent retailer's attempt to survive in e-commerce independent of Amazon:

[1565] *See* Production of Amazon, to H. Comm. on the Judiciary, 17 (Oct. 14, 2019) (on file with Comm.).

[1566] Production of Amazon, to H. Comm. on the Judiciary, AMAZON-HJC-0059575 (Nov. 22, 2010) (on file with Comm.).

[1567] SIMILARWEB, WORLDWIDE E-COMMERCE AND SHOPPING CATEGORY PERFORMANCE (July 2020), https://pro.similarweb.com/#/industry/overview/E-commerce_and_Shopping/999/1m/?webSource=Total (Amazon had 2.6 billion visits in July 2020 compared to 940.8 million visits for eBay).

[1568] Submission from Source 11, to H. Comm. on the Judiciary, 5 (Oct. 14, 2019) (on file with Comm.).

[1569] Lucy Koch, *Looking for a New Product? You Probably Searched Amazon*, EMARKETER (Mar. 31, 2019), https://www.emarketer.com/content/looking-for-a-new-product-you-probably-searched-amazon (citing FEEDVISOR, THE 2019 AMAZON CONSUMER BEHAVIOR REPORT 14 (2019)); *see also* WUNDERMAN THOMPSON, THE FUTURE SHOPPER REPORT 2020 11 (2020), https://insights.wundermanthompsoncommerce.com/hubfs/@UK/Landing%20Pages/2020/The%20Future%20Shopper%20 2020/WTC%20-%20The%20Future%20Shopper%20Report%202020.pdf?hsCtaTracking=24d37c38-db5d-4797-bd6c-2ea35127ad21%7C70cdff40-3236-48fb-a2ec-c4b298453df9).

As its customers moved online, so too did the company. Gazelle Sports built a robust e-commerce site. With scores of enthusiastic reviews on Google and Yelp, the site came right up in online searches, yielding a brisk stream of customers and sales.

But, in 2014, sales began to decline. The problem was that many people in Michigan and across the country were no longer starting their online shopping on a search engine, where they might find Gazelle Sports. Instead, they were going straight to Amazon. By 2016, the share of online shoppers bypassing search engines and beginning their product search on Amazon had grown to 55 percent. With sales flagging and staff reductions underway, the owner of Gazelle Sports . . . made what seemed like a necessary decision: Gazelle Sports would join Amazon Marketplace, becoming a third-party seller on the digital giant's platform. "If the customer is on Amazon, as a small business you have to say, 'That is where I have to go,'" he explained. "Otherwise, we are going to close our doors."[1570]

Interviews with sellers, as well as documents that Subcommittee staff reviewed, make clear that Amazon has monopoly power over most third-party sellers and many of its suppliers.[1571] Numerous sellers told Subcommittee staff in interviews that they cannot turn to alternative marketplaces, regardless of how much Amazon may increase their costs of doing business or how badly they are treated. David Barnett, the CEO and Founder of PopSockets, a former third-party seller and current Amazon supplier, testified about Amazon's coercive tactics at one of the Subcommittee's hearings:

I suspect that Amazon is accustomed to behaving this way because most brands cannot afford to leave Amazon. They evidently have no choice but to endure tactics that would be rejected out of hand in any ordinary relationship whereby the two parties enter into the relationship by preference rather than necessity.[1572]

Sellers feel forced to be on Amazon because that is where the buyers are.[1573] At the Subcommittee's sixth hearing, Representative Lucy McBath (D-GA) noted that the evidence the Subcommittee collected is at odds with how Amazon describes its relationship with third-party sellers. She asked Mr. Bezos:

[1570] Innovation and Entrepreneurship Hearing at 3–4 (statement of Stacy Mitchell, Co-Director, Inst. for Local Self-Reliance).

[1571] *See, e.g.*, Submission from Top Shelf Brands, to H. Comm. on the Judiciary, 49 (Oct. 26, 2019) ("98% of all of Top Shelf's transaction has taken place on Amazon's platform."); *see also* Dig. Competition Expert Panel Report at 30 ("Regardless of the view on dominance over a particular defined market, it is clear that for thousands of smaller independent online sellers in particular, Amazon's marketplace is a strategically important gateway to consumers.").

[1572] Competitors Hearing at 3 (statement of David Barnett, CEO and Founder, Popsockets LLC).

[1573] Submission from Source 11, to H. Comm. on the Judiciary, 5 (Oct. 14, 2019) (on file with Comm.).

[Y]ou referred to third party sellers today as "Amazon's partners" and that your success depends on their success. But, over the past year, we've heard a completely different story. As part of this investigation, we've interviewed many small businesses, and they use the words like "bullying," "fear," and "panic" to describe their relationship with Amazon. . . . . You said that sellers have many other attractive options to reach customers, but that's not at all what we found in our investigation . . . . If Amazon didn't have monopoly power over these sellers, do you think they would choose to stay in a relationship that is characterized by bullying, fear, and panic?"[1574]

Mr. Bezos responded that "there are a lot of options" for sellers, and that "[t]here are more and more every day."[1575] This claim is inconsistent with the Subcommittee's investigative record. In a submission to the Committee, the Online Merchants Guild, a trade association for small and medium-sized online sellers, said that its members who try to diversify sales across multiple platforms often report that they are unable to generate many sales outside of Amazon.[1576]

An important limit on a seller's ability to switch from Amazon to selling on its own site or a competing platform is that Amazon generally forbids sellers from contacting their customers.[1577] The packaging and even the order confirmation email for third-party sales feature the Amazon brand prominently and do not reference the seller. A typical Amazon customer is unaware of the source of the sale.[1578] According to the Online Merchants Guild, "Many Amazon sellers use websites such as

---

[1574] CEO Hearing Unofficial Transcript at 88–89 (question of Rep. Lucy McBath, Member, Subcomm. On Antitrust, Commercial and Admin. Law).

[1575] *Id.* at 91 (statement of Jeff Bezos, CEO, Amazon.com, Inc.).

[1576] Submission from Online Merchants Guild, to H. Comm. on the Judiciary, OMG-000005 (Oct. 23, 2019) (on file with Comm.) ("Members who sell across multiple platforms often report the amount of revenue generated outside of Amazon including their own eCommerce site, is insignificant, with over 90% of their sales being generated on the platform."); *see also* Submission from Top Shelf Brands, to H. Comm. on the Judiciary, 60–61 (Oct. 26, 2019) (explaining that it has "no viable alternatives" to Amazon, where 98% of its transactions have taken place on Amazon's platform, eBay accounts for 1% of its income, and Walmart accounts for less than 1%).

[1577] *Selling Polices and Seller Code of Conduct*, AMAZON SELLER CENTRAL, https://sellercentral.amazon.com/gp/help/external/G1801?language=en_US&ref=efph_G1801_cont_200386250 (last visited Sept. 28, 2020); *see also* Submission from Source 100, to H. Comm. on the Judiciary (Sept. 26, 2020) (raising concerns that Amazon permits itself to contact customers about negative reviews for Amazon branded products, while third-party sellers are largely barred from customer engagement).

[1578] Submission from Online Merchants Guild, to H. Comm. on the Judiciary, OMG-000005 (Oct. 23, 2019) (on file with Comm.); *see also* Submission from Source 11, to H. Comm. on the Judiciary, 3 (Oct. 14, 2019) (on file with Comm.) (explaining that "[w]henever an order is shipped through [Fulfillment by Amazon], even if the purchase is made through another marketplace, it is likely to arrive in an Amazon-branded box, creating confusion" for customers).

Shopify to try and establish their own eCommerce presence, but without the ability to market to their supposed core customer base, their Amazon customers, it's pretty futile."[1579]

Subcommittee staff heard from several market participants that Amazon also has significant market power over suppliers. For example, third-party sellers told Subcommittee staff that Amazon frequently ignores manufacturer policies that bind sellers.[1580] For example, brand manufacturers may establish minimum advertised pricing guidelines (MAP) to prevent online retailers from freeriding off brick-and mortar =-stores' investments in product display or expertise—such as how to fit a running shoe. Amazon's leverage over suppliers gives it the ability to "break" minimum advertised pricing rules and undercut competing sellers on price. In contrast, third-party sellers must abide by the rules. As a former third-party seller explained, "Given Amazon's immense clout, we believe that suppliers have no realistic threat to stop selling on Amazon in response to Amazon 'breaking' MAP."[1581] Amazon's internal documents suggest that it does not fear any consequences for failing to comply with most vendor policies.[1582]

Another way that Amazon leverages its market power is to force certain brand manufacturers that would prefer to be third-party sellers into being wholesalers. A discussion among Amazon executives suggests that certain brands may only be allowed to have a wholesale relationship with Amazon even if the brand would prefer to be a third-party seller. In 2016, Sebastian Gunningham, then senior vice president of Amazon Marketplace, commented on a list of proposed seller tenets, "I would add that there are x,000 suppliers around the world that do not get this choice... I am talking about the apple, nikes and p&g, etc... We don't want to open that door, relationship has to be reseller."[1583] Consistent with this stance, Popsockets CEO and Founder David Barnett testified that Amazon attempted to force him into maintaining a wholesale relationship with Amazon Retail despite his preference to be a third-party seller or make sales on the marketplace through an authorized distributor.[1584] A former Amazon employee confirmed that it was not uncommon for Amazon to use its

---

[1579] Submission from Online Merchants Guild, to H. Comm. on the Judiciary, OMG-000006 (Oct. 23, 2019) (on file with Comm.).

[1580] *See, e.g.*, Phone Interview with Source 84 (Mar. 4, 2020).

[1581] Submission from Source 48, to H. Comm. on the Judiciary, 8 (Nov. 8, 2019) (on file with Comm.).

[1582] *See, e.g.*, Production of Amazon, to H. Comm. on the Judiciary, AMAZON-HJC-00151722 (Feb. 9, 2009) (on file with Comm.) ("[P]lease audit that we are price matching . . . any diapers.com pricing. If this puts us in the soup with P&G on their pampers map price, so be it."); AMAZON-HJC-00206714 (Mar. 8, 2018) ("Why did Walmart break MAP and we didn't?").

[1583] Production of Amazon, to H. Comm. on the Judiciary, AMAZON-HJC-00190108 (June 6, 2016) (on file with Comm.).

[1584] Competitors Hearing at 3 (statement of David Barnett, CEO and Founder, Popsockets LLC).

brand standards policy to shut down a brand's third-party seller account and force brands into an exclusive wholesaler relationship.[1585]

Amazon also enjoys significant market power over online consumers. Amazon uses Prime and its other membership programs to lock consumers into the Amazon ecosystem. According to an internal analysis, Amazon was willing to pay a credit card company a significant sum in 2013 for signing up new Prime members under the assumption that each new member would contribute $527 to Amazon's gross merchandise sales and $46 of gross profit.[1586] Amazon estimated that the deal had a five-year net present value of $17 million, assuming that it delivered 100,000 paid Prime members.[1587]

Once Prime members pay the upfront annual membership fee, they are likely to concentrate their online purchases with Amazon.[1588] According to a recent survey, Prime members spend an average of $1,400 annually on Amazon, versus $600 for non-members.[1589] As one market participant observed, "Prime members will continue to use Amazon and not switch to competing platforms, despite higher prices and lower-quality items on Amazon compared to other marketplaces, and despite recent increases in the price of a Prime membership."[1590]

Other retailers are unable to match Amazon on its ability to provide free and fast delivery for such a large volume and inventory of products. Even Walmart, with its extensive, national distribution network, does not come close to matching Amazon on this measure.[1591] Amazon currently offers Prime members free, next-day delivery on over 10 million items anywhere in the continental United

---

[1585] Submission from Source 91, to H. Comm. on the Judiciary (Sept. 22, 2020) (on file with Comm.).

[1586] Production of Amazon, to H. Comm. on the Judiciary, AMAZON-HJC-00199845 (Oct. 23, 2013) (on file with Comm.).

[1587] *Id.*

[1588] *See* Submission from Source 11, to H. Comm. on the Judiciary, 3 (Oct. 14, 2019) (on file with Comm.) ("Amazon has been quite frank about the reality that once consumers invest in Prime, they do most of their online shopping on Amazon in order to gain value from the investment in shipping, whereas they might otherwise multisource.").

[1589] Tonya Garcia, *Amazon Prime membership exceeds 100 million*, MARKETWATCH (Jan. 17, 2019), https://www.marketwatch.com/story/amazon-prime-membership-exceeds-100-million-2019-01-17; *see also Q1 2020 Earnings Call,* Brian Olsavsky, Sr. Vice Pres. and Chief Fin. Officer, Amazon.com, Inc. (Apr 30, 2020, 5:30 PM) ("We see our Prime customers are shopping more often and they have larger basket sizes.").

[1590] Submission from Source 11, to H. Comm. on the Judiciary, 3 (Oct. 14, 2019) (on file with Comm.).

[1591] *See* J.P. MORGAN, RETAIL VS. AMAZON: LIFE IN A POST COVID-19 WORLD (2020), https://markets.jpmorgan.com/research/email/-lbk68f4/Alp1kP9tQUPS29jlzW_bOg/GPS-3397412-0 ("We believe there are no comparable unlimited free shipping offerings available at scale, with Amazon's large and growing infrastructure investments serving as a significant barrier to entry.")

States.[1592] Walmart, by contrast, has only about 200,000 products eligible for two-day shipping in select markets.[1593]

Amazon's market power is durable and unlikely to erode in the foreseeable future. There are several factors that make successful entry or expansion by a challenger to Amazon unlikely. Barriers to entry include: (1) network effects, which make it difficult for another marketplace to achieve a comparable number of buyers and sellers; (2) switching costs associated with consumers shopping outside of the Amazon ecosystem; and (3) the steep costs of building a logistics network comparable in size and scope to Amazon's massive international footprint in fulfillment and delivery. Amazon's internal documents recognize that entry into online commerce "require[s] significant incremental investments in brand development, inventory, and marketing/customer acquisition."[1594] Further, Amazon expanded its market power through avoiding taxes, extracting state subsidies, and engaging in anticompetitive conduct—tactics that have given the company an unfair advantage over actual and potential competitors.

As the COVID-19 pandemic pushes more American shoppers online, Amazon's market power has grown. Evidence shows that Amazon is willing to use its increased market power in e-commerce during this crisis to exert pressure on suppliers and favor its own first-party products over those sold by third-party sellers. Amazon initially responded to the sudden surge in sales by refusing to accept or deliver non-essential supplies from its third-party sellers—a stance that would seem reasonable except that Amazon continued to ship its own non-essential products while restricting third-party sellers' ability to use alternative distribution channels to continue selling through Prime.[1595] As for suppliers, Subcommittee staff heard concerns that the platform used its power as a large buyer to pressure suppliers into prioritizing Amazon over other retail customers such as independent grocers.[1596]

[1592] *Prime*, AMAZON, https://www.amazon.com/b?ie=UTF8&node=15247183011 (last visited Sept. 28, 2020) ("Free One-Day Delivery . . . Available coast-to-coast on more than 10 million items with no minimum purchase.").

[1593] Press Release, Marc Lore, Pres. and CEO, Walmart eCommerce US, Free NextDay Delivery Without a Membership Fee (May 14, 2019), https://corporate.walmart.com/newsroom/2019/05/14/free-nextday-delivery-without-a-membership-fee; *Walmart Help Center: NextDay Delivery*, https://www.walmart.com/help/article/nextday-delivery/fd3f1c5cf0ec4682abca8c83f5f0e977 (last visited Sept. 28, 2020) ("Currently, NextDay Delivery is only available in select markets.").

[1594] Production of Amazon, to H. Comm. on the Judiciary, AMAZON-HJC-00154659 (Nov. 23, 2010) (on file with Comm.).

[1595] Ron Knox & Shaoul Sussman, *How Amazon Used the Pandemic to Amass More Monopoly Power*, THE NATION (June 26, 2020), https://www.thenation.com/article/politics/amazon-bezos-pandemic-monopoly/.

[1596] Phone Interview with Nat'l Grocers Ass'n (May 28, 2020) (raising concerns that Amazon and some Big Box retailers may have used their buyer power over suppliers during the pandemic to secure inventory at the expense of smaller businesses); Letter from Int'l Bhd. Of Teamsters, Commc'n Workers of America, United Food & Commercial Workers Int'l Union & Change to Win to Comm'rs of the Fed. Trade Comm'n, at 6 (July 23, 2020) (stating that if seller reports are true, "Amazon's hold over sellers effectively took food from the shelves of neighborhood grocery stores . . . and moved it to Amazon's own warehouses, where it earned fees for Amazon."); *see also* Renee Dudley, *The Amazon Lockdown: How an Unforgiving Algorithm Drives Suppliers to Favor the E-Commerce Giant Over Other Retailers*, PROPUBLICA (Apr. 26,

Meanwhile, numerous reports suggest that Amazon is in talks to convert real estate in vacated malls into additional Amazon distribution centers, further highlighting how it will continue to amass further scale even as its brick-and-mortar counterparts crater.[1597]

b. Merger Activity

Amazon's acquisition strategy has primarily focused on purchasing its competitors and companies that operate in adjacent markets, providing access to additional valuable customer data. This strategy has effectively protected and expanded Amazon's market power in e-commerce and helped Amazon extend that power to other markets.

Over the past two decades, Amazon has acquired at least 100 companies.[1598] It has been particularly aggressive over the past few years, making deals that are bigger and more ambitious relative to its historic approach.[1599] In 2017, the company made its largest acquisition to date by purchasing Whole Foods for $13.7 billion.[1600] Amazon's other large purchases include Ring, which it bought for $1.2 billion in 2018; PillPack, which it bought for $1 billion in 2018; and Zappos, which it bought for $1.2 billion in 2009.[1601] Over the years, Amazon has acquired an assortment of highly recognizable companies, including IMDB.com, which it bought in 1998; Audible, which it bought in 2008; Goodreads, which it bought in 2013; and Twitch, which it bought in 2014.[1602]

Amazon's acquisition strategy has led to fewer choices for consumers in terms of differentiated online retail channels, as well as reduced competitive pressure in terms of price and quality. Additionally, Amazon's expansion into a diverse array of business lines—from brick-and-mortar supermarkets to home security—has reinforced its significant stockpile of consumer data. With more data about online and offline consumer behavior, Amazon's acquisitions set in motion a self-reinforcing cycle, creating an ever-widening gap between the platform and its competitors. As one

---

2020), https://www.propublica.org/article/the-amazon-lockdown-how-an-unforgiving-algorithm-drives-suppliers-to-favor-the-e-commerce-giant-over-other-retailers.

[1597] Esther Fung & Sebastian Herrera, *Amazon and Mall Operator Look at Turning Sears, J.C. Penney Stores Into Fulfillment Centers*, WALL ST. J. (Aug. 9, 2017), https://www.wsj.com/articles/amazon-and-giant-mall-operator-look-at-turning-sears-j-c-penney-stores-into-fulfillment-centers-11596992863.

[1598] *See infra* Appendix.

[1599] *Infographic: Amazon's Biggest Acquisitions,* CB INSIGHTS (June 19, 2019), https://www.cbinsights.com/research/amazon-biggest-acquisitions-infographic/.

[1600] *Id.*

[1601] *Id.*

[1602] *Amazon Acquisitions*, MICROACQUIRE, https://acquiredby.co/amazon-acquisitions/ (last visited Oct. 3, 2020).

former Amazon employee told Subcommittee staff, "Amazon is first and foremost a data company, they just happen to use it to sell stuff."[1603]

Over its history, Amazon has acquired a number of its rivals.[1604] A decade ago, Amazon acquired two of its direct competitors: Zappos and Quidsi.[1605] Documents reviewed by Subcommittee staff show that Amazon viewed both online retailers as competitive threats prior to acquiring them.

Amazon's 2009 acquisition of Zappos, an online shoe-retailer, marked the company's first $1 billion-plus purchase.[1606] Acquiring Zappos provided Amazon with two important advantages. First, it enabled Amazon to add significant selection to its category of shoes and other fashion-related items at a time when expanding its selection was critical to the company's success.[1607] The added selection included access to "hold-out" brands, which had previously refused to sell on Amazon.com or Amazon's other online retail store Endless.com.[1608] Second, Zappos' unique approach to customer service, marked by "a deeply felt connection with customers," added an emotional and psychological element to Amazon's relationship with consumers.[1609] An Amazon internal planning document from 2008 referred to Zappos as one of Endless's "primary competitors," and notes that "Zappos offers the

---

[1603] Interview with Source 91 (May 8, 2020); *see also* Submission from Artist Rights Alliance, to H. Comm. on the Judiciary, 2 (July 31, 2019) (on file with Comm.) ("With respect to the music world, at the heart of this problem lies a simple, economic truth – companies like . . . Amazon are not music businesses. They are advertising platforms and data machines. As our then-President, Melvin Gibbs, told the *New York Times* back in 2017, 'None of these companies that are supposedly in the music business are actually in the music business. They are in the data-aggregation business. They're in the ad-selling business. The value of music means nothing to them.'").

[1604] *See* Stigler Report at 75 n.152 ("The number of potential competitors purchased by the tech giants is large. For example, Amazon has purchased Zappos, Fabric, CDNow, Quorus, Audible, Goodreads, and Quidsi"); TIM WU, THE CURSE OF BIGNESS: ANTITRUST IN THE NEW GILDED AGE 124 (Columbia Global Reports ed., 2018) ("Amazon acquired would-be competitors like Zappos, Diapers.com, and Soap.com.").

[1605] *Amazon Closes Zappos Deal, Ends Up Paying $1.2 Billion*, TECHCRUNCH (Nov. 2, 2009), https://techcrunch.com/2009/11/02/amazon-closes-zappos-deal-ends-up-paying-1-2-billion/; *Confirmed: Amazon Spends $545 Million on Diapers.com Parent Quidsi*, TECHCRUNCH (Nov. 8, 2010, 9:04 AM), https://techcrunch.com/2010/11/08/confirmed-amazon-spends-545-million-on-diapers-com-parent-quidsi/.

[1606] Eric Engleman, *Amazon and Zappos, Six Months Later: How They're Fitting Together*, PUGET SOUND BUS. J. (May 21, 2010), https://www.bizjournals.com/seattle/blog/techflash/2010/05/amazon_and_zappos_how_theyre_fitting_together.html.

[1607] Bill Taylor, *Amazon and Zappos: A Savvy Deal*, HARV. BUS. REV. (July 23, 2009), https://hbr.org/2009/07/a-savvy-deal-from-amazon-to-za.

[1608] Alistair Barr, *Amazon to Close Fashion Website endless.com*, REUTERS: INDUS., MATERIALS AND UTILS. (Sept. 18, 2012), https://www.reuters.com/article/amazon-endless/amazon-to-close-fashion-website-endless-com-idUSL1E8KINKD20120918 (quoting an Amazon spokesman who stated that Amazon shut down Endless.com as an independent site in 2012 and incorporated it into Amazon's main website, Amazon.com, "in order to focus on the Amazon Fashion experience").

[1609] Bill Taylor, *Amazon and Zappos: A Savvy Deal*, HARV. BUS. REV. (July 23, 2009), https://hbr.org/2009/07/a-savvy-deal-from-amazon-to-za.

largest selection of brands and styles and carries all of our top holdouts including Nike, Merrell, Keen, Cole Haan and Michael Kors."[1610]

About a year later, Amazon acquired Quidsi, the parent company of Diapers.com and Soap.com, for about $540 million.[1611] Prior to buying it, Amazon identified Diapers.com as its "largest and fastest growing competitor in the on-line diaper and baby care space,"[1612] and its "#1 short term competitor."[1613] Amazon's internal documents said that Diapers.com "keep[s] the pressure on pricing on us" and provided extremely high customer services levels, which—prior to the merger—had forced Amazon to up its game.[1614] Amazon executives took swift and predatory action in response to this competitive threat. As Representative Mary Gay Scanlon (D-PA) summarized at the Subcommittee's sixth hearing, Amazon's internal documents "show that Amazon employees began strategizing about ways to weaken this company, and, in 2010, Amazon hatched a plot to go after Diapers.com and take it out."[1615] Specifically, Amazon's documents show that the firm entered into an aggressive price war, in which Amazon was willing to bleed over $200 million in losses on diapers in one month.[1616] Addressing Mr. Bezos, Representative Scanlon added, "Your own documents make clear that the price war against Diapers.com worked, and within a few months it was struggling, and so then Amazon bought it."[1617]

In 2017, Amazon shut down Diapers.com, citing profitability issues, though some industry experts questioned the legitimacy of this rationale.[1618] In shutting down the company, Amazon eliminated a differentiated online retailer that consumers loved[1619]—reducing the number of online

---

[1610] Production of Amazon, to H. Comm. on the Judiciary, AMAZON-HJC-00170649 (Sept. 23, 2008) (on file with Comm.).

[1611] Claire Cain Miller, *Amazon Has a Reported Deal to Buy Parent of Diapers.com*, N.Y. TIMES (Nov. 7, 2010), https://www.nytimes.com/2010/11/08/technology/08amazon.html.

[1612] Production of Amazon, to H. Comm. on the Judiciary, AMAZON-HJC-00142833 (May 12, 2009) (on file with Comm.).

[1613] *Id.* at AMAZON-HJC-00151722 (Feb. 9, 2009).

[1614] *Id.* at AMAZON-HJC-00151722–24 (Feb. 9, 2009).

[1615] CEO Hearing Transcript at 81–82 (question of Rep. Mary Gay Scanlon, Vice Chair, H. Comm. on the Judiciary).

[1616] Production of Amazon, to H. Comm. on the Judiciary, AMAZON-HJC-00057007 (Apr. 5. 2010) (on file with Comm.).

[1617] CEO Hearing Transcript at 82-83 (question of Rep. Mary Gay Scanlon, Vice Chair, H. Comm. on the Judiciary).

[1618] *See, e.g.*, Jason Del Rey, *Why Amazon's Explanation for Shutting Down Diapers.com and Quidsi Stunned Employees*, VOX: RECODE (Apr. 2, 2017), https://www.vox.com/2017/4/2/15153844/amazon-quidsi-shutdown-explanation-profits.

[1619] *See, e.g.*, Production of Amazon, to H. Comm. on the Judiciary, AMAZON-HJC-00034097 (Nov. 8, 2010) (on file with Comm.) (email from Diapers.com founder Vinit Bharara forwarding a customer testimonial in the form of a poem titled "An Ode to Diapers.com," beginning, "Oh how do I love thee, my Diapers.com?" and ending with "Don't ever leave me, my Diapers.com").

options for consumers in the diaper and baby care markets. Further, it eliminated a potential competitor in other verticals such as household goods, toys, and pets.[1620]

More recently, Amazon acquired Whole Foods, a strategic move to acquire both a competitor,[1621] and a new source of customer data.[1622] Amazon purchased Whole Foods at around $13.7 billion, more than 10 times the cost of its second-most expensive acquisition.[1623] In addition to bolstering its position in the grocery market, Amazon's purchase of Whole Foods expanded its touch points with Prime members and gave it access to a unique set of customer information.[1624] Specifically, the deal enabled Amazon to monitor and compile data on how the same person shops both online and in person, data that is particularly useful for targeted advertising and promotional campaigns.[1625]

While the deal was under review by the FTC, then-Ranking Member Cicilline raised concerns that "the proposed acquisition w[ould] result in additional consolidation in the retail sector, erode American jobs through increased automation, and threaten local communities through diminished economic opportunity for hardworking Americans."[1626] Amazon's acquisition of Whole Foods has added to the platform's market power in retail by increasing its buyer power over suppliers,[1627] adding to the platform's capabilities in online grocery, and expanding the company's brick-and-mortar retail

---

[1620] *Id.* at AMAZON-HJC-00154656 (noting that "[a]lthough Quidsi is still primarily an online baby care specialty retailer, it has recently begun selling new items such as household goods and personal-care products with the launch of Soap.com . . . . In the future, management intends to launch additional vertical shopping categories such as beauty, toys and pets."); AMAZON-HJC-00132026 (June 8, 2010) (email from Doug Herrington, Vice President of Consumables, to Jeff Bezos stating, "While we find no evidence that alice.com has gotten traction with vendors or customers, and can't see an economic model for them that pencils out, soap.com feels like a more credible threat").

[1621] *Id.* at AMAZON-HJC-00172932 (June 22, 2017) (showing analysis that for Amazon Fresh customers who don't do 100% shopping on Amazon Fresh, Whole Foods is consistently among the top 5 stand-alone national chains where Amazon Fresh customers do their grocery shopping).

[1622] Lauren Hirsch, *A year after Amazon announced its acquisition of Whole Foods, here's where we stand*, CNBC (June 15, 2018), https://www.cnbc.com/2018/06/15/a-year-after-amazon-announced-whole-foods-deal-heres-where-we-stand.html.

[1623] *Infographic: Amazon's Biggest Acquisition*, CBINSIGHTS (June 19, 2019), https://www.cbinsights.com/research/amazon-biggest-acquisitions-infographic/.

[1624] Production of Amazon, to H. Comm. on the Judiciary, AMAZON-HJC-00172090 (June 22, 2017) (on file with Comm.) ("[A] survey said about 45% of WFM customers are Prime; and about 20% of Prime members shop at [Whole Foods Market]."); Production of Amazon, to H. Comm. on the Judiciary, AMAZON-HJC-00173652 (June 23, 2017) (on file with Comm.) ("Based on our survey results, we estimate that approximately 46% of Prime members have shopped at a [Whole Foods] store in the last four weeks.").

[1625] Lauren Hirsch, *A Year After Amazon Announced Its Acquisition of Whole Foods, Here's Where We Stand*, CNBC (June 15, 2018), https://www.cnbc.com/2018/06/15/a-year-after-amazon-announced-whole-foods-deal-heres-where-we-stand.html.

[1626] Letter from Hon. David Cicilline, Chairman, Subcomm. on Antitrust, Commercial and Admin. Law of the H. Comm. on the Judiciary to Hon. Bob Goodlatte, Chairman, H. Comm. on the Judiciary, Hon. Tom Marino, Chairman, Subcomm. on Regulatory Reform, Commercial and Antitrust Law, 3 (July 13, 2017), https://cicilline.house.gov/sites/cicilline.house.gov/files/images/Amazon_Whole_Foods_Acquistion.pdf.

[1627] *See, e.g.*, Interview with Source 153 (May 11, 2020); Interview with Nat'l Grocers Ass'n (May 28, 2020).

footprint. In addition, it appears that concerns about diminished economic opportunities may have been well-founded as Amazon reportedly plans to implement cashierless technology across all of its Whole Foods stores.[1628]

In recent years, Amazon has also made several significant acquisitions of home security companies, further expanding its reach and visibility into Americans' homes. An Amazon executive described the company's in-home strategy by noting, "Two senses matter – eyes and ears."[1629] In 2017, Amazon paid $90 million to acquire Blink, a home-security camera company whose technology and energy-efficient chips could be used by Amazon in its Echo Speakers and other products.[1630] In 2018, Amazon spent $1.2 billion to acquire Ring, a home-security system spanning cameras, doorbells, and floodlights.[1631] Ring's "eyes and ears" add significant value to Amazon's smart home, allowing customers to virtually interact with Amazon delivery personnel and instruct them on where to drop off Amazon packages.[1632] Amazon's significant investments in the Internet of Things ecosystem and its strategy, centered on Amazon's voice assistant, Alexa, is discussed in other parts of this Report.

Other notable acquisitions include Kiva Systems in 2012, which provided Amazon with a robotics company that accelerated its ability to streamline picking, packing, and shipping e-commerce products;[1633] and PillPack in 2018, which equips Amazon with an online pharmacy and marks its entry into the pharmaceutical market.[1634]

Amazon's acquisition of Kiva gave it power over an important input for competitors. When Amazon bought the robotics company it was supplying technology to a large number of retailers, including Gap, Staples, and Walgreens.[1635] Many of these customers had invested a sunk cost of $4

[1628] Taylor Lyles, *Amazon Go's Cashierless Tech May Come to Whole Foods As Soon As Next Year*, THE VERGE (Aug. 24, 2020), https://www.theverge.com/2020/8/24/21399607/amazon-cashierless-go-technology-whole-foods-2021-rumor.

[1629] Production of Amazon, to H. Comm. on the Judiciary, AMAZON-HJC-00170877 (Oct. 11, 2017) (on file with Comm.).

[1630] Jeffrey Dastin, *Amazon Quietly Dropped $90 Million on a Camera Startup Last Year to Acquire its Unique Chip Technology*, BUS. INSIDER (Feb. 12, 2018, 8:54 AM), https://www.businessinsider.com/amazon-blink-camera-maker-acquisition-2018-2.

[1631] Dennis Green, *Amazon's $1 Billion Acquisition of the Door Camera Startup Ring is the Company Doing What It Does Best – and it Should Terrify Every Other Retailer*, BUS. INSIDER (Mar. 3, 2018), https://www.businessinsider.com/why-amazon-acquired-ring-2018-3.

[1632] *Id.*

[1633] Leena Rao, *Amazon Acquires Robot-Coordinated Order Fulfillment Company Kiva Systems For $775 Million In Cash*, TECHCRUNCH (Mar. 19, 2012), https://techcrunch.com/2012/03/19/amazon-acquires-online-fulfillment-company-kiva-systems-for-775-million-in-cash/.

[1634] Christina Farr, *The Inside Story of Why Amazon Bought PillPack in its Effort to Crack the $500 Billion Prescription Market*, CNBC (May 13, 2019), https://www.cnbc.com/2019/05/10/why-amazon-bought-pillpack-for-753-million-and-what-happens-next.html.

[1635] Evelyn M. Rusli, Amazon.com to Acquire Manufacturer of Robotics, N.Y. TIMES: DEALBOOK (Mar. 19, 2012), https://dealbook.nytimes.com/2012/03/19/amazon-com-buys-kiva-systems-for-775-million/.

million to $6 million per warehouse in order to make use of Kiva's technologies.[1636] Kiva had promised to keep shipping its technology to non-Amazon customers—regardless of whether they competed with Amazon—but in 2015, Amazon rebranded the company as Amazon Robotics and announced it would stop servicing other firms.[1637] Amazon stated that retailers seeking to use Kiva's robots would need to use Amazon Services to fulfill orders with Amazon's technology in Amazon's warehouses.[1638]

Documents Subcommittee staff reviewed relating to the PillPack deal, meanwhile, give insight into how Amazon views some acquisitions as opportunities to collect additional customer data and to cross-sell across its different business lines. One Amazon executive summarized a potential upside of the PillPack deal, asking "Is there a cross-selling opportunity with amazon.com based on known maladies from prescriptions? Or is this prohibited by privacy law? My understanding is there is a number of different ways we could cross-sell customers in both directions (Rx<>non-Rx)."[1639] Though it is unclear whether and the extent to which Amazon implemented this strategy, the exchange reveals how Amazon assesses potential acquisitions and the cross-business opportunities they create, suggesting that the firm views its vast operations in a highly integrated manner.

The FTC investigated several of these transactions, including Amazon's acquisition of Quidsi, the parent company of Diapers.com,[1640] and Whole Foods.[1641] The agency declined, however, to challenge any of them as a violation of antitrust law despite (1) strong evidence, in some cases, of direct head-to-head competition on price and quality between the merging firms; and (2) evidence that many of these mergers would enable Amazon to expand or entrench its market power, particularly in e-commerce. For most, if not all, of the acquisitions discussed in this Report, the FTC had advance notice of the deals, but did not attempt to block any of them.

In addition to eliminating competitive threats, Amazon's acquisition strategy has expanded and protected the company's dominance. The company's significant expansion into new markets, paired with Amazon's wealth of data from its retail business, has fueled the platform's increasing market power. Amazon Associate General Counsel Nate Sutton testified at the Subcommittee's hearing last July that "Amazon is proud to be a company of builders and we have built our company from within,

---

[1636] Mick Mountz, *Kiva the Disrupter*, HARV. BUS. REV. (Dec. 2012), https://hbr.org/2012/12/kiva-the-disrupter.

[1637] Adam Putz, M&A flashback: Amazon announces $775M Kiva Systems acquisition, PITCHBOOK (Mar. 19, 2018), https://pitchbook.com/news/articles/ma-flashback-amazon-announces-775m-kiva-systems-acquisition.

[1638] *Id.*

[1639] Production of Amazon, to H. Comm. on the Judiciary, AMAZON-HJC-00172665 (May 23, 2018) (on file with Comm.).

[1640] Letter from April Tabor, Acting Sec. of the Fed. Trade Comm'n, to Thomas Barnett (Aug. 22, 2012), https://www.ftc.gov/sites/default/files/documents/closing_letters/amazon.com-inc./quidsi-inc./110323amazonlubek.pdf.

[1641] Press Release, Federal Trade Comm'n, Statement of Federal Trade Commission's Acting Director of the Bureau of Competition on the Agency's Review of Amazon.com, Inc.'s Acquisition of Whole Foods Market Inc. (Aug. 23, 2017), https://www.ftc.gov/news-events/press-releases/2017/08/statement-federal-trade-commissions-acting-director-bureau.

not through acquisitions."[1642] But the evidence examined during the investigation demonstrates that Amazon's acquisitions—including of its direct competitors—have been key to Amazon's attainment, maintenance, and expansion of market power.

c. Conduct

i. Treatment of Third-Party Sellers

1) Bullying

While Amazon has referred to third-party sellers on its Marketplace as "partners," and "customers,"[1643] numerous small and medium-sized businesses told the Subcommittee that Amazon routinely bullies and mistreats them. The Online Merchants Guild, a trade association representing the interests of sellers engaged in online commerce, stated that they "have seen Amazon use their position of strength to take advantage of sellers."[1644]

Underlying Amazon's public-facing rhetoric is the reality that it views many of the sellers on its platform as competitors. In its internal documents, Amazon refers to third-party sellers as "internal competitors."[1645] At the Subcommittee's sixth hearing, Subcommittee Chairman Cicilline asked Mr. Jeff Bezos about Amazon's apparent doublespeak.[1646] In response, Mr. Bezos conceded, "[I]t wouldn't surprise me. In some ways, we are competing."[1647]

Over the course of the investigation, the Subcommittee heard from numerous sellers who described abusive tactics or mistreatment by Amazon in a variety of circumstances. For example, at the Subcommittee's fifth hearing, CEO and Founder of PopSockets David Barnett testified about Amazon's bullying tactics, which he said were enabled by "the asymmetry in power between Amazon

---

[1642] Innovation and Entrepreneurship Hearing Transcript at 39 (statement of Nate Sutton, Assoc. Gen. Counsel, Competition, Amazon.com, Inc.).

[1643] *See, e.g.*, CEO Hearing at 44 (response to Questions for the Record of Jeff Bezos, CEO, Amazon.com, Inc.) ("Amazon makes significant investments to support Amazon's selling partners."); CEO Hearing at 41 (response to Questions for the Record of Jeff Bezos, CEO, Amazon.com, Inc.) ("Amazon recognizes that third-party sellers are our customers too, and their trust is critical to Amazon's success.").

[1644] Submission from Online Merchants Guild, to H. Comm. on the Judiciary, 3 (Oct. 29, 2019) (on file with Comm.).

[1645] *See, e.g.*, Production from Amazon, to H. Comm. on the Judiciary, AMAZON-HJC-00206715 (Mar. 8, 2016) (on file with Comm.) (describing change to manual Pricing Rules when Amazon offer is competing with "internal 3P competitor" offers); AMAZON-HJC-00038917 (Sept. 2009) (describing proposal on "how to treat FBA sellers differently from other Buy Box (BB) eligible 3P sellers when we're matching *internal* competitors for non-media categories."); AMAZON-HJC-00142724 (defining Amazon's "Standard Price Matching Policy," and conditions when "Internal competitors (3P merchants) are matched" on price").

[1646] CEO Hearing Transcript at 93 (question of Rep. Cicilline (D-RI), Chairman, Subcomm. on Antitrust, Commercial and Admin. Law).

[1647] *Id.* (statement of Jeff Bezos, CEO, Amazon, Inc.)

and its partners."[1648] He stated that after the two companies decided on a minimum price at which Amazon would sell PopSockets, Amazon sold the products for a lower price and then demanded that PopSockets pay for the lost margin.[1649] As a result, PopSockets decided to end its relationship with Amazon Retail.[1650] When PopSockets communicated this intent to Amazon, its response was, "No, you are not leaving the relationship."[1651] PopSockets did sever its relationship with Amazon Retail for a period of time, but reestablished it about a year later.[1652] Mr. Barnett estimates that in 2019 his company incurred losses of $10 million in revenue from when he stopped selling to Amazon Retail and Amazon blocked one of his authorized distributors from selling on the marketplace.[1653]

Subcommittee staff learned about numerous other instances of Amazon employing strong-arm tactics in negotiations. A company that conducts business with multiple divisions of Amazon described how the platform leveraged its dominance in e-commerce to force acceptance of certain terms and conditions during negotiations over a different part of its business.[1654] According to this company, Amazon knows the power they have as a retailer. In the midst of negotiations, the platform repeatedly referenced its power to destock the company's products on Amazon.com as a "bargaining chip to force terms" unrelated to retail distribution on the company.[1655] The company added, "Amazon know[s] they have a lot of power [in retail e-commerce] and they are not afraid to use it to get terms they want in other markets."[1656]

Book publishers described a similar asymmetric power dynamic with Amazon. According to one publisher, "Amazon has used retaliation . . . to coerce publishers to accept contractual terms that impose substantial penalties for promoting competition" with Amazon's rivals.[1657] The publisher added that the platform's retaliatory conduct shows "Amazon's ability and willingness to leverage its market power to prevent publishers from working effectively with rival e-book retailers and, thereby, maintain and enhance its dominance in e-book distribution."[1658] Amazon's retaliatory tactics against publishers include removing the "buy" button, which blocks a customer's ability to purchase a publisher's current

---

[1648] Competitors Hearing at 5 (statement of David Barnett, CEO and Founder, Popsockets LLC),

[1649] *Id.* at 22 (statement of David Barnett, CEO and Founder, Popsockets LLC).

[1650] *Id.*

[1651] *Id.* at 23.

[1652] *Id.* at 3–4 (statement of David Barnett, CEO and Founder, Popsockets LLC).

[1653] *Id.* at 4 (statement of David Barnett, CEO and Founder, Popsockets LLC).

[1654] Interview with Source 148 (Aug. 26, 2020).

[1655] *Id.*

[1656] *Id.*

[1657] Submission from Source 17, to H. Comm. on the Judiciary, 13 (Nov. 14, 2019) (on file with Comm.).

[1658] *Id.* at 3 (Sept. 22, 2020) (on file with Comm.).

titles;[1659] and removing the "pre-order" button, which eliminates the ability for a consumer to pre-order a publishers' forthcoming titles.[1660] Another form of retaliation that Amazon reportedly engaged in was showing publishers' titles as out of stock or with delayed shipping times.[1661] According to credible reports, Amazon used these tactics in its public battle with Hachette Book Group in 2014 over e-book pricing,[1662] and has used them or threatened to use them in more recent negotiations.[1663] Publishers, authors, and booksellers have "significant fear" because of Amazon's dominance.[1664]

Amazon can treat sellers in this manner because it knows that sellers have no other realistic alternatives to the platform. As Mr. Barnett noted in his testimony:

> When there is bullying by an extremely successful company with all these partners that continue to do business with it, one has to ask how is it that such a successful business maintains partnerships with so many companies while bullying them. It is because of the power asymmetry . . . that companies tolerate this.[1665]

A recent complaint filed against Amazon described the situation as follows, "From the third-party retailers' perspective, Amazon Marketplace is like Hotel California, a lovely place to start or expand an online retail business, but check out from Amazon Marketplace and you can quickly find your business in bankruptcy."[1666] Additional comments from sellers that Subcommittee staff interviewed include, "We're stuck. We don't have a choice but to sell through Amazon,"[1667] and, referring to Amazon, "They've never been a great partner, but you have to work with them."[1668]

As Stacy Mitchell, Co-Director of the Institute for Local Self-Reliance, noted during the Subcommittee's hearing on Innovation and Entrepreneurship, "Among the most egregious examples of Amazon's arbitrary treatment of sellers are its abrupt suspensions of their accounts, frequently made

[1659] *See, e.g.*, David Streitfeld, *Amazon Pulls Thousands of E-Books in Dispute*, N.Y TIMES: Bits (Feb. 22, 2012), https://bits.blogs.nytimes.com/2012/02/22/amazon-pulls-thousands-of-e-books-in-dispute/?hpw.

[1660] *See, e.g.*, Polly Mosendz, *Amazon Blocks Pre-orders Of Hachette Books*, THE ATLANTIC (May 23, 2014), https://www.theatlantic.com/business/archive/2014/05/amazon-blacklists-hachette-books/371545/.

[1661] *See, e.g.*, David Streitfeld, *Writers Feel an Amazon-Hachette Spat*, N.Y. TIMES (May 9, 2014), https://www.nytimes.com/2014/05/10/technology/writers-feel-an-amazon-hachette-spat.html.

[1662] *Id.*

[1663] *See* Interview with Source 155 (Sept. 29, 2020); Submission from Source 17, to H. Comm. on the Judiciary, 13–18 (Nov. 14, 2019) (on file with Comm.).

[1664] Interview with Ass'n of American Publishers, The Authors Guild & American Booksellers Ass'n (Aug. 26, 2020).

[1665] Competitors Hearing at 23 (statement of David Barnett, CEO and Founder, Popsockets LLC).

[1666] Class Action Complaint at 20, Frame-Wilson v. Amazon.com, Inc., No. 20-cv-00424 (W.D. Wash. Mar. 9, 2020).

[1667] Interview with Source 150 (July 11, 2020).

[1668] Interview with Source 151 (July 2, 2020).

without explanation."[1669] Once Amazon suspends a seller's account or delists its products, the business is left with largely ineffective remedies as they watch their sales disappear. Sellers shared with Subcommittee staff that communications to Amazon's Seller Support Central generally prompt automated, unhelpful responses, which may be entirely unrelated to the specific case, question, or concern raised by the seller.[1670]

The founder of an infant product sold on Amazon told Subcommittee staff that after her products were mistakenly delisted, "[i]t would take weeks of repeated calls—at least 10 or 15 contacts with Seller Support—before somebody inside would determine that it was a mistake and error," and take action to fix the problem.[1671] She stated that this happened at least six times, and that in each instance her listings would be down for two to three weeks at a time.[1672] Describing how Amazon's mistakes can threaten a new business's survival, this small-business owner said:

> When you're a new company and Amazon suddenly delists you, it creates fear in the customer. "Where did it go? Is there something wrong with the product? What happened?" If a customer searched and it's no longer there, they're unlikely to ever come back and buy it . . . You've probably lost that customer for good.[1673]

In another example, a third-party bookseller told Subcommittee staff that Amazon delisted 99% of his business's inventory in September 2019.[1674] The bookseller requested that Amazon return its products, which were stored in Amazon's warehouses.[1675] As of July 2020, Amazon had only returned a small fraction of the bookseller's inventory and continued to charge him storage fees.[1676] Amazon blocked the bookseller both from selling its products on its marketplace and retrieving its inventory, precluding the seller from trying to recover some of his losses by making sales through another, albeit lesser, channel. At the Subcommittee's sixth hearing, Representative McBath presented the bookseller's story to Mr. Bezos, who responded that this treatment is "not the systematic approach that [Amazon] take[s]."[1677] However, evidence Subcommittee staff collected through extensive seller interviews shows that Amazon's poor treatment of sellers is far from an isolated incident—a fact

---

[1669] Innovation and Entrepreneurship Hearing at 9 (statement of Stacy Mitchell, Co-Director, Inst. for Local Self Reliance).

[1670] Interview with Source 125 (Jan. 9, 2020); *see also* Submission from Joel Hellmann, to H. Comm. on the Judiciary (July 31, 2019) (on file with Comm.) (responding to automated messaged, "If you were a person and not a robot you would have read that I already tried this and it failed.").

[1671] Interview with Source 149 (July 22, 2020).

[1672] *Id.*

[1673] *Id.*

[1674] Interview with Source 125 (July 7, 2020).

[1675] *Id.*

[1676] *Id.*

[1677] CEO Hearing Transcript at 89 (statement of Jeff Bezos, CEO, Amazon.com, Inc.).

supported both by public posts on Amazon's Seller Central forum,[1678] as well as pleas for help routinely sent directly to Mr. Bezos.[1679]

Because of the severe financial repercussions associated with suspension or delisting, many Amazon third-party sellers live in fear of the company.[1680] For sellers, Amazon functions as a "quasi-state," and many "[s]ellers are more worried about a case being opened on Amazon than in actual court."[1681] This is because Amazon's internal dispute resolution system is characterized by uncertainty, unresponsiveness, and opaque decision-making processes.

Additionally, the sellers interviewed by Subcommittee staff generally indicated that Amazon's customer service and treatment towards them has declined significantly in recent years. One business owner, who has been selling on Amazon for over a decade, told Subcommittee staff that in the past a seller could get meaningful assistance by talking to an Amazon representative over the phone.[1682] He said, "I used to think that Amazon was a partner," but, now, "I don't think they care about the third party seller . . . . They treat us as a commodity."[1683] Internal Amazon documents suggest that the company's hyper-focus on a cost-cutting strategy to adopt automated processes for nearly everything—which Amazon refers to as "HOTW" or "Hands off the wheel"[1684]—combined with the platform's monopoly power over sellers may be to blame for Amazon's atrocious levels of customer service for sellers.

[1678] *See, e.g.*, iNOVATECH_MEDICAL, *Inventory being held hostage by Amazon for 3 months*, AMAZON SERVICES SELLER FORUMS (Apr. 8, 2020, 10:30 PM), https://sellercentral.amazon.com/forums/t/inventory-being-held-hostage-by-amazon-for-3-months/607892.

[1679] *See* Josh Dzieza, *Prime and Punishment: Dirty Dealing in the $175 Billion Amazon Marketplace*, THE VERGE (Dec. 19, 2018), https://www.theverge.com/2018/12/19/18140799/amazon-marketplace-scams-seller-court-appeal-reinstatement ("Emailing the richest man in the world is actually the standard method of escalating an Amazon seller appeal. It's called a Jeff Bomb, or . . . a Jeff Letter."); Interview with Chris McCabe, Founder, ecommerceChris LLC (Dec. 30, 2019) ("Out of desperation, some sellers try to email Jeff Bezos directly."); Submission from Source 125, to H. Comm. on the Judiciary (Jan. 27, 2020) (on file with Comm.); Submission from Source 150, to H. Comm. on the Judiciary (Aug. 16, 2017) (on file with Comm.).

[1680] *See, e.g.*, Submission from Source 125, to H. Comm. on the Judiciary (July 17, 2020) (on file with Comm.) ("My pregnant wife had to visit the ER due to increased anxiety and fear for the future . . . . Due to Amazon's stature, influence, and bullying nature, we are afraid of retaliation."); Interview with Source 154 (July 2, 2019) ("[Amazon] know[s] that small sellers have no power and no ability to avoid them," because "they are the powerhouse giant in the transaction and they could crush us."). *See also* Submission from Nat'l Ass'n of Wholesaler-Distributors, to H. Comm. on the Judiciary, 3 (July 22, 2020) (on file with Comm.) ("Small businesses that depend upon Amazon for access to their markets, including many of our members, fear retribution by Amazon if they speak up.").

[1681] Josh Dzieza, *Prime and Punishment: Dirty Dealing in the $175 Billion Amazon Marketplace*, THE VERGE (Dec. 19, 2018), https://www.theverge.com/2018/12/19/18140799/amazon-marketplace-scams-seller-court-appeal-reinstatement.

[1682] Interview with Source 152 (Sept. 18, 2020).

[1683] *Id.*

[1684] *See, e.g.*, Production from Amazon, to H. Comm. on the Judiciary, AMAZON-HJC-00227277 (on file with Comm.) ("The implementation of Hands Off the Wheel in [Site Merchandising] will mean that through automation . . . there is less work for humans. . . . Project Tiger combines all Hands off the Wheel (HOTW) programs and Amazon spans of control guidelines."); AMAZON-HJC-00227278 (Apr. 27, 2017) ("We are pursuing three tracks to drive Productivity savings: 1) FCF initiatives; 2) HOTW; and 3) Defect Reduction & Catalog Improvement.").

Amazon has recently monetized the degradation of its seller services, rolling out a program where sellers can pay an extra fee for a dedicated account representative. Sellers are supposed to pay for representatives to help them solve the very problems that Amazon created in the first place. Many sellers say, however, that even with paid Amazon account managers they are often unable to get their issues resolved. One seller told Subcommittee staff, "It [i]s a problem that an algorithm can make a decision that just shuts off my income stream and there's nothing I can do to get it back . . . . The only thing I can do to get it back is pay $6,000 a month for a dedicated rep and even then, it doesn't always work."[1685]

The last resort for sellers facing these circumstances is the "Jeff Bomb," or "Jeff Letter," in which a seller sends an email to Mr. Bezos to plead their case.[1686] As the Online Merchants Guild explained in its submission, "a 'Jeff Letter' is almost like a Writ of Certiorari within Amazon's internal kangaroo court system."[1687] But by the time this point is reached, "a seller could be locked out of their account, or denied funds, for weeks, losing hundreds of thousands of dollars even if the mistake was Amazon's."[1688] Because of the large volume of sellers who reach this point of last resort, sending a "Jeff Letter" is not a realistic avenue for most sellers to get their issues addressed.

2) Forced Arbitration

All of Amazon's third-party sellers and most of its vendors are subject to a pre-dispute, binding ("forced") arbitration clause,[1689] requiring them to sign away the right to their day in court if a dispute with Amazon arises. Subcommittee staff heard from sellers who said that if it were not for Amazon's market power over them they would not agree to this term.[1690] As noted by the Online Merchants Guild, "Through arbitration, Amazon knows it holds all the cards, and in many ways has the final say

---

[1685] Interview with Source 149 (July 22, 2020). *See also* Submission from Source 100, to H. Comm. on the Judiciary (identifying one concern with Amazon's treatment of sellers as, "Pay or Die - Forcing sellers to pay for their support services to correct Amazon's wrong doings").

[1686] Josh Dzieza, *Prime and Punishment: Dirty Dealing in the $175 Billion Amazon Marketplace*, THE VERGE (Dec. 19, 2018), https://www.theverge.com/2018/12/19/18140799/amazon-marketplace-scams-seller-court-appeal-reinstatement ("Emailing the richest man in the world is actually the standard method of escalating an Amazon seller appeal. It's called a Jeff Bomb, or . . . a Jeff Letter."). *See also* Interview with Chris McCabe, Founder, ecommerceChris LLC (Dec. 30, 2019) ("Out of desperation, some sellers try to email Jeff Bezos directly."); Submission from Source 125, to H. Comm. on the Judiciary (Jan. 27, 2020) (on file with Comm.); Submission from Source 150, to H. Comm. on the Judiciary (Aug. 16, 2017) (on file with Comm.).

[1687] Submission from Online Merchants Guild, to H. Comm. on the Judiciary, 3 (Oct. 29, 2019) (on file with Comm.).

[1688] *Id.*

[1689] Data and Innovation Hearing at 49–50 (response to Questions for the Record, Nate Sutton, Assoc. Gen. Counsel, Amazon.com, Inc.); *Amazon Services Business Solutions Agreement*, AMAZON SELLER CENTRAL, https://sellercentral.amazon.com/gp/help/external/G1791 (last visited Sept. 29, 2020).

[1690] *See, e.g.*, Interview with Source 125 (Jan. 9, 2020) (explaining reason for agreeing to Amazon's terms, "What can I do? They don't give me much choice. You are so small that you don't have any leverage.").

whenever there is a dispute."[1691] As a result, sellers rarely initiate arbitration actions against Amazon. Between 2014 and 2019, even as the number of Amazon sellers continued to grow by hundreds of thousands per year, only 163 sellers and 16 vendors initiated arbitration proceedings.[1692] Because sellers are generally aware that the process is unfair and unlikely to result in a meaningful remedy, they have little incentive to bring an action.

As extensive scholarship has shown, forced arbitration often fails to provide a legitimate forum for resolving disputes and instead usually serves to insulate those engaging in wrongdoing from liability.[1693] The case of Amazon sellers is no different. In practice, arbitration functions as a way for Amazon to keep disputes within its control, with the scales tipped heavily in its favor. As such, Amazon can withhold payments from sellers, suspend their accounts without cause, and engage in other abusive behavior without facing any legal consequences for its actions.[1694]

3) Seller Fee Increases

Amazon's treatment of sellers indicates that it sees them as a source of profit, rather than "Amazon's treatment of sellers indicates that it sees them as a source of profit, rather than "partners."[1695] Individuals and small businesses who depend on access to the platform to make sales report that Amazon has raised seller fees significantly over the past decade. Over the past five years, a recent Institute for Local Self-Reliance report estimates that Amazon added an extra 11% to its cut of third-party sales.[1696] The platform now takes an average of 30% of each sale compared to 19% in 2015.[1697] In 2018, third-party sellers paid Amazon $39.7 billion in fees, which totaled about 25% of Amazon's $160 billion in Gross Merchandise Volume.[1698] This amount includes commissions,

---

[1691] Submission from Online Merchants Guild, to H. Comm. on the Judiciary, 3 (Oct. 29, 2019) (on file with Comm.).

[1692] Data and Innovation Hearing at 49–51 (response to Questions for the Record, Nate Sutton, Assoc. Gen. Counsel, Amazon.com, Inc.).

[1693] *See* Cynthia Estlund, *The Black Hole of Mandatory* Arbitration, 96 N.C. L. REV. 679, 684 (2018) (stating that mandatory arbitration "effectively enables employers to nullify employee rights and to insulate themselves from the liabilities that back up crucial public policies"); see also Judith Resnik, *Diffusing Disputes: The Public in the Private of Arbitration, the Private in Courts, and the Erasure of Rights*, 124 YALE L.J. 2804, 2873 (2015) ("Mandated arbitration is also common in web-based sales.").

[1694] *See* Submission from Online Merchants Guild, to H. Comm. on the Judiciary, 3 (Oct. 29, 2019) (on file with Comm.).

[1695] *See, e.g.*, Production of Amazon, to H. Comm. on the Judiciary, AMAZON-HJC-00206936 (Nov. 8, 2013) (on file with Comm.) ("Seems like we should be making more on the seller loans. . . . Net takeaway is that sellers may be getting too good of a deal... There are different ways to fix... commitment fees, higher rates, etc.. We should get rewarded for satisfying a timing spike like this.").

[1696] STACY MITCHELL, RON KNOX & ZACH FREED, INST. OF LOCAL SELF-RELIANCE, REPORT: AMAZON'S MONOPOLY TOLLBOOTH 3 (2020), https://ilsr.org/amazons_tollbooth/.

[1697] *Id. See also* Interview with Jason Boyce, Founder & CEO, Avenue7Media, LLC (Sept. 15, 2020) (estimating that most sellers are currently paying an average of 35% in fees to Amazon when you add up the referral fees and payments for ads based on his experience).

[1698] MARKETPLACE PULSE, MARKETPLACES YEAR IN REVIEW 4 (2019), https://cdn.marketplacepulse.com/misc/marketplaces-year-in-review-2019.pdf.

fulfillment and shipping fees, and other third-party seller services, but does not include revenue from the advertising fees for third-party sellers,[1699] which are often substantial.[1700] An internal Amazon document suggests the company can increase fees to third-party sellers without concern for them switching to another marketplace. The document notes that the amount of "seller attrition as a result of [2018] fee increases" for its Fulfillment by Amazon program was "[n]othing significant."[1701]

Amazon's pattern of exploiting sellers, enabled by its market dominance, raises serious competition concerns. For many sellers, there is no viable alternative to Amazon, and a significant number of sellers rely on its marketplace for their entire livelihood.[1702]

4) Appropriation of Third-Party Seller Data

One of the widely reported ways in which Amazon treats third-party sellers unfairly centers on Amazon's asymmetric access to and use of third-party seller data.[1703] During the investigation, the Subcommittee heard repeated concerns that Amazon leverages its access to third-party sellers' data to identify and replicate popular and profitable products from among the hundreds of millions of listings on its marketplace.[1704] Armed with this information, it appears that Amazon would (1) copy the product to create a competing private-label product;[1705] or (2) identify and source the product directly from the manufacturer to free ride off the seller's efforts, and then cut that seller out of the equation.[1706]

Amazon claims that it has no incentive to abuse sellers' trust because third-party sales make up nearly 60% of its sales and Amazon's first-party sales are relatively small.[1707] Amazon has similarly

---

[1699] *Id.*

[1700] *See, e.g.*, Interview with Top Shelf Brands (Sept. 29. 2020) (estimating Top Shelf paid Amazon over $1 million in fees for advertising in one year); Submission from Top Shelf, to H. Comm. on the Judiciary, Ex. 1 (Oct. 26, 2019) (on file with Comm.).

[1701] Production of Amazon, to H. Comm. on the Judiciary, AMAZON-HJC-00186540 (Jan. 30, 2018) (on file with Comm.).

[1702] *See, e.g.*, JUNGLESCOUT, THE STATE OF THE AMAZON SELLER 2020 4 (2020), https://www.junglescout.com/wp-content/uploads/2020/02/State-of-the-Seller-Survey.pdf ("More than a third (37%) of sellers [surveyed] earn income from Amazon sales alone.").

[1703] Innovation and Entrepreneurship Hearing at 5 (statement of Stacy Mitchell, Co-Director, Inst. for Local Self-Reliance) ("Amazon's [gatekeeper power] allows it to maintain a God-like view of the transactions of rival businesses and customers, and use this data to move into new markets with a built-in advantage.").

[1704] *See, e.g.*, Interview with Source 158 (July 2, 2020); Submission from Nat'l Ass'n of Wholesaler-Distributors, to H. Comm. on the Judiciary (July 22, 2020) (on file with Comm.).

[1705] *See, e.g.*, Interview with Jason Boyce, Founder & CEO, Avenue7Media (Sept. 15, 2020).

[1706] *See, e.g.*, Submission from Nat'l Ass'n of Wholesaler-Distributors, to H. Comm. on the Judiciary (July 22, 2020) (on file with Comm.).

[1707] CEO Hearing at 23 (response to Questions for the Record of Jeff Bezos, CEO, Amazon.com, Inc.).

pointed out that third-party listings far outnumber Amazon's first-party listings.[1708] In a recent shareholder letter, CEO Jeff Bezos wrote, "Third-party sellers are kicking our first party butt. Badly."[1709] In response to a question from the Subcommittee, however, Amazon admitted that by percentage of sales—a more telling measure—Amazon's first-party sales are significant and growing in a number of categories. For example, in books, Amazon owns 74% of sales, whereas third-party sellers only account for 26% of sales.[1710] At the category level, it does not appear that third-party sellers are kicking Amazon's first-party butt. Amazon may, in fact, be positioned to overtake its third-party sellers in several categories as its first-party business continues to grow.

Third-Party vs. First-Part Listings and Sales on Amazon[1711]

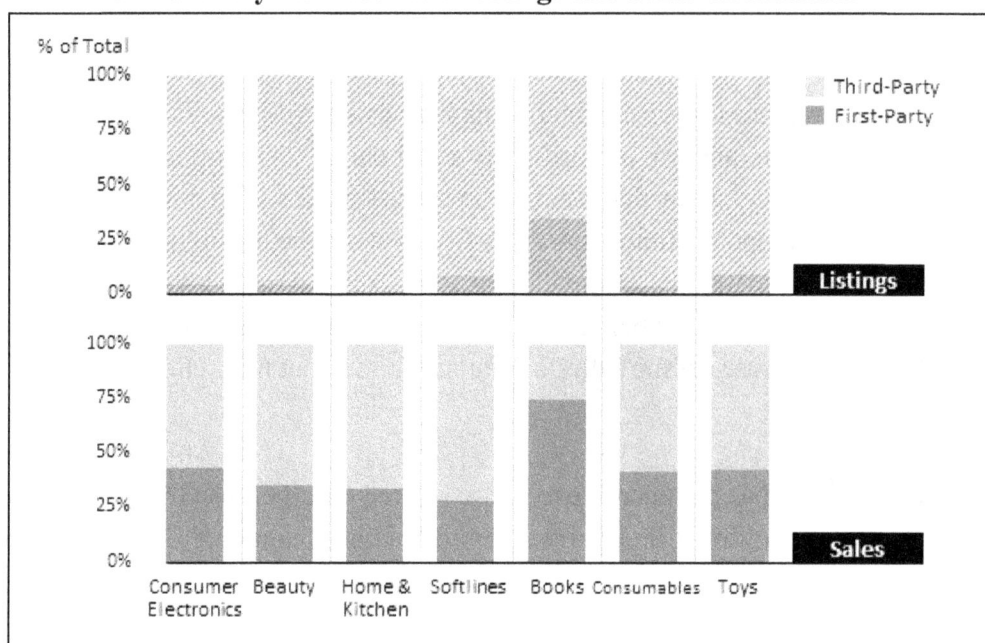

Amazon recognizes that it competes against many of its third-party sellers.[1712] In response to concerns about its unfair use of third-party seller data, Amazon points to its Seller Data Protection Policy, which it instituted in 2014.[1713] According to the company:

> Amazon recognizes that third-party sellers are our customers too, and their trust is critical to Amazon's success. In an effort to further this partnership, Amazon decided

---

[1708] *Id.* at 24.

[1709] Jeff Bezos, *2018 Letter to Shareholders*, THE AMAZON BLOG: DAY ONE (Apr. 11, 2019), https://blog.aboutamazon.com/company-news/2018-letter-to-shareholders.

[1710] CEO Hearing at 25 (response to Questions for the Record of Jeff Bezos, CEO, Amazon.com, Inc.).

[1711] *Id.* at 24–25 (response to Questions for the Record of Jeff Bezos, CEO, Amazon.com, Inc.).

[1712] Production of Amazon, to H. Comm. on the Judiciary, AMAZON-HJC-00142724 (on file with Comm.).

[1713] CEO Hearing at 2 (response to Questions for the Record of Jeff Bezos, CEO, Amazon.com, Inc.).

years ago to take additional voluntary steps to protect seller data by instituting its voluntarily-adopted Seller Data Protection Policy, which prohibits Amazon Retail teams from using non-public seller-specific data to compete against third-party sellers.[1714]

Following up on public reporting and information collected during the investigation suggesting that Amazon might be abusing its access to third-party sellers' data, Representative Pramila Jayapal (D-WA) asked Amazon lawyer Nate Sutton about this precise issue at a Subcommittee hearing in July 2019. Sutton testified: "We do not use [third-party sellers'] individual data when we're making decisions to launch private brands."[1715]

Since the July 2019 hearing, public reporting has made clear that, contrary to its own internal policy and testimony before Congress, Amazon routinely appropriates seller data to benefit its own private-label and retail businesses. After the hearing, according to a July 2019 report, a former employee who worked in product management told *The Capitol Forum*, "I used to pull sellers' data to look at what the best products were when I was there … That was my job."[1716] In September 2019, employees reported to *Yahoo Finance* that access to data is a "free-for-all" and that Amazon Retail and Marketplace teams "share the same access to the data warehouse, which makes it possible for the retail team to use the data from marketplace sellers to develop private labels."[1717]

Earlier this year, in a groundbreaking article, the *Wall Street Journal* reported that executives in Amazon's private-label division "had access to data containing proprietary information that they used to research bestselling items they might want to compete against, including on individual sellers on Amazon's website."[1718] In one case, Amazon employees reportedly used non-public sales data about a third-party seller of car-trunk organizers named Fortem to develop an Amazon private-label version of the very same product.[1719]

In light of the April 2020 report from the *Wall Street Journal*, the Committee requested that Jeff Bezos testify before Congress to address the possibility that Amazon's lawyer had misled

---

[1714] *Id.* 41 (response to Questions for the Record of Jeff Bezos, CEO, Amazon.com, Inc.).

[1715] Innovation and Entrepreneurship Hearing Transcript at 51 (statement of Nate Sutton, Assoc. Gen. Counsel, Competition, Amazon.com, Inc.).

[1716] *Amazon: Former Employee Challenges Executives' Denial About Company's Use of Sellers' Data*, THE CAPITOL FORUM (July 18, 2019).

[1717] Krystal Hu, *Amazon Uses Third-Party Seller Data to Build a Private Label Juggernaut*, YAHOO FIN. (Sept. 27, 2019), https://finance.yahoo.com/news/amazon-uses-thirdparty-sellers-data-to-build-private-labels-145813238.html.

[1718] Dana Mattioli, *Amazon Scooped Up Data From Its Own Sellers to Launch Competing Products*, WALL ST. J. (Apr. 23, 2020), https://www.wsj.com/articles/amazon-scooped-up-data-from-its-own-sellers-to-launch-competing-products-11587650015.

[1719] *Id.*

Congress.[1720] Despite significant public reporting on the issue and references to it in Amazon's internal documents, Mr. Bezos claimed to be unaware of these practices. According to Mr. Bezos, "Amazon first learned about the alleged violations of Amazon's voluntarily adopted Seller Data Protection Policy recently reported in the *Wall Street Journal* from the *Wall Street Journal*."[1721] When Representative Pramila Jayapal again asked in July 2020 about whether Amazon uses third-party seller data to benefit its private-label products, Bezos could only respond: "I can't answer that question yes or no . . . we have a policy against using seller-specific data to aid our private-label business, but I can't guarantee you that that policy has never been violated."[1722]

Representative Ken Buck (R-CO) similarly raised this issue with Mr. Bezos, stating, "I'm concerned that you've used Amazon's dominant market position to unfairly harm competition. We've heard from a number of companies that Amazon uses proprietary data from third-party companies to launch its own private-label products."[1723] Later in the hearing, Representative Kelly Armstrong (R-ND) described this as an "important issue," and asked whether "Amazon is conducting an internal investigation into the use of third-party data," to which Mr. Bezos answered in the affirmative. Mr. Bezos agreed to inform the Subcommittee of the outcome of that investigation.

In October 2020, approximately six months after Amazon said that it had initiated the investigation,[1724] the company informed the Committee that it had completed it.[1725] According to Amazon's Vice President of Public Policy, Brian Huseman, "Amazon's records of past data queries related to the two products cited in the *Wall Street Journal* report show that a single former employee pulled and analyzed only aggregate data for both products in compliance with the Seller Data Protection Policy."[1726] The results of this limited investigation do not alter the views of Subcommittee staff on Amazon's use of third-party seller data as set forth in this Report.

[1720] Letter from Hon. Jerrold Nadler, Chairman, H. Comm. on the Judiciary, Hon. David N. Cicilline, Chairman, Subcomm. on Antitrust, Commercial and Admin. Law of the H. Comm. on the Judiciary, Hon. F. James Sensenbrenner, Ranking Member, Subcomm. on Antitrust, Commercial and Admin. Law of the H. Comm. on the Judiciary, Hon. Joe Neguse, Vice-Chair, Subcomm. on Antitrust, Commercial and Admin. Law of the H. Comm. on the Judiciary, Hon. Pramila Jayapal, Member, Subcomm. on Antitrust, Commercial and Admin. Law of the H. Comm. on the Judiciary, Hon. Ken Buck, Member, Subcomm. on Antitrust, Commercial and Admin. Law of the H. Comm. on the Judiciary, Hon. Matt Gaetz, Member, Subcomm. on Antitrust, Commercial and Admin. Law of the H. Comm. on the Judiciary, to Jeff Bezos, CEO, Amazon.com, Inc. (May 1, 2020).

[1721] CEO Hearing at 1 (response to Questions for the Record of Jeff Bezos, CEO, Amazon.com, Inc.).

[1722] CEO Hearing Transcript at 66 (statement of Jeff Bezos, CEO, Amazon.com, Inc.).

[1723] *Id.* at 128 (question of Rep. Ken Buck, Member, Subcomm. on Antitrust, Commercial and Admin. Law of the H. Comm. on the Judiciary).

[1724] @AmazonPolicy, TWITTER (Apr. 24, 2020), https://twitter.com/amazon_policy/status/1253769684425625601.

[1725] Letter from Brian Huseman, Vice Pres., Public Pol'y, to Chairman Jerrold Nadler, Chairman David N. Cicilline, Ranking Member F. James Sensenbrenner, and Ranking Member Jim Jordan (Oct. 4, 2020).

[1726] *Id.*

Subcommittee staff uncovered evidence in interviews with former Amazon employees, as well as current and former sellers, that is consistent with the public reporting about Amazon's misuse of seller data.[1727] In a submission to the Subcommittee, a former employee said:

> In 2010, I started working on the Amazon marketplace team … It was widely known that many (10+) of my peers were running very successful [third-party] accounts, where they were pulling private data on Amazon seller activity, so they could figure out market opportunity, etc. Totally not legitimate, but no one monitored or seemed to care.[1728]

Referring to accessibility of third-party seller data, the same individual told Subcommittee staff, "It's a candy shop, everyone can have access to anything they want," and added, "There's a rule, but there's nobody enforcing or spot-checking. They just say, don't help yourself to the data … it was 'wink wink,' don't access."[1729]

Subcommittee staff interviewed a third-party seller who described how Amazon will use a request for proof of authenticity to collect proprietary information about a seller's business. According to the seller, Amazon will submit a product authenticity claim to sellers, forcing the retailer to submit their original sales receipts as proof that the items are authentic.[1730] Although a seller is supposed to be able to black out price information, sometimes the platform will reject a submission on the basis that is an "altered document."[1731] With insight into the seller's costs and supplier, combined with its knowledge of the seller's retail price among a virtually unfathomable amount of other data, it appears that Amazon Retail can easily replicate the seller's listing to offer a competing product.

A former third-party seller and retired U.S. Marine told Subcommittee staff about several instances over his seventeen years as a seller when Amazon leveraged his work, undercut him on price, and eventually drove him out of business. In each instance, he had to change his business model after Amazon took over the Buy Box for his listings, "killing" his sales.[1732] On at least two different occasions, his company did all the legwork to create a new, top-selling product or product line, as well as creating the product listings, only to have Amazon copy the idea and offer a competing product.

[1727] *See* Submission from Nat'l Ass'n of Wholesaler-Distributors, to H. Comm. on the Judiciary (July 22, 2020) (on file with Comm.) (describing a member's experience in which Amazon allowed a distributor to sell a product for about a year, "then went out and replicated the product and began selling their own branded product, terminating the distributor . . . Amazon became the winner and the distributor was left empty handed.").

[1728] Submission from Source 91, to H. Comm. on the Judiciary (Sept. 16, 2020) (on file with Comm.).

[1729] *Id.*

[1730] Interview with Source 154 (July 2, 2019).

[1731] *Id.*

[1732] Interview with Jason Boyce, Founder & CEO, Avenue7Media (Sept. 15, 2020).

Amazon used different tactics each time, but the result was always the same: Amazon profited from his work and made it impossible for him to fairly compete.[1733]

As part of his last attempt to sell on Amazon, his business created its own line of table game products with a unique design and color palette. Once these products became top sellers, Amazon again swooped in to reap the rewards of his work. Amazon copied his designs, down to the color palette, and started selling their competing products at unsustainable prices. Ultimately, he exited his seller business, gave up on trying to bring new products to consumers, and founded a consulting agency for Amazon sellers.[1734]

In addition to its private-label business, Amazon also uses third-party seller data to benefit its Amazon Retail business, where the company functions more like a retailer. At the Subcommittee's sixth hearing, Chairman David Cicilline (D-RI) asked Mr. Bezos about this conduct, recounting the story that a former third-party seller shared with Subcommittee staff:

> During this investigation, we have heard so many heartbreaking stories of small businesses who sunk significant time and resources into building a business and selling on Amazon, only to have Amazon poach their best-selling items and drive them out of business.

> So I want to talk to you about one company that really stood out from the rest. I want you to pay close attention to how they described your partnership, Mr. Bezos. We heard from a small apparel company that makes and sells what they call "useful apparel" for people who work on their feet and with their hands, like construction workers and firefighters.

> This particular business discovered and started selling a unique item that had never been a top seller for the brand. They were making about $60,000 a year on just this one item. One day, they woke up and found that Amazon had started listing the exact same product, causing their sales to go to zero overnight. Amazon had undercut their price, setting it below what the manufacturer would generally allow it to be sold so that, even if they wanted to, they couldn't match the price.[1735]

Amazon has tried to draw a meaningful distinction between individual and aggregate data, but this is largely beside the point when it comes to the concerns that Subcommittee members have about the platform's conduct and its effect on competition. Amazon says it only uses "aggregate" seller data

---

[1733] *Id.*

[1734] *Id.*

[1735] CEO Hearing Transcript at 117 (question of Rep. David N. Cicilline, Chairman, Subcomm. on Antitrust, Commercial and Admin. Law of the H. Comm. on the Judiciary).

across multiple sellers, not "individual" data about any specific seller.[1736] Importantly, though, it chooses how those terms are defined and uses various methods to deem seller data as aggregate rather than individual. According to the *Wall Street Journal* report, because Fortem accounted for 99.95% of total sales in the car-trunk organizer product category, not 100%, Amazon considered that data aggregate rather than individual.[1737] And at the Subcommittee's hearing in July 2020, Bezos confirmed that Amazon indeed allows the use of aggregate data to inform private-label brands when there are only two or three sellers of a product.[1738] Separately, if there is only one seller of an item, and Amazon is selling returned or damaged versions of that item through its Amazon Warehouse Deals program, that data is considered aggregate.[1739]

An Amazon "Frequently Asked Questions" (FAQ) document from 2014 suggests that Amazon was aware that the Seller Data Protection Policy had significant loopholes. For example, the document indicates that even seller-specific data can be used for "strategic business decision at the category level or above."[1740] The answer to an FAQ also makes clear that the line between "aggregated" data and "Seller-specific" data is fuzzy: "As a general rule, if information isn't directly tied or easily attributed to a specific Seller, it can be considered aggregated and non-Seller-specific." As to how aggregated information attributed to a small group of Sellers should be treated, the guidance is also ambiguous: "This is a high judgment area. If Seller-specific information could be easily derived from aggregated information, it should be treated as Seller-specific."[1741]

In addition to collecting data relating to sales, Amazon may also be able to reverse engineer third-party sellers' cost structures through the tools that it offers sellers to track profits, costs, ad spend, and other expenses, as well as fulfillment services through Fulfillment by Amazon (FBA). An internal document suggests that Amazon may use its FBA service as an avenue to identify popular third-party seller items and gather competitively sensitive information about them.[1742] FBA provides another avenue for Amazon to access competing sellers' third-party data.

[1736] Letter from David Zapolsky, Gen. Counsel, Amazon.com, Inc., to Rep. David N. Cicilline, Chairman, Subcomm. on Antitrust, Commercial and Admin. Law of the H. Comm. on the Judiciary (July 26, 2019) (on file with Comm.).

[1737] Dana Mattioli, *Amazon Scooped Up Data From Its Own Sellers to Launch Competing Products*, WALL ST. J. (Apr. 23, 2020), https://www.wsj.com/articles/amazon-scooped-up-data-from-its-own-sellers-to-launch-competing-products-11587650015.

[1738] CEO Hearing Transcript at 155 (statement of Jeff Bezos, CEO, Amazon.com, Inc.).

[1739] Dana Mattioli, *Amazon Scooped Up Data From Its Own Sellers to Launch Competing Products*, WALL ST. J. (Apr. 23, 2020), https://www.wsj.com/articles/amazon-scooped-up-data-from-its-own-sellers-to-launch-competing-products-11587650015.

[1740] Production of Amazon, to H. Comm. on the Judiciary, AMAZON-HJC-00221869 (June 30, 2014) (on file with Comm.).

[1741] *Id.*

[1742] *See, e.g.*, Production of Amazon, to H. Comm. on the Judiciary, AMAZON-HJC-00207035–36 (Sept. 19, 2013) (on file with Comm.) ("On the top selling Owl necklace . . . we should go deep and see what we can learn including how much it would costs [sic] to manufacture this?").

The documents and information that Subcommittee staff reviewed suggest that instances of Amazon's data misappropriation go beyond what is in the public domain. Furthermore, Subcommittee staff rejects Amazon's contention that Amazon's use of third-party seller data is no different from a traditional brick-and-mortar retailer's use of data. Subcommittee staff also does not believe that the marketplace-derived data the platform uses to inform Amazon Retail's product pipeline, among other decisions, is equally available to all Amazon Marketplace sellers.

On many fronts, Amazon makes inconsistent arguments depending on the forum and issue in support of its attempts to escape liability. In the context of lawsuits regarding liability for counterfeits and unsafe products sold on its site, Amazon insists it is a marketplace and not a retailer.[1743] By contrast, in his testimony before the Subcommittee, Mr. Bezos referred to Amazon as a "store" and a "retailer."[1744] Similarly, when Nate Sutton testified before the Subcommittee he stated, "Amazon is one of the leading retailers."[1745] In response to price gouging allegations, Amazon switches back to the position that it is just a marketplace. As Public Citizen observed in a recent report titled *Prime Gouging*:

> Amazon is trying to have the best of both worlds by enabling third-party sellers to exploit the crisis (and benefiting from facilitating those sales), but also seeking to immunize itself from responsibility for directly engaging in price gouging by shifting the focus on to the unscrupulous actions of third-party sellers, not only in the eye of the public but also in the eye of the law.[1746]

Amazon identified a few types of non-public seller data that it has access to, but which are supposed to be protected by its Seller Data Protection Policy.[1747] It is obvious from this small glimpse into the data Amazon has at its disposal that the type and scope of data the platform can access is very different from the information available to traditional brick-and-mortar stores. Physical stores have much less detailed information about the competing products they offer for sale alongside their private-

---

[1743] *See* Colin Lecher, *How Amazon escapes liability for the riskiest products on its site*, THE VERGE (Jan. 28, 2020), https://www.theverge.com/2020/1/28/21080720/amazon-product-liability-lawsuits-marketplace-damage-third-party.

[1744] *See generally* CEO Hearing (Jeff Bezos, CEO, Amazon.com, Inc.).

[1745] *See generally* Innovation and Entrepreneurship (Nate Sutton, Assoc. Gen. Counsel, Competition, Amazon.com, Inc.).

[1746] PUBLIC CITIZEN, PRIME GOUGING: HOW AMAZON RAISED PRICES TO PROFIT FROM THE PANDEMIC 5 (2020), https://www.citizen.org/article/prime-gouging/ (also noting "a pattern of significant price increases on essential products sold directly by Amazon, as well as price gouging by third-party sellers.").

[1747] Production of Amazon, to H. Comm. on the Judiciary, AMAZON-HJC-00221867 (June 30, 2014) (on file with Comm.) (listing information protected by the Seller Data Protection policy as "Seller pricing plans (e.g., future promotions), Seller inventory levels, Seller sourcing information, Seller sales (e.g., unit sales, GMS), [and] Seller performance (e.g., non-public metrics)").

label items. Physical stores also have far less information about customers' shopping habits and preferences.[1748]

5) Self-Preferencing

By virtue of its role as an intermediary in the marketplace, Amazon can give itself favorable treatment relative to competing sellers. It has done so through its control over the Buy Box, as well as by granting itself access to data and tools that are off limits for third-party sellers. Most recently, there have been reports that Amazon has given preferential treatment to its own non-essential products over competitors' non-essential products during the pandemic.

a) Critical Inputs

Amazon has control over critical inputs for competing sellers and other types of competitors—including consumer data, fulfillment and delivery services, and advertising and other marketing tools—that give it the ability to advantage itself over rivals. During the investigation, Subcommittee staff conducted numerous interviews with market participants that, along with credible public reporting and Amazon's documents, confirm that Amazon employed this business strategy as early as 2009 and continues to do so today.

b) Access to Market Data

Amazon has access to data that gives it greater insight into consumer behavior and preferences than competing sellers on its platform. A former Amazon employee that Subcommittee staff interviewed summarized the significance of this information asymmetry:

> It's important to understand that Amazon has access to every piece of data on what products each customer has searched and purchased [or] not purchased. . . . With information about what customers have searched, Amazon is able to create customized marketing [and] targeting of products for the individual customer. "Is Amazon using a particular [third-party] seller's data here? No," but it is using all of the aggregate site data to develop a highly targeted marketing plan for each customer. Should Amazon choose to use that targeting information to focus [on] its own products, it can, while [third-party] sellers don't have access to similar data.[1749]

[1748] *See* Stigler Report at 45 ("Traditional brick-and-mortar stores and online platforms differ greatly in their advertising and personalization capabilities.").

[1749] Submission from Source 91, to H. Comm. on the Judiciary (Sept. 22, 2020) (on file with Comm.).

Although Amazon provides its sellers with access to some helpful data and tools—which is a key differentiator from other marketplaces with no or limited seller tools—there is a large amount of data that is off limits, only available at a largely prohibitive cost, or unhelpful because it is outdated or inaccurate. One paid service that Amazon offered sellers was called Amazon Retail Analytics Premium. Sellers who paid extra to participate in this program could access some, but not all, of the data Amazon collected on marketplace activity. But the program was expensive: vendors reportedly had to pay a minimum of $30,000 to get access to this database.[1750]

Another example of this asymmetric access to data is evident from an Amazon internal email discussion. The discussion began with a consultant alerting Amazon employees about a problem with its Marketplace Web Services APIs that caused it to report information to sellers that is "disconnected from the reality and often misleading."[1751] According to the representative, "This is a huge issue and causes sellers losses and inconvenience."[1752] In response, an Amazon employee said that there was not a problem with the API functionality; rather, the Pricing APIs just do not provide sellers with information at the level of granularity requested. Further, she explained that this is "a feature request for adding location aware information to the Pricing APIs," which is "currently below the line for 2018 for the pricing team."[1753]

c) Marketing Tools

One tool that Amazon Retail uses to benefit its own business is Amazon Vine, a review-generating program.[1754] In interviews with market participants, many sellers said that good reviews are critical for a product to be successful online.[1755] Accordingly, sellers aim to obtain as many positive reviews as possible early in a product's life cycle. At one time, it was permissible for Amazon sellers to provide incentives such as free samples to reviewers. However, in 2016, it was widely reported that some sellers were generating fake reviews.[1756] In response to these reports, Amazon announced that it would ban incentivized reviews except for those obtained through its own incentivized review

---

[1750] Robyn Johnson, *Amazon Just Made the $30k Amazon Retail Analytics Premium Data Free*, SEARCH ENGINE J. (Feb. 26, 2020), https://www.searchenginejournal.com/amazon-retail-analytics-premium-data-free/350692/ (last visited Oct. 4, 2020).

[1751] Production of Amazon, to H. Comm. on the Judiciary, AMAZON-HJC-00188405–06 (Dec. 14, 2017) (on file with Comm.).

[1752] *Id.*

[1753] *Id.* at AMAZON-HJC-00188536 (Dec. 15, 2017).

[1754] Innovation and Entrepreneurship at 13 (response to Questions for the Record of Nate Sutton, Assoc. Gen. Counsel, Competition, Amazon.com, Inc.).

[1755] *See, e.g.*, Interview with Source 125 (July 7, 2020) (explaining that the inability to move customer reviews from Amazon to other marketplaces is a barrier to use of other marketplaces, due to the importance of customer feedback for seller reputation).

[1756] Elizabeth Weise, *Amazon Bans 'Incentivized' Reviews*, USA TODAY (Oct. 3, 2016), https://www.usatoday.com/story/tech/news/2016/10/03/amazon-bans-incentivized-reviews/91488702/.

program, Amazon Vine.[1757] As a result, sellers lost access to this program, regardless of whether they were engaged in bad conduct or not.

For many years, including after the incentivized-reviews ban, the Amazon Vine program was not available to third-party sellers, while Amazon continued to enjoy the program's ability to "minimize marketing costs associated with generating awareness early in a product's lifecycle," among other benefits.[1758] An Amazon internal document describes other advantages of the program as, "[d]rive conversion and sales with more insightful reviews on detail pages," and "can contribute to higher order counts and sales."[1759]

By both banning incentivized reviews and excluding third-party sellers from the Amazon Vine program, Amazon allocated to itself a significant marketing advantage over the other businesses with which it competes on its platform.

Amazon's dual position as both operator and seller on its online marketplace also provides it with the ability to disadvantage competitors that seek to sell or advertise on its platform. One way that Amazon does this is by limiting certain rivals' ability to buy Amazon.com search advertising—ads that present products at the top of the search results when consumers enter specific search terms or a product name. Although "search advertising is a lucrative part of the company's business," Amazon "won't let some of its own large competitors buy sponsored-product ads tied to searches for Amazon's own devices."[1760] The *Wall Street Journal* reported this month that Roku, Inc. "can't even buy [] Amazon ads tied to its own products."[1761] Consistent with this report, a competitor of Amazon that manufacturers voice-enabled devices told Subcommittee staff that Amazon prohibited it from buying ads on Amazon.com.[1762] The competitor expressed concerns about the harm this could cause consumers, who may be confused or deceived when they receive ads promoting Amazon products even when they specifically search for a competitor's product on Amazon.com.[1763]

[1757] *Id.*

[1758] Production of Amazon, to H. Comm. on the Judiciary, AMAZON-HJC-00146732 (Dec. 14, 2017) (on file with Comm.); Spencer Soper, *Amazon Doles out Freebies to Juice Sales of Its Own Brands*, BLOOMBERG NEWS (Oct. 16, 2018), https://www.bloomberg.com/news/articles/2018-10-16/amazon-doles-out-freebies-to-juice-sales-of-its-own-brands (last visited Oct. 4, 2020).

[1759] Production of Amazon, to H. Comm. on the Judiciary, AMAZON-HJC-00146732 (Dec. 14, 2017) (on file with Comm); *see also* AMAZON-HJC-0059576 (Nov. 22, 2010) (describing program as "[g]reat for new product launches - good for seeding").

[1760] Dana Mattioli, et al., *Amazon Restricts How Rival Device Makers Buy Ads on Its Site*, WALL ST. J. (Sept. 22, 2020), https://www.wsj.com/articles/amazon-restricts-advertising-competitor-device-makers-roku-arlo-11600786638.

[1761] *Id.*

[1762] Interview with Source 148 (Aug. 26, 2020).

[1763] *Id.*

The Subcommittee's investigation also uncovered internal documents showing that Amazon executives have long understood the competitive advantage Amazon wields due to the company's control over search advertising on Amazon.com. In an internal email describing an ad block against Groupon and other "deal site ecommerce competitors,"[1764] an Amazon executive wrote that "Groupon is blocked + let's keep a clear line on this. No deal site ecommerce competitors allowed to advertise on amazon.x sites."[1765]

Similarly, an email discussion in 2009 among high-level Amazon executives discussed the possibility of implementing an ad block against Diapers.com, saying:

> Do we really think it is ok that Diapers.com flipped from selling on the platform to being a large scale user of Product Ads totally unscrrutinized [sic]? I don't. . . . We're under no obligation to allow them to advertise on our site. I'd argue we should block them from buying Product Ads immediately or at minimum price those ads so they truly reflect the opportunity cost of a lost diaper buyer (or to reflect the true value of a new customer to such a competitor.).[1766]

The executive suggests that Amazon should maintain a "watch list" of strategic competitors and set up "[a]n automatic trigger when a merchant on [the] watch list . . . attempts to launch a significant quantity of product ads-with escalated approval required to allow their ads to launch."[1767] The *Wall Street Journal* report, based on discussions with Amazon employees, confirms that Amazon ultimately implemented a plan of this type. According to the report, "Tier 1 Competitors" are blocked from buying certain ads and employees are allegedly instructed to "mark any discussion of this practice . . . with 'privileged and confidential' to evade regulators."[1768]

In March 2020, Amazon announced that it would begin temporarily delaying shipments of all non-essential products from its warehouses, regardless of whether they were sold by Amazon or by competing third-party sellers.[1769] The company claimed it was doing so to better serve customers in need while also helping to ensure the safety of warehouse workers. The effect of this change was to block third-party sellers of items that Amazon designated "non-essential" from shipping new inventory using fulfillment by Amazon.

[1764] Production of Amazon, to H. Comm. on the Judiciary, AMAZON-HJC-00129156 (Dec. 14, 2017) (on file with Comm).

[1765] *Id.*

[1766] *Id.* at AMAZON-HJC-00065094 (May 28, 2009) (on file with Comm).

[1767] *Id.*

[1768] Dana Mattioli, et al., *Amazon Restricts How Rival Device Makers Buy Ads on Its Site*, WALL ST. J. (Sept. 22, 2020), https://www.wsj.com/articles/amazon-restricts-advertising-competitor-device-makers-roku-arlo-11600786638.

[1769] CEO Hearing Transcript at 7–8 (response to Questions for the Record of Jeff Bezos, CEO, Amazon.com, Inc.)

Amazon reportedly excepted itself from this policy and continued to ship non-essential items sold by Amazon Retail from its warehouses. According to a survey of Amazon workers conducted by Change to Win between April 29 and May 9, 2020, workers reported that Amazon had "continued to ship non-essential items such as hammocks, fish tanks, sex toys, and pool floaties."[1770] More than two-thirds of fulfillment center workers reported that 50% or more of the items they handled during this period were non-essential. Based on the survey results, Change to Win concluded that, "Amazon has continued to place workers in danger of contracting COVID-19 in order to ship non-essential goods."[1771] A number of market participants that Subcommittee staff interviewed also indicated that Amazon prioritized shipping its own items over those sold by third-party sellers.[1772] Amazon confirmed that it did give preferential treatment to its own products for a period of time, but claimed it was "unintentional."[1773]

6) <u>Tying and Bundling – Fulfillment by Amazon and Advertising</u>

a) Fulfillment by Amazon

There is a strong link between Amazon Marketplace and Fulfillment by Amazon (FBA), Amazon's paid logistics service. Amazon uses its dominance in each of these markets to strengthen and reinforce its position in the other.

Amazon's FBA program combines warehousing, packing, and shipping services, and most importantly, access to Prime customers.[1774] For a seller's products to get the Prime badge, which is essential to making sales on the platform, a seller must either qualify for Amazon's Seller Fulfilled Prime (SFP) program or use Amazon's FBA service. On August 18, 2020, Amazon informed sellers of changes to Seller Fulfilled Prime, which render it an entirely impractical option for most sellers.[1775]

[1770] CHANGE TO WIN, AMAZON COVID-19 WORKER SURVEY DATA BRIEF 3 (2020), https://static1.squarespace.com/static/5d374de8aae9940001c8ed59/t/5ec67b15a155792a0f9ef435/1590065963743/Amazon-Worker-COVID-19-Data-Brief.pdf.

[1771] *Id.*

[1772] *See, e.g.*, Submission from Source 91, to H. Comm. on the Judiciary (Sept. 16, 2020) ("When we looked at Amazon private-label products during April/early May, they were almost all available for immediate Prime delivery, while comparable national brands were not able to get the same shipment times. Definitely preference was given to many Amazon private-label products during times of "essential"/"non-essential" classification."); Interview with Source 152 (Sept. 18, 2020).

[1773] CEO Hearing at 8 (response to Questions for the Record of Jeff Bezos, CEO, Amazon.com, Inc.) ("After instituting these changes, Amazon became aware that shipments of certain Amazon devices that did not fall into the priority categories had been inadvertently included in the list of products with faster delivery promises. This was unintentional.").

[1774] *Fulfillment by Amazon*, AMAZON, https://sell.amazon.com/fulfillment-by-amazon.html (last visited Oct. 4, 2020).

[1775] Pascal, The Seller Fulfilled Prime Team, *Important Updates to Seller Fulfilled Prime*, AMAZON SERVICES SELLER FORUMS (Aug. 18, 2020), https://sellercentral.amazon.com/forums/t/important-updates-to-seller-fulfilled-prime/682240.

Even before this change, only a very small percentage of sellers could meet the onerous eligibility requirements for Seller Fulfilled Prime.[1776] This means FBA is functionally the only way for sellers to get the Prime badge for their product listings.[1777] A document setting forth draft Q&A before a 2018 earnings call for Amazon Chief Financial Officer Brian Olsavsky explained the connection between Prime and FBA: "Prime and FBA reinforce each other – they are inextricably linked. FBA adds Prime eligible selection. Prime member growth and purchasing habits attract sellers to FBA."[1778]

Due to a lack of alternatives, third-party sellers have no choice but to purchase fulfillment services from Amazon. More than 73% of all Marketplace sellers worldwide reportedly rely on FBA services.[1779] Numerous third-party sellers told the Subcommittee that they feel they have no choice but to pay for FBA to maintain a favorable search result position, to reach Amazon's more than 112 million Prime members, and to win the Buy Box—through which the vast majority of Amazon sales are made.[1780] A recent consumer survey indicated that 75% of Amazon Prime customers specifically search for products flagged as Prime-eligible.[1781] As a result, as the Online Merchant's Guild told Subcommittee staff, many sellers will "say that without Prime you are dead."[1782]

In response to concerns about Amazon tying a seller's ability to make sales on its platform to participation in FBA, Amazon has offered contradictory statements. In the Subcommittee's second hearing, Representative Lucy McBath (D-GA) asked Amazon's Associate General Counsel Nate Sutton whether Amazon "privileged vendors who use Amazon Fulfillment Services over those who chose not to."[1783] Mr. Sutton asserted that Amazon "do[es] not favor . . . products that use FBA over

---

[1776] *See, e.g.*, Interview with Jason Boyce, Founder & CEO, Avenue7Media, LLC (Sept. 15, 2020) ("It used to be possible, but hard, to be a Seller Fulfilled Prime seller. There were only 200 sellers that were able to meet the requirements. What's changing recently is that they used to allow you to have the Prime badge in certain regions, but now they say you need the Prime badge nationally, i.e., you need to have multiple warehouses across the country plus ship on Saturdays, etc.").

[1777] Regan McPhee, *How to Sell on Amazon Prime in 2020*, JUNGLESCOUT (May 27, 2020), https://www.junglescout.com/blog/how-to-sell-on-amazon-prime/.

[1778] Production of Amazon, to H. Comm. on the Judiciary, AMAZON-HJC-00186643 (July 23, 2018) (on file with Comm.).

[1779] *See* J. Clament, *Fulfillment by Amazon (FBA) Usage Among Top Marketplace Sellers Worldwide 2017–2018*, STATISTA (Jan. 7, 2020) https://www.statista.com/statistics/1020046/global-fba-usage-top-amazon-sellers/.

[1780] *See, e.g.*, Submission from Source 43, to H. Comm. on the Judiciary, 30 (Oct. 26, 2019) (on file with Comm.).

[1781] FEEDVISOR, THE 2019 AMAZON CONSUMER BEHAVIOR REPORT 10 (2019), https://fv.feedvisor.com/CN_2019_Amazon-Consumer-Behavior-Report.html.

[1782] Submission from Online Merchants Guild, to H. Comm. on the Judiciary, 7 (Oct. 23, 2019) (on file with Comm.).

[1783] Innovation and Entrepreneurship Hearing Transcript at 53 (question of Rep. Lucy McBath, Member, Subcomm. on Antitrust, Commercial and Admin. Law).

others."[1784] He also indicated that Fulfillment by Amazon is not a factor in Amazon's ranking algorithm.[1785]

At the Subcommittee's sixth hearing, Representative Mary Gay Scanlon (D-PA) asked Mr. Bezos about whether there is a connection between a seller's use of FBA and its ability to win the Buy Box.[1786] In response, Mr. Bezos said "I'm not sure if it's direct, but, indirectly, I think the Buy Box does favor products that can be shipped with Prime."[1787] Given that FBA is effectively the only way for sellers to get a Prime badge, this indicates that Amazon does favor sellers who use FBA over those who do not for both its search rankings and the Buy Box. Amazon claims that it favors sellers who use FBA because it is in the best interest of consumers and that it "does not consider profitability as part of the Featured Merchant Algorithm."[1788] Documents reviewed by Subcommittee staff, however, suggest that Amazon has used profitability—also referred to internally as "contribution profit" or "CP"—as a factor in awarding the Buy Box.[1789]

Furthermore, Amazon's own documents show that it has considered FBA participation for purposes of determining the Buy Box winner.[1790] An Amazon document that sets forth pricing rules for a pilot program appears to favor third-party sellers that use FBA over those who do not for awarding the Buy Box.

[1784] *Id.*

[1785] *Id.* at 3 (response to Questions for the Record of Nate Sutton, Associate Gen. Counsel, Competition, Amazon.com, Inc.).

[1786] CEO Hearing Transcript at 175 (question of Rep. Mary Gay Scanlon (D-PA), Vice Chair, H. Comm. on the Judiciary).

[1787] *Id.* (statement of Jeff Bezos, CEO, Amazon.com, Inc.).

[1788] CEO Hearing at 3 (response to Questions for the Record of Jeff Bezos, CEO, Amazon.com, Inc.).

[1789] Production of Amazon, to H. Comm. on the Judiciary, AMAZON-HJC-00141750 (Mar. 25, 2010) (on file with Comm).

[1790] Production of Amazon, to H. Comm. on the Judiciary, AMAZON-HJC-00142724 (on file with Comm).

Internal Pricing Strategy Document[1791]

From: Wales, Chance
To: VanDuine, Jason
Sent: 3/25/2010 11:26:35 AM
Subject: RE: SIGN OFF REQUESTED: Pre-WBR Follow-up: Healthcare Pricing Strategy

ok

From: VanDuine, Jason
Sent: Thursday, March 25, 2010 9:46 AM
To: Wales, Chance
Cc: VanDuine, Jason
Subject: SIGN OFF REQUESTED: Pre-WBR Follow-up: Healthcare Pricing Strategy

Chance – please sign off (or provide fdbk) before I send to Doug.

Jason

Doug,

You had asked me to help you understand the 'size of the issue' with regards to diverted product as well as clarification on pricing rules/matching for the image competitor simulation in the Healthcare category. Some current data (from February):

1. The top 25 negative CP ASINs in Health & Beauty (all Image ASINs) accounted for $265k in negative CP, 46k units and $1.6M in product revenue.
2. The diverted product ASINs (8 of the top 25) accounted for $109k in negative CP (41% of ttl), 14k units (31% of ttl) and $366k (21% of ttl) in product revenue.
3. Babycare products accounted for 14 of the top 25 ASINs (13 diaper and 1 wipe ASIN) and the remaining 3 ASINs are vendor or operational cost issues that are being addressed.
4. The image competitor pilot in Healthcare will address 6 of the 8 ASINs referenced in #2 (it will not address Align and Alli – both in Nutrition & Wellness)

We do not plan any manipulation to pricing rules in the Healthcare category other than the setting of number of image ASINs to zero.
Use cases (for Pricing Rules): using Prilosec as the example (CP neutral = $27)

Ref #	Use Case	Amazon Landed Cost	Comp Box Price	Comp Shipping Cost	Comp Landed Price	Amazon Match Price	Non-Prime (1% pad to FBA, 2% pad to 3P)	Prime (5% pad)
1	Walmart (Image Competitor)	$27.00	$28.00	$0.97	$28.97	$28.00	Amzn wins buy box	Amzn wins buy box
2	DAB Nutrition (3P) + FBA	$27.00	$26.50	$0.00	$26.50	$27.00	3P wins buy box	Amzn wins buy box
3	DAB Nutrition (3P) + no FBA	$27.00	$26.50	$0.00	$26.50	$27.00	Amzn wins buy box	Amzn wins buy box
4	AlltheTimeWholesale + no FBA	$27.00	$22.00	$4.50	$26.50	$27.00	Amzn wins buy box	Amzn wins buy box

The primary change coming is that we will now lose the buy box if 3P merchants continue to price below CP neutral (we will stop at CP neutral unless matching to an image competitor). As long as Prilosec is priced below $27 landed price (excluding buffers), we will lose the buy box. Currently, the lowest landed is under $20.

Estimated impact (based on simulation completed by the Pricing team) is a 6% negative impact on Healthcare category growth and a $.74/unit positive impact on CP. Using OP2 as the base, this would translate to ($750k) in revenue loss and ($775k) gain in CP. We will begin the pilot in April and will measure results on a weekly basis (with highlights in the pre-WBR as appropriate).

If you have any further questions, please let me know.

Jason

One third-party seller provided the Subcommittee with anecdotal evidence that Amazon favors sellers who participate in Amazon's fulfillment program over sellers who do not. The seller set up an experiment where he sold the same product, one self-fulfilled and the other fulfilled through FBA, and ran different test cases.[1792] The seller found that "Even when the consumer price of the self-fulfilled order was reduced and sold for a lower price (7% lower) than the FBA offer, the FBA still 'won' the 'Buy Box.'"[1793] The seller indicated that, without this favorable treatment for FBA, they would not choose to use FBA, as they found Amazon's fulfillment service was often slower and less reliable than self-fulfillment.[1794]

Although Jeff Bezos told the Subcommittee that Fulfillment by Amazon "is probably the greatest invention that we ever created for sellers," and that "it's working for sellers," information that Subcommittee staff reviewed suggests that it has significant shortfalls.[1795] One third-party seller told

[1791] Prepared by Subcomm. based on Production of Amazon, to H. Comm. on the Judiciary, AMAZON-HJC-00141750 (Mar. 25, 2010) (on file with Comm).

[1792] Submission from Source 43, to H. Comm. on the Judiciary, 29 (Oct. 26, 2019) (on file with Comm.).

[1793] *Id.*

[1794] *Id*; *see also* Interview with Source 920 (July 14, 2020); Interview with Source 100 (July 24, 2020).

[1795] CEO Hearing Transcript at 174 (statement of Jeff Bezos, CEO, Amazon.com, Inc.).

Subcommittee staff, "We use both FBA and self-fulfillment, all of our negative comments are on items shipped through FBA."[1796] According to another seller that uses FBA, at one point, Amazon decided to change the packaging on her products from cardboard boxes to padded envelopes, causing damage to her products in transit. When the damaged items started arriving at her customers' homes in a damaged state, this caused a surge of negative reviews and requests for returns. When she asked Amazon to remove these bad reviews, which were caused by FBA's shipping methods, Amazon refused.[1797]

A competing online marketplace described how Amazon effectively forcing sellers into its FBA program makes it more difficult to compete with Amazon for sellers, stating, "[T]hrough anticompetitive strategies and practices by Amazon, many . . . sellers are being pulled into Amazon's tied marketplace-and-ecommerce-fulfilment ecosystem in a manner that makes them not only less independent but directly dependent on Amazon."[1798] It further explained that because of Amazon's dominance in online commerce, "Even sellers who sell on other marketplaces are pushed into FBA, because it is the only practicable way to obtain sales on the Amazon marketplace.[1799] In addition to the Subcommittee's investigation, antitrust enforcement agencies are currently investigating Amazon for tying these two services together.[1800]

b) Advertising

Consistent with public reporting,[1801] evidence that Subcommittee staff reviewed suggests that Amazon may require sellers to purchase their advertising services as a condition of making sales on the platform. Because 44% of consumers tend to only look through the first two search pages when shopping on Amazon, a seller is practically invisible if it does not show up on one of the first two pages.[1802] Amazon's Sponsored Products and Sponsored Brand tools allow sellers to ensure they are prioritized in search results for specific key terms. A 2020 survey of large brands found that at least 73% used Amazon's advertising services, with 65% spending at least $40,000 a month on advertising

---

[1796] Interview with Source 89 (July 22, 2020).

[1797] Interview with Source 149 (Feb. 26, 2020).

[1798] Submission from Source 11, to H. Comm. on the Judiciary, 1 (Oct. 14, 2019) (on file with Comm.).

[1799] *Id.* at 2.

[1800] *See. e.g.*, Press Release, Ital. Competition Auth., Amazon: Investigation Launched on Possible Abuse of a Dominant Position in Online Marketplaces and Logistic Services (Apr. 15, 2019), https://en.agcm.it/en/media/press-releases/2019/4/A528 (announcing launch of investigation into whether "Amazon would unduly exploit its dominant position in the market for e-commerce platforms intermediary services in order to significantly restrict competition in the e-commerce logistics market, as well as - potentially - in the e-commerce platform market, to the detriment of final consumers").

[1801] *See, e.g.*, Shira Ovide, Amazon Advertising Is Just a Toll in Disguise, BLOOMBERG (July 15, 2019), https://www.bloomberg.com/opinion/articles/2019-07-15/amazon-advertising-is-just-a-toll-in-disguise.

[1802] FEEDVISOR, THE 2019 AMAZON CONSUMER BEHAVIOR REPORT 5 (2019), https://fv.feedvisor.com/CN_2019_Amazon-Consumer-Behavior-Report.html.

on the site.[1803] In just one year, the number of brands with this monthly advertising spend increased by 33%.[1804] A recent report issued by the Institute for Local Self-Reliance explained:

> Sellers that decline to advertise risk losing their place in Amazon's organic search results, no matter how many glowing customer reviews they have. That's because the Amazon algorithm that delivers the search results favors products with more sales. As more orders are driven by ads, sellers than don't advertise lose out on those sales and, as their share of sales declines, they also slip in the search rankings, further reducing their sales in a negative cycle.[1805]

Similarly, the Online Merchants Guild told the Subcommittee in a submission, "[i]t is now common belief in the Amazon seller community that the only way to sell on Amazon is through Amazon's Pay-Per-Click ('PPC') offering." The submission describes the situation as "pay-to-play," adding that "[Pay-Per-Click advertising] has become a major point of frustration for many sellers, with many sellers left feeling as if they are paying a mandatory fee, and have even described [Pay-Per-Click] as a way for Amazon to increase their seller fees without looking like they are increasing their seller fees."[1806]

At the same time that advertising services have become "less of an option and more of a requirement for sellers to compete" on the platform, Amazon's ads have also become more expensive.[1807] The ads' costs are determined by reverse auction—businesses bid on keywords that customers may use to search for a given product. In just a year, "the cost-per-click for sponsored ads increased by about 15% on average," and for some, by as much as 127%.[1808] A former third-party seller told Subcommittee staff that this harms both sellers and consumers, adding that "the good old days before [Pay-Per-Click], products would rise on the merits."[1809] Similarly, the Online Merchants Guild said, "[i]n the past, the belief was more reviews would create a trending product."[1810]

[1803] FEEDVISOR, BRANDS AND AMAZON IN THE AGE OF E-COMMERCE, 2020 EDITION 12 (2020), https://fv.feedvisor.com/CN_2020_Brands-and-Amazon-in-the-Age-of-E-Commerce.html.

[1804] Id.

[1805] STACY MITCHELL, RON KNOX & ZACH FREED, INST. OF LOCAL SELF-RELIANCE, REPORT: AMAZON'S MONOPOLY TOLLBOOTH 9 (2020), https://ilsr.org/amazons_tollbooth/.

[1806] Submission from Online Merchants Guild, to H. Comm. on the Judiciary, 8 (Oct. 23, 2019) (on file with Comm.); see also Interview with Jason Boyce, Founder & CEO, Avenue7Media, LLC (Sept. 15, 2020) ("Pay-Per-Click is now mandatory.").

[1807] Submission from Online Merchants Guild, to H. Comm. on the Judiciary, 8 (Oct. 23, 2019) (on file with Comm.).

[1808] STACY MITCHELL, RON KNOX & ZACH FREED, INST. OF LOCAL SELF-RELIANCE, REPORT: AMAZON'S MONOPOLY TOLLBOOTH 10 (2020), https://ilsr.org/amazons_tollbooth/.

[1809] Interview with Jason Boyce, Founder & CEO, Avenue7Media, LLC (Sept. 15, 2020).

[1810] Submission from Online Merchants Guild, to H. Comm. on the Judiciary, 8 (Oct. 23, 2019) (on file with Comm.).

In response to concerns about tying, Amazon claims that it provides non-discriminatory access to the Buy Box and that participation in fulfillment by Amazon and its pay-per-click advertising program is voluntary.[1811] Amazon's revenue from these sources is increasing, however, and sellers continue to raise concerns that increased fees for compulsory fulfillment and advertising services are squeezing their business.

7) Strategic Platform Management and Mismanagement

During the investigation, the Subcommittee also heard concerns that Amazon engages in strategic mismanagement of its platform by (1) allowing the proliferation of counterfeit and unsafe goods; (2) using its ability to control the flow of counterfeits as leverage; and (3) putting in place ineffective counterfeit prevention tools that result in the suspension of a large number of innocent sellers.[1812]

As Amazon's dominance in e-commerce has grown, so has the proliferation of dangerous and counterfeit products on its marketplace.[1813] A 2019 *Wall Street Journal* investigation found that Amazon had active listings for over 4,000 items "that have been declared unsafe by federal agencies [and] are deceptively labeled or are banned by federal regulators."[1814] In the worst cases, these products have even caused bodily injury or even death to unsuspecting consumers.[1815] As recently as September 2020, CNN released a report describing multiple instances in which Amazon's own private-label products, such as a phone charging cable, have caught fire while in use by consumers.[1816]

[1811] *See, e.g.*, CEO Hearing Transcript at 134 (statement of Jeff Bezos, CEO, Amazon.com, Inc.) ("I think what you're referring to is the fact that we offer an advertising service basically for third party sellers to drive additional promotion to their products. That is a voluntary program. Some sellers use it. Some don't.").

[1812] During the investigation, the Committee also heard concerns about Amazon using "brand gating" to block competitors from selling certain products on its platform. *See, e.g.*, Submission from Source 5, to H. Comm. on the Judiciary (Sept. 15, 2020) (on file with Comm.) (raising concerns about "brand gating," which allows Amazon, on its own, or in concert with "a trademark owner/manufacturer/seller, who is registered on the Brand Registry, to block other third party sellers from selling a particular brand, unless certain conditions are met."); Source 100, to H. Comm. on the Judiciary (Jan. 10, 2020) (on file with Comm.) (raising concerns that Amazon "gates" a brand when it decides that it wants to source items directly from the manufacturer and limit competition from third-party sellers and stating, "[w]e have lost literally millions of dollars on [inventory from] brands that Amazon has gated, purchases directly from manufacturers and we are no longer able to sell on Amazon.").

[1813] Alexandra Berzon, Shane Shifflett & Justin Scheck, *Amazon Has Ceded Control of Its Site. The Result: Thousands of Banned, Unsafe or Mislabeled Products*, WALL ST. J. (Aug. 23, 2019), https://www.wsj.com/articles/amazon-has-ceded-control-of-its-site-the-result-thousands-of-banned-unsafe-or-mislabeled-products-11566564990.

[1814] *Id.*

[1815] *Id.*

[1816] Blake Ellis & Melanie Hicken, *Dozens of Amazon's Own Products Have Been Reported As Dangerous – Melting, Exploding or Even Bursting Into Flames. Many Are Still on the Market*, CNN BUS. (Sept. 10, 2020), https://www.cnn.com/2020/09/10/business/amazonbasics-electronics-fire-safety-invs/index.html.

The spread of counterfeit products also has serious consequences for vendors and brand manufacturers who rely on consumer trust and their reputation to maintain successful businesses. Amazon's marketplace platform is designed in a way that makes it difficult for consumers to identify counterfeit products. As the Retail Industry Leaders Association (RILA) noted in a submission to the Subcommittee, "Where a platform both obfuscates the origin or source and provides fulfillment services, a seller of counterfeits is harder for consumers to uncover because the item appears to have the backing of the platform."[1817]

Although it claims to take its counterfeit problem seriously, Amazon's business model incentivizes it to do less, not more. Because Amazon's profits increase with the number of sales on the platform, the company has an incentive to turn a blind eye to counterfeit products that contribute to its increased sales volume. Regardless of the source, more sales generally result in more profits for Amazon because its typically "profits twice from a sale through purchase and fulfillment[,] and potentially three times through advertising."[1818]

For example, Subcommittee staff uncovered evidence during the investigation that Amazon has used its ability to police counterfeits more or less aggressively as leverage in contract negotiations with brands who attempt to resist Amazon pressure to sell on its platform—referred to internally at Amazon as "holdouts."[1819] This recently occurred when it agreed to increase efforts to crack down on counterfeit Apple products as part of Apple agreeing to establish a wholesale relationship with Amazon Retail.[1820] Documents received by the Subcommittee suggest that Apple was dissatisfied with Amazon's anti-counterfeiting program and sought the following as a condition of selling Apple products wholesale to Amazon: "Amazon must proactively monitor platform for counterfeits/knockoffs and cooperate with Apple to remove and prevent them."[1821]

At the Subcommittee's field hearing in Colorado, PopSockets founder David Barnett testified that "Amazon was aware that large quantities" of counterfeit PopSockets products were selling on its platform, but that Amazon allowed the problem to continue until PopSockets agreed to spend nearly two million dollars on Amazon marketing services.[1822] Mr. Barnett further testified that Amazon was not just facilitating the sale of counterfeit PopSockets products, but that Amazon itself was engaged in selling knockoffs. Representative Buck (R-CO) and Representative Johnson (D-GA) confronted Mr.

[1817] Submission from Retail Industry Leaders Ass'n, to H. Comm. on the Judiciary, 9 (July 16, 2019) (on file with Comm.).

[1818] *Id.*

[1819] Competitors Hearing Transcript at 2–3 (statement of David Barnett, CEO and Founder, Popsockets LLC); *see also* Laura Stevens & Sara Germano, *Nike Thought It Didn't Need Amazon – Then the Ground Shifted*, WALL ST. J. (June 28, 2017), https://www.wsj.com/articles/how-nike-resisted-amazons-dominance-for-years-and-finally-capitulated-1498662435.

[1820] Jouzas Kaziukenas, *Amazon's Apple Moment*, MARKETPLACE PULSE (Nov. 27, 2018), https://www.marketplacepulse.com/articles/amazon-apple-moment (last visited Oct. 4, 2020).

[1821] *See* Production of Amazon, to H. Comm. on the Judiciary, AMAZON-HJC-00190195 (Feb. 15, 2018) (on file with Comm.) ("We understand Apple's IP team may not be happy with elements of our anti-counterfeiting program.").

[1822] Competitors Hearing Transcript at 2–3 (statement of David Barnett, CEO and Founder, PopSockets LLC).

Bezos on Amazon's behavior towards PopSockets at the Subcommittee's sixth hearing. Mr. Bezos responded, "if those are the facts and if someone somewhere inside Amazon said, you know, 'Buy X dollars in ads, and then we'll help you with your counterfeit problem,' that is unacceptable. And I will look into that, and we'll get back to your office with that." To date, however, Amazon has not followed up with the Subcommittee to provide additional information.

In response to criticism and negative publicity about the proliferation of counterfeit products on its platform, Amazon announced several initiatives to combat fake products.[1823] During the Subcommittee's sixth hearing, Mr. Bezos testified that Amazon "invest[s] hundreds of millions of dollars in systems" that police counterfeits.[1824] However, Amazon's approach appears to be ineffective, resulting in suspensions of many innocent, third-party sellers, with devastating effects on some sellers' businesses.[1825]

For example, Subcommittee staff interviewed a former Amazon employee and current consultant for Amazon sellers who described recent unfair changes in Amazon's treatment of sellers suspected of being counterfeiters. He said that, in the past, Amazon would only suspend accounts and withhold funds from third-party sellers it confirmed were selling counterfeit goods.[1826] However, increasingly, "Amazon rejects invoices or fails to verify suppliers without any justification or basis as to why . . . and they are using that as a reason to hold funds indefinitely."[1827]

One third-party seller told the Subcommittee that Amazon blocked some of her listings, citing a number of her products as "inauthentic."[1828] The seller provided evidence to Amazon that, not only were her vendor's products authentic, but Amazon actively sold the same products, sourced from the same vendor, through its first-party sales.[1829] Despite elevating the issue to Amazon executives in July 2020, this issue has still not been resolved as of September 2020.[1830]

[1823] *See, e.g.*, Press Release, Amazon, Amazon Establishes Counterfeit Crimes Unit to Bring Counterfeiters to Justice (June 24, 2020), https://press.aboutamazon.com/news-releases/news-release-details/amazon-establishes-counterfeit-crimes-unit-bring-counterfeiters.

[1824] CEO Hearing Transcript at 132 (Jeff Bezos, CEO, Amazon.com, Inc.).

[1825] *See, e.g.*, Production of Amazon, to H. Comm. on the Judiciary, AMAZON-HJC-00173394 (Sept. 6, 2016) (on file with Comm.) ("Additional gating requirements were put in place to reduce counterfeit and improve product safety, but did not have the right processes in place to limit the number of false negatives (declining Seller applications despite the seller's ability to provide the correct documentation).").

[1826] Interview with Chris McCabe, Founder, ecommerceChris, LLC (June 12, 2020).

[1827] *Id.*

[1828] Submission from Source 100, to H. Comm. on the Judiciary (Sept. 18, 2020) (on file with Comm.).

[1829] *Id.*

[1830] *Id.*

ii. Most-Favored-Nation and Price Parity Provisions

Amazon also uses its dominant position in e-commerce as leverage with other businesses to require most-favored-nation (MFN) clauses or similar price parity provisions to guarantee that it will always receive the best prices and most favorable terms. While these clauses are not inherently anticompetitive, Amazon has a history of using MFN clauses to ensure that none of its suppliers or third-party sellers can collaborate with an existing or potential competitor to make lower-priced or innovative product offerings available to consumers.

The anticompetitive effects of Amazon's use of MFN clauses are particularly pronounced in the book market. According to a book publisher, Amazon used its market power in print and e-book sales to force a price MFN on it and other book publishers.[1831] As the publisher explained, the result has been that "publishers are completely handcuffed from stimulating platform competition because Amazon's price MFN causes publishers to incur significant financial penalties if they offer Amazon's rivals better pricing."[1832] Another publisher told the Subcommittee that "Amazon always has and still does require MFNs."[1833] According to this publisher, the MFN provisions prevent publishers from partnering with any of Amazon's competitors and reinforces Amazon's "stranglehold" and "control" over book distribution.[1834] Although Amazon has changed the name and specific mechanisms over the years, it appears that the company continues to impose contract provisions that effectively function as MFNs on book publishers.

In a joint letter to Subcommittee Chairman Cicilline following the Subcommittee's sixth hearing, a group of organizations representing authors, publishers, and booksellers wrote that Amazon's use of MFNs has "stifle[d] the emergence and growth of competitive alternatives in the book distribution marketplace."[1835] When Amazon entered the e-book market through its release of the Kindle and Kindle Store in 2007, it unseated incumbent booksellers in market position by offering steep discounts on best-selling books.[1836] Over a decade later, Amazon's dominance in e-books and its anticompetitive application of price parity clauses to its business relationships in this market

---

[1831] Submission from Source 17, to H. Comm. on the Judiciary, 9 (Nov. 15, 2019) (on file with Comm.).

[1832] *Id.* at 10 (Nov. 15, 2019).

[1833] Interview with Source 155 (Sept. 29, 2020).

[1834] *Id.*

[1835] Letter from Maria A. Pallante, Pres. and CEO, Ass'n of American Publishers, Mary E. Rasenberger, Executive Director, The Authors Guild, Allison K. Hill, CEO, American Booksellers Ass'n, to Hon. David. N. Cicilline, Chairman, Subcomm. on Antitrust, Commercial and Admin. Law of the H. Comm. on the Judiciary, 2 (Aug. 17, 2020), https://publishers.org/wp-content/uploads/2020/08/Joint-Letter-to-Rep-Cicilline-081720.pdf.

[1836] George Packer, *Cheap Words*, NEW YORKER (Feb. 10, 2014), https://www.newyorker.com/magazine/2014/02/17/cheap-words (last visited Oct. 4, 2020) (noting that in 2007, the prices of e-books on Kindle were "below wholesale in some cases, and so low that [they] represented a serious threat to the market . . . By 2010, Amazon controlled ninety per cent of the market in digital books—a dominance that almost no company, in any industry, could claim.").

"eliminate[s] the ability of rivals or new entrants to gain any meaningful competitive advantage relative to Amazon."[1837] Essentially, Amazon disrupted this market, dominated it, and now wields its immense power to effectively guarantee that no competitor could possibly do the same.

Amazon also aggressively enforces price parity rules on Amazon marketplace's third-party sellers. It imposed MFN provisions on U.S. sellers until 2019. In response to antitrust scrutiny, the platform replaced those provisions with a "Fair Pricing Policy," which has the same effect of blocking sellers from offering lower prices to consumers on other retail sites.[1838] To enforce the policy, Amazon uses "computer software to regularly scan listings on competitors' websites, and pressuring their sellers to change their price if their Amazon price is substantially higher."[1839] A violation, or even a perceived violation, of the policy can lead to suspension of a seller's account, with dire consequences for the seller. A former third-party seller explained that Amazon uses "Buy Box Suppression," where Amazon will remove a seller's ability to win the Buy Box, as a way to penalize sellers that offer products at a lower price on competing sites.[1840]

One of Amazon's competitors told the Subcommittee that "as Amazon raises the costs to sellers, and requires that Amazon have the lowest prices available, for a seller to be able to make significant sales on its marketplace, these sellers will raise the price on competitor sites to match Amazon's price."[1841] Amazon's "Fair Price Policy," which has been described as a "thinly-veiled MFN restriction," is likely anticompetitive with respect to blocking competition from other marketplaces, and does not result in lower prices for consumers as Amazon has claimed.[1842]

iii. Predatory Pricing

As part of its business strategy, Amazon has historically placed a higher premium on long-term growth at the expense of short-term profitability. As noted earlier in this Report, Amazon did not post

---

[1837] Letter from Maria A. Pallante, President and CEO, Ass'n of American Publishers, Mary E. Rasenberger, Executive Director, The Authors Guild, Allison K. Hill, CEO, American Booksellers Ass'n, to Hon. David. N. Cicilline, Chairman, Subcomm. on Antitrust, Commercial and Admin. Law of the H. Comm. on the Judiciary, 3 (Aug. 17, 2020), https://publishers.org/wp-content/uploads/2020/08/Joint-Letter-to-Rep-Cicilline-081720.pdf.

[1838] Submission from Online Merchants Guild, to H. Comm. on the Judiciary, 7 (Oct. 29, 2019) (on file with Comm.).

[1839] Id. at 8.

[1840] Submission from Jason Boyce, Founder & CEO, Avenue7Media (Sept. 25, 2020) (on file with Comm.).

[1841] Submission from Source 11, to H. Comm. on the Judiciary, 4 (Oct. 14, 2019) (on file with Comm.); see also Submission from Jason Boyce, Founder & CEO, Avenue7Media (Sept. 25, 2020) (on file with Comm.) ("Amazon prohibiting sellers from offering lower prices on other online retail platforms clearly hurts consumers if the only way for sellers to regain their listing on Amazon is to raise their prices on other platforms or remove their listings all together, therefore limiting competition.").

[1842] Submission from Int'l Bhd. Of Teamsters, Commc'n Workers of America, United Food & Commercial Workers Int'l Union, Service Employees Int'l Union & Change to Win, to H. Comm. on the Judiciary, 4 (March 10, 2020) (on file with Comm.).

its first full-year profit until 2003—a decade after the company was founded.[1843] Consistent with this trend, Amazon has adopted a predatory-pricing strategy across multiple business lines at various stages in the company's history.[1844]

Because of the nature of its marketplace business, Amazon's below-cost prices on products and services tend to lock customers into Amazon's full marketplace ecosystem. As a former Amazon employee told the Subcommittee, "[A]bove all else, Amazon's goal is to keep the customer shopping on Amazon."[1845] Once a customer is locked in, they are less likely to change their behavior even when Amazon's pricing is not competitive.

1) Prime

The most prominent example of Amazon's use of strategic losses to lock customers into the platform's ecosystem is its popular membership program, Amazon Prime. As of August 2020, a Prime membership costs $119 per year, up from its original $79 at its launch in February 2005 and $99 from March 2014 to April 2018. An Amazon executive wrote in 2013, in reference to pricing Prime, "the better course is to let the existing Prime program grow . . . and then raise prices later assuming a lower elasticity in future years,"[1846] once customers are locked in.

An Amazon internal document describes the rationale behind Amazon Prime and its other membership programs: "Membership programs are created with a long-term, company-wide perspective with the goal of increasing loyalty and cross-category shopping behavior. The programs do not optimize for short-term gain or profitability in a single category."[1847] Another internal Amazon document describes these membership programs as, "[d]oubl[ing] down on 'Big Moats,'" aiming to create an impenetrable barrier around its dominant position.[1848]

Despite Amazon Prime's popularity and wide membership base, it is a loss-leader for the company. Many industry analysts have estimated Amazon's Prime losses over the years, finding that it is unprofitable, and that Amazon is willing to spend significant amounts of money to prop up the

---

[1843] Saul Hansen, *Technology; Amazon Reports First Full-Year Profit*, N.Y. TIMES (Jan. 28. 2004), https://www.nytimes.com/2004/01/28/business/technology-amazon-reports-first-full-year-profit.html.

[1844] In this Report, the term "predatory pricing" should be understood in its broadest sense to refer to any situation where a dominant firm prices a good or service below cost in a way that is harmful to competition.

[1845] Submission from Source 91, to H. Comm. on the Judiciary (Sept. 22, 2020) (on file with Comm.).

[1846] Production of Amazon, to H. Comm. on the Judiciary, AMAZON-HJC-00216088 (Oct. 28. 2013) (on file with Comm.).

[1847] *Id.* at AMAZON-HJC-00068510 (Sept. 8, 2010).

[1848] *Id.*; *see also* Production of Amazon, to H. Comm. on the Judiciary, AMAZON-HJC-00184863 (May 7, 2015) (on file with Comm.) ("The value differentiation for Prime members accelerates the Prime flywheel creating an additional reason to become a Prime member and concentrate household spend with Amazon.").

program.[1849] In 2016, a Forrester Research analysis estimated that Prime costs Amazon $1 billion per year.[1850] In 2019, J.P. Morgan estimated that, though priced at $119, a Prime subscription is valued at about $860, up 10% from its estimated value in 2018.[1851] A Prime membership also includes access to Prime Video, its library of digital video content, and Amazon Music, its music streaming service.

The Artists Rights Alliance, an advocacy group for the digital rights of music creators, raised concerns that Amazon's inclusion of a streaming music services in its Prime program poses a severe risk of "driv[ing] down royalties in an uncompetitive way."[1852] According to its submission:

> Amazon's ongoing efforts to launch a streaming music service as part of its Prime family of products should be carefully scrutinized . . . . [W]e are concerned about the dangers of predatory/sub-market pricing in a service that Amazon operates as a "loss leader." In general, creators need an economy that more accurately sees and values their work; not one with cut-rate prices that entangles music even more deeply in a web of soulless data collection and 'content distribution' operations.[1853]

Although Amazon Prime is a loss leader for the company, it is one of Amazon's most effective drivers of growth. Amazon Prime members account for 65% of Amazon shoppers as of Q4 2019.[1854] While the average Amazon customer spends about $600 per year on Amazon.com, Prime members reportedly spend more than double that—an average of $1400 per year.[1855]

In 2010, Amazon started its Amazon Mom program, now called Amazon Family, another membership service that offers discounts on diapers and other items associated with parenthood.[1856] At the outset, Amazon was willing to lose money to ensure the success of this program. A 2010 document outlining the lead-up to the official launch of Amazon Mom included a plan to discount diapers and

---

[1849] *See, e.g.*, Stu Woo, *Amazon 'Primes' Pump for Loyalty*, WALL ST. J. (Nov. 14, 2011), http://www.wsj.com/articles/SB10001424052970203503204577036102353359784.

[1850] Nanette Byrnes, *How Amazon Loses on Prime and Still Wins*, MIT TECH. REV. (July 12, 2016), https://www.technologyreview.com/2016/07/12/158869/how-amazon-loses-on-prime-and-still-wins/ (last visited Oct. 4, 2020).

[1851] J.P. MORGAN, RETAIL VS. AMAZON: LIFE IN A POST COVID-19 WORLD 26 (June 11, 2020), https://markets.jpmorgan.com/research/email/-lbk68f4/Alp1kP9tQUPS29jlzW_bOg/GPS-3397412-0; Production of Amazon, to H. Comm. on the Judiciary, AMAZON-HJC-00184863 (May 7, 2015) (on file with Comm.).

[1852] Submission from Artist Rights Alliance, to H. Comm. on the Judiciary, 5 (July 31, 2019) (on file with Comm.).

[1853] *Id.*

[1854] Fareeha Ali, *Amazon Prime Has 112 Million Members in the U.S.*, DIG. COMMERCE 360 (Jan. 24, 2020) https://www.digitalcommerce360.com/article/amazon-prime-membership/.

[1855] Jack Houston & Irene Anna Kim, *How Amazon Gets You to Spend More Money*, BUS. INSIDER (Sept. 17, 2020), https://www.businessinsider.com/amazon-prime-members-spend-more-money-sneaky-ways-2019-9.

[1856] Production of Amazon, to H. Comm. on the Judiciary, AMAZON-HJC-00130737 (Aug. 31, 2010) (on file with Comm.).

wipes at a rate that would "put [their] product below cost."[1857] And selling diapers was not the goal of this program—instead Amazon recognized that "a long-lasting, sticky relationship" with Amazon Mom members was the source of its true value.[1858] Additionally, an internal presentation observed that "[e]arly results from our Amazon Mom program" showed that "[n]ew Amazon customers, whose first purchase included diapers, spend over three times as much ($292 vs. $91) during their first year as the average new Amazon customer."[1859]

Some of Amazon's rivals view this dynamic as harmful to competition, saying that Amazon is "[u]nderpricing Prime to consumers to build a huge and highly targetable share of ecommerce demand."[1860] Once consumers have paid the yearly fee for Prime, they are incentivized to use it as much as possible to maximize return on their investment, "whereas they might otherwise multisource."[1861]

2) Diapers.com

The Amazon Mom program served another important function and had a central role in one of Amazon's early applications of its predatory-pricing strategy. In 2009, Bezos and other Amazon executives noticed and began discussing the rise of Diapers.com, a competitor in the baby and personal-care product markets.[1862] What followed was a year-long price war, ending in Amazon's eventual acquisition of Quidsi, the parent company of Diapers.com.

At the Subcommittee's hearing, Mr. Bezos testified that Amazon was always a price follower in its war with Diapers.com.[1863] However Amazon's "'plan to win' against [D]iapers.com" explicitly included price-leading on diapers.[1864] Recognizing that Diapers.com was the company's "#1 short term competitor," Amazon executives decided that going after them required a "need to match pricing . . . no matter what the cost."[1865] Amazon internal documents indicate that Amazon was willing to lose $200 million in one month alone on products in the relevant competitive categories.[1866] Offering 30% cash back on diapers and a free year's worth of Prime membership to Amazon Mom members, an

---

[1857] *Id.* at AMAZON-HJC-00159560 (Apr. 2010).

[1858] *Id.* at AMAZON-HJC-00035545 (July 20, 2010) ("[W]e can see that Moms . . . have a favorable year one downstream value relative to the average customer.").

[1859] *Id.* at AMAZON-HJC-00154656.

[1860] Submission from Source 11, to H. Comm. on the Judiciary, 2 (Oct. 14, 2019) (on file with Comm.).

[1861] *Id.* at 3.

[1862] Production of Amazon, to H. Comm. on the Judiciary, AMAZON-HJC-00151723 (Feb. 9, 2009) (on file with Comm.).

[1863] CEO Hearing Transcript at 83 (statement of Jeff Bezos, CEO, Amazon.com, Inc.).

[1864] Production of Amazon, to H. Comm. on the Judiciary, AMAZON-HJC-00132026 (June 8, 2010) (on file with Comm.).

[1865] *Id.* at AMAZON-HJC-00151722 (Feb. 9, 2009).

[1866] *Id.* at AMAZON-HJC-00057007 (Apr. 5, 2010)

Amazon executive predicted in November 2010 that it would seriously wound Quidsi, stating, "[T]hey expect to lose lots of money over the nxt [sic] few yrs [sic]-this will make it worse."[1867] Quidsi explicitly identified "Predatory Pricing" as a "Near-Term Risk" in a 2009 presentation.[1868] In November 2010, Amazon acquired its self-described "largest and fastest growing competitor in the on-line diaper and baby care space."[1869]

3) "Can't Realize Any Profit"

Once Amazon succeeds in trapping enough customers in its "flywheel" to secure dominant position across varied markets, it can then raise prices or remove incentives or allowances for Marketplace sellers to sell products at favorable prices for consumers. One example of the latter is Amazon's treatment of "CRAP," a term coined internally which refers to products on which Amazon "Can't Realize Any Profit."[1870] CRAP products are low-priced items that are heavy and expensive to ship—often consumables, like packs of bottled water.[1871]

These items were integral to Amazon's pursuit of dominance in the e-commerce market. But once Amazon began to switch its focus from pure growth to profitability, it reversed course on these products, engaging in an ongoing "CRAP-Out Process," by which Amazon attempts to make CRAP profitable through a variety of methods, such as raising delivery fees or requiring vendors to repackage products.[1872] This increases costs for sellers and brands, who have no choice but to acquiesce to the changed shipping and packaging rules given their dependence on Amazon for e-commerce sales. Amazon executives acknowledged that CRAP was an element of its plan for growth, noting in a strategy session that, "We want to ensure that if despite all our efforts to improve our cost structure, we lose money on an ASIN [Amazon Standard Identification Number] it is for the long term strategic growth of Amazon."[1873]

Amazon documents provided in response to the Committee's requests show the extent to which Amazon was committed to below-cost pricing. A 2010 review of its baby formula business identified Amazon's "most frequently matched internal competitor" as ABCBabyFormula, which "typically [ ]

[1867] *Id.* at AMAZON-HJC-00009716 (Sept. 21, 2010)

[1868] *Id.* at AMAZON-HJC-00009596 (Nov. 2, 2010).

[1869] *Id.* at AMAZON-HJC-00142833 (May 12, 2009).

[1870] *Id.* at AMAZON-HJC-00167480.

[1871] Laura Steven, Sharon Terlep & Annie Gasparro, *Amazon Targets Unprofitable Items, with a Sharper Focus on the Bottom Line*, WALL ST. J. (Dec. 16, 2018), https://www.wsj.com/articles/amazon-targets-unprofitable-items-with-a-sharper-focus-on-the-bottom-line-11544965201.

[1872] Production of Amazon, to H. Comm. on the Judiciary, AMAZON-HJC-00167484 ("How to deal with CRAP.") (on file with Comm.).

[1873] *Id.*

price[d] 15-20% below [Amazon's] cost."[1874] Identifying this company as the most significant influence on Amazon's baby formula profit loss, the document notes of ABCBabyFormula that "[m]anufacturers do not sell to them directly and believe they are sourcing black market stolen goods."[1875] Amazon frequently price-matched, at significantly below-cost, a competitor that it had reason to believe was sourcing baby formula from illegal and potentially dangerous sources—indicating the lengths to which Amazon was willing to go to ensure product selection and, in turn, growth.

4) Amazon Devices

Finally, Amazon sells its own branded hardware devices on its Marketplace and has often priced those devices below cost in an attempt to corner the market for those devices and adjacent markets. In Amazon's effort to "own the smart home," for example, Amazon sometimes prices its Echo Speaker below-cost. Market estimates suggest that Amazon's Echo Dot third generation materials cost is $37.68,[1876] while the company listed it at $22 during its 2019 Prime Day.[1877] Other market research of Amazon products found that Amazon Echo products are on sale as often as they are at full price.[1878] Illustrating how low prices may not always be in consumers' best interest, Patrick Spence, the CEO of Sonos, testified before the Subcommittee that these pricing habits "hamstring[] those companies that have better products that cannot be sold at a loss."[1879] At the Subcommittee's hearing, Representative Jamie Raskin (D-MD) raised this concern with Mr. Bezos.[1880] In response, Mr. Bezos responded that the Amazon Echo is "often on promotion, and sometimes when it's on promotion it may be below cost."[1881]

[1874] *Id.* at AMAZON-HJC-0014302 (Sept. 30, 2010).

[1875] *Id.*

[1876] Submission from Source 38, to H. Comm. on the Judiciary, 19 (Sept. 1, 2019) (citing TECHINSIGHTS).

[1877] *Id.*; *see also* Samantha Gordon, *Prime Day is Almost Over—These Are the Best Deals You Can Still Get*, USA TODAY (July 15, 2019), https://www.usatoday.com/story/tech/reviewedcom/2019/07/15/prime-day-2019-best-amazon-deals-you-can-get-during-massive-sale/1683589001/ (last visited Oct. 4, 2020) ("Echo Dot—$22").

[1878] Sean Hollister, *Amazon Doesn't Sell Echo Speakers at a Loss, Says Bezos — Unless They're on Sale*, THE VERGE (July 29, 2020), https://www.theverge.com/2020/7/29/21347121/amazon-echo-speaker-price-undercut-rivals-loss-sale-antitrust-hearing.

[1879] Competitors Hearing at 4–5 (statement of Patrick Spence, CEO, Sonos, Inc.).

[1880] CEO Hearing Transcript at 107 (question of Rep. Jamie Raskin (D-MD, Member, Subcomm. On Antitrust, Commercial and Admin. Law).

[1881] *Id.* (statement of Jeff Bezos, CEO, Amazon.com, Inc.).

3. Fulfillment and Delivery

a. Market Power

As Amazon's e-commerce business has grown, it has also developed a significant logistics business surrounding fulfillment and delivery of third-party orders with its Fulfillment by Amazon (FBA) program. More than 73% of all Amazon Marketplace sellers reportedly rely on this program to fulfill their orders.[1882] Because of this, a trade association that represents third-party sellers refers to Amazon's fulfillment operation "as the railroad of [e-commerce]."[1883] In addition to its fulfillment operation, Amazon is also one of the largest shippers in the world. The company provides global shipping services for its own products and independent sellers that sell on Amazon.com, as well as other e-commerce sites.[1884]

Amazon's ground shipping infrastructure consists of "trucks, trailers, intermodal containers, and delivery vehicles."[1885] Its truck fleet consists of more than 10,000 trailers.[1886] It also has its own freight airline, Amazon Air, with about 50 leased aircraft,[1887] and plans to expand its fleet to 70 by 2021.[1888] Amazon has also built hundreds of package sorting and delivery centers across the United States and has established its own network of contracted delivery providers exclusively dedicated to delivering packages for Amazon.[1889]

In recent years, the size and scope of Amazon's delivery services and network has grown significantly. When Amazon first launched Fulfillment by Amazon, it stored products and packed

---

[1882] *See Fulfillment by Amazon Usage Among Top Sellers Worldwide 2017–2018*, STATISTA, https://www.statista.com/statistics/1020046/global-fba-usage-top-amazon-sellers/ (last visited Oct. 4, 2020).

[1883] Submission from Online Merchants Guild, to H. Comm. on the Judiciary, OMG-000009 (Oct. 23, 2019) (on file with Comm.).

[1884] *Fill Orders from Other Sales Channels (Multi-Channel Fulfillment)*, AMAZON SELLER CENTRAL, https://sellercentral.amazon.com/gp/help/external/200332450#:~:text=Multi%2DChannel%20Fulfillment%20(MCF),ships%20them%20to%20your%20customers (explaining that "Multi-Channel Fulfillment (MCF) is a program within Fulfillment by Amazon (FBA)," that fills orders from sales channels placed on sites other than Amazon.com) (last visited Oct. 4, 2020).

[1885] Innovation and Entrepreneurship Hearing at 19 (response to Questions for the Record of Nate Sutton, Assoc. Gen. Counsel, Competition, Amazon.com, Inc.).

[1886] Press Release, Amazon, Continued Growth for Amazon's Air Network (June 28, 2019), https://press.aboutamazon.com/news-releases/news-release-details/continued-growth-amazons-air-network-expand-prime-fast-free.

[1887] Innovation and Entrepreneurship Hearing at 19 (response to Questions for the Record of Nate Sutton, Assoc. Gen. Counsel, Competition, Amazon.com, Inc.).

[1888] Press Release, Amazon, Continued Growth for Amazon's Air Network (June 28, 2019), https://press.aboutamazon.com/news-releases/news-release-details/continued-growth-amazons-air-network-expand-prime-fast-free.

[1889] INST. FOR LOCAL SELF-RELIANCE, AMAZON'S MONOPOLY TOLLBOOTH 8 (2020), https://cdn.ilsr.org/wp-content/uploads/2020/07/ILSR_Report_AmazonTollbooth_Final.pdf.

orders in its warehouses, but relied on other carriers to handle shipping and delivery. Today, Amazon ships a growing number of products itself. In 2019, "Amazon delivered about half of its own packages, up from 15 percent just two years before."[1890] Amazon has also lessened its use of large delivery companies during this time, using "800 small, independent contractors [which] are now responsible for around 48 percent of Amazon's last mile deliveries."[1891] These smaller providers are economically-dependent on Amazon, and "many are in fact reliant on Amazon for 100 percent of their business."[1892]

Parcel volume handled by Amazon's delivery service now rivals the top carriers, including UPS, FedEx, and the U.S. Postal Service. "In 2019, Amazon delivered 2.5 billion parcels, or about one-fifth of all e-commerce deliveries,"[1893] and anticipates growth. In a July 2020 investor call, Amazon CFO Brian Olsavsky stated that Amazon "expect[s] a meaningfully higher year-over-year square footage growth of approximately 50%," which includes "strong growth in new fulfillment center space as well as sort centers and delivery stations."[1894]

An analysis by Morgan Stanley concluded that Amazon will overtake UPS and FedEx in market share for delivery by 2022. Amazon has already surpassed the U.S. Postal Service, which has been downsized dramatically under its current leadership.[1895] Last year, the U.S. Postal Service had a decrease in parcel volume for the first time in nearly a decade.[1896]

b. Monopsony Power

Amazon exercises monopsony power in labor markets directly and indirectly. As one of the largest employers in America, Amazon exercises direct power over hundreds of thousands of workers across the United States.[1897] Amazon employees 22% of the U.S. labor market in warehousing and

---

[1890] *Id.*

[1891] Submission from Int'l Bhd. Of Teamsters, Commc'n Workers of America, United Food & Commercial Workers Int'l Union, Service Employees Int'l Union & Change to Win, to H. Comm. on the Judiciary, 13 (March 10, 2020) (on file with Comm.).

[1892] *Id.* at 14.

[1893] INST. FOR LOCAL SELF-RELIANCE, AMAZON'S MONOPOLY TOLLBOOTH 8 (2020), https://cdn.ilsr.org/wp-content/uploads/2020/07/ILSR_Report_AmazonTollbooth_Final.pdf.

[1894] Rachel Premack, *Amazon Is Piling Up Fulfillment Center Square Footage, and It Shows Bezos Thinks the Pandemic-Driven Online Shopping Surge Is Here to Stay*, BUS. INSIDER: MKTS. (Jul 31, 2020), https://markets.businessinsider.com/news/stocks/amazon-fulfillment-center-growth-reveals-pandemic-online-ordering-surge-2020-7-1029456709# (last visited Oct. 4, 2020).

[1895] INST. FOR LOCAL SELF-RELIANCE, AMAZON'S MONOPOLY TOLLBOOTH 8 (2020), https://cdn.ilsr.org/wp-content/uploads/2020/07/ILSR_Report_AmazonTollbooth_Final.pdf.

[1896] *Id.*

[1897] Submission from Int'l Bhd. Of Teamsters, Commc'n Workers of America, United Food & Commercial Workers Int'l Union, Service Employees Int'l Union & Change to Win. to H. Comm. on the Judiciary, 12 (March 10, 2020) (on file with Comm.).

storage, excluding seasonal workers.[1898] There has been a growing amount of public reporting in recent years regarding Amazon's treatment of warehouse employees, including strenuous working conditions, unforgiving packing and sorting quotas, and unfair firings.[1899] Amazon warehouses also have a tendency to depress wages when they enter a local labor market. For example, since Amazon opened a warehouse in Lexington County, South Carolina in 2011, the county has seen average annual wages for warehouse workers fall more than 30%, from $47,000 to $32,000 annually.[1900]

Indirectly, Amazon has wage-setting power through its ability to set route fees and other fixed costs for independent contractors in localities in which it dominates the delivery labor market. These entities are dependent on Amazon for a large majority—or even 100%—of their delivery business.[1901] As a result, they have little choice but to "submit to Amazon's prices and other terms."[1902] Amazon's dominance also enables it to compel logistics employees to quit their jobs and instead act as independent contractors, removing employment protections. A group of labor unions stated in their submission to the Subcommittee, "By virtue of its size and power as a buyer of delivery services, Amazon can impose monopolistic restraints on the treatment of workers within its supply chain while, at the same time, avoiding legal responsibility for their fair treatment."[1903]

Despite the loss of jobs and economic activity in the wake of the COVID-19 pandemic, Amazon's monopsony power has likely increased. In response to higher demand for goods and services, Amazon hired 175,000 temporary workers in March and April of 2020, making 125,000 of those jobs permanent in May 2020.[1904]

[1898] *What Amazon Does to Wages*, THE ECONOMIST (Jan. 20, 2018), https://www.economist.com/united-states/2018/01/20/what-amazon-does-to-wages.

[1899] *See, e.g.*, Colin Lecher, *How Amazon Automatically Tracks and Fires Warehouse Workers for 'Productivity,'* THE VERGE (Apr. 25, 2019), https://www.theverge.com/2019/4/25/18516004/amazon-warehouse-fulfillment-centers-productivity-firing-terminations.

[1900] *What Amazon Does to Wages*, THE ECONOMIST (Jan. 20, 2018), https://www.economist.com/united-states/2018/01/20/what-amazon-does-to-wages.

[1901] Submission from Int'l Bhd. Of Teamsters, Commc'n Workers of America, United Food & Commercial Workers Int'l Union, Service Employees Int'l Union & Change to Win, to H. Comm. on the Judiciary, 14 (March 10, 2020) (on file with Comm.).

[1902] *Id.*

[1903] *Id.* at 13.

[1904] Sebastian Herrera, *Amazon to Keep Most of the Jobs It Added During Pandemic*, WALL ST. J. (May 28, 2020). https://www.wsj.com/articles/amazon-to-keep-most-of-the-jobs-it-added-during-pandemic-11590661802 (last visited Oct. 4, 2020).

4. Alexa's Internet of Things Ecosystem

    a. Overview

    Amazon has significant investments in the Internet of Things ecosystem, centering its strategy around Amazon's voice assistant, Alexa. In 2014, Amazon launched the Alexa-enabled Echo smart speaker.[1905] Since then, Amazon has built the largest ecosystem of devices and applications connected to the Internet of Things,[1906] creating a broad portfolio of services, development tools, and devices for its Alexa platform. Amazon's research and development team, Lab126, leads the development of Amazon's Internet of Things hardware expansion, including the development of Amazon Echo and Fire TV.[1907] These devices represent a "critical touchpoint that generates insights into user behavior, which can then be used to deepen the relationship with consumers and expose them to new products through personalized recommendations."[1908] Amazon encourages consumers to use Alexa through its Echo smart speakers and other Alexa compatible devices, ranging from smart microwaves to its Echo Frames.[1909]

    In 2015, Amazon launched a kit for independent developers to access Alexa in the cloud and create new Alexa apps, which Amazon refers to as "skills."[1910] Two years later, in an effort to expand its ecosystem of devices, Amazon launched Alexa Voice Service. This suite of services allows manufacturers of hardware with microphones and speakers to receive and respond to Alexa voice commands, making the device "Alexa-enabled,"[1911] or "Alexa built-in."[1912] Additionally, Amazon oversees Works with Alexa, an Alexa-compatible device certification program for devices that receive

---

[1905] See e.g., Chris Welch, *Amazon just surprised everyone with a crazy speaker that talks to you*, THE VERGE (Nov. 6, 2014), https://www.theverge.com/2014/11/6/7167793/amazon-echo-speaker-announced; Nick Statt, *Amazon wants Alexa to be the operating system for your life*, THE VERGE (Sept. 27, 2018), https://www.theverge.com/2018/9/27/17911300/amazon-alexa-echo-smart-home-eco-system-competition.

[1906] See infra Section IV.

[1907] *Amazon Jobs, Lab126*, AMAZON, https://amazon.jobs/en/teams/lab126/ (last visited Sept. 29, 2020).

[1908] See Johanna Ambrosio, *Amazon smart devices to expand in homes and businesses*, TechTarget (Mar. 23, 2020), https://searchaws.techtarget.com/feature/Amazon-smart-devices-to-expand-in-homes-and-businesses

[1909] *Echo Frames – Eyeglasses with Alexa – Black – A Day 1 Editions product*, AMAZON, https://www.amazon.com/dp/B07W72XKPJ. *See also AmazonBasics Microwave, Small, 0.7 Cu. Ft, 700W, Works With Alexa*, AMAZON, https://www.amazon.com/dp/B07894S727 (last visited Sept. 29, 2020).

[1910] David Isbitski, *Introducing the Alexa Skills Kit, Enabling Developers to Create Entirely New Voice Driven Capabilities*, AMAZON DEVELOPER (June 25, 2015), https://developer.amazon.com/blogs/post/Tx205N9U1UD338H/Introducing-the-Alexa-Skills-Kit-Enabling-Developers-to-Create-Entirely-New-Voic.

[1911] Satish Iyer, *Introducing the Alexa Voice Service Device SDK for Commercial Device Makers*, AMAZON ALEXA (Aug. 17, 2017), https://developer.amazon.com/blogs/alexa/post/7a72f14e-66d6-42fb-b369-c60af364489a/introducing-the-alexa-voice-service-avs-device-sdk-for-commercial-device-makers.

[1912] *What are Alexa Built-in Devices?*, AMAZON ALEXA, https://developer.amazon.com/en-US/alexa/devices/alexa-built-in (last visited Sep. 29, 2020).

commands through an Alexa-enabled device, such as a smart speaker.[1913] Amazon does not charge third-party device manufacturers for access to its integration services, which promotes rapid adoption of Alexa in a larger number of devices, which, in turn, drives greater adoption by consumers.[1914]

These programs indicate that Amazon is focused on expanding Alexa's reach rather than short-term profitability, consistent with the early stages of its marketplace strategy. Amazon CFO Brian Olsavsky confirmed this in an earnings call in July 2019, saying that the company's "emphasis is around expanding the reach of Alexa and the usefulness."[1915] He added that at the time, Alexa had "over 45,000 skills" and was in "over 13,000 smart home devices from 2,500 unique brands."[1916]

Lastly, Amazon's Alexa ecosystem is a major source of consumer data; it tracks if the home owner's lights are off and the events on their calendar.[1917] Amazon is also building a series of devices that allow people to have "Alexa in [their] ears, on [their] eyes, and around [their] fingers."[1918]

b. Market Power

Amazon's Alexa represents one of three emerging voice assistant platforms domestically, along with Google Assistant and Apple's Siri, but has a more expansive collection of integrated devices and voice applications than its competitors.[1919] The Echo collection of smart speakers—the hub of Alexa's ecosystem—captures over 60% of the smart speaker market in the U.S.[1920]

As of September 2019, there were 85,000 Works with Alexa devices available for consumers to purchase.[1921] The current network of Alexa-enabled devices includes companies like Sonos, Hewlett-Packard, and BMW.[1922] The U.S.-based Alexa Skills Store as of January 2020 includes 70,729

[1913] *Works with Alexa Program*, AMAZON ALEXA, https://developer.amazon.com/en-US/alexa/connected-devices/launch/works-with-alexa (last visited Sept. 29, 2020).

[1914] Class Action Complaint at 8, B.F. v. Amazon.com, Inc., Case No.: 2:19-cv-910 (W.D. Wash. June 11, 2019).

[1915] Production of Amazon, to H. Comm. on the Judiciary, AMAZON-HJC-00200464 (July 26, 2018) (on file with Comm.).

[1916] *Id.*

[1917] Innovation and Entrepreneurship Hearing at 40 (response to Questions for the Record of Nate Sutton, Assoc. Gen. Counsel, Competition, Amazon.com, Inc.).

[1918] Daniel Newman, *Opinion: Amazon's Alexa is about to become even more of a fixture in our lives*, MARKETWATCH (Sept. 30, 2019), https://www.marketwatch.com/story/amazons-alexa-is-about-to-become-even-more-of-a-fixture-in-our-lives-2019-09-27.

[1919] *See infra* Section IV.

[1920] Submission from Source 38, to H. Comm. on the Judiciary, 7 (Sept. 1, 2019).

[1921] Kyle Wiggers, *The Alexa Skills Store now has more than 100,000 voice apps*, VENTUREBEAT (Sept. 25, 2019), https://venturebeat.com/2019/09/25/the-alexa-skills-store-now-has-more-than-100000-voice-apps/.

[1922] Production of Amazon, to H. Comm. on the Judiciary, AMAZON-HJC-00200465 (July 26, 2018) (on file with Comm.).

skills.[1923] In comparison, as of December 2019, Google's voice application ecosystem had just over 18,826 Google Actions.[1924]

The voice assistant market has strong entry barriers due to the significant investments required to compete in the market. These include investments in artificial intelligence, voice-enabled hardware, and cloud computing infrastructure, which are critical inputs Amazon has been developing for years. Amazon's Alexa Voice Service is also hosted on Amazon Web Services, allowing it to bind products and developers to its cloud platform. [1925] In turn, this relationship gives Amazon a potential head-start on turning its Alexa business partners into customers through the cross-sale of Amazon Web Services and other Amazon products and services down the line.

Voice assistants collect significant amounts of personal data and learn users' preferences over time. For example, when Alexa users add more devices that integrate with Alexa, they often manage the settings for these devices through mobile applications and websites that are tied to their Amazon credentials, thereby creating a robust user profile. [1926] As Amazon continues to expand Alexa's reach, this customization of features allows Amazon to better "understand" its users, which may affect their willingness to retrain a new voice assistant.[1927] In addition to the cost of replacing their devices, this friction—retraining a new voice assistant—may increase costs associated with switching to another voice assistant ecosystem.

c. Merger Activity

Amazon has expanded its voice assistant ecosystem by acquiring artificial intelligence companies to strengthen Alexa's functionality and voice-enabled device manufactures to expand Alexa's reach.[1928] In 2011, Amazon acquired Yap, a speech recognition platform.[1929] The next year, in 2012, Amazon acquired Evi, a technology for understanding natural language.[1930] Over the years, Amazon has continued to acquire other businesses engaged in natural language processing, machine

---

[1923] H. Tankovska, *Total number of Amazon Alexa skills in selected countries as of January 2020*, STATISTA (Aug. 27, 2020), https://www.statista.com/statistics/917900/selected-countries-amazon-alexa-skill-count/.

[1924] Shanhong Liu, *Number of Google Assistant Actions Worldwide 2019, by Language*, STATISTA (June 17, 2020), https://www.statista.com/statistics/1062722/worldwide-google-action-disappearance-by-language/.

[1925] *Build the future of the connected home with AWS IoT and Amazon Alexa*, AWS, https://aws.amazon.com/iot/solutions/connected-home/iot-and-alexa/ (last visited Sept. 29, 2020).

[1926] Production of Amazon, to H. Comm. on the Judiciary, AMAZON-HJC-00172104 (Mar. 9, 2018) (on file with Comm.).

[1927] Submission from Source 39, to H. Comm. on the Judiciary, Source 39-00000098, 19 (Sept. 16, 2019) (on file with Comm.).

[1928] *See Appendix*

[1929] Sam Byford, *Amazon Acquires Yap, move into Speech Recognition?*, THE VERGE (Nov. 9, 2011), https://www.theverge.com/2011/11/9/2550764/amazon-acquires-yap-speech-recognition-siri.

[1930] Emma Bryce, *How Amazon's Alexa was 'born' and where voice-controlled tech will take us next*, WIRED (Feb. 14, 2017), https://www.wired.co.uk/article/amazon-alexa-ai-evi.

learning, and other related technologies in support of its continued efforts to improve Alexa's artificial intelligence functionality.[1931]

One of Amazon's strategic goals for Alexa has been to use its voice assistant to reinforce the company's dominance in e-commerce and strengthen its presence in offline retail. In 2017, Amazon acquired Graphiq, a technology company that collects and organizes details about "products, places, and people to simplify online research."[1932] This acquisition appears to have been part of Amazon's effort to improve Alexa's overall search capabilities, most notably product search, as the technology includes "features to tailor comparisons around individual preferences."[1933]

In 2017, Amazon purchased Blink, followed by Ring in 2018—both to solidify its position in the home security market.[1934] In an internal document, Amazon recognized that security could "feed our flywheels (Prime, Alexa) while being a large, profitable business in its own right."[1935] Prior to these acquisitions Jeff Helbling, Vice President at Amazon, emailed a group of Amazon executives, recapping a discussion on the transactions he had with Mr. Bezos. There, he detailed the twin justification for the acquisitions, saying that "two senses matter—eyes and ears."[1936] Amazon had already locked down "ears" through its continued development of Alexa. Ring and Blink would act as Amazon's "eyes" right outside the home.

Amazon's internal documents show that, in large part, it purchased Ring to capture the company's share of the smart home security market. In December 2017, Mr. Bezos wrote to Dave Limp, the Senior Vice President of Devices & Services, that Amazon was really "buying market position" by acquiring Ring.[1937] During the Subcommittee's sixth hearing, Representative Jamie Raskin (D-MD) asked Mr. Bezos about this exchange.[1938] Mr. Bezos responded:

> Sir, market position is valuable in almost any business, and it's one of the primary
> things that one would look at in an acquisition. There are multiple reasons that we might

---

[1931] *See infra* Appendix.

[1932] Paresh Dave, *Amazon acquires Santa Barbara start-up Graphiq to try to bolster Alexa*, L.A. TIMES (July 20, 2017), https://www.latimes.com/business/technology/la-fi-tn-graphiq-amazon-20170719-story.html.

[1933] *Id.*

[1934] Jacob Kastrenakes, *Amazon buys smart camera and doorbell startup Blink*, THE VERGE (Dec. 22, 2017), https://www.theverge.com/circuitbreaker/2017/12/22/16810516/amazon-blink-acquisition-smart-camera-doorbell-company; *see also* Samuel Gibbs, *Amazon buys video doorbell firm Ring for over $1bn*, THE GUARDIAN (Feb. 28, 2018), https://www.theguardian.com/technology/2018/feb/28/amazon-buys-video-doorbell-ring-smart-home-delivery.

[1935] Production of Amazon, to H. Comm. on the Judiciary, AMAZON-HJC-00169702 (Mar. 9, 2018) (on file with Comm.).

[1936] *Id.* at AMAZON-HJC-00170877. (Oct. 11, 2017).

[1937] *Id.* at AMAZON-HJC-00173560 (Dec. 15, 2017).

[1938] CEO Hearing Transcript at 108 (question of Rep. Jamie Raskin (D-MD), Member, Subcomm. on Antirust, Commercial and Admin. Law).

buy a company. Sometimes we're trying to buy some technology or some IP. Sometimes it's a talent acquisition. But the most common case is market position, that the company has traction with customers, they've built a service, maybe they were the first mover. There could be any number of reasons why they have that market position. But that's a very common reason to acquire a company.[1939]

This response suggests that adding Ring's users to the Alexa ecosystem quickly was also important to Amazon's rationale.

A 2017 internal memorandum further explains Amazon's strategy behind these acquisitions. As the memorandum notes, while acquiring each company independently would make Amazon stronger, acquiring both "would put us in a meaningfully better position than we are today (and we would not want to stake our chances in the segment on closing any one opportunity)."[1940] Douglas Booms, the Vice President of Corporate Development at Amazon, sent an email summarizing the thoughts of other senior executives at the company, which included: "I don't know how we can get big fast in that segment without an [sic] acquiring someone."[1941]

The documents and other relevant information reviewed by Subcommittee staff demonstrate that Amazon acquiring Ring and Blink was in part to expand and reinforce its market power for its other business lines. Internally, Amazon executives discussed how home surveillance acquisitions would help them implement unattended package delivery. Similarly, they discussed the idea that the acquisitions would help Amazon develop its Alexa Doorbell application program interface, an AWS service that allows Alexa Skills developers to build apps that respond to a ringing doorbell.[1942] Amazon referred to this strategy as an "integration approach" to "remove impediments to future growth."[1943]

More recently, Amazon purchased Eero, a mesh networking company, for $97 million in 2019.[1944] The purchase was part of Amazon's strategy to offer "frustration-free setup" for smart home devices in the Alexa ecosystem, another move aimed at removing impediments to growing the platform's presence in the home.[1945] "Amazon Wi-fi Simple Setup" scans the user's Eero network

---

[1939] *Id.* (statement of Jeff Bezos, CEO, Amazon.com, Inc.).

[1940] Production of Amazon, to H. Comm. on the Judiciary, AMAZON-HJC-00169706 (Mar. 9, 2018) (on file with Comm.).

[1941] *Id.* at AMAZON-HJC-00170869 (Nov. 1, 2017).

[1942] *Id.* at AMAZON-HJC-00169706 (Mar. 9, 2018); *Alexa.DoorbellEventSource Interface*, AMAZON ALEXA, https://developer.amazon.com/en-US/docs/alexa/device-apis/alexa-doorbelleventsource.html (last visited Sept. 30, 2020).

[1943] Production of Amazon, to H. Comm. on the Judiciary, AMAZON-HJC-00172104 (Mar. 9, 2018) (on file with Comm.).

[1944] Lisa Eadicicco & Alexei Oreskovic, *Amazon paid $97 million to acquire Eero in a fire sale deal that left some shareholders with practically nothing, according to leaked documents*, BUS. INSIDER (Apr. 5, 2019), https://www.businessinsider.com/amazon-paid-97-million-to-acquire-eero-in-fire-sale-leaked-documents-2019-4.

[1945] *See* Lisa Eadicicco, *A year after selling to Amazon for $1 billion, the chief inventor of the Ring video doorbell explains how he's bringing his entrepreneurial spirit to the online retailer*, BUS. INSIDER (Apr. 9, 2019),

during initial set-up of an Alexa-enabled device, applying the user's stored credentials to automatically connect to other smart devices, such as outlets and Fire TV devices.[1946] To achieve this, Eero must continually understand which devices are connected to the network, including the IP addresses of those devices.[1947] This acquisition gives Amazon access to another important input for consumer data.[1948]

d. Conduct

During the Subcommittee's investigation, market participants raised concerns about Amazon's business practices in the smart home market. As these market participants note, Amazon uses Alexa to favor its own goods and services, including AmazonBasics and Prime Music. Amazon has also imposed barriers to entry for other voice-enabled device manufactures through predatory pricing of Alexa-enabled devices, and through its dominance as a leading distribution channel for smart home devices.

i. Self-Preferencing

Amazon has the largest voice application "store" of third-party skills, as well as first-party services that represent popular voice assistant applications, such as Amazon Music and an e-commerce platform that it can favor over third-party applications.[1949] Amazon favors its services in Alexa by making them defaults for common voice commands. For example, Amazon.com is the default store for basic voice commands related to shopping. "Alexa, add milk to my cart" adds milk to the user's Amazon shopping cart.[1950]

Besides favoring Amazon services with default voice commands, Alexa also allows Amazon to favor its retail products over products offered by third-party sellers. When users shop via voice command, they are presented with one spoken offer, and an option for a follow-up question, which is

---

http://static7.businessinsider.com/ring-founder-jamie-siminoff-life-after-amazon-acquisition-2019-4 (quoting Jamie Siminoff, Founder of Ring, describing the importance of Eero and his support of Amazon's acquisition, "[Ring is] a product that requires great Wi-Fi connectivity. We use a lot of bandwidth so we we're certainly very sensitive to Wi-Fi networks.").

[1946] *Amazon Frustration-Free Setup Frequently Asked Questions,* AMAZON, https://www.amazon.com/gp/help/customer/display.html?nodeId=GMPKVYDBR223TRPY (last visited Oct. 4, 2018).

[1947] *Legal: Privacy policy for eero Devices, Applications and Services*, Eero, https://eero.com/legal/privacy (last visited Sept. 29, 2020); *Legal: Privacy policy for eero Websites*, Eero, https://eero.com/legal/privacy-website (last visited Sept. 29, 2020).

[1948] Innovation and Entrepreneurship Hearing at 41 (response to Questions for the Record of Nate Sutton, Assoc. Gen. Counsel, Competition, Amazon.com, Inc.).

[1949] Competitors Hearing at 4 (statement of Patrick Spence, CEO, Sonos, Inc.).

[1950] *Do more with Alexa*, AMAZON, https://www.amazon.com/alexa-voice-shopping/b?ie=UTF8&node=14552177011 (last visited Sept. 30, 2020).

distinct from an online user interface that shows the additional offers ranked. This increases the importance of being Alexa's featured offer.[1951]

For example, *The New York Times* reported in 2018 that when a user says, "Alexa, buy batteries," Alexa responds with the AmazonBasics option[1952] Similarly, a study conducted by Bain & Company found that for categories in which Amazon offered a private-label product, Alexa recommended those products 17% of the time, despite its private-label goods representing only about 2% of total volume sold.[1953] During the Subcommittee's sixth hearing, Congressman Jamie Raskin (D-MD) asked Mr. Bezos "[H]as Alexa ever been trained to favor Amazon products when users shop by voice?"[1954] Mr. Bezos responded that he didn't "know if it's been trained in that way," but "it wouldn't surprise me if Alexa sometimes does promote our own products."[1955]Amazon chooses the products Alexa suggests based on a range features, including products that "customers frequently purchase based on their past orders" and Amazon's Choice designation.[1956] Amazon's method for determining "Amazon's Choice" is opaque.[1957]

Amazon minimizes concerns about favoring its first-party goods through voice shopping by highlighting how rare it is for people to purchase goods through Alexa.[1958] Reporting suggests, however, that there is an increasing number of queries from users who expect to hear product information or to complete a transaction while interacting with a voice assistant.[1959] Amazon also justified the fact that third-party sales through Alexa are lower than third-party sales on Amazon.com—42% compared to 58%—by saying that "customers disproportionately use Alexa to order household consumable items (like paper towels or batteries) for which Amazon's offers are

---

[1951] Submission from Source 39, to H. Comm. on the Judiciary, Source 39-00000097, 19 (Sept. 16, 2019) (on file with Comm.).

[1952] Julie Creswell, *How Amazon Steers Shoppers to Its Own Products*, N.Y. TIMES (June 23, 2018), https://www.nytimes.com/2018/06/23/business/amazon-the-brand-buster.html.

[1953] Aaron Cheris, Darrell Rigby & Suzanne Tager, *Dreaming of an Amazon Christmas*, BAIN & CO. (Nov. 9, 2017), https://www.bain.com/insights/retail-holiday-newsletter-2017-issue-2/.

[1954] CEO Hearing Transcript at 120 (question of Rep. Jamie Raskin (D-MD, Member, Subcomm. on Antitrust, Commercial and Admin. Law).

[1955] *Id.* at 121 (statement of Jeff Bezos, CEO, Amazon.com, Inc.) .

[1956] CEO Hearing at 5 (response to Questions for the Record of Jeff Bezos, CEO, Amazon.com, Inc.); *see also* Aaron Cheris, Darrell Rigby & Suzanne Tager, *Dreaming of an Amazon Christmas*, BAIN & CO. (Nov. 9, 2017), https://www.bain.com/insights/retail-holiday-newsletter-2017-issue-2/.

[1957] Aaron Cheris, Darrell Rigby & Suzanne Tager, *Dreaming of an Amazon Christmas*, BAIN & CO. (Nov. 9, 2017), https://www.bain.com/insights/retail-holiday-newsletter-2017-issue-2/.

[1958] Amazon QFR response 128 What percentage of consumers purchase the product that Amazon recommends when a consumer is voice shopping through Alexa?"

[1959] Khari Johnson, *Voicelabs ditches analytics service to launch Alpine.ai for ecommerce voice apps*, VENTUREBEAT (Jan. 29, 2018), https://venturebeat.com/2018/01/29/voicelabs-ditches-analytics-service-to-launch-alpine-ai-for-ecommerce-voice-apps/.

particularly competitive."[1960] This demonstrates the problem, however, given that voice shopping is most useful for products in which consumers do not have to do much research or engage in price comparison. Alexa's algorithm, in conjunction with the AmazonBasics business model, provides a convenient avenue for Amazon to favor first-party products.

Although it is technically possible for Alexa users to voice shop on other stores, there is significant friction. Users must first enable the shopping skills for other online retailers, which then requires the user to set up a completely separate billing profile, even though it contains similar information to their Amazon user profile.[1961] Alexa-enabled devices are tied to the user's Amazon account, which populates the user's saved credit card and shipping information for use during general shopping commands.[1962]

ii. Predatory Pricing and Bundling

Amazon uses a predatory pricing strategy to increase its sales of smart home devices by pricing its products below cost.[1963] It is common for Amazon to sell these products in bundles at steep discounts. Several smart home device manufacturers told the Subcommittee that when Amazon sells certain devices in a bundle or at a steep discount, it makes it nearly impossible for companies who specialize in making one piece of voice-assistant enabled hardware to compete on its merits.[1964] Furthermore, as described earlier in this Report, aggressive pricing of smart home devices— specifically "hubs" such as the Echo—has created a significant barrier to entry for companies that want to compete with the leading voice assistant platforms.

iii. Use of Gatekeeper Power

Amazon Marketplace is an important distribution channel for voice-enabled electronics in its Alexa ecosystem. Amazon decides the availability and placement of products on its site. As a result, Amazon can use the threat of delisting a product on its marketplace to ensure that Alexa is enabled on other company's devices, or to secure other favorable contractual terms.

In an interview with Subcommittee staff, a seller that sells a significant number of its device on Amazon.com said that during contract negotiations Amazon repeatedly refers to its power to delist the

---

[1960] CEO Hearing at 5 (response to Questions for the Record of Jeff Bezos, CEO, Amazon.com, Inc.).

[1961] *See Alexa Skills: Shopping,* AMAZON, https://www.amazon.com/s/ref=lp_13727921011_nr_n_16?fst=as%3Aoff&rh=n%3A13727921011%2Cn%3A%2113727279 22011%2Cn%3A14284862011&bbn=13727922011&ie=UTF8&qid=1600864849&rnid=13727922011 (last visited Sept. 30, 2020).

[1962] *Set Up Your Echo,* AMAZON, https://www.amazon.com/gp/help/customer/display.html?nodeId=GKFJXZCLQ83HGHQZ (last visited Oct. 3, 2020).

[1963] *Id.* at 119 (statement of Jeff Bezos, CEO, Amazon.com, Inc.) .

[1964] Competitors Hearing at 3–4 (statement of Patrick Spence, CEO, Sonos, Inc.).

313

company's product if Amazon's services are not prominent enough on the device.[1965] In 2017, Amazon also reportedly informed one of its main home security competitors—the Google-owned smart home company Nest—that it would not list any of its recently announced products, including its latest smart thermostat and home security system.[1966] Notwithstanding its own market power, Google's internal communications describe Amazon as having "changed the dynamics," observing that there is a "built in incentive to partner with Alexa, since [Amazon] will pull you from their store if you don't support it."[1967]

Additionally, Amazon controls the prominence of competing voice-enabled devices on its marketplace and promotes its first-party voice-enabled devices on Amazon.com. In an internal memorandum to Amazon executives about the Ring acquisition, Michael Deal, Amazon's Vice President and Associate General Counsel, said that Amazon "can promote Ring's products and subscription plans heavily on our sites as we do with our current [first-party] devices."[1968]

Relatedly, Amazon can also use advertisement placement as leverage during negotiations with other device manufactures. In interviews with Subcommittee staff and submissions to the Subcommittee, several market participants said that ad placement was used as leverage in negotiations. In one instance, Amazon placed a competing brand's ad beneath the product of the firm it was negotiating with "to influence negotiations."[1969] Additionally, Subcommittee staff heard from a voice-enabled device manufacturer that offers a competitive product to Amazon's first-party devices that it was prohibited from buying ads on Amazon.com.[1970] The competitor expressed concern about the harm this causes consumers, who may be confused or deceived when they receive ads promoting Amazon products even when they specifically search for a competitor's product on Amazon.com.[1971]

Even Google, which ranks just behind Amazon in online shopping queries, believes it has a disadvantage with Amazon. In an internal email about smart speakers, a Google employee noted that "fighting Amazon with a very-hard-to-differentiate product and a channel disadvantage and a huge economic disadvantage (due to channel mix margin differences) is already like fighting a shark on a surfboard."[1972]

[1965] Interview with Source 148 (Aug. 26, 2020).

[1966] Steve Kovach, *Amazon Will Stop Selling Nest Smart Home Devices, Escalating Its War With Google*, BUS. INSIDER (Mar. 2, 2018, 7:20 PM), https://www.businessinsider.com/amazon-wont-sell-nest-products-from-google-2018-3.

[1967] Production of Google, to H. Comm. on the Judiciary, GOOG-HJC- 04258793-993 (Jan. 29, 2019) (on file with Comm.).

[1968] Production of Amazon, to H. Comm. on the Judiciary, AMAZON-HJC-00172104 (Mar. 9, 2018) (on file with Comm.).

[1969] Submission from Source 38, to H. Comm. on the Judiciary, 27 (Sept. 1, 2019) (on file with Comm.).

[1970] Interview with Source 148 (Aug. 26, 2020).

[1971] *Id.*

[1972] Production of Google, to H. Comm. on the Judiciary, GOOG-HJC-04261582-85 (Nov. 27, 2018) (on file with Comm.).

iv. Misuse of Data

Amazon has access to information about consumer use of third-party applications on Alexa-enabled devices and uses its dominant position in the voice assistant market to collect more data from within the Alexa ecosystem.

Amazon has insight into which Alexa skills are invoked by Alexa users and the frequency of usage.[1973] Considering Amazon's use of third-party seller's data in e-commerce and cloud customer's data on Amazon Web Services, Amazon may use the same tactics with other firms' voice application data to determine which voice assistant skills it should invest in.

Additionally, Amazon uses its market power to collect third-party voice application data. According to July 2020 reporting by the *Wall Street Journal*, Amazon told Vivint, a manufacturer of smart-home devices that, "it would only allow the company to remain on the Echo if Vivint agreed to give it not only the data from its Vivint function on Echo, but from every Vivint device in those customers' homes at all times."[1974]

Amazon has also faced civil suits related to its storage of voice data.[1975] When Alexa hears a "wake" word— such as "Alexa" or "Echo"—it records the user's voice command, including conversations in the background, and saves a permanent recording of the user's voice to its own servers, as opposed to temporary storage for artificial intelligence training purposes.[1976]

v. Copying Nascent Competitors Technology

The Subcommittee's investigation produced evidence consistent with public reporting that Amazon uses information collected through Alexa Fund investments to inform and improve Amazon's smart home ecosystem. When Amazon invests in a startup, it obtains access to the company's non-public financial information, strategic plans, and other proprietary information.[1977] According to a recent *Wall Street Journal* report, eight months after Alexa Fund invested in Nucleus, Amazon

---

[1973] Innovation and Entrepreneurship Hearing at 40 (response to Questions for the Record of Nate Sutton, Assoc. Gen. Counsel, Competition.com, Amazon, Inc.).

[1974] Dana Mattioli & Cara Lombardo, *Amazon Met With Startups About Investing, Then Launched Competing Products*, WALL ST. J. (July 23, 2020), https://www.wsj.com/articles/amazon-tech-startup-echo-bezos-alexa-investment-fund-11595520249.

[1975] *See* Tice v. Amazon.com, Inc., No. 5:10-cv-1311, (C.D. Cal. Mar. 25, 2020); C.O. v. Amazon.com, Inc., No. C19-910 (W.D. Wash. Sept. 23, 2019).

[1976] *Id.*

[1977] Dana Mattioli & Cara Lombardo, *Amazon Met With Startups About Investing, Then Launched Competing Products*, WALL ST. J. (July 23, 2020, 12:08 PM), https://www.wsj.com/articles/amazon-tech-startup-echo-bezos-alexa-investment-fund-11595520249.

announced the Echo Show, a very similar Alexa-enabled video-chat device.[1978] This report described several other examples, including Vocalife, the inventors of a "speech-detection technology," which filed a lawsuit against Amazon alleging it improperly used proprietary technology.[1979] At the Subcommittee's sixth hearing, Representative Ken Buck (R-CO) said that allegations that Amazon incorporated features demonstrated to it by Vocalife's founders during an investment meeting "are serious, especially because the size and scope of these practices couldn't happen without Amazon's monopolistic control of the marketplace."[1980]

Prior to Amazon's acquisition of Ring, Amazon invested in Ring through the Alexa Fund, and internal emails about meetings during this time demonstrate how Amazon is able to obtain crucial insights into young companies. Amazon was able to learn about Ring's "roadmap, future products, [and] two acquisitions they have done."[1981] While Amazon often denies public reporting that it steals and copies technology from young startups, Amazon's emails suggest that it does replicate some of the startups it meets with or invests in. An email out of Amazon's Lab 126 regarding Ring indicated that Amazon "could easily replicate all of their hardware to be better, [and] operate in a more secure and robust infrastructure, for a LOT less than [the] cost of buying them."[1982] In the same email chain, Amazon employees wondered "if we move forward with due diligence, then decide not to buy [Ring], could we have legal issues if we go into the market by ourselves as a competitor and materially impact their business?"[1983]

5. Amazon Web Services

a. Overview

Amazon Web Services (AWS) is considered the pioneer of cloud computing and has sustained a first-mover advantage for over a decade.[1984] AWS officially launched in 2006 featuring two of its core IaaS offerings, Simple Storage Service (S3) and Elastic Compute Cloud (EC2).[1985] While Amazon.com was AWS's first customer, in the early 2000s AWS began creating cloud offerings for third-party merchants, who could use AWS to "build online shopping sites on top of Amazon's e-

---

[1978] *Id.*

[1979] *Id.*

[1980] CEO Hearing Transcript at 102 (statement of Rep. Ken Buck (R-CO), Member, Subcomm. on Antitrust, Commercial and Admin. Law of the H. Comm. on the Judiciary).

[1981] Production from Amazon, to H. Comm. on the Judiciary, AMAZON-HJC-00214240 (Oct. 18, 2017) (on file with Comm.).

[1982] *Id.* at AMAZON-HJC-00220705 (Nov. 4, 2017).

[1983] *Id.* at AMAZON-HJC-00220703 (Nov. 4, 2017).

[1984] Ron Miller, *How AWS Came To Be*, TECHCRUNCH (July 2, 2016), https://techcrunch.com/2016/07/02/andy-jassys-brief-history-of-the-genesis-of-aws/.

[1985] *What's New*, AMAZON WEB SERVICES (Oct. 4, 2006), https://aws.amazon.com/about-aws/whats-new/2006/.

commerce engine."[1986] For AWS, meanwhile, this partnership with third parties gave the company experience in creating well-documented APIs for internal developers.[1987] Over the next few years, AWS rolled out additional programs to expand its network of third-party software vendors and implementation partners, including AWS Marketplace[1988] and the AWS Partnership Network (APN) in 2012.[1989]

Over the last decade, AWS has also secured significant government contracts. Most notably, in 2014 AWS signed a $600 million Commercial Cloud Services (C2S) contract to build the AWS Secret Region, a cloud offering tailored for the U.S. intelligence community.[1990] The deal marked the largest cloud infrastructure contract at the time and signaled the government's shift from investing in on-premise server capacity to cloud services.[1991] Today, AWS boasts work "with over 6,500 government agencies" and states that Amazon has been "among the first to solve government compliance challenges facing cloud computing," while also "consistently help[ing] our customers navigate procurement and policy issues related to adoption of cloud computing."[1992]

AWS contributes immense value to Amazon's overall business. In each quarter since Amazon began publicly reporting its financials for cloud, AWS has accounted for an outsized share of Amazon's operating profits. While AWS contributes to less than 15% of Amazon's annual revenue, it consistently accounts for over 50% of the company's operating income. In 2017, AWS accounted for over 100% of Amazon's operating income, due to losses in the company's international business.[1993] In the first quarter of 2020, AWS accounted for 13.5% of Amazon's total revenues yet 77% of its operating income.[1994]

[1986] *Id.*

[1987] Ron Miller, *How AWS Came To Be*, TECHCRUNCH (July 2, 2016), https://techcrunch.com/2016/07/02/andy-jassys-brief-history-of-the-genesis-of-aws/.

[1988] *Introducing AWS Marketplace*, AMAZON WEB SERVICES (Apr. 19, 2012), https://aws.amazon.com/about-aws/whats-new/2012/04/19/introducing-aws-marketplace/.

[1989] Jeff Barr, *Announcing the AWS Partner Network*, AWS NEWS BLOG (Apr. 17, 2012), https://aws.amazon.com/blogs/aws/announcing-the-aws-partner-network/. (in beta).

[1990] Frank Konkel, *Federal Cloud Spending Trends Toward All-Time High*, NEXTGOV (Sept. 12, 2018), https://www.nextgov.com/it-modernization/2018/09/federal-cloud-spending-trends-toward-all-time-high/151221/.

[1991] *Id.*

[1992] *The Trusted Cloud for Government*, AMAZON WEB SERVICES, https://aws.amazon.com/government-education/government/ (last visited Sept. 30, 2020).

[1993] Amazon.com, Inc., Annual Report (Form 10-K) 26 (Feb. 1, 2018), https://s2.q4cdn.com/299287126/files/doc_financials/annual/Amazon_AR.PDF.

[1994] Amazon.com, Inc., Quarterly Report (Form 10-Q) 17 (Apr. 30, 2020), http://d18rn0p25nwr6d.cloudfront.net/CIK-0001018724/708a19c5-7d8c-4fc9-ab37-bfaa7a31629b.pdf.

Contributions to Amazon's Revenue and Operating Profit over Time[1995]

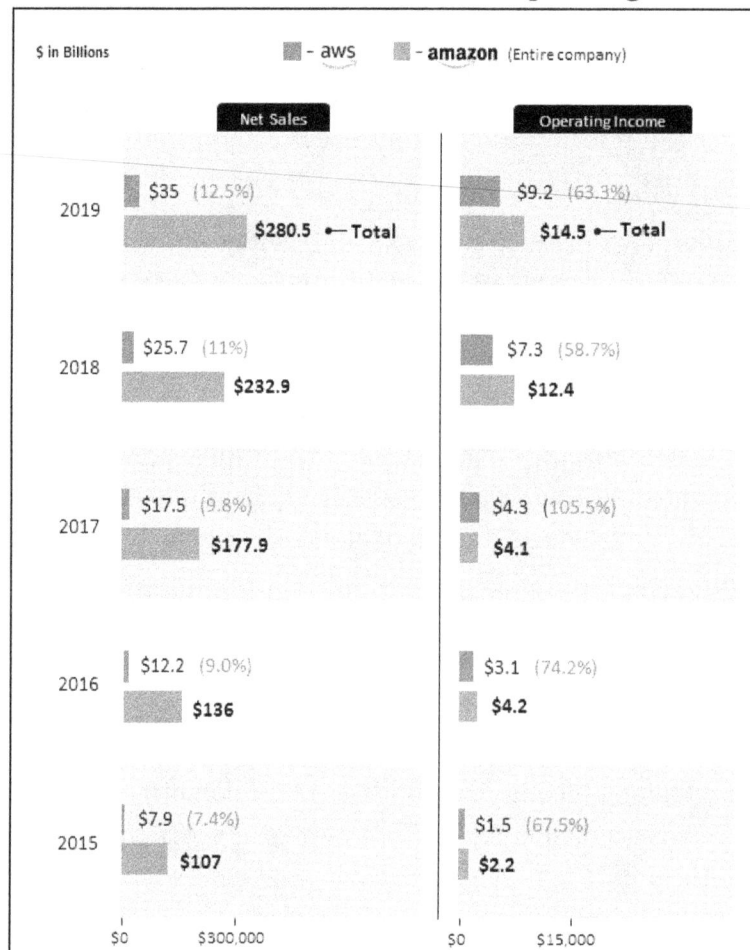

Profits earned through its cloud services enable Amazon to invest heavily into expanding its cloud operation, as well as to support its other lines of business. Several market participants expressed concerns to Subcommittee staff that Amazon uses its high and steady profits from AWS to subsidize these other lines of business, including its retail operation.[1996] In an internal document produced in response to the Committee's requests for information, Amazon instructs its employees to rebut this claim by referring to it as a "myth."[1997] However, Amazon failed to produce the financial data that would have enabled Subcommittee staff to make an independent assessment.[1998]

[1995] Prepared by the Subcomm. based on Amazon.com, Inc., Annual Report (Form 10-K) (2015-2019), https://www.sec.gov/Archives/edgar/data/1018724/000101872419000004/amzn-20181231x10k.htm

[1996] Submission from Source 48, to H. Comm. on the Judiciary, 8 (Nov. 8, 2019) (on file with Comm.).

[1997] Production of Amazon, to H. Comm on the Judiciary, AMAZON-HJC-00216209 (Aug. 24, 2018) (on file with Comm.).

[1998] Letter from Hon. Jerrold Nadler, Chairman, H. Comm. on the Judiciary, Hon. Doug Collins, Ranking Member, H. Comm on the Judiciary, Hon. David N. Cicilline, Chairman, Subcomm. on Antitrust, Commercial and Admin. Law of the H. Comm. on the Judiciary, Hon. F. James Sensenbrenner, Ranking Member, Subcomm. on Antitrust, Commercial and Admin. Law of the H. Comm. on the Judiciary, to Jeff Bezos, CEO, Amazon.com, Inc., 2 (on file with Comm.).

b. Market Power

As discussed earlier in this Report, AWS is the largest provider of cloud computing services, capturing approximately 24% of the U.S. spend in 2018 on cloud computing services, including IaaS, PaaS, and SaaS.[1999] AWS represents close to half of global spending on cloud infrastructure services, with three times the market share of Microsoft, its closest competitor.[2000] Its growth continues to soar. In the first quarter of 2020, AWS crossed $10 billion in quarterly revenue while growing 33% on an annualized basis.[2001]

Amazon has a "lion's share of the government cloud infrastructure market."[2002] Exact data on AWS's share of government cloud expenditure is opaque because most of AWS's public sector revenue comes through subcontracts, which are harder to track, and contracts related to the intelligence community, which are listed as classified spending and are rarely reported. Market participants, however, emphasize that AWS is considered a major player in federal cloud contracts.[2003]

In its submissions to the Subcommittee, Amazon describes itself as a relatively small player representing "less than 1% of IT spending globally and less than 2% in the United States."[2004] Amazon states that AWS competes with a large array of offerings including on-premise computing.[2005] In other contexts, however, Amazon has highlighted its leading position, describing itself as the "largest cloud software marketplace" and the "only cloud provider with existing classified infrastructure."[2006]

Through a careful review of Amazon's internal documents and other evidence during the investigation, Subcommittee staff found that Amazon has a dominant position in cloud computing. Amazon's dominance in cloud computing traces in part to its first-mover advantage and the high fixed

---

[1999] Letter from David Zapolsky, Gen. Counsel, Amazon.com, Inc., to Hon. David N. Cicilline, Chairman, Subcomm. on Antitrust, Commercial and Admin. Law of the H. Comm. on the Judiciary, 6 (July 26, 2019) (on file with Comm.).

[2000] *Id.*; Press Release, Katie Costello, Gartner, *Gartner Forecasts Worldwide Public Cloud Revenue to Grow 17.5 Percent in 2019* (Apr. 2, 2019), https://www.gartner.com/en/newsroom/press-releases/2019-04-02-gartner-forecasts-worldwide-public-cloud-revenue-to-g.

[2001] Jordan Novet, *AWS Tops $10 Billion in Quarterly Revenue for the First Time,* CNBC (Apr. 30, 2020) https://www.cnbc.com/2020/04/30/aws-earnings-q1-2020.html.

[2002] David Ramel, *AWS vs. Azure Heats Up in Federal Market,* WASH. TECH. (Sept. 14, 2018) https://washingtontechnology.com/articles/2018/09/14/aws-vs-azure-public-sector.aspx.

[2003] Interview with Source 31 (May 27, 2020).

[2004] Letter from David Zapolsky, Gen. Counsel, Amazon.com, Inc., to Hon. David N. Cicilline, Chairman, Subcomm. on Antitrust, Commercial and Admin. Law of the H. Comm. on the Judiciary, 6 (July 26, 2019) (on file with Comm.).

[2005] *Id.*

[2006] Complaint at 5, Amazon Web Servs, Inc. v. United States, 147 Fed. Cl. 146 (2020) (No. 1:19-cv-01796), https://www.courthousenews.com/wp-content/uploads/2019/12/amazon-trump-cafc.pdf.

319

costs and economies of scale associated with this market.[2007] But evidence suggests that Amazon has also taken steps to lock in and extend this dominance in ways that risk harming customers, businesses, and the broader public.

Network effects incentivized Amazon to build out AWS offerings quickly. As with other sectors of the digital economy, the value of Amazon's cloud offerings increases with the number of businesses and customers that use it. Introducing more services and partnership programs draws more customers, attracts more developers and implementation partners, which, in turn, draws additional customers.[2008]

AWS is considered to have the largest collection of cloud offerings. Its AWS Management Console and supporting technologies span many categories, including storage and computing, databases, migration services, and machine learning tools.[2009] Many of these products are based on open-source software or on the technology of companies that Amazon acquired.[2010] In addition to selling cloud offerings directly, AWS also runs a cloud marketplace where third-party vendors can list their products. The AWS Marketplace enjoys over 1,300 vendors as of 2018, and over 9,000 products, functioning as the largest cloud marketplace in the sector.[2011]

The widespread adoption of AWS's developer certification programs, partner networks, and student programs has meant that there are far more engineers familiar with AWS technology than with any other platform.[2012] Several market participants listed the availability of AWS-trained engineers as a reason for selecting AWS over other cloud vendors and as a barrier for switching platforms or attempting to multi-cloud.[2013]

High switching costs reinforce Amazon's dominance in the cloud market.[2014] A cloud-based application company interviewed by Subcommittee staff explained these costs:

> We've looked at other services (Google, Microsoft, Oracle) but we've relied on AWS for so long that we couldn't just flip a switch, and we've run down a lot of engineering problems with AWS . . . There are other providers we could go to, but it would take

---

[2007] *See infra* Section IV.

[2008] Production of Google, to H. Comm. on the Judiciary, GOOG-HJC-04260401 (Aug. 25, 2016) (on file with Comm.).

[2009] *AWS Marketplace*, AMAZON WEB SERVICES, https://aws.amazon.com/marketplace (last visited Sept. 30, 2020).

[2010] CEO Hearing at 6 (response to Questions for the Record of Jeff Bezos, CEO, Amazon.com, Inc.).

[2011] *AWS Marketplace*, AMAZON WEB SERVICES, https://aws.amazon.com/marketplace(last visited Sept. 30, 2020); Brad Lyman, *See What's New for AWS Marketplace Sellers*, AWS PARTNER NETWORK BLOG (Mar. 9, 2018), https://aws.amazon.com/blogs/apn/see-whats-new-for-aws-marketplace-sellers.

[2012] Interview with Source 736 (June 10, 2020).

[2013] Interview with Source 126 (June 29, 2020).

[2014] *See infra* Section IV.

work. We could also build some functionality internally, but that would also take a lot of work.[2015]

For cloud-based application developers, whose entire product is dependent on AWS, the fears of lock-in are even greater. One marketplace participant said:

"[A]ny transition of the cloud services currently provided by AWS to another cloud service provider would be difficult to implement and would cause us to incur significant time and expense and could disrupt or degrade our ability to deliver our products and services. Our business relies on the availability of our services for [users] and advertisers.[2016]

Amazon has also taken steps to lock-in its position, including through long-term contracts, volume minimums, and the use of fees to move data to other cloud providers, which are also known as egress fees. In submissions to the Subcommittee, numerous market participants noted that AWS often seeks multi-year contracts during negotiations.[2017] These contracts are also commonplace in companies' investor statements. For example, according to Lyft's 2020 investor filing, they agreed to pay "an aggregate of at least $300 million between January 2019 and December 2021 on AWS services."[2018] According to Slack's investor filling, in 2018 it committed to a five-year contract with minimum annual commitments of $50 million.[2019]

Subcommittee staff also uncovered evidence that Amazon sometimes requires a volume agreement when a large company seeks to negotiate lower prices. In an internal email discussion on this topic, a senior executive at AWS wrote that Amazon has "a private rate card which has a commit level for bandwidth pricing. Rates at or above the private rate card are pre-approved. Anything below that has to be first approved by me and then the price goes to service GM."[2020]

When an Amazon customer chooses to move data to another cloud provider, they are charged an egress fee. Market participants told Subcommittee staff that they view these fees less as a cost for

---

[2015] Interview with Source 111 (Apr. 6, 2020).

[2016] Submission from Source 32, to H. Comm. on the Judiciary, Source 32-000009 (Oct. 29, 2019) (on file with Comm.).

[2017] *Id.* at Source 32-000017.

[2018] Lyft, Annual Report (Form 10-K) 7 (Feb. 28, 2020), https://investor.lyft.com/static-files/981ad93a-5d97-4f7f-8937-5682ca83cba7.

[2019] Slack, Registration Statement (Form S-1) 90 (Apr. 26, 2019), http://d18rn0p25nwr6d.cloudfront.net/CIK-0001764925/b6da15ae-25c5-4447-ba38-c287bf11e624.pdf.

[2020] Production of Amazon, to H. Comm. on the Judiciary, AMAZON-HJC-00206893 (May 11, 2017) (on file with Comm.).

Amazon to transport data and more as friction imposed by Amazon for switching providers, noting that Amazon charges egress fees even when data is staying locally within the same data center.[2021]

The COVID-19 pandemic has underscored the centrality of cloud computing to the functioning of an increasing swath of businesses—highlighting how cloud services have come to resemble critical infrastructure. Reporting by *The Information* in April 2020 discussed how the major cloud providers are facing requests from many customers for financial relief, while the demand for cloud computing has increased.[2022] As this reporting noted, "AWS has been the least willing to offer flexible terms on customer bills, according to numerous customers. That stands in contrast to Microsoft and Google which have shown some flexibility, partners say."[2023]

c. Merger Activity

Amazon has acquired a significant number of cloud computing firms over the past decade. Although a full discussion of this activity is beyond the scope of this Report, Amazon's acquisition activity in the cloud market appears to be part of a broader trend among dominant cloud providers to make serial acquisitions, any one of which may seem insignificant but which collectively serve to solidify and expand their dominance.[2024] In some instances AWS has acquired cloud technologies that previously integrated with multiple clouds, only for AWS to make it an AWS-specific product after acquisition, foreclosing competitors and increasing consumers' switching costs.[2025]

d. Competitive Significance of AWS to Amazon's Other Lines of Business

Amazon's dual role as a dominant provider of cloud infrastructure and as a dominant firm in other markets creates a conflict of interest that Amazon has the incentive and ability to exploit.

Amazon's dominance in cloud computing alongside its integration across an array of businesses—online retail, music and video, and smart home devices—creates a core conflict of interest. Cloud computing customers like Netflix and Target are in the position of competing with Amazon while also relying on AWS. Firms in their position effectively have to choose between switching to one of the alternative cloud infrastructure providers or funding their primary

---

[2021] Interview with Source 170 (May 27, 2020).

[2022] Kevin McLaughlin & Amir Efrati, *AWS Holds the Line on Cloud Bills as Customers Ask for Relief*, THE INFO. (Apr. 17, 2020) https://www.theinformation.com/articles/aws-holds-the-line-on-cloud-bills-as-customers-ask-for-relief.

[2023] *Id.*

[2024] *See infra* Section IV.

[2025] Ron Miller, *Update: Amazon Has Acquired Israeli Disaster Recovery Service CloudEndure for Around $200M*, TECHCRUNCH (Jan. 8, 2019), https://techcrunch.com/2019/01/08/amazon-reportedly-acquired-israeli-disaster-recovery-service-cloudendure-for-around-200m/. *See also CloudEndure deprecation.* GOOGLE CLOUD, https://cloud.google.com/compute/docs/deprecations/cloudendure (last visited Oct. 4, 2020).

competitor.[2026] One venture capitalist described Amazon as "useful but dangerous" because "it's hard to predict what Amazon wants to get into . . . you can't know."[2027] Similarly, a business-to-business application developer told Subcommittee staff that they felt pressure to switch their entire product to Microsoft Azure because of its client's concerns with Amazon's anticompetitive conduct in the online retail sector.[2028]

Amazon acknowledges that cloud customers that are also its competitors are wary of using AWS. One internal document had guidance on how to discuss the issue with customers. An FAQ sheet listed: "What do you say to customers who are worried that using AWS services will support Amazon's competitive growth in the retail space?" Amazon's sample answer stated, "How can you afford to not compete with the best possible tools in such a tough market like retail?"[2029]

Subcommittee staff also spoke with market participants that expressed concern about how this conflict of interest shapes Amazon's behavior in its other lines of business. For example, in 2015 Amazon kicked Google Chromecast and Apple TV—direct competitors with the Amazon Fire Stick and Fire TV cube—out of its retail store.[2030] AWS is also positioned to use customer and seller data from one line of business to inform decisions in other lines of business, analogous to its conduct in Amazon Retail. At least one market participant who spoke with Subcommittee staff had evidence that AWS engaged in this cross-business data sharing.[2031] In another internal document with guidance for staff on "AWS Competitive Messaging," employees were advised to offer the following response:

Q.   Walmart is warning its suppliers that they don't want them to be running on
     AWS because they don't want Amazon.com, a competitor of Walmart's, to have
     access to their data. How are you addressing that?

A: Even though Amazon's consumer business has no access to any customer data
     in AWS, I can understand why Walmart would be paranoid in making sure that

---

[2026] Christina Farr & Ari Levy, *Target Is Plotting a Big Move Away From AWS As Amazon Takes Over Retail*, CNBC (Aug. 29, 2017), https://www.cnbc.com/2017/08/29/target-is-moving-away-from-aws-after-amazon-bought-whole-foods.html); *See also Netflix on AWS,* AMAZON WEB SERVICE, https://aws.amazon.com/solutions/case-studies/netflix/ (last visited Sept. 30, 2020).

[2027] Interview with Source 146 (May 28, 2020).

[2028] Interview with Source 126 (June 29, 2020).

[2029] Production of Amazon, to H. Comm. on the Judiciary, AMAZON-HJC-00216210 (Aug. 24, 2018) (on file with Comm.).

[2030] Barb Darrow, *Why Cloud Users Should Care That Amazon Just Kicked Apple TV to the Curb*, FORTUNE (Oct. 2, 2015), http://fortune.com/2015/10/02/why-aws-users-should-care-that-amazon-nixed-apple-tv/.

[2031] Interview with Source 126 (June 29, 2020).

their data is private. So, I think it's a pretty reasonable expectation for them to ask their suppliers to encrypt that data in AWS.[2032]

Engineers and market participants have also raised concerns that AWS employees may have access to Amazon's Key Management Services (KMS), which customers can use to store encryption keys.[2033] If an employee were able to access a customer's encryption keys, they could potentially see the contents of a customer's application, including proprietary code, business transactions, and data on their user's. In response to questions from the Subcommittee, Amazon said that the company's "policies prohibit employees from accessing and reading customer keys in KMS. KMS is designed such that customer keys in the service cannot be retrieved in plain text (unencrypted) form by anybody, including AWS employees."[2034] Even if AWS employees can never access the content of their customers applications, AWS tracks a host of commercially sensitive metrics, including any changes in demand for storage and compute services, the components of their application's architecture, the requests to a specific database per second, database size, and the types of requests.[2035] One industry expert told Subcommittee staff:

> They don't need to see the encrypted content of a movie to see that there are a ton of requests to particular data. If Netflix announced five new movies this weekend and there's a ton of data to five new objects. So, you don't need all the information to know what's happening.[2036]

Finally, AWS provides Amazon with unparalleled insights into the trajectory of startups using its services, information that it can use to guide acquisitions and to replicate promising technology. Data that AWS collects on cloud computing customers can provide unique business intelligence, information that investors, other firms, and entrepreneurs lack.

A report from 2011 published in *Reuters,* profiling the AWS Start-up Challenge, describes cases where AWS has used insights gleaned from its cloud computing service to inform its venture capital investment decisions.[2037] Adam Selipsky, then Vice President of AWS, told *Reuters*, "AWS has great relationships with many young companies and there have been cases where we've been able to

---

[2032] Production of Amazon, to H. Comm. on the Judiciary, AMAZON-HJC-00216213 (Aug. 24, 2018) (on file with Comm.).

[2033] Interview with Source 146 (May 28, 2020).

[2034] CEO Hearing at 17 (response to Questions for the Record of Jeff Bezos, CEO, Amazon.com, Inc.).

[2035] Interview with Source 146 (May 28, 2020); Innovation and Entrepreneurship Hearing at 44 (response to Questions for the Record of Nate Sutton, Assoc. Gen. Counsel, Competition, Amazon.com, Inc.).

[2036] Interview with Source 146 (May 28, 2020).

[2037] Alistair Barr, *Amazon Finds Startup Investments in the 'Cloud,'* REUTERS (Nov. 9, 2011), http://www.reuters.com/article/amazon-cloud-idUSN1E7A727Q20111109.

help with investment opportunities."[2038] Today, one way Amazon leverages AWS is through relationships with startups. The AWS Activate program provides startups with free credits, technical support, and training.[2039]

Subcommittee staff interviewed a startup and beneficiary of AWS Activate that had engaged in partnership conversations with Amazon. During these discussions, the startup shared information about how its product was built with AWS. Within a few years, the startup learned that Amazon had introduced a replica product. This company said that Amazon "had so many incentives. Rate cuts, and free services. Not having a lot of resources, it's hard to turn that down. But fast forward, we basically helped them build their offering that they copied from us."[2040]

As part of its investigation, the Subcommittee asked Amazon whether it uses or has ever used AWS usage patterns or data to inform its investment decisions. Amazon responded:

> AWS uses data on individual customers' use of AWS to provide or improve the AWS services and grow the business relationship with that customer. This data may inform AWS's decisions about how AWS invests in infrastructure, such as data centers, edge networks, hardware, and related software solutions in order improve the customer experience.[2041]

Amazon's response leaves unclear whether it would view it appropriate to use a firm's AWS data to develop products competing with that firm, so long as Amazon could identify some benefit to the broader "customer experience."

Prior to 2017, Amazon also required that AWS customers agree "not to assert any intellectual property claim against any AWS service used by that customer."[2042] Amazon removed that condition from the AWS online customer agreement on June 28, 2017.[2043]

In addition to creating a significant information advantage for Amazon, AWS may also reinforce its market power in other ways. Because startups often rely heavily on AWS, Amazon is a natural choice when pursuing a sale or seeking investment. In an internal email produced to the Subcommittee, Peter Krawiec, Amazon's Vice President of Worldwide Corporate Development, recapped a meeting with a recently acquired company, noting that the company was, "[s]uper excited

---

[2038] *Id.*

[2039] *AWS Activate*, AMAZON WEB SERVICES, https://aws.amazon.com/activate/ (last visited Sept. 30, 2020).

[2040] Interview with Source 126 (June 29, 2020).

[2041] Innovation and Entrepreneurship Hearing at 45 (response to Questions for the Record of Nate Sutton, Assoc. Gen. Counsel, Competition, Amazon.com, Inc.).

[2042] *Id.* at 43.

[2043] *Id.* at 42.

about Amazon and relieved that Walmart will not be the buyer. Engineering team thrilled that they won't have to unplug from AWS under a Walmart world."[2044]

e. Conduct

The leading position AWS enjoys in the market traces in part to its first-mover advantage, network effects, and steep investments that the company made in building out the physical infrastructure on which cloud resides. However, AWS has also engaged in a series of business practices designed to maintain its market dominance at the expense of choice and innovation. Through a combination of self-preferencing, misappropriation, and degradation of interoperability, Amazon has sought to eliminate cross-platform products with Amazon-only products. Amazon's conduct has already led several open-source projects to become more closed, a move driven by a need for protection from Amazon's misappropriation. If unchecked, Amazon's tactics over the long-term risk solidifying lock-in and diminishing the incentive to invest. Because cloud is the core infrastructure on which the digital economy runs, ensuring its openness and competitiveness is paramount.

i. Misappropriation of Data

As described earlier in this Report, cloud platform vendors compete by expanding their first-party cloud offerings, such as those offered through the AWS Management Console.[2045] Market participants note that one way AWS has expanded its offerings is by creating proprietary versions of products that have been developed under open-source licenses.[2046]

Open-source licenses allow software to be freely used, modified, and shared.[2047] Open-source software can run on any infrastructure, local machine, server room, or on the cloud, reducing lock-in to a specific hardware vendor.[2048] Companies based on open-source software bring in revenue by selling additional features under proprietary licenses or services.[2049] In recent years, open-source development has been a leading model for software development, attracting significant venture capital investment.[2050]

[2044] Production of Amazon, to H. Comm. on the Judiciary, AMAZON-HJC-00225832 (June 15, 2018) (on file with Comm.).

[2045] *See infra* Section IV.

[2046] Interview with Source 152 (Apr. 15, 2020).

[2047] *Open Source Licenses by Category*, OPEN SOURCE INITIATIVE, https://opensource.org/licenses/category (last visited Sept. 30, 2020).

[2048] Nicholas Loulloudes et al., *Enabling Interoperable Cloud Application Management Through an Open Source Ecosystem*, 19 IEEE INTERNET COMPUTING, 54 (2015), https://ieeexplore.ieee.org/document/7111887.

[2049] Max Schireson & Dharmesh Thakker, *The Money in Open-Source Software*, TECHCRUNCH (Feb. 9, 2016), https://techcrunch.com/2016/02/09/the-money-in-open-source-software/.

[2050] Interview with Source 152 (Apr. 15, 2020).

Market participants note that the rise of cloud computing services has led to a shift in the way open-source software is delivered and used. Many open-source software companies allowed engineers to download free versions of their software from their website, often without collecting any personal data about their users. As engineers outgrew the functionality of the free version, they would purchase more powerful versions.[2051] As cloud computing grew in popularity, open-source software vendors began offering versions of their software on the AWS Marketplace, where application developers could easily integrate the software. Market participants explain that AWS was able to use the data collected on their customers, including usage metrics, to learn which third-party software was performing well and ultimately to create their own proprietary version offered as a managed service. Creating a "knock-off" version of software was particularly easy when the product was using an open-source license, which provides more visibility to the underlying code.[2052]

In interviews with Subcommittee staff, market participants repeatedly said that AWS relied on innovations from open-source software communities to gain dominance. A venture capitalist told Subcommittee staff that "open-source is critical for AWS getting market power. They're standing on the shoulders of giants and they're not paying the giants."[2053] A long-time cloud vendor likewise said that "Amazon never built a database, never built cloud services, never built any of their AWS offerings. They took open source and offered it out on cloud. At the time that was innovative."[2054]

AWS has developed many of its offerings using this practice and has created products that are only accessible as first-party offerings through the AWS Management Console.[2055] An example frequently cited by market participants is Amazon Elasticsearch Service (AESS), a tool for searching and analyzing data, and a first-party product listed on the AWS Management Console.[2056] According to public reporting and interviews with market participants, this product is a copy of Elastic's, Elasticsearch open-source product that was available for purchase on the AWS Marketplace.[2057] According to public reporting, within a year of introducing the product, Amazon was generating more money from its replica of Elasticsearch than Elasticsearch itself was generating. One key advantage that Amazon's "knock-off" had was that Amazon had given it superior placement in AWS

[2051] *Id.*

[2052] *Id.*

[2053] Interview with Source 146 (May 28, 2020).

[2054] Interview with Source 31 (May 27, 2020).

[2055] *What Is the AWS Management Console*, AMAZON WEB SERVICES, https://docs.aws.amazon.com/awsconsolehelpdocs/latest/gsg/getting-started.html#learn-whats-new (last visited Sept. 30, 2020).

[2056] Daisuke Wakabayashi, *Prime Leverage: How Amazon Wields Power in the Technology World*, N.Y. TIMES (Dec. 16, 2019), https://www.nytimes.com/2019/12/15/technology/amazon-aws-cloud-competition.html. *See also* Interview with Source 152 (Apr. 15, 2020).

[2057] *Id.*

Management Console.[2058] Additionally, as described in the *Elasticsearch vs Amazon* case, AWS can name their open-source "knock-off" products in a way that can mislead customers into believing that the "knock-off" product is sponsored by the open-source software vendor.[2059]

The Subcommittee's investigation uncovered evidence relating to numerous instances in which Amazon has offered proprietary managed services based on knock-offs of open-source code. One open-source market participant interviewed by Subcommittee staff said that because of this conduct, the benefits of open source "weren't accruing to [the] open-source community. People were feeling, we develop all this work and then some large company comes and monetizes that."[2060] MongoDB, a document-based database, has similarly commented that "once an open source project becomes interesting, it is too easy for large cloud vendors to capture all the value but contribute nothing back to the community."[2061]

When the Subcommittee inquired about this practice, Amazon responded, that "Projects where AWS has developed distributions on top of OSS [open-source software], like Open Distro for Elasticsearch and Amazon Corretto, add to, not supplant, the set of capabilities provided by the upstream open-source projects… it allows them to move between deploying OSS themselves and using managed services for open-source."[2062] Market participants told Subcommittee staff, however, that in the instances when AWS creates a "knock-off" version of an open-source software by adding "additional developments," those additional developments often only work with AWS infrastructure and are no-longer cross-platform—heightening the risk of lock-in.[2063] As one third-party explains, "So, the earlier benefits of open-source go out the window as Amazon takes over each of these product areas."[2064]

For example, while MongoDB is an open-source document-based database project, Amazon offers a proprietary product called Amazon DocumentDB. According to AWS, DocumentDB implements the open-source MongoDB API and is designed to "emulate the responses that a MongoDB client expects from a MongoDB server."[2065] When a cloud customer chooses to build an

[2058] *Id.*

[2059] Complaint at 2, Elasticsearch, Inc. v. Amazon.com, Inc., No. 4:19-cv-06158 (N.D. Cal. Sept. 27, 2019), http://ipcasefilings.com/wp-content/uploads/2019/10/ElasticSearch_Amazon.pdf.

[2060] Interview with Source 144 (Apr. 17, 2020).

[2061] *Server Side Public License FAQ*, MONGODB, https://www.mongodb.com/licensing/server-side-public-license/faq (last visited Sept. 30, 2020).

[2062] CEO Hearing at 6 (response to Questions for the Record of Jeff Bezos, CEO, Amazon.com, Inc.).

[2063] Interview with Source 152 (Sept. 24, 2020).

[2064] *Id.*

[2065] Jeff Barr, *New-Amazon DocumentDB (with MongoDB Compatibility): Fast, Scalable, and Highly Available*, AMAZON WEB SERVICES: AWS NEWS BLOG (Jan. 9, 2019), https://aws.amazon.com/blogs/aws/new-amazon-documentdb-with-mongodb-compatibility-fast-scalable-and-highly-available/.

application using DocumentDB they are tied to AWS's infrastructure. If they ever wanted to switch to another provider they would have to extensively re-engineer their product in another software, whereas, had they built their application using MongoDB—on AWS or any other cloud provider's infrastructure—their applications could move to other platforms.[2066]

ii. Harms to Innovation

Amazon's practice of offering managed service versions of open-source software has prompted open-source software companies to make defensive changes, such as closing off advanced features and changing their open-source license to be less permissive.[2067] One open-source vendor that recently started offering premium closed-sourced features said they were "paranoid" in light of Amazon cloning Elastic's features, noting that if this had happened to them they "would not have a business."[2068] Amazon's conduct has also reduced the availability of features in open-source software. Confluent,[2069] Redis Labs,[2070] and CochroachDB,[2071] along with several other open-source software vendors, have made similar license and business model changes, reducing the level of access to their software.[2072]

Market participants believe these changes significantly undermine innovation. Several noted that more closed-off licenses will result in fewer free, open-source features available to startups building prototypes and research labs that cannot afford access to paid features.[2073] Subcommittee staff also spoke with cloud computing customers in the public sector who worry about the changes and ambiguity in open-source licenses. One cloud computing customer told Subcommittee staff that three pieces of open-source software that they use underwent license changes in the last year and that, due to strict "open source only" policies, they are "now stuck using older versions of the software [from] before the license change which requires additional work to improve the code base, implement the same functionality in-house or switch to a competitive product."[2074]

[2066] Interview with Source 152 (Sept. 24, 2020).

[2067] *Open Source Licenses by Category*, OPEN SOURCE INITIATIVE, https://opensource.org/faq#permissive (last visited Sept. 30, 2020) ("A 'permissive' license is simply a non-copyleft Open source license – one that guarantees the freedoms to use, modify, and redistribute, but that permits proprietary derivative works.")

[2068] Interview with Source 144 (Apr. 17, 2020).

[2069] *Confluent Community License FAQ*, CONFLUENT, https://www.confluent.io/confluent-community-license-faq/ (last visited Sept. 30, 2020).

[2070] Frederic Lardinois, *Redis Labs Changes Its Open-Source License – Again*, TECHCRUNCH (Feb. 21, 2019), https://techcrunch.com/2019/02/21/redis-labs-changes-its-open-source-license-again/.

[2071] Tom Krazit, *Another Open-Source Database Company Will Tighten Its Licensing Strategy, Wary of Amazon Web Services*, GEEKWIRE (Jun. 4, 2019), https://www.geekwire.com/2019/another-open-source-database-company-will-tighten-licensing-strategy-wary-amazon-web-services/.

[2072] Interview with Source 152 (Apr. 15, 2020).

[2073] Interview with Source 146 (May 28, 2020).

[2074] Interview with Source 49 (May 20, 2020).

iii. Self-Preferencing

According to market participants, once a product—based on open source or otherwise—is available in the AWS Management Console, it becomes an easier choice for existing AWS customers relative to purchasing a managed service from a third-party vendor or self-managing open-source software. In an interview with Subcommittee staff , one startup said they purchased software services through the AWS Management Console as opposed to identical or nearly identical software from a third-party vendor because they were a small company and "instead of us managing everything, it was hit a button . . . they are all in one, it was easier."[2075] As with all cloud services offered through the AWS Management Console, customers benefit from a single sign-on with billing information already in place.[2076]

Market participants also note that Amazon makes certain functionality available to its first-party products that it doesn't make available to the companies managing the original version of the open-source software.[2077] For example, AWS services can run inside Amazon's Virtual Private Could (Amazon VPC) offering, which allows users to provision an "isolated section of the AWS Cloud," but third-party services cannot do so.[2078]

While Amazon failed to provide the Subcommittee with financial data identifying what AWS makes in revenue from individual cloud offerings, many marketplace participants believe that AWS makes more from managed versions of open-source software than the third-party vendors and managers of the software. In 2019, *The New York Times* reported that the Chief Executive of MariaDB, an open-source relational database company, estimated that "Amazon made five time more revenue from running MariaDB software than his company generated from all of its businesses."[2079] Market participants suggest this multiple of difference in income is likely for other AWS products based on open-source projects.[2080]

[2075] Interview with Source 126 (June 29, 2020).

[2076] Interview with Source 146 (May 28, 2020).

[2077] Interview with Source 152 (Sept. 24, 2020).

[2078] *Amazon Virtual Private Cloud*, AMAZON WEB SERVICES, https://aws.amazon.com/vpc/ (last visited Sept. 30, 2020).

[2079] Daisuke Wakabayashi, *Prime Leverage, How Amazon Wields Power in the Technology World,* N.Y. TIMES (Dec. 16, 2019), https://www.nytimes.com/2019/12/15/technology/amazon-aws-cloud-competition.html.

[2080] Interview with Source 146 (May 28, 2020).

D. Apple

1. Overview

Apple was incorporated in 1977, and is headquartered in Cupertino, California.[2081] Apple was an early pioneer in designing and marketing mass-produced personal computers.[2082] Today, the company "designs, manufacturers, and markets smartphones, personal computers, tablets, wearables, and accessories, and sells a variety of related services."[2083] Apple's hardware products include the iPhone, iPad, Mac, Apple TV, and AirPods; its Services business segment includes the App Store, iCloud, AppleCare, Apple Arcade, Apple Music, Apple TV+, and other services and software applications.[2084] Apple tightly integrates its services and software applications with its products to ensure a seamless experience for consumers.[2085]

[2081] Apple Inc., Annual Report (Form 10-K) 1 (Sept. 28, 2019), https://s2.q4cdn.com/470004039/files/doc_financials/2019/ar/_10-K-2019-(As-Filed).pdf.

[2082] *See* Angelique Richardson & Ellen Terrell, *Apple Computer, Inc.*, LIB. OF CONGRESS (Apr. 2008), https://www.loc.gov/rr/business/businesshistory/April/apple.html.

[2083] Apple Inc., Annual Report (Form 10-K) 1 (Sept. 28, 2019), https://s2.q4cdn.com/470004039/files/doc_financials/2019/ar/_10-K-2019-(As-Filed).pdf.

[2084] *Id.* at 1–2.

[2085] *See* Apple, *Apple: Distinctive Products with a Seamless, Integrated User Experience* 1 (July 13, 2020) (on file with Comm.)

Apple's Ecosystem: Hardware, Software Infrastructure, Apple & Third-Party Apps[2086]

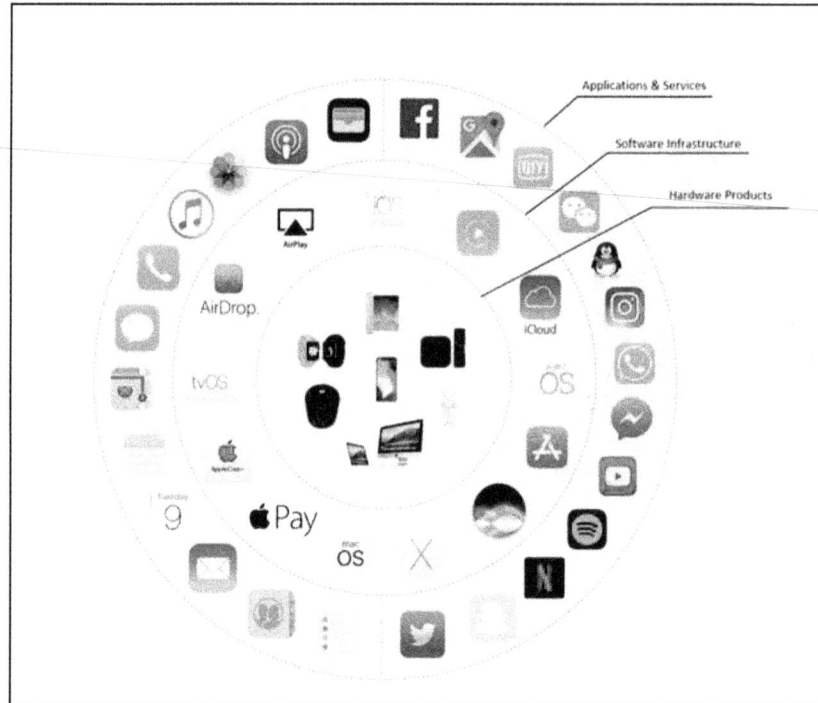

Apple reports financial information for two business categories: Products and Services.[2087] For fiscal year 2019, Apple reported total revenue of approximately $260 billion, down 2% from 2018, but up nearly 13.5% from 2017.[2088] Apple's total margins were 37.8%, with profits of $98.3 billion.[2089] As of September 2020, Apple is the most valuable public company in the world, and in August 2020 became the first publicly traded U.S. firm to be valued at $2 trillion.[2090] Apple's stock rose by 60% in the first 8 months of 2020.[2091]

[2086] *Are domestic investors missing out?*, SWELL, (June 22, 2018), https://swellasset.com.au/2018/06/domestic-investors-missing/.

[2087] Apple Inc., Annual Report (Form 10-K) 19 (Sept. 28, 2019), https://s2.q4cdn.com/470004039/files/doc_financials/2019/ar/_10-K-2019-(As-Filed).pdf.

[2088] *Id.* at 17–19; *see also Apple's 1 Crazy Number Key to $800 Billion in Stock Growth*, FORBES (July 13, 2020), https://www.forbes.com/sites/greatspeculations/2020/07/13/how-did-apple-add-800-billion-in-value-over-3-years/#5b9250df20f8.

[2089] *Id. at* 21, 29.

[2090] Jessica Bursztynsky, *Apple becomes first U.S. company to reach a $2 trillion market cap*, CNBC (Aug. 19, 2020), https://www.cnbc.com/2020/08/19/apple-reaches-2-trillion-market-cap.html.

[2091] Kifi Leswing, *Apple's $2 trillion value is proof that Tim Cook's services plan worked*, CNBC (Aug. 19, 2020), https://www.cnbc.com/2020/08/19/apples-2-trillion-value-proof-that-tim-cooks-services-plan-worked.html.

Apple is the leading smartphone vendor in the U.S., accounting for approximately 45% of the domestic market,[2092] with more than 100 million iPhone users worldwide.[2093] Apple's iOS is also one of two dominant mobile operating systems—the other operating system, Android, is discussed elsewhere in this Report. iOS runs on more than half of U.S. smartphones and tablets.[2094] Globally, Apple accounts for less than 20% of the smartphone market, and roughly 25% of smartphones and tablets run on iOS worldwide.[2095] In 2018, Apple sold its 2 billionth iOS device, and is projected to sell its 2 billionth iPhone by 2021.[2096]

Apple also owns and operates the App Store for iOS devices. Launched in 2008, Apple highlights that the App Store allows app developers to reach consumers in 155 countries, and that more than 27 million app developers have published millions of apps in the App Store. Apple credits the App Store with creating 1.5 million jobs in the United States, and more than $120 billion in worldwide revenue for app developers.[2097] According to Apple, the App Store ecosystem, including direct sales of apps, sales of goods and services inside of apps, and in-app advertising facilitated more than $138 billion in economic activity in the U.S. last year.[2098]

[2092] *See* S. O'Dea, *Manufacturers' market share of smartphone sales in the United States from 2016 to 2020*, STATISTA (Sept. 3, 2020), https://www.statista.com/statistics/620805/smartphone-sales-market-share-in-the-us-by-vendor/; S. O'Dea, *Manufacturers' market share of smartphone subscribers in the United States from 2013 and 2019, by month**, STATISTA (June 9, 2020), https://www.statista.com/statistics/273697/market-share-held-by-the-leading-smartphone-manufacturers-oem-in-the-us/; *US Smartphone Market Share: By Quarter*, COUNTERPOINT RESEARCH (Aug. 17, 2020), https://www.counterpointresearch.com/us-market-smartphone-share/; S. O'Dea, *Share of smartphone users that use an Apple iPhone in the United States from 2014 to 2021*, STATISTA (Sept. 10, 2020), https://www.statista.com/statistics/236550/percentage-of-us-population-that-own-a-iphone-smartphone/.

[2093] S. O'Dea, *Share of smartphone users that use an Apple iPhone in the United States from 2014 to 2021*, STATISTA (Sept. 10, 2020), https://www.statista.com/statistics/236550/percentage-of-us-population-that-own-a-iphone-smartphone/.

[2094] *See* S. O'Dea, *Subscriber share held by smartphone operating systems in the United States from 2012 to 2020*, STATISTA (Aug. 17, 2020), https://www.statista.com/statistics/266572/market-share-held-by-smartphone-platforms-in-the-united-states/; *Mobile Operating System Market Share United States of America Aug. 2019 – Aug. 2020*, GLOBALSTATS (on file with Comm).

[2095] *See Global Smartphone Market Share: By Quarter*, COUNTERPOINT RESEARCH, (Aug. 18, 2020), https://www.counterpointresearch.com/global-smartphone-share/; *Mobile Operating System Market Share Worldwide Aug. 2019 – Aug. 2020*, GLOBALSTATS (on file with Comm).

[2096] Malcolm Owen, *How Apple has hit 2 billion iOS devices sold, and when it will hit 2 billion iPhones*, APPLE INSIDER (Sept. 13, 2018), https://appleinsider.com/articles/18/09/13/how-apple-has-hit-2-billion-ios-devices-sold-and-when-it-will-hit-2-billion-iphones.

[2097] *See* Letter from Kyle Andeer, Vice Pres. Legal & Chief Compliance Officer, Apple Inc., to Hon. Jerrold Nadler, Chairman, H. Comm. on the Judiciary, Hon. Doug Collins, Ranking Member, H. Comm. on the Judiciary, Hon. David N. Cicilline, Chairman, Subcomm. on Antitrust, Commercial and Admin. Law of the H. Comm. on the Judiciary, Hon. F. James Sensenbrenner, Ranking Member, Subcomm. on Antitrust, Commercial and Admin. Law of the H. Comm. on the Judiciary, 2 (Oct. 14, 2019) (on file with Comm.); Letter from Kyle Andeer, Vice Pres., Corp. Law and Chief Compliance Officer, Apple Inc., to Hon. Jerrold Nader, Chairman, H. Comm. on the Judiciary, Hon. Jim Jordan, Ranking Member, H. Comm. on the Judiciary, Hon. David N. Cicilline, Chairman, Subcomm. on Antitrust, Commercial and Admin. Law of the H. Comm. on the Judiciary, Hon. F. James Sensenbrenner, Ranking Member, Subcomm. on Antitrust, Commercial and Admin. Law of the H. Comm. on the Judiciary, 3 (Sept. 21, 2020) (on file with Comm.).

[2098] Letter from Kyle Andeer, Vice Pres., Corp. Law and Chief Compliance Officer, Apple Inc., to Hon. Jerrold Nader, Chairman, H. Comm. on the Judiciary, Hon. Jim Jordan, Ranking Member, H. Comm. on the Judiciary, Hon. David N. Cicilline, Chairman, Subcomm. on Antitrust, Commercial and Admin. Law of the H. Comm. on the Judiciary, Hon. F.

In addition to the Subcommittee's investigation of Apple's market power and conduct, federal antitrust authorities are investigating it for potential violations of the U.S. antitrust laws. In June 2019, *The New York Times* and the *Wall Street Journal* reported that the Justice Department had opened investigations into potential violations of the antitrust laws by Apple.[2099] Apple is also under investigation by multiple international competition authorities for antitrust violations and anticompetitive practices,[2100] as well as private antitrust lawsuits in the U.S.[2101]

Previously, the Justice Department and Attorneys General of 33 states sued Apple for orchestrating a conspiracy to fix prices in the eBooks market in 2012.[2102] Apple was found to have violated state and federal antitrust law and forced to pay $450 million.[2103] In 2010, Apple settled an antitrust complaint with the Department of Justice that it conspired with several other technology

---

James Sensenbrenner, Ranking Member, Subcomm. on Antitrust, Commercial and Admin. Law of the H. Comm. on the Judiciary, 2 (Sept. 21, 2020) (on file with the Subcomm.) (citing JONATHAN BORCK ET AL., AG ANALYSIS GRP., HOW LARGE IS THE APPLE APP STORE ECOSYSTEM: A GLOBAL PERSPECTIVE FOR 2019, 4 (2020), https://www.apple.com/newsroom/pdfs/app-store-study-2019.pdf).

[2099] *See* Celia Kang et al., *Antitrust Troubles Snowball for Tech Giants as Lawmakers Join In*, N.Y. TIMES (June 3, 2019), https://www.nytimes.com/2019/06/03/technology/facebook-ftc-antitrust.html; Brent Kendall & John McKinnon, *Congress, Enforcement Agencies Target Tech*, WALL ST. J. (June 3, 2019), https://www.wsj.com/articles/ftc-to-examine-how-facebook-s-practices-affect-digital-competition-11559576731.

[2100] *See e.g.*, Press Release, Eur. Comm'n, Antitrust: Commission opens investigation into Apple practices regarding Apple Pay (June 16, 2020), https://ec.europa.eu/commission/presscorner/detail/en/ip_20_1075; Foo Yun Chee, *Apple in Dutch Antitrust Spotlight for Allegedly Promoting Own Apps*, REUTERS (Apr. 11, 2019), https://www.reuters.com/article/us-apple-antitrust-netherlands/apple-in-dutch-antitrust-spotlight-for-allegedly-promoting-own-apps-idUSKCN1RN215; *Italy Antitrust Opens Inquiry into Google, Apple, Dropbox on Cloud Computing*, REUTERS (Sept. 7, 2020), https://www.reuters.com/article/us-google-italy-antitrust/italy-antitrust-opens-inquiry-into-google-apple-dropbox-on-cloud-computing-idUSKBN25Y0YM; Tim Hardwick, *Apple and Amazon Under Investigation By Italian Watchdog for Alleged Price Fixing*, APPLE INSIDER (July 22, 2020), https://www.macrumors.com/2020/07/22/apple-amazon-italy-alleged-price-fixing/.

[2101] *See e.g.*, Nick Statt, *Epic Games is suing Apple*, THE VERGE (Aug. 13, 2020), https://www.theverge.com/2020/8/13/21367963/epic-fortnite-legal-complaint-apple-ios-app-store-removal-injunctive-relief; Reed Albergotti, *Apple suppressed competitors in its App Store – until it got caught, a lawsuit alleges*, WASH. POST (Dec. 20, 2019), https://www.washingtonpost.com/technology/2019/12/20/apple-suppressed-competitors-its-app-store-until-it-got-caught-lawsuit-alleges/; Bob Van Voris and Peter Blumberg, *Apple App Developers Jump on Silicon Valley Antitrust Bandwagon*, BLOOMBERG (June 4, 2019), https://www.bloomberg.com/news/articles/2019-06-04/apple-inc-sued-by-app-developers-claiming-antitrust-violations; David G. Savage and Suhauna Hussain, *Supreme Court Rules Apple can face antitrust suits from iPhone owners over App Store sales*, L.A. TIMES (May 13, 2019), https://www.latimes.com/politics/la-na-pol-supreme-court-apple-smart-phone-20190513-story.html.

[2102] *See* Complaint, U.S. v. Apple Inc., No. 12-02826-UA (S.D.N.Y. 2012).

[2103] *See* U.S. v. Apple Inc., 952 F.Supp.2d 638 (S.D.N.Y. 2013), *aff'd by* U.S. v. Apple Inc., 791 F.3d 209 (2d Cir. 2015); Dawn Chmielewski, *Apple to Pay $450 Million E-Book Settlement After Supreme Court Waves Off Case*, RECODE (Mar. 7, 2016), https://www.vox.com/2016/3/7/11586748/apple-to-pay-450-million-e-book-settlement-after-supreme-court-waves; *see also* August 27, 2013 Hr'g Tr. at 17:1-6, U.S. v. Apple Inc. , No. 12-cv-2826 (S.D.N.Y 2012) ("The record at trial demonstrated a blatant and aggressive disregard at Apple for the requirements of the law. Apple executives used their considerable skills to orchestrate a price-fixing scheme that significantly raised the prices of E-books. This conduct included Apple lawyers and its highest level executives."); *see also* Philip Elmer-Dewitt, *'I'd do it again,' says the man at the center of Apple's e-book case*, FORTUNE (Dec. 2, 2014), https://fortune.com/2014/12/02/id-do-it-again-says-the-man-at-the-center-of-apples-e-book-case/.

companies to eliminate competition in hiring for employees,[2104] and it later settled a class action lawsuit by the affected employees through a $415 million joint settlement agreement with other firms.[2105]

2. iOS and the App Store

a. Market Power

Apple has significant and durable market power in the market for mobile operating systems and mobile app stores, both of which are highly concentrated.[2106] Apple's iOS mobile operating system is one of two dominant mobile operating systems, along with Google's Android, in the U.S. and globally.[2107] Apple installs iOS on all Apple mobile devices and does not license iOS to other mobile device manufacturers. More than half of mobile devices in the U.S. run on iOS or iPadOS, an iOS derivation for tablets introduced in 2019.[2108] Apple's market power is durable due to high switching costs, ecosystem lock-in, and brand loyalty. It is unlikely that there will be successful market entry to contest the dominance of iOS and Android.

As a result, Apple's control over iOS provides it with gatekeeper power over software distribution on iOS devices. Consequently, it has a dominant position in the mobile app store market and monopoly power over distribution of software applications on iOS devices.[2109]

[2104] Press Release, U.S. Dep't of Justice, Department Requires Six High Tech Companies to Stop Entering into Anticompetitive Employee Solicitation Agreements (Sept. 24, 2010), https://www.justice.gov/opa/pr/justice-department-requires-six-high-tech-companies-stop-entering-anticompetitive-employee.

[2105] Dawn Chmielewski, *Silicon Valley Companies Agree to Pay $415 Million to Settle "No Poaching" Suit*, RECODE (Jan. 15, 2015), https://www.vox.com/2015/1/15/11557814/silicon-valley-companies-agree-to-pay-415-million-to-settle-no.

[2106] *See* Stigler Report at 78 ("[T]he evidence thus far does suggest that current digital platforms face very little threat of entry. … [T]he key players in this industry remained the same over the last two technology waves, staying dominant through the shift to mobile and the rise of AI. In the past, dominant businesses found it difficult to navigate innovation or disruption waves. By contrast, Facebook, Google, Amazon, Apple, and even Microsoft were able to ride these waves without significant impact on market share or profit margins. This indirect evidence corroborates the argument that these companies are facing few competitive threats.").

[2107] *See infra* Section IV.

[2108] *See* S. O'Dea, *Subscriber share held by smartphone operating systems in the United States from 2012 to 2020*, STATISTA (Aug. 17, 2020), https://www.statista.com/statistics/266572/market-share-held-by-smartphone-platforms-in-the-united-states/; *Mobile Operating System Market Share United States of America Aug. 2019 – Aug. 2020*, GLOBALSTATS (on file with Comm); Jason Cipriani, *iPad turns 10: Why did it take a decade for Apple's tablet to get its own operating system*, ZDNET (Jan. 24, 2020), https://www.zdnet.com/article/a-decade-old-device-why-did-it-take-nine-years-for-the-ipad-to-get-its-own-operating-system/.

[2109] *See infra* Section IV.

Apple's App Store is the only method to distribute software applications on iOS devices.[2110] It does not permit alternative app stores to be installed on iOS devices, nor does it permit apps to be sideloaded. As discussed earlier in this Report, consumers have a strong preference for native apps to web apps,[2111] and Apple has acknowledged key differences between them. Developers have explained that Apple actively undermines the open web's progress on iOS "to push developers toward building native apps on iOS rather than using web technologies."[2112] As a result, Apple's position as the sole app store on iOS devices is unassailable. Apple fully controls how software can be installed on iOS devices and CEO Tim Cook has explained that the company has no plan to permit an alternative app store.[2113] The former director of the app review team for the App Store observed that Apple is "not subject to any meaningful competitive constraint from alternative distribution channels."[2114]

In response to these concerns, Apple has not produced any evidence that the App Store is not the sole means of distributing apps on iOS devices and that it does not exert monopoly power over app distribution. Apple says it does not create—nor is it aware of third-party data—that tracks market share in the app distribution market.[2115] Apple claims the App Store competes in a larger software distribution market that includes other mobile app stores, as well as the open internet, personal computers, gaming consoles, smart TVs, and online and brick-and-mortar retail stores.[2116] While consumers can access software and developers can distribute software through those platforms, none of those platforms permit consumers to access apps on an iOS device, or for developers to distribute apps to iOS devices.

Apple's monopoly power over software distribution on iOS devices appears to allow it to generate supra-normal profits from the App Store and its Services business. Apple CEO Tim Cook set a goal in 2017 to rapidly double the size of the Services business by the end of 2020.[2117] Apple met this goal by July 2020, six months ahead of schedule.[2118] The Services business accounted for nearly 18%

[2110] CEO Hearing Transcript at 50 (statement of Tim Cook, CEO, Apple Inc.) (responding to Representative Johnson's question about whether Apple alone determines whether apps are admitted to the App Store Mr. Cook replied "If it's a native app, yes, sir. If it's a web app, no.").

[2111] *See infra* Section IV.

[2112] Owen Williams, *Apple Is Trying to Kill Web Technology*, ONEZERO (Nov. 7, 2019), https://onezero.medium.com/apple-is-trying-to-kill-web-technology-a274237c174d.

[2113] CEO Hearing Transcript at 3 (response to Questions for the Record of Tim Cook, CEO, Apple Inc.).

[2114] Phillip Shoemaker, *Apple v. Everybody*, MEDIUM (Mar. 29, 2019), https://medium.com/@phillipshoemaker/apple-v-everybody-5903039e3be.

[2115] Production of Apple, to H. Comm. on the Judiciary, HJC-APPLE-000008 (Oct. 14, 2019) (on file with Comm.).

[2116] *See* CEO Hearing Transcript at 52, 164 (statement of Tim Cook, CEO, Apple Inc.). *See also* Production of Apple, to H. Comm. on the Judiciary, HJC-APPLE-000012-13 (Oct. 14, 2019) (on file with Comm.).

[2117] Anita Balakrishnan, *Tim Cook: Goal is to double Apple's services revenue by 2020*, CNBC (Jan. 31, 2017), https://www.cnbc.com/2017/01/31/tim-cook-on-apple-earnings-call-double-services-revenue-by-2020.html.

[2118] *See Apple (AAPL) Q3 2020 Earnings Call Transcript*, MOTLEY FOOL (July 31, 2020), https://www.fool.com/earnings/call-transcripts/2020/07/31/apple-aapl-q3-2020-earnings-call-transcript.aspx.

of total revenue ($46.2 billion) in fiscal year 2019. Services grew faster than Products in recent years, increasing by more than 41% since 2017.[2119] The Services category is also Apple's highest margin business at 63.7% in fiscal year 2019 and 67.2% for Apple's quarter ending in June 2020.[2120]

Annual Revenue by Segment[2121]

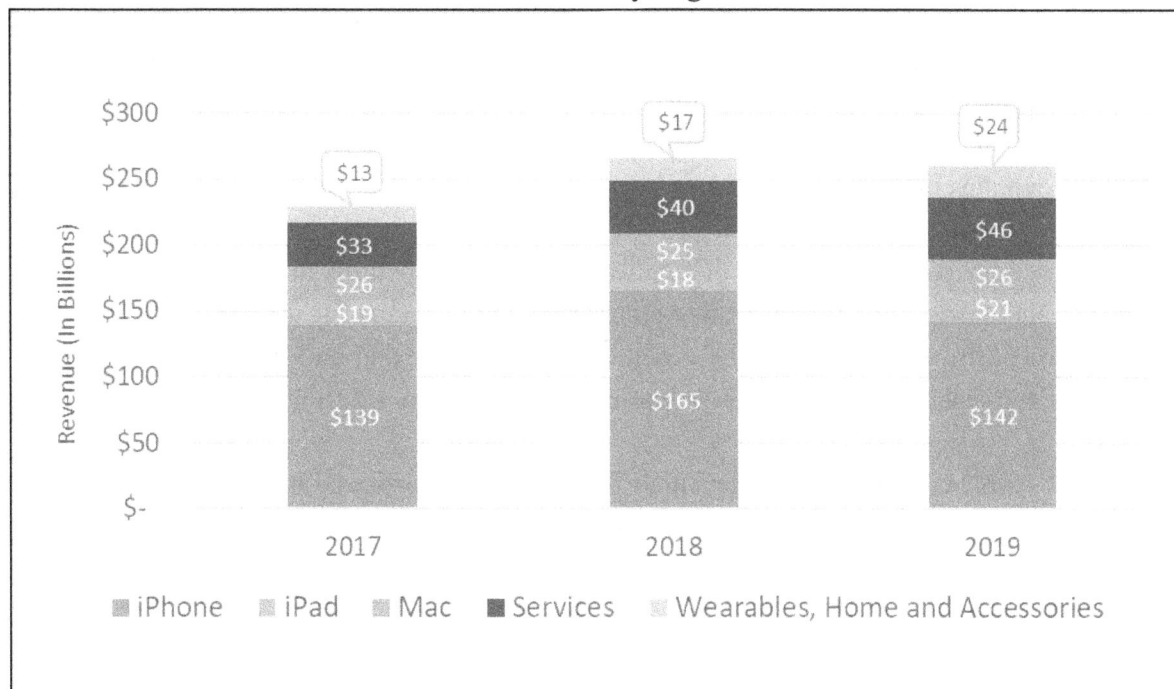

Industry observers credit Apple's rising valuation and future long-term value to its successful focus on growing the Services business.[2122] Apple has attributed the growth of Services as a driver of the firm's profits from sales and an important factor supporting Apple's overall margins as hardware

---

[2119] Apple Inc., Annual Report (Form 10-K) 19 (Sept. 28, 2019), https://s2.q4cdn.com/470004039/files/doc_financials/2019/ar/_10-K-2019-(As-Filed).pdf.

[2120] Apple Inc., Annual Report (Form 10-K) 21 (Sept. 28, 2019), https://s2.q4cdn.com/470004039/files/doc_financials/2019/ar/_10-K-2019-(As-Filed).pdf; Apple Inc., Quarterly Report (Form 10-Q) 28 (June 27, 2020), https://s2.q4cdn.com/470004039/files/doc_financials/2020/q3/_10-Q-Q3-2020-(As-Filed).pdf.

[2121] Prepared by the Subcomm. based on Apple Inc., Annual Report (Form 10-K) (2017–2019), https://www.sec.gov/Archives/edgar/data/320193/000032019318000145/a10-k20189292018.htm.

[2122] See e.g., Kifi Leswing, *Apple's $2 trillion value is proof that Tim Cook's services plan worked*, CNBC (Aug. 19, 2020), https://www.cnbc.com/2020/08/19/apples-2-trillion-value-proof-that-tim-cooks-services-plan-worked.html; Anne Sraders, *As Apple stock tops $500, bulls cite these key reasons it could still go higher*, FORTUNE (Aug. 24, 2020), https://fortune.com/2020/08/24/apple-stock-tops-500-can-it-go-higher/.

sales slowed or declined.[2123] The company has consistently credited the App Store, licensing sales, and AppleCare for the success of Services.[2124]

b. Merger Activity

In 2019, Apple CEO Tim Cook told CNBC that Apple buys a new company every two to three weeks, with a focus on acquiring "talent and intellectual property."[2125] In July 2020, Mr. Cook explained that Apple's "approach on acquisitions has been to buy companies where we have challenges, and IP, and then make them a feature of the phone."[2126] An Apple submission to the Subcommittee explains that it:

> [H]as not embarked on a strategy of acquiring nascent competitors in service of its growth and market position. Instead, Apple's acquisitions generally are meant to complement its product business by accelerating innovation and building out new features and technologies for Apple's hardware and software offerings.[2127]

In 2020, Apple continued acquiring small firms, including artificial intelligence and virtual reality startups, an enterprise software maker, a contactless payment startup, and a weather application,

---

[2123] Apple Inc., Annual Report (Form 10-K) 22, 26 (Sept. 29, 2018), https://www.sec.gov/Archives/edgar/data/320193/000032019318000145/a10-k20189292018.htm; Apple Inc., Annual Report (Form 10-K) 22, 26 (Sept. 30, 2017), https://www.sec.gov/Archives/edgar/data/320193/000032019317000070/a10-k20179302017.htm.

[2124] Apple Inc., Annual Report (Form 10-K) 19 (Sept. 28, 2019), https://s2.q4cdn.com/470004039/files/doc_financials/2019/ar/_10-K-2019-(As-Filed).pdf.; Apple Inc., Annual Report (Form 10-K) 25 (Sept. 29, 2018), https://www.sec.gov/Archives/edgar/data/320193/000032019318000145/a10-k20189292018.htm; Apple Inc., Annual Report (Form 10-K) 25 (Sept. 30, 2017), https://www.sec.gov/Archives/edgar/data/320193/000032019317000070/a10-k20179302017.htm. AppleCare is Apple's extended warranty products for Apple devices. *See* Jason Cross, *AppleCare+: Everything you need to know about Apple's extended warranty program*, MACWORLD (Sept. 16, 2020), https://www.macworld.com/article/3227045/applecare-warranty-faq.html. In addition to the markets discussed in this section, the Committee sought information and continues to investigate competition and conduct in the resale and repair markets for Apple products.

[2125] Lauren Feiner, *Apple buys a company every few weeks, says CEO Tim Cook*, CNBC (May 6, 2019), https://www.cnbc.com/2019/05/06/apple-buys-a-company-every-few-weeks-says-ceo-tim-cook.html.

[2126] Kif Leswing, *Tim Cook says Apple buys innovation, not competitors*, CNBC (July 31, 2020), https://www.cnbc.com/2020/07/31/tim-cook-contrasts-apple-ma-with-other-big-tech.html.

[2127] Apple, *Apple: Distinctive Products with a Seamless, Integrated User Experience* 2 (July 13, 2020) (on file with Comm.).

among others.[2128] One of Apple's largest transactions occurred in 2019, when it paid $1 billion to acquire Intel's smartphone modem business.[2129]

Apple has also recently acquired software companies to create a foundation from which it could launch new apps. After purchasing the digital magazine subscription service Texture in 2018, for example, Apple integrated most of Texture's functionality into its own Apple News+ service, which debuted the following year.[2130] Similarly, one of Apple's largest purchases to date—its $3 billion acquisition of Beats Electronics in 2014—was instrumental to the 2015 launch of Apple Music.[2131] Apple sought to grow Apple Music quickly after its introduction. Apple pre-installed the service on iPhones and made it the only music service accessible through Siri, Apple's virtual assistant. Apple also offered Apple Music with a free month trial period and made it available on Android devices. The strategy saw Apple gain 10 million paying subscribers within six months.[2132] Apple supplemented its music services business in 2018 by acquiring the music recognition app Shazam, and most recently in 2020 by acquiring podcast app Scout FM.[2133]

It is common for Apple to integrate apps it purchases into its own pre-existing apps or into the iOS mobile operating system. Examples include acquisitions of Swell, a podcast app that Apple acquired in 2014, and HopStop, a transit navigation app it acquired in 2013.[2134]

[2128] *See* Jordan Novet, *Apple buys an A.I. start-up that came from Microsoft co-founder Paul Allen's research lab*, CNBC (Jan. 15, 2020), https://www.cnbc.com/2020/01/15/apple-acquires-xnor-ai-startup-that-spun-out-of-allen-institute.html; Mark Gurman, *Apple Acquires AI Startup to Better Understand Natural Language*, BLOOMBERG (Apr. 3, 2020), https://www.bloomberg.com/news/articles/2020-04-03/apple-acquires-ai-startup-to-better-understand-natural-language; Kif Leswing, *Apple buys virtual reality company NextVR*, CNBC (May 14, 2020), https://www.cnbc.com/2020/05/14/apple-buys-virtual-reality-company-nextvr.html; Kif Leswing, *Apple buys Fleetsmith, a company making it easier to deploy iPhones and Macs at workplaces*, CNBC (June 24, 2020), https://www.cnbc.com/2020/06/24/apple-acquires-device-management-company-fleetsmith.html; Jessica Bursztynsky, *Apple buys popular weather app Dark Sky and plans to shut down Android versions*, CNBC (Mar. 31, 2020), https://www.cnbc.com/2020/03/31/apple-buys-popular-weather-app-dark-sky.html; Mark Gurman, *Apple Buys Startup to Turn iPhones Into Payment Terminals*, BLOOMBERG (July 31, 2020), https://www.bloomberg.com/news/articles/2020-08-01/apple-buys-startup-to-turn-iphones-into-payment-terminals.

[2129] Press Release, Apple, Apple to acquire the majority of Intel's smartphone modem business (July 25, 2019), https://www.apple.com/newsroom/2019/07/apple-to-acquire-the-majority-of-intels-smartphone-modem-business/.

[2130] Anita Balakrishnan, *Apple buys Texture, a digital magazine subscription service*, CNBC (Mar. 12, 2018), https://www.cnbc.com/2018/03/12/apple-buys-texture-a-digital-magazine-subscription-service.html.

[2131] Billy Steele, *Apple's $3 billion purchase of Beats has already paid off*, ENGADGET (May 28, 2019), https://www.engadget.com/2019-05-28-apple-beats-five-years-later.html.

[2132] Neth. Auth. For Consumers & Mkts. Study at 62.

[2133] Press release, Apple, *Apple acquires Shazam, offering more ways to discover and enjoy music* (Sept. 24, 2018), https://www.apple.com/newsroom/2018/09/apple-acquires-shazam-offering-more-ways-to-discover-and-enjoy-music/; Mark Gurman, *Apple Buys Startup That Creates Radio-Like Stations for Podcasts*, BLOOMBERG (Sept. 24, 2020), https://www.bloomberg.com/news/articles/2020-09-24/apple-buys-startup-that-creates-radio-like-stations-for-podcasts.

[2134] Chris Gayomali, *Swell Shuts Down Following Apple Acquisition*, FAST CO. (July 29, 2014), https://www.fastcompany.com/3033698/swell-shuts-down-following-apple-acquisition; Andrew Nusca, *Apple Maps vs. Google Maps heats up as Apple shuts down HopStop*, FORTUNE (Sept. 12, 2015), https://fortune.com/2015/09/12/hopstop-apple-shutdown/.

Apple has followed a similar strategy for integrating the Dark Sky weather app. Apple shut down Dark Sky's Android app in August 2020 and plans to integrate the app's features with the iPhone's Weather widget on iOS 14.[2135] In addition to its app, Dark Sky supplied data to independent weather apps, like Carrot, Weather Line, and Partly Sunny. As a result of Apple's takeover of Dark Sky, independent weather apps will lose access to the inexpensive, hyper-local weather data that Dark Sky supplied, leading some weather apps to shut down and others to rely on higher-priced suppliers for forecast data.[2136]

c. Conduct

i. Commissions and In-App Purchases

The Subcommittee sought information regarding Apple's policy of collecting commissions from apps sold through the App Store and purchases made in iOS apps. Apple charges a 30% commission on paid apps—those that charge a fee for users to download—downloaded from the App Store. It also takes a 30% fee on in-app purchases (IAP) of "digital goods and services."[2137] App subscriptions are charged a 30% commission for the first year and a 15% commission for subsequent years.[2138] Apps are not permitted to communicate with iOS users that the app may be available for purchase at a lower price outside the App Store, provide links outside of the app that may lead users to find alternative subscription and payment methods, or offer their own payment processing mechanism in the app to avoid using Apple's IAP.[2139] Apps that violate Apple's policies can be removed from the App Store, losing access to the only means of distributing apps to consumers with iOS devices.[2140]

[2135] Hannah Klein, *The Dark Sky Android App Is Officially Kaput*, SLATE (Aug. 4, 2020), https://slate.com/technology/2020/08/dark-sky-app-android-shuts-down.html.

[2136] Jared Newman, *Apple's Dark Sky acquisition could be bad news for indie weather apps*, FAST COMPANY (Apr. 2, 2020), https://www.fastcompany.com/90485131/apples-dark-sky-acquisition-could-be-bad-news-for-indie-weather-apps; *but see* CEO Hearing Transcript at 9 (response to Questions for the Record of Tim Cook, CEO, Apple) (noting Dark Sky will "continue to make its API available to Dark Sky's existing customers until the end of 2021.").

[2137] *App Store: Dedicated to the best store experience for everyone*, APPLE, https://www.apple.com/ca/ios/app-store/principles-practices/ (last visited Oct. 4, 2020).

[2138] *Id.*

[2139] *See* Innovation and Entrepreneurship Hearing at 1–2 (response to Questions for the Record of Kyle Andeer, Vice Pres., Corp. Law, Apple Inc.); Submission from ProtonMail, to H. Comm. on the Judiciary, 5 (Aug. 22, 2020) (on file with Comm.); Interview with Source 143 (Aug. 27, 2020).

[2140] *See e.g.*, Sara Morrison, *Apple's Fortnite ban, explained*, VOX: RECODE (Sept. 8, 2020), https://www.vox.com/recode/2020/8/20/21373780/fortnite-epic-apple-lawsuit-app-store-antitrust; Nick Statt, *Apple doubles down on controversial decision to reject email app Hey*, THE VERGE (June 18, 2020), https://www.theverge.com/2020/6/18/21296180/apple-hey-email-app-basecamp-rejection-response-controversy-antitrust-regulation.

Apple describes its policies as a standard industry practice and says that other app stores charge the same fees.[2141] In 2020, Apple funded a study that concluded that other software distribution platforms run by Google, Amazon, Samsung, Microsoft, and others charge identical or similar commissions on software downloads and transactions, and that commissions are common in other digital markets.[2142] Apple also highlighted that its commissions are lower than the cost of software distribution by brick-and-mortar retailers, which dominated the marketplace prior to the introduction of the App Store.[2143] The Apple-commissioned study explained Apple funds the App Store through a $99 annual fee it charges to developers and $299 for developers building enterprise apps, as well as the commission and fees collected on apps and in-app purchases.[2144]

Apple also noted that 84% of all apps distributed through the App Store pay no commissions or fees.[2145] Apple does not take a commission on purchases from apps like Uber or Etsy that sell "physical goods or services that will be consumed outside the app."[2146] Apple also makes some exceptions to its rules and may change or update its rules.[2147] For example, Apple has an exception for "Reader" apps such as Netflix and Kindle that permit users to access content purchased outside the

---

[2141] Innovation and Entrepreneurship Hearing at 2 (Response to Questions for the Record of Kyle Andeer, Vice Pres., Corp. Law, Apple Inc.), https://docs.house.gov/meetings/JU/JU05/20190716/109793/HHRG-116-JU05-20190716-SD037.pdf. *See also* Mark Gurman, *Apple Defends App Store Revenue Take Ahead of Antitrust Hearing*, BLOOMBERG (July 22, 2020), https://www.bloomberg.com/news/articles/2020-07-22/apple-defends-app-store-revenue-cut-ahead-of-antitrust-hearing; David Pierce and Emily Birnbaum, *Apple defends its App Store tax ahead of antitrust hearings*, PROTOCOL (July 22, 2020), https://www.protocol.com/apple-app-store-commission-study.

[2142] *See* JONATHAN BORCK ET AL., APPLE'S APP STORE AND OTHER DIGITAL MARKETPLACES: A COMPARISON OF COMMISSION RATES 2, 5-6 (2020), https://www.analysisgroup.com/globalassets/insights/publishing/apples_app_store_and_other_digital_marketplaces_a_comparison_of_commission_rates.pdf.

[2143] *See* CEO Hearing Transcript at 30 (statement of Tim Cook, CEO, Apple Inc.); Letter from Kyle Andeer, Vice Pres., Corp. Law and Chief Compliance Officer, Apple Inc., to Hon. Jerrold Nader, Chairman, H. Comm. on the Judiciary, Hon. Jim Jordan, Ranking Member, H. Comm. on the Judiciary, Hon. David N. Cicilline, Chairman, Subcomm. on Antitrust, Commercial and Admin. Law of the H. Comm. on the Judiciary, Hon. F. James Sensenbrenner, Ranking Member, Subcomm. on Antitrust, Commercial and Admin. Law of the H. Comm. on the Judiciary, 3 (Sept. 21, 2020) (on file with Comm.).

[2144] *See* JONATHAN BORCK ET AL., APPLE'S APP STORE AND OTHER DIGITAL MARKETPLACES: A COMPARISON OF COMMISSION RATES 4, n.5, Appendix A-3 (2020), https://www.analysisgroup.com/globalassets/insights/publishing/apples_app_store_and_other_digital_marketplaces_a_comparison_of_commission_rates.pdf.

[2145] *See e.g.*, Innovation and Entrepreneurship Hearing at 68 (statement of Kyle Andeer, Vice Pres., Corp. Law, Apple Inc.); Letter from Timothy Powderly, Apple Inc., to Hon. David N. Cicilline, Chairman, Subcomm. on Antitrust, Commercial and Admin. Law of the H. Comm. on the Judiciary, and Hon. F. James Sensenbrenner, Ranking Member, Subcomm. on Antitrust, Commercial and Admin. Law of the H. Comm. on the Judiciary, 3 (July 15, 2019).

[2146] *App Store Review Guidelines 3.1.3(e): Goods and Services Outside of the App*, APPLE, https://developer.apple.com/app-store/review/guidelines/#goods-and-services-outside-of-the-app (last visited Sept. 27, 2020).

[2147] *See e.g.*, Sarah Perez & Anthony Ha, *Apple revises App Store rules to permit game streaming apps, clarify in-app purchases and more*, TECHCRUNCH (Sept. 11, 2020), https://techcrunch.com/2020/09/11/apple-revises-app-store-rules-to-permit-game-streaming-apps-clarify-in-app-purchases-and-more/; Phillip Shoemaker, *Apple v. Everybody*, MEDIUM (Mar. 29, 2019), https://medium.com/@phillipshoemaker/apple-v-everybody-5903039e3be.

app, but do not allow for in-app subscriptions or purchases.[2148] Apple also makes exceptions for "third-party premium video apps" that integrate with Apple TV and other Apple services.[2149] Mr. Cook explained, "[t]oday, there are over 130 apps that participate in this program," and "[t]he reduced 15% commission is available to all developers offering premium video content on the same terms as Amazon Prime Video, with the same qualification criteria."[2150] Amazon Prime Video, Altice One, and Canal+ have been publicly confirmed as participants.[2151]

During the investigation, the Subcommittee received evidence from app developers regarding Apple's commissions and fees for IAP. ProtonMail, a secure email provider, explained that Apple's justification of its 30% commission overlooks the dynamics of the marketplace for distributing software to consumers with iOS devices—conflating practices that may be unremarkable in competitive markets but abusive in monopoly markets.[2152]

For example, personal computer (PC) users can install software from app stores run by Microsoft, Google, Amazon and others, or they can download software directly from the software developer's website and bypass app stores altogether. Similarly, Apple's Mac App Store is one of many options for Mac users to download software. While Samsung is a global leader in smartphones, the Samsung Galaxy Store is one of several app stores available on Samsung's mobile devices. Google's Play Store dominates app distribution on Android devices and is the most apt comparison to the App Store, but Google permits some competition via sideloading and alternative app stores.[2153]

In contrast, Apple owns the iOS operating system as well as the only means to distribute software on iOS devices. Using its role as operating system provider, Apple prohibits alternatives to the App Store and charges fees and commissions for some categories of apps to reach customers. It responds to attempts to circumvent its fees and commissions with removal from the App Store.[2154] Because of this policy, developers have no other option than to play by Apple's rules to reach customers who own iOS devices. Owners of iOS devices have no alternative means to install apps on

---

[2148] *App Store Review Guidelines 3.1.3(a): "Reader" Apps*, APPLE, https://developer.apple.com/app-store/review/guidelines/#reader-apps (last visited Sept. 27, 2020).

[2149] CEO Hearing Transcript at 8 (response to Questions for the Record of Tim Cook, CEO, Apple Inc.)

[2150] *Id.*

[2151] Nick Statt, *Apple now lets some video streaming apps bypass the App Store cut*, THE VERGE (Apr. 1, 2020), https://www.theverge.com/2020/4/1/21203630/apple-amazon-prime-video-ios-app-store-cut-exempt-program-deal. *See also*, Production of Apple, to H. Comm. on the Judiciary, HJC-APPLE-015111 (Nov. 1, 2016) (showing details of negotiations between Eddy Cue, Senior Vice President, Internet Software and Services, Apple, and Jeff Bezos, CEO, Amazon.) (on file with Comm.).

[2152] *See* Submission from ProtonMail, to H. Comm. on the Judiciary, 11–12 (Aug. 22, 2020) (on file with Comm.).

[2153] *See id.* Apple has pointed to these as benchmarks for the App Store. *See* JONATHAN BORCK ET AL., APPLE'S APP STORE AND OTHER DIGITAL MARKETPLACES: A COMPARISON OF COMMISSION RATES 4–6 (2020), https://www.analysisgroup.com/globalassets/insights/publishing/apples_app_store_and_other_digital_marketplaces_a_comparison_of_commission_rates.pdf.

[2154] *See* Submission from ProtonMail, to H. Comm. on the Judiciary, 5 (Aug. 22, 2020) (on file with Comm.).

their phones. Apple notes that its 30% commission has remained static for most apps for more than a decade.[2155] A group of developers that filed a lawsuit against Apple because of this policy argue that the persistence of Apple's 30% rate over time, particularly "despite the inevitable accrual of experience and economies of scale," indicates there is insufficient competition.[2156] Additionally, as previously noted, there is little likelihood for new market entry in the mobile operating system or mobile app store markets to compel Apple to lower its rates.[2157]

Industry observers have also challenged Apple's implicit claim that the iPhone was the start of the online software distribution market. For example, Mac and iOS developer Brent Simmons remarked that "when the App Store was created, developers were selling and distributing apps over the web, and it worked wonderfully," noting that he began distributing software over the internet in the 1990s.[2158] Software designer and technology writer John Gruber agreed, explaining that in the mid-1990s there was "a thriving market for software sold directly over a thing called 'The Internet,'" and that Apple's omission of the fact that "direct downloads and sales over the web" pre-dated the iPhone by more than a decade "is flat-out dishonest."[2159]

Many developers have stressed that because Apple dictates that the App Store is the only way to install software on iOS devices and requires apps offering "digital goods and services" implement the IAP mechanism, that Apple has illegally tied IAP to the App Store.[2160] Consumers with iOS devices account for a disproportionately high amount of spending on apps—spending twice as much as Android users.[2161] Further, iOS users seldom switch to Android.[2162] Thus, developers cannot abandon

---

[2155] *See* CEO Hearing Transcript at 52 (statement of Tim Cook, CEO, Apple Inc.); Letter from Kyle Andeer, Vice Pres., Corp. Law and Chief Compliance Officer, Apple Inc., to Hon. Jerrold Nader, Chairman, H. Comm. on the Judiciary, Hon. Jim Jordan, Ranking Member, H. Comm. on the Judiciary, Hon. David N. Cicilline, Chairman, Subcomm. on Antitrust, Commercial and Admin. Law of the H. Comm. on the Judiciary, and Hon. F. James Sensenbrenner, Ranking Member, Subcomm. on Antitrust, Commercial and Admin. Law of the H. Comm. on the Judiciary, 3 (Sept. 21, 2020) (on file with Comm.).

[2156] Class Action Complaint at 2, Cameron v. Apple Inc., No. 5:19-cv-3074 (N.D. Cal. June 4, 2019).

[2157] *See infra* Section IV.

[2158] *See* Rob Pegoraro, *What Tim Cook Left Out Of His Version of App Store History*, FORBES (July 29, 2020), https://www.forbes.com/sites/robpegoraro/2020/07/29/what-tim-cook-left-out-of-his-version-of-app-store-history/.

[2159] John Gruber, *Parsing Tim Cook's Opening Statement from Today's Congressional Antitrust Hearing*, DARING FIREBALL (July 29, 2020), https://daringfireball.net/2020/07/parsing_cooks_opening_statement.

[2160] *See e.g.*, Submission from Source 711, to H. Comm. on the Judiciary, Appendix A 4–8 (Oct. 15, 2019) (on file with Comm.); Submission from Source 202, to H. Comm. on the Judiciary, 22–41 (Oct. 18, 2018); Submission from Source 736, to H. Comm. on the Judiciary, 6–10 (Oct. 31, 2019) (on file with Comm.).

[2161] *See Global App Revenue Grew 23% Year-Over-Year Last Quarter to $21.9 Billion*, SENSORTOWER (Oct. 23, 2019), https://sensortower.com/blog/app-revenue-and-downloads-q3-2019; Prachi Bhardwaj & Shayanne Gal, *Despite Android's growing market share, Apple users continue to spend twice as much money on apps as Android users*, BUS. INSIDER (July 6, 2018), https://www.businessinsider.com/apple-users-spend-twice-apps-vs-android-charts-2018-7.

[2162] *See Mobile Operating System Loyalty: High and Steady*, CONSUMER INTEL. RESEARCH PARTNERS (Mar. 8, 2018), http://files.constantcontact.com/150f9af2201/4bca9a19-a8b0-46bd-95bd-85740ff3fb5d.pdf; *iPhone vs. Android – Cell Phone Brand Loyalty Survey 2019*, SELLCELL (Aug. 20, 2019), https://www.sellcell.com/blog/iphone-vs-android-cell-phone-brand-loyalty-survey-2019/; *see also* MORNINGSTAR EQUITY ANALYST REPORT, APPLE INC 3 (Aug. 6, 2020) (on file

the App Store—it is where the highest value customers are and will remain. As a result, developers say that Apple abuses its control of its valuable user base by prohibiting alternative payment processing options to compete with Apple's IAP mechanism.

Developers further argue that Apple's 30% commission from IAP is a "payment processing" fee, and not a distribution fee.[2163] In a submission to the Subcommittee, Match said "Apple distorts competition in payment processing by making access to its App Store conditional on the use of IAP for in-app purchases, thus excluding alternative payment processors. IAP eventually becomes the vessel through which Apple extracts its extraordinary commissions."[2164] Two app developers that offer services that compete with Apple explained that IAP is a payment processing fee and not a distribution fee. Both pointed out that Apple does not charge apps for distribution, evidenced by the fact Apple admits distributing most apps for free. Instead, Apple generates revenue by adding a 30% processing fee on transactions in the App Store and using IAP.[2165] Apple's Developer Program website explains that Apple does charge for distribution—it requires enrollment in the Apple Developer Program and payment of a $99 fee to distribute apps on the App Store.[2166]

Apple responded that its "commission is not a payment processing fee" and that it "reflects the value of the App Store as a channel for the distribution of developers' apps and the cost of many services" it incurs to maintain the App Store.[2167] It said that "[t]he commission also enables Apple to

---

with Comm.) ("Recent survey data shows that iPhone customers are not even contemplating switching brands today. In a December 2018 survey by Kantar, 90% of U.S.-based iPhone users said they planned to remain loyal to future Apple devices."); Martin Armstrong, *Most iPhone Users Never Look Back*, STATISTA (May 22, 2017), https://www.statista.com/chart/9496/most-iphone-users-never-look-back/.

[2163] *See e.g.*, Competitors Hearing at 9 (statement of David Heinemeier Hansson, Founder and CTO, Basecamp); Interview with Source 143 (Aug. 27, 2020); Submission from Match Group, to H. Comm. on the Judiciary, MATCH-GRP_00000168 (July 1, 2019) (on file with Comm.); Submission from Source 482, to H. Comm. on Judiciary, 9 (Oct. 15, 2019) (on file with Comm.).

[2164] Submission from Match Group, to H. Comm. on the Judiciary, MATCH_GRP_00000238 (Nov. 1, 2019) (on file with Comm.).

[2165] *See* Submission from ProtonMail, to H. Comm. on the Judiciary, 11 (Aug. 22, 2020) (on file with Comm.); Submission from Spotify, to H. Comm. on the Judiciary, Appendix A at 7–8 (Oct. 15, 2019) (on file with Comm.).

[2166] *See Apple Developer Program, How the Program Works*, APPLE, https://developer.apple.com/programs/how-it-works/ (last visited Sept. 27, 2020) ("If you're new to development on Apple Platforms, you can get started with our tools and resources for free. If you're ready to build more advanced capabilities and distribute your apps on the App Store, enroll in the Apple Developer Program. The cost is 99 USD per membership year.").

[2167] Letter from Kyle Andeer, Vice Pres., Corp. Law & Chief Compliance Officer, Apple Inc. to Hon. Jerrold Nadler, Chairman, H. Comm. on the Judiciary, Hon. Doug Collins, Ranking Member, H. Comm on the Judiciary, Hon. David N. Cicilline, Chairman, Subcomm. on Antitrust, Commercial and Admin. Law of the H. Comm. on the Judiciary, and Hon. F. James Sensenbrenner, Ranking Member, Subcomm. on Antitrust, Commercial and Admin. Law of the H. Comm. on the Judiciary, 3 (Feb. 17, 2020) (on file with Comm.), https://docs.house.gov/meetings/JU/JU05/20200117/110386/HHRG-116-JU05-20200117-SD004.pdf; *see also* Letter from Kyle Andeer, Vice Pres., Corp. Law and Chief Compliance Officer, Apple Inc., to Hon. Jerrold Nader, Chairman, H. Comm. on the Judiciary, Hon. Jim Jordan, Ranking Member, H. Comm. on the Judiciary, Hon. David N. Cicilline, Chairman, Subcomm. on Antitrust, Commercial and Admin. Law of the H. Comm. on the Judiciary, and Hon. F. James Sensenbrenner, Ranking Member, Subcomm. on Antitrust, Commercial and Admin. Law of the H. Comm. on the Judiciary, 3 (Sept. 21, 2020) (on file with Comm.).

realize a return on its investment in the App Store and in Apple's intellectual property, and to fund future App Store innovation."[2168] Similarly, a study commissioned by Apple in 2020 explained that the annual fees paid by developers, commissions, and charges for in-app purchases fund investments in the App Store ecosystem, such as app review, developer tools, marketing, search functionality, application program interfaces, and software development kits.[2169] Apple has also argued that its App Store Developer Guidelines—including its requirement to use Apple's in-app purchase mechanism—is "designed to keep the store safe for our users."[2170]

Apple's rationale for its commissions and fees has evolved over time. Its recent explanations of the basis for its 30% commission differs significantly from its explanation of its fee and revenue expectations in the early years of the App Store. Prior to the App Store's debut in 2008, then-Apple CEO Steve Jobs explained "We don't intend to make any money off the App Store . . . We're basically giving all the money to the developers and the 30 percent that pays for running the store, that'll be great."[2171] In 2011, Apple Chief Financial Officer Peter Oppenheimer explained to Apple's shareholders that Apple runs the App Store "just a little over break even."[2172]

Apple's financial reports indicate that the App Store is faring far better than the modest business Apple originally contemplated. According to a 2019 market analysis, Apple's net revenue from the App Store is projected to be $17.4 billion for fiscal year 2020.[2173] CNBC estimated the App Store had total sales of nearly $50 billion in 2019, generating "about $15 billion in revenue for Apple."

[2168] Apple, *Apple: Distinctive Products with a Seamless, Integrated User Experience* 14 (July 13, 2020) (on file with Comm.). *See also* Letter from Kyle Andeer, Vice Pres., Corp. Law and Chief Compliance Officer, Apple Inc., to Hon. Jerrold Nader, Chairman, H. Comm. on the Judiciary, Hon. Jim Jordan, Ranking Member, H. Comm. on the Judiciary, Hon. David N. Cicilline, Chairman, Subcomm. on Antitrust, Commercial and Admin. Law of the H. Comm. on the Judiciary, and Hon. F. James Sensenbrenner, Ranking Member, Subcomm. on Antitrust, Commercial and Admin. Law of the H. Comm. on the Judiciary, 3 (Sept. 21, 2020) (on file with Comm.).

[2169] *See* JONATHAN BORCK ET AL., APPLE'S APP STORE AND OTHER DIGITAL MARKETPLACES: A COMPARISON OF COMMISSION RATES 2–3 (2020), https://www.analysisgroup.com/globalassets/insights/publishing/apples_app_store_and_other_digital_marketplaces_a_comparison_of_commission_rates.pdf; *see also* Letter from Kyle Andeer, Vice Pres., Corp. Law & Chief Compliance Officer, Apple Inc. to Hon. Jerrold Nadler, Chairman, H. Comm. on the Judiciary, Hon. Doug Collins, Ranking Member, H. Comm on the Judiciary, Hon. David N. Cicilline, Chairman, Subcomm. on Antitrust, Commercial and Admin. Law of the H. Comm. on the Judiciary, and Hon. F. James Sensenbrenner, Ranking Member, Subcomm. on Antitrust, Commercial and Admin. Law of the H. Comm. on the Judiciary, 2 (Feb. 17, 2020) (on file with Comm.), https://docs.house.gov/meetings/JU/JU05/20200117/110386/HHRG-116-JU05-20200117-SD004.pdf.

[2170] Kif Leswing, *Apple sued by Fortnite maker after kicking the game out of the App Store for payment policy violations*, CNBC (Aug. 13, 2020), https://www.cnbc.com/2020/08/13/apple-kicks-fortnite-out-of-app-store-for-challenging-payment-rules.html.

[2171] Peter Cohen, *'App Store' will distribute iPhone software*, MACWORLD (Mar. 6, 2008), https://www.macworld.com/article/1132402/appstore.html.

[2172] Daniel Eran Dilger, *Inside Apple's shareholder meeting and Q&A with Tim Cook*, APPLE INSIDER (Feb. 23, 2011), https://appleinsider.com/articles/11/02/23/tim_cook_presides_over_annual_apple_shareholder_meeting.

[2173] Eric J. Savitz, *App Stores Could Be Ripe for Regulation. Here's Who Benefits if Commissions Fall*, BARRONS (July 25, 2019), https://www.barrons.com/articles/news-updates-51599747657.

With $50 billion in annual sales, CNBC explained "the App Store alone would be no. 64 on the Fortune 500, ahead of Cisco and behind Morgan Stanley."[2174] An analytics firm concluded that Apple likely made $15.5 billion from the App Store in 2018, and estimated $18.8 billion for 2022. *Bloomberg* reported that analysts forecasting Apple's third-quarter 2020 performance predicted growth from Services "up 15% from a year earlier," and that growth would largely be attributable to the App Store and licensing, not new services.[2175] In addition to Apple's commissions and fees for IAP, App Store revenue also includes an $2.67 billion Apple would make through the $99 annual fee paid by Apple's 27 million iOS developers.[2176] Apple also reportedly made $9 billion in 2018 and $12 billion in 2019 to set Google as the default search engine on the Safari browser.[2177] Revenue from setting Google as Safari's default search engine is attributed to Apple's Services business, which is the business unit that includes the App Store.[2178]

In an interview with Subcommittee staff , Phillip Shoemaker, former director of app review for the App Store, estimated that Apple's costs for running the App Store is less than $100 million. Other analysts estimate that the App Store has significantly higher profits. A gaming developer explained that the fees it pays Apple's add up to millions of dollars—or even tens or hundreds of millions of dollars for some developers—far in excess of the developer's estimate of Apple's costs of reviewing and hosting those apps.[2179] Although only estimates, these figures indicate that as the mobile app economy has grown, Apple's monopoly power over app distribution on iPhones permits the App Store to generate supra-normal profits. These profits are derived by extracting rents from developers, who either pass on price increases to consumers, or reduce investments in innovative new services. Apple's ban on rival app stores and alternative payment processing locks out competition, boosting Apple's profits from a captured ecosystem of developers and consumers.[2180]

[2174] Kif Leswing, *Apple's App Store had gross sales around $50 billion last year, but growth is slowing*, CNBC (Jan. 8, 2020), https://www.cnbc.com/2020/01/07/apple-app-store-had-estimated-gross-sales-of-50-billion-in-2019.html.

[2175] Mark Gurman, *Apple's New Services Off to a Slow Start in First Year*, BLOOMBERG (July 28, 2020), https://www.bloombergquint.com/business/apple-s-new-services-off-to-a-slow-start-in-first-year.

[2176] *See* Letter from Kyle Andeer, Vice Pres., Corp. Law and Chief Compliance Officer, Apple Inc., to Hon. Jerrold Nader, Chairman, H. Comm. on the Judiciary, Hon. Jim Jordan, Ranking Member, H. Comm. on the Judiciary, Hon. David N. Cicilline, Chairman, Subcomm. on Antitrust, Commercial and Admin. Law of the H. Comm. on the Judiciary, and Hon. F. James Sensenbrenner, Ranking Member, Subcomm. on Antitrust, Commercial and Admin. Law of the H. Comm. on the Judiciary, 3 (Sept. 21, 2020) (on file with Comm.). ("[T]here are more than 1.8 million apps on the App Store, and a thriving community of more than 27 million iOS developers."); *Developer Support, Purchase and Activation*, APPLE, https://developer.apple.com/support/purchase-activation/ (last visited Sept. 27, 2020) ("The Apple Developer Program annual fee is $99 USD and the Apple Developer Enterprise Program annual fee is $299 USD").

[2177] *See* Lisa Marie Segarra, *Google to Pay Apple $12 Billion to Remain Safari's Default Search Engine in 2019: Report*, FORTUNE (Sept. 29, 2018), https://fortune.com/2018/09/29/google-apple-safari-search-engine/.

[2178] *See* Mark Gurman, *Apple's New Services Off to a Slow Start in First Year*, BLOOMBERG (July 28, 2020), https://www.bloombergquint.com/business/apple-s-new-services-off-to-a-slow-start-in-first-year.

[2179] Interview with Source 143 (Aug. 27, 2020).

[2180] Dr. Carl Shapiro of the University of California, Berkeley—the former top economist for the Justice Department's Antitrust Division under the Obama Administration—has noted that persistently high corporate profits that are not eroded by competitive forces over time are an indicator of market power. It also suggests the rise of incumbency rents, or the earning of excess profits "by firms whose positions are protected by high barriers to entry." Carl Shapiro, *Antitrust in a*

346

To address this concern without compromising the security or quality of the App Store, some developers argue in favor of allowing third-party payment processors like PayPal, Square, and Stripe to compete in the App Store. They explain that the most likely competitors are already trusted and widely used for e-commerce transactions.[2181] David Heinemeier Hansson, the Founder and CTO of Basecamp, testified at the Subcommittee's fifth hearing that Apple's market power allows it to keep fees "exorbitantly high."[2182] By comparison, he noted that other markets, such as credit card processes, are "only able to sustain a 2 percent fee for merchants. Apple, along with Google, has been able to charge an outrageous 30 percent for years on end."[2183] Several other firms observed that Apple's control over app distribution allows it to extract high fees on a minority of apps, and that competition for processing payments would drive prices down. For example, developers explain that payment processing typically costs less than 5% of the transaction value.[2184] Before the App Store, one developer reportedly explained that "[w]e typically paid about 5%—not 30%—to a payment processor," and it "worked just as well for small developers as for large."[2185]

Other developers have noted that alternative payment processing providers charge significantly lower rates than Apple's fee for IAP. Match estimates that Apple's expenses related to payment processing "justify charging no more than 3.65% of revenue."[2186] Some app developers would prefer to implement in-house payment processing. In August 2020, Epic Games introduced a direct payment option in its Fortnite app, allowing gamers to elect to use Apple's IAP or pay Epic directly. Epic's payment processing option that charged consumers 10%, a 20% discount from purchases using IAP.[2187] In response, Apple disabled updates for Fortnite for violating the App Store Guidelines.[2188]

Time of Populism, 61 INT'L J. INDUS. ORG. 714, 733–737 (2018), https://faculty.haas.berkeley.edu/shapiro/antitrustpopulism.pdf.

[2181] Submission from ProtonMail, to H. Comm. on the Judiciary, 13 (Aug. 22, 2020) (on file with Comm.).

[2182] Competitors Hearing at 8 (statement of David Heinemeier Hansson, Founder and CTO, Basecamp); *see also* Interview with Source 88 (May 12, 2020).

[2183] Competitors Hearing at 8 (statement of David Heinemeier Hansson, Founder and CTO, Basecamp); *see also* Interview with Source 873 (May 12, 2020).

[2184] *See e.g.*, Competitors Hearing at 8 (statement of David Heinemeier Hansson, Founder and CTO, Basecamp); Submission from Source 202, to H. Comm. on the Judiciary, 15 (Oct. 18, 2018) (on file with Comm.).

[2185] Rob Pegoraro, *What Tim Cook Left Out Of His Version of App Store History*, Forbes (July 29, 2020), https://www.forbes.com/sites/robpegoraro/2020/07/29/what-tim-cook-left-out-of-his-version-of-app-store-history/.

[2186] Submission of Source 736, to H. Comm. on the Judiciary, 6 (Oct. 31, 2019) (on file with Comm.).

[2187] *See* Andrew Webster, *Epic offers new direct payment in Fortnite on iOS and Android to get around app store fees*, THE VERGE (Aug. 13, 2020), https://www.theverge.com/2020/8/13/21366259/epic-fortnite-vbucks-mega-drop-discount-iphone-android.

[2188] Nick Statt, *Apple just kicked Fortnite off the App Store*, THE VERGE (Aug. 13, 2020), https://www.theverge.com/2020/8/13/21366438/apple-fortnite-ios-app-store-violations-epic-payments.

Developers have also detailed that Apple attempts lock in its fees by preventing apps from communicating with customers about alternatives. Under the App Store Guidelines, apps may not provide any information "that direct[s] customers to purchasing mechanisms other than in-app purchase."[2189] They also cannot communicate with iOS app customers about purchasing methods other than IAP.[2190]

In an interview with Subcommittee staff , one developer that offers a "freemium" app—a popular business model where the app is available for free but users can purchase upgrades—recalled that it sent an email to customers with iOS devices with information about how to upgrade to a paid subscription, including a link to the service's website where customers could upgrade their subscription. Apple responded by threatening to remove the app from the App Store and blocked its updates, including security patches.[2191] A game developer described Apple's rules as reaching outside the App Store itself to police the communications that an app can have with its own customers, including communications intended to improve customer experience and offer discounts.[2192]

In his questions for the record for the Subcommittee's second hearing, Representative W. Gregory Steube (R-FL) asked Apple about banning communications to customers by app providers. Apple responded that its restrictions on communications between apps and customers are to ensure Apple can collect commissions and "prevent free-riding."[2193] Apple explained that it restricts developers from using the iOS ecosystem to "direct customers they have acquired through Apple to purchase content elsewhere for the purpose of avoiding Apple's rightful commission."[2194] The company described its policy as a prohibition "on developers promoting, *via* the App Store, transactions outside the App Store," and said Apple's policies were no different than most other retailers.[2195]

In June 2020, the European Commission announced that it had opened a formal antitrust investigation of Apple's App Store rules and conduct, including "the mandatory use of Apple's own

---

[2189] *App Store Developer Guidelines 3.1.1: In-App Purchase*, APPLE, https://developer.apple.com/app-store/review/guidelines/#in-app-purchase (last visited Sept. 27, 2020).

[2190] *Apple, App Store Developer Guidelines 3.1.3: Other Purchase Methods*, APPLE, https://developer.apple.com/app-store/review/guidelines/#other-purchase-methods (last visited Sept. 27, 2020).

[2191] Submission from ProtonMail, to H. Comm. on the Judiciary, 5 (Aug. 22, 2020) (on file with Comm.).

[2192] Interview with Source 143 (Aug. 27, 2020).

[2193] Innovation and Entrepreneurship Hearing at 2 (Response to Questions for the Record of Kyle Andeer, Vice Pres., Corp. Law, Apple Inc.).

[2194] *Id.* at 1.

[2195] *Id.* at 1–2.

proprietary in-app purchase system and restrictions on the availability of developers to inform iPhone and iPad users of alternative cheaper purchasing possibilities outside of apps."[2196]

As Apple has emphasized growing its Services business, app developers and technology writers have observed Apple is increasingly insistent that apps implement IAP—cutting Apple in on revenue from more developers—and threatening apps that do not comply with expulsion from the App Store.[2197] In June 2020, an email app developed by Basecamp called HEY was approved by the App Store and then abruptly told it would have to implement Apple in-app purchasing or face removal from the platform.[2198] While HEY's app updates were eventually allowed, Apple did force it to create a free trial option for iOS customers.[2199] Basecamp Founder and CTO David Heinemeier Hansson observed that Apple threatened and abused small app developers for years, and that the conflict with HEY amounted to a "shakedown."[2200] In August 2020, Apple denied WordPress the ability to update its app unless it implemented IAP, even though the WordPress app does not sell anything. Apple ultimately backed off its demands only after the issue received negative attention on social media.[2201] ProtonMail told the Subcommittee that its privacy-focused email app competes with an Apple's email app, and after being in the App Store for two years, Apple demanded the ProtonMail implement IAP or be removed from the App Store. ProtonMail complied to avoid damage to its business.[2202]

Internal Apple communications reviewed by Subcommittee staff indicate that Apple has leveraged its power over the App Store to require developers to implement IAP or risk being thrown

---

[2196] Press Release, Eur. Comm'n, Antitrust: Commission opens investigations into Apple's App Store rules (June 16, 2020), https://ec.europa.eu/commission/presscorner/detail/en/ip_20_1073.

[2197] *See e.g.*, Jeremy Howitz, *Apple's antitrust woes stem from its obsessions with control and money*, VENTURE BEAT (Aug. 7, 2020), https://venturebeat.com/2020/08/07/apples-antitrust-woes-stem-from-its-obsessions-with-control-and-money/ ("Apple might act like it's too large to care about money, but the company has recently sniped at developers who have succeeded on iOS without paying Apple anything, while doing as much as possible to push other developers — and users — into coughing up recurring subscription fees for both apps and games.").

[2198] *See e.g.*, Nilay Patel, *Apple approves Hey email app, but the fight's not over*, THE VERGE (June 22, 2020), https://www.theverge.com/2020/6/22/21298552/apple-hey-email-app-approval-rules-basecamp-launch; Rob Pegoraro, *Apple To Basecamp's Hey: Expect to Pay Us If You Want To Sell Privacy*, FORBES (June 17, 2020), https://www.forbes.com/sites/robpegoraro/2020/06/17/apple-to-basecamps-hey-expect-to-pay-us-if-you-want-to-sell-privacy/.

[2199] Chaim Gartenberg, *Hey opens its email service to everyone as Apple approves its app for good*, THE VERGE (June 25, 2020), https://www.theverge.com/2020/6/25/21302931/hey-email-service-public-launch-apple-approves-app-fight-policy-price.

[2200] *Apple v. Hey*, HEY, https://hey.com/apple/ (last visited Sept. 27, 2020).

[2201] *See* Sean Hollister, *WordPress founder claims Apple cut off updates to his completely free app because it wants 30 percent*, THE VERGE (Aug. 21, 2020), https://www.theverge.com/2020/8/21/21396316/apple-wordpress-in-app-purchase-tax-update-store; Sean Hollister, *Apple apologizes to WordPress, won't force the free app to add purchases after all*, THE VERGE (Aug. 23, 2020), https://www.theverge.com/2020/8/22/21397424/apple-wordpress-apology-iap-free-ios-app.

[2202] Submission from ProtonMail, to H. Comm. on the Judiciary, 5 (Aug. 22, 2020) (on file with Comm.).

out of the App Store.[2203] Then-Apple CEO Steve Jobs once explained, "there will be some roadkill because of it. I don't feel guilty" when confronted with developer complaints about Apple's commission and requirement to use IAP.[2204] The Netherlands Authority for Consumers and Markets (ACM) has noted that some app developers attribute Apple's inconsistent application of its rules to inattention to apps that are infrequently updated, and that Apple likely focuses on requiring IAP for high revenue-generating apps.[2205]

In response to the COVID-19 pandemic, some businesses moved physical events online, often booking through an app and holding the event through a video chat application. Educators have also shifted resources online, including through apps. *The New York Times* reported that Apple demanded a 30% commission from these virtual class offerings. As a result, one company stopped offering virtual classes to users of its iOS app. The *Times* reported that Apple threatened Airbnb that it would remove its app from the App Store if Airbnb did not comply with Apple's demand for a share of its revenues.[2206]

In interviews with Subcommittee staff , multiple app developers confirmed the *The New York Times'* reporting.[2207] Airbnb spoke with Subcommittee staff and described conversations with the App Store team in which Apple said it had observed an uptick in the number of apps offering virtual classes in lieu of in-person classes due to the COVID-19 pandemic. As a result, Apple began canvassing the App Store to require app developers implement IAP, entitling Apple to take 30% of in-app sales. Airbnb explained that Apple's commission, plus compliance with Apple's pricing tiers for in-app purchases would ultimately result in a 50-60% price increase for consumers.[2208]

Technology industry observers have reported similar conduct. On June 17, 2020, Ben Thompson, a prominent business analyst, wrote that app developers told him that Apple was demanding 30% commissions from businesses that have had to change their business models from live, in-person events to virtual events as a result of the COVID-19 pandemic. Mr. Thompson quoted one developer that explained Apple was taking advantage of small businesses in the midst of the ongoing public health crisis.[2209]

[2203] *See* Production of Apple, to H. Comm. on the Judiciary, HJC-APPLE-014701-702 (Nov. 23, 2010) (on file with Comm.).

[2204] Patrick McGee & Javier Espinoza, *Apple conflict with developers escalates ahead of worldwide conference*, FINANCIAL TIMES (June 22, 2020) https://www.ft.com/content/733ae8d4-e516-4418-9998-30414c368c6f.

[2205] *See* Neth. Auth. for Consumers & Mkts. at 89, 92–93.

[2206] Jack Nicas & David McCabe, *Their Business Went Virtual. Then Apple Wanted a Cut.*, N.Y. TIMES (July 28, 2020), https://www.nytimes.com/2020/07/28/technology/apple-app-store-airbnb-classpass.html.

[2207] *See e.g.*, Interview with Airbnb; Interview with Source 147 (Sept. 10, 2020).

[2208] *See* Interviews with Airbnb.

[2209] *See* Ben Thompson, *Xscale and ARM in the Cloud, Hey Versus Apple, Apple's IAP Campaign*, STRATECHERY (June 17, 2020), https://stratechery.com/2020/xscale-and-arm-in-the-cloud-hey-versus-apple-apples-iap-campaign/.

At the Subcommittee's hearing on July 29, 2020, Chairman Jerrold Nadler (D-NY) asked Mr. Cook about the allegations that Apple was canvassing the App Store to extract commissions from businesses that have been forced to change their business model in order to survive during the pandemic. Mr. Cook responded that Apple "would never take advantage" of the pandemic, but justified the conduct, explaining that the app developers were now offering what Apple defined as a "digital service" and Apple was entitled to commissions.[2210] Responding to *The New York Times'* reporting on the mater, Apple defended its conduct, explaining "[t]o ensure every developer can create and grow a successful business, Apple maintains a clear, consistent set of guidelines that apply equally to everyone."[2211]

App developers affected by these changes said that after Apple's conduct became public it created an exception to its policies until the end of 2020. However, on January 1, 2021 those businesses will be required to implement IAP or remove the ability to book virtual classes in their apps.[2212]

Developers have submitted evidence that Apple's commissions and fees, combined with the lack of competitive alternatives to the App Store and IAP harm competition and consumers. For instance, Match called Apple's fee for IAP "unreasonable," leading to higher prices for consumers and "an inferior user experience and a reduction of innovation."[2213] One developer that offers an app that directly competes with Apple told the Subcommittee that it was forced to raise prices to pay Apple's commission.

As a result, it was less competitive and fewer iOS users purchased its service. The company said that because apps often have small margins, they cannot absorb Apple's fees, so the price consumers pay for its app is more than 25% higher than it would otherwise be.[2214] Small developers described Apple's 30% cut "onerous."[2215] Epic Games, which recently filed an antitrust complaint against Apple, has told a federal court that Apple's fees and commissions force developers "to increase the prices they charge in order to pay Apple's app tax. There is no method app developers can use to

---

[2210] CEO Hearing Transcript at 156 (statement of Tim Cook, CEO, Apple Inc.)

[2211] Jack Nicas & David McCabe, *Their Business Went Virtual. Then Apple Wanted a Cut.*, N.Y. TIMES (July 28, 2020), https://www.nytimes.com/2020/07/28/technology/apple-app-store-airbnb-classpass.html.

[2212] Interview with Airbnb (Aug. 31, 2020).

[2213] Submission by Match Group, to H. Comm. on the Judiciary, MATCH_GRP_00000236, MATCH_GRP_00000238 (Oct. 23, 2019) (on file with Comm.).

[2214] Submission from ProtonMail, to H. Comm. on the Judiciary, 6 (Aug. 22, 2020) (on file with Comm.); *see also* Neth. Auth. for Consumers & Mkts. Study at 91.

[2215] Interview with Source 143 (Aug. 27, 2020).

avoid this tax."[2216] Mac and iOS app developer Brent Simmons explained Apple's fees reduce innovation and lead to fewer apps in the marketplace, observing:

> [T]he more money Apple takes from developers, the fewer resources developers have. When developers have to cut costs, they stop updating apps, skimp on customer support, put off hiring a graphic designer, etc. They decide not to make apps at all that they might have made were it easier to be profitable.[2217]

In Apple's internal documents and communications, the company's senior executives previously acknowledged that IAP requirement would stifle competition and limit the apps available to Apple's customers. For example, in an email conversation with other senior leaders at Apple about whether to require IAP for e-Book purchases, then-CEO Steve Jobs concluded, "I think this is all pretty simple—iBooks is going to be the only bookstore on iOS devices. We need to hold our heads high. One can read books bought elsewhere, just not buy/rent/subscribe from iOS without paying us, which we acknowledge is prohibitive for many things."[2218]

International competition authorities have also examined the competitive effects of Apple's App Store commissions and fees. The Australian Competition and Consumer Commission (ACCC) observed that Apple's control over app distribution on iOS devices gives it leverage to extract commissions from apps, reducing the revenue that app providers like media businesses can invest in content.[2219] The ACM, which completed a comprehensive study of mobile app stores in 2019, noted that developers have increased prices to account for commissions and fees.[2220] The ACM also remarked that Apple's 30% commission on in-app purchases may distort competition because Apple's requirement to use IAP often applies to apps competing directly against Apple's apps. As a result, app developers with small margins cannot simply absorb the cost of Apple's commission, so they increase their price, which gives Apple's competing service an advantage.[2221] Developers ACM spoke with "mentioned that it is highly unlikely that it is a coincidence that these digital services that are required to use IAP face competition from Apple's own apps, or possibly will do in the future."[2222]

[2216] Complaint at 3, Epic Games, Inc. v. Apple Inc., 4:20-cv-05640 (N.D.Cal. 2020), https://cdn2.unrealengine.com/apple-complaint-734589783.pdf.

[2217] Brent Simmons, *I Got Teed Off and Went on a Long Rant About This Opinion Piece on the App Store,* INESSENTIAL (July 28, 2020), https://inessential.com/2020/07/28/untrue.

[2218] Production of Apple, to H. Comm. on the Judiciary, HJC-APPLE-014816-18 (Feb. 6, 2011) (on file with Comm.).

[2219] *See* Austl. Competition & Consumer Comm'n at 223, 225 (2019); *see also* Ben Thompson, *Antitrust, the App Store, and Apple,* STRATECHERY (Nov. 27, 2018), https://www.stratechery.com/2018/antitrust-the-app-store-and-apple ("Apple makes a huge amount of money, with massive profit margins, by virtue of its monopolistic control of the App Store. It doesn't make the games or the productivity applications or the digital content, it simply skims off 30%, and not because its purchasing experience is better, but because it is the only choice.").

[2220] Neth. Auth. for Consumers & Mkts. Study at 91.

[2221] *See id.* at 7.

[2222] *Id.* at 89.

ii. Pre-Installed Apps, Default Settings, Private App Programming Interfaces (APIs), and Device Functionality

In addition to investigating whether Apple abuses its monopoly power over app distribution to leverage high commissions and fees from app developers, Subcommittee also examined whether Apple abuses its role as iOS and App Store owner to preference its own apps or harm rivals. The Committee requested information regarding Apple's practice of locking-in Apple's apps as defaults on the iPhone, and Subcommittee Chairman Cicilline requested information from Apple regarding its practice of pre-installing its own apps on the iPhone. Subcommittee Chairman Cicilline also sought input on whether Apple's policy of reserving certain application programing interfaces (APIs) and access to certain device functionalities for its apps gives Apple's services a competitive advantage.

It is widely understood that consumers usually do not change default options.[2223] This is the case "even if they can freely change them or choose a competitive alternative."[2224] Subcommittee staff reviewed communications between Apple employees that demonstrate an understanding inside Apple that pre-loading apps could be advantageous when competing against third-party apps.[2225]

Apple pre-installs about 40 Apple apps into current iPhone models.[2226] Several of these apps are set as defaults and are "operating system apps" that are "integrated into the phone's core operating system and part of the combined experience of iOS and iPhone."[2227] According to Apple, users can delete most of these pre-installed apps.[2228] Apple does not pre-install any third-party apps, and until the September 2020 release of iOS 14, it did not allow consumers to select third-party web browser or email apps as defaults.[2229] Apple says that it is making "more than 250,000 APIs available to developers in iOS 14."[2230]

[2223] *See e.g.,* Dig. Competition Expert Panel Report at 36 ("[C]onsumers in digital markets display strong preferences for default options and loyalty to brands they know."); Stigler Report at 8, 41 ("Consumers do not replace the default apps on their phones... and take other actions that may look like poor decisions if those consumers like to choose among options and experience competition.").

[2224] JOHN BERGMAYER, PUBLIC KNOWLEDGE, TENDING THE GARDEN: HOW TO ENSURE THAT APP STORES PUT USERS FIRST 19 (2020), https://www.publicknowledge.org/wp-content/uploads/2020/06/Tending_the_Garden.pdf.

[2225] *See* Production of Apple, to H. Comm. on the Judiciary, HJC-APPLE-011035–36 (Mar. 12, 2019) (on file with Comm.) (noting that Apple pre-loading software products on to iOS devices "would clearly be even more problematic" than "Apple releasing its apps via the App Store....").

[2226] CEO Hearing Transcript at 1 (response to Questions for the Record of Tim Cook, CEO, Apple Inc.).

[2227] *Id.* at 2.

[2228] *Id.*

[2229] *Id. See also* Press Release, Apple, Apple reveals new developer technologies to foster the next generation of apps (June 22, 2020), https://www.apple.com/newsroom/2020/06/apple-reveals-new-developer-technologies-to-foster-the-next-generation-of-apps/ ("Email and browser app developers can offer their apps as default options, selectable by users.").

[2230] CEO Hearing Transcript at 3 (response to Questions for the Record of Tim Cook, CEO, Apple Inc.).

A report by the Netherlands Authority for Consumers and Markets (ACM) on mobile app stores recently observed that app providers believe they "have a strong disadvantage" when competing with Apple's apps due to the fact that those services are often pre-installed on iOS devices.[2231] The study also noted that "pre-installation of apps can create a so-called status-quo bias. Consumers are more likely to use the apps that are pre-installed on their smartphones."[2232] Consumers will download apps that compete with pre-installed apps only when there is a noted quality difference, and even then, lower-quality pre-installed apps will still enjoy an advantage over third-party apps.[2233] The European Commission's 2019 report on competition in digital markets explained that privileging access to APIs can provide an advantage to those with greater access over those with more innovative products.[2234] Public Knowledge concluded that Apple's control of iOS and the App store enables it to advantage its own apps and services by pre-installing them on iOS devices, leading consumers to rely on the pre-installed apps rather than looking for alternatives in the App Store.[2235]

Mobile operating system providers develop APIs to permit apps to access a device's features, such as the microphone, camera, or GPS, or other software programs and determine what information on the device apps can access.[2236] Public APIs for iOS are made available to app developers to ensure apps are integrated with the device and function as intended. These public APIs also control the services that are opened via default when users click a link to open a webpage or an address to open a map application. Private APIs access functionality that is not publicly released. Apple is permitted to use the private APIs on iOS devices, but third-party developers are not.[2237]

Apple's public APIs default to Apple's pre-installed applications. As a result, when an iPhone user clicks on a link, the webpage opens in the Safari Browser, a song request opens in Apple Music, and clicking on an address launches Apple Maps.[2238] With some recent exceptions, iPhone users are

---

[2231] Neth. Auth. for Consumers & Mkts. Study at 5, 15, 85–86.

[2232] *Id.* at 84 (citing Press Release, Eur. Comm'n, Antitrust: Commission Fines Google €4.34 Billion for Illegal Practices Regarding Android Mobile Devices to Strengthen Dominance of Google's Search Engine (July 18, 2018), https://ec.europa.eu/commission/presscorner/detail/en/ip_18_4581).

[2233] *Id.*

[2234] Eur. Comm'n Competition Report at 34.

[2235] JOHN BERGMAYER, PUBLIC KNOWLEDGE, TENDING THE GARDEN: HOW TO ENSURE THAT APP STORES PUT USERS FIRST 20 (2020), https://www.publicknowledge.org/wp-content/uploads/2020/06/Tending_the_Garden.pdf. *See also* DIG. COMPETITION EXPERT PANEL, PUBLIC RESPONSES TO CALL FOR EVIDENCE FROM ORGANISATIONS, RESPONSE OF BRITISH BROAD. CORP. 44 (2018), https://assets.publishing.service.gov.uk/government/uploads/system/uploads/attachment_data/file/785549/DCEP_Public_re sponses_to_call_for_evidence_from_organisations.pdf ("Apple's control of devices and operating system allows it to pre-load and favour its own services i.e. Apple Podcasts.").

[2236] Competition & Mkts. Auth. Report at 42; Neth. Auth. for Consumers & Mkts. Study at 59.

[2237] *See* Thomas Claburn, *Apple Frees a Few Private API, Makes them Public*, THE REGISTER (June 13, 2017), https://www.theregister.com/2017/06/13/apple_inches_toward_openness/.

[2238] Neth. Auth. for Consumers & Mkts. Study at 59–60.

unable to change this default setting;[2239] however they are able to send app-specific links from inside many popular apps. For example, a person can share a link to a song in a third-party music streaming app such that it would open that song in the same app if it is already downloaded on the recipient's smartphone. One app developer has argued, however, that Apple uses its control over iOS to give its own apps and services advantages that are not available to competitors. For example, the developer explained that for years it was barred from integrating with Siri, Apple's intelligent virtual assistant that is built into Apple devices. Although Siri can now integrate with the app, users must explicitly request Siri launch the third-party app, otherwise it will default to launch Apple's service.[2240]

Like setting advantageous defaults and pre-installing its own apps, Apple is also able to preference its own services by reserving access to APIs and certain device functionalities for itself. ACM and technology reporters have both noted that "private APIs have the potential to give Apple apps a competitive advantage," and that "Apple has for a long time favored its own services through APIs."[2241] For example, from the release of iOS 4.3 until iOS 8, "third-party developers had to rely on the UIWebView API to render web pages in iOS apps, while Apple gave its own apps access to a private, faster API," and as a result, "Google's mobile version of Chrome for iOS could not compete with Apple's mobile version of Safari in terms of speed."[2242]

Apple's mobile payments service, Apple Pay, is an example of an in-house app that enjoys an advantage due to its ability to access certain functionalities, such as near-field communication (NFC), on the iPhone that are off limits to third-party apps. According to Apple, "NFC is an industry-standard, contactless technology" that enables communications between the mobile device and payment terminal.[2243] Apple Pay uses the iPhone's NFC chip to allows users to make contactless payments at retail outlets that use the technology.[2244] However, Apple blocks access for third-party apps. In June 2020 the European Commission opened a formal antitrust investigation into Apple's conduct in the mobile payments market, including "Apple's limitation of access to the Near Field Communication (NFC) functionality ('tap and go') on iPhones for payments in stores."[2245] In response to questions

---

[2239] *See* Press Release, Apple, *Apple Reveals New Developer Technologies to Foster the Next Generation of Apps* (June 22, 2020), https://www.apple.com/newsroom/2020/06/apple-reveals-new-developer-technologies-to-foster-the-next-generation-of-apps/ ("Email and browser app developers can offer their apps as default options, selectable by users.").

[2240] Submission from Source 711, to H. Comm. on the Judiciary, Source 711-00000080 at 23 (Oct. 15, 2019) (on file with Comm.).

[2241] Thomas Claburn, *Apple Frees a Few Private API, Makes them Public*, THE REGISTER (June 13, 2017), https://www.theregister.com/2017/06/13/apple_inches_toward_openness/. *See also* Neth. Auth. for Consumers & Mkts. Study at 82.

[2242] Thomas Claburn, *Apple Frees a Few Private API, Makes them Public*, THE REGISTER (June 13, 2017), https://www.theregister.com/2017/06/13/apple_inches_toward_openness/.

[2243] *Apple Pay Security and Privacy Overview*, APPLE, https://support.apple.com/en-us/HT203027 (last visited Oct. 4, 2020).

[2244] *Id.*

[2245] Press Release, Eur. Comm'n, Antitrust: Commission Opens Investigation into Apple Practices Regarding Apple *Pay* (June 16, 2020) https://ec.europa.eu/commission/presscorner/detail/en/ip_20_1075.

from Subcommittee Chairman Cicilline and Representative Kelly Armstrong (D-ND) about Apple's treatment of third-party mobile payment apps and access to the iPhone's NFC chip, Apple said that it limits access to the NFC chip to protect the security of the iPhone and has detailed the differences between Apple's treatment of Apple Pay and third-party mobile payment apps.[2246]

The advantage Apple provides Apple Pay may be heightened during the COVID-19 pandemic. Due to the novel coronavirus, consumers have accelerated their adoption of contactless payments, with more than half of global consumers preferring contactless payments over cash or traditional credit cards.[2247] In April 2020, MasterCard reported a 40% rise in use of contactless payments, with the trend expected to continue after the pandemic. MasterCard CEO Ajay Banga explained the trend was driven by shoppers "looking for a quick way to get in and out of stores without exchanging cash, touching terminals, or anything else."[2248] Apple itself has capitalized on the perception that contactless is the safest way to make transactions, marketing Apple Pay as "a safer way to pay that helps you avoid touching buttons or exchanging cash."[2249]

Like Apple Pay, Safari is another pre-installed app that enjoys advantages over rivals. Safari is Apple's default browser on iOS and Mac devices. When someone using an Apple device clicks on a website link, the webpage opens in the Safari browser.[2250] Until the September 2020 release of iOS 14, Apple did not allow consumers to select third-party web browser as a default.[2251] This was unique to iOS. Other mobile device operating systems allow the user to set a default browser across all applications.[2252]

[2246] CEO Hearing Transcript at 1, 3 (response to Questions for the Record of Tim Cook, CEO, Apple Inc.).

[2247] *See* DYNATA, GLOBAL CONSUMER TRENDS: COVID-19 EDITION, THE NEW NORMAL, A BREAKTHROUGH FOR CONTACTLESS PAYMENTS 2 (2020), http://info.dynata.com/rs/105-ZDT-791/images/Dynata-Global-Consumer-Trends-COVID-19-The-New-Normal-Breakthrough-for-Contactless-Payments.pdf. *See also* Press Release, Eur. Comm'n, Antitrust: Commission Opens Investigation into Apple Practices Regarding Apple Pay (June 16, 2020) https://ec.europa.eu/commission/presscorner/detail/en/ip_20_1075 ("Executive Vice-President Margrethe Vestager, in charge of competition policy, said: 'Mobile payment solutions are rapidly gaining acceptance among users of mobile devices, facilitating payments both online and in physical stores. This growth is accelerated by the coronavirus crisis, with increasing online payments and contactless payments in stores.'").

[2248] Kate Rooney, *Contactless payments jump 40% as shoppers fear germs on cash and credit cards, Mastercard says*, CNBC (Apr. 29, 2020) https://www.cnbc.com/2020/04/29/mastercard-sees-40percent-jump-in-contactless-payments-due-to-coronavirus.html.

[2249] *Apple Pay*, APPLE, https://www.apple.com/apple-pay/ (last visited Sept. 26, 2020).

[2250] Neth. Auth. for Consumers & Mkts. Study at 59–60.

[2251] *See* Mark Gurman, *Apple's Default iPhone Apps Give It Growing Edge Over App Store Rivals*, BLOOMBERG (Oct. 2, 2019), https://www.bloomberg.com/news/articles/2019-10-02/iphone-ios-users-can-t-change-default-apps-safari-mail-music; Press Release, Apple, Apple reveals new developer technologies to foster the next generation of apps (June 22, 2020), https://www.apple.com/newsroom/2020/06/apple-reveals-new-developer-technologies-to-foster-the-next-generation-of-apps/ ("Email and browser app developers can offer their apps as default options, selectable by users.").

[2252] *See e.g., Google Chrome Help*, GOOGLE https://support.google.com/chrome/answer/95417?co=GENIE.Platform%3DAndroid&hl=en-GB (last visited Sept. 26, 2020); *Support*, MOZILLA, https://support.mozilla.org/en-US/kb/make-firefox-default-browser-android (last visited Sept.

Apple's policies require alternative browsers apps for iOS (iPhone) to use Apple's WebKit browser engine. As a result, all competing web browser companies must rebuild their product to make it available for iOS users.[2253] Additionally, browser engines are used in other applications that link to web content, such as email applications.[2254] Market participants explained to Subcommittee staff that these guidelines cost significant internal resources and create a hurdle for market entry on iOS. These requirements also make alternative browsers on iOS less technically distinct from Safari limiting product differentiation.[2255] Further, market participants expressed concern that because Apple mandates the use of WebKit, as opposed to allowing developers an option, that WebKit has become slower to innovate and adopt standards.[2256]

At the Subcommittee's second hearing, Chairman Cicilline asked Apple about its policies related to web browser engines. Apple responded: "By requiring use of WebKit, Apple can provide security updates to all our users quickly and accurately, no matter which browser they decide to download from the App Store." [2257] While market participants agree that Apple's WebKit mandates would allow for easier updates to browser apps, there is disagreement about whether WebKit is measurably less secure than other browser engines.[2258]

The ACM has noted app providers have limited access to some APIs "that are essential for the functioning of apps. In certain cases, these functionalities are, however, used by Apple for their own apps,"[2259] which may limit competitive alternatives to Apple's products and services.[2260]

26, 2020); *Support*, MICROSOFT, https://support.microsoft.com/en-us/help/4028606/windows-10-change-your-default-browser (last visited Sept. 26, 2020).

[2253] *App Store Review Guidelines 2.5.6*, APPLE: DEVELOPER, https://developer.apple.com/app-store/review/guidelines/#software-requirements (last visited Sept. 26, 2020) ("Apps that browse the web must use the appropriate WebKit framework and WebKit Javascript.").

[2254] *See* Michael Krasnov, *Browser Engine Diversity or Internet of Google*, EVERDAY.CODES (Dec. 15 2019), https://everyday.codes/google/browser-engine-diversity-or-internet-of-google/.

[2255] Interview with Source 269 (July 23, 2019) ("Apple prohibits competitors from deploying their own web browsing engines on its mobile operating system. Web browsing engines provide the distinctive features of a web browser. Apple forces competitors to base their web browsers on a reduced version of its own web browser engine, 'WebKit'.").

[2256] *See* Owen Williams, *Apple is Trying to Kill Web Technology*, ONEZERO (Nov. 7, 2019), https://onezero.medium.com/apple-is-trying-to-kill-web-technology-a274237c174d.

[2257] Innovation and Entrepreneurship Hearing at 2 (response to Questions for the Record of Kyle Andeer, Vice Pres., Corp. Law, Apple Inc.).

[2258] *See* Andy Greenberg, *How Safari and iMessage Have Made iPhones Less Secure*, WIRED (Sept. 9, 2019), https://www.wired.com/story/ios-security-imessage-safari/.

[2259] Neth. Auth. for Consumers & Mkts. Study at 85–86.

[2260] *Id.* at 103.

In January 2020, Kirsten Daru, Chief Privacy Office and General Counsel of Tile offered testimony to Subcommittee about this dynamic.[2261] Tile is a company that makes hardware and software that helps people find lost items.[2262] Tile testified that for years it successfully collaborated with Apple. However, in 2019 reports surfaced that Apple planned a launch a hardware product to compete with Tile.[2263] In her testimony, Ms. Daru said that Apple's 2019 release of iOS 13 harmed Tile's service and user experience while simultaneously introducing a new pre-installed Apple finder app called Find My.[2264] Changes to iOS 13 made it more difficult for Tile's customers to set up the service, requiring several confusing steps to grant Tile permission to track the phone's location.[2265] Meanwhile, Apple's Find My app was pre-installed on iOS devices and activated by default during iOS installation. Users are unable to opt out of Find My's location tracking "unless they go deep into Apple's labyrinthine menu of settings."[2266] Tile's response to the Subcommittee's Questions for the Record included detailed location permission flow comparisons between Tile and Find My.[2267] Tile explained that as a result of Apple's changes to iOS 13 it saw significant decreases in users and a steep drop off in users enabling the proper settings on iOS devices.[2268]

A group of app developers wrote to Apple CEO Tim Cook in 2019 arguing that Apple's new location notification permission polices will hurt their businesses and accused Apple of acting anticompetitively because it was treating its own services differently:

> The developers conclude their email by asserting that Apple's own apps don't have to jump through similar hoops to get access to user location. An Apple app called Find My for tracking the location of other iPhone users, for example, bypasses the locating tracking requests that apps from outside developers must go through, the email reads.

[2261] *See* Competitors Hearing (statement of Kirsten Daru, Chief Privacy Officer & Gen. Counsel, Tile, Inc.).

[2262] *Id.* at 1.

[2263] *See* Guilherme Rambo, *Apple revamping Find My Friends & Find My iPhone in unified app, developing Tile-like personal item tracking*, 9TO5MAC (Apr. 17, 2019), https://9to5mac.com/2019/04/17/find-my-iphone-revamp/.

[2264] Competitors Hearing at 2 (statement of Kirsten Daru, Chief Privacy Officer & Gen. Counsel, Tile, Inc.).

[2265] *Id.*

[2266] Reed Albergotti, *Apple says recent changes to operating system improve user privacy, but some lawmakers see them as an effort to edge out its rivals*, WASH. POST (Nov. 26, 2019), https://www.washingtonpost.com/technology/2019/11/26/apple-emphasizes-user-privacy-lawmakers-see-it-an-effort-edge-out-its-rivals/; *see also* Competitors Hearing at 3 (statement of Kirsten Daru, Chief Privacy Officer & Gen. Counsel, Tile, Inc.).

[2267] Competitors Hearing at 4–14 (response to Questions for the Record of Kirsten Daru, Chief Privacy Officer & Gen. Counsel, Tile, Inc.).

[2268] Competitors Hearing at 6 (response to Questions for the Record of Kirsten Daru, Chief Privacy Officer & Gen. Counsel, Tile, Inc.); Interview with Kirsten Daru, Vice President and General Counsel, Tile Inc. (July 10, 2020).

Instead, Find My gains location access through a process that occurs as users install the new operating system.[2269]

The app developers—including Tile, Arity, Life360, Happn, Zenly, Zendrive, and Twenty—explained that this gives Apple products that compete against their apps an advantage. "Apple says Find My and other apps are built into iOS and that it doesn't see a need to make location-tracking requests from users for the apps after they install the operating system."[2270] Apple also differentiates Find My by pointing out that "'Find My' stores user location data *locally* on the user's iPhone, and Apple only transmits the location up on the user's request."[2271]

In response to the Subcommittee's questions at its second hearing in July 2019, Apple responded and explained that the iOS 13 changes give users more control over background location tracking by apps. Apple also explained that turning on location tracking to Apple's Find My service was "essential" for users, and that the disparate treatment between Find My and Tile was due to the fact that data from Find My remains on the device, while Tile stores data externally.[2272] Additionally, during Apple's June 2020 World Wide Developers Conference, Apple announced that the Find My app would work with third-party finder hardware like Tile's.[2273] However, Apple's service would require companies like Tile to abandon their apps and the ability to differentiate their service from Apple's and other competitors.[2274] Apple's solution would continue to put Tile and other apps and hardware developers offering finder services at a competitive disadvantage.[2275]

[2269] Aaron Tilley, *Developers Call Apple Privacy Changes Anti-Competitive*, THE INFO. (Aug. 16, 2019), https://www.theinformation.com/articles/developers-call-apple-privacy-changes-anti-competitive.

[2270] *Id.*

[2271] Letter from Kyle Andeer, Vice Pres., Corp. Law & Chief Compliance Officer, Apple Inc., to Hon. Jerrold Nadler, Chairman, H. Comm. on the Judiciary, Hon. Doug Collins, Ranking Member, H. Comm on the Judiciary, Hon. David N. Cicilline, Chairman, Subcomm. on Antitrust, Commercial and Admin. Law of the H. Comm. on the Judiciary, and Hon. F. James Sensenbrenner, Ranking Member, Subcomm. on Antitrust, Commercial and Admin. Law of the H. Comm. on the Judiciary, 3 (Feb. 17, 2020), https://docs.house.gov/meetings/JU/JU05/20200117/110386/HHRG-116-JU05-20200117-SD004.pdf.

[2272] *See id.* at 2.

[2273] *See* Ben Lovejoy, *Comment: This week's keynote quietly tackled five of Apple's antitrust issues*, 9TO5MAC (Jun. 24, 2020), https://9to5mac.com/2020/06/24/apples-antitrust-issues-2/.

[2274] *See* Interview with Kirsten Daru, Vice President and General Counsel, Tile Inc. (July 10, 2020); APPLE, FIND MY NETWORK ACCESSORY SPECIFICATION, DEVELOPER PREVIEW: RELEASE R1, 14, https://images.frandroid.com/wp-content/uploads/2020/06/Find_My_network_accessory_protocol_specification.pdf (prohibiting "an accessory that supports the Find My network accessory protocol" from "operat[ing] simultaneously on the Find My network and another finder network....").

[2275] Interview with Kirsten Daru, Vice Pres. and Gen. Counsel, Tile Inc. (Jun. 26, 2020). *See* Reed Albergotti, *Amid antitrust scrutiny, Apple makes quiet power moves over developers*, WASH. POST (July 24, 2020), https://www.washingtonpost.com/technology/2020/07/24/apple-find-my-competition/.

iii. App Search Rankings

In response to extensive reporting on the subject, Subcommittee staff has also examined the competitive effects of Apple's search rankings in its App Store. In 2019, the *Wall Street Journal* and *The New York Times* both conducted extensive investigations and reported that Apple appeared to be favoring its apps in the App Store search results.[2276] The *Wall Street Journal* explained that "Apple's mobile apps routinely appear first in search results ahead of competitors in its App Store, a powerful advantage that skirts some of the company's rules on search rankings."[2277] *The New York Times* reported that six years of analysis of App Store search rankings found Apple-owned apps ranked first for at least 700 common search terms. "Some searches produced as many as 14 Apple apps before showing results from rivals," although app developers could pay Apple to place ads at the top of the search results.[2278] Searches for the app titles of competing apps even resulted in Apple's apps ranked first.[2279]

Apple's apps "ranked first in more than 60% of basic searches, such as for 'maps'" and "Apple apps that generate revenue through subscriptions or sales, like Music or Books, showed up first in 95% of searches related to those apps."[2280] *The Wall Street Journal* noted that growing revenue from its apps is core to Apple's strategy of offsetting sluggish hardware sales by increasing revenue from its Services business.[2281]

Rival app developers slipped down the search rankings as Apple introduced new services in their product categories. For example, Spotify had long been the top search result for the query "music," but Apple Music quickly became the top search result shortly after it joined the App Store in June 2016. By the end of 2018, eight of Apple's apps appeared in the first eight search results for "music," and Spotify had fallen to the 23rd result. Similarly, Audiobooks.com was the top ranked result for "audiobooks" for nearly two years but was overtaken by Apple Books shortly after Apple began marketing for Books. Audiobooks explained to the *Wall Street Journal* that losing the top search ranking to Apple "triggered a 25% decline in Audiobooks.com's daily app downloads."[2282]

[2276] *See* Tripp Mickle, *Apple Dominates App Store Search Results, Thwarting Competitors*, WALL ST. J (July 23, 2019), https://www.wsj.com/articles/apple-dominates-app-store-search-results-thwarting-competitors-11563897221; Jack Nicas & Keith Collins, *How Apple's Apps Topped Rivals in the App Store it Controls*, N.Y. TIMES (Sept. 9, 2019), https://www.nytimes.com/interactive/2019/09/09/technology/apple-app-store-competition.html.

[2277] Tripp Mickle, *Apple Dominates App Store Search Results, Thwarting Competitors*, WALL ST. J (July 23, 2019), https://www.wsj.com/articles/apple-dominates-app-store-search-results-thwarting-competitors-11563897221.

[2278] Jack Nicas & Keith Collins, *How Apple's Apps Topped Rivals in the App Store it Controls*, N.Y. TIMES (Sept. 9, 2019), https://www.nytimes.com/interactive/2019/09/09/technology/apple-app-store-competition.html.

[2279] Tripp Mickle, *Apple Dominates App Store Search Results, Thwarting Competitors*, WALL ST. J (July 23, 2019), https://www.wsj.com/articles/apple-dominates-app-store-search-results-thwarting-competitors-11563897221.

[2280] *Id.*

[2281] *Id.*

[2282] *Id.*

The reporting on App Store search also revealed that Apple may also advantage its apps by holding them to a different standard when they appear in the App Store search rankings. Apple told *The Wall Street Journal* "it uses 42 factors to determine where apps rank," and that the four most important factors are "downloads, ratings, relevance, and 'user behavior,'" with user behavior the most important factor because it measures how often users select and download an app.[2283] Approximately forty of Apple's apps come preinstalled on iPhones. These apps do not have reviews and consumers cannot rate them. Mr. Cook explained at the Subcommittee's hearing that Apple's "apps that are integrated into the iPhone are not reviewable by users on the App Store."[2284] Apple has also said that its search algorithm works the same for all apps, including its own.[2285]

Despite the fact that Apple's pre-installed apps do not have ratings or reviews—factors that Apple says are most influential in determining app ranking—many of Apple's pre-installed apps "still tend to be ranked first, even when users search for exact titles of other apps."[2286] For example, Apple Books has no reviews or rankings and appears first in a search for "books," while competing apps have tens-of-thousands of customer reviews and ratings of 4.8 or 4.9 stars on Apple's five-star rating system.[2287] A search by Subcommittee staff of terms "music," "news," "TV," and "podcast" returned Apple Music, News, TV, and Podcasts as top ranked search results although those apps do not have any reviews or ranking.[2288]

Despite the lack of reviews or rankings, Apple told the *Wall Street Journal* that "the No. 1 position for Books in a 'books' search is reasonable, since it is an exact name match."[2289] Philip Schiller, Apple's Senior Vice President, Worldwide Marketing who oversees the App Store and Eddy Cue, Apple's Senior Vice President Internet and Software Services said "there was nothing underhanded about the algorithm the company had built to display search results in the store,"[2290] and

---

[2283] *Id.*

[2284] CEO Hearing Transcript at 2 (response to Questions for the Record of Tim Cook, CEO, Apple Inc.).

[2285] *See* Tripp Mickle, *Apple Dominates App Store Search Results, Thwarting Competitors*, WALL ST. J (July 23, 2019), https://www.wsj.com/articles/apple-dominates-app-store-search-results-thwarting-competitors-11563897221.

[2286] *Id.*

[2287] Search Results: "books," IOS APP STORE (Sept. 17, 2020).

[2288] Search Results: "music," "news," "TV," "podcast," IOS APP STORE (Sept. 17, 2020).

[2289] Tripp Mickle, *Apple Dominates App Store Search Results, Thwarting Competitors*, WALL ST. J (July 23, 2019), https://www.wsj.com/articles/apple-dominates-app-store-search-results-thwarting-competitors-11563897221.

[2290] Jack Nicas & Keith Collins, *How Apple's Apps Topped Rivals in the App Store it Controls*, N.Y. TIMES (Sept. 9, 2019), https://www.nytimes.com/interactive/2019/09/09/technology/apple-app-store-competition.html.

that Apple's apps tend to rank highly because they are popular and their generic names like Books and Music closely match common search terms.[2291]

It appears that Apple does not apply the same rule to third-party apps. Documents reviewed by Subcommittee staff show that Apple previously punished non-Apple apps that attempted to "cheat" the app store rankings. Apple determined that at least one third-party app had achieved its high search ranking because its name was a generic name that was also a common search term. Apple's employees determined it was cheating to give an app the name of common search term.

In February 2018, Apple's App Store search team noted that an app named "Photo Editor— Stylo" was the top ranked result when users searched the App Store for "photo editor."[2292] In an email thread with Philip Schiller, Apple's Senior Vice President, Worldwide Marketing, an Apple employee wrote that "[s]ince the app name matched a broad query term like 'photo editor' the developer was able to game the query with a direct name match."[2293] The Apple employee explained that "[t]he app has been added to the Search Penalty Box for rank demotion," and the action was labeled as complete.[2294] Additional action was slated to disable the initial boost that new apps are given in the app store if the app name is an "exact match to broad queries."[2295] Here, Apple punished an app for the same conduct it said justified Apple's position atop the App Store rankings.

Apple's position as the provider of iOS enabled it to designate the App Store as the sole means for app developers to distribute software to iPhone users. Apple's public statements, including testimony by Mr. Cook that Apple's apps "go through the same rules" as more than 1.7 million third-party apps appear to be inconsistent with Apple's actual practices.[2296] In this case, Apple leveraged its control of iOS and the App Store to give its own apps preferential treatment, and applied a different set of rules than third-party apps, punishing them for the very conduct Apple engaged in. Subcommittee staff did not have access to additional evidence from Apple to determine how widespread this practice is within the company.

iv. Competitively Sensitive Information

In addition to investigating allegations Apple engages in self-preferencing in the App Store, the Committee sought information regarding whether Apple exploits third-party developers that rely on

---

[2291] *Id.*; *see also* Apple, *Apple: Distinctive Products with a Seamless, Integrated User Experience* 23 (July 13, 2020) (on file with Comm.) ("Because many of Apple's apps are named after generic topics (such as Music, Maps, and Podcasts), those apps benefit from functional queries that have essentially become navigational.").

[2292] Production of Apple, to H. Comm. on the Judiciary, HJC-APPLE-008082–86 (Feb. 9, 2018) (on file with Comm.).

[2293] *Id.*

[2294] *Id.*

[2295] *Id.*

[2296] CEO Hearing Transcript at 176 (statement of Tim Cook, CEO, Apple Inc.).

distribution in the App Store. Developers have alleged that Apple abuses its position as the provider of iOS and operator of the App Store to collect competitively sensitive information about popular apps and then build competing apps, or integrate the popular app's functionality into iOS.[2297] The practice is known as "Sherlocking." The antitrust laws do not protect app developers from competition, and platforms should continue to innovate and improve their products and services. However, Sherlocking can be anticompetitive in some instances.[2298]

Some app developers have complained that Apple leverages its control of iOS and the App Store to glean business intelligence that enables it to better compete against third-party apps.[2299] For example, after a stress relief app called Breathe was Sherlocked in 2016, the app's developers said that Apple used third-party developers "as an R&D arm."[2300] *The Washington Post* reported on the phenomenon, explaining:

> Developers have come to accept that, without warning, Apple can make their work obsolete by announcing a new app or feature that uses or incorporates their ideas. Some apps have simply buckled under the pressure, in some cases shutting down. They generally don't sue Apple because of the difficulty and expense in fighting the tech giant—and the consequences they might face from being dependent on the platform.[2301]

At the Subcommittee's fifth hearing, Representative Joe Neguse (D-CO) asked Ms. Daru of Tile about how Apple used competitively sensitive information it collects as owner of the iOS ecosystem to compete against third-party apps. She explained that as operating system provider and App Store operator, Apple knows who Tile's customers are, the types of apps those customers preferred, and the demographics of iOS users that look at Tile's app or search for similar apps—information that would give Apple a competitive advantage against Tile.[2302] Ms. Daru testified that

---

[2297] *See e.g.*, Brian Heater, *The makers of Duet Display and Luna on life after Apple's Sidecar*, TECHCRUNCH (Jun. 7, 2019), https://techcrunch.com/2019/06/07/the-makers-of-duet-display-and-luna-on-life-after-apples-sidecar/.

[2298] *See* JOHN BERGMAYER, PUBLIC KNOWLEDGE, TENDING THE GARDEN: HOW TO ENSURE THAT APP STORES PUT USERS FIRST 21, 58 (2020), https://www.publicknowledge.org/wp-content/uploads/2020/06/Tending_the_Garden.pdf.

[2299] *See e.g.*, Reed Albergotti, *How Apple uses its App Store to copy the best ideas*, WASH POST (Sept. 5, 2019), https://www.washingtonpost.com/technology/2019/09/05/how-apple-uses-its-app-store-copy-best-ideas/.

William Gallagher, *Developers talk about being 'Sherlocked' as Apple uses them 'for market research'*, APPLE INSIDER (Jun. 6, 2019), https://appleinsider.com/articles/19/06/06/developers-talk-about-being-sherlocked-as-apple-uses-them-for-market-research; John Patrick Pullen, *Why These People Are Upset About Apple's Latest Updates*, TIME (Jun. 21, 2016), https://time.com/4372515/apple-app-developers-wwdc-sherlock-sherlocked/; Adi Robertson, *Apple restores mail app after developer tries to rally 'Sherlocked' victims*, THE VERGE (Feb. 11, 2020), https://www.theverge.com/2020/2/11/21133023/apple-bluemail-blix-restored-mac-app-store-sherlocking-patent-lawsuit.

[2300] John Patrick Pullen, *Why These People Are Upset About Apple's Latest Updates*, TIME (Jun. 21, 2016), https://time.com/4372515/apple-app-developers-wwdc-sherlock-sherlocked/.

[2301] Reed Albergotti, *How Apple uses its App Store to copy the best ideas*, WASH POST. (Sept. 5, 2019), https://www.washingtonpost.com/technology/2019/09/05/how-apple-uses-its-app-store-copy-best-ideas/.

[2302] Competitors Hearing Transcript at 53 (statement of Kirsten Daru, Chief Privacy Officer & Gen. Counsel, Tile, Inc.).

Apple had harmed Tile's service and user experience, while simultaneously introducing a rival app and preparing to launch a rival hardware product.[2303] Blix, developer of email management app BlueMail, has sued Apple in federal court claimed Apple has engaged in Sherlocking and infringed the patents underlying BlueMail:

> Apple frequently takes other companies' innovative features, adds those ideas to Apple's own software products without permission, and then either ejects the original third-party application from the App Store (as it did with Blix's software) or causes the third-party software developer to close its doors entirely.[2304]

In response to the requests for information, Match Group, Inc. told the Subcommittee that Apple has a history of "closely monitoring the success of apps in the App Store, only to copy the most successful of them and incorporate them in new iPhones" as a pre-installed app.[2305] Phillip Shoemaker, former director of app review for the App Store, similarly told Subcommittee staff that during his time at Apple an app developer proposed an innovative way to wirelessly sync the iPhone and Mac.[2306] The app did not violate any of Apple's Guidelines, but it was rejected from the App Store nonetheless.[2307] Apple then appropriated the rejected app's feature for its own offerings.[2308]

During the Subcommittee's sixth hearing, Rep. Neguse asked Mr. Cook about Tile's testimony. In particular, he asked if Apple has access to the confidential information of app developers, and whether Apple's Developer Agreement explicitly authorizes Apple to use developers' information to build apps to compete against them.[2309] Mr. Cook's answer was non-responsive regarding allegations of Sherlocking. Instead, he said that Apple does not violate other companies' intellectual property rights.[2310]

[2303] *See* Competitors Hearing at 4 (statement of Kirsten Daru, Chief Privacy Officer & General Counsel, Tile, Inc.); Guilherme Rambo, *Apple revamping Find My Friends & Find My iPhone in unified app, developing Tile-like personal item tracking*, 9TO5MAC (Apr. 17, 2019), https://9to5mac.com/2019/04/17/find-my-iphone-revamp/.

[2304] Amended Complaint at 4, Dkt No. 13, Blix Inc. v. Apple Inc., No. 1:19-cv-1869-LPS (D. Del Dec. 20, 2019).

[2305] Submission from Source 736, to H. Comm. on the Judiciary, Source 736_00000243 (Oct. 23, 2019) (on file with Comm.).

[2306] Interview with Phillip Shoemaker, former Senior Dir., App Store Review, Apple Inc. (Sept. 21, 2020).

[2307] *Id.*

[2308] *Id.*

[2309] CEO Hearing Transcript at 177 (question of Rep. Neguse (D-CO), Vice Chairman, Subcomm. on Antitrust, Commercial and Admin. Law).

[2310] *Id.* at 177–78 (statement of Tim Cook, CEO, Apple Inc.) ("[Apple] run[s] the App Store to help developers, not hurt them. We respect innovation. It's what our company was built on. We would never steal somebody's IP.").

In contrast, Apple co-founder and former CEO Steve Jobs once noted that "[w]e have always been shameless about stealing great ideas."[2311] The Apple Developer Agreement, which Apple requires every app developer to agree to, appears to warns developers that in exchange for access to the App Store, Apple is free to build apps that "perform the same or similar functions as, or otherwise compete with" apps in the App Store.[2312] Additionally, "Apple will be free to use any information, suggestions or recommendations you provide to Apple pursuant to this Agreement for any purpose, subject to any applicable patents or copyrights."[2313]

Mr. Cook's statement that Apple's apps play by the same rules as other apps appears contrary to Apple's stated policies. While the Apple Developer Agreement provides Apple the right to replicate third-party apps, Apple's Guidelines direct developers not to "copy another developer's work" and threaten removal of apps and expulsion from the Developer Program for those that do.[2314] Further, the Guidelines instruct developers to "[c]ome up with your own ideas," and admonishes them "[d]on't simply copy the latest popular app on the App Store, or make some minor changes to another app's name or UI and pass it off as your own."[2315] Lastly, Apple differentiates between—rather than conflates or confuses—copycat apps and intellectual property infringement, which are both prohibited in the App Store.[2316]

v. Excluding Rival Apps

During the Subcommittee's sixth hearing, Representatives Val Demings (D-FL) and Lucy McBath (D-GA) asked questions regarding Apple's conduct in 2018 and 2019 removing parental control apps from the App Store. In 2018, Apple announced its Screen Time app, a new feature bundled with iOS 12 that helped iOS users limit the time they and their children spent on the iPhone. Thereafter, Apple began to purge many of the leading rival parental control apps from the App Store. Apple explained the apps were removed because they used a technology called Mobile Device Management (MDM). The MDM technology allowed parents to remotely take over their children's

---

[2311] Reed Albergotti, *How Apple uses its App Store to copy the best ideas*, WASH POST. (Sept. 5, 2019), https://www.washingtonpost.com/technology/2019/09/05/how-apple-uses-its-app-store-copy-best-ideas/.

[2312] *Apple Developer Agreement, Clause 11: Apple Independent Development*, APPLE, https://developer.apple.com/terms/apple-developer-agreement/Apple-Developer-Agreement-English.pdf.

[2313] *Id.*

[2314] *App Store Review Guidelines: Introduction*, APPLE: DEVELOPER, https://developer.apple.com/app-store/review/guidelines/ (last visited Sept. 27, 2020).

[2315] *App Store Review Guidelines 4.1: Copycats*, APPLE: DEVELOPER, https://developer.apple.com/app-store/review/guidelines/#copycats (last visited Sept. 27, 2020).

[2316] *App Store Review Guidelines 4.1: Copycats, 5.2: Intellectual Property*, APPLE: DEVELOPER, https://developer.apple.com/app-store/review/guidelines/ (last visited Sept. 27, 2020).

phones and block content. Apple noted that MDM could allow the app developer to access sensitive content on the device.[2317]

According to *The New York Times*, the parental control apps using MDM had been offered in the App Store for years, and hundreds of updates to those apps had been approved by Apple.[2318] As a result, many apps were forced to shut down,[2319] although some were given a reprieve.[2320] Two parental control apps filed a complaint with the European Commission, alleging Apple's App Store policies were anticompetitive. The complaint alleged that as Apple purged competitors it introduced Screen Time, pre-installed Screen Time on iOS 12 and activated it by default, and gave Screen Time access to iOS functionalities it denied to competing third-party apps.[2321]

Subcommittee staff reviewed emails from parents who contacted Apple to complain about the removal of one of the purged parental control apps.[2322] They said that Screen Time was a comparably worse option for consumers—and described it as "more complicated" and "less restrictive" than competitors.[2323] In emails to the company reviewed by Subcommittee staff, parents complained about Apple's monopoly power over app distribution on iOS and self-interest in promoting Screen Time

---

[2317] *See* Jack Nicas, *Apple Cracks Down on Apps that Fight iPhone Addiction*, N.Y. TIMES (Apr. 27, 2019), https://www.nytimes.com/2019/04/27/technology/apple-screen-time-trackers.html. *See also* Sarah Perez, *Apple puts third-party screen time apps on notice*, TECHCRUNCH (Dec. 5, 2018), https://techcrunch.com/2018/12/05/apple-puts-third-party-screen-time-apps-on-notice/.

[2318] Jack Nicas, *Apple Cracks Down on Apps that Fight iPhone Addiction*, N.Y. TIMES (Apr. 27, 2019), https://www.nytimes.com/2019/04/27/technology/apple-screen-time-trackers.html. *See also* Production of Apple, to H. Comm. on the Judiciary, HJC-APPLE-012255–59 (Apr. 28, 2019); HJC-APPLE-013251–53 (Apr. 28, 2019).

[2319] *See e.g.*, Nick Kuh, *Mute App: Startup to Shutdown*, MEDIUM (Oct. 22, 2018), https://medium.com/@nick.kuh/mute-app-startup-to-shutdown-a1db01440c56; Georgie Powell, *In the Kill Zone – Update for Space on iOS*, SPACE (Nov. 6, 2018), https://findyourphonelifebalance.com/news/2018/11/6/in-the-kill-zone-an-update-for-space-on-ios; *Is Apple Systematically Destroying the Time Management Industry?*, KIDSLOX (Nov. 8, 2018), https://kidslox.com/blog/apple-destroying-screen-time-industry/; OurPact, *There Used to Be an App for That*, MEDIUM (May 1, 2019), https://medium.com/@ourpactapp/there-used-to-be-an-app-for-that-41344f61fb6f; Justin Payeur, *Letter to Users About Apple Parental Controls*, BOOMERANG (Jan. 31, 2020), https://useboomerang.com/2020/01/31/letter-users-apple-parental-controls/.

[2320] *See* Nick Kuh, *Apple Called...*, MEDIUM (Oct. 27, 2018), https://medium.com/@nick.kuh/apple-called-a229d86ece30; Georgie Powell, *Space is Back! An Update on our Discussions with Apple.*, SPACE (Nov. 7, 2018), https://findyourphonelifebalance.com/news/2018/11/7/space-versus-apple.

[2321] Press Release, Qustodio & Kidslox File a Complaint Against Apple with the European Commission over Abuse of Dominant Position, GLOBENEWSWIRE (Apr. 30, 2019), https://www.globenewswire.com/news-release/2019/04/30/1812192/0/en/Qustodio-Kidslox-File-a-Complaint-Against-Apple-with-the-European-Commission-over-Abuse-of-Dominant-Position.html#.

[2322] *See e.g.*, Production of Apple, to H. Comm. on the Judiciary, HJC-APPLE-012242–43 (May 6, 2019) (on file with Comm.); HJC-APPLE-012245–46 (May 6, 2019); HJC-APPLE-012247–48 (June 5, 2019); HJC-APPLE-013220 (May 14, 2019); HJC-APPLE-013219 (May 5, 2019); HJC-APPLE-013251–53 (Apr. 28, 2019).

[2323] Jack Nicas, *Apple Cracks Down on Apps That Fight iPhone Addiction*, N.Y. TIMES (Apr. 27, 2019), https://www.nytimes.com/2019/04/27/technology/apple-screen-time-trackers.html.

motivated Apple's actions.[2324] In response, Apple Senior Vice President Worldwide Marketing, Phil Schiller explained that Screen Time was "designed to help parents manage their children's access to technology."[2325] He added that Apple would "work with developers to offer many great apps on the App Store for these uses, using technologies that are safe and private for us and our children."[2326]

Internally, Apple's Vice President of Marketing Communications, Tor Myhren concurred, responding "[t]his is quite incriminating. Is it true?" to an email with a link to *The New York Times'* reporting.[2327] Apple's communications team asked CEO Tim Cook to approve a "narrative" in that Apple's clear-out of Screen Time's rivals was "not about competition, this is about protecting kids privacy."[2328]

Developers of the purged apps also contacted Apple, outraged that they had been removed from the App Store while other apps that used MDM remained.[2329] One developer explained it had invested more than $200,000 building its parental control app, then another $30,000 to fix the problem Apple identified, only to be told that Apple would no longer support parental control apps in the App Store.[2330]

Although Apple claimed its conduct was motivated to protect privacy and not intended to clear out competitors to Screen Time, Apple reinstated many of the apps the same day that it was reported the Department of Justice was investigating Apple for potential antitrust violations.[2331] Apple's solution to address privacy concerns was to ask the apps to promise not to sell or disclose user data to third parties, which could have been achieved through less restrictive means and without removing those apps from the App Store.[2332]

[2324] *See e.g.*, Production of Apple, to H. Comm. on the Judiciary, HJC-APPLE-013210–11 (Apr. 27, 2019) (on file with Comm.); HJC-APPLE-013215 (May 17, 2019); HJC-APPLE-013216 (May 6, 2019); HJC-APPLE-013221–23 (Apr. 29, 2019); HJC-APPLE-013265–66 (Apr. 27, 2019).

[2325] *See e.g.*, *id.* at HJC-APPLE-013210–11 (Apr. 27, 2019) (on file with Comm.); HJC-APPLE-013217 (Apr. 27, 2019); HJC-APPLE-013221–23 (Apr. 29, 2019).

[2326] *Id.* at HJC-APPLE-013221–23 (Apr. 29, 2019).

[2327] *Id.* at HJC-APPLE-013175 (Apr. 27, 2019).

[2328] *Id.* at HJC-APPLE-012223 (June 2, 2019). *See also* CEO Hearing Transcript at 127 (statement of Tim Cook, CEO, Apple Inc.) ("It was that the use of technology called MDM, mobile device management, placed kids' data at risk, and so we were worried about the safety of kids."); CEO Hearing Transcript at 139 (statement of Tim Cook, CEO, Apple Inc.) ("We were concerned, Congresswoman, about the privacy and security of kids.").

[2329] *See, e.g.*, Production of Apple, to H. Comm. on the Judiciary, HJC-APPLE-012255–59 (Apr. 28, 2019) (on file with Comm.); HJC-APPLE-012275–79 (Jan. 17, 2019); Production of Apple, to H. Comm. on the Judiciary, HJC-APPLE-012286–87 (Jan. 17, 2019).

[2330] *Id.* at HJC-APPLE-012286–87 (Jan. 17, 2019) (on file with Comm.).

[2331] Jack Nicas, *Apple Cracks Down on Apps that Fight iPhone Addiction*, N.Y. TIMES (Apr. 27, 2019), https://www.nytimes.com/2019/04/27/technology/apple-screen-time-trackers.html.

[2332] *Id. See App Store Review Guidelines 5.5: Mobile Device Management*, APPLE, https://developer.apple.com/app-store/review/guidelines/#mobile-device-management (last visited Sept. 27, 2020).

Developers of parental control apps asked Apple to "release a public API granting developers access to the same functionalities that Apple's native 'Screen Time' uses."[2333] Eventually, Apple did grant some apps access to APIs,[2334] but only after rival app developers were accused of being a risk to children's privacy, removed from the App Store, forced to incur significant costs, only for Apple to change its mind.[2335] As one developer noted, Apple's new MDM privacy policies resulted in "really nothing much changing from the developer side as far as the technology goes."[2336]

Here, Apple's monopoly power over app distribution enabled it to exclude rivals to the benefit of Screen Time. Apple could have achieved its claimed objective—protecting user privacy—through less restrictive means, which it ultimately did only after significant outcry from the public and a prolonged period of harm to rivals.[2337] Apple's conduct here is a clear example of Apple's use of privacy as a sword to exclude rivals and a shield to insulate itself from charges of anticompetitive conduct.

Subcommittee staff learned that Apple has engaged in conduct to exclude rivals to benefit Apple's services in other instances. For example, Mr. Shoemaker explained that Apple's senior executives would find pretextual reasons to remove apps from the App Store, particularly when those apps competed with Apple services.[2338]

vi. Opaque Guidelines and Arbitrary Enforcement

At the Subcommittee's sixth hearing, Representative Henry C. "Hank" Johnson, Jr. (D-GA) asked Mr. Cook about how the App Store Developer Guidelines are interpreted and applied to developers in the App Store. Subcommittee Chairman Cicilline requested similar information about the Guidelines as well, including how they have evolved and whether there are "unwritten rules" developers must comply with.

The Guidelines are rules for the more than 20 million iOS app developers and more than 1.8 million apps in the App Store must comply with to reach "hundreds of millions of people around the

---

[2333] SCREEN TIME API, https://screentimeapi.com/ (last visited Sept. 27, 2020).

[2334] *See* Joe Rossignol, *Apple Reverses Course and Allows Parental Control Apps to Use MDM Technology With Stricter Privacy Requirements*, MACRUMORS (Jun. 4, 2019), https://www.macrumors.com/2019/06/04/apple-lets-parental-apps-use-mdm-strict-privacy/.

[2335] *See, e.g.*, Production of Apple, to H. Comm. on the Judiciary, HJC-APPLE-012275-79 (Jan. 17, 2019) (on file with the Comm.); HJC-APPLE-013210–11 (Apr. 27, 2019).

[2336] Production of Apple, to H. Comm. on the Judiciary, HJC-APPLE-012273–74 (June 4, 2019) (on file with Comm.).

[2337] *See* Damien Geradin & Dimitrios Katsifis, *The Antitrust Case Against the Apple App Store* 55–56 (Apr. 22, 2020), https://papers.ssrn.com/sol3/papers.cfm?abstract_id=3583029.

[2338] Interview with Phillip Shoemaker, former Senior Dir., App Store Review, Apple Inc. (Sept. 21, 2020).

world."[2339] Apple notes that the App Store is "highly curated" and that "every app is reviewed by experts."[2340] The introductory section of the Guidelines warns that Apple can create new rules at any time, and explains "[w]e will reject apps for any content or behavior that we believe is over the line. What line, you ask? Well as a Supreme Court Justice once said, 'I'll know it when I see it.' And we think that you will also know it when you cross it."[2341]

App developers the Subcommittee spoke with expressed frustration with Apple's curation of the App Store. David Heinemeier Hansson testified before the Subcommittee and explained:

> It's complete tyranny, and the rules are often interpreted differently by different reviewers because they're intentionally left vague. So we live in constant fear we may have violated these vague rules, and that the next update to our applications will be blocked by Apple. There are countless examples where developers large and small have been denied access to publish their applications without explanation for days or even weeks at a time. It's insufferable.[2342]

One social media platform expressed concern that Apple has absolute discretion about whether to approve apps or accept updates.[2343] Developers are frustrated that Apple's interpretation and enforcement of the Guidelines have changed over time, despite prior precedents and the fact developers rely on understanding the Guidelines to operate their businesses. One developer described Apple's Guidelines as "arbitrarily interpreted," and another party that called it "opaque and arbitrary."[2344] Internally, after an app was rejected from the App Store an Apple employee wrote to the leadership of the App Store that Apple's decision "still isn't obvious to people inside the company that work directly on the App Store."[2345]

In 2017, *Gizmodo* reported that iOS app maker Deucks saw its Finder for AirPods app removed from the App Store. The app used the iPhone's Bluetooth signal to locate lost AirPods, helping its users find a missing earbud and save money by not having to purchase replacements. After the app was reviewed and approved, it disappeared from the App Store. Deucks told Gizmodo that Apple's app

---

[2339] *App Store Review Guidelines: Introduction*, APPLE: DEVELOPER, https://developer.apple.com/app-store/review/guidelines/ (last visited Sept. 27, 2020).

[2340] *Id.*

[2341] *Id.*

[2342] Competitors Hearing at 9 (statement of David Heinemeier Hansson, Chief Technology Officer & Co-Founder, Basecamp).

[2343] Submission from Source 247, to H. Comm. on the Judiciary, Source 247_0000000002 (Oct. 14, 2019) (on file with Comm.).

[2344] Submission from Source 736, to H. Comm. on the Judiciary, Source 736_00000236 (Oct. 23, 2019) (on file with Comm.); Interview with Source 88 (May 12, 2020).

[2345] Production of Apple, to H. Comm. on the Judiciary, HJC-APPLE-014848 (May 30, 2018) (on file with Comm.).

review team "didn't find anything wrong with the app itself, but rather they didn't like the 'concept' of people finding their AirPods and hence [the app] was deemed 'not appropriate for the App Store.'"[2346] At the time, Deucks had several other finder apps, such as Finder for Fitbit and Finder for Jawbone, that remained available in the App Store.[2347]

Developers also say that Apple uses its power over the App Store to change the Guidelines when convenient in ways that benefit Apple. The Guidelines—along with their interpretation and enforcement—all change over time in ways that always appear to benefit Apple.[2348] Spotify noted, "[t]he reality is Apple continues to move the goal posts and change the rules to its advantage and the detriment of developers," and that the company's "selective and capricious enforcement [of its App Store policies] is designed to put companies like [Spotify] at an untenable competitive disadvantage."[2349] ProtonMail explained it offered a free version of its app in the App Store for years, but then Apple abruptly changed the way it applied its IAP requirement and demanded the app add the ability for consumers to purchase upgraded functionality through the app—giving Apple a 30% cut from those subscriptions. ProtonMail noted that its app competes with an Apple service and that requiring it to implement IAP would increase its customer acquisition costs and make it less competitive, benefitting Apple.[2350] Another party Subcommittee staff spoke with said when Apple introduces a new app, developers with rival apps know they may be targeted for a violation of a rule Apple has suddenly decided to interpret or enforce differently.[2351] Another app developer that competes with an Apple services noted the Guidelines are constantly shifting, that Apple arbitrarily decides when an app no longer complies with the rules, and those decisions always favor Apple's interests.[2352]

Others have noted that Apple unilaterally determines if, how, and when to apply its Guidelines, and that it also freely makes up "unwritten rules" when convenient.[2353] For example, Apple's

---

[2346] Michael Nunez, *'Finder for AirPods' App Mysteriously Disappears From App Store Without Much Explanation from Apple*, GIZMODO (Jan. 9, 2017), https://gizmodo.com/finder-for-airpods-app-mysteriously-disappears-from-app-1790999059.

[2347] *Id.*

[2348] *See* Dieter Bohn, *Apple's App Store policies are bad, but its interpretation and enforcement are worse*, The VERGE (June 17, 2020), https://www.theverge.com/2020/6/17/21293813/apple-app-store-policies-hey-30-percent-developers-the-trial-by-franz-kafka ("The key thing to know is that the text of this policy is not actually the policy. Or rather, as with any law, the text is only *one* of the things you need to understand. You also need to know how it is *enforced* and how the enforcers *interpret* that text.").

[2349] Kara Swisher, *Is It Finally Hammer Time for Apple and Its App Store*, N.Y. TIMES (June 19, 2020, https://www.nytimes.com/2020/06/19/opinion/apple-app-store-hey.html?referringSource=articleShare.

[2350] Submission from ProtonMail to H. Comm. on the Judiciary, 5 (Aug. 22, 2020) (on file with Comm.).

[2351] Interview with Source 88 (May 12, 2020).

[2352] Interview with Source 766 (July 2, 2020).

[2353] *See* JOHN BERGMAYER, PUBLIC KNOWLEDGE, TENDING THE GARDEN: HOW TO ENSURE THAT APP STORES PUT USERS FIRST 27 (2020), https://www.publicknowledge.org/wp-content/uploads/2020/06/Tending_the_Garden.pdf; Bapu Kotapati,

distinction between "business" and "consumer" apps to justify its June 2020 decision to require Basecamp to redesign its app to permit in-app signups—and attempt to require implementation of IAP—was not a distinction that appeared in Apple's Guidelines until an update on September 11, 2020.[2354] Apple said that it has a "set of standard terms for Amazon, and every other video-streaming service that met the criteria, to launch their service on Apple TV and iOS."[2355] One of Apple's business partners told Subcommittee staff that it suspects Amazon receives preferential treatment by being exempt from sharing revenue for some categories of transactions.[2356]

Subcommittee staff reviewed communications between Apple CEO Tim Cook and an executive from Baidu regarding whether Apple would provide Baidu with preferential treatment. At the Subcommittee's sixth hearing, Rep. Johnson questioned Mr. Cook whether Apple differentiates in how it treats app developers. Rep. Johnson also asked if it was true that Apple assigned Baidu two employees to help it navigate the App Store bureaucracy, and whether other app developers receive the same access to Apple personnel. Mr. Cook responded, "we treat every developer the same," and explained the App Store Guidelines "apply evenly to everyone."[2357] He also said "I don't know about that, sir," in response to Mr. Johnson's inquiry about Baidu, adding, "We do a lot of things with developers including looking at their beta test apps regardless of whether they're large or small."[2358]

Communications reviewed by Subcommittee staff show that in 2014 Baidu requested, among other things, that Apple "set up a fast track for the review process for Baidu APPs," along with setting Baidu as the default search and mapping services on "all Apple devices in China."[2359] Mr. Cook solicited feedback from Apple's senior executives regarding these and other requests from Baidu, and also noting, "I think we should have someone focus on them as we have done with Facebook. Thoughts?"[2360] Responding to the email thread with Mr. Cook's request that Apple focus on Baidu as it had with Facebook, one executive explained, "Engineering proposal is for extensions to be our path

---

et al., *The Antitrust Case Against Apple*, YALE UNIV., THURMOND ARNOLD PROJECT, DIGITAL PLATFORM THEORIES OF HARM PAPER SERIES: PAPER 2, 22 (2020), https://som.yale.edu/sites/default/files/DTH-Apple-new.pdf.

[2354] *See* Ben Thompson, *Xscale and ARM in the Cloud, Hey Versus Apple, Apple's IAP Campaign*, STRATECHERY (Jun. 17, 2020) https://stratechery.com/2020/xscale-and-arm-in-the-cloud-hey-versus-apple-apples-iap-campaign/; John Gruber, *The Flimsiness of 'Business vs. Consumer' as a Justification for Apple's Rejection of Hey From the App Store for Not Using In-App Purchases*, DARING FIREBALL (June 16, 2020), https://daringfireball.net/2020/06/hey_app_store_rejection_flimsiness; Sarah Perez & Anthony Ha, *Apple revises App Store Rules to permit game streaming apps, clarify in-app purchases and more*, TECHCRUNCH (Sept. 11, 2020), https://techcrunch.com/2020/09/11/apple-revises-app-store-rules-to-permit-game-streaming-apps-clarify-in-app-purchases-and-more/.

[2355] CEO Hearing Transcript at 8 (response to Questions for the Record of Tim Cook, CEO, Apple Inc.).

[2356] Interview with Source 77 (Sept. 10, 2020).

[2357] CEO Hearing Transcript at 51 (statement of Tim Cook, CEO, Apple Inc.).

[2358] *Id.*

[2359] Production of Apple, to H. Comm. on the Judiciary, HJC-APPLE-011082 (June 3, 2015) (on file with Comm.).

[2360] *Id.* at HJC-APPLE-011081 (Aug. 3, 2014).

for integration," and responded to Baidu's app review fast track request, "I believe we put a lot of work into having a fast review process for all apps."[2361]

Within two weeks, Mr. Cook responded to the Baidu executive's requests. "I'd like Apple to have a deeper relationship with Baidu," Cook wrote, noting that "some of" the Baidu executive's requests were "great starts."[2362] In response to the Baidu executive's request for "APP Review Fast Track," Mr. Cook wrote "We can set up a process where Baidu could send us a beta app for review and this can often speed up the process."[2363] Mr. Cook then noted he had assigned Baidu two employees from App Store chief Phil Schiller's team to "help manage through Apple."[2364]

When asked about these issues in questions submitted for the record following the hearing, Mr. Cook explained his view that "There is no 'fast track' for App Review special to Baidu," that "any developer can request expedited review from App Review by submitting a formal expedite request," and "[t]he beta app review process I referenced in my email has been available to developers since 2009."[2365] Mr. Cook also noted "The key contacts referenced in my email were focused on other strategic opportunities outlined by Baidu. Neither individual had responsibility for App Store review."[2366]

In a subsequent interview with Mr. Shoemaker, the former Director of App Review for the App Store, Subcommittee staff asked about Apple's treatment of app developers. Mr. Shoemaker responded that Apple "was not being honest" when it claims it treats every developer the same.[2367] Mr. Shoemaker has also written that the App Store rules were often "arbitrary" and "arguable," and that "Apple has struggled with using the App Store as a weapon against competitors."[2368] He has noted that "Apple has complete and unprecedented power over their customers' devices. The decisions they make with regards to third-party apps needs to be above reproach, and currently are not."[2369]

Mr. Shoemaker also admitted that Apple advantages its own apps over third-party apps. In an interview with Subcommittee staff, he described it as inaccurate to say Apple does not favor its own

---

[2361] *Id.* at HJC-APPLE-011079-80 (Aug. 3, 2014).

[2362] *Id.* at HJC-APPLE-011083 (June 3, 2015).

[2363] *Id.* at HJC-APPLE-011084 (June 3, 2015).

[2364] *Id.*

[2365] CEO Hearing Transcript at 8 (response to Questions for the Record of Tim Cook, CEO, Apple Inc.).

[2366] *Id.* at 9.

[2367] Interview with Phillip Shoemaker, former Senior Dir., App Store Review, Apple Inc. (Sept. 21, 2020).

[2368] Phillip Shoemaker, *A Modern Content Store*, MEDIUM (Dec. 12, 2017), https://medium.com/@phillipshoemaker/a-modern-content-store-3344bbe79edc.

[2369] Phillip Shoemaker, *Apple v. Everybody*, MEDIUM (Mar. 29, 2019), https://medium.com/@phillipshoemaker/apple-v-everybody-5903039e3be.

apps over third-party apps.[2370] He has previously noted that apps that compete against Apple's services have a track record of problems getting through the App Store's review process. For example, Apple's gaming service, Apple Arcade, is a type of app that was "consistently disallowed from the store," when offered by third-party developers, but Apple allowed its own app in the store "even though it violates existing [App Store] guidelines."[2371] Mr. Shoemaker explained to Subcommittee staff that Apple's new Guideline 3.1.2a related to streaming game services was likely written to "specifically exclude Google Stadia," describing the decision as "completely arbitrary."[2372] Similar conduct has been commented on by the courts,[2373] as well as international antitrust authorities.[2374]

Apple disputes that its rules are opaque and arbitrarily applied. In response to questions from Rep. Johnson, Mr. Cook insisted the Guidelines are "open and transparent," and that Apple "treat[s] every developer the same."[2375] In response to questions submitted for the record from Subcommittee Chairman Cicilline (D-RI), Mr. Cook reiterated that "[t]he Guidelines provide transparency and act as a practical guide to help developers better understand the app approval process. . . . Apple attempts to apply the Guidelines uniformly to all developers and all types of apps."[2376]

Apple appears to have recently revised some of its App Store policies under the scrutiny of the Subcommittee, the Department of Justice, and global competition authorities. In June 2020, Apple announced new policies for its App Store review that will allow app developers to appeal decisions by app reviewers and even challenge the Guidelines governing the App Store. Apple also announced that app updates with bug fixes will no longer be held up due to a violation of an App Store guideline. Additionally, on September 11, 2020 Apple changed its App Developer Guidelines to address some of the questions raised about the Guidelines arising from many recent controversies described earlier in this Report.[2377]

[2370] Interview with Phillip Shoemaker, former Senior Dir., App Store Review, Apple Inc. (Sept. 21, 2020).

[2371] Phillip Shoemaker, *Apple v. Everybody*, MEDIUM (Mar. 29, 2019), https://medium.com/@phillipshoemaker/apple-v-everybody-5903039e3be.

[2372] Interview with Phillip Shoemaker, former Senior Dir., App Store Review, Apple Inc. (Sept. 21, 2020).

[2373] U.S. v. Apple Inc., 952 F. Supp. 2d 638, 662 (S.D.N.Y. 2013), *aff'd* 791 F.3d 290 (2d Cir. 2015).

[2374] *See e.g.*, Neth. Auth. for Consumers & Mkts. Study at 5–6, 68, 79; Killian Bell, *Apple Rejects Samsung Pay app for iOS*, CULT OF MAC (Dec. 12, 2016), https://www.cultofmac.com/457916/apple-rejects-samsung-pay-app-ios/; Gil Jaeshik & Park Sora, *Apple Rejects Samsung Pay Mini to Be Registered on Its App Store*, KOREA IT NEWS (Dec. 12, 2016), http://english.etnews.com/20161212200003.

[2375] CEO Hearing Transcript at 61 (statement of Tim Cook, CEO, Apple Inc.).

[2376] CEO Hearing Transcript at 5 (response to Questions for the Record of Tim Cook, CEO, Apple Inc.).

[2377] *See* Sarah Perez and Anthony Ha, *Apple Revises App Store Rules to permit game streaming apps, clarify in-app purchases and more*, TECHCRUNCH (Sept. 11, 2020), https://techcrunch.com/2020/09/11/apple-revises-app-store-rules-to-permit-game-streaming-apps-clarify-in-app-purchases-and-more/.

3. <u>Siri Intelligent Voice Assistant</u>

a. <u>Market Power</u>

Apple describes Siri as "an intelligent assistant that offers a faster, easier way to get things done on Apple devices," helping users to "make calls, send text messages or email, schedule meetings and reminders, make notes, search the Internet, find local businesses, get directions, get answers, find facts, and more just by asking."[2378] Apple integrated Siri into iPhone 4S at its release in October 2011. As of January 2018, Apple said Siri was active on over 500 million devices, making Siri one of the most widely used voice assistants in the world.[2379]

In a submission to the Subcommittee, Apple states that it neither creates market share data for Siri nor tracks third-party market share data for integrated voice assistants.[2380] Market research firm FutureSource Consulting found that as of December 2019 Siri was the leading intelligent virtual assistant with a 35% market share globally.[2381] A third-party supplied the Subcommittee with additional market research that reported in the first half of 2018 Apple's Siri was built into 42% of virtual assistant-enabled devices sold worldwide.[2382] Apple, along with Google, Amazon, and Microsoft are the leading providers of intelligent virtual assistants.[2383] Siri's success reflects its integration into the iPhone and other Apple hardware, such as the iPad, Mac, Apple Watch, Apple TV, and HomePod.[2384] Siri is the hub of Apple's ecosystem of smart-home devices. Users can control Apple HomeKit-compatible devices using Siri on an Apple device.[2385]

b. <u>Merger Activity</u>

[2378] Production of Apple, to H. Comm. on the Judiciary, HJC-APPLE-000007 (Oct. 14, 2019) (on file with Comm.).

[2379] Press Release, Apple, HomePod arrives February 9, available to order this Friday (Jan. 13, 2018), https://www.apple.com/newsroom/2018/01/homepod-arrives-february-9-available-to-order-this-friday/.

[2380] Production of Apple, to H. Comm. on the Judiciary, HJC-APPLE-000011 (Oct. 14, 2019) (on file with Comm.).

[2381] Press Release, FutureSource Consulting, Virtual Assistants to Exceed 2.5 Billion Shipments in 2023 (Dec. 18, 2019), https://www.futuresource-consulting.com/press-release/consumer-electronics-press/virtual-assistants-to-exceed-25-billion-shipments-in-2023/.

[2382] Submission from Source 918, to H. Comm. on the Judiciary, Source 918-0001578 (Nov. 4, 2019) (on file with Comm.).

[2383] *See e.g.*, Press Release, FutureSource Consulting, Virtual Assistants to Exceed 2.5 Billion Shipments in 2023 (Dec. 18, 2019), https://www.futuresource-consulting.com/press-release/consumer-electronics-press/virtual-assistants-to-exceed-25-billion-shipments-in-2023/; Submission from Source 918, to H. Comm. on the Judiciary, Source 918-0001578 (Nov. 4, 2019) (on file with Comm.).

[2384] *See* Press Release, FutureSource Consulting, Virtual Assistants to Exceed 2.5 Billion Shipments in 2023 (Dec. 18, 2019, https://www.futuresource-consulting.com/press-release/consumer-electronics-press/virtual-assistants-to-exceed-25-billion-shipments-in-2023/; Juli Clover, *Siri: Everything You Need to Know*, MAC RUMORs (July 27, 2020), https://www.macrumors.com/guide/siri/.

[2385] Daniel Wroclawski, *How to Use Siri and Apple HomeKit to Control Your Smart Home*, CONSUMER REPS. (Oct. 5, 2019), https://www.consumerreports.org/home-automation-systems/how-to-use-siri-to-control-smart-home/.

The startup Siri, Inc launched the Siri app for iOS in February 2010 based on a prototype developed by Adam Cheyer while working at SRI International Research Lab.[2386] Apple acquired the company two months later.[2387] Apple has followed up on its acquisition of Siri with a series of additional acquisitions to strengthen Siri's underlying technology and natural language processing. For example, in 2019, Apple acquired Laserlike, technology to help Siri improve at delivering personalized results for users.[2388] In 2020, Apple acquired Inductiv, an AI technology for correcting data flaws, Xnor.ai which specializes in low-power, edge-based artificial-intelligence tools needed for smart home devices, and Voysis to increase Siri's speech recognition accuracy.[2389]

c. Conduct

As with many of Apple's other products and services, Apple has taken a walled garden approach to the intelligent voice assistant market by, among other things, limiting interoperability by restricting how digital voice assistants work on Apple devices and how Siri works with non-Apple devices, and by using Siri to guide users to its own products and services.

Apple does not allow competing digital voice assistants to replace Siri as the default on Apple devices. On iOS devices the user must download the app for a competing digital voice assistant and then either use Siri to access that voice assistant, or use that app directly.[2390] Additionally, Apple does not have a program where third-party device manufactures can install a speaker that receives Siri commands; only Apple devices can respond to the "hey Siri" prompt.[2391] While third-party hardware manufactures can make their products Siri-compatible through the Works with Apple HomeKit, the voice commands needed to control the smart devices must still be directed to Siri on an Apple device, such as an iPhone or iPad.[2392]

[2386] Catherine Clifford, *Here's how Siri made it onto your iPhone*, CNBC (Jun. 29, 2017), https://www.cnbc.com/2017/06/29/how-siri-got-on-the-iphone.html.

[2387] Jenna Wortham, *Apple Buys a Start-Up for Its Voice Technology*, N.Y. TIMES (Apr. 29, 2010), https://www.nytimes.com/2010/04/29/technology/29apple.html.

[2388] Jeremy Horwitz, *Apple acquires Laserlike, an ML startup that might make Siri smarter*, VENTURE BEAT (Mar. 13, 2019), https://venturebeat.com/2019/03/13/apple-bought-laserlike-an-ml-startup-that-might-make-siri-smarter/.

[2389] *See* Lisa Eadicicco, *Apple just bought another AI startup to help Siri catch up to rivals Amazon and Google*, BUS. INSIDER (May 28, 2020), https://www.businessinsider.com/apple-buys-ai-startup-inductiv-siri-catch-up-amazon-google-2020-5; Mark Gurman, *Apple Acquires AI Startup to Better Understand Natural Language*, BLOOMBERG (Apr. 3, 2020), https://www.bloomberg.com/news/articles/2020-04-03/apple-acquires-ai-startup-to-better-understand-natural-language; Charlie Wood, *Apple has acquired the artificial-intelligence startup Xnor.ai for a reported $200 million*, BUS. INSIDER (Jan. 16, 2020), https://www.businessinsider.com/apple-reportedly-buys-xnor-ai-200-million-2020-1.

[2390] *See, e.g.*, Ben Lovejoy, *Alexa iPhone app can now operate hands-free — with a little help from Siri*, 9TO5MAC (July 8, 2020), https://9to5mac.com/2020/07/08/alexa-iphone-app/; Chris Welch, *Google Assistant just got much better and more convenient on iOS thanks to Siri Shortcuts*, THE VERGE (Nov. 20, 2018), https://www.theverge.com/2018/11/20/18105693/google-assistant-siri-shortcuts-feature-iphone-ios.

[2391] *How 'Hey Siri' works with multiple devices*, APPLE, https://support.apple.com/en-us/HT208472 (last visited Sept. 27, 2020).

[2392] *Homekit*, APPLE, https://developer.apple.com/homekit/ (last visited Oct. 3, 2020).

In addition to keeping Siri closely tied to Apple hardware, Apple has used its voice-enabled devices to strengthen consumer engagement with its own services and apps. For example, as of the writing of this Report, by default requests to Siri to play music open the Apple Music app; requests for directions open the Apple Maps app; and requests for web searches open the Safari app.[2393] To use a competing service through Siri a user must adjust the device's settings and identify the service in the command to Siri (e.g., "Hey Siri, play the National Anthem on Spotify").[2394] For streaming music services, this integration only became possible with the introduction of iOS 13 in 2019.[2395] Previously, even when a user said the name of a third-party streaming service in the voice command, Apple opened an Apple-branded alternative.[2396] In June 2020 Apple announced that it would update its HomePod smart speaker system to support third-party music services.[2397] It remains unclear how seamless the integration will be and if Apple Music will remain the pre-installed default service.[2398]

One third party that spoke with Subcommittee staff described Siri as a "closed" intelligent virtual assistant that limits the types of voice interactions voice app developers have access to.[2399] The app developer explained that SiriKit, which allows iOS apps to work with Siri, relies on a pre-deigned list of basic interactions that third parties can use, such as messaging, calling, payments, etc. The very limited set of interactions permitted by Apple can make it impossible to launch an app for the third-party's services, including applications that compete with an Apple service.[2400]

These practices have recently come under scrutiny by antitrust authorities. In March 2019, Spotify filed a complaint against Apple before the European Commission, reportedly alleging, among

---

[2393] *E.g.*, *Use Siri to play music or* podcasts, APPLE, https://support.apple.com/en-us/HT208279 (last visited Sept. 27, 2020); David Phelan, *Apple Mulls Letting You Choose Default iOS 14 Apps: Why it Matters*, FORBES (FE. 21, 2010) https://www.forbes.com/sites/davidphelan/2020/02/21/apple-mulls-letting-you-switch-default-iphone-apps-in-ios-14/#70330c9c11f8.

[2394] Kate Kozuch, *How to Use Siri to Control Spotify in iOS 13*, TOM'S GUIDE (Oct. 7, 2019), https://www.tomsguide.com/how-to/how-to-use-siri-to-control-spotify-ios-13.

[2395] Jason Cross, *iOS 13 enables Siri support in third party media apps: Spotify, Pandora, Overcast, and much more*, MACWORLD (Jun. 7, 2019), https://www.macworld.com/article/3400881/ios-13-enables-siri-support-in-third-party-media-apps.html.

[2396] *See* Submission from Source 301, to H. Comm. on the Judiciary, Source 301-00000080 at 23 (Oct. 15, 2019) (on file with Comm.)

[2397] Kif Leswing, *Apple will let iPhone users change default mail and browser apps, addressing antitrust concerns*, CNBC (June 22, 2020), https://www.cnbc.com/2020/06/22/apple-allows-users-to-change-default-mail-and-browser-apps-at-wwdc.html.

[2398] Filipe Esposito, *iOS 14 includes option to change default services on HomePod for each user*, 9TO5MAC (July 7, 2020), https://9to5mac.com/2020/07/07/ios-14-includes-option-to-change-default-services-on-homepod-for-each-user/.

[2399] Submission from Source 711, to H. Comm. on the Judiciary, Source 711-00000080 at 6–7 (Oct. 15, 2019) (on file with Comm.).

[2400] *Id.*

other things, that Apple is restricting Spotify's access to Siri.[2401] July 2020, the European Commission's antitrust authority announced that it had opened an inquiry into the use of digital assistants and smart home products by Apple, Google, and Amazon, among other companies.[2402] In her statement accompanying the announcement, Margrethe Vestager, the Commission's Executive Vice President, identified interoperability and self-preferencing as areas of concern.[2403]

VI.   RECOMMENDATIONS

As part of its top-to-bottom review of competition in digital markets, the Subcommittee examined whether current laws and enforcement levels are adequate to address the market power concerns identified through this investigation. In pursuit of this goal, on March 13, 2020, the Subcommittee requested submissions from antitrust and competition policy experts. These experts were chosen on a careful, bipartisan basis to ensure the representation of a full range of views. Throughout the investigation the Subcommittee received additional submissions and written statements from antitrust enforcers and other leading experts, including Margrethe Vestager, the Executive Vice President of the European Commission, and Rod Sims, the Chair of the Australian Competition and Consumer Commission. Most recently, the Subcommittee held an oversight hearing on October 1, 2020 on "Proposals to Strengthen the Antitrust Laws and Restore Competition Online," its seventh and final hearing as part of the investigation.

Subcommittee Chairman David N. Cicilline requested that staff provide Members of the Subcommittee with a series of recommendations, informed by this investigation, on how to strengthen the antitrust laws and restore competition online. As he noted in remarks to the American Antitrust Institute in June 2019:

> No doubt, other branches of government have a key role to play in the development of antitrust law. But Congress—not the courts, agencies, or private companies—enacted the antitrust laws, and Congress ultimately decides what the law should be and whether the law is working for the American people. As such, it is Congress' responsibility to conduct oversight of our antitrust laws and competition system to ensure that they are properly working and to enact changes when they are not. While I do not have any preconceived ideas about what the right answer is, as Chairman of the Antitrust Subcommittee, I intend to carry out that responsibility with the sense of urgency and serious deliberation that it demands.[2404]

[2401] Thomas Ricker, *Apple to be formally investigated over Spotify's antitrust complaint, says report*, THE VERGE (MAY 6, 2019), https://www.theverge.com/2019/5/6/18530894/apple-music-monopoly-spotify-app-store-europe.

[2402] *Statement by Executive Vice-President Margrethe Vestager on the launch of a Sector Inquiry on the Consumer Internet of Things*, EUR. COMM'N (July 16, 2020), https://ec.europa.eu/commission/presscorner/detail/en/speech_20_1367.

[2403] *Id.*

[2404] David N. Cicilline, Chairman, Subcomm. on Antitrust, Commercial and Admin. Law of the H. Comm. on the Judiciary, Keynote Address at American Antitrust Institute's 20th Annual Policy Conference (June 20, 2019),

In response to this request, Subcommittee staff identified a broad set of reforms for further examination by the Members of the Subcommittee for purposes of crafting legislative and oversight responses to the findings of this Report. These reforms include proposals to: (1) promote fair competition in digital markets; (2) strengthen laws relating to mergers and monopolization; and (3) restore vigorous oversight and enforcement of the antitrust laws.

Subcommittee staff intends for these recommendations to serve as a complement, not a substitute, to strong enforcement of the antitrust laws. This is particularly true for acquisitions by dominant firms that may have substantially lessened competition or tended to create a monopoly in violation of the Clayton Act. In these cases, Subcommittee staff supports as a policy matter the examination of the full range of remedies—including unwinding consummated acquisitions or divesting business lines—to fully restore competition that was harmed as a result of these acquisitions and to prevent future violations of the antitrust laws.[2405]

A. Restoring Competition in the Digital Economy

For more than a century, Congress has addressed the market power of dominant intermediaries using a robust antitrust and antimonopoly toolkit.[2406] The antitrust laws prohibit anticompetitive mergers and monopolistic conduct in order to promote open markets and prevent undue concentration of economic power. In many critical sectors of the economy—including financial services, telecommunications, and transportation—Congress has also relied on a broad set of policies to create the conditions necessary for fair competition, even when economies of scale may favor concentration.

In a similar vein, the remedies identified in this section seek to restore competition online by addressing harmful business practices as well as certain features of digital markets that tend to tip the market towards concentration.

1. Reduce Conflicts of Interest Thorough Structural Separations and Line of Business Restrictions

In addition to controlling one or multiple key channels of distribution, the dominant firms investigated by the Subcommittee are integrated across lines of business. When operating in adjacent markets, these platforms compete directly with companies that depend on them to access users, giving

---

https://cicilline.house.gov/press-release/cicilline-delivers-keynote-address-american-antitrust-institute%E2%80%99s-20th-annual-policy.

[2405] Due to separation of powers concerns and other relevant considerations, we do not take a position on the outcome of any individual matter before the Justice Department or Federal Trade Commission.

[2406] See, e.g., Subcomm. on Study of Monopoly Power of the H. Comm. on the Judiciary, 81st Cong. 2d Sess., *The Antitrust Laws: A Basis for Economic Freedom* iii (1950) (identifying an extensive list of statutes "dealing directly with the preservation of the American competitive economy" and reflecting the legislative policy that "under no circumstances should [laws] foster the growth of monopoly.").

rise to a conflict of interest. As discussed earlier in this Report, the Subcommittee's investigation uncovered several ways in which Amazon, Apple, Facebook, and Google use their dominance in one or more markets to advantage their other lines of business, reducing dynamism and innovation.

First, the investigation revealed that the dominant platforms have misappropriated the data of third parties that rely on their platforms, effectively collecting information from customers only to weaponize it against them as rivals. For example, the investigation produced documents showing that Google used the Android operating system to closely track usage trends and growth patterns of third-party apps—near-perfect market intelligence that Google can use to gain an edge over those same apps. Facebook used its platform tools to identify and then acquire fast-growing third-party apps, thwarting competitive threats at key moments. A former Amazon employee told the Subcommittee that Amazon has used the data of third-party merchants to inform Amazon's own private label strategy, identifying which third-party products were selling well and then introducing copycat versions. These and other examples detailed in this Report demonstrate a dangerous pattern of predatory conduct that, if left unchecked, risk further concentrating wealth and power.

Some have suggested that there is little difference between the dominant platforms' access to and use of this data and the way that brick-and-mortar retailers track popular products. The Subcommittee's investigation, however, produced evidence that the platforms' access to competitively significant market data is unique. Specifically, the dominant platforms collect real-time data which, given the scale of their user-base, is akin to near-perfect market intelligence. Whereas firms with a choice among business partners might seek to protect their proprietary data, the platforms' market power lets them compel the collection of this data in the first place.

Second, dominant platforms can exploit their integration by using their dominance in one market as leverage in negotiations in an unrelated line of business. For example, evidence produced during the investigation showed that Amazon has leveraged its dominance in online commerce as pressure during negotiations with firms in a separate line of business. Market participants that depend on Amazon's retail platform are effectively forced to accept its demands—even in markets where Amazon would otherwise lack the power to set the terms of commerce.

Third, dominant platforms have used their integration to tie products and services in ways that can lock in users and insulate the platform from competition. Google, for example, required that smartphone manufacturers seeking to use Android also pre-install and give default status to certain Google apps—enabling Google to maintain its search monopoly and crowd out opportunities for third-party developers.

And fourth, these firms can use supra-competitive profits from the markets they dominate to subsidize their entry into other markets. Documents uncovered during the Subcommittee's investigation indicate that the dominant platforms have relied on this strategy to capture markets, as startups and non-platform businesses tend to lack the resources and capacity to bleed billions of dollars over multiple years in order to drive out rivals. For dominant platforms, meanwhile, this strategy appears to be a race to capture ecosystems and control interlocking products that funnel data back to the platforms, further reinforcing their dominance.

Through using market power in one area to advantage a separate line of business, dominant firms undermine competition on the merits. By functioning as critical intermediaries that are also integrated across lines of business, the dominant platforms face a core conflict of interest. The surveillance data they collect through their intermediary role, meanwhile, lets them exploit that conflict with unrivaled precision. Their ability both to use their dominance in one market as negotiating leverage in another, and to subsidize entry to capture unrelated markets, have the effect of spreading concentration from one market into others, threatening greater and greater portions of the digital economy.

To address this underlying conflict of interest, Subcommittee staff recommends that Congress consider legislation that draws on two mainstay tools of the antimonopoly toolkit: structural separation and line of business restrictions.[2407] Structural separations prohibit a dominant intermediary from operating in markets that place the intermediary in competition with the firms dependent on its infrastructure. Line of business restrictions, meanwhile, generally limit the markets in which a dominant firm can engage.

Congress has relied on both policy tools as part of a standard remedy for dominant intermediaries in other network industries, including railroads and telecommunications services.[2408] In the railroad industry, for example, a congressional investigation found that the expansion of common carrier railroads' into the coal market undermined independent coal producers, whose wares the railroads would deprioritize in order to give themselves superior access to markets. In 1893, the Committee on Interstate and Foreign Commerce wrote that "[n]o competition can exist between two producers of a commodity when one of them has the power to prescribe both the price and output of the other."[2409]

Congress subsequently enacted a provision to prohibit railroads from transporting any goods that they had produced or in which they held an interest.[2410] Congress has legislated similar prohibitions in other markets. The Bank Holding Company Act of 1956 broadly prohibited bank

---

[2407] *See* Submission from Sally Hubbard, Dir. of Enforcement Strategy, Open Mkts. Inst. et al., to H. Comm. on the Judiciary, 7–8 (Apr. 17, 2020) (on file with Comm.) [hereinafter Hubbard Submission]; Submission from Stacy Mitchell, Co-Dir., Inst. for Local Self-Reliance, to H. Comm. on the Judiciary, 4 (May 4, 2020) (on file with Comm.) [hereinafter Mitchell Submission]; Submission from Zephyr Teachout, Assoc. Professor of Law, Fordham Law School, to H. Comm. on the Judiciary, 6 (Apr. 23, 2020) (on file with Comm.) [hereinafter Teachout Submission]; Submission from Americans for Fin. Reform, to H. Comm. on the Judiciary, 3–4 (Apr. 17, 2020) (on file with Comm.).

[2408] Mitchell Submission at 4.

[2409] H.R. REP. NO. 52-2278, vii–viii (1893).

[2410] Hepburn Act, Pub. L. No. 59-337, § 1, 34 Stat. 584, 585 (1906).

holding companies from acquiring nonbanking companies.[2411] Vertically integrated television networks, meanwhile, were subject to "fin-syn" rules, which prohibited networks from entering production and syndication markets.[2412]

Both structural separations and line of business restrictions seek to eliminate the conflict of interest faced by a dominant intermediary when it enters markets that place it in competition with dependent businesses. In certain cases, structural separations have also been used to prevent monopolistic firms from subsidizing entry into competitive markets and to promote media diversity.[2413]

At a general level, there are two forms of structural separation: (1) ownership separations, which require divestiture and separate ownership of each business; and (2) functional separations, which permit a single corporate entity to engage in multiple lines of business but prescribe the particular organizational form it must take.[2414] Importantly, both forms of structural limits apply on a market-wide basis while divestitures in antitrust enforcement generally apply to a single firm or merging party.

A benefit of these proposals is their administrability. By setting rules for the underlying structure of the market—rather than policing anticompetitive conduct on an *ad hoc* basis—structural rules are easier to administer than conduct remedies, which can require close and continuous monitoring.[2415]

The challenges of crafting and implementing structural solutions vary by market and market participants. In response to the Subcommittee's requests for comments on potential reforms, some antitrust experts have cautioned that crafting separations can pose a major cost and challenge, especially in dynamic markets.[2416] Others have responded by identifying certain principles that can make identifying the fault lines easier. In the case of separations that are undoing vertical mergers, the fault lines designating the separate companies are likely to still be apparent, even in the new

---

[2411] Bank Holding Company Act of 1956, Pub. L. No. 84-511, § 2(a), 70 Stat. 133, 133 (codified as amended at 12 U.S.C. § 1841(a) (2012)).

[2412] Competition & Responsibility in Network Television Broad., 23 F.C.C.2d 382, 398, para. 30 (1970) (report and order).

[2413] Mitchell Submission at 4.

[2414] John Kwoka & Tommaso Valletti, *Scrambled Eggs and Paralyzed Policy: Breaking Up Consummated Mergers and Dominant Firms* 22 (forthcoming Oct. 2020) (on file with Comm.).

[2415] OECD, STRUCTURAL SEPARATION IN REGULATED INDUSTRIES: REPORT ON IMPLEMENTING THE OECD RECOMMENDATION 9 (2016) ("[S]eparation limits the need for regulation that is difficult and costly to devise and implement, and may be only partly effective; it improves information; and it eliminates the risk of cross-subsidies by the incumbent from its non-competitive to its competitive segments."), https://www.oecd.org/daf/competition/Structural-separation-in-regulated-industries-2016report-en.pdf.

[2416] *See, e.g.*, Submission from Maureen K. Ohlhausen, Partner, Baker Botts L.L.P., to H. Comm. on the Judiciary, 5 (Apr. 17, 2020) (on file with Comm.).

structure.[2417] In cases where a firm grew through internal expansion, or when the constituent parts are no longer clearly distinguishable, scholars have suggested identifying distinct business operations.[2418] Experts have also noted that business-initiated corporate restructuring and divestitures may in some cases also provide a guide to designing and implementing successful break-ups.[2419]

Several enforcement bodies around the world are exploring the use of structural separations in digital markets. In July 2020, the United Kingdom's Competition and Markets Authority recommended that its digital regulatory body have powers to "implement ownership separation or operational separation," concluding that "there could be significant benefits if there were more formal separation between businesses with market power" in digital advertising markets in particular.[2420] Meanwhile the OECD in 2001 adopted recommendations to structurally separate vertically integrated regulated firms that operate in concentrated markets.[2421] In its 15-year overview, the OECD concluded that "structural separation remains a relevant remedy" and identified other market areas where it might be adopted.[2422]

2. Implement Rules to Prevent Discrimination, Favoritism, and Self-Preferencing

As discussed throughout this Report, the Subcommittee identified numerous instances in which dominant platforms engaged in preferential or discriminatory treatment. In some cases, the dominant platform privileged its own products or services. In others, a dominant platform gave preferential treatment to one business partner over others. Because the dominant platform was, in most instances, the only viable path to market, its discriminatory treatment had the effect of picking winners and losers in the marketplace.

Google, for example, engaged in self-preferencing by systematically ranking its own content above third-party content, even when its content was inferior or less relevant for users. Web publishers of content that Google demoted suffered economic losses and had no way of competing on the merits. Over the course of the investigation, numerous third parties also told the Subcommittee that self-preferencing and discriminatory treatment by the dominant platforms forced businesses to lay off employees and divert resources away from developing new products and towards paying a dominant platform for advertisements or other ancillary services. They added that some of the harmful business

---

[2417] John Kwoka & Tommaso Valletti, *Scrambled Eggs and Paralyzed Policy: Breaking Up Consummated Mergers and Dominant Firms* 11 (forthcoming Oct. 2020) (on file with Comm.).

[2418] *Id.* at 15.

[2419] *Id.*; Rory Van Loo, *In Defense of Breakups: Administering a 'Radical' Remedy*, 105 CORNELL L. REV (forthcoming 2020), https://ssrn.com/abstract=3646630.

[2420] Competition & Mkts. Auth. Report at 405–06.

[2421] OECD, STRUCTURAL SEPARATION IN REGULATED INDUSTRIES: REPORT ON IMPLEMENTING THE OECD RECOMMENDATION 9 (2016), https://www.oecd.org/daf/competition/Structural-separation-in-regulated-industries-2016report-en.pdf.

[2422] *Id.* at 3.

practices of the platforms discouraged investors from supporting their business and made it challenging to grow and sustain a business even with highly popular products. Without the opportunity to compete fairly, businesses and entrepreneurs are dissuaded from investing and, over the long term, innovation suffers.

In response to these concerns, the Subcommittee recommends that Congress consider establishing nondiscrimination rules to ensure fair competition and to promote innovation online. Nondiscrimination rules would require dominant platforms to offer equal terms for equal service and would apply to price as well as to terms of access. As several experts noted, nondiscrimination has been as a mainstay principle for governing network intermediaries, especially those that play essential roles in facilitating transportation and communications.[2423]

The 1887 Interstate Commerce Act, for example, prohibited discriminatory treatment by railroads.[2424] In the century years since, Congress and policymakers have continued to apply nondiscrimination principles to network monopolies, even as technologies have rapidly evolved. Most recently, the Open Internet Order written by the Federal Communications Commission (FCC) in 2015 was effectively a nondiscrimination regime, prohibiting internet service providers from picking winners and losers among content providers and other users.[2425] Other jurisdictions have begun to apply nondiscrimination principles to digital markets. For example, after determining that Google had engaged in illegal self-preferencing, the European Commission required that Google follow "the simple principle of equal treatment."[2426]

Historically, Congress has implemented nondiscrimination requirements in a variety of markets. With railroads, the Interstate Commerce Commission oversaw obligations and prohibitions applied to railroads designated as common carriers.[2427] More recently, the Cable Act of 1992 included a provision requiring the Federal Communications Commission to oversee a nondiscrimination

---

[2423] *See, e.g.*, Submission from Harry First, Charles L. Denison Professor of Law, N.Y.U. School of Law & Eleanor Fox, Walter J. Derenberg Professor of Trade Reg., N.Y.U. School of Law, to H. Comm. on the Judiciary (Aug. 6, 2020) ("[Google, Amazon, Facebook, and Apple] are akin to essential facilities for many smaller businesses. Many businesses, to do business, must use the platform. They have almost no choice. The GAFA compete with the businesses on their platforms.") (on file with Comm.) [hereinafter First & Fox Submission]; Submission from Albert A. Foer, Founder and Senior Fellow, Am. Antitrust Inst., to H. Comm. on the Judiciary, 1–2 (Apr. 14, 2020)(on file with Comm.) [hereinafter Foer Submission]; Hubbard Submission at 5–7; Remedies Hearing 6–7 (statement of K. Sabeel Rahman, President, Demos).

[2424] Hubbard Submission at 4–5.

[2425] Protecting and Promoting the Open Internet, 30 FCC Rcd. 5601, 5603, para. 4 (2015) ("[C]arefully-tailored rules that would prevent specific practices we know are harmful to Internet openness—blocking, throttling, and paid prioritization—as well as a strong standard of conduct designed to prevent the deployment of new practices that would harm Internet openness.").

[2426] Press Release, Eur. Comm'n, Antitrust: Commission Fines Google €2.42 Billion for Abusing Dominance as Search Engine by Giving Illegal Advantage to Own Comparison Shopping Service (June 27, 2017), https://ec.europa.eu/commission/presscorner/detail/en/MEMO_17_1785.

[2427] Hubbard Submission at 5.

requirement for cable operators.[2428] Some experts have proposed establishing a similar venue to adjudicate discrimination disputes between dominant platforms and the third parties that depend on them.[2429] Others note that the Federal Trade Commission could also use its existing competition rulemaking authority to "require dominant gatekeepers to apply a rule of neutrality in operating their platforms."[2430]

Finally, on several occasions, nondiscrimination rules have been treated as an important complement to divestitures in antitrust enforcement. For example, the Justice Department combined AT&T's divestiture of the Regional Bell Operating Companies with an equal access obligation, requiring AT&T to offer independent long-distance providers access to its network on equal terms of quality and price.[2431] The DOJ argued that requiring equal access without mandating divestiture would be insufficient due to AT&T's incentive and ability to discriminate against local carriers.[2432]

3. Promote Innovation Through Interoperability and Open Access

As discussed elsewhere in the Report, digital markets have certain characteristics—such as network effects, switching costs, and other entry barriers—that make them prone to tipping in favor of a single dominant firm. As a result, these markets are no longer contestable by new entrants,[2433] and the competitive process shifts from "competition *in* the market to competition *for* the market."[2434]

This dynamic is particularly evident in the social networking market. As discussed earlier in the Report, Facebook's internal documents and communications indicate that due to strong network effects and market tipping, the most significant competitive pressure to Facebook is from within its own family of products—Facebook, Instagram, Messenger, and WhatsApp—rather than from other social

---

[2428] *See, e.g.,* Submission from Hal Singer, Managing Dir., Econ One Research, to H. Comm. on the Judiciary, 4–5 (Mar. 30, 2020) (on file with Comm.) [hereinafter Singer Submission].

[2429] *Id.*

[2430] First & Fox Submission at 12.

[2431] *See* United States v. AT&T Co., 552 F. Supp. 131 (D.D.C. 1982).

[2432] Mitchell Submission at 4 ("It's important to note here that applying this kind of [nondiscrimination-based] regulatory oversight to the big tech firms will not be effective unless it's done in conjunction with breakups. In the case of Amazon, it's my view that several factors make it virtually impossible to establish a system of oversight and adjudication that would be robust enough to protect competition and fair market access, absent spinning off its shopping platform from its other divisions. These factors include the enormous number of sellers and transactions, the low dollar value of most transactions, and the many subtle and hard-to-detect ways that Amazon can skew outcomes to favor its own interests. Therefore, oversight must be combined with structural separation, which would do much of the work by removing the underlying conflicts of interest, thus allowing for an effective and less bureaucratic system of oversight.").

[2433] Competition & Mkts. Auth. Report at 10–11.

[2434] *See* Stigler Report at 29; Michael Kades & Fiona Scott Morton, *Interoperability as a Competition Remedy for Digital Networks*, WASH. CTR. FOR EQUITABLE GROWTH 1 (Sept. 2020) ("The monopolist operates in a market with significant network effects, scale and scope economies, and low distribution costs. Therefore, the competition that matters most is often *for* the market not *within* the market. Anticompetitive conduct is more likely to succeed. And, the harm to consumers greater because the market tends to be winner-take-all, or most.") (on file with Comm.).

apps in the market, such as Snapchat or Twitter. In the case of messaging apps, Facebook's documents show that network effects can be even more extreme. And because Facebook is not interoperable with other social networks, its users have high costs to switch to other platforms, locking them into Facebook's platform.

High switching costs are also present in other markets. In the smartphone market, switching costs include learning a new operating system, which can discourage users from leaving Google or Apple due to familiarity with their distinct operating systems, as well as the inability to easily port all of their data, such as messages, call history, and photos. In online commerce, sellers have high switching costs associated with their reputation. Sellers can be locked into an incumbent platform for online commerce if they are unable to transfer their reputation—ratings and customer reviews accrued over a long period of time—to a different platform. Switching costs involving data for other services, such as email, can also contribute to user lock-in.[2435] In response to these concerns, Subcommittee staff recommends that Congress consider data interoperability and portability to encourage competition by lowering entry barriers for competitors and switching costs by consumers. These reforms would complement vigorous antitrust enforcement by spurring competitive entry.

a. Interoperability

Interoperability is fundamental to the open internet.[2436] It is present in email, which is an open, interoperable protocol for communicating online regardless of a person's email service or the type of device they use to send the email.[2437] It has also been built into numerous other services online[2438] and is a "core technical structure of the Internet."[2439] Interoperability standards are also present in other communications systems, from telephones to telegraphs.[2440] Telecommunications would not work without the ability of users on one carrier's network to interconnect with other carriers.[2441] And in the absence of interoperability, dominant carriers could foreclose new entrants from offering lower prices or better services, reinforcing their monopoly power while harming consumers and competition.[2442]

[2435] Chris Riley, *A Framework for Forward-Looking Tech Competition Policy*, MOZILLA 10 (2019), https://blog.mozilla.org/netpolicy/files/2019/09/Mozilla-Competition-Working-Paper.pdf.

[2436] *See generally id.* at 18–24.

[2437] Michael Kades & Fiona Scott Morton, *Interoperability as a Competition Remedy for Digital Networks* 14 (Sept. 2020) (on file with Comm.).

[2438] Becky Chao & Russ Schulman, *Promoting Platform Interoperability*, NEW AM. FOUND. (May 13, 2020), https://www.newamerica.org/oti/reports/promoting-platform-interoperability/.

[2439] Chris Riley, *A Framework for Forward-Looking Tech Competition Policy*, MOZILLA 18 (2019), https://blog.mozilla.org/netpolicy/files/2019/09/Mozilla-Competition-Working-Paper.pdf.

[2440] Becky Chao & Russ Schulman, *Promoting Platform interoperability*, NEW AM. FOUND. (May 13, 2020), https://www.newamerica.org/oti/reports/promoting-platform-interoperability/.

[2441] Michael Kades & Fiona Scott Morton, *Interoperability as a Competition Remedy for Digital Networks* 13–14 (Sept. 2020) (on file with Comm.).

[2442] *Id.*

An interoperability requirement would allow competing social networking platforms to interconnect with dominant firms to ensure that users can communicate across services.[2443] Foremost, interoperability "breaks the power of network effects" by allowing new entrants to take advantage of existing network effects "at the level of the market, not the level of the company."[2444] It would also lower switching costs for users by ensuring that they do not lose access to their network as a result of switching.

The implementation cost of requiring interoperability by dominant firms would be relatively low. Unlike interconnecting in traditional communications markets, there is little direct cost associated with interoperating with dominant platforms.[2445]

Finally, interoperability is an important complement, not substitute, to vigorous antitrust enforcement. As discussed in this Report, Facebook has tipped the social network toward a monopoly, and due to its strong network effects, does not face competitive pressure. On its own, interoperability is unlikely to fully restore competition in the social networking market due to the lack of meaningful competition in the market today. On the other hand, in the absence of pro-competitive policies like interoperability, it is also possible that enforcement alone may provide incomplete relief due to future market tipping.[2446]

b. Data Portability

Data portability is also a remedy for high costs associated with leaving a dominant platform. These costs present another barrier to entry for competitors and a barrier to exit for consumers. Dominant platforms can maintain market power in part because consumers experience significant

---

[2443] *Competition in Digital Technology Markets: Examining Self-Preferencing by Digital Platforms: Hearing Before Subcomm. on Antitrust, Competition Policy and Consumer Rights of the S. Comm. on the Judiciary*, 116th Cong. 21 (2020) (statement of Sally Hubbard, Dir. of Enforcement Strategy, Open Mkts. Inst.) ("Interoperability is an anti-monopoly tool that has been used successfully many times to promote innovation by reducing barriers to entering markets.") (on file with Comm.).

[2444] Michael Kades & Fiona Scott Morton, *Interoperability as a Competition Remedy for Digital Networks* 13–14 (Sept. 2020) (on file with Comm.).

[2445] *Id.* at 15 ("Unlike the familiar AT&T example, there would be no cost to interconnection in the digital platform context. The standard is simply a way to present and transfer information that is already being presented and transferred. No wire needs to be connected to achieve it, nor do machines need to be co-located, or special workers employed. Transferring digital files has almost zero cost, but regardless of that cost, Facebook would be transferring those files to serve its users in any case. Facebook might need to pay some costs to redesign the format in which it transfers text and images, but if it has been found liable for monopolization by a court, it is expected that a remedy will have costs. The real cost of ongoing interoperability to Facebook.com is the possibility that it loses customers once the barriers to entry fall. But that risk is what every firm faces in a competitive market and represents a benefit to consumers.").

[2446] *Id.* at 10. ("A divestiture may reduce the existing market power of the dominant network but not eliminate the market power due to network effects that was achieved through anticompetitive conduct. And, alone, divestiture may not prevent future tipping. Thus, on their own, they risk being insufficient to fully restore the lost competition.").

frictions when moving to a new product.[2447] Users contribute data to a platform, for example, but can find it hard to migrate that data to a rival platform.[2448] The difficulty of switching tends to keep users on incumbent platforms.[2449] Providing consumers and businesses with tools to easily port or rebuild their social graph, profile, or other relevant data on a competing platform would help address these concerns.[2450] Although complementary to interoperability, data portability alone would not fully address concerns related to network effects since consumers would still need to recreate their networks on a new platform and would not be able to communicate with their network on the incumbent platform.[2451]

4. Reduce Market Power Through Merger Presumptions

The firms investigated by the Subcommittee owe part of their dominance to mergers and acquisitions. Several of the platforms built entire lines of business through acquisitions, while others used acquisitions at key moments to neutralize competitive threats. Although the dominant platforms collectively engaged in several hundred mergers and acquisitions between 2000-2019, antitrust enforcers did not block a single one of these transactions. The Subcommittee's investigation revealed that several of these acquisitions enabled the dominant platforms to block emerging rivals and undermine competition.

Despite a significant number of ongoing antitrust investigations, the dominant platforms have continued to pursue significant deal-making. Over the last year, for example, Google purchased Fitbit for $2.1 billion and Looker for $2.6 billion; Amazon purchased Zoox for $1.3 billion; and Facebook

---

[2447] *See* JOSHUA GANS, THE HAMILTON PROJECT, ENHANCING COMPETITION WITH DATA AND IDENTITY PORTABILITY 5 (June 2018), http://www.hamiltonproject.org/assets/files/Gans_20180611.pdf.

[2448] *See id.*

[2449] *See* Josh Constine, *Friend Portability Is the Must-Have Facebook Regulation*, TECHCRUNCH (May 12, 2019), https://technologycrunch.com/2019/05/12/friends-wherever; Chris Dixon, *The Interoperability of Social Networks*, BUS. INSIDER (Nov. 10, 2010), https://www.businessinsider.com/the-interoperability-of-social-networks-2011-2; Data and Privacy Hearing at 2 (statement of Dina Srinivasan, Fellow, Thurman Arnold Project).

[2450] Submission from Charlotte Slaiman, Competition Policy Dir., Public Knowledge, to H. Comm. on the Judiciary (May 14, 2020) (on file with Comm.); Appendix I at 3–4 (statement of Gene Kimmelman, Senior Advisor, Public Knowledge) [hereinafter Slaiman Submission].

[2451] *Competition in Digital Technology Markets: Examining Self-Preferencing by Digital Platforms: Hearing Before Subcomm. on Antitrust, Competition Policy and Consumer Rights of the S. Comm. on the Judiciary*, 116th Cong. 21 (2020) (statement of Sally Hubbard, Dir. of Enforcement Strategy, Open Mkts. Inst.) (on file with Comm.). Last year, Senators Mark R. Warner (D-VA), Josh Hawley (R-MO), and Richard Blumenthal (D-CT) introduced S.2648, the "Augmenting Compatibility and Competition by Enabling Service Switching (ACCESS) Act," bipartisan legislation to require that dominant platforms make user data portable and their services interoperable. Additionally, this proposal would also allow users to delegate management of their privacy preferences to a third-party service. Press Release, Sen. Mark R. Warner, *Senators Introduce Bipartisan Bill to Encourage Competition in Social Media* (Oct. 22, 2019), https://www.warner.senate.gov/public/index.cfm/2019/10/senators-introduce-bipartisan-bill-to-encourage-competition-in-social-media.

acquired Giphy for an undisclosed amount.[2452] Meanwhile, all four of the firms investigated by the Subcommittee have recently focused on acquiring startups in the artificial intelligence and virtual reality space.[2453]

Ongoing acquisitions by the dominant platforms raise several concerns. Insofar as any transaction entrenches their existing position, or eliminates a nascent competitor, it strengthens their market power and can close off market entry. Furthermore, by pursuing additional deals in artificial intelligence and in other emerging markets, the dominant firms of today could position themselves to control the technology of tomorrow.

It is unclear whether the antitrust agencies are presently equipped to block anticompetitive mergers in digital markets. The record of the Federal Trade Commission and the Justice Department in this area shows significant missteps and repeat enforcement failures. While both agencies are currently pursuing reviews of pending transactions, it is not yet clear whether they have developed the analytical tools to challenge anticompetitive deals in digital markets. For example, the Justice Department in February permitted Google's acquisition of Looker, a data analytics and business intelligence startup, despite serious risks that the deal would eliminate an independent rival and could allow Google to cut off access to rivals.[2454] These concerns are especially acute today, given the combined national health and economic crises, which have widened the gap between the dominant platforms and businesses across the rest of the economy.

To address this concern, Subcommittee staff recommends that Congress consider shifting presumptions for future acquisitions by the dominant platforms. Under this change, any acquisition by a dominant platform would be presumed anticompetitive unless the merging parties could show that the transaction was necessary for serving the public interest and that similar benefits could not be achieved through internal growth and expansion. This process would occur outside the current Hart-Scott-Rodino Act (HSR) process, such that the dominant platforms would be required to report *all* transactions and no HSR deadlines would be triggered. Establishing this presumption would better reflect Congress's preference for growth through ingenuity and investment rather than through acquisition.

[2452] Chaim Gartenberg, *Google buys Fitbit for $2.1 billion*, THE VERGE (Nov. 1, 2019), https://www.theverge.com/2019/11/1/20943318/google-fitbit-acquisition-fitness-tracker-announcement; Lauren Feiner & Jordan Novet, *Google cloud boss Thomas Kurian makes his first big move — buys Looker for $2.6 billion*, CNBC (June 6, 2019), https://www.cnbc.com/2019/06/06/google-buys-cloud-company-looker-for-2point6-billion.html; Karen Weise & Erin Griffith, *Amazon to Buy Zoox, in a Move Toward Self-Driving Cars*, N.Y. TIMES (June 26, 2020), https://www.nytimes.com/2020/06/26/business/amazon-zoox.html; Kurt Wagner & Sarah Frier, *Facebook Buys Animated Image Library Giphy for $400 Million*, BLOOMBERG (May 15, 2020), https://www.bloomberg.com/news/articles/2020-05-15/facebook-buys-animated-image-library-giphy-to-boost-messaging.

[2453] *See infra* Appendix.

[2454] Letter from Diana L. Moss, President, Am. Antitrust Inst., to Hon. Makan Delrahim, Assistant Att'y Gen., Dep't of Justice, Antitrust Div. (July 8, 2019), https://www.antitrustinstitute.org/wp-content/uploads/2019/07/AAI-Ltr-to-DOJ_Google-Looker_7.8.19.pdf.

5. Create an Even Playing Field for the Free and Diverse Press

The free and diverse press—particularly local press—is the backbone of a healthy and vibrant democracy. But as discussed in this Report, the rise of market power online has corresponded with a significant decline in the availability of trustworthy sources of news.[2455] Through dominating both digital advertising and key communication platforms, Google and Facebook have outsized power over the distribution and monetization of trustworthy sources of news online,[2456] creating an uneven playing field in which news publishers are beholden to their decisions.[2457]

To address this imbalance of bargaining power, we recommend that the Subcommittee consider legislation to provide news publishers and broadcasters with a narrowly tailored and temporary safe harbor to collectively negotiate with dominant online platforms.

In April 2019, Subcommittee Chairman Cicilline and Doug Collins (R-GA), the former-Ranking Member of the Committee on the Judiciary, introduced H.R. 2054, the "Journalism Competition and Preservation Act of 2019."[2458] H.R. 2054 would allow coordination by news publishers under the antitrust laws if it (1) directly relates to the quality, accuracy, attribution or branding, or interoperability of news; (2) benefits the entire industry, rather than just a few publishers, and is non-discriminatory to other news publishers; and (3) directly relates to and is reasonably necessary for these negotiations, instead of being used for other purposes. As Subcommittee Chairman Cicilline noted at the time of the bill's introduction:

> The free press is a cornerstone of our democracy. Journalists keep the public informed, root out corruption, and hold the powerful accountable. This bill will provide a much-needed lifeline to local publishers who have been crushed by Google and Facebook. It's about time we take a stand on this issue.[2459]

[2455] Free and Diverse Press Hearing at 3 (statement of David Chavern, Pres.and CEO, News Media Alliance) ("In effect, a couple of dominant tech platforms are acting as regulators of the digital news industry.").

[2456] Submission of Source 52, to H. Comm. on the Judiciary, 12 (Oct. 30, 2019) (on file with Comm.).

[2457] Submission from Source 53, to H. Comm. on the Judiciary, 7 (Oct. 14, 2019) (on file with Comm.). Although Apple News and Apple News Plus are increasingly popular news aggregators, most market participants that the Subcommittee received evidence from during the investigation do not view it as a critical intermediary for online news at this time. Some publishers raised competition concerns about the tying of payment inside Apple's news product.

[2458] Press Release, Cicilline, Collins Introduce Bill to Provide Lifeline to Local News, Congressman David. N. Cicilline (Apr. 3, 2019), https://cicilline.house.gov/press-release/cicilline-collins-introduce-bill-provide-lifeline-local-news.

[2459] *Id.*

Mr. Collins added that the proposed legislation would allow "community newspapers to more fairly negotiate with large tech platforms that are operating in an increasingly anti-competitive space," which would "help protect journalism, promote competition and allow communities to stay informed."[2460]

We recommend the consideration of this legislation as part of a broader set of reforms to address the rise of market power online. This proposed legislation follows a long congressional tradition of allocating coordination rights to individuals or entities that lack bargaining power in a marketplace.[2461] Although antitrust exemptions have been disfavored, at various times lawmakers have created exemptions in order to rectify imbalances of power or to promote non-competition values.[2462] In this instance, the risk associated with antitrust exemptions to preserve the free and diverse press—a bedrock constitutional value—is low, while the benefits of preserving access to high-quality journalism are difficult to overstate. As discussed earlier in the Report, the bill would follow steps that other jurisdictions are similarly taking to rebalance the power between news publishers and the dominant platforms.

6. Prohibit Abuse of Superior Bargaining Power and Require Due Process

By virtue of functioning as the only viable path to market, dominant platforms enjoy superior bargaining power over the third parties that depend on their platforms to access users and markets. Their bargaining leverage is a form of market power,[2463] which the dominant platforms routinely use to protect and expand their dominance.

Through its investigation, the Subcommittee identified numerous instances in which the dominant platforms abused this power. In several cases, dominant platforms used their leverage to extract greater money or data than users would be willing to provide in a competitive market. While a firm in a competitive market would lose business if it charged excessive prices for its goods or services because the customer would switch to a competitor, dominant platforms have been able to charge excessive prices or ratchet up their prices without a significant loss of business. Similarly, certain dominant platforms have been able to extort an ever-increasing amount of data from their customers and users, ranging from a user's personal data to a business's trade secrets and proprietary content. In the absence of an alternative platform, users effectively have no choice but to accede to the platform's demands for payment whether in the form of dollars or data.

[2460] *Id.*

[2461] *See generally* Submission from Sanjukta Paul, Assistant Professor of Law, Wayne State Univ., to H. Comm. on the Judiciary, 2–4 (Apr. 21, 2020) (on file with Comm.) [hereinafter "Paul Submission"].

[2462] *See, e.g.*, Clayton Act, 15 U.S.C. § 17 (1914); Capper-Volstead Act, ch. 57, 42 Stat. 388–89 (1922) (codified as amended at 7 U.S.C. §§ 291, 292 (2012)).

[2463] Aviv Nevo, Deputy Assistant Att'y Gen. for Econ., Dep't of Justice, Antitrust Div., "Mergers that Increase Bargaining Leverage," Remarks at the Stanford Institute for Economic Policy Research, 7 (Jan. 22, 2014), https://www.justice.gov/atr/file/517781/download ("[A]s a matter of economic theory and case law bargaining leverage is a source of market power.").

The Subcommittee's investigation found that dominant platforms have also leveraged their market power in negotiations with businesses and individuals to dictate the terms of the relationship. The dominant platforms frequently impose oppressive contractual provisions or offer "take-it-or-leave-it" terms in contract negotiations—even when dealing with relatively large companies represented by sophisticated counsel.[2464] Lacking bargaining power, dependent third parties often find themselves at the whims of the platform's arbitrary decisions. Subcommittee staff encountered numerous instances in which a third party had been abruptly delisted or demoted from a platform, without notice or explanation, and often without a clear avenue for recourse.

The dominant platforms' ability to abuse their superior bargaining power in these ways can cause long-term and far-reaching harm. To address these issues, the Subcommittee recommends that Congress consider prohibiting the abuse of superior bargaining power, including through potentially targeting anticompetitive contracts, and introducing due process protections for individuals and businesses dependent on the dominant platforms.[2465]

B. Strengthening the Antitrust Laws

1. Restore the Antimonopoly Goals of the Antitrust Laws

The antitrust laws that Congress enacted in 1890 and 1914—the Sherman Act, the Clayton Act, and the Federal Trade Commission Act—reflected a recognition that unchecked monopoly power poses a threat to our economy as well as to our democracy.[2466] Congress reasserted this vision through subsequent antitrust laws, including the Robinson-Patman Act of 1936, the Celler-Kefauver Act of 1950, and the Hart-Scott-Rodino Act of 1976.[2467]

In the decades since Congress enacted these foundational statutes, the courts have significantly weakened these laws and made it increasingly difficult for federal antitrust enforcers and private plaintiffs to successfully challenge anticompetitive conduct and mergers.[2468] Through adopting a

---

[2464] *See, e.g.*, Dig. Competition Expert Panel Report at 45 (noting how a report commissioned by the UK's Department for Digital, Culture, Media & Sport found that as "a consequence of their high market share, ownership of key technologies and strong user data assets, Google and Facebook are, to some extent, able to set their own terms to advertisers and publishers").

[2465] Foer Submission at 2–3; Submission from Marshall Steinbaum, Assistant Professor of Econ., Univ. of Utah, to H. Comm. on the Judiciary, 8 (Apr. 2020) (on file with Comm.) [hereinafter Steinbaum Submission]. *See generally* Austl. Competition & Consumer Comm'n Report at 205–79; Commission and Mkts. Auth. Report at 328–49.

[2466] *See generally* First & Fox Submission at 10–11; Steinbaum Submission; Submission from Robert H. Lande, Venable Professor of Law, Univ. of Balt. School of Law, to H. Comm. on the Judiciary (Apr. 16, 2020) (on file with Comm.) [hereinafter Lande Submission]; Paul Submission at 2-4; Submission from Maurice Stucke, Douglas A. Blaze Distinguished Professor of Law, Univ. of Tennessee, to H. Comm. on the Judiciary, 2 (Mar. 13, 2020) (on file with Comm.) [hereinafter Stucke Submission].

[2467] Thomas J. Horton, *Rediscovering Antitrust's Lost Values*, 16 U.N.H. L. REV. 179 (2018).

[2468] *See generally* Submission from Tim Wu, Julius Silver Professor of Law, Columbia Law School, to H. Comm. on the Judiciary (Apr. 25, 2020) (on file with Comm.) [hereinafter "Wu Submission"]; Submission from Spencer Weber Waller,

narrow construction of "consumer welfare" as the sole goal of the antitrust laws, the Supreme Court has limited the analysis of competitive harm to focus primarily on price and output rather than the competitive process[2469]—contravening legislative history and legislative intent.[2470] Simultaneously, courts have adopted the view that under-enforcement of the antitrust laws is preferable to over-enforcement, a position at odds with the clear legislative intent of the antitrust laws, as well as the view of Congress that private monopolies are a "menace to republican institutions."[2471] In recent decades, the Justice Department and the Federal Trade Commission have contributed to this problem by taking a narrow view of their legal authorities and issuing guidelines that are highly permissive of market power and its abuse. The overall result is an approach to antitrust that has significantly diverged from the laws that Congress enacted.

In part due to this narrowing, some of the anticompetitive business practices that the Subcommittee's investigation uncovered could be difficult to challenge under current law.[2472] In response to this concern, this section identifies specific legislative reforms that would help renew and rehabilitate the antitrust laws in the context of digital markets. In addition to these specific reforms, the Subcommittee recommends that Congress consider reasserting the original intent and broad goals of the antitrust laws, by clarifying that they are designed to protect not just consumers, but also workers, entrepreneurs, independent businesses, open markets, a fair economy, and democratic ideals.[2473]

2. Invigorate Merger Enforcement

Section 7 of the Clayton Act of 1914 prohibits any transaction where "the effect of such acquisition may be substantially to lessen competition, or to tend to create a monopoly."[2474] In 1950, Congress passed the Celler-Kevauver Anti-Merger Act to broaden the types of transactions covered by

---

John Paul Stevens Chair in Competition Law, Loyola Univ. Chicago School of Law, to H. Comm. on the Judiciary (Apr. 28, 2020) (on file with Comm.) [hereinafter "Waller Submission"].

[2469] Jonathan Sallet, *Protecting the "Competitive Process"—The Evolution of Antitrust Enforcement in the United States*, WASH. CTR. FOR EQUITABLE GROWTH (Oct. 31, 2018), https://equitablegrowth.org/competitive-edge-protecting-the-competitive-process-the-evolution-of-antitrust-enforcement-in-the-united-states/.

[2470] Submission from John Newman, Assoc. Professor of Law, Univ. of Miami School of Law, to the Subcomm. on Antitrust, Commercial and Admin. Law of the H. Comm. on the Judiciary, 2 (Apr. 1, 2020) (on file with Comm.) [hereinafter Newman Submission]; Stucke Submission at 2.

[2471] 21 CONG. REC. 3146 (1890) (statement of Sen. Hoar).

[2472] *See* Wu Submission at 2 ("If read broadly, the prohibitions on 'monopolization,' 'unfair means of competition,' and 'restraints on trade' could be used to handle the challenges of our time. But 'broadly' is manifestly not how the laws are read by the judiciary at this point. For the courts have grafted onto these laws burdens of proof, special requirements and defenses that are found nowhere in the statutes, and that have rendered the laws applicable only to the narrowest of scenarios, usually those involving blatant price effects. And it is this that makes the laws inadequate for the challenges presented by digital markets.").

[2473] *See generally* First & Fox Submission at 10–11; Stucke Submission at 2; Wu Submission; Waller Submission.

[2474] Clayton Act, 15 U.S.C. § 18 (1914).

the Clayton Act, specifically to include vertical mergers, conglomerate mergers, and purchases of assets.[2475]

As noted above, since 1998, Amazon, Apple, Facebook, and Google collectively have purchased more than 500 companies.[2476] The antitrust agencies did not block a single acquisition. In one instance—Google's purchase of ITA—the Justice Department required Google to agree to certain terms in a consent decree before proceeding with the transaction.[2477]

The Subcommittee's review of the relevant documents revealed that several of these acquisitions lessened competition and increased market power. In several cases, antitrust enforcers permitted dominant platforms to acquire a competitive threat. For example, documents produced during the investigation demonstrate that Facebook acquired Instagram to neutralize an emerging rival, while Google purchased Waze to eliminate an independent provider of mapping data. In other instances, the platform engaged in a series of acquisitions that enabled it to gain a controlling position across an entire supply chain or ecosystem. Google's acquisitions of DoubleClick, AdMeld, and AdMob, for example, let Google achieve a commanding position across the digital ad tech market.

In light of this, Subcommittee staff recommends that Congress considers a series of reforms to strengthen merger enforcement.

a. Codify Bright-Line Rules and Structural Presumptions in Concentrated Markets

A major change in antitrust enforcement over the last few decades has been the shift away from bright-line rules in favor of "rule of reason" case-by-case analysis. Although the rule of reason approach is said to reduce errors in enforcement through fact-specific analysis, in practice the standard tilts heavily in favor of defendants.[2478] The departure from bright-line rules and presumptions has especially affected merger enforcement, where enforcers seeking to challenge a merger must fully prove that it will have anticompetitive effects, even in cases where the merging parties are dominant firms in highly concentrated markets. Scholarship by Professor John Kwoka of Northeastern University shows that the antitrust agencies acted in only 38% of all mergers that led to price increases, suggesting that the current approach to merger review is resulting in significant under-enforcement.[2479]

[2475] Celler-Kefauver Anti-Merger Act, 64 Stat. 1125 (1950).

[2476] *See* Appendix.

[2477] Stipulation and Order, United States v. Google Inc. & ITA Software Inc. (D.D.C. 2011) (No. 1:11-cv-00688).

[2478] Michael A. Carrier, *The Rule of Reason: An Empirical Update for the 21st Century*, 16 GEO. MASON L. REV. 827 (2009).

[2479] JOHN KWOKA, MERGERS, MERGER CONTROL, AND REMEDIES 155 (2014).

To respond to this concern, the Subcommittee recommends that Members consider codifying bright-line rules for merger enforcement, including structural presumptions.[2480] Under a structural presumption, mergers resulting in a single firm controlling an outsized market share, or resulting in a significant increase in concentration, would be presumptively prohibited under Section 7 of the Clayton Act.[2481] This structural presumption would place the burden of proof upon the merging parties to show that the merger would not reduce competition. A showing that the merger would result in efficiencies should not be sufficient to overcome the presumption that it is anticompetitive. It is the view of Subcommittee staff that the 30% threshold established by the Supreme Court in *Philadelphia National Bank* is appropriate, although a lower standard for monopsony or buyer power claims may deserve consideration by the Subcommittee.

By shifting the burden of proof to the merging parties in cases involving concentrated markets and high market shares, codifying the structural presumption would help promote the efficient allocation of agency resources and increase the likelihood that anticompetitive mergers are blocked.

b. Protect Potential Rivals, Nascent Competitors, and Startups

The Subcommittee's investigation produced evidence that several of the dominant platforms acquired potential rivals and nascent competitors. Potential rivals are firms that are planning to enter or could plausibly enter the acquirer's market. Nascent competitors are firms whose "prospective innovation represents a serious future threat to an incumbent."[2482] In digital markets, potential rivals and nascent competitors play a critical role in driving innovation, as their prospective entry may dislodge incumbents or spur competition. For this reason, incumbents may view potential rivals and nascent competitors as a significant threat, especially as their success could render the incumbent's technologies obsolete.

To strengthen the law relating to potential rivals and nascent competitors, Subcommittee staff recommends strengthening the Clayton Act to prohibit acquisitions of potential rivals and nascent competitors. This could be achieved by clarifying that proving harm on potential competition or nascent competition grounds does not require proving that the potential or nascent competitor would

---

[2480] For support of codifying the structural presumption, *see* Submission from John Kwoka, Finnegan Professor of Econ., Northeastern Univ., to H. Comm. on the Judiciary, 3 (Apr. 17, 2020) (on file with Comm.) [hereinafter Kwoka Submission]; Submission from Michael Kades, Dir., Mkts. & Competition Policy, Wash. Ctr. for Equitable Growth et al., to H. Comm. on the Judiciary, 9 (Apr. 30, 2020) (on file with Comm.) [hereinafter "Kades Submission"]; Lande Submission at 5; Slaiman Submission at 3; Foer Submission at 9. *See also* Herbert Hovenkamp & Carl Shapiro, *Horizontal Mergers, Market Structure, and Burdens of Proof*, 127 YALE L.J. 1996 (2018); Steven C. Salop, *The Evolution and Vitality of Merger Presumptions: A Decision-Theoretic Approach*, 80 ANTITRUST L.J. 269 (2015).

[2481] Although some courts still follow the structural presumption adopted by the Supreme Court in *Philadelphia National Bank*, it is not universally followed, especially given the D.C. Circuit's decision in *United* States v. Baker Hughes Inc., 908 F.2d 981 (D.C. Cir. 1990).

[2482] Wu Submission at 4–5; *see also* C. Scott Hemphill & Tim Wu, *Nascent Competitors*, 168 U. PA. L. REV. (forthcoming 2020); Kades Submission at 14.

have been a successful entrant in a but-for world.[2483] Given the patchwork of cases that are unfavorable to potential- and nascent competition-based theories of harm, this amendment should also make clear that Congress intends to overrides this case law.[2484]

Since startups can be an important source of potential and nascent competition, the antitrust laws should also look unfavorably upon incumbents purchasing innovative startups. One way that Congress could do so is by codifying a presumption against acquisitions of startups by dominant firms, particularly those that serve as direct competitors, as well as those operating in adjacent or related markets.[2485]

Lastly, Subcommittee staff's review of relevant documents produced by the Federal Trade Commission and Justice Department demonstrated that the antitrust agencies consistently underestimated—by a significant margin—the degree to which an acquisition would undermine competition and impede entry. In light of this tendency, Subcommittee staff recommends that Congress consider strengthening the incipiency standard by amending the Clayton Act to prohibit acquisitions that "may lessen competition or tend to increase market power."[2486] Revising the law would "arrest the creation of trusts, conspiracies, and monopolies in their incipiency and before consummation." [2487]

c. Strengthen Vertical Merger Doctrine

The Subcommittee's investigation identified several ways in which vertical integration of dominant platforms enabled anticompetitive conduct. For this reason, the Subcommittee recommends that Congress examine proposals to strengthen the law relating to vertical mergers. The current case law disfavors challenges to vertical mergers. Specifically, courts tend to defer to claims from the merging parties that the transaction will yield efficiencies through the "elimination of double marginalization" and are skeptical about claims that the merger will result in foreclosure.

To address this concern, the Subcommittee recommends that Congress explore presumptions involving vertical mergers, such as a presumption that vertical mergers are anticompetitive when either

---

[2483] Wu Submission at 6; Kwoka Submission at 6.

[2484] *See, e.g.*, United States v. Marine Bancorporation, Inc., 418 U.S. 602 (1974).

[2485] Submission from Mark Lemley, William H. Neukom Professor of Law, Stanford Law School, to H. Comm. on the Judiciary, 7–8 (Apr. 8, 2020) (on file with Comm.) [hereinafter Lemley Submission].

[2486] Submission from Consumer Reports, to H. Comm. on the Judiciary, 5 (Apr. 17, 2020) (on file with Comm.) [hereinafter Consumer Reports Submission]; Submission from Richard M. Steuer, Adjunct Professor, Fordham School of Law, to H. Comm. on the Judiciary (Apr. 8, 2020) (on file with Comm.) [hereinafter Steuer Submission]; Peter C. Carstensen & Robert H. Lande, *The Merger Incipiency Doctrine and the Importance of 'Redundant' Competitors*, 2018 WIS. L. REV. 783 (2018).

[2487] S. Rep. No. 698 (1914) in EARL W. KINTNER, THE LEGISLATIVE HISTORY OF THE FEDERAL ANTITRUST LAWS AND RELATED STATUTES 1744–52 (1978) (noting that the Senate Judiciary Committee report stated that the purpose of the bill was to supplement the Sherman Act "by making these practices illegal, to arrest the creation of trusts, conspiracies, and monopolies in their incipiency and before consummation").

of the merging parties is a dominant firm operating in a concentrated market, or presumptions relating to input foreclosure and customer foreclosure.[2488]

3. Rehabilitate Monopolization Law

Section 2 of the Sherman Act makes it illegal to "monopolize, or attempt to monopolize, or combine or conspire with any other person or persons, to monopolize any part of the trade or commerce among the several States."[2489] Over recent decades, courts have significantly heightened the legal standards that plaintiffs must overcome in order to prove monopolization. Several of the business practices the Subcommittee's investigation uncovered should be illegal under Section 2. This section briefly identifies the relevant business practices and the case law that impedes effective enforcement of section 2 of the Sherman Act.

a. Abuse of Dominance

The Subcommittee's investigation found that the dominant platforms have the incentive and ability to abuse their dominant position against third-party suppliers, workers, and consumers. Some of these business practices are a detriment to fair competition, but they do not easily fit the existing categories identified by the Sherman Act, namely "monopolization" or "restraint of trade." Since courts have shifted their interpretation of the antitrust law to focus primarily on the formation or entrenchment of market power, and not on its exploitation or exercise, many of the business practices that Subcommittee staff identified as undermining competition in digital markets could be difficult to reach under the prevailing judicial approach.

To address this concern, Subcommittee staff recommends that Congress consider extending the Sherman Act to prohibit abuses of dominance.[2490] Furthermore, the Subcommittee should examine the creation of a statutory presumption that a market share of 30% or more constitutes a rebuttable presumption of dominance by a seller, and a market share of 25% or more constitute a rebuttable presumption of dominance by a buyer.[2491]

b. Monopoly Leveraging

The Subcommittee's investigation found that the dominant platforms have engaged in "monopoly leveraging," where a dominant firm uses its monopoly power in one market to boost or

---

[2488] Kades Submission at 5; Jonathan Baker et al., *Five Principles for Vertical Merger Enforcement Policy*, 33 ANTITRUST 3 (2019).

[2489] Sherman Act, 15 U.S.C. § 2 (1890).

[2490] First & Fox Submission at 2; Foer Submission at 2–4; Newman Submission at 7–8; Stucke Submission at 14; Waller Submission at 13.

[2491] Waller Submission at 12.

privilege its position in another market. For example, Google's use of its horizontal search monopoly to advantage its vertical search offerings is a form of monopoly leveraging. Although monopoly leveraging was previously a widely cognizable theory of harm under antitrust law, courts now require that use of monopoly power in the first market "actually monopolize" the secondary market or "dangerously threaten[] to do so."[2492] The Subcommittee's investigation identified several instances in which use of monopoly power in one market to privilege the monopolist's position in the second market injured competition, even if the conduct did not result in monopolization of the second market. For this reason, Subcommittee staff recommends overriding the legal requirement that monopoly leveraging "actually monopolize" the second market, as set out in *Spectrum Sports, Inc. v. McQuillan.*[2493]

c. <u>Predatory Pricing</u>

The Subcommittee's investigation identified several instances in which a dominant platform was pricing goods or services below-cost in order to drive out rivals and capture the market. For example, documents produced during the investigation revealed that Amazon had been willing to lose $200 million in a single quarter in order to pressure Diapers.com, a firm it had recognized as its most significant rival in the category. Amazon cut prices and introduced steep promotions, prompting a pricing war that eventually weakened Diapers.com. Amazon then purchased the company, eliminating its competitor and subsequently cutting back the discounts and promotions it had introduced.

Predatory pricing is a particular risk in digital markets, where winner-take-all dynamics incentivize the pursuit of growth over profits, and where the dominant digital platforms can cross-subsidize between lines of business. Courts, however, have introduced a "recoupment" requirement, necessitating that plaintiffs prove that the losses incurred through below-cost pricing subsequently were or could be recouped. Although dominant digital markets can recoup these losses through various means over the long term, recoupment is difficult for plaintiffs to prove in the short term. Since the recoupment requirement was introduced, successful predatory pricing cases have plummeted.[2494]

The Subcommittee recommends clarifying that proof of recoupment is not necessary to prove predatory pricing or predatory buying, overriding the Supreme Court's decisions in *Matsushita v. Zenith Ratio Corp.*,[2495] *Brooke Group Ltd. v. Brown & Williamson Tobacco Corp.*,[2496] and *Weyerhaeuser Company v. Ross-Simmons Hardwood Lumber Company.*[2497]

[2492] 506 U.S. 447 (1993).

[2493] *Id. See also* Alaska Airlines, Inc. v. United Airlines, Inc., 948 F.2d 536 (9th Cir. 1991).

[2494] Hubbard Submission at 20; Stucke Submission at 7; Teachout Submission at 12; Christopher R. Leslie, *Predatory Pricing and Recoupment*, 113 COLUM. L. REV. 1695 (2013).

[2495] 475 U.S. 574 (1986).

[2496] 509 U.S. 209 (1993).

[2497] 549 U.S. 312 (2007).

d. Essential Facilities and Refusals to Deal

The Subcommittee's investigation uncovered several instances in which a dominant platform used the threat of delisting or refusing service to a third party as leverage to extract greater value or more data or to secure an advantage in a distinct market. Because the dominant platforms do not face meaningful competition in their primary markets, their threat to refuse business with a third party is the equivalent of depriving a market participant of an essential input. This denial of access in one market can undermine competition across adjacent markets, undermining the ability of market participants to compete on the merits.

To address this concern, the Subcommittee recommends that Congress consider revitalizing the "essential facilities" doctrine, or the legal requirement that dominant firms provide access to their infrastructural services or facilities on a nondiscriminatory basis.[2498] To clarify the law, Congress should consider overriding judicial decisions that have treated unfavorably essential facilities- and refusal to deal-based theories of harm.[2499]

e. Tying

The Subcommittee's investigation identified several instances in which a dominant platform conditioned access to a good or service that the dominant platform controlled on the purchase or use of a separate product or service. This business practice undermines competition on the merits, by enabling a firm with market power in one market to privilege products or services in a distinct market.

Although antitrust law has long treated tying by a monopolist as anticompetitive, in recent decades, courts have moved away from this position. Subcommittee staff recommends that Congress consider clarifying that conditioning access to a product or service in which a firm has market power to the purchase or use of a separate product or service is anticompetitive under Section 2, as held by the Supreme Court in *Jefferson Parish Hosp. Dist. v. Hyde*.[2500]

f. Self-Preferencing and Anticompetitive Product Design

The Subcommittee's investigation uncovered several instances in which a dominant platform used the design of its platform or service to privilege its own services or to disfavor competitors. This practice undermines competition by enabling a firm controlling an essential input to distort competition in separate markets. The Subcommittee recommends that Congress consider whether

---

[2498] Submission from the Am. Antitrust Inst., to H. Comm. on the Judiciary, 4 (Apr. 17, 2020) (on file with Comm.) [hereinafter "AAI Submission"]; Waller Submission at 13.

[2499] Verizon Commc'ns Inc. v. Law Offices of Curtis V. Trinko, *LLP*, 540 U.S. 398 (2004); Pacific Bell Telephone Co. v. linkLine Communications, Inc., 555 U.S. 438 (2009).

[2500] 466 U.S. 2 (1984).

making a design change that excludes competitors or otherwise undermines competition should be a violation of Section 2, regardless of whether the design change can be justified as an improvement for consumers.[2501]

4. Additional Measures to Strengthen the Antitrust Laws

In response to the Subcommittee's requests for submissions, experts identified other proposals that Subcommittee staff believes warrant review by Congress. These include:

- Overriding *Ohio v. American Express* by clarifying that cases involving platforms do not require plaintiffs to establish harm to both sets of customers;[2502]

- Overriding *United States v. Sabre Corp.*, clarifying that platforms that are "two-sided," or serve multiple sets of customers, can compete with firms that are "one-sided";[2503]

- Clarifying that market definition is not required for proving an antitrust violation, especially in the presence of direct evidence of market power;[2504] and

- Clarifying that "false positives" (or erroneous enforcement) are not more costly than "false negatives" (erroneous non-enforcement), and that, when relating to conduct or mergers involving dominant firms, "false negatives" are costlier.[2505]

C. Strengthening Antitrust Enforcement

1. Congressional Oversight

As discussed earlier in the Report, Congress has a strong tradition of performing vigorous oversight of the enforcement and adequacy of the antitrust laws. Over the last century, Congress at key

---

[2501] This would require overriding Allied Orthopedic Appliances, Inc. v. Tyco Health Care Group LP, 592 F.3d 991 (9th Cir. 2010).

[2502] AAI Submission at 4; Submission from Herbert Hovenkamp, James G. Dinan Univ. Professor, Univ. of Pa. Law School, to H. Comm. on the Judiciary, 3 (Apr. 17, 2020) (on file with Comm.) [hereinafter "Hovenkamp Submission"]; Hubbard Submission at 20; Kades Submission at 8.

[2503] United States v. Sabre Corp., 452 F.Supp.3d 97 (D. Del. 2020). *See also* Kades Submission at 10.

[2504] Hovenkamp Submission at 3–4; Newman Submission at 5–6.

[2505] Subcommittee staff believes that Congress could clarify that the views set out by then-Professor Frank Easterbrook in *The Limits of Antitrust*, 63 TEX. L. REV. 1 (1984) do not reflect the views of the Congress in enacting the antitrust laws. *See also* Submission from Bill Baer, Visiting Fellow, The Brookings Institution, to H. Comm. on the Judiciary, 3 (May 19, 2020) (on file with Comm.) [hereinafter "Baer Submission"] ("That is my fundamental concern with the state of antitrust enforcement today. It is too cautious, too worried about adverse effects of "over enforcement" (so called Type I errors).").

moments responded forcefully to the courts' narrowing of antitrust laws, the rising tide of economic concentration, or other challenges to the sound and effective administration of the antitrust laws.[2506]

This tradition includes the creation of the Federal Trade Commission and concurrent enactment of the Clayton Antitrust Act in 1914, as both a response to the Supreme Court's narrow construction of the Sherman Act in 1911 and an effort to limit the discretion of the courts.[2507] It also includes Congress's broadening of merger enforcement to cover non-horizontal acquisitions and other transactions in the Celler-Kefauver Antimerger Act of 1950 as well as establishing a mechanism for judicial oversight of consent decrees in response to political interference in merger enforcement with the Tunney Act of 1974.[2508] Additionally, Congress has regularly investigated the rise and abuse of market power in important markets.[2509] In support of these efforts, Congress dedicated substantial congressional and agency resources to perform the task of identifying and responding to anticompetitive conduct.[2510]

In recent decades, Congress has departed from this tradition, deferring largely to the courts and to the antitrust agencies in the crafting of substantive antitrust policy.[2511] Its inaction has been read as acquiesce to the narrowing of the antitrust laws and has contributed to antitrust becoming "overly technical and primarily dependent on economics."[2512]

In other cases, congressional attention has fallen short as lawmakers tried to address competition problems without sustained efforts to implement enforcement changes, leading some reform efforts in recent decades to have misfired.[2513] Responding to these concerns, Congress has

---

[2506] *See generally,* Marc Winerman, *The Origins of the FTC: Concentration, Cooperation, Control, and Competition*, 71 ANTITRUST L.J. 1 (2003).

[2507] Clayton Act, 15 U.S.C. § 12; Fed. Trade Comm'n Act, 15 U.S.C. § 41.

[2508] 5 U.S.C. § 16. *See also Consent Decree Program of the Dep't of Justice: Hearings Before the Subcomm. on Antitrust of the H. Comm. on the Judiciary, 85th Cong.* (1957); REPORT OF THE SUBCOMM. ON ANTITRUST OF THE H. COMM. ON THE JUDICIARY, CONSENT DECREE PROGRAM OF THE DEP'T OF JUSTICE, 86TH CONG., 1ST SESS. (1959).

[2509] In the 1990s, the Committee on the Judiciary conducted significant oversight of competition in the telecommunications market in the wake of the breakup of Ma Bell and through oversight of the 1982 consent decree. These efforts culminated in the passage of H.R. 3626, the "Antitrust and Communications Reform Act," by the House of Representatives in 1994 by a vote of 423 to 5. Chairman Jack B. Brooks introduced this bill—a precursor to the Telecommunications Act of 1996—to address monopolization in the telecommunications market. *See generally* H. Rept. 103-559; Robert M. Frieden, *The Telecommunications Act of 1996: Predicting the Winners and Losers*, 20 HASTINGS COMM. & ENT. L.J. 11, 57 n.8 (1997).

[2510] Submission from Alison Jones & William E. Kovacic, to H. Comm. on the Judiciary, 4 (Apr. 17, 2020) (on file with Comm.) [hereinafter Jones & Kovacic Submission].

[2511] Harry First & Spencer Weber Waller, *Antitrust's Democracy Deficit*, 81 FORDHAM L. REV. 2543, 2556 (2013) ("[D]espite a history of bipartisan congressional support for the importance of the antitrust laws and their enforcement, of late Congress has done little. And when it has done something, it has focused on the micro rather than the macro changes that have occurred in the field.").

[2512] *Id.* at 2559.

[2513] Submission of Alison Jones & William E. Kovacic at 4 (Apr. 17, 2020) (on file with Majority staff of the Subcomm.) [hereinafter "Jones & Kovacic Submission"] ("The miscalculation of Congress (and the agencies) about the magnitude of

increased appropriations and provided modest improvements to the Federal Trade Commission's budget and remedial authority during this period. But these efforts were insufficient without sustained support in the face of "ferocious opposition" from large defendants and businesses lobbying Congress.[2514]

To remedy these broader trends, Subcommittee staff recommends that Congress revive its long tradition of robust and vigorous oversight of the antitrust laws and enforcement, along with its commitment to ongoing market investigations and legislative activity. Additionally, greater attention to implementation challenges will enable Congress to better see its reform efforts through.

2. Agency Enforcement

Over the course of the investigation, the Subcommittee uncovered evidence that the antitrust agencies consistently failed to block monopolists from establishing or maintaining their dominance through anticompetitive conduct or acquisitions. This institutional failure follows a multi-decade trend whereby the antitrust agencies have constrained their own authorities and advanced narrow readings of the law. In the case of the Federal Trade Commission, the agency has been reluctant to use the expansive set of tools with which Congress provided it, neglecting to fulfill its broad legislative mandate. Restoring the agencies to full strength will require overcoming these trends.

As a general matter, Congress created the FTC to police and prohibit "unfair methods of competition,"[2515] and to serve as an "administrative tribunal" that carefully studied ongoing business practices and economic conditions.[2516] To enable the agency to carry out these functions, Congress assigned the Commission powers to "make rules and regulations for the purpose of carrying out the [FTC Act's] provisions," as well as broad investigative authority to compel business information and conduct market studies.[2517] Notably, Congress established the provision prohibiting "unfair methods of competition" to reach beyond the other antitrust statutes, "to fill in the gaps in the other antitrust laws,

---

implementation tasks in this earlier period came at a high price. Implementation weaknesses undermined many investigations and cases that the federal agencies launched in response to congressional guidance. The litigation failures raised questions about the competence of the federal agencies, particularly their ability to manage large cases dealing with misconduct by dominant firms and oligopolists. The wariness of the federal agencies since the late 1970s to bring cases in this area—a wariness that many observers today criticize as unwarranted—is in major part the residue of bitter litigation experiences from this earlier period.").

[2514] Jones & Kovacic Submission at 6.

[2515] "The committee gave careful consideration to the question as to whether it would attempt to define the many and variable unfair practices which prevail in commerce and to forbid [them] . . . or whether it would, by a general declaration condemning unfair practices, leave it to the commission to determine what practices were unfair. It concluded that the latter course would be better, for the reason . . . that there were too many unfair practices to define, and after writing 20 of them into the law it would be quite possible to invent others." S. REP. NO. 63-597, 13 (1914).

[2516] Neil W. Averitt, *The Meaning of "Unfair Methods of Competition" in Section 5 of the Federal Trade Commission Act*, 21 B.C. L. REV. 227 (1980); *see also* Marc Winerman, *The Origins of the FTC: Concentration, Cooperation, Control, and Competition*, 71 ANTITRUST L.J. 1 (2003).

[2517] 15 U.S.C. § 46.

to round them out and make their coverage complete."[2518] Lawmakers delegated to the FTC the task of defining what constituted an "unfair method of competition," recognizing that an expert agency equipped to continuously monitor business practices would be best positioned to ensure the legal definition kept pace with business realities.

In practice, however, the Commission has neglected to play this role. In its first hundred years, the FTC promulgated only one rule defining an "unfair method of competition."[2519] In 2015 the Commission adopted a set of "Enforcement Principles" stating that the FTC's targeting of "unfair methods of competition" would be guided by the "promotion of consumer welfare," a policy goal absent from any legislative directive given to the Commission.[2520] Since the adoption of this framework, the FTC has brought only one case under its standalone section 5 authority.[2521] The agency has also failed to regularly produce market-wide studies, having halted regular data collection in the 1980s.[2522]

Together with the DOJ, the FTC has also chosen to stop enforcing certain antitrust laws entirely. For two decades, neither agency has filed a suit under the Robinson-Patman Act, which Congress passed in order to limit the power of large chain retailers to extract concessions from independent suppliers.[2523] In 2008, the Justice Department issued a report recommending that section 2 of the Sherman Act be curbed dramatically.[2524] Although the report was subsequently rescinded, the Justice Department has not filed a significant monopolization case in two decades. Meanwhile, both

---

[2518] Neil W. Averitt, *The Meaning of "Unfair Methods of Competition" in Section 5 of the Federal Trade Commission Act*, 21 B.C. L. REV. 227, 251 (1980) ("Section 5 is not confined to conduct that actually violates, or that threatens to violate, one of the other antitrust statutes. If it were limited to this extent it would be a largely duplicative provision. The legislative purpose instead assigned to Section 5 a broader role. It was to be an interstitial statute: it was to fill in the gaps in the other antitrust laws, to round them out and make their coverage complete. In addition to overt violations, therefore, Section 5 would reach closely similar conduct that violates the policy or 'spirit' of the antitrust laws, even though it may not come technically within its terms.").

[2519] Discriminatory Practices in Men's and Boys' Tailored Clothing Industry, 16 C.F.R. pt. 412 (1968).

[2520] Fed. Trade Comm'n, Statement of Enforcement Principles Regarding "Unfair Methods of Competition" Under Section 5 of the FTC Act (Aug. 13, 2015), https://www.ftc.gov/system/files/documents/public_statements/735201/150813section5enforcement.pdf.

[2521] The one exception is FTC's recent suit against Qualcomm. Fed. Trade Comm'n v. Qualcomm Inc., 411 F.Supp.3d 658 (N.D. Cal. 2019) (5:17-cv-00220).

[2522] FED. TRADE COMM'N, BUREAU OF ECON., ANNUAL LINE OF BUSINESS REPORT 1977 (1985), https://www.ftc.gov/reports/us-federal-trade-commission-bureau-economics-annual-line-business-report-1977-statistical.

[2523] In a memo submitted on behalf of the United States to the OECD, the Justice Department stated that "a shift in emphasis based on economic analysis resulted in a significant reduction in enforcement actions brought by the Agencies under the Robinson-Patman Act. As a result, current enforcement of the Act occurs mainly through private treble damages actions." Note by the United States, Roundtable on "Price Discrimination," OECD (Nov. 2016), https://www.justice.gov/atr/case-document/file/979211/download.

[2524] Thomas O. Barnett & Hill B. Wellford, *The DOJ's Single-Firm Conduct Report: Promoting Consumer Welfare Through Clearer Standards for Section 2 of the Sherman Act* (Sept. 8, 2008), https://www.justice.gov/sites/default/files/atr/legacy/2009/05/11/238599.pdf.

agencies have targeted their enforcement efforts on relatively small players—including ice skating teachers and organists—raising questions about their enforcement priorities.[2525]

The agencies have also been hamstrung by inadequate budgets. In 1981, FTC Chairman Jim Miller won steep budget cuts at the Commission, a drastic rollback from which the agency has not yet recovered. Prior to this Congress, appropriations for both agencies have reached historic lows.[2526] To restore the antitrust agencies to full strength, Subcommittee staff recommends that Congress consider the following:

- Triggering civil penalties and other relief for violations of "unfair methods of competition" rules, creating symmetry with violations of "unfair or deceptive acts or practices" rules;

- Requiring the Commission to regularly collect data and report on economic concentration and competition in sectors across the economy, as permitted under section 6 of the FTC Act;

- Enhancing the public transparency and accountability of the antitrust agencies, by requiring the agencies to solicit and respond to public comments for merger reviews, and by requiring the agencies to publish written explanations for all enforcement decisions;[2527]

- Requiring the agencies to conduct and make publicly available merger retrospectives on significant transactions consummated over the last three decades;

- Codifying stricter prohibitions on revolving door between the agencies and the companies that they investigate, especially with regards to senior officials;[2528] and

- Increasing the budgets of the Federal Trade Commission and the Antitrust Division.[2529]

3. Private Enforcement

Private enforcement plays a critical role in the nation's antitrust system. The Sherman Act and Clayton Act both include a private right of action. This reflected lawmakers' desire to ensure that those

---

[2525] Sandeep Vaheesan, *Accommodating Capital and Policing Labor: Antitrust in the Two Gilded Ages*, 78 MD. L. REV. 766 (2019). *See also* Brief for the United States and the Fed. Trade Comm'n as Amicus Curiae in Support of Appellant and in Favor of Reversal, Chamber of Commerce of the United States of America and Rasier, LLC, v. City of Seattle, 890 F.3d 769 (9th Cir. 2018) (No. 17-35640).

[2526] MICHAEL KADES, WASH. CTR. FOR EQUITABLE GROWTH, THE STATE OF U.S. FEDERAL ANTITRUST ENFORCEMENT (2019), https://equitablegrowth.org/wp-content/uploads/2019/09/091719-antitrust-enforcement-report.pdf.

[2527] Mitchell Submission at 9–10.

[2528] *See* submission from Source 17.

[2529] *See* Baer Submission at 7–8; Kades Submission at 12–13.

abused by monopoly power have an opportunity for direct recourse.[2530] It also reflected a recognition that public enforcers would be susceptible to capture by the very monopolists that they were supposed to investigate, necessitating other means of enforcement.

Empirical surveys of trends in antitrust enforcement indicate that private enforcement deters anticompetitive conduct and strengthens enforcement overall.[2531] In recent decades, however, courts have erected significant obstacles for private antitrust plaintiffs, both through procedural decisions and substantive doctrine.

One major obstacle is the rise of forced arbitration clauses, which undermine private enforcement of the antitrust laws by allowing companies to avoid legal accountability for their actions.[2532] These clauses allow firms to evade the public justice system—where plaintiffs have far greater legal protections—and hide behind a one-sided process that is tilted in their favor.[2533] For example, although Amazon has over two million sellers in the United States, Amazon's records reflect that only 163 sellers initiated arbitration proceedings between 2014 and 2019.[2534] This data seem to confirm studies showing that forced arbitration clauses often fails to provide a meaningful forum for resolving disputes and instead tend to suppress valid claims and shield wrongdoing.[2535]

Several other trends in judicial decisions have hampered private antitrust plaintiffs, including in cases involving dominant platforms. To address these concerns, the Subcommittee recommends that Congress consider:

[2530] *See, e.g.*, 51 CONG. REC. 9073 (1914) (remarks of Rep. Webb that private Section 7 remedies "open the door of justice to every man, whenever he may be injured by those who violate the antitrust laws, and give the injured party ample damages for the wrong suffered.").

[2531] Joshua P. Davis & Robert H. Lande, *Toward an Empirical and Theoretical Assessment of Private Antitrust Enforcement*, 36 SEATTLE U. L. REV. 1269, 1276 (2013).

[2532] *Justice Denied: Forced Arbitration and the Erosion of our Legal System: Hearing Before the Subcomm. on Antitrust, Commercial and Admin. Law of the H. Comm. on the Judiciary*, 116th Cong. 2 (2019) (statement of Myriam Gilles, Paul R. Verkuil Research Chair in Public Law & Professor of Law, Benjamin N. Cardozo School of Law).

[2533] *Justice Denied: Forced Arbitration and the Erosion of our Legal System: Hearing Before the Subcomm. on Antitrust, Commercial and Admin. Law of the H. Comm on the Judiciary*, 116th Cong. 2 (2019) (statement of Deepak Gupta, Founding Principal, Gupta Wessler PLLC).

[2534] Innovation and Entrepreneurship Hearing at 49 (response to Questions for the Record of Nate Sutton, Assoc. Gen. Counsel, Amazon).

[2535] Judith Resnik, *Diffusing Disputes: The Public in the Private of Arbitration, the Private in Courts, and the Erasure of Rights*, 124 YALE L. J. 2804 (2015).

- Eliminating court-created standards for "antitrust injury"[2536] and "antitrust standing,"[2537] which undermine Congress's granting of enforcement authority to "any person . . . injured . . . by reason of anything forbidden in the antitrust laws;"[2538]

- Reducing procedural obstacles to litigation, including through eliminating forced arbitration clauses[2539] and undue limits on class action formation;[2540] and

- Lowering the heightened pleading requirement introduced in *Bell Atlantic Corp. v. Twombly*.[2541]

* * *

[2536] *Brunswick Corp. v. Pueblo Bowl-O-Mat, Inc.*, 429 U.S. 477 (1977).

[2537] *Associated Gen. Contractors v. California State Council of Carpenters*, 459 U.S. 519 (1983).

[2538] Clayton Act, 15 U.S.C. § 15 (1914).

[2539] *American Express v. Italian Colors*, 570 U.S. 228 (2013); *AT&T Mobility v. Concepcion*, 563 U.S. 333 (2011).

[2540] *Comcast v. Behrend*, 569 U.S. 27 (2013).

[2541] 550 U.S. 544 (2007).

VII. APPENDIX: MERGERS AND ACQUISITIONS BY DOMINANT PLATFORMS[2542]

A. Amazon

Amazon			
Company	**Year Acquired**	**Categories**	**Acquisition Value (USD)**
Zoox	2020	Autonomous Vehicles, Robotics, Transportation	1,200,000,000
Health Navigator	2019	Health Care	--
Internet Gaming Database (IGDB)	2019	Video Games, Content, Media and Entertainment	--
INLT	2019	Enterprise Applications, Freight Service, Logistics, SaaS, Shipping, Transportation	--
E8 Storage	2019	Cloud Computing, Enterprise Software, Flash Storage, Software	50,000,000
Bebo	2019	Internet, Video Games	25,000,000
Sizmek Ad Server	2019	Advertising, Marketing	--
CANVAS Technology	2019	Robotics	--
Eero	2019	Internet, IoT, Wireless	97,000,000
CloudEndure	2019	Cloud Computing, Cloud Storage, Enterprise Software, SaaS	200,000,000

[2542] Prepared by Subcomm. based on *The Acquisition Takeover by the 5 Tech Giants*, https://people.ischool.berkeley.edu/~neha01mittal/infoviz/dashboard/, (last visited Oct 4, 2020); *see also* BIG TECH MERGERS, AMERICAN ECON. LIBERTIES PROJ., https://www.economicliberties.us/big-tech-merger-tracker/ (last visited Oct 4, 2020); *see also* Search: Acquisitions, CRUNCHBASE, https://www.crunchbase.com/ (last visited Oct 4, 2020).

Amazon			
Company	**Year Acquired**	**Categories**	**Acquisition Value (USD)**
TSO Logic	2019	Analytics, Cloud Computing, Cloud Management, Data Center, Software	--
Tapzo	2018	E-Commerce, Mobile, Software	40,000,000
PillPack	2018	Pharmacy, E-Commerce	753,000,000
Ring	2018	Consumer Electronics, Security, Smart Home	--
Immedia	2018	Semiconductors	--
Sqrrl	2018	Cybersecurity	40,000,000
Dispatch	2017	Robotics	--
Blink	2017	Consumer Electronics, Electronics, Hardware, Security	90,000,000
Goo Technologies	2017	3D Technology, Internet, Software, Web Development	--
Body Labs	2017	3D Technology, Artificial Intelligence, Computer Vision, Developer APIs, Machine Learning	50,000,000
Wing	2017	Information Technology, Logistics, Mobile, SaaS	--
GameSparks	2017	E-Commerce, Mobile, Software	10,000,000
Graphiq	2017	Artificial Intelligence, Big Data, Data Visualization, Market Research, Search Engine, Semantic Web	50,000,000

Amazon			
Company	**Year Acquired**	**Categories**	**Acquisition Value (USD)**
Souq.com	2017	Consumer Electronics, E-Commerce, Shopping	580,000,000
Whole Foods	2017	Food and Beverage, Grocery, Organic Food	13,700,000,000
Do.com	2017	Internet, Meeting Software, Software	--
Thinkbox Systems	2017	Software	--
Colis Privé	2017	Shipping & Delivery, Logistics	--
Harvest.ai	2017	Artificial Intelligence, Cloud Security, Cyber Security, Predictive Analytics	19,000,000
Biba Systems	2016	Apps, Messaging, Mobile	--
Partpic	2016	Photo Recognition	--
Westland	2016	Publishing	--
Curse Inc.	2016	Digital Media, Gaming, Video Games	--
Cloud9 IDE	2016	Cloud Computing, Enterprise Software, Mobile, Open Source, Software	--
Orbeus	2016	Artificial Intelligence, Photo Recognition	--
NICE	2016	Cloud Infrastructure, Enterprise Software, Power Grid	--

Amazon			
Company	**Year Acquired**	**Categories**	**Acquisition Value (USD)**
Emvantage Payments	2016	Mobile Payments, Payments	--
Elemental Technologies	2015	Content Delivery Network, Enterprise Software, Video, Video Streaming	500,000,000
Safaba Translation Systems	2015	Software	--
AppThwack	2015	Android, Cyber Security, iOS, Mobile, SaaS, Test and Measurement	--
Shoefitr	2015	E-Commerce, Fashion, Personalization, Software	--
ClusterK	2015	Software	--
Amiato	2015	Analytics, Real Time, Service Industry	--
2lemetry	2015	Cloud Computing, IoT, Software	--
Annapurna Labs	2015	Cloud Computing, Cloud Storage, Data Storage	350,000,000
GoodGame	2014	Video Games, Social Media	--
Rooftop Media	2014	Content, Digital Entertainment, Audio	--
ComiXology	2014	Cloud Data Services, Comics, Digital Entertainment, Digital Media, Reading Apps	--
Twitch	2014	Social Media, Video, Video Games, Video Streaming	970,000,000

Amazon			
Company	Year Acquired	Categories	Acquisition Value (USD)
Double Helix Games	2014	Developer Platform, PC Games, Video Games	--
TenMarks Education	2013	E-Learning, EdTech, Education	--
Liquavista	2013	Electronics, Hardware, Manufacturing, Software	--
Goodreads	2013	E-Learning, Social Media	--
INOVA Software	2013	Software	--
UpNext	2012	3D Mapping	--
Evi	2012	Mobile, Search Engine	26,000,000
Avalon Books	2012	Books, Education	--
Kiva Systems	2012	Hardware, Mobile, Robotics, Software	775,000,000
Teachstreet	2012	Charter Schools, Education	--
Yap	2011	Artificial Intelligence, Audio, Messaging, Mobile, Speech Recognition, Telecommunications	--
Pushbutton	2011	Content, Digital Entertainment, TV	--
The Book Depository	2011	E-Commerce, Retail	--

	Amazon		
Company	**Year Acquired**	**Categories**	**Acquisition Value (USD)**
Toby Press	2010	Books	--
Quidsi	2010	Beauty, Child Care, E-Commerce	545,000,000
BuyVIP	2010	E-Commerce, Marketing, Shopping	96,500,000
Amie Street	2010	Media and Entertainment, Music, Music Streaming	--
Woot.com	2010	Electronics, Fashion, Wine And Spirits	110,000,000
Touchco	2010	Hardware, Software	--
Zappos	2009	E-Commerce, Retail, Shoes	1,200,000,000
SnapTell	2009	Advertising, Marketing, Mobile	--
Lexcycle	2009	iOS, Mobile, Software	--
AbeBooks	2008	E-Commerce, Marketplace, Shopping	--
Reflexive Entertainment	2008	Gaming, Mobile, Video Games	--
Shelfari	2008	Social Media	--
Box Office Mojo	2008	Analytics, Film, Media and Entertainment	--

Amazon			
Company	**Year Acquired**	**Categories**	**Acquisition Value (USD)**
Fabric.com	2008	E-Commerce, Fashion, Retail	--
LoveFilm	2008	Digital Entertainment, Gaming, Internet	312,000,000
Without A Box	2008	Video	--
Audible	2008	Audio, Audiobooks, Digital Entertainment, E-Commerce, Media and Entertainment	300,000,000
Brilliance Audio	2007	E-Commerce	--
Digital Photography Review	2007	E-Commerce, News, Publishing	--
Text Pay Me	2006	Messaging, Payments	--
Shopbop.com	2006	E-Commerce, Lifestyle, Shopping	--
CustomFlix	2005	Digital Media, DVDs	--
Small Parts Inc.	2005	3D Printing, E-Commerce, Manufacturing, Retail	--
MobiPocket	2005	Shopping	--
Createspace	2005	Digital Media, Printing, Publishing	--
Joyo.com	2004	E-Commerce, Internet, Music, Video	75,000,000

Amazon			
Company	**Year Acquired**	**Categories**	**Acquisition Value (USD)**
Egghead.com	2002	E-Commerce, Retail	6,100,000
OurHouse	2001	E-Commerce, Retail	--
Leep Technology	1999	CRM, Information Technology, Software	--
Back to Basics	1999	Internet, Toys, Video Games	--
Tool Crib	1999	Tools, E-Commerce	--
Convergence Corp.	1999	Enterprise Software, Internet, Wireless	23,000,000
Accept.com	1999	E-Commerce Platforms, Photography, Retail	101,000,000
Alexa	1999	Digital Marketing, SEO, Web Development	250,000,000
LiveBid	1999	Auctions	--
Exchange.com	1999	Books, Music	--
MindCorps	1999	Web Development, Consulting	--
Bookpages	1998	E-Commerce, Internet	--
Internet Movie Database (IMDb)	1998	Content, Media and Entertainment, TV	55,000,000

Amazon			
Company	**Year Acquired**	**Categories**	**Acquisition Value (USD)**
Junglee	1998	E-Commerce, Retail, Shopping	250,000,000
PlanetAll	1998	Internet, Social Media, Web Development	--
Telebook	1998	E-Commerce, Internet	--

B.   Apple

Apple			
Company	**Year Acquired**	**Categories**	**Acquisition Value (USD)**
Spaces	2020	AR/VR	--
Mobeewave	2020	Software	100,000,000
Fleetsmith	2020	Software, Security	--
NextVR	2020	AR/VR	100,000,000
Inductiv	2020	AI, Machine Learning, Software	--
Voysis	2020	AI, Machine Learning, Software	--
Dark Sky	2020	Software, Apps	--

Apple			
Company	**Year Acquired**	**Categories**	**Acquisition Value (USD)**
Xnor.ai	2020	AI, Machine Learning, Software	200,000,000
Spectral Edge	2019	Photography, Software, Artificial Intelligence	--
iKinema	2019	Graphics, 3D Animation, Digital Media	--
Intel Smartphone Modem Business	2019	Hardware	1,000,000,000
Drive.ai	2019	Autonomous Vehicles	--
Tueo Health	2019	Health Care, Information Technology	--
Laserlike	2019	Machine Learning	--
Stamplay	2019	Cloud Computing, Data Integration, Developer Tools, SaaS, Sales Automation	5,600,000
DataTiger	2019	Marketing	--
PullString	2019	Voice Recognition	--
Platoon	2018	Talent Search/Acquisition	--
Silk Labs	2018	AI, Machine Learning, Software	--
Dialog	2018	Semiconductors	300,000,000

Apple			
Company	**Year Acquired**	**Categories**	**Acquisition Value (USD)**
Shazam	2018	Android, iOS, Music, Audio Recognition	400,000,000
Akonia	2018	Glasses, AR	--
Texture	2018	Content, Digital Entertainment, Digital Media	--
Buddybuild	2018	Developer Tools, Mobile, Software	--
Pop Up Archive	2017	Audio, Podcasts, Software	--
Spektral	2017	Photography, Software, AR	30,000,000
InVisage	2017	Photography, Software	--
Vrvana	2017	Computer, Hardware, Information Technology, Virtual Reality	30,000,000
Init.ai	2017	Artificial Intelligence, B2B, Developer Platform, Developer Tools, Machine Learning, Messaging, Natural Language Processing, Virtual Assistant	--
PowerbyProxi	2017	Consumer Electronics, Industrial, Wireless	--
Regaind	2017	Artificial Intelligence, Computer Vision, Photo Sharing, Photography	--
SensoMotoric Instruments	2017	Computer Vision, Image Recognition, Psychology, Software	--

Apple			
Company	**Year Acquired**	**Categories**	**Acquisition Value (USD)**
Beddit	2017	Fitness, Health Care, Wellness	--
Lattice Data	2017	Big Data, Information Technology, Machine Learning	200,000,000
Workflow	2017	Mobile, Productivity Tools, Software	--
RealFace	2017	Facial Recognition	--
Indoor.io	2016	Mapping Services, Navigation, Service Industry, Internet	--
Tuplejump	2016	Analytics, Artificial Intelligence, Big Data, Data Visualization, Machine Learning, Software	--
Turi	2016	Analytics, Artificial Intelligence, Big Data, Machine Learning, Software	200,000,000
Gliimpse	2016	Health Care, Information Technology	--
Emotient	2016	Artificial Intelligence, Machine Learning, Software, Video	--
LearnSprout	2016	Analytics, Big Data, EdTech, Education, Predictive Analytics	--
Flyby Media	2016	Augmented Reality, Computer Vision, Internet, Location Based Services, Mobile, Social Media, Video	--
Faceshift	2015	Broadcasting, Content Creators, Digital Media, Facial Recognition, Information Technology, Video Conferencing	--

Apple			
Company	**Year Acquired**	**Categories**	**Acquisition Value (USD)**
LegbaCore	2015	Consulting, Information Technology, Security	--
VocalIQ	2015	Artificial Intelligence, Audio, Automotive, Machine Learning, Mobile, Wearables	--
Perceptio	2015	Artificial Intelligence, Digital Media, Machine Learning	--
Mapsense	2015	Geospatial, Location Based Services, Web Hosting	25,000,000
Coherent Navigation	2015	Apps, Software	--
Metaio	2015	Advertising, Augmented Reality, Mobile, Software	--
LinX	2015	Mobile, Social Media	20,000,000
Dryft	2015	Hardware, Software	--
FoundationDB	2015	Analytics, Database, Enterprise Software	--
Camel Audio	2015	Audio, Music	--
Semetric	2015	Analytics, Content Discovery, Predictive Analytics	50,000,000
Prss	2014	iOS, Publishing	--
Beats Electronics	2014	Consumer Electronics, Hardware, Manufacturing, Media and Entertainment, Music, Software	3,000,000,000

Apple			
Company	**Year Acquired**	**Categories**	**Acquisition Value (USD)**
BookLamp	2014	Content Discovery, Reading Apps, Software	--
Spotsetter	2014	Big Data, Social Media	--
Swell	2014	Content Discovery, Machine Learning, Mobile, Personalization	30,000,000
LuxVue Technologies	2014	Consumer Electronics, Hardware, Software	--
Burstly	2014	Advertising, Analytics, iOS, Mobile Advertising	--
SnappyLabs	2014	Photography	--
Acunu	2013	Analytics, Big Data, Software	--
Topsy	2013	Analytics, Internet, Real Time, Search Engine, Social Media	200,000,000
BroadMap	2013	Geospatial, Software	--
PrimeSense	2013	3D Technology, Consumer Electronics, Hardware	345,000,000
Cue	2013	Internet, Mobile Apps	35,000,000
Passif Semiconductor	2013	Manufacturing, Semiconductor, Wireless	--
Matcha	2013	Content, Online Portals, Video	--

Apple			
Company	**Year Acquired**	**Categories**	**Acquisition Value (USD)**
Embark	2013	Mobile, Mobile Apps, Public Transportation	--
AlgoTrim	2013	Mobile	--
Catch.com	2013	Android, iOS, Mobile	--
Locationary	2013	Analytics, Crowdsourcing, Location Based Services	--
HopStop.com	2013	Android, iOS, Navigation	--
OttoCat	2013	Apps, Internet, Mobile	--
WiFiSlam	2013	Location Based Services, Mobile, Wireless	20,000,000
Novauris Technologies	2013	Information Services, Mobile, VoIP	--
Anobit	2012	Electronics, Flash Storage, Semiconductor	390,000,000
Chomp	2012	Mobile	50,000,000
AuthenTec	2012	Biometrics, Cyber Security, Identity Management, NFC, Security, Semiconductor, Sensors	356,000,000
Particle	2012	Developer Platform, Mobile, Web Development	--
Redmatica	2012	Music, Music Streaming	--

		Apple	
Company	**Year Acquired**	**Categories**	**Acquisition Value (USD)**
C3 Technologies	2011	Assistive Technology, Enterprise Software, Information Technology	240,000,000
Quattro Wireless	2010	Ad Network, Advertising, Advertising Platforms, Mobile, Publishing	275,000,000
Intrinsity	2010	Manufacturing, Mobile, Semiconductor	121,000,000
Siri	2010	Consumer Electronics, iOS, Software, Virtualization	--
Gipsy Moth Studios	2010	App Localization	--
Poly9	2010	Geospatial, Software	--
Polar Rose	2010	Internet, Browser Extensions, Image Recognition, Photography	22,000,000
IMSense	2010	Image Recognition, Photography, Software	--
Placebase	2009	Database, Developer APIs, Developer Tools	--
Lala	2009	Internet, Music, Music Streaming	17,000,000
P.A. Semi	2008	Electronics, Manufacturing, Semiconductor	278,000,000
Silicon Color	2006	Film, Software, Video	--
Proximity	2006	Media Asset Management	--

	Apple		
Company	**Year Acquired**	**Categories**	**Acquisition Value (USD)**
SchemaSoft	2005	Software	--
FingerWorks	2005	Hardware, Human Computer Interaction, Software	--
Nothing Real	2002	Software	--
Zayante	2002	Software	13,000,000
Emagic	2002	Software	30,000,000
Prismo Graphics	2002	Robotics, Software, Video	20,000,000
Silicon Grail Corp-Chalice	2002	Software	20,000,000
Propel Software	2002	Computer, Internet, Software	--
PowerSchool	2001	EdTech, Education, SaaS, Software	62,000,000
Spruce Technologies	2001	Information Technology	15,000,000
Bluebuzz	2001	Internet Service Provider	--
Bluefish Labs	2001	Database, Mobile Apps, Web Apps	--
Astarte	2000	DVD Authoring	--

Apple			
Company	**Year Acquired**	**Categories**	**Acquisition Value (USD)**
NetSelector	2000	Information Technology, Internet, Software	--
SoundJam MP	2000	MP3 Player, Audio Player, Software	--
Raycer Graphics	1999	3D Technology, Graphic Design, Information Technology	15,000,000
Xemplar Education	1999	Education	5,000,000
NeXT	1997	Education, Hardware, Software	404,000,000
Power Computing Corp.	1997	Manufacturing, Software	100,000,000
Coral Software	1989	Artificial Intelligence, Information Technology, Software	--
Nashoba Systems	1988	Software	--
Network Innovations	1988	Information Technology, Software, Virtualization	--
Orion Network Systems	1988	Communications Infrastructure, Satellite Communication	--
Styleware	1988	Internet, IoT, Software, Web Hosting	--

C.   Facebook

Facebook			
Company	**Year Acquired**	**Categories**	**Acquisition Value (USD)**
Giphy	2020	Software	400,000,000
Ready at Dawn	2020	VR, Video Games	--
Mapillary	2020	Software, Mapping	--
Sanzaru Games	2020	VR, Video Games	--
Scape Technologies	2020	AR/VR, Computer Vision, Software	40,000,000
PlayGiga	2019	Digital Media, Video Games	--
Beat Games	2019	VR, Video Games	--
Packagd	2019	E-Commerce, Shopping	--
GrokStyle	2019	Artificial Intelligence	--
CTRL-labs	2019	Augmented Reality	--
Servicefriend	2019	AI, Messaging	--
Chainspace	2019	Apps, Blockchain, Information Technology	--
Vidpresso	2018	Broadcasting, Software	--

Facebook			
Company	**Year Acquired**	**Categories**	**Acquisition Value (USD)**
Redkix	2018	Productivity, Enterprise Collaboration	--
Bloomsbury AI	2018	AI, Machine Learning	30,000,000
Confirm.io	2018	Identity Management	--
Tbh	2017	iOS, Mobile Apps, Social, Social Media	--
Fayteq	2017	Software	--
Source3	2017	Content Rights Management	--
Ozlo	2017	Artificial Intelligence, Computer, Information Services, Mobile	--
Zurich Eye	2017	AR/VR, Computer Vision, Robotics	--
CrowdTangle	2016	Brand Marketing, Non-Profit, Social Media	--
FacioMetrics	2016	Machine Learning, Mobile Apps, Social Media, Software	--
InfiniLED	2016	Lighting, Hardware	--
Nascent Objects	2016	Manufacturing, Product Design, Software	--
Two Big Ears	2016	Audio, Consumer Electronics, Software, Virtual Reality	--

Facebook			
Company	**Year Acquired**	**Categories**	**Acquisition Value (USD)**
Masquerade	2016	Consumer Applications, Mobile, Photo Editing	--
Endaga	2015	Communications Infrastructure, Impact Investing, Infrastructure, Mobile, Telecommunications	--
Pebbles Interfaces	2015	Digital Media, Hardware, Mobile	60,000,000
Surreal Vision	2015	Software	--
TheFind	2015	Coupons, E-Commerce, Lifestyle, Local, Mobile, Search Engine, Shopping	--
QuickFire Networks	2015	Cloud Data Services, Video	--
Wit.ai	2015	Artificial Intelligence, Computer, Developer APIs, Machine Learning, Software	--
WaveGroup Sound	2014	Music, Product Design	--
PRYTE	2014	Mobile Devices, Emerging Markets	--
PrivateCore	2014	Cyber Security, Security	--
LiveRail	2014	Advertising, Enterprise Software, Video	500,000,000
ProtoGeo Oy	2014	Mobile	--
Ascenta	2014	Aerospace, Manufacturing	20,000,000

Facebook			
Company	**Year Acquired**	**Categories**	**Acquisition Value (USD)**
WhatsApp	2014	Android, Messaging, Mobile, Subscription Service	19,000,000,000
Oculus VR	2014	Augmented Reality, Consumer Electronics, Hardware, Video Games, Virtual Reality, Virtualization	2,000,000,000
Branch	2014	Internet, Messaging, Social	15,000,000
Little Eye Labs	2014	Android, Mobile, Test and Measurement	15,000,000
SportStream	2013	Consumer Electronics, Mobile, Sports	--
Onavo	2013	Finance, Mobile, Social Network	--
Jibbigo	2013	Apps, Audio, Big Data, Language Learning, Mobile	--
Monoidics	2013	Analytics, Enterprise Software, Information Technology	--
Parse	2013	Android, Cloud Computing, Enterprise Software, iOS, Mobile, PaaS	85,000,000
Hot Studio	2013	Internet, Social Media, Web Design	--
Spaceport	2013	Gaming, Mobile, Mobile Devices, Online Games, Web Development	--
Atlas Solutions	2013	Advertising, Advertising Platforms, Internet	100,000,000

Facebook			
Company	**Year Acquired**	**Categories**	**Acquisition Value (USD)**
Osmeta	2013	Hardware, Software	--
Storylane	2013	Social Media	--
Threadsy	2012	Messaging, Social Media, Social Network	--
Spool	2012	Enterprise Software, Mobile, Social Bookmarking, Video	--
Acrylic Software	2012	Software	--
Karma	2012	Gifts, Mobile, Social	--
Face.com	2012	Artificial Intelligence, Cloud Storage, Facial Recognition, Machine Learning, Photography, Social Network	100,000,000
TagTile	2012	Direct Marketing, Loyalty Programs, Mobile, Social Media	--
Glancee	2012	Android, Dating, iOS, Location Based Services, Mobile, Public Relations, Search Engine	--
Lightbox.com	2012	Android, Mobile, Photo Sharing	--
Instagram	2012	Mobile, Photo Sharing, Photography, Social Media	1,000,000,000
Caffeinated Mind	2012	File Transfer, Big Data	--

Facebook			
Company	**Year Acquired**	**Categories**	**Acquisition Value (USD)**
Gowalla	2011	Location Based Services, Photography, Private Social Networking, Travel, Internet	--
Strobe	2011	iOS, Mobile, Software, Web Development	--
Friend.ly	2011	Blogging Platforms, Social Media	--
Push Pop Press	2011	Advertising, Digital Media, Marketing	--
MailRank	2011	Email, CRM, Information Technology, Software	--
DayTum	2011	Analytics, Big Data, Database	--
Sofa	2011	Developer Tools, Software	--
RecRec	2011	Computer Vision	--
Beluga	2011	Messaging, Mobile, Social Media	--
Rel8tion	2011	Advertising, Advertising Platforms	--
Snaptu	2011	Mobile	70,000,000
ShareGrove	2010	Real Time, Social Network, Web Hosting	--
Drop.io	2010	EdTech, Education, Email, File Sharing, Finance, FinTech, Flash Storage, Mobile	10,000,000

Facebook			
Company	**Year Acquired**	**Categories**	**Acquisition Value (USD)**
Hot Potato	2010	Social, Social Media, Social Media Marketing	10,000,000
Nextstop	2010	Digital Entertainment, Social, Travel	2,500,000
Chai Labs	2010	Software	10,000,000
Zenbe	2010	Android, Email, Location Based Services, Messaging, Mobile, Software, Web Apps	--
Divvyshot	2010	Photo Sharing, Social Network, Web Hosting	--
Octazen	2010	Enterprise Software, Social Network, Web Browsers	--
FriendFeed	2009	Social Media	47,500,000
ConnectU	2009	Social Media	--
Parakey	2007	Social Media, Web Browsers, WebOS	--
AboutFace	2007	Internet	--

D.   Google

Google			
Company	**Year Acquired**	**Categories**	**Acquisition Value (USD)**
Stratozone	2020	Cloud, Platform Migration	--
North	2020	Hardware, Glasses	180,000,000
Looker	2020	Big Data, Analytics	2,600,000,000
Cornerstone Technology	2020	Cloud, Platform Migration	--
AppSheet	2020	Enterprise Software	--
Pointy	2020	Software, Inventory	163,000,000
Fitbit	2019	User Data, Mobile Devices, Fitness Tracking, Health Care	2,100,000,000
Typhoon Studios	2019	Video Games, Video Streaming	--
CloudSimple	2019	Cloud	--
Elastifile	2019	Cloud, Storage	--
Nightcorn	2019	Internet, Social Media, Video Streaming	--
Alooma	2019	Data Integration, Cloud, Platform Migration	--

Google			
Company	**Year Acquired**	**Categories**	**Acquisition Value (USD)**
Superpod	2019	Software	60,000,000
DevOps Research and Assessment	2018	Cloud	--
Sigmoid Labs	2018	Software	--
Workbench	2018	Software, Education	--
Onward	2018	AI, Customer Service, Sales	--
GraphicsFuzz	2018	Graphics Drivers, Security	--
Velostrata	2018	Cloud Migration, Data Centers	--
Cask Data	2018	Big Data, Analytics	--
Lytro	2018	Photography, Film, Hardware, VR	--
Tenor	2018	Messaging, Social Media, Video	--
Socratic	2018	AI, Software	--
Xively	2018	Enterprise Software, IoT, SaaS	--
Redux	2018	Speakers, Mobile Devices	--

	Google		
Company	**Year Acquired**	**Categories**	**Acquisition Value (USD)**
HTC Smartphone Division	2018	Consumer Electronics, Manufacturing, Mobile	1,100,000,000
Banter	2017	Mobile Software, Messaging	--
Relay Media	2017	Analytics	--
60db	2017	Audio, Media and Entertainment, Social Media, Video Streaming	--
Bitium	2017	Cloud Computing, Cyber Security, Identity Management, SaaS, Security, Software	--
AIMatter	2017	Artificial Intelligence, Computer Vision, Software	--
Senosis Health	2017	Health, Mobile Device, Software	--
Halli Labs	2017	Artificial Intelligence, Machine Learning, Software Engineering	--
Owlchemy Labs	2017	Gaming, Software Engineering, Virtual Reality	--
Kaggle	2017	Analytics, Big Data, Data Mining, News, Predictive Analytics	--
AppBridge	2017	Apps, Data Storage, Google	--
Crashlytics	2017	Android, iOS, Mobile, SaaS	--
Fabric	2017	Cloud Infrastructure, Developer APIs, Developer Tools, Enterprise Software, Mobile Apps, Real Time	--

Google			
Company	**Year Acquired**	**Categories**	**Acquisition Value (USD)**
Limes Audio	2017	Audio, Communication Hardware, Telecommunications	--
Cronologics	2016	Hardware, Software, Wearables	--
LeapDroid	2016	Software	--
Qwiklabs	2016	Cloud Computing, Information Technology, Software	--
FameBit	2016	Internet, Music, Video	--
Eyefluence	2016	Consumer Electronics, Manufacturing, Wearables	--
Apigee	2016	Cloud Data Services, Enterprise Software, Information Technology	625,000,000
Urban Engines	2016	Analytics, Big Data, GovTech, Mobile, Software, Transportation	--
Api.ai	2016	Natural Language Processing, Voice Recognition	--
Orbitera	2016	Analytics, Cloud Computing, E-Commerce, Marketing Automation, SaaS, Software	100,000,000
Apportable	2016	Developer Tools, Enterprise Software, Mobile, iOS	--
Moodstocks	2016	Artificial Intelligence, Hardware, Image Recognition, Machine Learning, Mobile, QR Codes, Real Time, Visual Search	--

Google			
Company	**Year Acquired**	**Categories**	**Acquisition Value (USD)**
Anvato	2016	Software, Video Conferencing, Video Streaming	--
Kifi	2016	Analytics, Artificial Intelligence, Big Data, Content Discovery, Knowledge Management	--
LaunchKit	2016	Developer Tools, Mobile Apps	--
Webpass	2016	Internet, ISP, Wireless	--
Synergyse	2016	Apps, Search Engine, Software, Training	--
BandPage	2016	Consumer, Facebook, Marketplace, Music	--
Pie	2016	Automotive, Incubators	--
Fly Labs	2015	iOS	--
Bebop	2015	Business Development, Enterprise, Enterprise Software	380,000,000
Digisfera	2015	Images	--
Oyster	2015	Email, Web Design, Web Hosting	--
Jibe Mobile	2015	File Sharing, Messaging, Mobile, Social Media	--
Pixate	2015	Computer, Enterprise Software, Mobile	--

Google			
Company	**Year Acquired**	**Categories**	**Acquisition Value (USD)**
Timeful	2015	Analytics, Artificial Intelligence, Database, Machine Learning, Task Management	--
Pulse.io	2015	Apps, Mobile	--
Thrive Audio	2015	Audio, 3D Technology	--
Skillman & Hackett	2015	Software, Virtual Reality	--
Launchpad Toys	2015	Apps, Education, iOS	--
Odysee	2015	Enterprise Software, Mobile Apps, Photo Sharing	--
Softcard	2015	Apps, Mobile Payments	--
Red Hot Labs	2015	Advertising Platforms, Apps, Mobile, Software	--
Granata Decision Systems	2015	Analytics, Artificial Intelligence, Machine Learning	--
Vidmaker	2014	Collaboration, Social Media, Video	--
Lumedyne Technologies	2014	Consumer Electronics, Information Technology, Semiconductors	--
RelativeWave	2014	Apps, Developer Tools	--
Agawi	2014	EdTech, Gaming, Mobile Apps, Mobile Devices	--

436

Google			
Company	**Year Acquired**	**Categories**	**Acquisition Value (USD)**
Firebase	2014	Cloud Infrastructure, Developer APIs, Developer Tools, Enterprise Software, Mobile Apps, Real Time	--
Dark Blue Labs	2014	Artificial Intelligence, Data Visualization, Machine Learning	--
Vision Factory	2014	Artificial Intelligence, Computer Vision, Machine Learning, Search Engine, Software	--
Revolv	2014	Internet of Things, Smart Home, Software	--
Lift Labs	2014	Hardware, Health Care, Medical, Software	--
Polar	2014	Fitness, Health Care, Wearables	--
Skybox Imaging	2014	Cloud Security, Cyber Security, Enterprise Software, Network Security, Security, Software	500,000,000
Emu	2014	E-Commerce	--
Directr	2014	Energy, Solar	--
Jetpac	2014	AI, ML	--
Gecko Design	2014	Product Design	--
Zync Render	2014	Digital Media, Flash Storage, Social Media	--
Dropcam	2014	Consumer Electronics, Hardware, SaaS	555,000,000

Google			
Company	**Year Acquired**	**Categories**	**Acquisition Value (USD)**
Songza	2014	Music	--
DrawElements	2014	Enterprise Software	--
mDialog	2014	Advertising, Information Technology, Video Streaming	--
Aplental Technologies	2014	Information Technology, Wireless	--
Baarzo	2014	Video, Search	--
Appurify	2014	Android, Apps, iOS, Mobile, Test and Measurement	--
Rangespan	2014	Analytics, E-Commerce, Supply Chain Management	--
Adometry	2014	Advertising, Analytics, SaaS	--
Appetas	2014	Network Security, Restaurants, SaaS	--
Stackdriver	2014	Apps, Cloud Computing, Enterprise Software, Infrastructure	--
Quest Visual	2014	Data Visualization, iOS, Software	--
Gridcentric	2014	Software, Virtualization	--
Divide	2014	Enterprise Software, Information Technology, Mobile, SaaS, Software	--

Google			
Company	**Year Acquired**	**Categories**	**Acquisition Value (USD)**
Titan Aerospace	2014	Aerospace, Manufacturing	--
GreenThrottle	2014	Console Games, Consumer Electronics, Mobile	--
Nest Labs	2014	Sensor, Manufacturing, Smart Home	3,200,000,000
SlickLogin	2014	Mobile, Mobile Apps, Security	--
Spider.io	2014	Advertising, Analytics, Fraud Detection, Internet, Security	--
Bitspin	2014	Apps, Web Development	--
Impermium	2014	Security	--
DeepMind Technologies	2014	AI, ML	500,000,000
Flutter	2013	Content, Software	40,000,000
FlexyCore	2013	Software	23,000,000
Calico	2013	Biotech, Genetics, Health Care	--
Bump	2013	Mobile, Contact Sharing	--
WIMM Labs	2012	Hardware, Software, Wearables	--

Google			
Company	Year Acquired	Categories	Acquisition Value (USD)
Waze	2013	Mobile Apps, Navigation, Transportation	966,000,000
Makani Power	2013	Energy	--
MyEnergy	2013	Clean Energy, Energy Efficiency	--
Behavio	2013	Software	--
Wavii	2013	ML, AI	30,000,000
Channel Intelligence	2013	Manufacturing, Product Search, Shopping	125,000,000
DNNresearch	2013	AI	--
Talaria Technologies	2013	Software, Web Design, Web Development	--
Schaft	2013	Hardware, Robotics	--
Industrial Perception	2013	AI	--
Redwood Robotics	2013	Robotics	--
Meka Robotics	2013	Robotics	--
Holomni	2013	Mobile, Robots	--

		Google	
Company	**Year Acquired**	**Categories**	**Acquisition Value (USD)**
Bot & Dolly	2013	Software, Robotics	--
Autofuss	2013	Product Design	--
Incentive Targeting	2012	Public Relations, Retail	--
BufferBox	2012	E-Commerce, Marketplace, Shopping	17,000,000
Viewdle	2012	Analytics, Augmented Reality, Computer Vision, Mobile, Facial Recognition	45,000,000
VirusTotal.com	2012	Security	--
Nik Software	2012	Image Recognition, Software	--
Sparrow	2012	Email, Messaging	25,000,000
Wildfire Interactive	2012	Consulting, Content, Data Integration, Developer Tools	450,000,000
Cuban Council	2012	Consulting, Consumer Electronics, Search Engine	--
Meebo	2012	Internet, Messaging, Web Development	100,000,000
Quickoffice	2012	Enterprise Software, iOS, Mobile	--
TxVia	2012	Finance, FinTech, Mobile, PaaS	--

Google			
Company	**Year Acquired**	**Categories**	**Acquisition Value (USD)**
Milk, Inc	2012	Apps, Mobile, Software	--
RightsFlow	2011	Accounting, Music, Legal	--
Clever Sense	2011	ML, AI	--
Apture	2011	Advertising	--
Katango	2011	Social Media	--
Anthony's Robots	2011	Autonomous Vehicles	--
510 Systems	2011	Autonomous Vehicles, Software	--
SocialGrapple	2011	Analytics, Social Media	--
Zave Networks	2011	Apps, Mobile	--
Zagat	2011	Consumer Reviews	151,000,000
DailyDeal	2011	Beauty, Shopping	114,000,000
Dealmap	2011	Coupons, Local, Mobile, Search Engine, Social Media	--
Motorola Mobility	2011	Mobile Apps	12,500,000,000

Google			
Company	**Year Acquired**	**Categories**	**Acquisition Value (USD)**
Punchd	2011	Android, iOS, Loyalty Programs, Mobile	--
Fridge	2011	Photo Sharing	--
PittPatt	2011	Facial Recognition	--
PostRank	2011	Analytics, Social Media, Test and Measurement	--
Admeld	2011	Advertising, Auctions, Software	400,000,000
SageTV	2011	Digital Entertainment, Events, Media and Entertainment	--
Modu	2011	Mobile, Telecommunications, Wireless	--
Sparkbuy	2011	Consumer Electronics, E-Commerce, Shopping	--
PushLife	2011	Digital Media, E-Commerce, Mobile	25,000,000
ITA Software	2011	Information Technology	676,000,000
TalkBin	2011	Messaging	--
BeatThatQuote.com	2011	Auto Insurance, E-Commerce, Price Comparison	65,000,000
Next New Networks	2011	Video, Video Streaming	--

Google			
Company	**Year Acquired**	**Categories**	**Acquisition Value (USD)**
Green Parrot Pictures	2011	Digital Media, Enterprise Software, Video	--
Zynamics	2011	Security	--
eBook Technologies	2011	Content, E-Books	--
SayNow	2011	Messaging, Social Network, Telecommunications	--
Phonetic Arts	2010	Software	--
Widevine Technologies	2010	Digital Entertainment, Digital Media, Video	--
Zetawire	2010	Mobile Payments, NFC	--
BlindType	2010	Mobile	--
Plannr	2010	Mobile	--
Quiksee	2010	Digital Media	10,000,000
MentorWave Technologies	2010	Software, 3D Visualization	--
Slide.com	2010	Developer Tools, Software	228,000,000
Jambool	2010	Apps, Internet	70,000,000

Google			
Company	**Year Acquired**	**Categories**	**Acquisition Value (USD)**
Like.com	2010	Image Recognition	100,000,000
Angstro	2010	Enterprise Software, Facebook, Social Network	--
SocialDeck	2010	Mobile, Social Website	--
Metaweb	2010	Database, Infrastructure	--
Invite Media	2010	Advertising	81,000,000
Instantiations	2010	Software	--
Global IP Solutions	2010	Software	68,200,000
Simplify Media	2010	Digital Entertainment, Digital Media, Mobile	--
Ruba.com	2010	Guides, Internet	--
PinkArt	2010	Software	--
Agnilux	2010	Hardware	--
LabPixies	2010	Software	--
BumpTop	2010	Software	30,000,000

Google			
Company	**Year Acquired**	**Categories**	**Acquisition Value (USD)**
Picnik	2010	Photosharing	--
DocVerse	2010	Document Management	25,000,000
Episodic	2010	Broadcasting, Internet	--
reMail	2010	Email, Messaging, Mobile Apps	--
Aardvark	2010	Internet, Search Engine, Social	50,000,000
AdMob	2009	Ad Network, Advertising, Apps, Marketing, Mobile	750,000,000
Gizmo5	2009	Public Relations, VoIP	30,000,000
Teracent	2009	Advertising, Machine Learning	--
AppJet	2009	Software, Web Development	--
reCAPTCHA	2009	Security	--
On2	2009	Content, Internet, SaaS, Software, Video	133,000,000
Eluceon Research	2009	Internet, Software	--
TNC	2008	Google, Web Browsers, Web Hosting	--

	Google		
Company	**Year Acquired**	**Categories**	**Acquisition Value (USD)**
Begun	2008	Advertising	--
Omnisio	2008	File Sharing, Video	15,000,000
Jaiku	2007	Mobile	--
Zingku	2007	Digital Media, Social Media, Social Network	--
Postini	2007	Cyber Security, Internet, Security	625,000,000
ImageAmerica	2007	Software, Document Scanning	--
FeedBurner	2007	Blogging Platforms, Internet, Podcast	100,000,000
PeakStream	2007	Apps, Developer APIs, GPU, Software	--
Zenter	2007	Content, E-Commerce, Web Hosting	--
GrandCentral	2007	Mobile, Telecommunications, VoIP	45,000,000
GreenBorder	2007	Computer, Internet, Software	--
Panoramio	2007	Photo Sharing, Photography, Social Media	--
Crusix	2007	Social Networking	--

Google			
Company	Year Acquired	Categories	Acquisition Value (USD)
DoubleClick	2007	Advertising	3,100,000,000
Tonic Systems	2007	Web Development	--
Marratech	2007	Software, Video Conferencing	15,000,000
Trendalyzer	2007	Visual Statistics, Data Visualization, Software	--
Adscape	2007	Advertising, Digital Media, Marketing	23,000,000
Endoxon	2006	Information Technology	28,000,000
JotSpot	2006	Collaboration, Enterprise Software, Software	--
YouTube	2006	Internet, Music, Video	1,650,000,000
Neven Vision	2006	Software	--
2Web Technologies	2006	Software	--
Orion	2006	Content, Search Engine, Web Hosting	--
Upstartle	2006	Software	--
@Last Software	2006	3D Technology, Developer Tools	--

Google			
Company	**Year Acquired**	**Categories**	**Acquisition Value (USD)**
Measure Map	2006	Advertising, Analytics, Big Data	--
dMarc Broadcasting	2006	Advertising, Advertising Platforms, Internet Radio	102,000,000
Phatbits	2005	XML Desktop Applications	--
allPAY GmbH	2005	Mobile	--
bruNET GmbH	2005	Digital Entertainment, Social Media	--
Skia	2005	Graphic Design	--
Akwan Information Technologies	2005	Information Technology, IT Management, Search Engine	--
Android	2005	Linux, Mobile, Search Engine	50,000,000
Reqwireless	2005	Wireless	--
Dodgeball	2005	Mobile Devices, Software	--
Urchin Software Corporation	2005	Software	--
Where 2 Technologies	2004	Software	--
Keyhole	2004	Geospatial, Software	--

Google			
Company	Year Acquired	Categories	Acquisition Value (USD)
ZipDash	2004	Automotive, E-Commerce, Mobile, Real Time, Travel	--
Picasa	2004	Photos, Photo Editing	--
Ignite Logic	2004	Internet, Software, Web Design	--
Sprinks	2003	Online Advertising	--
Genius Labs	2003	Developer APIs, Developer Tools, Software	--
Neotonic Software	2003	CRM, Software	--
Applied Semantics	2003	Developer APIs, Enterprise Software, Mobile Apps	102,000,000
Kaltix	2003	SEO, Web Hosting	--
Pyra Labs	2003	Blogging Platforms, Developer APIs, Developer Tools, Enterprise Software, Project Management, Social Media	--
Outride	2001	Energy, Information Technology, Online Portals	--
Deja	2001	Information Technology, Internet, Web Development	--

www.ingramcontent.com/pod-product-compliance
Lightning Source LLC
Chambersburg PA
CBHW081436190326

41458CB00020B/6224